(Re)constructing communities

design participation in the face of change

The 5th Pacific Rim Conference on Participatory Community Design

Edited by

Jeffrey Hou
Mark Francis
Nathan Brightbill

Center for Design Research
University of California, Davis

(Re)constructing Communities

Funded in part by Grant 03T-PRRP-3-12 from the University of California Pacific Rim Research Program

To order copies:

Center for Design Research
Landscape Architecture Program
University of California, Davis
142 Walker Hall
Davis, CA 95616
(530) 752-3907
lda@ucdavis.edu

For more information on the Pacific Rim Community Design Network, please visit http://faculty.washington.edu/jhou/pacrim.htm

Cover design by Nathan Brightbill, Chia-Lin Molly Ma and Jeffrey Hou.
    Cover illustrations adapted from Hester, R. and C. Kweskin, Eds. 1999. Democratic Design in the Pacific Rim: Japan, Taiwan and the United States. Mendocino: Ridge Times Press, and Adams, E. and I. Kinoshita, Eds. 2000. Machi-Work: Education for Participation. Tokyo: Fudosya.

Illustrations credited by photographs and artwork except when created by the author of the article.

Printed in the USA by Reprographics, University of California, Davis.

(Re)constructing Communities: Design Participation in the Face of Change
    edited by Jeffrey Hou, Mark Francis and Nathan Brightbill

ISBN 0-9764420-0-0(paper)

ACKNOWLEDGEMENTS

The 5th Pacific Rim Conference on Participatory Community Design was organized through collaboration between the Landscape Architecture Program at University of California, Davis (UCD) and the Department of Landscape Architecture at University of Washington (UW). We wish to thank the Pacific Rim Research Program of the University of California Office of President, University of California Agricultural Experiment Station, the Northwest Center for Livable Communities and Taiwan Ministry of Education for supporting the conference and printing of the proceedings. Shenglin Chang, Randy Hester, Liling Huang, John Liu, Marcia McNally, Tamesuke Nagahashi and Tianxin Zhang provided invaluable feedbacks for the preparation of the conference. Yukio Nishimura provided important input for the grant proposal. Isami Kinoshita and Shenglin Chang led the demonstration of 'keywords' in the closing session. The conference could not have successfully been held without the assistance of the following students at University of Washington—William Buckingham, Richard Cochrane, Brian Hammer, Yamani Hernandez, Katherine Idziorek, Laurie Karlinsky, Vanessa Lee, Chia-Lin Molly Ma, Elizabeth Maly, Jayde Lin Roberts, Lee Roberts, Keiko Shimada, Makie Suzuki, Candy Wang and Kaila Yun. Yamani Hernandez and Daniele Spirandelli designed and produced the conference booklet. Chia-Lin Molly Ma provided the graphic design of the conference materials. Leah Briney provided additional conference support. We are grateful for the administrative support from Heath Schenker, Chair, Landscape Architecture Program, UC Davis; Debbie Johnson, Meredith Sypolt and Victoria Whitworth in the Landscape Architecture Program at UC Davis and JoAnne Edwards, Dean Robert Mugerauer, Victoria Reyes, Department of Landscape Architecture Chair Iain Robertson, and Department of Landscape Architecture Chair Fritz Wagner at the University of Washington. Finally, we would like to extend a special thanks to Jim Diers, Tom Im, Milenko Matanovic, Joyce Moty, Bob Santos and Daniel Winterbottom for their assistance in organizing a special panel and field tours during the conference. Over the last six years, we have benefited from the sharing of lessons and experiences through the conferences. This volume represents a collective work that celebrates the efforts of everyone who has participated and contributed to the conference series since its inception in 1998.

CONTENTS

*Abstracts only

INTRODUCTION
(RE)CONSTRUCTING COMMUNITY DESIGN

Jeffrey Hou, Mark Francis and Nathan Brightbill

What do community designers across the Pacific Rim share in common? How can practices in the different political, institutional and social contexts inform each other? What lessons can be drawn from an increasing array of cross-cultural and transnational collaboration in design and planning? This collection of papers is an outcome of a three-day conference held in Seattle in September 2004 that brought together a dynamic group of activists/scholars from eight countries to answer and reflect on these critical questions concerning the growing practice of community design in the Pacific Rim.

'Community' and Community Design in the Face of Change

In recent decades, community design and planning has become a common part of urban planning and design practice in the Pacific Rim. With deep roots in advocacy planning and citizen participation developed in the United States, citizen participation and community planning can now also be found in Japan, Taiwan, Hong Kong and even China. The movement toward citizen participation and community revitalization in the United States has been echoed by the Machizukuri Movement in Japan, the Community Building Movement (Sher-chu-zong-ti-yin-zhao)[1] in Taiwan, and an emerging challenge to the top-down urban planning and redevelopment process in Hong Kong. More recently, decentralization of decision-making in China has led to more government-led community building programs, and some experiments in participatory planning processes.

The parallel movements across the Pacific Rim reflect a shared aspiration of democratic decision-making and community building. However, while the idealism of community building begins to take roots, recent social changes across the Pacific Rim have also challenged the traditional notion of 'community' and the practice of community design and planning. In the United States, demographic shifts and other socio-economic forces have changed the composition, identity and definitions of communities in cities and regions. In Japan and Taiwan, influx of urban population as a result of continued urbanization is also changing the demographic makeup of traditional communities leading to competing interests and ideologies and often pitting newcomers against long-time residents. In Hong Kong, the traditional consultation process is no longer adequate in addressing conflicts and contentions in the redevelopment of

aging urban communities. In China, the drive toward economic development outpaces institutional and social adjustments. Across the region, globalization and its influence on economic activities and cultural change are contributing to transformations in the meanings, identities and spatial structure of urban landscapes. These changes provide the collective context for the papers included in this volume.

Why the Pacific Rim?

The growing practice of community planning and the conditions of changing communities present both revealing parallels and differences across the Pacific Rim.[2] They also provide opportunities for critical comparisons and analysis. First, with the establishment and institutionalization of citizen participation and community planning in the United States and Canada, the practice of participatory design and planning is becoming increasingly parochial, focusing more on methods than social and environmental change (see Hou and Rios, 2003; Francis, 1999; Hester, 1999b). In contrast, community design in the form of social movements in Taiwan and Japan can provide lessons and help reinvigorate the institutionalized practice of community design in North America. Conversely, the issues of institutionalization in North America can offer forewarnings on future problems to its Asian counterparts.

Secondly, the growth of new immigrant and multicultural communities in North American cities has put new strains on many traditional institutions of democratic participation, and requires a re-envisioning of the democratic process in response to the new multicultural and cross-cultural context. Similarly, debates concerning multiculturalism are also beginning to emerge in Asian countries as a result of growing acknowledgement of cultural differences and the politics of pluralism and democracy. The experience in North America may offer important lessons for the Asian countries and communities. Third, the changes in the Pacific Rim are increasingly transnational and interrelated. A cross-cultural and transnational examination of the experience across the Pacific Rim will contribute to a better understanding of the ongoing transformation in cities and communities as the result of increasing economic and social ties across the Pacific Rim. In an age of globalization, the focus on the Pacific Rim would transcend geographical and cultural boundaries and make critical comparison and understanding of cross-cultural influences possible.

The "Pacific Rim Conferences"

The "Democratic Design in the Pacific Rim" conferences have been convened to address across countries and communities the changing context and nature of community design. The conference that produced this collection of papers was the fifth in this series of working conferences that began in Berkeley in 1998. The purpose of these meetings has been to provide practitioners and scholars working in the field of participatory design and planning across the Pacific Rim region with an opportunity to share and compare each other's experiences and advance their practice and research (Hester, 1999b). In addition to the conferences, a network of conference participants called "The Pacific Rim Community Design Network"

Figure 1. Berkeley conference, 1998.

Figure 2. Taiwan conference, 2001.

was launched in Berkeley in 1998. Inspired by shared interests and experiences, members have undertaken collaborative research to investigate differences and shared lessons in community design in their respective institutional, political and social contexts. Some have taken a deliberately cross-cultural framework to bridge community design practices through joint studios and comparative research. Over the years, many have participated in each other's community-based work. Through regular conferences and joint projects, the network has provided a vehicle for collaboration and mutual support, as well as a forum for comparative understanding of community design in the Pacific Rim.

In many ways, the Seattle conference represents a milestone for this growing network. By returning to the United States six years later, it marks the completion of the first round of conferences in Berkeley (1998), Japan (1999), Taiwan (2001) and Hong Kong (2002). Second, it attracted the largest and most diverse group of participants, including scholars, practitioners, faculty and students, as well as local government officials and staff, from Canada, China, Japan, Indonesia, Singapore, Taiwan and the United States. The number of papers presented is also the largest of all the conferences, with topics ranging from new actors and institutions to community art and engaging marginalized groups. This large pool of papers and presentations provide an opportunity for more in-depth discussions into the different subject categories of community design. As the fifth conference in the series, it also provides a chance to look back at what the network and the working conferences have accomplished in its first six years. The theme of the Seattle conference "(Re)constructing Communities: Design Participation in the Face of Change" reflects the need to re-examine the theory and practice of community design in the changing political and social landscapes of the Pacific Rim.

With the large number of papers, the grouping of papers in a meaningful and practical way presented a formidable challenge for the editors. We have attempted to group them into major themes in order for the reader to understand critical issues and advances in community design taking place through-

Figure 3. Seattle conference, 2004.

out the Pacific Rim. The organization of papers here largely follow the conference program but also highlight the overarching and crisscrossing themes during the three days of papers and discussions. In addition, we include some photos and graphics generated during the conference to give a flavor of the spirited and collegial exchange that took place.

Re-examining Community Design

In the spirit of a critical re-examination, the conference opened with a panel of papers in Chapter 1 that provided different observations on methods of evaluating community design practice. Mark Francis argues that participatory community design has developed to a point where critical and more systematic reexamination is needed. To document and critique the work in more rigorous ways, he suggests the use of the case study method to help designers and planners tell stories to practitioners, clients, students and each other, using a shared language and comparative framework. Echoing Francis' critique of the lack of reflection, Michael Rios further suggests the use of Participatory Action Research (PAR) in meeting the goals of both communities and universities in the context of service learning and community-university partnership. As a teaching and community outreach approach, PAR would offer the potential to improve current methods of service learning. Specifically, the shift from 'expert' to 'local' knowledge under PAR "creates new sites of inquiry and discovery outside the traditional academic settings." Mayumi Hayashi offers a case study on the effectiveness of workshops in connecting citizen organization and the management of green spaces. In the case of a post-earthquake rebuilding effort in Takarazuka, Japan, she observes that workshops in which citizens made proposals and undertook actual activities allowed them to gradually take ownerships of the planning process and expressed higher degrees of satisfaction.

An important part of examining the practice of community design is to reflect on the role and responsibility of professionals themselves. In Chapter 2, John Liu examines the epistemological challenges facing professionals engaged in trans-cultural planning and design activities. Based on participant observations of the tension between professional judgment, local cultural practice and political interests in the case of a temple expansion on Matzu, he argues that professional knowledge needs to incorporate the multiple realities and diversity of values in the local context. Ching-Fen Yang describes the role of professionals as both an interface and agents of disturbance in a power structure in the case of a campus planning in Taiwan. Through events and proactive negotiation, planners were able to mobilize resources and opportunities within an institutionalized participatory process. Similarly, members of the DaYuanZi Studio at National Taiwan University describe the multiple and sometimes conflicting roles facing planners in working with institutions and in addressing the need for social actions and advocacy in the case of preserving colonial-era Japanese houses in Taipei.

Institutions and Citizen Movements

Faced with socio-political changes and restructuring of government, new actors and institutions with important roles in the practice of community design have emerged across the Pacific Rim. Chapter 3 discusses the context for growing influences of non-profit organizations (NPOs) in Japan and the institutionalization of 'community planners' in Taiwan. Yasuyoshi Hayashi describes the conversion from a vertical society to a horizontal social structure in Japan through the formation of a "new public" in the 1990s. In contrast to the "traditional public," the new public is a public in which citizens, NPOs, businesses and administrative authorities support each other. He argues that while many government authorities in Japan are still struggling to cope with this new paradigm, the growth of NPOs has already given rise to the formation of a new societal model. In Taiwan, democratization and social movements in the past decades have given rise to the power of citizens in urban decision-making. The transformation has been reflected in the institutionalization of community planning practice in cities such as Taipei. Pao-Chi Sung, a city planner in Taipei, assesses the current successes and problems facing the 'Community Planner' program in Taipei particularly in relation to the limited resources, ambiguous roles, and conflicting expectations from the communities. Despite the advancement of citizen involvement in Japan and Taiwan, much of the urban redevelopment processes in Asia still lies beyond the reach of average citizens. Perry Yang contrasts two models of redevelopment planning in Singapore and Kaohsiung in terms of citizen involvement in influencing the outcomes of the proposed plans.

In Seattle, local government's support has been critical to the growth of citizen initiatives and community-based programs. In Chapter 4, Jim Diers, former Director of Seattle's Department of Neighborhoods, describes the approach Seattle has undertaken since 1988 to empower local communities and foster community-government partnerships. Specifically, he describes how the city's Neighborhood Matching Funds program has spurred community self-help projects, such as building new parks and playgrounds, renovating community facilities, recording oral histories and creating public art. As an important point of departure, he distinguishes strongly between citizen participation and community empowerment. The former implies government control over priority and process, whereas the latter means, "giving citizens the tools and resources they need to address their own priorities." The institutional process in supporting the citizen initiatives is described in more detail in Hilda Blanco's evaluation on neighborhood planning in Seattle.

Figure 4. Forum on Empowering Seattle's Communities (Center: Jim Diers; from right: Former Mayor Paul Schell and activist Joyce Moty).

While institutionalization of citizen involvement has become a trend across the Pacific, citizen movements continue to be an important feature of urban planning and politics. In Chapter 5, Mintai Kim describes the influence of the environmental NGOs (non-governmental organizations) on government policies and decisions in South Korea. He also describes the role of the landscape architecture profession in supporting the movement through both leadership and practice in creating ecologically friendly open spaces that raise the consciousness of the public. Even in Seattle, citizen movements continue to be an important force in the design of the city. Kristina Hill describes and assesses the strategies used by a grassroots movement in Seattle to create a 14-mile monorail line through three successful citywide ballots. However, although citizen movement can represent progressive thinking and actions, it also faces many internal challenges. Satoko Asano examines a citizen movement against the building of arterial roads in Kobe following the Great Hanshin Earthquake. The case of Kobe, in which gender stereotype and hierarchy has prevented women from taking on a greater leadership role, reminds us that social movements face both the external and internal forces and are not without flaws. As reflective practitioners, community designers working in the context of social movement have greater responsibility in critically addressing such internal injustice.

Community Change and Differences

From Japan to the United States, small rural towns have been facing new economic challenges ranging from agricultural decline, new tourism economy and land development pressure. Chapter 6 includes papers that examine community design efforts at the small town scale . Patsy Eubanks Owens describes the case of a park master plan for the town of Knights Landing in California in which a participatory planning process brought together new and old residents in the town to envision a new park. Douglas Kot and Deni Ruggeri examine another Californian town, Westport, in which structured participatory process allows the town's residents to collectively plan for a new development that is expected to bring new economic development opportunities while preserving and reinforcing the town's physical identity. Soshi Higuchi, Haruhiko Goto and Nobuyuki Sekiguchi describe the case of community planning in Kinosaki, Japan—a hot spring resort town faced with the challenge of municipal merger. Through a series of workshops, faculty and students from Waseda University have worked with local residents to enact future scenarios of the community and develop ideas for local governance. In these projects, participatory community design process has been critical in helping local residents envision the future of the community and identify practical steps including design of physical places and development of new organizations.

Figure 5. Tour of Danny Woo Community Garden in Seattle's International District.

Another aspect of changes that are occurring in communities across the region is the increasing presence of differences within the so-called communities. The papers in Chapter 7 all address the implications of differences in community design practice. Michael Rios examines recent theoretical debates centered on the concept of multiple publics and differences as a way to problematize the normative approach of participatory design. Using the design of Plaza del Colibrí in San Francisco as a case study, he demonstrates how an inclusive approach in involving local non-profit organizations, residents, public agencies and different park users, including the homeless, youth and transit passengers, was critical to an understanding of the multiple identities, interests and needs of the users, which then led to the design of an inclusive public space. Based on a similar body of literature, Jeffrey Hou and Isami Kinoshita compare the processes of negotiating community differences in Seattle's International District and the Kogane District in Matsuo, Japan.

They further suggest the importance of informal activities in navigating the political and cultural nuances in the participatory process. In addition to differences within the communities, the gap in perspectives between locals and professional remains a barrier in participatory design. Carey Knecht discusses the techniques that can either widen or narrow the gap in the case of a town center design in Caspar, California.

Engaging Marginalized Communities

An important characteristic of community design is the strong sense of social responsibility that distinguishes it from more traditional design and planning practice. In particular, community designers often play a critical role in engaging and empowering marginalized populations and individuals. In Chapter 8, Antonio Ishmael Risianto describes a three-pronged strategy—MPE (meta-development, physical/environmental development and "people's economic development)—to address the multiple needs of marginalized poor in Indonesia. Sergio Palleroni discusses a similar effort in Mexico using models of community-based social banks and sustainable technologies in helping an indigenous community maintain their cultural/social value while developing their capacity to survive in a new economy. The problems of marginalized communities exist not only in poor developing countries, but also in wealthy, industrialized countries such as Japan and the United States. Yuko Hamasaki discusses the intermediary role of an NPO in Fukuoka, Japan that fills the gaps between wide-ranging needs of the residents and the formal welfare service system. The NPO provides critical services for seniors, people with mental illness, newcomers from rural areas, and children in the community. Lynne Manzo examines the process in engaging a group of ethnically diverse and low-income residents in the redevelopment of a public housing site in Seattle.

Reflecting a growing array of participatory practices, art has also become an alternative medium through which marginalized communities can be empowered. In Chapter 9, Min Jay Kang provides a critical examination of the practice of community artivism ("a conscious combination of art and activism") as a form and instrument of resistance and community empowerment. Specifically, he examines the creative power of art as well as the tension between the community and art in the case of Treasure Hill, a squatter settlement in Taipei, under the threat of demolition to make way for a new park. Kimura et al. describes a collaborative art project conducted with the residents of "Izumi no Ie", a welfare facility for people with physical disability in Setagaya, Tokyo. They examine how a carefully structured program based on trust in people's creative power can bring people independent self-expression and empower them to take part in collective actions. Milenko Matanovic presents a seven-fold 'community gathering place' model as a way of creating inclusive places and connecting environment, civic

involvement, education, the arts, economy and ethics—"combining justice with beauty."

Power and Representation

Other than art, what techniques do most community designers use in creating places with people? How are they different from the conventional tools of the design and planning profession? In Chapter 10, reflecting on the literature and papers presented in the past Pacific Rim conferences, Randy Hester presents a typology and a critique of techniques commonly used by community designers. Specifically, he examines how 'drawings' help to exchange complex ideas, science, and technical information with diverse publics and allow for collaborative imagination of the environment. In reviewing the papers from past conferences, he observed the frequent use of techniques to emphasize the experience of a location. In addition, there seems to be "a concerted effort to overcome modern abstraction and post-modern deconstruction of life space" to capture its sensual and experiential nuances. However, he also argues that for a group of designers, there have been few spatially explicit collaborative design techniques precisely described in the previous proceedings. Specifically, he argues that the workshop seems to have become "the participatory 'black box' through which community designers are as inarticulate as traditional designers are about creative form making."

Echoing the theme of Hester's paper on co-authoring and drawing with the public, Masato Dohi argues that it is only through participation that 'lines' have meanings and begin to create spaces which then give meaning to people and to which people give meanings. He also argues for a need to take risks, to trust people's ability to express their own world. In examining participatory techniques to search for collective urban memories in the disappearing public sphere, Annie Chiu examines the case of a commemorative park design as part of a mall development in Taipei on the site of a former paper mill. Specifically, the paper examines a series of workshops with former factory workers that provided a process of searching, exchanging ideas, producing and finally transforming voices of wound/trauma into landscape. She argues that participatory design workshops provide the chance to tell the story and turn the story into representation that people can continue to imagine.

Nature(s) and Place

In recent years, community design is no longer practiced solely in the context of empowering disenfranchised communities. Increasingly, environmental learning and connecting people to places has also become an important realm of community design practice. The papers in Chapter 11 all discuss a social connection to place and imply multiple views of 'nature' that facilitate the connections. Sawako Ono analyzes the case of

Rikugien Garden in Tokyo in the 18th Century. Through intermediaries such as the relatives, servants, friends, and gardeners, the private garden of an aristocratic clan became accessible to a wide of range of people including samurai, neighbors, farmers, priests, women and children, and served as a 'public' space for the appreciation of 'nature' in a strongly hierarchical Japanese society. Julie Johnson examines children's learning potentials in nature and school landscapes. Through the case study of Dearborn Elementary in Seattle, she illustrates how the development of an ecologically designed school landscape can support learning and foster community. Complementing Johnson's paper on children's environmental learning, I-Chun Kuo presents the results of her study in Taipei showing that an increase in children's experiences of nearby nature has translated into increased participation in environment-related activities as adults. She argues that designers, educators and parents should value the importance of nearby nature and create neighborhoods with rich experiences of nature. Shifting to the context of low-income communities, Amy Dryden looks at two affordable housing developments in Oakland, California and evaluates the relationships between sustainable site design and residents' preference and values regarding outdoor space. She argues that understanding user preferences is particularly important when advancing sustainable design in a non-market based system such as affordable housing.

Through fostering people's connection to place, participatory mechanisms have also become increasingly recognized in engaging people in environmental stewardship and activism. The papers in Chapter 12 examine different forms of citizen engagement with a common focus on the protection of creeks and watersheds. Victoria Chanse and Chia-Ning Yang provide an overview on how stewardship of urban nature has changed

Figure 6. Children's Garden at Bradner Garden Park, Seattle.

from "a top-down, distant, centralized, professionals-leading regime to a local, participatory, grassroots movement." They further examine how two modes of engaging people—volunteerism and spontaneous use—can together create a participatory culture of urban nature stewardship. Demonstrating the importance of volunteerism, Louise Mozingo reviews the essential role and ongoing challenges of citizen activism and NGOs in restoration advocacy of urban creeks in the East Bay of San Francisco Bay Area. The complex web of citizen organizations provides important science support, training, and sources of volunteer labor in restoring and protecting the neighborhood creeks. Echoing the argument for spontaneous use, Asano, et al., describe the current challenges facing the protection of the Yoshino River and Daiju Weir in Tokushima City, Japan. To reinvigorate and sustain the local citizen movement, they present a proposal for tangible hands-on activities that recognize the opportunities for diverse uses on the river and the ecological and social connections these activities provide. They argue that the hands-on projects would stimulate citizen use and understanding of the place.

Engaging Students and Youths

One of the many challenges facing community design lies in the planning and design education and in engaging youths in community development. The papers in Chapter 13 examine different models and cases of service learning. Christopher Campbell and Dennis Ryan argue that recent social and political changes around the globe call for a new paradigm of engagement where "learning is simultaneously acting in the world." Using the Community and Environmental Planning program at University of Washington as a case study, they argue for a trans-disciplinary and collaborative model of community design education. Nancy Rottle describes the unique benefits and limitations of service learning studios based on two recent community planning studios at University of Washington. She also examines the challenges and sometime conflicting goals of 'service' and 'learning' from the perspective of a studio. Addressing service learning at a different scale, Daniel Winterbottom examines students' hands-on involvement in a design/build studio model at University of Washington that connects design, community participation and construction. Based on observations of three studios conducted in different cultural and social contexts (immigrant women in Mexico, children with HIV/AIDS in New York City, and cancer patients in Seattle), he describes the values of "educational outreach, cultural exchange, community understanding and shared endeavor" in addition to the tangible result of built work. Shifting to the other side of the Pacific Rim, Koichi Kobayashi describes the involvement of students in producing an advocacy proposal to rehabilitate an urban greenway in Osaka, Japan.

Figure 7. Children's art at Bradner Garden Park.

In community development and design, youths represent a frequent group of constituents and participants. It is widely assumed that youth involvement can contribute positively to the society and instill a sense of civic responsibility and citizenship among youths. However, participation of youths in community design also faces numerous challenges. In Chapter 14, Jonathan London describes a lack of linkage between youth and community development in practice. To address this issue, he presents a method of youth-led research, evaluation and planning in linking youths and community development. In the face of commercialism and commodification of youth culture, Isami Kinoshita also argues that the nexus between youth participation and community planning is important in restructuring the relationship between youth and community. On the need to engage and empower youths, Elijah Mirochnik reflects on his role as a teacher and experiences in working with children. Specifically, he explores the use of a transgressive vocabulary that challenges old notions about knowledge, teaching and learning. To demonstrate a critical approach to youth involvement, Michael Rios presents the case of a youth art project in the North Cheyenne reservation in the United States to illustrate the use of community-based design and art as a vehicle to explore issues of identity, landscape and civic engagement.

Cross-cultural Perspectives and Collaboration

As a forum on community design in the Pacific Rim, cross-cultural perspectives have been a main focus of the conference series. Chapter 15 includes papers from a self-organized panel on cross-cultural understanding and the linkages between professional expertise and local knowledge. Focusing on multicultural communities, Margarita Hill describes a participatory community process to create a more walkable community in West Hyattsville in Maryland, USA, in which multiple methodologies were deployed to engage a multicultural population. She also examines the different perspectives of the multiple actors in the process—students, faculty, and community members and

Figures 8 through 10. Groups working on reflections of the conference through 'keywords' at closing workshop.

leaders. Presenting a case study of a community design studio on the remote islands of Matzu, John Liu, Hsing-Rong Liu and Shenglin Chang examine the multiple layers of tensions—between the views of the insiders and outsiders, professionals and locals, and between teamwork and individuals. With growing concern on the global environment, international collaboration and partnership have grown rapidly in recent years providing alternative models of environmental and resource management. Based on the case study of IEGC (Organization for International Exchange of Green Culture), Takayoshi Yamamura, Tianxin Zhang and Aijun He describe the benefits and challenges of a collaborative framework consisting of tourists, residents, international NGOs and local administration in sustainable environmental management and education in Lijiang, China. The challenges include opposing value systems and tensions between universal science and local perspectives.

Since the Berkeley conference 1998, several collaborative projects have been launched among members of the Pacific Rim network, including an ongoing collaborative project between National Taiwan University and University of California, Berkeley in developing an ecological conservation and sustainable economic development plan for the coastal region of Tainan County, Taiwan, and a collaborative neighborhood design studio between University of Washington and Chiba University in 2003, among others. The final chapter includes

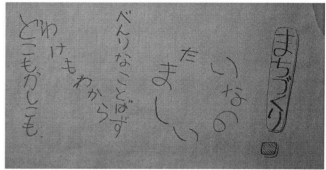

Figure 13. With "No Machizukuri!" the research team from the Tokyo Institute of Technology critiques the institutionalization of the community building movement in Japan.

Figures 11 and 12. Performing the keywords.

two collaborative projects involving researchers and research sites across the Pacific Rim. Liling Huang, Marcia McNally and Louise Mozingo undertook a comparative study of the planning and design of neighborhood open space in Taipei, Kyoto, Berkeley, Oakland and Los Angeles. They have found that the production of neighborhood spaces in these cities share two phenomena—standardization and community action, and argue that neighborhood has become the "basic landscape unit of globalization and resistant local action." In examining recent changes at the neighborhood level, they also point out three important forces—local government policy, global capital, and demographic shifts that influence the making of neighborhood and neighborhood open space across the Pacific Rim. Echoing the focus on neighborhood space, Daniel Abramson, Jeffrey Hou and their students from a summer field studio present the results of a cross-cultural, interdisciplinary, community-based planning studio in Quanzhou, China. As a community design studio that brought together students from North America, Taiwan and Chinese universities and working on issues of preservation and neighborhood change, the experience exemplifies the opportunities and challenges facing cross-cultural community designers as intermediaries to bridge the multiple gaps of values, knowledge and perspectives in the collective region of the Pacific Rim.

山城藝驚太平洋

hill/town/art/surprise/Pacific Ocean

川流不息內外間

river/flows/non-stop/between inside and outside

聚集廟後蛙將軍

gathering/together/temple/behind/frog/general

落日樓頭茶當酒

setting/sun/building/front/tea as wine

風馬牛間談認同

wind/horse/cattle/in-between/talk/identities

貌與神移風雲動

face/change/wind/cloud/move

轉首評估社區夢

turn/head/evaluate/community/dream

'Keywords': Shenglin Chang
Translation: Jeffrey Hou

A Conclusion and a Beginning: Toward a Reflexive Practice of Community Design

As the papers in this proceedings demonstrate, the practice of community design today reflects the multiple and pluralistic realities in the fast-changing region of the Pacific Rim. Community designers today, including practitioners, researchers and students, work with diverse constituents and issues in a wide range of contexts, from slums of the developing countries to trans-local communities and small rural towns in industrialized nations, from protest movements to working as intermediaries between governments and citizens, and from shopping malls of global cities to streams and schoolyards in urban neighborhoods. Community designers utilize a wide array of methods and techniques to engage citizens and navigate the political and social process, from workshops and charrettes to walking tours and drinking at a neighborhood pub, from drawing on the feet to Geographical Information Systems, and from ethnographic fieldwork to artivism. The practice of community design today is also informed by a growing body of knowledge, from feminist and post-structuralist discourses to various forms of local knowledge, and from evaluation of existing cases to ongoing participatory action research. Community designers benefit from growing cross-cultural and interdisciplinary perspectives and collaboration that allow them to become more aware of the critical differences and common values, as well as a broader range of techniques. The growing body of knowledge and experiences has also made them become more critical and reflexive of the external and internal challenges.

The collection of papers in this volume celebrates the pluralism and differences in the contexts and approaches of community design in a changing world. The papers also reflect the shared values of democracy, justice, and diversity. Working at the local level and in trans-local contexts, community designers are at the forefront of profound changes that are occurring both locally and globally. In the face of the continued and dynamic changes in the society, is our knowledge and repertoire of tools today adequate in addressing the growing array of issues and constituents? How can the practice of community design respond to a broad range of external and internal challenges? We hope that this collective body of work offers important lessons and reflections that can enable community designers to become more effective and reflective in their everyday practice.

ENDNOTES

[1] This term has been translated in several other ways such as 'Community Empowerment Project' (See Hsia, 1999).
[2] Our definition of the Pacific Rim includes countries and regions that shared strong economic, social and political ties in the region, which are not limited to those mentioned in this article.

REFERENCES

Francis, M. 1999. "Proactive Practice: Visionary Thought and Participatory Action in Environmental Design," Places 12:2 (1999): 62.

Hester, R. 1999a. "A Refrain with a View," Places 12:2 (1999): 12.

Hester, R. 1999b. Introduction: A Struggle to Improve Each Other's Work. Hester, R. and C. Kweskin (eds.), Democratic Design in the Pacific Rim: Japan, Taiwan and United States. Mendocino, CA: Ridge Times Press.

Hou, J. and M. Rios. 2003. Community-driven Place Making: the Social Practice of Participatory Design in the Making of Union Point Park. Journal of Architectural Education, 57 (1): 19-27.

Hsia, C-J. 1999. Theorizing Community Participatory Design in a Developing Country: the Historic Meaning of Democratic Design in Taiwan. Hester, R. and C. Kweskin (eds.), Democratic Design in the Pacific Rim: Japan, Taiwan and United States. Mendocino, CA: Ridge Times Press.

Photos: Makie Suzuki, Katherine Idziorek.

evaluating
community design

COMMUNITY DESIGN (RE)EXAMINED

Mark Francis

ABSTRACT

Participatory community design has matured to a point where more critical examination is needed for further advancement of this important area of design practice. As community designers, we need to find more rigorous ways to document and critique our work. Furthermore, we need to be able to look across projects and methods to develop a more shared language and comparative way of working especially in the context of more global practice. The case study method is one way for community design to further establish itself as part of mainstream professional design practice. This paper briefly reviews recent advances in community design and some of its most common and closely held beliefs. It argues for a more research-based approach to our work based on looking at projects and core values based on a common set of questions and criteria. A framework for thinking more critically about what we do and being more systematic in looking at the results and impacts of our projects is suggested. A case study method is proposed for ongoing evaluation and improvement of community design projects, issues, methods, and teaching. This is based on recent work commissioned as part of the Landscape Architecture Foundation's "Case Study Initiative in Land and Community Design" (Francis 2001, 2003). Developed specifically for landscape architecture, the method may have value for design and planning projects involving user and community participation. The goal is to adapt this method to help advance theory development, practice, and teaching in democratic design.

INTRODUCTION

Significant progress has been made in the area of professional practice now commonly know as community design.[1] There are clear signs that community design has established itself as a forceful and mainstream part of environmental design (Bell, 2003; Dean, 2002). Interest in this area of practice among environmental designers and the public has been increasing and there is a need for more dissemination of the results of community design. A strong network now exists of people working internationally.[2] Community design has also become institutionalized in many schools of architecture, planning and landscape architecture.[3]

Figure 1. Community design has developed into a lively and mainstream form of environmental design practice.

Changes in community and public life are forcing a rethinking of more traditional design activity (Oldenburg, 1989; Putnam, 2001; Brill, 2002). The social and environmental problems of our time demand a more thoughtful and proactive approach to community design (MacCannell, 1993). This is required due to changes in social structure and public life and globalization of everyday life (Carr et. al., 1992). The movement toward more democratic and participatory design has been enlivened by recent popular debates on design, architecture and ecology including global warming, smart growth, new urbanism and post world September 11, 2001. The events of 9-11 have led to an interest in more participatory architecture. Community input into architecture and urban design has become almost a daily feature in The New York Times after September 11, 2001. While some may see this as a more fashionable and less democratic form of city design, we need to pay better attention to these larger social movements as they can inform and redirect our work in new and positive ways.

The values of community design have also found themselves in new paradigms of design and planning practice including "activist practice" (Feldman, 2003), the "reflective practitioner" (Schon, 1983), the "deliberative practitioner" (Forester, 1999) and "proactive practice" (Francis, 1999). While the titles vary, they share a common of approach of design and planning practice based on reflection, empowerment, participation, vision and activism (Dean 2002).

Critical Reflection in a Global Context

Community design is well suited for critical reflection.[4] Historically community designers have been among the most reflective and critical minded of design practitioners.[5] Yet there is an ongoing need for more systematic ways to know what works and does not work in community design, especially across countries and cultures.

Figure 2. Central Park in New York City has been the subject of many case studies.

Several useful guides for knowledge development and application can be found in environmental design research. One example is recent studies of the relationship between health and the built and natural environment (Frank et. al., 2003; Jackson et. al., 2001; Torres et. al., 2001). The participation of children and youth in shaping the designed environment also serves as a useful model for community design evaluation (Hart, 1997; Owens, 1988; Francis and Lorenzo, 2002). Studies of new urbanism (Calthorpe, 1993; Kelbaugh, 1997), regional planning (Calthorpe and Fulton, 2001; Thayer, 2003) and community-based place history (Hayden, 1995) and design (Hou and Rios, 2003) also are useful evaluation prototypes.

The case study method is a useful way to organize ongoing studies on the importance and impact of community design. Case studies are the primary way that community designers tell their stories and pass them on to other practitioners, clients and students. Case studies are often used to describe a project or process. They can also be used to critically evaluate the success and failure of projects as we often learn more through our failures than our successes.

Figure 3. Seaside, Florida is an example of a community design project that been documented as a case study and compared with others such as Sea Ranch in Northern California.

Case studies can also explain or even develop new theory. Case studies are a way to build a body of criticism and critical theory and to disseminate project results more broadly. They also can integrate best practices into a comprehensive and coherent body of practice and theory.

The Case Study Method

A case study is a well-documented and systematic examination of the process decision-making and outcomes of a project, which is undertaken for the purpose of informing future practice, policy, theory, and/or education (Francis 2001).

The case study method has great potential in informing and advancing practice and education in community design. Case studies often serve to make concrete what are often generalizations or purely anecdotal information about projects and processes. They also bring to light exemplary projects and concepts worthy of replication. For community design practitioners, they can be a source of practical information on potential solutions to difficult problems. For professional education, case studies are an effective way to teach by example, to learn problem-solving skills, and to develop useful evaluation strategies.

I recently developed a case study method for landscape architecture that may also have value for community design (Francis, 2001, 2003). Commissioned by the Landscape Architecture Foundation (LAF), the method uses a common format and template for case studies. LAF has developed a broad "Case Studies in Land and Community Design Initiative" to develop a more critical mass of cases useful for practice and education that allows for more analysis across cases. The method is being used in several landscape architecture programs in lecture and seminar courses and is now required as the format for student thesis work at some schools.

The case study method was reportedly first used as a teaching tool at Harvard Law School in 1870 by then Dean Christopher Langdell (Garvin, 2003). It has since become the standard method of teaching and research in many professions such as business, law, medicine and engineering. Case studies are also now commonly used in science education, the arts and humanities and public policy. There is currently a large and useful literature on how to develop and apply cases (Yin, 1993, 1994; Stake, 1995), using cases in teaching (Barnes et. al., 1994), and how to evaluate the effectiveness of cases (Lundeberg et. al., 2000). The case study method is similar to the post occupancy evaluation (POE) method used in environmental design research but differs from POEs as it is focused more on design process and practice.

The design professions have been slower to adopt the case study method, but there are encouraging signs it is becoming more of a core teaching method in architecture, planning, ur-

Figure 4. The health benefits of community gardens has been well documented.

ban design and landscape architecture. Recently it has found its way more into environmental design education, research and publications. Many designers and design researchers now conduct or present their work in terms of "case studies." Case studies are continuing to be part of teaching and research in environmental design (Spirn 1999; Hester 1990). Presentations at American Society of Landscape Architects (ASLA), the American Institute of Architects (AIA), Environmental Design Research Association (EDRA) and the Council of Educators in Landscape Architecture (CELA) often have "case study" as their focus. One continuing limitation is that many of these cases are descriptive in nature and lack a critical or evaluative dimension.

Case studies can be utilized to develop several kinds of information for design practice. For example, they can test design assumptions against the actual built results. In addition they can inform design patterns that could or should not be used in future projects. While much of the information generated during a case study may be unique to the given project and its context, cases are useful for advancing knowledge in the profession in general. The elements that a full case study should include are: baseline information; the roles of key participants; financial aspects; process; problem definition and response; goals; program; design; site visit(s); use; maintenance and management; and perception and meaning. Additional critical dimensions to include in a case study are: scale; time; unique constraints; community and cultural impacts of the project; environmental sensitivity and impact; impact on the profession; infrastructure impacts; lessons learned and theory. In addition, it is useful to examine outside critiques, reports of the projects in the popular media, and peer reviews in the form of awards and honors. These dimensions are discussed in further detail in Table 1.

Case study analysis typically involves designing the case study, conducting the case study, analyzing the results, and disseminating the results. Case studies can be done alone or together to compare across projects (Yin, 1994). Case studies in community design can be organized around the type of project, the problem, the geographical region, or the designer. Each has its own unique purpose and benefits. Information for case studies can be gathered in a variety of ways. It is impor-

---

Abstract/Fact Sheet

Photo(s)
Project background
Project significance and impact
Lessons learned
Contacts
Keywords

Full Case Study

Project name
Location
Date designed/planned
Construction completed
Cost
Size
Community Designer(s)
Client
Consultants

Managed by
Context
Site analysis
Project background and history
Genesis of project
Design, development, participatory
　　and decision-making processes
Role of community designer(s)
Program elements
Maintenance and management
Photograph(s)
Site/Context plans to scale
User/use analysis
Peer reviews
Criticism
Significance and uniqueness of the
　　project
Limitations
General features and lessons
Future issues/plans

Bibliography of project citations/related
　　references
Web sites/links
Contacts for further information.

In-depth Analysis

Archival research (e.g., project re-
　　cords, newspaper articles, etc.)
Awards or special recognition for the
　　project
Copies of articles or reports on the
　　project
Interviews with client
Interviews with managers and mainte-
　　nance people
Interviews with users
Interviews with non-users
Longitudinal studies of the place over
　　time

Table 1. A suggested format for case studies in community design.

tant to be systematic and consistent in using these methods. Most successful case studies incorporate a variety of methods such as site visits; site analysis; historical analysis; design process analysis; behavioral analysis; interviews with designer(s), developer(s), manager(s), and public officials; interviews with users and non-users; archival material searches including project files, newspaper articles, public records; bibliographic searches; and internet searches.

CASE STUDIES FOR COMMUNITY DESIGN

At least four types of case studies are useful for community design. They include place or project specific cases, studies of community design methods, issue case studies that cut across several projects or places and case studies for teaching community design. They are discussed in more detail in Table 2.

Place-based

Most community design case studies have been developed of specific projects. For example, past cases include studies of community-based projects including parks, playgrounds, and neighborhoods. There is a need for a larger array of community design project case studies. One recent example of a place-based case study is Village Homes in Davis California, which shows how the case study method can be used to evaluate an entire community (Francis, 2003). Challenges in developing this case study included fully documenting the designers goals in the project and testing them against residents experience of living in the neighborhood. It was also difficult to fully assess the economic impacts of the project. Yet it was useful to examine why this largely successful example of neighborhood design has not been replicated elsewhere.

Method-based

A fewer number of studies have been conducted of the methods typically used in community design. For example, the workshop method is a common and even sacred method used in community based design and planning. Yet rarely has it been described or evaluated.[6] Other methods in need of case study evaluation include scored walks, mapping exercises, surveys and web-based methods. It would be especially useful to examine these in combination.

Issue-based

There are many issues that typically face community design projects. These include power relationships between participants, how projects are initiated, and the difference between local versus expert knowledge in community design. In addition, the impact of participation on project quality and participants needs to be examined in more detail. The resulting form and aesthetics of built projects also need to be studied.

Place-based

Identify types of projects to evaluate in different countries – need New urbanist projects
Public spaces in community development
Integration rather than separation of design, technology, ecology and community

Issue-based

Develop community design typologies
Test assumption that participation creates more humane environments
How does community design empower participants
Do community design projects result in distinctly different aesthetics than traditional design

Method-based

Describe and evaluate the workshop technique
Asses methods such as scored walks, surveys and interviews, etc.
How much does community design cost as compared to traditional practice

Teaching-based

Develop studio based projects that can be used in different schools
Develop both real and hypothetical teaching cases
New forms of practice including "proactive practice"

Table 2. Types of case studies needed for community design.

Figure 5. Village Homes in Davis, California has been extensively documented as a case study.

Figure 6. The workshop method is in critical need of documentation and evaluation.

Figure 8. Both large and small-scale projects need to be documented and evaluated such as the Hudson River Parkway in Manhattan. (Source: Carr, Lynch and Sandell)

Teaching-based

Community design continues to be an expanding part of environmental design education. This is evidenced by the large number of community design centers attached to schools of architecture, landscape architecture and planning. As community service continues to be a focus of public universities, engaging design faculty and students in community projects will be popular. We need to develop cases both real and hypothetical to aid in the training of community designers. These can include teaching cases that can be used in different school and locations to compare results and impacts.

Community Design Reexamined

The case study method provides an opportunity to advance the state of the art of community design. It is particularly helpful in examining practice and its impact on community and public life.

Figure 7. Children's access and use of the environment is an example of research that can benefit design practice.

Even more importantly, case studies can force a reexamination of the core assumptions and values in community design.

We also will need to find ways to build case study analysis into everyday practice. A critical mass of case studies is needed in community design. These can include cases of specific projects or places, issues that cut across places, methods commonly used in practice, and cases that can be used in teaching environmental design in undergraduate and graduate programs.

There are some challenges facing the development of future case studies in community design. Issues include who does the case study, how is feedback made to participants, and the need for redesign of projects based on case studies. A chronic problem for community designers is finding the time to organize the information for case studies. Community designers are often too busy doing it to reflect on what they do or examine the impact of their projects. Also who pays for community design studies? We need to find ways to build evaluation into the fee structure of community design projects as well as find new funding sources for preparing cases.

Case studies offer great promise for community design. They will help this realm of practice develop and mature. Community designers need to work together to define and refine the dimensions they want included in cases and use this method as a core way of working.

ENDNOTES

[1] My purpose here is not to offer a full review of the area of community design. There are several reviews that provide more complete historical (Sanoff 2000; Francis 1983) and contemporary overviews of community design (Bell 2003; Comerio 1983; Hester 1999).

[2] There are several organizations and informal networks committed to advancing research and practice in community design. These include The Planners Network, the Association for Community Design, and

the Participation Network within the Environmental Design Research Association (EDRA) (See websites at end). Reflective meetings such as these Pacific Rim meetings, and seminars at annual meetings of the AIA, CELA, ACSA, etc. are providing a useful way to examine issues across projects.

[3] The experience of Community Design Centers has been well documented (see for example Blake 2003; Cary 2000) and comprises a strong network organized by the Association of Community Design (see useful websites). Community design as a part of environmental design education has also been widely surveyed (Forsyth et. al. 2000).

[4] A group of us developed a critical framework for community participation to aid research and evaluation (Cashdan et. al. 1979). Dimensions we identified as critical included genesis of project, role of the professional, and the quality of built results. It is useful to identify on a continuing basis the core criteria and questions we use to assess community design.

[5] Some suggest that community designers may have been too critical in their work at the risk of not being forceful or proactive enough about advancing their own design solutions (Hester 1999; Francis 1999).

[6] An exception is the work of planner Daniel Iacofano who has provided an extensive description of how he uses meetings and workshops to facilitate participation in a wide range of projects (Iacofano 2003).

REFERENCES

Barnes, L. B., C. R. Christensen, and A. J. Hansen, (Eds.) 1994. Teaching and the Case Method. Boston, MA: Harvard Business School Press.

Bell, B. (Ed.). 2003. Good Deeds, Good Design: Community Service Through Architecture. New York: Princeton Architectural Press.

Blake, S. 2003. Community Design Centers: An Alternative Practice. in D. Watson, (Ed.), Time-Saver Standards for Urban Design. New York: McGraw-Hill.

Brill, M. 2002. Mistaking Public Life for Community Life. Places.

Calthorpe, P. 1993. The Next American Metropolis: Ecology, Community and the American Dream, New York: Princeton Architectural Press.

Calthorpe P. & W. Fulton. 2001. The Regional City. Washington, DC: Island Press.

Carr, S., M. Francis, L. Rivlin and A. Stone. 1992. Public Space. New York: Cambridge University Press.

Cary J. (Ed.). 2000. The ACSA Sourcebook of Community Design Programs at Schools of Architecture in North America. Washington, D.C.: Association of Collegiate Schools of Architecture Press.

Cashdan, L., B. Fahle, M. Francis, S. Schwartz and P. Stein. 1979. A Critical Framework for Participatory Approaches to Environmental Change. In M. Francis (Ed.), Participatory Planning and Neighborhood Control. New York: Center for Human Environments, CUNY.

Comerio, M. C. 1984. Community Design: Idealism and Entrepreneurship. Journal of Architecture and Planning Research. 1, 1: 227-43.

Dean, A. O. 2002. Rural Studio: Samuel Mockbee and the Architecture of Decency. New York: Princeton Architectural Press.

Feldman, R. M. 2003. Activist Practice. pp. 109 - 114. in B. Bell, (Ed.). Good Deeds, Good Design: Community Service Through Architecture. New York: Princeton Architectural Press.

Forester, J. 1999. The Deliberative Practitioner. Encouraging Participatory Planning Processes. Cambridge: MIT Press.

Forsyth, A., H. Lu, and P. McGirr. 2000. Service Learning in an Urban Context: Implications for Planning and Design Education. Journal of Architectural and Planning Research. 17, 3: 236 -259.

Francis, M. 1983. Community Design. Journal of Architectural Education. 3: 14-9.

Francis, M. 1999. Proactive Practice: Visionary Thought and Participatory Action in Environmental Design. Places. 12, 1: 60 – 68.

Francis, M. 2001. A Case Study Method for Landscape Architecture. Landscape Journal. 19, 2: 15-29.

Francis, M. 2003. Village Homes: A Community by Design. Landscape Architecture Foundation Case Studies Series in Land and Community Design. Washington DC: Island Press. 2003.

Francis, M. and R. Lorenzo. 2002. Seven Realms of Children's Participation. Journal of Environmental Psychology. 22: 157-169.

Frank, L. D., P. O. Engelke, and T. L. Schmid. 2003. Health and Community Design: The Impact of the Built Environment on Physical Activity. Washington, DC: Island Press.

Garvin, D. A. 2003. Making the Case: Professional Education for the World of Practice. Harvard Magazine. 106, 1: 56 –65.

Hart, R. 1997. Children's Participation: The Theory and Practice of Involving Young Citizens in Community Development and Environmental Care. London: Earthscan Publications Ltd.

Hayden, D. 1995. The Power of Place: Urban Landscapes as Public History. Cambridge: MIT Press.

Hester Jr., R. T. 1983. Process Can Be Style: Participation and Conservation in Landscape Architecture. Landscape Architecture. May.

Hester, R. T. 1990. Community Design Primer. Mendocino, CA: Ridge Times Press.

Hester, R. T. 1999. Participation with a View. Places. 12, 1.

Hou, J. and M. Rios. 2003. Community-Driven Placemaking: The Social Practice of Participatory Design and the making of Union Point Park. Journal of Architectural Education, 57: 1.

Iacofano, D. 2003. Meeting of the Minds: A Guide to Successful Meeting Facilitation. Berkeley: MIG.

Jackson, R. J. and C. Kochtitzky. 2001. Creating A Healthy Environment: The Impact of the Built Environment on Public Health. Atlanta: Centers for Disease Control and Prevention.

Kelbaugh, D. 1997. Common Place: Toward Neighborhood and Regional Design. Seattle: University of Washington Press.

Lundeberg, M. A., B. B. Levin and H. L. Harrington (Eds.) 2000. Who Learns What from Cases and How?: The Research Base for Teaching and Learning With Cases. Mahwah, NJ: Lawrence Erlbaum.

MacCannell, D. 1993. Empty Meeting Grounds. New York: Routledge.

Oldenburg, R. 1989. The Great Good Place. New York: Paragon.

Owens, P. E. 1988. Natural Landscapes, Gathering Places, and Prospect Refuges: Characteristics of Outdoor Places Valued by Teens. Children's Environments Quarterly. 5, 2: 17-24.

Putnam, R. D. 2001. Bowling Alone: The Collapse and Revival of American Community. New York: Simon and Schuster.

Sanoff, H. 2000. Community Participation Methods in Design and Planning. New York: Wiley.

Schon, D. 1983. The Reflective Practitioner. New York: Basic Books.

Spirn, A. 1999. The Language of Landscape. New Haven: Yale University Press.

Stake, R. E. 1995. The Art of Case Study Research. Thousand Oaks, CA: Sage.

Thayer, R. 2003. LifePlace. Berkeley: University of California Press.

Torres, G. W., M. K. Kraft and E. Henry. 2001. Active Living Through Community Design. Princeton, NJ: Robert Wood Johnson Foundation.

Ulrich, R. S. 1993. Biophilia, Biophobia, and the Natural Landscape. pp. 73-137 in S. R. Kellert & E. O. Wilson (Eds.). The Biophilia Hypothesis. Washington: Island Press.

Yin, R. F. 1993. Applications of Case Study Research. Thousand Oaks, CA: Sage.

Yin, R. F. 1994. Case Study Research: Design and Methods. Thousand Oaks, CA: Sage.

Zeisel, J. 1990. Inquiry by Design. New York: Cambridge University Press.

Some Useful Websites

American Planning Association: www.planning.org

American Society of Landscape Architects: www.asla.org

Association of Community Design: www.communitydesign.org

Children's Environments Research Group, CUNY: http://web.gsuc.cuny.edu/che

Children and Youth Environments: www.colorado.edu/journals/cye

Congress for New Urbanism: www.cnu.org

Environmental Design Research Association: www.edra.org

Landscape Architecture Foundation: www.lafoundation.org

Local Government Commission: www.lgc.org

Planners Network: www.plannersnetwork.org

Project for Public Spaces: www.pps.org

The Rural Studio: www. ruralstudio.com

Trust for Public Land: www.tpl.org

Urban Land Institute: www.uli.org

Urban Parks Institute: www.pps.org/urbanparks

WHERE DO WE GO FROM HERE?
An Evaluative Framework for Community-based Design[1]

Michael Rios

ABSTRACT

Initiated in the late 1960s as an alternative to the traditional practice of architecture and planning, community design can be defined by a commitment to building local capacity and providing technical assistance to low- and moderate-income communities through participatory means. While community design, built on a rich history of participatory practice is growing, substantive dialogue and reflection about its contribution to community development is lacking. This paper examines the efforts of university-based programs and presents an evaluative framework for community-based projects as a starting point. Treating universities and communities as coequals, a framework is proposed to measure the impacts of community-based projects for each.

INTRODUCTION

Community-based design is taught in many schools and practiced by numerous organizations and individuals in the public and private sector alike.[2] A 1997 survey conducted by the Association of Collegiate Schools of Architecture identified over one hundred community design programs, centers, and nonprofit organizations in the United States and Canada (ACSA, 2000). Of the 123 architecture schools that offer a professional degree in North America, over 30 percent run university-based community design and research centers. Technical assistance, community outreach, and advocacy characterize much community design work emanating from university campuses. Despite these efforts, little has been done to assess this work as a whole. As an initial response, this paper presents an evaluative framework for community-based projects.[3] Measurements of organizational capacity building, policy generation and implementation, and the quality of service and input through community involvement are some examples. The proposed framework suggests that methods such as participatory action research hold promise in meeting the goals of both communities and universities.

Practitioners of community design identify and solve particular environmental problems where the problem is some combination of social, economic, or political in nature (Comerio, 1984). As such, community design is a distinctive form of professional practice—linking issues of social equity, the environment, and economic advancement. More than eighty community design and research centers are currently in operation nationwide, surpassing the number of centers in the early seventies that reached a peak with sixty centers.[4] Unlike the community design activity that grew out of the social activism of the sixties or the economic pragmatism that followed, today's centers are more diverse as a whole.[5]

One core value of community design is participatory decision-making. The participation of locally-vested groups and individuals is understood as a critical component in building capacity for community decision making, implementation of local programs, and successful outcomes on the ground.[6] Participatory decision making can include conducting community charrettes, utilizing user-friendly models and technology such as GIS and web-based delivery systems, inviting suggestions from the community throughout the design and development process, and offering technical assistance as a way to empower residents.

Changes in federal policy, economic restructuring, the emergence of sustainability as a design paradigm, and a move toward integrating public service into design curricula are several of the reasons academics and practitioners give for contemporary attention to community design. A review of recent surveys echoes these findings.[7] Regardless of the underlying reasons for an increased focus on community design, the number of university-based programs suggests a desire and need for this type of activity at institutions of higher education. To date, evaluation of community-based design has been conducted in relationship to mainstream architectural practice, without consideration of its own body of work.[8] Although community-based design has been at the leading edge of integrating teaching with community outreach for years, as a whole it has contributed little to the growing literature on service learning and public scholarship.[9]

If the community-based design movement is to grow, it will be critical for its proponents to share knowledge that can help guide design and planning education. The dissemination of knowledge and promising practices, opportunities for education and training, assessment of the movement's long-term impacts, and the creation of commonly accepted standards are urgently needed. The recent focus on university-based activity raises several questions related to the broader field of community-based design:

- What goals do community-based projects serve for institutions of higher education?

- What contributions to community development are being made by university-based programs and initiatives?

- How is quality defined for community-based design education and practice?

In the following sections, I argue the need for evaluating community-based design. After giving a brief overview of approaches to assessment in community settings, I present a working framework for evaluation.[10] I conclude with several challenges to university-based programs vis-à-vis communities and the factors affecting the quality of evaluation.

WHY EVALUATE?

Evaluation is a key element of successful community development. In this context, evaluation is used to measure neighborhood impacts, and to assess the process of activities and the role of intermediaries and local stakeholders.[11] Increasingly common is the use of indicators that measure the progress of project-defined goals that link benchmarks to desired outcomes.[12] Most indicator-driven projects use data and information readily accessible to the public, but can also include volunteer programs to generate data and measure progress as a form of citizen science. Community indicator projects range in scale from metropolitan regions to cities and municipalities.[13] Indicators that focus on community development are typically practice-based and include identifiable categories and themes such as housing, economic development, and community building.[14]

Most efforts to assess and document design projects utilize the case study method.[15] This method is a descriptive approach to evaluation initiated after project implementation, which makes concrete what are often generalizations and anecdotal information about projects and processes (Yin, 1994). Used as a staple of teaching in business and law schools, the case study method can provide useful information to practitioners looking for project precedents and can be a form of continuing education. Although it is beneficial in providing an in-depth analysis of a particular project, there are several limitations to the case study method. One difficulty is comparing across cases, especially when different types of information are being gathered. Evaluating projects comparatively is a critical first step before knowledge be can generated more systematically.

One alternative to the case study method that holds promise in evaluating community-based design is participatory action research (PAR). PAR has emerged as an important approach to citizen participation in guiding and, upon completion, evaluating community projects. As an alternative to the scientific method of research, PAR is "a way of creating knowledge that involves learning from investigation and applying what is learned to collective problems through social action" (Park, 1992: 30). Efforts in PAR have focused on community development, resource management, organizational decision-making, and community health, among other aspects.[16] Within schools of architecture, PAR offers the possibility of combining sound methods with the knowledge and scholarship of practice. As a teaching and community outreach approach, PAR also offers the potential to improve current models of service learning that emphasize pre-professional assistance and pro bono services at the expense of research.

If they are assessed using a PAR approach, the results of community-based projects can also serve the interests of community groups as a tool to advocate for political resources (Nyden and Wiewel, 1992). This is a vital area of assistance given that many community groups turn to university-based design programs due to the lack of capacity and resources of grassroots organizations. Many university-based centers get involved in projects at the initial conceptual stages of a project and help groups frame issues and problems, taking into account complex social, economic, and political considerations. Project designs, reports, maps, and other technical documents can serve a political purpose to highlight resource disparities, articulate environmental concerns such as the prevalence of toxic sites in low-income neighborhoods, or help to organize a community in support of neighborhood improvements such as public parks and recreational facilities.[17] As such, PAR provides a means to measure results against early-defined goals and to identify critical elements within a project to help further a community's agenda or desired outcome. In addition to measuring tangible benefits as a result of university involvement, a PAR approach can also "put less powerful groups at the center of the knowledge creation process (and) move people and their daily experiences of struggle and survival from the margins of epistemology to the center" (Hall, 1992: 15-16). Shifting from expert to local knowledge creates the possibility for new sites of inquiry and discovery outside traditional academic settings—for both faculty and students alike. However, the collective benefits of work accrued by service learning projects can only be realized if knowledge is shared between schools *and* communities.

An important distinction between the case study method and PAR is that the latter includes a theory- or goal-driven form of evaluation (Chen and Rossi, 1992). While the method-driven evaluation of the case study approach follow a series of steps that are designed according to a predetermined set of criteria, theory-driven evaluation begins with a working hypothesis or goal established at a project's inception. It is important to note that the case study method does not assume a given outcome, or explicitly state an objective in evaluating the results of a project. For theory-driven evaluation such as PAR, hypotheses can be generated from abstract constructs, as well as hunches, to determine what is to be collected and what is to be measured to identify emergent patterns that match hypotheses. This approach allows tracking of the actual experience over time against the theory and allows for the testing of alternative

hypotheses.[18] The decision to use theory-driven instead of method-driven evaluation in community design projects depends on the overall goal of evaluation—what the evaluation is to be used for, its audience, and potential benefits derived from the assessment

Take, for example, the creation of a community facility on the site of an abandoned, trash-strewn lot. One theory that underlies this change could assert that as a result of the intervention, the surrounding physical environment would begin to improve. Thus, one would develop a series of benchmarks to measure this hypothesis, both prior to and after completion of the project. One relevant benefit of this form of evaluation is that it provides a framework from which to plan a project from conception through implementation. Also, evaluation. could be used as an argument for procuring resources from city agencies if crime rates dropped in the surrounding area, or as a strategy to attract private investment if a heightened sense of pride and ownership among local residents resulted in property improvements adjacent to the community facility site.

A WORKING FRAMEWORK FOR EVALUATION

The discussion thus far has focused on evaluation used outside the field of community-based design, and how the adoption of such methods could be beneficial to community-based design at universities. Given the emphasis on outreach by many university-based programs, one of the challenges in the future will be the ability to integrate service learning activities into the language of university research. A review of university-based programs conducted by the Hamer Center for Community Design at Penn State identified only seven of forty-one programs, or 17 percent, that evaluate projects (2003). However, new paradigms in community-based research that emphasize mutual engagement and collaboration, such as PAR, suggest an unprecedented opportunity to do so without compromising core values of community service and advocacy, while at the same time meeting pedagogical goals and curricular objectives. The following section presents a framework to evaluate the work of community-based design that proposes a twofold approach to assessment: 1) *centrifugal knowledge*: activities aimed toward the external goals of community groups and related community development intermediaries; and 2) *centripetal knowledge:* activities that are directed toward the internal goals particular to university-based community design programs.[19] For each, questions are posed as guides to evaluating community-based design projects and programs.

Centrifugal Knowledge

Given their historical roots in the civil rights movement in the sixties, many community-based projects have focused on the needs of low-income neighborhoods and disadvantaged populations. Although increasingly diverse in its focus, the emphasis of this work is to serve community organizations and anticipated users of designed environments. These projects range significantly– from design-build affordable housing to streetscape designs, neighborhood plans to model code policy tools– and include both short- and long-term relationships with government agencies, non-profit organizations, and community groups. Within this context, projects aim to support community

AN EPISTEMOLOGY OF COMMUNITY DESIGN	
CENTRIFUGAL KNOWLEDGE *aimed toward the external goals of community groups and related community development intermediaries*	**CENTRIPETAL KNOWLEDGE** *directed toward the internal goals particular to community design practitioners, educators, and students*
1) technical assistance Whose interests have been served and with what results?	1) community involvement To what degree did citizens participate in a community design project, and what were the significant outcomes of their participation?
2) capacity building How do capacity building efforts further the mission and goals of community groups and individuals?	2) service learning How does service learning in community-based design education benefit students as future practitioners?
3) policy support To what degree did a community-based project shape regulatory or policy change?	3) promising practices What are the standards used in community-based design projects and how do those standards compare with those established by the profession?

Figure 1. Source: Rios, Michael (forthcoming). "Where Do We Go From Here? An Evaluative Framework for Community-based Design" in Service Learning in Architecture and Planning, The American Association for Higher Education.

goals and priorities, and can be part of a triad focused on *technical assistance, capacity building*, and *policy support.*[20]

Technical assistance often takes the form of plans, drawings, studies, and reports that enable community organizations to carry out their mission and/or objective. Often, activities will be concentrated at the beginning stages of a project to help gather information, frame issues, and provide documentation of the results. As such, technical assistance helps community groups to make key decisions and identify resources for implementation, and serves as a mechanism for developing consensus and support for a project. Thus, a key question is: *Whose interests have been served and with what results?*

Activities conducted by faculty and students fulfill an important educational and advisory role in helping groups develop their own capacity. Grant writing, development of budgets, zoning and data analyses, the use of technology, and meeting facilitation are some of the skills that can be shared with community groups. Several outcomes that measure *capacity building* include the strengthening of local institutions, increasing the ability of organizations and individuals to identify and secure resources for staffing or project implementation, gaining legal nonprofit status, or implementing a successful community-driven project or campaign. A challenge is to identify gaps and weaknesses in organizational capacity and utilize projects as vehicles to strengthen these areas. Thus, a key question is: *How do capacity building efforts further the mission and goals of community groups?*

Projects and studies carried out by service learning activities often include recommendations that lead to changes in policy and regulation. Policy support varies significantly and can also include recommendations for changes to city services, code enforcement, and other aspects of community regulation. A goal of *policy support* might be to educate community members, elected officials, and municipal staff about resource disparities, discrepancies in existing regulations, problems with procedural matters, or other policy-related issues. Outcomes to evaluate the role of policy support in community design activities could include changes to existing policies, reallocation of municipal resources, or the creation of new tools that address regulatory barriers. Thus, a key question is: *To what degree did a community-based project shape regulatory or policy change?*

Centripetal Knowledge

In addition to furthering the goals of community groups, an additional objective of university-based projects and programs is to improve the pedagogy and practice of design. In this way, community engagement allows students to utilize feedback to make better design choices, leading to decisions that are responsive to both the physical and social context of a given project. Community engagement also provides a space for experimentation leading to promising practices that emphasize mutual engagement between universities and communities. Additionally, service learning experiences conducted through mechanisms such as community design centers can also help advance research unachievable in professional and classroom settings. For example, the application of on-site building methods related to straw bale and rammed earth allow for problem-based learning while providing a vehicle for research in community settings. As such, it is valuable to evaluate what is being created and tested, and how service learning experiences enhance pedagogy, practice, and research collectively. Assessing *community involvement, service learning,* and the identification of *promising practices* are three considerations that can be directed to the internal goals of community design projects and programs.

One of the primary components of any community design process is public involvement. Designers often solicit input, ideas, and criticism from neighborhood groups, municipal officials, and local residents in order to establish project goals and to guide the refinement of specific design proposals. Given the time and energy devoted to service learning activities to ensure adequate citizen participation, faculty and students should assess how successful they are in engaging communities in their work. Resident participation becomes a crucial element through various phases of the process and can contribute to the success of a project. One goal that bridges the external goals of community groups and those of professional practice is *community involvement.* Outcomes in the assessment of participatory projects could include the level of public involvement from project inception through implementation, increased levels of trust and volunteerism, skills development, or community awareness of a given issue. Thus, a key question is: *To what degree did citizens participate in a community design project, and what were the significant outcomes of their participation?*

As an increasingly critical element of university curricula, *service learning* has been identified as an important vehicle in creating a scholarship of engagement (Boyer and Mitgang, 1996). The service learning model of community design education teaches professionals the civic relevance of design, facilitates interdisciplinary learning and collective problem solving, fosters professional ethics, and introduces diversity issues into practice. Service learning is also an important vehicle for research and outreach to communities that lack resources. Assessing university-based service learning could include measures that benchmark civic and professional development, volunteerism, and social responsibility. Thus, a key question is: *How does service learning in community-based design education benefit students as future practitioners?*

The quality of community-based design can be measured by the number of awards and commendations received, as well as other forms of recognition such as publishing in peer-reviewed journals and securing external funding for community-based projects. However, the impact of community design can also be measured in terms of new methods and techniques that may be developed in the course of design, and the quality of completed projects. Outcomes in the assessment of *promising practices* could include the adoption of new methods, the durability and usability of built works and community environments, or the long-term sustainability of proposed strategies. Thus, a key question is: *What are the standards used in community-based design projects and how do those standards compare with those established by the profession?*

CONCLUSION

The purpose in proposing this framework is not to prescribe particular forms of measurement, but rather to define a starting point—from which architecture schools, community-based programs, faculty, and students alike can begin to develop goals to assess the outcomes of projects and related activities in community settings. Nor does the proposed framework suggest an exhaustive list of criteria. To do so would not acknowledge the diversity within the field and the varying sizes and organizational capacities among curricular programs and university-based design centers. Given the absence of an alternative, the evaluative framework suggested here should be viewed as an initial sketch open to interpretation, critique, and further development. It is also an invitation to design faculty to be more reflective and critical of their work in communities, and to help contribute to the growing body of knowledge in community-based design.

While what is suggested here may appear to be straightforward, there are several challenges to this form of evaluation, as there are when conducting any community-based project. Although community-based design projects are growing in schools of architecture, these activities are undertaken for different reasons and reflect different interests and values among faculty. For some they are to provide an enriching learning experience for students. For others community projects are either an outlet for alternative practice or a form of advocacy. Regardless of the motivation for creating such projects, it appears that service learning presents challenges for faculty, students, and communities when it comes to time commitments and meeting expectations for the overall quality of work.[21] It is also important to note that although university-based programs and projects may appear in line with work conducted by nonprofit community-based organizations, the organizational goals and priorities of nonprofits are often different than the institutional goals of universities and colleges. Faculty should be cognizant about the limitations of institutions of higher education especially when it comes to resource and liability issues, while community organizations should understand that the primary function of universities and colleges is education, not solely service delivery.[22]

Beyond these general observations, there are several specific challenges to academic programs conducting evaluation of community-based projects. Conflicting goals between researchers and practitioners and methodological issues such as the objectivity of the evaluator when the same person is a participant need to be considered, as do questions of context and scale. For example, how is the community defined and what is the scale for assessment (e.g., building, block, neighborhood, etc.)? Additionally, evaluation is often shaped by external factors, such as public agencies and foundations that fund community-based projects.[23] How do these entities influence the goals of a project and the types of assessment to be conducted? Lastly, the issue of time is critical. Consideration for differences between 'university time' and 'community time' needs to be accounted for in the planning and implementation of curriculum-based projects. Evaluating both effective process and project outcomes can ensure greater success in community-based design projects.

In sum, evaluation of community-based projects should not be entered into lightly and takes a considerable amount of effort on the part of individual faculty members. However, the presence of programs at universities and colleges suggests that community-based design is here to stay. In order to deepen the knowledge within the field, community-based projects need to be viewed as an integral part of scholarship in teaching, research, and service. More reflective practice is needed in service learning—to illuminate the actions and activities of practitioners, both academic and professional. In the words of the late educator, Donald Schön, we must "discover what (we) already understand and know how to do" (Schön, 1991: 5). The changing landscape of our cities, towns, and neighborhoods provide an unprecedented opportunity for faculty and students alike to engage in issues of public significance through service learning. Now is the time.

ENDNOTES

[1] An earlier version of this manuscript will be published in *Service Learning in Architecture and Planning* by The American Association for Higher Education.

[2] In this paper, community design and community-based design are used interchangeably. The emphasis here is working with communities in local contexts. This is not to be confused with the term used to describe broad land use and settlement patterns.

[3] I would like to thank Sam Dennis for his thoughtful comments on an earlier version of this manuscript, in particular for helping me to refine the evaluation framework proposed in this paper.

[4] See Pearson 2002; Curry 1998.

[5] A 2003 survey of university-based community design conducted by the Penn State Hamer Center for Community Design Assistance categorized over forty programs by service area, type of mission, projects and services, and funding support.

[6] See Kretzman and McKnight 1993.

[7] See Gabler 1999; ACSA 2000; Hamer Center 2003.

[8] Comerio 1984 was the first published article that alluded to "defining success" in community design. However, the central focus of the paper was to evaluate community design vis-à-vis traditional professional practice.

[9] However, see Forsyth, Lu, and McGirr 2000.

[10] This framework grew out of a roundtable discussion at the Association for Community Design's annual conference held in Indianapolis in June, 2000; and further developed during a 2003 graduate seminar taught with Dr. Ian Baptiste, PSU Associate Professor of Adult Education.

[11] See Hyland 2000.

[12] For a definition of sustainable community indicators, see, for example, Kline 1995.

[13] 2000 review of community indicator initiatives conducted by the PSU Hamer Center for Community Design Assistance identified twenty projects nationwide.

[14] See Development Leadership Network 2001.

[15] See, for instance, Francis 1999.

[16] See Reardon, Welsh, Kreiswirth, and Forester 1993; Chambers 1993; Whyte, Greenwood, and Lazes 1989; Wallerstein, Sanchez-Merki, and Dow 1997.

[17] For example, see Hou and Rios 2003.

[18] Presentation by Scott Hebert, Abt Associates, *Structuring Case Studies and Other Forms of Self-Evaluation: Recommendations Regarding a Theory-Driven Approach.* New York: Pratt Institute Center for Community and Environmental Development, March 2, 2001.

[19] This is not to suggest that the goals are mutually exclusive, but rather they reinforce each other to meet the needs of both communities and universities.

[20] This triad was developed by the Pratt Institute for Community and Environmental Development, one of the oldest community design centers in the country. See also Blake 2003.

[21] For a full discussion of challenges of service learning in planning and design education, see Forsyth, Lu, and McGirr 2000.

[22] There has been an increase in the reliance on universities to provide services for low-income communities. Although federal programs such as HUD's Community Outreach Partnership Center provide an avenue for community engagement and service learning, universities run the risk of creating dependency when they replace programs and forms of assistance once provided by government.

[23] See Jenkins and Halcli, 1999.

REFERENCES

ACSA Sourcebook of Community Design Programs. 2000. Washington, D.C.: ACSA Press.

Blake, S. 2003. Community Design Centers: An Alternative Practice. In Time-Saver Standards for Urban Design, 4.11-1 – 4.11-8. New York: McGraw-Hill.

Boyer, E., and Mitgang, L. D. 1996. Building Community: A New Future for Architecture Education and Practice: A Special Report.

Princeton, NJ: Carnegie Foundation for the Advancement of Teaching.

Chambers, R. 1993. Participatory Rural Appraisal (PRA): Challenges, Potentials and Paradigms. World Development 22: 10.

Chen, H-T., and Rossi P. H. 1992. Using Theory to Improve Program and Policy Evaluations. New York: Greenwood Press.

Comerio, M. 1984. Community Design: Idealism and Entrepreneurship. The Journal of Architecture and Planning Research 1: 227–243.

Curry, R. 1998. History of the Association for Community Design. New York: Pratt Institute Center for Community and Environmental Development.

Development Leadership Network. 2001. Success Measures Project. Available on DLN's website at <http://www.developmentleadership.net/smp/index.htm>. Accessed June 11, 2001.

Gabler, M. 1999. Survey of National Community Design Centers. University Park: PSU School of Architecture and Landscape Architecture. April.

Forsyth, A., Lu, H. and McGirr, P. 2000. Service Learning in an Urban Context: Implications for Planning and Design Education. Journal of Architectural and Planning Research 17(3): 236–259.

Francis, M. 1999. A Case Study Method for Landscape Architecture. Washington, D.C.: Landscape Architecture Foundation. September.

Hall, B. L. 1992. From Margins to Center? The Development and Purpose of Participatory Research. The American Sociologist volume 23: 15–28.

Hamer Center for Community Design Assistance. 2003. Survey of University-Based Community Design. University Park: PSU School of Architecture and Landscape Architecture.

Hou, J. and Rios, M. 2003. Community-Driven Place Making: The Social Practice of Participatory Design in the Making of Union Point Park. Journal of Architectural Education 57(1): 19–27.

Hyland, S. E. 2000. Issues in Evaluating Neighborhood Change: Economic and Community Building Indicators. Cityscape: A Journal of Policy Development and Research 5: 209–219.

Jenkins, J. C. and Halcli, A. 1999. Grassrooting the System? The Development and Impact of Social Movement Philanthropy, 1953–1990. In Philanthropic Foundations, edited by Ellen Condliffe Lagemann, pp. 229-256. Bloomington and Indianapolis: Indiana University Press.

Kline, E. 1995. Sustainable Community Indicators. Medford, MA: Tufts University Press.

Kretzman, J. P., and McKnight, J. L. 1993. Building Communities from the Inside Out: A Path toward Finding and Mobilizing a Community's Assets. Evanston, IL: The Asset-Based Community Development Institute, Institute for Policy Research, Northwestern University.

Nyden, P., and Wiewel, W. 1992. Collaborative Research: Harnessing the Tensions between Researcher and Practitioner. The American Sociologist volume 23: 43–55.

Park, P. 1992. The Discovery of Participatory Research as a New Scientific Paradigm: Personal and Intellectual Accounts. The American Sociologist 23(4): 29–42.

Pearson, J. 2002. University-Community Partnerships: Innovations in Practice. Washington, D.C.: National Endowment for the Arts.

Reardon, K., Welsh, J., Kreiswirth, B. and Forester, J. 1993. Participatory Action Research from the Inside: Community Development in East St. Louis. The American Sociologist 24(1): 69–106.

Schön, D. 1991. The Reflective Turn: Case Studies In and On Educational Practice. New York and London: Teachers College Press: 1–12.

Wallerstein, N., Sanchez-Merki V. and Dow, L. 1997. Freirian Praxis in Health Education and Community Organizing. In Community Organizing and Community Building for Health, edited by Meredith Minkler. New Brunswick, NJ: Rutgers University Press: 195–211.

Whyte, W. F., Greenwood, D. J. and Lazes, P. 1989. Participatory Action Research: Through Practice to Science in Social Research. American Behavioral Scientist 32(5): 513–551.

Yin, R. 1994. Case Study Research: Design and Methods. Thousand Oaks, CA: Sage Publications.

The Effects of Workshops to Promote Revitalization of an Urban Area After the Great Hanshin Awaji Earthquake

Mayumi Hayashi

Hyogo Prefecture
Takarazuka City
Yamamoto
District

Figure 1. Map of Japan and the Yamamoto district of Takarazuka.

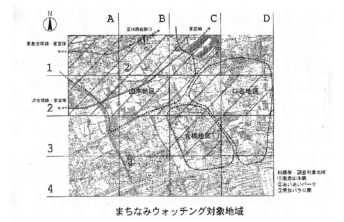

Figure 2. Division of Yamamoto District for community observation workshop.

ABSTRACT

The Yamamoto District, a part of Takarazuka City, is a residential area that is famous for being one of the three big horticultural production areas of Japan. After the Great Hanshin Awaji Earthquake devastated this area, however, reconstruction of town houses, promotion of the horticultural industry and improvement of the environment have been serious issues. In this research, I investigated the effects of workshops held from 2000 on for the improvement of the environment of this area. I investigated the process of the workshops and examined the opinions of the participants to study group characteristics, expectations about participation, and evaluation of the workshop results. I found that expectations about large-scale issues were greater than those for specific issues, but that participants took greater concern with the programs to make specific improvements and evaluated them more highly. Furthermore, communication and understanding were increased as a result of the programs. I also examined the results of citizen efforts and analyzed the connection between citizen organizations and the management of green spaces. From this study, I gained new understanding about the relationships between citizen organizations and the forms of participation in urban regeneration.

INTRODUCTION: RESEARCH BACKGROUND

Since the reconstruction after the Great Hanshin Awaji Earthquake of 1995, the use of various consensus-based methods for the design and planning of parks and public facilities created the foundation for participatory community design in Hyogo Prefecture. One of the methods frequently used in recent years to achieve consensus among citizen participants in the field of community design is the workshop. This method encourages the participation of citizens in making plans for new construction and policies and other activities that had been conducted mainly by government officials and professionals in the past. Workshops allow citizens, government officials, and professionals to discuss issues and work together on an equal level.

Prior research and the relevance of this research

Workshops have been used to decide goals for many projects related to landscape architecture and environmental improvement, including park planning, community mapping, consensus building for landscape plans and, in particular, increasing community greenery. Chiba, et al (2003) have evaluated the planning stages of participatory workshops. They conclude that planning through workshops has an influence on the management and the maintenance of parks afterwards. Sakano et al (2000) have evaluated program designs and the effects of workshops on participants, but this type of research is still lacking. Furthermore, most workshops have been conducted by government officials who guide the participants in programs based on goals for various themes that the officials have decided in advance.

No research has been done previously about workshops in which the participants first decided the issues themselves, implemented their own action programs, and finally evaluated the results. In other words, in Japan at least, there has been no research on the process and effects of this kind of workshop.

I examined several such workshops in which the participants chose themes and made appropriate action plans by themselves. I also consider how local citizens can work together with government bodies to plan and take action more effectively to achieve better urban landscapes of their own devising.

METHODS AND RESULTS

This research proceeded as follows. First, I invited participants to a variety of workshops in which they examined community issues and proposed solutions. After that, we summarized the issues and examined their shared perceptions of them. Following this, we implemented action plans based on the consensus among participants about proposed solutions. Then, I examined the effectiveness of the workshops through analysis of questionnaires about the series of activities, while considering such factors as the passage of time since the implementation of the action plans. From this analysis, I also considered possibilities for more effective workshop program design. At the same time, I examined the roles and responsibilities of the workshop participants. Finally, using these results, I analyzed the effectiveness of the program for the workshop process and developed some possibilities for the future.

Identification of issues through workshops

The Yamamoto district of Takarazuka (Figures 1 and 2) has been famous for its horticultural industry since the Muromachi Era (1392-1573), the Japanese medieval period (Takarazuka City, March 2001). In recent years, this area has developed as a residential area for commuters who work in Osaka, creating a mixture of residential and agricultural uses. At present, many horticultural nurseries have been legally designated as Productive Green Lands in order to preserve these important green spaces within the city. However, after suffering heavy damage in the Great Hanshin Awaji Earthquake in 1995, much small-scale housing development, including individual residences and condominiums, has started to appear among the nurseries, putting stress on the quality of the local environment. One of the reasons for environmental quality decline is that the horticultural industry has stagnated, making maintenance of nurseries difficult. A foundation to promote the horticulture industry, including the 1.2-hectare Aiai Park and the Takarazuka Horticulture Promotion Center were opened in Yamamoto in April 2000 with city and regional financial support.

As my goal was to help improve the local environment, for this research I used Aiai Park as the focal point for the workshops. My goals for holding the workshops included, 1) improvement of the local environment, 2) activation of the community, and 3) promotion of the traditional horticultural industries of the area.

Figure 3 shows the main workshops conducted between 2000 and 2002. In the first year, the focus was on identifying local issues and clarifying the possible ways to respond to them. In this way, I sought to develop shared understanding of the issues among the participants. One way this was done was by having the workshop members conduct observations of the community.[1] The community was divided into 8 main areas and groups inspected each of these for about an hour. Within each area, they identified, good points (attractions), problem points (issues), and future prospects (proposed reforms for issues) and marked them on maps (Takarazuka City, March 2001), sometimes with photos and illustrations. At the same time that this work was undertaken, we attempted to develop consensus about the issues. Next, action plans were developed. Figure 4 shows, as an example, key words that were identified in the first workshop.

We used the KJ Method to organize the keywords and prospects identified in the first three workshops. Figure 5 shows the action plans we developed (Hayashi, 2003). We organized the issues into long-term, medium-term, and short-term categories. Most of the long-term issues were government-level issues requiring urban planning projects and infrastructure improvements. Medium-term issues included those related to the nursery industry, community development, the neighborhood environment and other local level issues. Short-term issues were mostly related to the immediate

Year	Date	Contents	
2000	June 6	1st workshop	Town observation 1
	July 22	2nd workshop	Town observation 2 Proposals for improvement
	Nov.11	3rd workshop	Town observation 3 Planning for the action programs
2001	Jan. 29	4th workshop	Planning for the park of Yamamoto Naka 2 Chome
	May 9	5th workshop	Planting the flowerbeds of Shinike Park, Yurinoki Road and other activities
	Sep. 1	6th workshop	Walking map and open gardens
	Sep. 22	Planting activity for the Yurinoki road	
	Oct. 8	Open garden	
	Dec. 8	7th workshop	Planting flower bed s of Shinike Park
	Dec.16	Open garden	
2002	Mar. 16	8th workshop	About the activities and open garden
	Apr. 21 - June 2	Takarazuka open garden festival	
	May 7	Party for garden owners	
	Sep. 24	Meeting for core members	
	Oct. 5, 6	Open garden meeting for participants from throughout the country (Awaji Landscape and Planning Horticultural Academy)	
	May 27, 28	Gardening summit	
	June 24	Party for garden owners	
	Nov. 24	9th workshop	Planning for Tenjin River
	Feb. - Mar.	Association for open gardens	

Figure 3. Sequence of workshops and action programs.

About this town . . .

	Good points and likable points	Issues	Hopes and ideals
A-1	Beautiful landscapes, including, nursery gardens and productive green spaces View of the Rokko Mountains Takarazuka cherry-lined streets Yakushido Temple Rare stone paving First American Dogwood trees in Japan	Burden on nurseries and others to maintain scenic beauty Uncared for Jizo Bodhisattva statues Use of signage along the pilgrimage route Gloominess of Yakushi Temple	Tea shop at the herb nursery Peony and rhododendron garden at Yakushi Temple
A-2	Beauty of the gardens of people involved in the landscape business Large trees, including a Japanese-style pine Nurseries Views Garden rocks	area under the elevated JR tracks Reinforcement of the river on three sides	Improve cherry tree-lined streets Replace three-sided river reinforcement with a more natural reinforcement
B-1	River landscape and view from river Beauty of nursery gardens Bamboo grove along the embankment weir Flower plantings in the rotary and flowers in barrels Flower around the monument to Kitugidayu Pilgrimage route guideposts	River pollution Along the 176 National Highway, there are no traffic signals, crosswalks, sidewalks or signs, and the pedestrian bridges are not used Abandoned bicycles	Path around the retention pond Make the shopping street wider and provide signs to Aiai Park National Highway needs improvement Improve sidewalks Move Aiai Park sign at the North Entrance Reform the bus rotary Preserve areas through the rules of the Productive Green Land Law.
B-2	Singing birds Green treasures Symbolic camphor tree Pretty stream Black pine grove Beauty of private gardens	Iron fence blocks passage Amount of traffic Use of area around pond and slope	Green market Path along the stream Open nurseries Natural garden and spaces with plants and water connected with community center
C-1	Plantings in front of apartment buildings Plantings in parking lots View of the Rokko Mountains Foliage and large trees of the nurseries	Adjacent parks without character Heaps of scrap wood Unrefined bare wood River, parking without plants Vegetable gardens along the river	Parks with character Make nurseries attractive Increase plantings along river
C-2	Beauty of the gardens of professional landscape businesses Tulip trees on Yurinoki Road Stone paving	Poor consideration for children going to school Town appearance is haphazard in places Professional gardeners have stone piles that are in disarray and dangerous Parks are dull Open space is 1.2 m below road level, making it dangerous	Harmony between new and old housing Townscape that considers growing children Use of plants as suitable for a town of nurseries Improve landscape and add paths along waterways Increase attractiveness of park Increase street trees and planters
C-3	Traditional buildings Well planted home gardens Well planted housing estates Nursery plantings can be enjoyed from the road side Attractive lanes Apartment buildings with roof gardens that connect to an area park	Land left out of replanning Wall color of housing estates harm the view Field Swell Scrap piles Steel towers and high voltage power lines damage view Housing sprawl and possibility of more Narrow roads Dead-end streets from small-scale Uneven sidewalks	Illumination of Yurinoki Road and low Improvement of sidewalks Make steel towers into columns, bundle multiple power lines together Permanent protection of greenery
D-2/3	Bamboo-lined road Large *kuroganemochi* trees	Gloomy plantation woods Parks lack sense of openness	

Figure 4. Keywords from the workshop.

neighborhood landscapes. Most of these issues are concerned the nurseries and the use of local resources. Proposals to deal with these included consideration of a long-term master plan and medium-term cooperation between nursery businesses and local residents to achieve tax system reforms for designated Productive Green Lands. Other medium term goals include increasing the appeal of the nursery industry, making use of the watersides and investigating potential locations for planting new vegetation. Finally, the citizens developed possible short-term action plans that they could undertake themselves. See the following figures for more details of these plans.

Implementation and evaluation of short-term programs

In the following year, we considered action plans for several of the identified issues that could be improved with short-term efforts. The action plan development was achieved through a process of organizing the keywords identified in the workshops. As a result, 7 overall goals were established for the Yamamoto District, including 1) street and urban planting and scenic improvement, 2) Aiai Park planting and scenic improvement, 3) planning an area park within the district, 4) Tenjin River scenic improvement, 5) holding open gardens and open nurseries, 6) improving the promenade to Aiai Park, 7) repairing the local Matsuo Shrine and improving the surrounding scenery.

The last two goals, however, were judged to be difficult to tackle with just workshops. For the promenade to Aiai Park, compliance with plans to redevelop the area in front of the station would be necessary. Matsuo Shrine, while being a public open space, is particularly important to the local parishioners, therefore, consensus regarding shrine repair and scenic alterations would be hard to achieve.

We held workshops for the other 5 goals in which discussions deepened consensus that lead to the development and implementation of action plans: 1) For street planting and scenic improvement, we made a planting plan along the Prefectures Road (known as Yurinoki Road) so that flowers would be in bloom throughout the year. 2) For Aiai Park planting, we planted flowers in 120 square meters of flower beds that had been abandoned and planned for continuous planting. 3) For the district neighborhood area park plan we did all planning and design in workshops and made a proposal to the city. 4) For Tenjin River scenic improvement, we conducted repeated observations of the river and made a scenic improvement proposal to the city water bureau. 5) We held the first open garden event in 2001 and are preparing for the fourth this year. From the second year, the open gardens program was expanded to include the entire city. This citywide event is still run through workshops in which core members form a council and leaders are chosen.

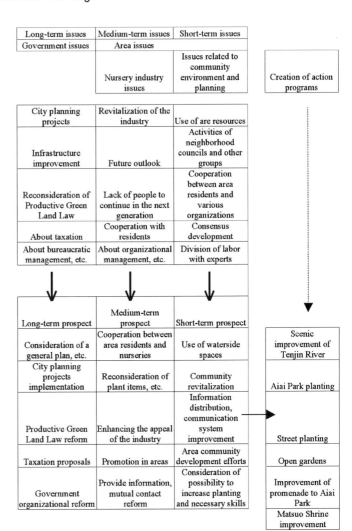

Figure 5. Long, medium, and short-term issues, prospects, and action programs.

Questionnaire

In September 2002, I sent questionnaires to all of the participants of the workshops to investigate the effects and to reflect on community design activities. Professionals and government officials participated as equals with other citizens, and so were also given the same questionnaire. Of the 120 sent out 65 were returned with usable responses. The main items covered in the questionnaire are as follows.

Respondent data

The percentage of men responding was 38% and of women was 62%. The ages of the respondents were in a wide range, with 8% in their 70s, 33% in their 60s, 26% in their 50s, 11% in their 40s, 5% in their 30s, and 8% in their 20s (9% unknown). People from a variety of occupations responded with 20% homemakers, 15% company workers, 15% self-employed, 12% unemployed, 8% working part-time, 5% government employees, and 8% others (17% unknown). The wide range of ages and occupations is probably a result of our initial efforts to publicize the workshops widely. Groups that the respondents belong to include those working for the improvement of the area environment (3 groups), residents associations, elderly groups, NPOs from the wider area (2 groups) and horticulture industry professionals.

Participant's expectations for the workshops

For the first question set, "What did you expect from the workshop?" I provided 16 questions and asked for ranked responses with 5 as the highest evaluation. The answers given were quite high with an average of around 4 points, meaning people expected much from the workshops (Fig. 6).

The highest points were for the items like "make the town more beautiful quickly with ornamental flowers in the parks and along the streets" (4.27), "draw more visitors to Yamamoto and make the town more lively" (4.24), and "publicize the history and the splendid resources of the town and make them last into the future" (4.31). These and other items show that expectations to make the entire town more attractive were high.

In contrast, people did not have high expectations for specific themes such as "make a map of Yamamoto" (3.63), "plant flowers on Yurinoki Road" (3.46) or "make Matsuo Shrine more inviting" (3.43). This shows that participants had high expectations for abstract purposes, rather than for specific targeted concrete activities. Standard deviation was between 1.16 and 0.69.

Reflections and evaluations of the activities so far

Tangible results were achieved for 4 of the action plans, 1) Walking through and rediscovering the town to find issues and make proposals for improvement, 2) Aiai Park flower bed planting, 3) flower planting along the tree-lined Yurinoki Road, and 4) holding the Yamamoto District open gardens. For these 4, I asked about individual participation, overall activity evaluation and evaluation of the results of the implemented plans. First,

I asked the individuals to rate their own participation on a 5-point scale from 5, made sincere efforts and have a sense of satisfaction, to 1, no efforts or satisfaction. The Yamamoto District open gardens, at 3.7 was the highest, with Yurinoki Road planting and Aiai Park flower bed planting close behind at 3.4. Walking through the town averaged only 2.9 with some range of responses. Although there was not much difference in the average scores, the open gardens and Yurinoki Road planting, projects that required a lot of actual work had a high rate, around 40%, of 5 ratings. These projects also received high numbers of 5s in evaluation of their action plans. Overall evaluations of the results were fairly good, ranging from 3.7 to 3.9 (walking through town 3.7, flower bed planting 3.7, Yurinoki planting 3.9, open gardens 3.9).

Good points about conducting activities using the workshop method

Throughout all the workshops, many people thought that, (2) thinking with others was valuable (57.8%) and a good point of the workshops. Other frequently noted good points were (1) rediscovering the attractions of Yamamoto (50.0%), (3) being happy to have been lead by outside professionals from Awaji Landscape Planning and Horticulture Academy and elsewhere (37.5), and (7) having the cooperation of people from outside (32.8).

Everything that had to do with interaction and cooperation with people was evaluated highly. On the other hand, the scores for the actual implementation activities, including the improvement of greenery in open spaces and flower planting were lower.

Impressions about each of the action plans (multiple response)

Regarding their thoughts about each of the action plans (Fig. 7), 100% of the participants were satisfied to work with others on planting flowers along Yurinoki Road. 91.3% of the participants were satisfied with working together during flower planting at Aiai Park. 70.8% thought that it was good to think things through with others for planning a new area park in Yamamoto Naka 2 Chome. Overall doing things with other people was evaluated highly.

Furthermore, for the open gardens, good points identified include "revealing gardens more widely" (77.8%) and "it was nice to have many guests" (72.2%). Overall it is clear that the interaction and co-operation between people was evaluated more highly than the actual improvements to the environment.

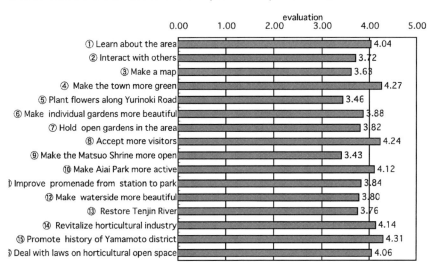

Figure 6. Expectations for workshops.

① Town observation and making proposals for improvement	① Get new information	② Good to make many proposals	③ Wished for more proposals	④ Unrealistic proposals	⑤ Othe rs		
	52.8%	44.4%	27.8%	13.9%	19.4%		
② Planning the park in Yamamoto Naka 2 Chome	① Good to think together	② Good to make many proposals	③ Wished for more proposals	④ Planning process is not clear	⑤ Others		
	70.8%	37.5%	4.2%	8.3%	25.0%		
③ Flower planting at the Shinike Park,	① Good to think together	② Enjoyed planting flowers	③ Continuing this work	④ Wish to attend planning	⑤ Work was too hard	⑥ Doubts about the work	⑦ Others
	91.3%	52.2%	73.9%	17.4%	4.3%	13.0%	43.5%
④ Flower planting along Yurinoki Road	① Good to think together	② Enjoyed planting flowers	③ Continuing this work and do it wider	④ Wish to attend planning	⑤ Work was too hard	⑥ Others	
	100.0%	50.0%	50.0%	25.0%	0.0%	18.8%	
⑤ Open gardens	① Good to do activities more widely	② Good to have many people	③good to have the relation to garden summit	④ Wish to have it regularly	⑤ Could not see other gardens; taking care of my own	⑥ Others	
	77.8%	72.2%	55.6%	77.8%	16.7%	44.4%	

Figure 7. Evaluation for the activities (plural answers).

Comparison of expectations, participation and evaluation of activities over time

In order to clarify the changes in the awareness and the desires of the participants over the course of three years and four action plans that lead to verifiable results, I compared the results of the evaluations of the participants for each action plan to identify 1) expectations for the workshops, 2) the degree of each individual's participation and sense of achievement, and 3) the overall evaluation of the workshops.

At first, from the score for (2) the degree of participation, I subtracted the score for (1) expectations for the workshops, to verify correspondence between expectations and participation. Then, to measure the correspondence between evaluation and expectations, from the score for (3), overall evaluation, I subtracted the score for (1) expectation of the workshops. Finally, I calculated (2) the degree of participation and achievement minus (3) the overall evaluation of the workshop in order to verify whether individuals participated actively even when their evaluation of the activities was lower. (Fig. 8) As a result, I found that expectation and participation levels differed slightly from evaluation. Most of these scores were negative, indicating that most people expected a lot at the start.

The ratings for town observation, Aiai Park planting, Yurinoki Road planting, and the open gardens, respectively, were 4.16, 4.25, 3.79 and 4.27 for starting expectations, 3.58, 3.55, 3.57 and 4.27 for participation, and 2.90, 3.75, 4.00 and 4.13 for evaluation. Looking at the figures for expectation, participation and evaluation over time, people had relatively high expectations for the first workshop in June 2002, (1) walking through the town and making proposals for improvement (4.16), but the evaluation for the program was not so high (2.90). The difference between participation (3.58) and evaluation is 0.68, which means that the whole program was not so valuable but many of the respondents thought that they personally did well. (3) The next two, flower planting in Aiai Park (May 2001), and (4) flower planting along Yurinoki Road (September 2001)

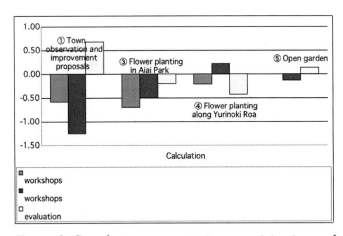

Figure 8. Gaps between expectations, participation and evaluation.

did not have significant differences between expectation, participation (3.55, 3.57) and evaluation (3.75, 4.00) ratings. The difference between participation and evaluation were +.20 and +.43, respectively. These results may be because these two activities required sustained participation. For the open gardens (December 2001), there was almost no difference between the expectation, participation and evaluation scores.

From these results, I can say that at first people held high expectations relative to their weak consciousness about participation. In other words, people were expecting someone else to do the work. Gradually, as the activities continued, the differences between expectations and participation became smaller, showing that people became more proactive in their attitudes toward participation to work for good community design.

Next I analyzed the human element in the workshops. In order to gather a diversity of opinions, involvement of a variety of groups and individuals was necessary in the workshop process. Participation of experts was hoped for because specialized knowledge and skills were necessary in order to draw out issues, prospects and action plans, to make preparations and

to provide equipment, coordination and analysis. Oversight of coordination and cooperation among citizens, government officials and specialists was also important in order to move from prospects and proposals to action plans, through publicity, planning and design, preparation of materials, gathering of opinions, consensus development, etc. For the workshops it was necessary to divide work, strengthen networks and work effectively not only with local citizens with deep affection for the area, but also with citizens with an interest in community improvement from the broader area, government officials, government related agencies, businesses, specialists with coordination skills, experienced specialist NPOs, and educational and research institutions (Fig. 9).

I can summarize the progress in working toward solutions to local issues and changes in participants' perspectives through the workshops as follows. At the start of the activities, workshop participants had high expectations for dealing with large issues, such as "making the town more beautiful," "making the town more lively" and "communicating the history and valuable resources of the Yamamoto District," while expectations for more localized issues were relatively low. At this point, participants seem to have been counting on government officials and specialists to bring about community improvement, rather than doing it by them. However, as a result of making proposals and undertaking actual activities in the workshops, in contrast to their original attitudes, they expressed higher evaluations and senses of personal satisfaction with individual concrete activities rather than abstract large-scale improvements. Furthermore, through repeated activities, the desire to be involved in such activities seems to have grown. At first, small actions were taken, such as replanting flower beds in the park and planting flowers along Yurinoki Road. Later, in order to implement the open gardens event, citizens took lead roles cooperatively in both preparation and implementation, including holding an open café, distributing maps and making signs. From these results, we can conclude that it is important to start workshop programs with short-term activities that have tangible results.

Government officials and academics announced and coordinated the workshops at first, and each workshop was planned and directed by a

Open Garden Program Workshops	Contents	Participating groups	Roles
Starting point	Initial planning among coordinators (ALPHA staff), City Hall (Aiai Park) and local residents seeking to improve their community environment	Some local residents	Already independently active
		City Hall	Revitalization of Nursery Industry
		Aiai Park	
		Coordinators	Consult with citizens and City Hall
Workshop to identify issues	Discussion between coordinators and local residents; clarification of places for improvement through community observations and other methods	Residents	Sponsor workshops
		Coordinators	
		Specialist NPOs	Participate in workshops Facilitation roles
Workshop to identify issues		Citizen NPOs	
		City Hall	Participate in workshops
		Aiai Park	
Proposals	Develop concrete plans through workshops involving residents from the wider community and NPOs	Residents	Local coordination
		Coordinators	Prepare report materials
		Specialist NPOs	Think about plan proposal
		Citizen NPOs	Internal coordination
		City Hall	Handle publicity, etc.
		Aiai Park	
Preparation and implementation	Cooperation among citizens and city agencies; publicity efforts; NPOs, coordinators and other supporting agencies (ALPHA) create preparatory materials	Residents	Invite garden owners
		Coordinators	Synthesize overall plan, map-making, etc.
		Specialist NPOs	Cooperate with map-making, etc.
		Citizen NPOs	Cooperate making plan proposal
		City Hall	
		Aiai Park	Inform local residents, etc.
Future sustained activity	Continue community development by building local networks and leadership, as well as by raising area awareness among residents	Residents	Inform and invite local residents to workshops
		Coordinators	Create a sustainable arrangement
		Specialist NPOs	Support various programs
		Citizen NPOs	
		Aiai Park	Coordinate publicity for Open Garden Program, etc.
		City Hall	Financial support, etc.

Figure 9. Participant groups and roles.

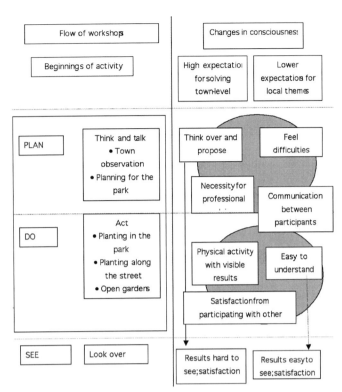

Figure. 10 The flow and changes of activities.

Figure 12. Making flowerbeds.

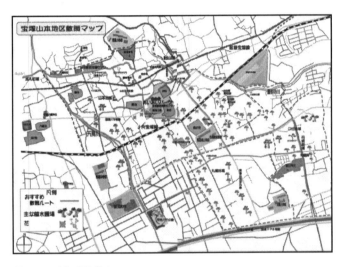

Figure 13. Walking map.

coordinator, but after participating several times the citizens became more proactive. The participants happily took on the rolls in the workshops that they could. The following figure shows the results of the workshops and the flow in the change of consciousness toward participation (Fig. 10).

This research also shows that in the future we can expect highly motivated citizens to continue to expand on these efforts. All of these results are because of the increased consciousness of participation and the will to take action that many participants developed.

FOR FUTURE DEVELOPMENT

As a result of accomplishing a variety of action plans, I observed a deepening and widening of community planning activities. The current state and possibilities for future developments as I see them follows.

Beginning with town observations, along with issues, prospects, and action plan execution for each theme, the development and

Figure 11. Discussion in workshop.

organization of local citizens progressed. The walking map that was made for town observation and improvement proposals was made even more valuable as the basis for a new idea of viewing the town as a tree museum with map making, events, permanent exhibitions and other local revitalization plans being made. As for the Yurinoki Road plantings, local groups have undertaken continuous planting and maintenance. For the planting in Aiai Park, in order to sustain it into the future, there is a proposal to offer plant cultivation, design and other courses in coordination with the maintenance conducted by TGC. For preparation of a scenic improvement plan for the Tenjin River, a committee seems to be forming.

The open garden program that started in the Yamamoto District expanded to include the whole city in 2002. In 2003, an executive committee was formed, and now it is held as the Takarazuka Garden Festival. The workshop created awareness of the possibility and allowed local citizens to develop a consensus for action, which in turn lead to stimulating the support of government officials.

*Figure 14.
Traditional
heritage for
open garden.*

As the open garden program has developed to a citywide level, it has expanded to include not only gardens, but also community planting and promotion of important spots around the city. From 50 private gardens and gardens affiliated with nurseries, the nurseries themselves, and local planting projects in the first year, last year there were 200. Furthermore, the city agricultural and the park and open space divisions, TGC, Inc., Awaji Landscape Planning and Horticulture Academy, various specialists, NPO groups, and other organization are now involved in the executive committee.

Along with the increasing the breadth and depth of the activities, a core member committee for handling workshops is being held with coordinators being chosen along themes. Furthermore, a single locality or agency cannot undertake a large-scale project alone. For this reason, round table meetings have been proposed in order to promote participation and involvement from all relevant government agencies. In order to implement plans, participation and cooperation among government officials, citizens, specialists, and a variety of organizations is indispensable. As a result of action plans implemented through workshops, local self-reliance for community planning and improvement is continuing to deepen in the Yamamoto area.

CONSIDERATION OF FUTURE PROSPECTS

To summarize the entire flow of the series of workshops, we first established long, medium, and short-term issues. Then we settled goals and action programs. Participants shared their opinions and made issues and prospects clear together, and a common sense about the issues developed among the residents, which provided the impetus for the action programs. My conclusion is that, for citizen participation activities, the process of determining the purpose is important.

By participating in the action programs for short-term issues, the consciousness of the residents changed. The expectations for the workshops, the degree of participation, and the evaluation of the whole workshop became more balanced. To solve the issues of the locals and residents, the participation of residents, administrators, and professionals are important, as is sharing of the rolls. Government agencies need to have flexibility and systems to respond to citizen needs to achieve some of the goals of the workshops. Local residents need to have the understanding and willingness to seek independent

and sustained solutions to issues, but they are not always successful on their own. Continuous support and oversight are desirable.

In the future, systems to support more partnerships between residents, administrators, and professionals, and educational programs to raise awareness of issues and determine goals among the participant groups are necessary. Management of the support from the government is still in a trial phase. We should observe the development of similar activities in many places in the future.

ENDNOTES

[1] The holding of workshops was announced in newspapers by the city council, by passing a circular notice around the community, and to the members of a wide range of professional NPOs, and an NPO made of graduates from Awaji Landscape Planning and Horticulture Academy.

REFERENCES

Chiba, N., Shinozawa, K. and Miyagi, S. 2003. The Process Of Citizen Participation And Its Potential Application In The Planning And Management Of Ishikawa River Park, Landscape Research Japan, Japan Institute of Landscape Architecture, 66 (5) 753-758.

Hayashi, M. 2003. The Result And Evaluation Of Workshops For Environmental Improvement Of A Local Community, Japan Landscape Journal Hokkaido Branch: 10-11.

Kimura, T., and Hayashi, M. 2000. The Organization And Human Factor In Community Design Workshops In The Yamamoto District Of Takarazuka. October: 39-40.

Sakano, Y., Kyoniwa, S. and Sato, S. 2000. Research About The Role Of Participatory Workshops In Planned Town Areas, City Planning, No. 35: 13-18.

Takarazuka City, March 2001. Research on Horticulture and the Development of the Regional Environment.

**rethinking
professionals**

INSPIRATIONAL

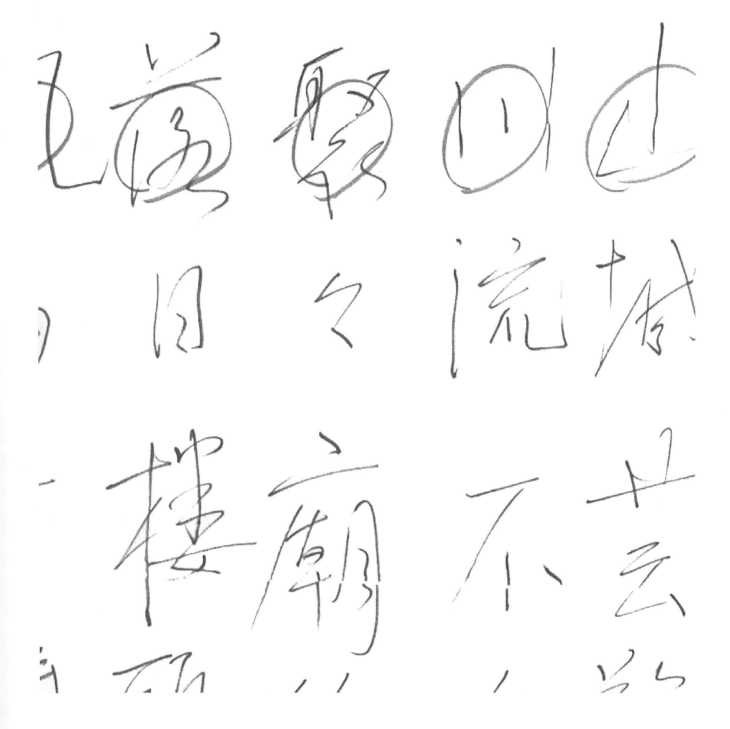

WHEN PROFESSIONAL KNOWLEDGE MEETS LOCAL WISDOM
A Dilemma in Trans-cultural Participatory Design

John K-C. Liu

ABSTRACT

It's the summer of 2003. In a remote fishing village on the island of Matzu off the coast of Mainland China province of Fujian, professional planners and designers from Taiwan were inadvertently mired in a conflict with a highly revered local deity, the Armoured General. As the metamorphosis of a frog, the Armoured General has long been worshipped and trusted for his wisdom in community affairs. A proposed extension of the temple plaza and a new entrance gate to the plaza brought the conflict into focus. The planners commissioned by the county government to preserve the cultural landscape of Chinbe village exercised their professional judgement with regard to the proposed temple plaza and gate. The proposal was too large, out of scale with the neighboring buildings, and inappropriate in form and material. The temple committee, acting as the medium through which the Armoured General speaks, insisted that it was the wishes of the god to build a large plaza and gate. Should the outside professionals acquiesce and respect the wishes of the god or should they remain firm in their best judgement? How will a local deity respond to disrespect and irreverence? What are the lessons for engaged and progressive professionals in a trans-cultural context? This paper will first tell the story of the Chinbe Village Frog and the events leading up to the conflict. The story will examine the key issues of contention between the interested parties, including the professionals, the deity, as well as the local people and the politicians. It will document how the conflict was resolved and what questions remain. Then the paper will address the general issues that are pervasive when professionals engage in trans-cultural planning and design activities where communities strive to preserve and develop their own local distinctiveness. Specifically, this paper intends to explore the essential dilemma of a generalized system of environmental knowledge in the face of local belief systems. The paper will try to demonstrate that in a local community setting, there are multiple realities that embody values and functions necessary to the maintenance and promotion of local environments. Professional knowledge needs to incorporate this multiplicity and diversity in the process of making plans and designs. The enrichment of professional knowledge in this regard remains a challenging epistemological subject matter.

EVERYDAY HAPPENINGS[1]

When you turn the corner in the road and see the austere village of Chin-be below teased by the gentle waves of the South China sea and nestled up against the steep banks of the rocky hill, a single colorful and exuberant building stands out among the subdued gray clusters of stone houses. This is the temple of the Sea Goddess, Matzu, or the Queen of the Heavens. What is not visible, until you get close to it, is a tiny little stone structure hidden behind the temple. In it sits a 30-cm. tall green frog with an ear-to-ear smile, the Frog deity worshipped by the local community. The Frog had been designated the Armored Commander and later elevated to the status of General, a high-ranking figure in the local Taoist belief system.

It so happens that Matzu's domain is far and wide and she must constantly be out tending to the needs of her believers that she could not pay too much attention to the local village affairs in Chin-be. Consequently the Sea Goddess delegates the Armored General (the Frog) to look after the needs of the villagers. This is a most satisfactory arrangement since the villagers feel closer to the Frog anyway. With power vested from the Sea Goddess, the Armored General now has absolute authority over the affairs of the community.

For an individual in the village, if there is a question of a personal nature, such as some ailment or distress, the Armored General would provide guidance. For a family in the village, questions regarding such decisions as building a new house, marriage arrangements, business opportunities, etc., would all be answered. For the village community, major events such as the building of a new road or a new fishing pier, the timing for a festivity or a ceremony, etc., would also require the approval of the Armored General. More importantly, anyone who aspires to a public position, whether it's the village chief, the town council, or even the county magistrate, would all adhere to the admonishments of the Armored General. Local politics, as such, is definitely within the purview of the Frog.

And how does the Armored General dispense his authority and by what means does he convey his wishes? First, the individual, a family, or public figures in the community asks for a hearing with the Armored General. At the assigned time, the petitioner presents the deity with a question either in written form, (including pictorial forms of drawings, diagrams, pictures, models, etc.) or simply by asking the question orally. The response from the Armored General is always in a written form, including drawings and sketches. This is done with a wooden sedan chair wherein sits a personified statue of the Armored General and is held up in motion by four villagers who, in unison, compose the response by dipping an arm of the sedan chair in wine and immediately proceeding to write on a flat board so that the writing is visible. To be qualified as a carrier of the sedan chair, a male member of the community must undergo a lengthy period of training in order to be able to enter into a collective trance-like state and the motions of the sedan chair are therefore results of the direct will of the Armored General. Every question to the god is answered in this fashion, and incense is burned and offerings made to thank him for taking the time.

In this way, individual questions are answered, family disputes are resolved, and community decisions made. The Frog, in the form of an Armored General, dispenses power and resources to keep peace and harmony. Ordinary daily life in this fringe and mundane village continues to revolve around the symbolic figure of the Frog, proprietor of local wisdom in its totality.

SETTLEMENT PRESERVATION AS PUBLIC POLICY

Socio-political and economic transformations over the past decade contributed to the public intervention in preserving Chin-be village as a historic settlement. The single most important development during this period was the demilitarization of the Matzu Islands by the central government in Taiwan. This was done partly as a gesture towards the relaxation of animosity across the Taiwan strait and partly due to the realistic acknowledgement of the uselessness of the outdated military installations defending the front lines against a possible invasion by the mainland communists. As a result of increasing cutbacks in military spending on the islands, the heart of the local economy, businesses catering to the servicemen declined drastically as fewer and fewer soldiers remain stationed here. Restaurants, pool halls, barber shops, internet cafes, convenience stores, etc., all faced closures.

Prior to the military occupation of the islands, of course, the people of these islands were fishermen off the coast of China. Here at the mouth of the Ming River in northern Fujian Province, one of the richest fishing grounds in the Asian Pacific is located nearby, fought over by not only the Chinese themselves, but by foreigners over the centuries to lay claim to its wealth and its strategic location. Living witnesses to this history of contestation are two lighthouses built by the British in the late 1800's situated at the northern and southern tips of the islands to guide British ships in and out of the treaty ports along the China coast. These lighthouses were manned by the British well into the 20th century up until the military takeover in 1949.

The other important evidence of the contestation over these islands is the physical settlements which record materially the history of the villages through the traces of form and construction, and of family clans in their rises and falls in fortune and piracy, and in political allegiance and cultural identity. I will come back to the settlements later.

As the number of servicemen dwindled, so did the local residents. True, over the past fifty years since military occupation, at least three generations of residents have sent their young people to Taiwan for higher education. As there is only one high-school and no college on the islands, young people seeking higher education must leave home to go to school in Taiwan. Over the years many have settled in Taiwan and have raised the next generation. Some have returned, working as teachers in elementary schools, as government workers, and as local business owners. But overall, there has been a general decline in local residents over the past decade largely due to the dwindling number of soldiers who had been the main customers of local businesses. The visible consequence of this trend is the gradual dilapidation of houses in the villages and of whole villages now deserted and overgrown with weeds.

About ten years ago, with the pull-out by the military and the erosion of both the physical and social fabric of the villages, a few of the local intellectuals, including teachers, artists, and council representatives, began to discuss the alarming situation of this precipitous decline. At that time, on Taiwan proper, there was already a movement towards the historic preservation of buildings, places, streets, and villages through the strategy of community participation. Progressive planners and activists in the academy forged an alliance of public agencies, budding non-governmental organizations, and local community residents to promote preservation. This movement evolved into what we now know as the Comprehensive Community Development program. On Matzu, these few thoughtful people sought a program of cultural revitalization through the preservation of old and abandoned villages.

On a particular occasion in 1994, a seminar was held in Matzu to introduce historic preservation ideas to the local people. Several academics were present and afterwards the group visited Chin-be village. It was at this moment when the wide-eyed outsiders first saw the extraordinary beauty of Chin-be that the concrete idea of preserving its entirety came into being. Thereafter, as the name of Chin-be spread, more and more people came to marvel at its rugged setting, the particular fit of the stone houses into a clustered settlement, the narrow winding paths and stairways which open up to small interior courtyards with long views out to the calm waters of the protected cove. From the small wooden windows of houses in the village, one can see a framed picture of Turtle Island (a rock outcropping in the cove) alive from every angle. The picturesque reminiscence of Italian hill-towns and Greek fishing villages is unmistakable, as people are generally familiar with the images of the Mediterranean. The romancing of Chin-be had begun in earnest.

Given all the attention, Chin-be was chosen by the county government to be the first village designated as a historic settlement. Resources from the central government including the Construction Bureau and the Council for Cultural Development were allocated towards the planning for its preservation. Most of the initial planning was undertaken by the county staff planners and was focused mainly on physical surveys, measurements, typological studies of buildings, and methods of construction, etc. From these materials, a new term, the "Ming-dong" (eastern Fujian) building type was coined to distinguish it from what is generally known as the northern Fujian type. Some of the distinguishing characteristics of this type are the thick masonry enclosures of each house, the independently constructed wooden structure for the interior with traditional Chinese post and lattice beam assembly, and the red clay roof tiles augmented with rows of granite stones as weights. Small openings in the stone walls are suggestive of the necessary protections against the natural elements and against possible intrusions by pirates and thieves. Houses are huddled together so as to form clusters set into the steep rocky landscape of the cove.

During the Spring of 2001, eight houses were selected for renovation. With agreements from all the house owners, the County embarked on a fast-track effort that completed the work in two months in time to host an international symposium. At the end of May, over eighty people from Japan, the United States, Hong Kong, and Taiwan, came to Chin-be for three days. One large house which had a front court was rebuilt as a restaurant and bar. Another large house with a two-story space was renovated as the main meeting room. The other houses were refurbished, complete with every item of fixtures and furnishings imported from the IKEA store in Taiwan, as sleeping quarters for guests.

The conference was a great success by all accounts as the international participants fully appreciated the breath-taking setting and the newly completed effort to use the old buildings. As an example of preservation and reuse of historic settlements, this appeared to fulfill the aspirations of all parties concerned. Throughout this effort, one particular individual played a crucial role. With the encouragement of local cultural elites, a young architect enthralled by the unique and distinctive beauty of the vernacular houses decided to stay in Matzu after completing his mandatory tour of military duty. The county government was just embarking on the renovation of the first group of houses, and this young man was hired to be a staff planner to manage this project.

Over the next year of intensive planning and organizing, this staff architect, Mr. Z, managed to not only successfully complete the renovation on time, but also to introduce to Matzu, for the first time, a new aesthetic of the Taipei modern, ala IKEA. The subtlety of the spatial manipulations which juxtaposed modern forms of consumption with the roughness of the vernacular buildings was unmistakable to the visitors as well as the local residents. What was crafted out of the ruins of this abandoned village matched well with the imaginations of a possible future where cosmopolitan visitors would consume the exotic beauty of a traditional settlement while fully enjoying the material comforts of the city. Once the script had been played out during the international symposium, visions of a bustling tourism destination where local people as entrepreneurs find glamour and money at their doorsteps took hold. Not only did the remaining residents of the village begin to think of ways to capitalize on this new development, even the gods in the temple were stirring for a piece of the action.

Subsequently, Chin-be has indeed turned into an exotic tourist destination catering to individuals looking for a different experience and to various groups holding retreats. By the late summer in 2002, a gathering of all the directors of culture departments of counties and cities in Taiwan was held here. Thus only one year after the initial conference Chin-be was already a very well known destination.

The county planners, buoyed by this early success, embarked on the second phase of renovations. By now, more absentee home-owners were eager to participate in the preservation program. Agreements between the local government and the home-owners were refined to accommodate individual needs such as using a graduated formula to calculate the subsidy to each house depending on the size of the house and the extent of repairs. In addition, more study was focused on the possible reuse of the houses as well as the management aspects of the preservation project.

Within the last year, four other villages in Matzu have been designated as historic settlements. Preservation plans are being prepared and work will be underway to rehabilitate and reuse them. The local county government's active intervention in saving these villages reflects a shift in public policy away from the traditional new development strategies towards transforming what is already there. By building upon traditions and local cultural resources, it is envisioned that a more enlightened and sustainable future will be gradually realized.

EXPANDING THE PLAZA AND BUILDING A NEW GATE FOR THE TEMPLE

Meanwhile, at the temple to the Sea Goddess, the governing committee including the village chief has also been busy sprucing up the temple as more and more visitors come to the village. A few years ago, an unsuccessful attempt was made to beautify the temple by applying a shining facia of marble and granite to the existing front of the temple which resulted in accusations of corruption and ridicules of bad taste. Some suggested knocking down the fake stone work and cutting back the plaza which protrudes menacingly over the main pathway in the village. However, nobody wished to offend the god and nothing was done to repair the damage.

In the summer of 2003, the temple committee informed the county government that, with the funds promised by the new county magistrate during last year's elections, it is now ready with plans for an expansion of the temple plaza and the building of a new gate. In accordance with the dictates of the god, in this case the Armored General, a local architect had drawn up plans. When the county planners saw these plans, which entailed building a 10-meter high retaining wall to hold up the expanded plaza, and also an even taller gate situated down-slope from the plaza, they realized that the temple committee was about to repeat what they had done before.

Had the county planners not intervened, the project for the expansion of the plaza and the construction of the gate would have proceeded. When the county planners voiced concerns that these new and clearly exaggerated spatial gestures would seriously impact the settlement landscape, the magistrate had to take notice. But what could he do? He had promised the temple these public funds, and in return, the local village had given him the decisive edge in winning the election. He negotiated with the temple to no avail. They were not budging, the will of the god must be carried forward.

The stalemate lasted for several months while informal negotiations continued. When it became apparent that neither side was willing to compromise, it was then suggested that the experts and scholars be brought in to be the detached and independent judges. While we, as experts and scholars, were not entirely objective, since we had earlier expressed our displeasure with the previous fiasco, and had backed the county planners opposing the new plans, we were still considered to be fair mediators. Thus finally after some arrangements, we were invited to be part of the process.

Originally the temple issued an invitation to us, represented by a professor at the most prestigious university in Taiwan, to come to Chin-be and to be part of the ceremony to directly discuss the issue of the plaza with the god. Of course for academics trained in western ways of thinking, we look upon traditional beliefs with curiosity and interest, but would consider them as unrelated to the concerns of planning and environmental quality. We initially did not see a role in actually communicating with the god, and thus were reluctant to go to Chin-be. Later, the temple decided to advance their quest by saying that if we did not wish to go to Chin-be, then the god would come to us!

This they did by flying the statue of the Armored General from Matzu to Taiwan in order to meet us in Taipei.

On the appointed afternoon, the entourage from Matzu accompanied the Armored General came into a crowded apartment in a suburb of Taipei. Along with four of us from the university, there was also the legislator and his assistants all gathered to have a face-to-face negotiation with the god over the design of the plaza/gateway. The local architect, who had previously drawn up plans according to the wishes of the god, brought his power-point presentation and proceeded to project it on the wall. A brief ceremony was performed where the sedan carriers drank from a bowl of liquor while incense was lit as an offering. The Armored General, sitting in his sedan chair held by his four carriers, looked on the diagrams and drawings, and conversation began. Incense and smoke filled the tight room and everyone spoke at the same time, in different dialects. When there was a lull, I quickly injected my opinion that what we were really concerned about was the scale and massing of the proposed plaza/gateway, that we worry they would adversely impact the plain and subdued landscape of the stone houses nestled together against the steep bank of the rocky hillside. This was translated into the local dialect for the Armored General to consider. After a moment, the carriers began to dance the sedan chair back and forth, swinging it from side to side. Then it stopped abruptly and as if of its own will, the chair, using one of its wooden arms, started to write on a wooden tablet previously prepared and placed on a table, in Chinese. One of the four carriers, being the chief interpreter, read out the words and everyone shouted his own understanding of what the god was trying to say. Well, the god said the plaza needs to be larger because he is planning for a big party, and the gateway needs to be taller because it must be of the same height as the Sea Goddess temple. The conversation continued in this fashion for the next two hours without much progress. While trying not to offend the god, we the professionals also did not acquiesce to his wishes. On the other hand, the god, being who he is, remained steadfast in his position. He not only made verbal/written wishes known to us, but was conversant with spatial/visual ideas as well. At one point, perhaps becoming impatient with our insistence, he proceeded to draw the shape and form of the gateway himself. It was a large, ornamental gateway of three arches which extended far beyond the restricted space in front of the temple. It was late afternoon and was apparent that we were at an impasse.

Not knowing how to further engage the god in a reasonable discussion, and not wanting a decision made de facto on his wishes, we initiated a final attempt to try to stall the decision. We made two suggestions: the first that the arches the god had drawn seemed un-Chinese, not part of the tradition, and second that what had been shown to him by the use of the power-point projection is two-dimensional and did not reflect the three-dimensional qualities of the hillside location. Would the god kindly consider looking at a 3-D model which we would prepare for him, and defer from making a decision that day. To our relief, the god replied readily that this would be fine. We then arranged to meet again in three weeks with a model of the site along with the proposed plaza and the gateway.

During the next three weeks, we mobilized to make a cardboard model of the site with the existing temple and the new plaza extension and the new gateway. Behind the scenes, our staff engaged the community leaders and the chief interpreter for the god in intensive negotiations on what would likely be acceptable to both sides. We made several models of the gateway, each to be revised and changed according to informal conversations. Finally, when the three-weeks time was up, we had come up with a design which both sides could agree to. We flew the model to Matzu and a formal audience with the Armored General was held in the Temple of the Sea Goddess. This time, many more people were present including many prominent professionals and academics, many more local residents were present, as well as many more government officials. It was more of a gala event with an air of festive excitement surrounding it.

While the county magistrate and the professors looked on, the model was shown to the Armored General. It was clear that the model was helpful in engaging the god in discussing the specifics of the design. For example, he asked specific questions about the height of the gateway. After we answered, he would make a point of finalizing the height in specific numbers. The dialogue went smoothly and a decision was reached in a short time. Everyone was happy and relieved.

Drawings and construction documents for the revised plaza/gateway were prepared, ready for implementation. The work was expected to be completed within six months. End of story.

THE KEY ACTORS AND THEIR ROLES

The first set of actors are what we call public figures. These are individuals who, besides being members of the community, assume functions and roles as either representatives of the people, or serve the people in different capacities. Here we identify the following:

The County Magistrate Mr. C who is not from this village but who, as the highest-ranking political figure in the county, oversees the distribution of resources to the local communities. He is the one who promised the Ma-tsu temple in Chin-be sufficient funds to build a new and enlarged plaza with a ceremonial entrance gate. The promise of funds was made in return for the support in the previous county-wide elections. Now Mr. C must deliver on his promises. However, the disagreements over the plan have put him in an awkward position. He cannot offend the Armoured General by reneging on the promise, and he doesn't want to disregard the advice of the staff and professionals opposed to the plan. Mr. C is in a bind and the natural outlet is to go to the Armoured General (the Frog) for a decision on what to do with the plaza and the gate. Being an astute politician, he knows when to relinquish his power and to let the local deity take on the difficult task of resolving the dispute. In this instance, secular public authority over the management of public funds is handed over to the local religious authority.

Within the community, it is the village chief, Mr. W, who is most powerful in channeling public funds. In the case of the temple plaza and the gate, because it involves construction, it is naturally a project of high visibility with potentially good profits. Local contractors and builders would be vying to do the work. Because it is a project using public funds, county procurement procedures must be adhered to, at least on the surface. Thus, bidding and the selection of the builder, etc., would all appear to be open and fair. Here the village chief, through his position, can be very influential in determining the outcome of any public process. Yet again, the village chief would most likely defer to the wishes of the Armoured General with regard to what is to be done and how it will be done.

Besides the village chief, there is also the head of the community association, Ms. W, who, in her own right is the leader of a powerful faction of the Upper Village community. She has aligned herself with the village chief forming an alliance to determine the future course of the village. Similarly, she and the Upper-village community are devout followers of the Armored General. To be close to the General, all of above public figures have to pay homage to those who manage the temple, the keepers of the Frog deity.

Typically, a local temple is managed by a governing council elected by the worshippers. Here in the village of Chin-be, the Matzu temple's governing council is chaired by a Mr. T who apparently has direct access to the Armored General. To illustrate the importance of this person, by reviewing the origin of the plaza/gateway project, we find that it was Mr. T who first proposed the project in the name of the Armored General. Mr. T conveyed to the county magistrate that the General wants to enlarge the plaza in front of the temple and that there should be a new ceremonial gate. Thus, in return for support in the local elections, the county magistrate promised funding for the project. While his position as the chair of the council does not have the status of a public official, but it is easy to see that he holds the key to access the General.

There are other players in the public realm, though they may not seem as crucial to the events as those mentioned above. There is the national legislature representative, Mr. Tsao who is responsible for ensuring the continual flow of federal funds into the county. He is often present at crucial audiences with the Armored General when major decisions are made. At these occasions, Mr. Tsao tends to be passive and remain as only a witness to the decision making process. But his absence would be noticed and often a pronouncement by the General would have to wait for his arrival.

Then there is the local county legislature representative, Mr. C, who represents the township of Bei-gan wherein the village of Chin-be is located. He is not an active participant in this episode since his stated position is to try to get a more equal distribution of resources to all the villages in the township. He feels that there is already too much attention on Chin-be and too much funds going into it. He would like to divert some of it to other villages. Thus he tends to stay away from the internal maneuverings in the village. Yet he is not ignorant of what's happening in the village. He has ways of keeping a tap on the village and he knows how to manage the needs of all of his constituents. For example, he knows how to deal with people in the other villages who complain about the favored status of Chin-be.

The next group of actors is the community. In Chin-be there are basically two neighborhoods: one is the so-called Upper Village which now dominates the community association and the temple council, and the other is the North Village which numbers only four families. The North Village people feel strongly that their needs have not been met by the village and county officials, and that the Armored General has been taken hostage by the Upper Village faction. Specifically, they complain that the General is no longer a fair and just god.

There are other people in the community, the house-owners who no longer reside in the village. These are people who have left the village to live elsewhere in the county or have moved further away to Taiwan where there is now a substantial community of ex-patriots from Matzu. Even though these people no longer participate in the daily affairs in the village, their consent on certain issues affecting the community is necessary. For example, a house-owner must sign an agreement with the county government in order for the county to repair and use this person's house for some public purpose.

An important actor in the community is the manager of the restaurant/hotel at Chin-be. Ms. Z is a daughter of a north village family who grew up in Taiwan and has now returned to become an entrepreneur in running the restaurant/hotel. As a business woman, she is keenly aware of the internal dynamics and the local politics. She cannot afford to offend anybody and she pays her due respects to the Armored General. She has a contract with the county government on the management of the restaurant/hotel and she needs to work hard to keep that contract.

The third group of actors is the professionals. By professionals I mean those individuals and organizations who use specialized knowledge to intervene in the daily life of the village. Here the professionals include planners and designers such as the Foundation, which is an academic-based non-profit professional service group, outside architects, county staff professionals in community planning, advisor/consultants such as professors and experts, and others, notably a self-styled psychic claiming to be able to communicate directly with the Frog, who are involved in one way or another. These people are all outsiders and none of them speak the local dialect. The professionals know a great deal about their own respective specializations such as vernacular building, community planning, historic preservation, and management of local businesses. But each only knows a very little about the village community and how it functions.

TOWARDS CROSS-CULTURAL COMMUNICATIONS

(To be continued)

ENDNOTES

[1] The writing of this story began in Fall 2003 while on sabbatical at U.C. Berkeley Department of Landscape Architecture. I wish to thank Randy Hester for listening to this story and for his insightful comments.

CAMPUS DREAMLAND
A Case Study for a Campus Participatory Design Project

Ching-Fen Yang[1]

ABSTRACT

September 2002, TM College started its participatory venture for redesigning the campus public spaces. The process not only has produced better environments but also changed the school bureaucratic system temporarily. This paper describes the practice process: what techniques have been adopted to motivate people, how participatory process disturbed the existing school bureaucratic system, and what opportunities and factors assisted reaching the goals. This paper evaluates the whole process then suggests strategies for TM's next try on participatory design: authorize participants first, provide feedback, refer to existing cases, and link partnership as outside force against the existing power structure.

BACKGROUND: TO STIMULATE A TRADITIONAL SCHOOL

TM College is a conservative and obedient school. The school follows the guidelines of the Ministry of Education (MOE). The principal has to execute the orders from the trustee board. Teachers listen to the principal and college students obey the teachers. The school takes the role as a traditional institution– a homogeneous body that reproduces for the society. As Touraine (2003) describes, "This conception of education is centered not on the individual, but on society, on what are known as values and on rational knowledge in particular. . .The individual of classical modernity learns to serve progress, the nation and knowledge."

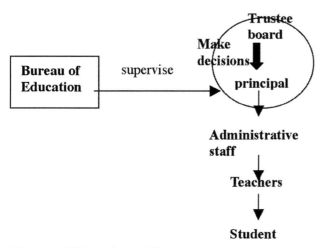

Figure 1. TM traditional bureaucratic structure.

However, two projects TM executed since 2002 provided the opportunity to transform TM from a traditional school to a school for the Subject: "community renaissance pedagogical studies" and "creative campus renew project." These two projects were both commissioned by the MOE. TM, being a private school and planning to upgrade to the university level,[2] needs to perform well to impress the MOE.

"Community renaissance pedagogical studies", handled by the Department of General Studies, basically was a seminar to introduce community renaissance/participatory design projects to facilitate teachers to conduct new classes regarding community issues. The "creative campus renew project" aimed at transforming some (forgotten) campus locations to be "creative" spaces. In 2002 six universities/colleges were reimbursed by MOE and each school had to face different difficulties. In TM's case, the main scope of the work was to create public spaces through participatory design process. Therefore, the above two projects were combined later.

Regarding the public spaces, according to the ideas of Lefebvre's production of space and Soja's the third space, there are three kinds of spaces to be considered, physical public space (the first space), the representation of public space (the second space), and the living space (the third space) (Hsia, 1997). These spaces aim to meet others, exchange ideas, and conduct discourses for public affairs. Ideally, by way of participatory design, the three spaces should be integrated.

When a school starts building public spaces, it is very likely to change its traditional reproduction role. Touraine describes an ideal school as a school for the Subject, that communicates, and that democratizes an educational system that "defines its mission as enhancing the capacity and will of individuals to become actors and learn to recognize that the Other enjoys the same freedom, the same right to individuation and the same right to defend social interests and cultural values that he or she enjoys is a democratizing system" (Touraine, 2003). In all, a school's role should be beyond an administrative service institution!

Then, how did TM create these spaces? How did a rigid school like TM start its participatory venture?

DESIGN PROCESS

Forming public discourse spaces

Principal Shen was the key person. In the private school system, the principal is the interface between the educational system and the trustee board. He/she needs to integrate the manpower and the ideas of both the administrative system and the trustee board. Therefore, the principal takes a critical role. In TM's case, Principal Shen initiated the "TM creative campus renew project." She then assigned the Department of General Studies to handle the project and invited the Building and

Figure 2. "Give me a name." Students voted for their favorite names (Left). Ballots on the first prize - Greeting Sunrise Boulevard (Below).

Planning Research Foundation (BPRF) to join the planning team. In the next step, the principal assembled a "Creative Campus Task Force" under the "Campus Planning Committee," as MOE's Request For Proposal requested. The Task Force, chaired by the principal and recruited administrative chiefs, teachers, students, and professional consultants (the BPRF team), was intended to incorporate broader opinions, which took a different way of its regular decision making process. Meanwhile, another related project—community renaissance pedagogical studies, took this project as a hands on practice, and thus recruited the main manpower to execute this project. The name of this study group was "the Wish Group (WG)," under the Creative Campus Task Force.

WG met once a week. The members came from various departments, which provided opportunities for teachers to communicate among different fields—the establishment of a primary public forum. Besides, these members were responsible to reach out through their networks to incorporate more opinions from the larger body. For example, Director Lin (for the student activities) conducted a student survey regarding the impressions of TM.[3] In addition, toward the end of the project, Director Lin also assisted arranging student clubs holding activities on the planning sites to claim as students' space. Teacher Joy Wu and Director Ko, core members, prepared a "TM creative campus" homepage as MOE requested and also invited a computer teacher to write a questionnaire program for students to fill out through the internet. However, WG evaluated that all the above methods still followed the existing teacher-student top-down power structure, which certainly could not guarantee motivating students to participate.

Therefore, WG changed the strategy to involve students by conducting several events. On the School Anniversary Day, WG held three events: "Wish Pool," "Speak Up'" and "Give Me a Name." The first two were for students to state their suggestions to the site planning. While the last one was intended to attract students' attention to a certain space—an alley between two building complexes, and also to increase the place attachment by naming it. In "Give Me a Name," WG invited all classes to give the space a name and a rationale so that we can also see how students thought about a certain space. Partly owing to an award provided, this event turned out to be a hot campaign! 56 names were submitted for the competition.[4] The first prize named "Greeting Sunrise Boulevard." "We, being students, to study hard is our responsibility and to work contentedly is our goal. Just so hopeful as being sun shined. We also wish more activities to be held on this boulevard in the future," the class stated.

Designing public spaces

The main purpose for TM's creative campus renew project was to create spaces to meet Others—to break the boundaries among different people to experience multicultural campus. The needs also came from upgrading the school. When TM is changing from a professional high school level to a college/university, the class system is also changed from a whole-day-class to the class electing system. That is, students did not need to stay at their home base classrooms for a whole day anymore. There is free time for them to hang out on campus during the class breaks. It was necessary to create more spaces other than classrooms for students. Based on a primary survey by the Task Force, WG chose three locations for planning:

a) "The Green Island,[5]" – an old three-floor building that stands alone by the main gate, which was perfect to be the bridge between TM and the community. As the name described, it was a "forgotten lonely island." It has been planned to be demolished for a new building. Therefore, it was empty for years, then changed to be student club bases. Since this space seemed to be abandoned, it had the potential for various usages, as Teacher Joy Wu's poem described:

Figure 3. A space planned for students to display their ideas in the future "Imaging the basement exit to be changed." (sketches by Y. C. Lee)

Let's play with the Green Island

Let's play with the Green Island, from ground floor to the third floor, from inside to the outside, from corridor to bathroom, from bathroom to façade, from façade to outdoor, from Latte to Spaghetti, from gallery to hip-hop, from now to renew. Let's play with the Green Island.

b) The newly named "Greeting Sunrise Boulevard." It is an alley between the old Service Hall (south face of Quadrangle) and the new Renew Hall. This area constitutes students' main living area on campus: it was one of the main walkways on campus; the basement of Service Hall was a convenience store; the old cafeteria was next to Renew Hall; many events were held on the stair flat by the Service Hall in the courtyard. The above functions could be integrated by renewing the "Greeting Sunrise Boulevard." This space was full of energy and should not be merely a walkway.

c) The courtyard of Quadrangle. Quadrangle is the very first building on TM campus that deserves a landmark. The courtyard was landscaped by various kinds of trees that contained no passage or places to stop. It was only used when students held events that gathered people, otherwise most people just passed by. The change of Quadrangle means a new start for the school. Owing to limited manpower, WG put more emphasis on Green Island and Greeting Sunrise Boulevard, and provided primary suggestions to the courtyard.

Besides the above spaces, WG tried to leave some small spaces for students to decorate in the future so that each year you will see different images of the space. More importantly, the event will motivate more students to be involved in the campus planning process, which will hopefully empower them.

Opportunities

Were there any chances to achieve our goal in this private school? As this paper describes above, private schools need to evaluate the efficiency of each investment before spending. And the decision making process is always top-down. Under this condition, we were not so sure that we could execute this bottom-up process. Luckily there were opportunities which promised the right time, right place and right person: First, on the School Anniversary Day, people "speak up" for their wish in front of the chair of the trustee board. Secondly, the creative campus renew project followed the basic concepts of TM campus planning guidelines for upgrading, which was on the process of preparation and had been discussed in the planning committee for a long time. Besides, this renew project matched the future construction schedule. For example, TM had already budgeted for remodeling the Quadrangle in early 2003, which would be an opportunity to create a better courtyard at the same time. Thirdly, owing to the construction schedule for the campus, TM would precede relocating spaces at the same

Figure 4. Claiming for usage through an event.

time, for example, the basement and first floor of the Service Hall would change from a convenience store and classrooms to student club offices and convenience store respectively. This was the rationale to renew the surrounding area.

Lastly, frequent communications within the Task Force, especially between WG and the principal, could integrate forces from both trustee board and administrative system instantaneously. Take Green Island planning as an example: WG planned this site to be "TM House'" to provide everyday needs for both school members and the neighborhood, including a cafeteria, galleries, and meeting lounge. WG took an existing case—YM Square, as reference, planned to recruit a company to operate it by way of Build-Operate-Transfer. As soon as WG had this idea, Director Ko explained it to Principal Shen, and invited Task Force members to visit the case in order to promote the idea. This should be a tri-win situation for students, the school (the trustee board mainly), and the neighborhood. The more people understand it, the more chances there are to accomplish it.

Design methods

In our minds, there were three considerations for the design of these spaces: claim for students spaces, design for proper usage, manage for multi-usage. First, claiming territory: During the planning phase, Director Lin suggested the student union use Green Island for an annual big event—White Valentine's Day. On that day, Green Island and the surroundings became a student living area again. WG did the same thing at Greeting Sunrise Boulevard. During the School Anniversary Day, the naming ballot and "Speak Up" were held at the Boulevard. After that, Director Ko arranged another ceremony over there to try to transform this alley from a walkway to a plaza.

Secondly, designing for the usage: Since students' living area was rarely included on TM campus, we visited other campuses as case studies. As a result, we introduced Yang-ming University's YM Square for our TM House at Green Island. We also used "A pattern language" to express individual concepts of the spaces for better communication. Then, we simulated our ideas on the models: For Green Island and Greeting Sunrise Boulevard, we added platforms to connect inside areas with the outdoors; for the courtyard, we suggested creating a hallway to let people easily walk through the courtyard, and build a stage for holding events.

Thirdly, managing for multi-usage: WG planned to conduct a series of events for multiple uses of the spaces being remodeled, which hopefully would re-claim the usage for the future. These examples were Green Island Festival,[6] Cheer Squad Contest, and Christmas Eve Party. In addition, a students' decorating competition for a façade and a basement exit would be held. These were the spaces for the continuation of the participatory spirit. Since these spaces were basically for students, we hoped the students would maintain the role of future management. WG had discussed this possibility with the chair of the student union for their involvement.

RESULTS AND DISCUSSIONS

Storms in a Pot

Among our target sites, Green Island was radically planned; the courtyard remained in similar usage; and Greeting Sunrise Boulevard transformed to be a real Boulevard. Consequently, the courtyard and the Boulevard were successfully remodeled; Green Island was rejected. The first two projects matched the Quadrangle remodeling schedule so that part of our ideas could be integrated into the final designs. After the contractor was commissioned, TM held one "Creative Campus Task Force" meeting and invited all WG members to comment on the design alternatives. The contractor agreed with some ideas for the courtyard, and fully followed our design for the Boulevard. As for the Green Island, even though the collaborative company had almost been decided, TM still maintained the use as classrooms for Extension Education but only adopted part of our landscape design for "decoration" without considering its original concept. Therefore, the new landscape became redundant and even awkward. Lastly, the plan to leave spaces for students to get involved was halted. The school made everything controllable and predictable as before.

Now there are more people hanging out at the courtyard and Boulevard.[7] You will meet more people other than your classmates and teachers. It seems people have more chances to interact and communicate with others on campus. Perhaps we can argue that public spaces have been established at TM.

Have these two projects successfully changed the school bureaucratic structure after all? There are several phenomena to be considered:

a) All of TM's temporary groups were dismissed after finishing these two projects. The "Creative Campus Task Force" turned in their final report and was dismissed, WG finished its mission and the pedagogical studies wrapped up its one-year seminar. It was planned that the participating teachers would conduct new classes regarding the issues of community renaissance. Those teachers had planned and reached a consensus to conduct classes collaboratively because they hope this tiny participation experiment will be continued through classes.[8] Unfortunately, this idea was objected to by some senior teachers who had never participated in the seminars and any event. Therefore, the department could not support teachers to conduct the community renaissance classes. Director Ko resigned from this position, too.

b) The whole process was a struggle between top-down and bottom-up. It is a paradox that the MOE, which supervises schools, (top-down) requests schools to execute a bottom-up process. This kind of institutionalized participatory process will be easily trapped by the existing power structure. It surely has been the largest defeat to the WG. "Our ideas were totally distorted in the construction. The spaces for students to display their ideas were destroyed by the school." "Our ideas cannot compete with one word by the trustee board." In TM's case, ways to solve the above difficulties were to use personal relationships for obtaining first hand information immediately and then trying to negotiate with different voices before making final decisions. Sometimes WG would need to seek the principal's support in order to integrate forces from different parties. It was the same case when bargaining with the trustee board. As I described before, frequent communication through the principal was needed. These strategies were repeatedly used at the end of the project to match the schedule/budget for remodeling Quadrangle. As described before, for the courtyard, WG explained the considerations for the spaces in a "public forum"—the Task Force meeting. Because Director Ko had discussed WG's ideas with the principal earlier, the Task Force meeting could wrap up with concrete conclusions, which helped to push the project forward.

This top-down/bottom-up conflict also happened when WG tried to recruit students to participate in the whole process. It was a big challenge to WG to let students take equal status during discussions. One presumption was the teachers' awareness to be open to all ideas. The other way was to use outsiders (of the power structure), in this case, BPRF, to be the interface and disturbance to the existing power structure. Therefore, the two parties would have a new equal status for the public discourse.

c) The participatory spirit seems to have evaporated. Ideally, the product (in this case, physical spaces) of this participatory process will meet the needs of the users, which provides

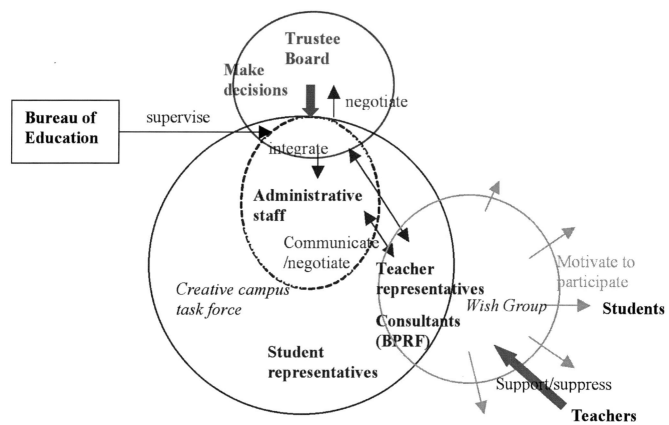

Figure 5. TM Creative Campus Renew Project bureaucratic structure.

feedback to follow the same process to form a public forum in the future. However, when this participatory power is institutionalized, can it remain public? I think it depends on whether the structure has been reconstructed or not, for example, recruit new outside forces, form a partnership with other schools. All these methods help to open up the existing structure. But it is an ideal situation. Usually when the project finishes, the participatory process will pause. TM is still under this situation. In the worst case, the process becomes institutionalized. It is pseudo-participation that is still controlled by the original hegemony, and the school remains an administrative institution.

Therefore, to answer the previous question, strictly speaking, the projects TM executed have disturbed the original bureaucratic structure but are still under the control of a conservative power. Even though we introduced the idea of participatory design, toward the end, we had to admit that it seemed like storms in a pot. Whenever the water threatens to overflow, a conservative power—as Touraine (2003) describes, existing among the teachers and administrative staff raises to hold the lid in order to maintain the existing power structure in the school, which lets the school remain in its traditional role.

Epilogue

Even though the results were not fully satisfying, I am still optimistic that the people of TM will continue implementing the

participatory design process in the future. Two phenomena support my points: a) Teachers were independent enough to stand against the mainstream. b) The results of the physical space remodeling provided positive feedback. According to Touraine's (2003) idea of democratized school, he indicates the needs of the independence of teachers. In TM's case, although WG teachers were at the existing power structure, they still tried to fight against the main stream to create new spaces through a participatory process. They were independent from the traditional structure. Next, the remodeling turned out to be acceptable, people love to use it. This positive feedback perhaps also urged proceeding with the next creative space. It is always the best encouragement for facing further challenges.

In conclusion, according to TM's previous experience, there were factors to increase the efficiency of the process of participation. I believe it will be true as well for their future practice.

a) When participants are authorized, they will have a better position to contest with the existing structure. In TM's case, WG members were authorized, which facilitated them to express their ideas efficiently. But this authorization should be carefully used not to be another hegemony but a tool for empowerment.

b) Positive feedback will enhance participants' confidence to continue their efforts. In TM's case, after the courtyard was remodeled, WG members then believed that their efforts could be realized, which gave them more confidence to carry on.

c) Taking cases as examples is a good way to persuade people for certain concepts. During the design process, WG members visited other campuses that not only inspired them but also became references for future design.

d) Link partnership as an outside force to disturb the existing structure. In this case, BPRF being the consultant was especially useful to be the interface among different parties. Under this condition, people will be released from the existing hierarchy system to form a public forum on equal positions.

TM's next round of participation process needs to expand the influences to the larger school body. As WG expresses in the report "When school upgrades, the characters of students will change. We hope students will learn to take over the management of their campus." Now that the mechanism of empowerment has been prepared, we hope TM is ready to take another journey.

ENDNOTES

[1] Planning Team members: TM University (Wish Group): C. H. Ko, C. L. Joy Wu, C. L. Lin, etc. BPRF consultants: Ching-fen Yang, Su-chun Lin, Yu-chung Lee

[2] The MOE takes the responsibility to decide which college is qualified to upgrade.

[3] Who has a strong relationship with the students.

[4] The alley is between two buildings: Service Hall and Renew Hall. Therefore, most names used the synonyms and connotations of the two buildings. One other naming type reflected its orientation—east-west. The other naming type expressed students' wishes for the future usage on this space.

[5] In Taiwanese connotation, "green island" refers to a place that stands alone as in the real world that Green Island is located East to Taiwan island.

[6] This event was planned to combine the forces of school and neighborhood. The programs would be a neighborhood flea market, story telling about the history of this area, computer aid booth, etc. All the programs would claim Green Island to be the bridge between TM and the neighborhood.

[7] Somehow it is odd, by observing, there are more first year students than others. Perhaps higher classes have more choices than the freshmen and would rather choose to go out of the school during the break.

[8] Teachers specialize in history studies, geography, civil education, arts, and public health.

REFERENCES

Hsia, C. 1994.〈(重)建構公共空間─理論的反省〉。《台灣社會研究季刊》16，21-54。

Hsia, C. 1997.〈再理論公共空間〉。《城市與設計學報》2/3，63-76。

《TM校園創意空間期末報告書》2003.。

Douglass, M. 2002. Civic spaces in a global Age: An agenda for pacific Asia cities. In IPS-Nus Forum on Civic Spaces in the Cities of the Asia-Pacific The Institute of Policy Studies, 4-5 March, 2002. Singapore.

Douglass, M. 2003. Civic society for itself and in the public sphere: Comparative Research on Globalization, Cities and Civic Space in Pacific Asia. In Second GRAD Conference, June 14-16, 2003. Vancouver.

Soja, E. 2004.《第三空間》（王志弘、張華蓀、王玥民譯）。台北：桂冠。

Touraine, A. 2003.《我們能否共同生存》（狄玉明、李平匯譯）。北京：商務印書館。

A PLANNER OR AN ACTOR
The Experience of Preserving Japanese Houses in Taipei

DaYuanZi Studio[1]

ABSTRACT

Due to the illegal razing on April 10th 2003, of two Japanese houses of National Taiwan University (NTU) located in Wen-Chou Street, the issue of preserving Japanese houses built in the colonial era has received significant social attention. We (DYZ studio) were assigned two projects by NTU and the Culture Bureau of the Taipei City Government, to do the general research and investigation of Japanese houses in Da-An, Zhong-Zheng, Zhong-Shan districts of Taipei City. The mission is to create a database of houses and trees in the area. At the same time, we took a variety of actions against the Central Government Policy. In the process of research and actions from last April, we realized the importance of the role of professionals, which are the main points of discussion in this paper:

1. When facing the nation, communities, and the limitation of structural position, professionals are often faced by the choice of being a planner or an actor. We found that switching back and forth between these two roles may be a better choice. Here we will discuss the model of progressive planners.

2. In undertaking the social action of preserving Japanese houses and the construction of preservation discourse, we will also discuss how professionals deal with the multiple conflicts and contradictions between complex colonial history and ethnic identities.

ENDNOTES

[1] The authors of the paper are Weishui Cheng, Huishin Huang, Lichin Kuo, Yenju Lee, Chiamin Cheng, members of DYZ studio.

new actors and
institutions

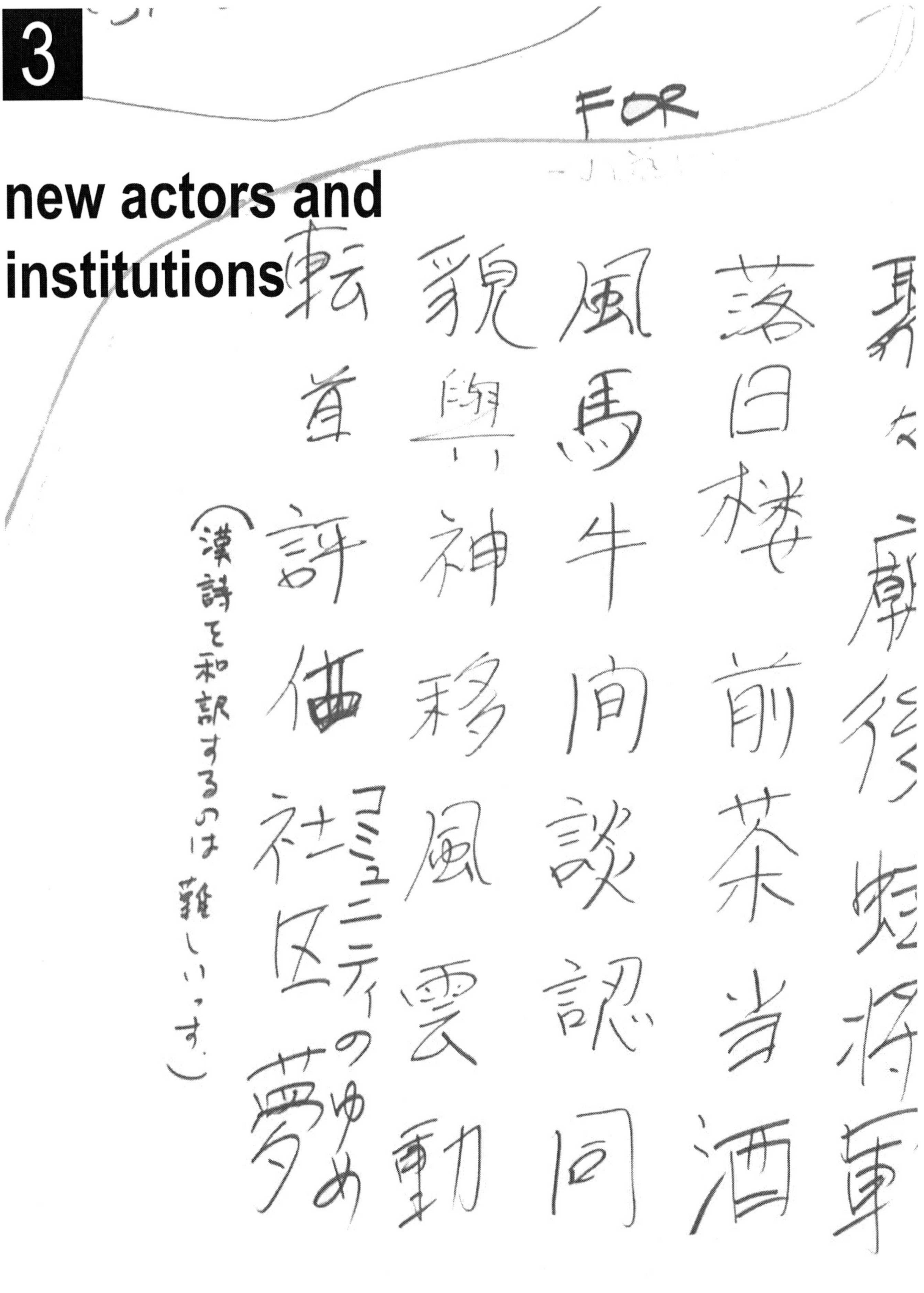

FOR

男
々
廟
後
短
将
軍

落
日
楼
前
茶
当
酒

風
馬
牛
向
談
認
同

貌
興
神
移
風
雲
動

轉
首
評
伍
社
区
夢

コミュニティの ゆめ

（漢詩を和訳するのは難しいです）

CHANGING CONTEXT OF COMMUNITY DEVELOPMENT IN JAPAN AND A FUTURE VIEW

Yasuyoshi Hayashi

ABSTRACT

This paper examines the features of social and economic change after the 1990s in Japan, specifically in terms of changes in civic consciousness, administrative system, economic and industrial structure, as well as community change. It also looks at the emergence of a new social image corresponding to the incompatibility and conflicts of economic and social system. Three examples of new systems to support community development are compared: Yamato City (ordinance to promote citizen's activity for creating 'new public'; Tsukisara District ('Cheer-up Support Program' to provide opportunities to realize creative and cooperative society); and Kuki City (conversion from centralized administration to collaboration between citizens and administration).

NOTABLE FEATURES OF THE SOCIAL AND ECONOMIC CHANGES OF JAPAN SINCE THE 90s

Changes in the consciousness of citizens

Citizens' consciousness in Japan has greatly changed since the 1990s from dependence on the administrations to independence and autonomy. An inclination toward heavy dependence on the administrative authorities, a marked feature in the way the Japanese behave, has rapidly changed since the 1990s. In the field of community development, a tendency has spread around the country to improve and sustain the quality of community life and environments by the hands of citizens, and citizens with a variety of backgrounds willingly take part in activities everywhere, working to realize the collaboration between community residents and local authorities.

Historically, the power relations between the central and local governments, as well as between administrative authorities and the private, have been understood as vertical ones in Japan where decisions are passed from the former/top to the latter/bottom, something we call the "structure of a vertical society." A conversion from this vertical society to a horizontal social structure was asserted by many citizen movements after the 60s, and the expansion of community development on the initiative of citizens in the 90s simultaneously fostered the growth of a horizontally-oriented consciousness at a grass roots level.

The Great Hanshin-Awaji Earthquake of 1995, with the relief activities by an estimated one million volunteer people, drastically changed the perception of citizen activities in Japanese society. Prompted by this, the so-called NPOs Law proposed by a group of lawmakers passed the Diet in 1998. The law allows citizens to give nonprofit organizations a legal status as juridical persons. Approximately 17,000 NPOs were founded in the five years after the law took effect, and more than 3,000 have been created every year since, thus creating a new social sector. A sense of reassurance that citizens can create a new sector by their own hands is further accelerating their participation in society.

In the 90s, the idea of a "new public" was born out of localities where citizens made the effort to realize the formation of a "horizontal social structure." Now recognition has spread among citizens that "small publics" are being created in their everyday activities, and they grow to become an "extensive public," against a traditional "public" monopolized by the governments and administrations. The "new public" is a "public" in which citizens, NPOs, businesses and administrative authorities support each other, under an agreement to realize a "horizontal social structure." This idea has quickly penetrated Japanese society since 2000.

The idea of a "new public," combined with the birth of the NPO Law, gives power to citizens working for positive change and prompts the emergence of a new social sector thereby transforming the civil society of Japan.

Features of changes in the communities

Local communities of Japan now stand at a crossroads of revitalization with the following processes:

1) Increase of the rate of senior people

The rate of citizens over 65 years old nationally reached 19.0% in 2003 and is expected to keep growing rapidly to an estimated 22.5% in 2010 and 35.7% in 2050. This change will have a significant influence on communities, whether in cities or in rural areas.

2) Desolation of communities

Desolation of both cities and rural areas is in progress nationwide, accompanied by the deterioration of communities as witnessed in the decrease of population and rapid rise of crime. In some respects, this urban desolation and community deterioration are similar to what a number of cities in America and Europe have experienced since the 60s.

3) Community development for revitalization takes root

To address these situations, management of local communities by communities themselves has become a major concern of citizens. Community development projects by citizens' own initiative as well as the launching of diverse local businesses are flourishing around the country.

4) Emergence of new methods to express citizens' will in the society.

Residents of communities facing difficulties make use of two new methods for the rebirth of their own communities. One is the method of participation including "community development workshops," which became popular in the 90s. The other is the utilization of advanced information technology and information systems, which spread in the late 90s. Both methods have the potential to create horizontal social structures in this vertical society.

In rural, mountain villages and small cities particularly, great efforts are made by residents, overcoming geographical disadvantages, to make full use of natural environments and historical resources to create new community cultures, develop tourist resources, promote exchanges with outside communities and generate diverse business opportunities.

Features of changes in the economic and industrial structures

Since the 90s, the destruction of the local economy caused by the penetration of the global economy has prompted the widening of debilitated areas both in cities and in rural areas. While Japan underwent depopulation in rural and mountainous areas during a period of economic growth (1950 to 75), this nationwide generation of debilitated areas is what the nation has never experienced. To alleviate this, political measures for community revitalization are under exploration.

Attempts of new communal economies intended for the revitalization of communities have been spreading since the late 90s. The interest in small businesses, or "community businesses" as they are called in Japan, is heightening among citizens and NPOs and a wide variety of projects are given a try throughout the country. With this, revaluation, rediscovery and creation of social resources and social capital within communities have become a big concern in citizen activities. Formation of multiple networks on a global scale, made possible by advanced IT, serves to widen the possibility of community revitalization.

The revaluation of social resources and social capital inside communities is giving birth to 'community banks,' financial systems run by citizens, and reutilization of existing local credit unions. The issuance and use of local currencies unique to individual communities is also being tried, thus generating new networks through which resources within communities are exchanged.

Since the 80s, an assertion has been made by the market sector that Japan, a globally notorious 'bureaucrat-regulated state,' should be changed to an open, market-oriented state with a small government, and political pressures for this change have also intensified. In response, reform has been in progress since the 90s designed to abolish the existing bureaucratic regulations.

In the market sector, recognition of social responsibilities of businesses has been heightening since the 90s and there is a gradually spreading tendency of businesses to engage in social-related activities. Also, appropriate forms are being sought in which businesses willing to take part in the "new public" can work in collaboration with the social sector.

Features of changes in the administrative systems

Since the deterioration of the Japanese "bubble economy" in the early 1990s, it has become apparent that inefficiency and rigidity of the administrative systems make it impossible for the nation to catch up with new global situations and international economic competition.

Due to the failed economic policies of the 90s, the government now faces a situation where it can no longer ignore the huge accumulation of financial deficits. It has proved evident that to solve the problems a small government is the only possible choice. To boost the conversion to a market-oriented state with a small government, the government sector cannot avoid collaboration with social sectors that take care of social services inconsistent with market principles.

Reform for decentralization to transform the centralized, bureaucrat-dominated state has remained a big political issue since the 1950s. The first step was made toward the reform by the enactment of the Comprehensive Decentralization Law in 2000. Prompted by this, waves of establishing the autonomous, self-governing bodies are further spreading. The actual effects of these measures have yet to be proved, however.

As already stated, resulting from the malfunctioning administrative systems and financial shrinkage of both the central and local governments, dependence on the authorities has rapidly lowered in the minds of citizens. The administrations, on the contrary, have become more dependent on NPOs. Some local governments have announced that, in the future, they will curtail the number of personnel by half while giving up a number of jobs, trusting them to citizens and NPOs. Reflecting expanding citizen activities, new social sectors have been mushrooming since the 1990s, while the market sector has at last started to catch up with the changing global economy, as earlier mentioned. The fact that the administrative sector is the most backward one is now recognized by many people.

FORMATION OF A NEW SOCIETY MODEL RESPONDING TO THE EMERGENCE OF A COMPREHENSIVE ISSUE: DIVISION AND STRUGGLE

Resulting from the afore-mentioned notable features of changes, a few new notions have spread among citizens. One notion is that *"community"* becomes a matter of grave concern for themselves. *"A comprehensive issue of community revitalization"* is now a major concern shared by a broad scope of people connected with community development. Another is a model for a new economy, a new society, which has been formed in the consciousness of citizens. The model has not necessarily acquired an expression sufficiently accurate to become a shared idea in the society, and therefore has not been distinctly described in its whole image yet. Nevertheless, images and concepts of the several elements that constitute the model, it seems, are graphically inscribed in the minds of citizens. Some of these elements are important particularly for the current stage of Japan, while others are commonly recognized by people in many countries. It can be said the clear image is expressed in various activities of citizens.

The comprehensive issue of community revitalization which encompasses cities and rural areas of the whole country contains some factors that require radical changes in the existing political, administrative, social and economic systems. Faith was lost, as early as in the 90s, in a central government which could provide solutions to all economic and social problems. The solution instead lies in how a given community takes the initiative to discover, create, nurture and utilize social capital, namely networks of people, and latent social resources within itself. This notion has diffused on a broad scale since the late 90s from rural, mountain and fishing villages to communities in major cities.

Several elements that constitute the new society model: their concepts and images

What is recognized by citizens as the goal of community revitalization is a society model of collaboration and symbiosis. The concepts and images of the elements constituting the model are listed as follows:

- Social systems to ensure collaboration on community scenes supported by the principles of "horizontal social structure" and a "new public."

- Windows of opportunity open to the community which ensures that a variety of citizens are allowed to give full attention to their potential.

- Diverse and multiple networks unique to individual communities which are accessible within and without.

- Creation of sustainable nonprofit communal economies.

- Creation of unique systems to ensure recycling of resources and symbiosis with the environment.

- Assurance that a community life, made by the hands of citizens utilizing the above-mentioned systems and devices, possesses unique and diverse functions, environments and expansion. Also assurance that this community life possesses a sustainable high quality.

- Acquisition of distinct identities, created through the above mentioned means, of which communities can be proud.

Division and struggle between two economies

Stratification of society caused by the global economy, the struggle between the global and local economies within communities, and the underlying conflict between society models are simultaneously the division, struggle and conflicts between participants in community revitalization.

Actors in social and economic activities in Japan over the last two decades were, first, certain groups in the business sector which believe in market principles, and, second, autonomous and independent citizens in the social sector and emerging NPOs as the social organizations they form. The administrative sector, the third central actor, has remained basically a negative one over the same period of time.

Figure 1. (Left) The selection open to public at the ex-bank building of a hundred years ago. Figure 2. (Right) Farmers' group explaining their proposal for a food processing business.

Figure 3. (Left) An example of small business: tourists practicing traditional salt manufacturing. Figure 4. (Right) An example of small business: tourists practicing MISO making with soy bean.

Where do powers to create social systems revitalization needs lie? While part of the social systems needed for community revitalization are being created by some innovative forces in the social sector, their powers are still weak and inadequate. While part of the administrative sector, particularly local administrations, are highly interested in revitalization, they are constrained by vertically split administrative systems, remains of the past centralism. Moreover, the grave financial difficulties they suffer are bound to make their roles in revitalization limited ones for a long time to come. Without the assistance of NPOs, the conception and materialization of effective social systems for revitalization by the administrations will not be successful.

In the market sector, there has been a heightening concern for the social responsibility of business as well as for social contribution-oriented activities since the late 80s. Attracting the attention of businesses to community revitalization through appropriate means of promotion is an issue of actual importance. Also as actors in communal economies, businesses presently are the most distinguishable actors in revitalization.

Given the current situation of conflicts and struggles, collaboration between these participants in community revitalization is an issue of vital importance.

EXAMPLES: CREATING NEW SYSTEMS SURROUNDING COMMUNITY DEVELOPMENT

Under the afore-mentioned circumstances, a diversity of interesting activities of community development have been carried out everywhere around the country. Appearance of NPOs has increased the social importance of community development. A number of social projects beyond the traditional concept of Machizukuri are mushrooming, and "community businesses," as community economic development is referred to in Japan, are expanding as a new area of Machizukuri.

The following examples reflect these recent situations – A society of creativity and collaboration born out of the window of opportunity open to community businesses; and collaboration versus division between citizens and the authorities.

Tsukisara Cheer-up Support Program

This is an example where promotion of community businesses was carried out as a means of community development in a semi-mountainous area through the collaboration between the local administration and NPOs.

Ordinance on promotion of citizen activities to create new public: Yamato City

Based on an ordinance adopted through full citizen participation, "authentic collaboration between citizens and the administration," unprecedented in Japan, has started and social frameworks supporting activities of citizens and NPOs

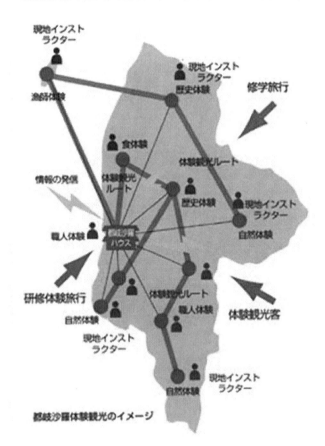

Figure 5. Tourism business; visiting sites of proposers; practicing farm works or shopping for native products.

are steadily taking shape. An example which shows the level that citizen participation in Japan has attained.

Fundamental ordinance on autonomy: City of Kuki

A draft drawn up and put forward by citizens, a product of full participation, was considerably rewritten by an opposing group inside the city hall, thus losing the idea of new autonomy and collaboration proposed by citizens. Here a fundamental issue that the current Japanese administrative systems do not recognize participation as a right of citizens has emerged.

In the contrasting cases of Yamato and Kuki, we see unstable relations between citizens and authorities in community development. At the same time, the reality in Japan is revealed that authorities do not give an appropriate institutional position to the public necessity of citizens' participation as a right of the citizen. Such situations explain the decisions authorities make that surprisingly deviate from citizens' idea in actual communities.

GOVERNMENT INSTITUTION AND LOCAL PRACTICE OF PROFESSIONAL PLANNING
Community Planners in Taipei

Pao-Chi Sung

ABSTRACT

Beginning in 1999, the Taipei City Government started to promote a 'Community Planner Program' in an effort to encourage residents to take part in creating a city of self-identity. This is the sixth year since the program was launched. With the central government's support and promotion by academia, more than half of all administrative divisions in the country have introduced the program. Specifically, the program has been introduced to earthquake-hit areas to speed up reconstruction. Through review of past experiences, compilation of existing firsthand data and applicable literature, the implementation of the 'Taipei Community Planner Program' is described, current successes are examined and hurdles encountered during the process are detailed. It is also my objective to explore the future of the program. Study results indicate that the Community Planner profession needs to be respected while the success of the program lies in good resident participation. In the long run, community planners are to act as defenders of the interest of the general public by assuming an active role in the participatory planning system. They should shoulder heavier responsibilities in the construction and maintenance of 'urban redevelopment.' It is hoped that with the description of the design concept of this program, those who are concerned about participatory community planning and design may gain an insight into the program.

THE PRACTICE PROCESS OF THE 'COMMUNITY PLANNER'

This is the sixth year since Taipei took the lead in introducing 'Community Planners' into the local planning process. The history of and reasons for the design and revision of this program are described below.

Growth of Community Consciousness and Rise of Grassroots Strength

As income rises and political reforms are implemented, the Taiwanese society is becoming more and more open. Since the 1980s, community energy has been growing gradually.

Communities have begun the methods of controlling and expressing themselves. In particular, mayors of state-governed cities were elected by city residents for the first time in 1995. The political restructuring enabled manifestation of grassroots forces in Taipei.

In response, 'The Neighborhood Improvement Program (NIP)' in the mid 1990s became the policy of Chen Shui-bian, then mayor of Taipei, in an attempt to meet community needs and solicit votes from middle-class communities. In the meantime, the 'Community Construction and Management or CCM (Sher-chu-zong-ti-yin-zhao)' policy by the Council for Cultural Affairs of the central government intended to turn community forces into a mechanism for community building nationwide. Taipei's NIP and the central government's CCM became the two major strategies for undertaking local planning in the mid 1990s. They also became the channels for communities to obtain government support and more resources. This urban reform through community participation helps to bridge– government institutions and local communities.

Predicaments and breakthroughs experienced while promoting NIP

Since 1995, the Taipei City Government began promoting NIP in an attempt to consolidate community energy and vigor into the public sector's implementation mechanism in order to reshape the cities.

Challenges and predicaments arise as NIP is implemented. The last year Chen was in office, despite the pressure of getting reelected, many NIPs were unable to be completed by their target date. Therefore, the Development Bureau began thinking about how to strengthen the function and role played by professional planners in terms of environmental renewal and their work with the public sector in the area of community planning. The drawbacks of the NIP implementation mechanism are detailed below:

- Little Communication and Cooperation between the Bureaucracy and the Community—

'NIP' is performed by non-governmental organizations under contract to the city government. However, once planning is completed, difficulties follow as ideas are implemented by the public segment. Examples include extremely high costs and difficult subsequent management and maintenance and design changes or revisions. Complicated by the difficulties posed by horizontal communication and division of work between different branches of the public sector, the community's expectations turn into disappointment and discontent. Many communities are therefore discouraged. In some cases, the community and the public segment criticize each other for not doing enough.[1]

- Lack of Intervention by Professionals in Communicating and Consolidating Community Opinions—

Impacted by local politics and elections, 'Li' (a unit of neighborhood) offices and community development associations often share conflicting interests. Since the government does not sign contracts with Li offices, it is difficult for the government to implement Lin/Li renewal programs without support by local opinion leaders and residents.[2]

- Disadvantaged Communities Are Not Receiving Enough Attention—

Most of the communities actively participating in submitting proposals for environmental renewal are middle-class communities. Many disadvantaged, low-class, edge-of-the-city communities are in more need of improvement of living quality through bettering the environment than middle-class communities. However, they haven't been able to find suitable professionals to help them.[3]

For the above-said three reasons, the Development Bureau in 1999 began asking the community and the professionals to form partnerships when promoting NIPs. The Bureau also hopes that the professional team may become representative of Party B in order to assist the community in consolidating opinions and in strengthening the feasibility of implementing NIPs. Meanwhile, the Bureau is thinking about how to encourage more professional planning teams to work in the field of community services. This is the how the 'Community Planner' program began.

THE INITIAL FRAMEWORK OF TAIPEI CITY COMMUNITY PLANNER PROGRAM 1999

The Roles Community Planners Play and Their Qualifications

According to 'Rules Governing Recruitment of Community Planners 1999 by the Urban Development Bureau, Taipei City Government (hereinafter referred to as the Rules)' the roles community planners play and their qualifications are:

- Professional knowledge in space planning and design

- The passion to serve the community

- Community planners play the role of a liaison between the community and the government. They deal with issues that are related to "public space."

- Community planners are to be very familiar with the environment of the area they serve and feel strongly about the place.

What Community Planners Do

What community planners do, as stated in the Rules, have much to do with the handling of issues relating to the community's public space. They include providing professional consultation services, making proposals to improve community environments and participating in seminars by the city government on urban development issues and giving advice.[4]

The Way Community Planners Work

Setting up a 'Community Planner Office' – Community planners are to open their offices in the communities they serve or set up a Community Planner Office at an adequate location for easy access by community residents to discuss various issues relating to urban public space and construction within the community. The Office is to provide professional consultation services or be made available for the participation and discussion of the planning and design work.

Use of the Internet – Internet service is to be available for easy access by residents to obtain relevant information. Questions by residents may be answered through the discussion areas of websites or via email. The Development Bureau and Community Planners may communicate with each other via email, simplifying the administrative operating procedure between the city government and community planners. The city government may thus support community planners' work in a more efficient manner.

Measures Taken by the City Government

Qualifications of Community Planners – According to the Rules, individuals specializing in urban planning, urban design, urban renewal, community construction planning, community environmental planning, community design, architectural planning, architectural design, landscape design, transportation engineering, civil engineering, and environmental engineering are eligible to apply. However, they also have to have a certain degree of knowledge of the community they are to serve and be willing to devote themselves to the community. It is obvious that the Development Bureau already believes that the educational background of community planners is not to be limited to environmental planning. Nevertheless, their backgrounds still show traces of 'Development Bureau Character.'

Selection of Community Planners – Selection of community planners is conducted in several ways. Community groups or local opinion leaders may recommend candidates of their choice. Trade associations and academic organizations also have the right to make recommendations. Individuals who think that they are qualified may apply as well. To select the right space planning professionals in order to build a community planning human-resources database and help community residents conduct environment renewal, the city government has decided that community planners are to be selected in the following three-step procedure: preliminary examination, on-location inspection and panel review as stated in Table 1.

Procedure		Description
1	Preliminary Examination	The Bureau conducts preliminary examination of applications according to the Rules (including the required content and format) and the purpose of community planners.
2	On-location Inspection	The Bureau sends personnel to office of applicant to conduct on-location inspection in order to determine whether it is easily accessible, whether it provides adequate discussion room, whether it has Internet access and whether applicant understands fully the role of community planner.
3	Initial Review	The Bureau reviews information obtained in the first two steps and submits "The List of Semifinalists" to the Panel. Thirty applicants are to be selected from the List.
4	Panel Review (Final Review)	1. The Bureau invites experts/scholars, representatives from relevant organizations and members of responsible departments of the city government to form the Panel (the number of representatives from the government is not to exceed one half of all panelists.) The Panel is to review the semifinalists. 2. During the review process, applicant is to provide relevant information requested by the Panel. 3. The Panel has the option to ask applicant to make presentations in the process. 4. Applicant may submit supplementary written information voluntarily during the process or when requested by the Panel. Once adopted, the information is to be used as the basis for implementing program by recruited community planners. 5. Applicants failed the preliminary examination are to be reported to the Panel for confirmation and necessary adjustments.

Table 1. Taipei City Community Planner Selection Procedure 1999. (Source: Bureau of Urban Development, Taipei City Government; compiled by the author)

Community Planner Meeting – To enhance communication with community planners, the Bureau holds a Community Planner Meeting every two to three months. The purposes of the meeting are:

- Community planners report progress of their work and discussion with each other.

- Assist community planners to solve problems raised by residents that cannot be solved by planners immediately; discussing proposals made at the meeting.

- Feasible environmental improvement suggestions that need to be dealt with immediately are resolved at the meeting and turned over to concerned government offices for speedy handling.

- Provide community planners an opportunity to exchange work experiences.

- Review the operating procedure and implementation mechanism of the community planner program.

- Offer residents, community organizations and news media the opportunity to gain knowledge of the operations and progress of the community planner program.

Assistance to Community Planners –

• Funding:

The amount paid by the Bureau to the community planner depends on the content and quantity of services listed in the written proposal by the community planner. The amount is NT $500,000 (U.S. $15,000) or thereabouts. The exact amount is to be agreed upon by both parties through negotiations. During the period the community planner is hired, the Bureau is to negotiate with the planner the amount to be paid for extra work done.

• Information:

For the information needed by the community planner when carrying out community services, the Bureau is to assist the planner in obtaining from various departments of the city government information needed and provide relevant reference books.

• Website:

As the Internet transmits data, provides interactive discussions and posts the latest information, the Bureau has set up the first community planner website: www.communityplanner.taipei. gov.tw.

The website is:

a) Professional: With community planners of different professional backgrounds, consultations on urban and community public space are made possible through the Internet.

b) Real-time: With the Internet, community planners are able to respond quickly and in a timely manner to residents' inquiries. Internet-surfers are able to obtain opinions and information through the website.

c) Multilateral: Through the website, city residents, community planners, different departments of the city government, district government offices, Li offices and community organizations are able to discuss issues regarding environmental improvement.

d) Participatory: City residents are encouraged to participate through the Internet public forums.

The Bureau creates a communication channel between the government, the community planner and residents through the website. In addition, community planners are offered individual website space to use. Meanwhile, the Bureau is able to monitor the quantity and quality of work done by community planners through the website's back-end management and statistics mechanisms.

Concurrent Outsourced Study and Review – To avoid a lack of external input, in the same year the Organization of Urban Re's (OURs) was commissioned by the Bureau to conduct 'Evaluation of the Operating Strategy and Mechanism of the Taipei Community Planner Program.' The results were used to make amendments for the promotion of the community planner program.

REVISIONS OF AND CHANGES TO THE 'TAIPEI COMMUNITY PLANNER' PROGRAM

It's been six years since Taipei City began promoting 'Community Planner.' As government officials keep being replaced, the program has undergone many modifications and expansions. Table 2 is a summary of the changes.

Honorary Community Planners

According to the Bureau's plan, Serving Community Planners are selected by the city government based on applicable rules. They sign contracts with the Bureau and accept funding from it to perform community planning duties according to the contract. Honorary Community Planners, though also selected by the city government, don't sign contracts with the Bureau. They work as community planners according to their skills and interests. In a word, Serving Community Planners are paid while Honorary Community Planners are not.

With their professional skills, community planners help residents and disadvantaged groups to conduct environmental renewal and make suggestions for improvement of public open spaces. There is no doubt about their role as service providers. Nevertheless, there is a competitive yet cooperative relationship between community planners and the planning department of the government. As community planners are paid by the city government, their stance is questioned by some residents when the city government's policy differs with residents' needs. As a result, some of the first group of community planners said they would rather not get paid by the city government in return for more freedom to do what they wanted. This is why the Bureau began the Honorary Community Planner pilot program.

As the 'Community Planner' program is in its experimental stage, it is completely funded by the Construction and

Year	1999	2000	2001	2002	2003	2004
# of Applicants	62	47	63	56	58	
# of Applicants Selected	28	42	52	53	51	50
Nature	Serving: 28	Serving: 29 Honorary: 13	Honorary: 52	Honorary: 53	Honorary: 51	Honorary: 50
Funding	NT$500,000	NT$300,000	Honorary	Honorary	Honorary	Honorary
Job Description	Professional Consulting	Professional Consulting	Professional Consulting	Professional Consulting	Professional Consulting	Professional Consulting
		Neighborhood Development Projects	X	X	X	X
Professional Exchange Platform	Community Planner Meeting	Community Planner Meeting	Community Planner Meeting	Community Planner Meeting	Community Planner Meeting	Community Planner Meeting
	X	Neighborhood Community Planner Work Meeting	X	X	X	X
	X	X	Community Planning Service Center	Community Planning Service Center	Community Planning Service Center	Community Planning Service Center
Professional Training	X	Young Community Planner Training Program	Young Community Planner Training Program	Young Community Planner Training Program	Young Community Planner Training Program	Young Community Planner Training Program
	X	X	Community Planning Service Center	Community Planning Service Center	Community Planning Service Center	Community Planning Service Center
Community Resources	X	X	Community Colleges	Community Colleges	Community Colleges	Community Colleges
	X	X	X	Children Environment Experience Camps (4)*	Children Environment Experience Camps (2)	X
Websites	V	V	V	V	V	V
Liaison	X	V	V	V	X	X
Outsourced Studies	Taipei City Community Planner Program Operating Strategy and Mechanism Evaluation and Study	Taipei City Neighborhood Development Plan and Community Planner Program Operation Evaluation and Strategy Study 2000	Review of Taipei City Community Planner Program and Selection of Community Planners; Review of Taipei City Neighborhood Development Plan and suggestions	X	Taipei City Community Building Center Establishment Project	(about Community Planner)

*: Number of Camps

Table 2. Taipei Community Planners.

Planning Agency, at the Ministry of the Interior. So far, the city government doesn't have regular funding for the 'Community Planner' program. As the funding from the central government decreases by the year, the city government is thinking about how to use limited funding to hire more community planners in order to meet residents' expectations of the 'Community Planner' program. The objective is that every community has a community planner. Consequently, the second year (2000) the Honorary Community Planner pilot program was conducted, nearly half of the first group of planners and new planners supported the program. The Bureau in the third year (2001) turned all the planners into honorary planners. Meanwhile, the soliciting and adopting of environmental renewal plans and neighborhood development plans were added to reinforce the 'Community Planner' program. These changes not only gave planners enough room to apply their specialties to their work but also allowed individuals other than community planners to contribute to the cause of community development and renewal.

It is found that with the implementation of the 'Community Planner' program, administrative resources may be effectively taken advantage of. The promotion of honorary community planners should encourage passionate professionals interested in serving their communities to work with their fellow residents to realize planning and design ideas and to cooperate with the public segment to maintain environmental justice. Looking from a different perspective, the phenomenon fully demonstrates the support by the public segment in terms of funding and its impact on the promotion of other relevant work.

Promoting the 'Neighborhood Development Plan (NDP)'

The promotion of the NDP is aimed at improving regular NIP. Rather than focusing on short-term goals, the NDP stresses long-term objectives in an effort to gradually eliminate the disadvantages of traditional urban planning. It is hoped that, through participation by residents and partnership between the public and private sectors, a new resource consolidation model may be established in order to improve government decision-making, upgrade urban living quality and strengthen the city's competitiveness in the globalization process.

Expectations and needs of community residents are more likely to be met if community planners (local professionals) are to assist community residents in reaching a consensus in terms of the development of the community with their professional knowledge. The community planner is to work with residents to draw up an NDP with community living, environmental quality and public interest taken into consideration.

Therefore, the Bureau's plan to include community planners in the promotion of urban reform policy is observable. It is also observable how the government officials' understanding of

community planners impacts the establishment and revision of the system.

Establishing Community Planner Experience Exchange Platform: From 'Neighborhood Community Planner Work Meeting' to 'Community Planning Service Center' –

Many community planners told the Bureau that they became community planners so they could use their leisure time to provide the community with their services. Therefore, the Community Planner Meeting held by the Bureau once every two to three months requires that they submit formal reports, which has created excessive administrative work for them. The Bureau also discovered that though the subjects of discussion of the meeting center around 'The Old City Center,' 'The City Center' and 'The Area Neighboring the City Center,' subtler community needs are usually not dealt with. For this reason, having those who are willing and popular with community residents convene the Neighborhood Community Planner Work Meeting encourages exchange between community planners of the same neighborhood. By doing so, professionals are encouraged to conduct in-depth studies of the common issues of the neighborhood and reflect the needs of the neighborhood.

The 'Community Planner' program has entered its third year. Since some planners of some communities have been replaced, the Bureau finds it necessary to help communities to set up permanent offices in order to provide residents with a relatively more stable space of discussion and assembly. Residents are encouraged to participate in community affairs with the establishment of permanent offices. As it is hard to find suitable locations and personnel as well as raise enough funds in a short time, it is the Bureau's plan to encourage colleges to have space planning departments and non-governmental or non-profit organizations to sponsor the establishment of Community Planning Service Centers.

For schools, this move encourages teachers and students alike to care more about neighboring communities. Young professionals may learn about the specifics of becoming a community planner. For the public sector, the abundant teaching and human resources as well as the hardware of the private sector may be utilized to provide the community with long-term community planning services. For the community itself, more passionate professionals are willing to contribute to the cause. For community planners, there are plenty of opportunities for dialogue between profession practice and learning. Because of the win-win advantage, the Community Planning Service Center replaces the Neighborhood Community Planner Work Meeting, becoming the platform of experience exchange between community planners.

The Young Community Planner Training Program and Community Empowerment

The purpose of the 'Young Community Planner Training Program' is to recruit passionate, creative, young, space planning professionals who are willing to devote themselves to community planning and to offer them opportunities of systematic learning and practical training. Their abilities in communication, coordination and consolidation are to be nurtured until they possess the knowledge and skills needed to promote community planning affairs. The goal is that they are committed to becoming community planners, devoting themselves to the work of community building and sustainable development.

Since it was launched, many from different segments of the society have responded with much interest. As experiences accumulate, new recruits are no longer limited to space planning professionals and community operators. The Program has even become the role model of other counties and cities. Miaoli County, for example, copied the Program and gradually set up a community planning and building mechanism while Tainan City developed unique Tainan Studies in the process. The successes of the application of the Program to other counties and cities should be attributed to the conscientious and careful attitude of the study of Professor Huang Ding-kuo.[5] He not only compiled the handouts of lecturers and placed them in one book but also published the details of how the Program was conducted and reviewed.

Since residents are of different social, economic and cultural backgrounds, the Taipei city government needs individuals who not only possess professional knowledge in community planning but also have the passion for community work. That's how the Program was conceived.

In order to practice 'community empowerment', the Bureau has joined forces with community colleges and community planning service centers to offer a series of seminars on urban planning and community building. 'Children Environmental Experience Camps' have also been launched to make residents more aware of the environment so that the ideas of community planning and perpetual development may take root.

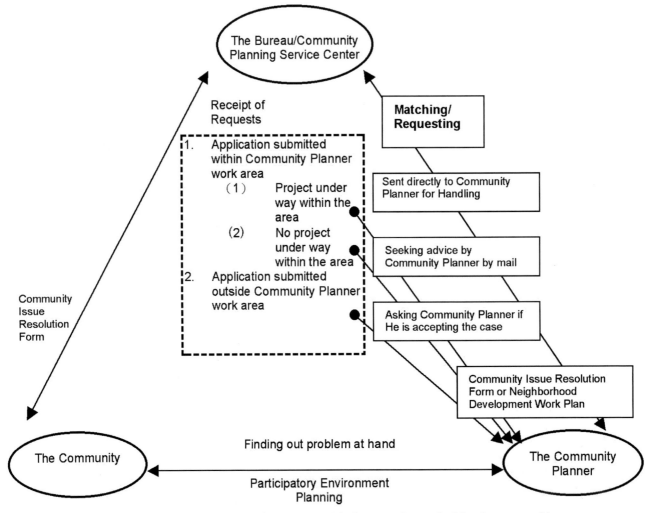

Figure 1. The Community Planner Matching/Requesting Mechanism (compiled by the research).

The Community Planner Matching/Requesting Mechanism

All Taipei community planners are now honorary planners. In order to better serve disadvantaged communities, encourage participation by residents and help establish the link between community planning service centers and community planners, the Bureau consulted the Professionals Dispatch System established after the Kobe earthquake to facilitate after-quake restoration and reconstruction. The result was establishment of the Community Planner Matching/Requesting Mechanism as illustrated in Figure 1.

With the establishment of the Community Issue Resolution mechanism, the Planning Service Center becomes the community planning workstation within the administrative division that is responsible for communication and coordination. Its main task is to find the right community planner to help community residents to eliminate flaws in the community public spaces.

The Community Liaison Mechanism

Mr. Zeng Xuzheng wrote an article titled 'The City Government Needs Prodding? Community Autonomy, the City Machine is yet to be Fine-Tuned.' It was published in Liberty Times on December 30, 1999. He said, 'The community's overall needs once and again accentuate the absurdity of the self-centeredness of different departments of the city government. The community is a base of actual living. With the community as the center, many issues are involved and intertwined. When the community tries to solve a problem, many departments of city government are involved. However, the departments are so used to their self-centeredness; they are not able to effectively solve the problem. In some cases, they even damage the morale of the community.'

For this reason, the Bureau is considering encouraging resident participation and to effectively increase its departments' efficiency. It has been decided that a "community liaison" will be instated for every department that interacts with the community. The idea is borrowed from the liaison office between the President's Office and the Legislature. The liaison will be the consolidated contact point between the department and the community, while the Bureau will be the coordinator between different departments and the community. Through Internet interactions and seminars, the exchange and understanding between the community planner and the community liaison are reinforced. Meanwhile, the horizontal communication between different departments is expected to be improved.

Unfortunately, the mechanism failed to eliminate the self-centeredness of the departments and stopped being promoted in 2003.

REASONS FOR INITIAL SUCCESSES AND BOTTLENECKS CURRENTLY FACED

Taipei City Community Planner Program's Achievements

1. Improving the Use of Public Spaces

Through the environmental renewal plans and neighborhood development plans proposed by the joint efforts of community planners and community residents, public spaces and living quality have been improved. The improvements include bettering neighborhood parks, widening and renewing sidewalks for schoolchildren and pedestrians, utilizing idle spaces, building thematic spaces and invigorating industries. The Program contributes much to creating activity spaces that meet community needs and have community characteristics.

2. Encouraging Participation by Residents

Throughout the entire environmental renewal process, community planners play an important role in the communication between the government and community residents. (Sometimes they even become the targets of criticism.) In the participatory planning and design process, community planners materialize the ideas of residents in terms of the use of spaces. Residents see the process and results of the spatial changes that are created by themselves. They therefore realize the true meaning of participation and community autonomy is thus accomplished.

3. Improving the Public Segment's Efficiency

The communication and interaction among different parties during the environmental renewal process may not be entirely satisfactory, but the process does bring new ideas to those government officials who work strictly by the book. The process makes breakthroughs and creates an "everyone wins" situation. In addition, the fact that community planners deal with different departments of the city government to assist them in implementing many projects indirectly encourages competition between the departments and results in their improvement.

The Reasons behind the Success of Promoting the Initial-Stage Community Planner Program

The Taipei Community Planner Program is successful because it receives support from the central government. The Program was later introduced to other parts of the country and to the disaster-stricken areas in order to rebuild communities. The Program is the first of its kind in the nation. There were no previous examples to follow. Nevertheless, the Bureau set up a four-person taskforce to lay the firm foundation of the Program. The main reasons behind its success are:

1. A Well-Thought Out Strategy and Procedure

- Experts, scholars and trade association representatives were invited to give their opinions.

- A conscientious and careful selection process.

- Letters of appointment were handed out by the mayor to community planners.

- Thematic community planner conferences were held on several separate occasions. The mayor's good image and the media's power were used to promote the community planner program.

- The community planner website was set up at the same time to increase the Program's visibility.

- Outsourced studies were evaluated concurrently.

- The Program was publicized through all sorts of channels.

2. Leadership of consensus and support from high-ranking officials of the city government.

Under the leadership of Chen Weiren and Xu Zhijian, the former and current chiefs of the Bureau, the Program has been one of the Bureau's top priorities. Community planners were invited to participate in the review and change of urban plans, and consultation of urban design reviews. Efforts have been made to continually promote neighborhood renewal plans, neighborhood development plans, improvement of public spaces and urban renewal. In the event of trouble when Mayor Ma goes on his field trips, he often instructs his assistants that community planners are consulted first.

3. Support by the Central Government

In the initial stage, the Program was an experimental project. The city government had no funding for the Program. It was until a $20 million subsidy was received from the "Expanding Domestic Demand - Creating a New Look of the City" program sponsored by Construction and Planning Agency, Ministry of the Interior, that the Program was able to be launched.

4. Support by Academia

Long before the Program was launched, academia had proposed Community Planning, Community Architecture and Community Design. Many scholars offered precious suggestions to the Bureau when the Bureau first proposed the Program.

5. Response from Professionals

Taipei Architect Union is an example. Soon after Architect Zhang Junzhe became president, he wrote an article saying he would encourage architects to become more involved in the community they lived in. He said architects should actively participate in community building and become a "community architect." They should take part in renewing the environment and help to create a community not only suitable for living and working in but is beautiful. So far, community planners

and members of community planning service centers have consisted of individuals of architecture, urban planning, urban design, landscape design, environmental education, community work and other occupational backgrounds.

Bottlenecks

As time progresses, it is found that the number of community planners stagnates and the visibility of their work decreases. The chief reasons are:

1. Fewer Resources from the Government

Taking a close look at the community building projects now under way, it is obvious that whether there is funding from the government determines whether the project will be successful. As a result, the operations of the Program still rely heavily on funding from the government.

Community planning concerns the interests of residents of different stances in the community. For the government, who habitually considers resident participation as the mere communication with neighborhood chiefs or local opinion leaders, community planners are more likely to face the complex community issues than be the bridge between the public and the private sectors. Having become used to judging performance from the perspective of funding or time, the government thinks less of the sub-standard "performance" of environmental renewal than some "invisible construction projects." Many issues urgently waiting to be dealt with emerge after the usually "quiet" communities have been "stirred up" by community planners. The public segment is unable to tackle so many problems within a short time, which leads residents to think that the public segment is slow to react. The conflicting opinions within the community further aggravate the problem as a result of the loss of votes in coming elections. All the above-mentioned factors make the public segment even slower in the promotion of the "community building" work. When recessions strike, some community planners are unable to continue to contribute to community planning. This is because they have to work hard to make ends meet.

2. The Obscure Role Community Planners Play

According to my personal experience and observation, some community planners think the reason that their work is often obstructed is simply because they lack the authority. It never occurs to them that the role they play is different from that of the planners of the government. What they should do is assist the public and the private segments in solving problems with their professional skills. Some community planners consider themselves "directors" of the community, causing discontent among community residents and tension felt by opinion leaders. Some others accept residents' suggestions without giving enough thought to the importance of the environment and public interests.

When the program was first launched, Associate Professor Chen Liangquan once said, "If an architect or a consultant is chosen by the city government or the Bureau, it is questionable whether the architect may become 'the community architect.' Though he is called "the community architect" or is chosen to serve the community, his boss is still the Bureau or the city government. In fact, the needs and opinions of the community are not necessarily the same as those of the city government or the Bureau. Whose side is 'the community architect' to choose when that happens? The community architect certainly should play a role of coordination. However, since he is chosen by the Bureau, he tends to get into an 'awkward' position. The Phase-1 Architects the Bureau proposed recently could only become duty-bound 'architects stationed by the city government in various administrative divisions' rather than 'community architects.'" No matter whether community planners are planners of residents or planners of the city government, they are planners of the Bureau rather than planners of the city government even though they get the letter of appointment from the mayor.

3. Awakening of Community Awareness - The Transitional Period

At the beginning of the Program, the Program was aimed at solving problems the city government faced when promoting neighborhood environmental renewal. The much-hyped Program led residents to believe that community planners were able to solve all their problems. Residents were disappointed to find that they were not while planners felt enormous pressure.

The problem was further aggravated by incomplete awakening of community awareness, personal interests in disguise of community planning, different aesthetic ideas and folk beliefs. Community planners therefore face questioning and challenges from all sides when conducting planning. Some left their posts after unsuccessful cooperation with the community.

Furthermore, the idea of community building itself has not taken root. Most people think community planners offer their services for free. Full-time community planners therefore cannot make a living without funding from the public segment. The situation has prevented many professionals interested in becoming community planners from doing so. The phenomenon can only be corrected by efforts in the longer term.

CONCLUSIONS AND PROSPECTS

The Success of the Program Relies on Solidifying Resident Participation

Establishment of the Program is not for the design profession itself. As a result, the prerequisite for promoting the Program is the realization that the Program is after all a supplementary mechanism to solidify "resident participation."

Residents have the right to determine how the environment and space is used. Only with their participation can the environment and space be planned and designed in a way that meets their requirements and a humane, hospitable living space created.

Consider the issue from the resident, the planning profession and the public sector angles. Residents should fight for their rights and abilities of space planning. Planning professionals should think about how to help residents to fight for their rights of space planning and what should be left for residents to decide. The so-called "rights" have much to do with "abilities." Without abilities, the rights or power are likely to be dominated by those who have abilities. Therefore, the community planner's job is obvious. His responsibilities include reinforcing residents' power in controlling their environment. This is closely related to the community planner's abilities. The more able a community planner is, the more he can do to help residents take back their lost rights. His job is to discover the deepest needs and most basic requirements of residents.

What the public segment (the planner) has to do is very similar to what the community planner has to do. The only difference is that the planner of the public segment has more power than the community planner. Therefore, the public segment should think about how to share some of its power with others so that residents have more say in deciding what their environment should be like. Once residents have the power, the community planner naturally has something to do and goals to set. When the Program was first launched, some planners in the public segment already thought of using existing resources to train community planners and correct the biased or erroneous ideas of some planners in the public segment.

Promotion of the Program Depends Largely on Government Authority

The community planner programs now promoted in other counties and cities are directed by the public segment. The reasons are:

- The Program was originally initiated by professionals in the public sector.

- The community force is not powerful enough to create a need for the Program.

- The community planning profession does not pay well enough for professionals to earn a living.

- Residents trust community planners because they know the planners are hired by the government, not because they trust their professional knowledge and skills.

- The planning profession, when it comes to community planning, has not become a real profession. (At present, community planners are not from within the community. Rather, they are individuals interested in participating in community affairs.) Consequently, when the planning professional returns to or enters the community, it is easier for him to claim that he has the government's certification.

The Most Important Qualities of a Community Planner are Passion and Professionalism

The author thinks the difference between a community planner and a regular planning professional is not that a community planner is selected and certified by the government. Rather, it is that a community planner has the passion to serve the community and the professional knowledge required.

Moreover, when the community planner is conducting community planning, he faces not the person who pays him but residents of the community who have different ideas about community planning and different interest groups and political factions. Without the passion to serve the community, it is hard for anyone to face the different needs and questioning from all sides. The biggest challenge the community planner faces is how to find the solution to the problem through creativity of the planning profession and how to carry out the solution with utmost sincerity and the best communication (another aspect of the profession.) Both passion and profession are indispensable.

Suggestions

1. Legislation of the Community Building Act

Both the Taipei city government and the central government are currently working on legislation for community building. The author suggests that, in the legislation process, more stress is laid on the public sector than the private sector in order to urge the public sector to invest steadily in community building. Meanwhile, existing administrative mechanisms should be adjusted to give residents more opportunities to participate in running their communities. Businesses may be encouraged to sponsor maintenance of community public spaces in return for tax credits. By doing so, more funds could be raised to finance community building.

2. The Urban Planning Review Process should be More Open

Reviews of and changes to urban planning concern residents' interests. The pursuit of public welfare and the upgrading and improvement of the quality of the living environment require much professional knowledge. However, the existing evaluation method that focuses on the target population is becoming ineffective and unsatisfactory as the structures of industry and population change rapidly. As a result, many European and US cities are managing their communities with vision. An open urban planning review process is helpful in creating a process similar to advocacy planning under the development permit system. Community planners are good candidates for managers of community opinions, working with the public

segment in helping community residents to determine the rationality and adequacy of reviews of and changes to urban planning.

In the short term, the Bureau is advised to modify the operating procedure of the Neighborhood Development Plan. The suggestion is that it thinks about how to include community residents' visions of community development in the review process of urban planning in a more conscientious and careful manner. For community planners, they should endeavor to improve their professional knowledge and skills in order to be able to play the role of community manager. At a time of financial difficulties, they are advised to take the initiative to become organized in an effort to exchange experiences among themselves and to shake off the image of being representatives of the public sector. By doing so, they may expand their workroom from public spaces to "the private domain." They can play the key supporting role in the urban renewal projects now under way so they can find a way to make a living in the existing Taipei urban setting.

ENDNOTES

[1] At that time, many NIPs were handled by local non-governmental organizations such as Li offices, community development associations, etc. They were not handled by planning professionals. As a result, most communities sought assistance from professionals while these professionals played a role of participant or assistant.
[2] Would it be more suitable for professionals (the third party) to play the role of communication and coordination and provide professional opinion?
[3] Where are the professionals? Professionals, you should take the initiative to help them!
[4] Such as consultation of applicable laws and regulations, consultation of improvement and sponsorship of public space and explanation of applicable civic administrative operations.
[5] Professor of Institute of Architecture and Urban Design, National Taipei University of Technology, 1945-2003.

REFERENCES

Bureau of Urban Development, Taipei City Government. 1999. Rules Governing Recruitment of Community Planners 1999.

Sung, P-C. 2002. Implementation of citizen participation mechanism for improvement of public spaces- Neighborhood improvement program at Taipei, Proceedings of The 6th Asia-Pacific NGO's Environmental Conference, November 1-4, 2002, Kaohsiung, Taiwan.

中華民國專業者都市改革組織，1999.，「台北市社區規劃師制度運作策略及機制評估研究案」，台北市：台北市政府都市發展局。

中華民國都市設計學會，2002.，「台北市推動社區規劃與社區營造相關制度設計與檢討」，台北市：台北市政府都市發展局。

台北市政府都市發展局，1999.，台北市政府都市發展局八十八年度徵聘「社區規劃師」甄選作業須知。

台北市政府都市發展局，2000.，妳/你是台北社區夢想的引

擎：台北市政府都市發展局八十九年度徵聘「社區規劃師」－「八十九年度社區規劃師制度擴大實施計畫」甄選作業須知。

台北市政府都市發展局88.3.22.北市都秘字第8820492800號函。

李得全、宋寶麒，2001.，社區規劃師之意義、功能與角色，「台北市青年社區規劃師培訓班講義」，台北市：台北市政府都市發展局。

夏鑄九，〈1999〉，社區規劃師對都市發展的重要性，社區規劃師會議專題演講大綱。

許志堅、宋寶麒，2002.，民眾參與城市空間改造之機制－以台北市推動「地區環境改造計畫」與「社區規劃師制度」為例，第九屆（2002年）海峽兩岸城市變遷與展望研討會論文集，2002.8.24.，台南市國立成功大學。

陳亮全，1999.1.27.，致台北市政府都市發展局陳局長威仁信函。

陳威仁、宋寶麒，2001.，都市空間改造DIY－台北市推動「地區環境改造計畫」與「社區規劃師制度」經驗談，第二屆「上海－台北兩岸城市論壇」，上海。

曾旭正，1999.12.30.，市府團隊不點不亮？，「自由時報」，第十三版。

謝慶達、林賢卿譯，1993.，「社區建築－人民如何創造自我的環境」，台北市：創興。

TWO ASIAN MODELS OF PLANNING DECISION MAKING Case Studies of the Planning Process in Singapore New Downtown and Kaohsiung Multifunctional Business District

Perry Pei-Ju Yang and Ze Li

ABSTRACT

Singapore and Kaohsiung, two major port cities in East Asia, have been facing urban physical changes through large-scale urban initiatives in the central city areas during the past decade. This paper explores how the distinctive planning systems in the two cities affect the local actions and help shape the physical environment and future scenarios. Two central city areas are investigated and taken as different Asian models for understanding the processes behind urban transformation. In Singapore, urban form making follows a top-down planning control system. In the 1990s, a new downtown plan was proposed at the reclaimed land, Marina South, using the concepts of through-block linkages, all weather comfort and separated multimodal pedestrian and transportation circulation. The ambitious plan is supported by the three tiers of Singapore's urban planning system from the island-wide conceptual plan, district-wide land use plan to the site specific urban design guidelines. In the Kaohsiung City central area, we observe a different urban pattern of street networks, block systems and building types generated through an evolutionary process of urban growth from the north to the south over a few decades. At almost the same period, a new business center was proposed on a piece of large-scale industrial land along the waterfront near the existing central area. A relatively loose spatial and regulatory framework was provided in Kaohsiung, where an incremental process was adopted for dealing with the multiple and complex landholdings on the new waterfront business center. A recent governmental-initiated planning mechanism of "community architect" plays a certain role in the process through participation. The article finally raises the issue of participation in the shaping of better environment in the Asian urban context. The two Asian models of planning provide some bases for discussing the fundamental questions of the participatory approach.

INTRODUCTION: A BACKGROUND OF TWO ASIAN DOWNTOWNS

Singapore New Downtown

In 1996, a new generation "New Downtown" on reclaimed land was proposed by the Singapore government with the policy intention to create a new downtown environment combining work, play and living in a single space in a planning area of 372 acres at Marina Bay (Singapore URA, 1996).

Figure 1. Aerial view of Marina South, 1997. (Source: Singapore URA)

According to the urban vision from Singapore's government, the downtown at Marina Bay is planned as a "city-within-a-garden" and a "distinctive location for business, living, working and leisure, around-the-clock." Envisioned as an extension of office development from the existing CBD at Shenton Way area, the area will be developed to provide prime office space for global business and financial institutions, which is to be complemented with a full range of residential, shopping, dining, cultural, and entertainment facilities for the provision of a total live-work-play environment (Singapore URA, 1996). Different from the concept of traditional CBD planning such as the Shenton Way district, the area will offer a variety of housing near the waterfront and parks with all the city's attractions and conveniences close at hand. The unique location of the new Downtown provides the opportunity to expand the existing uses within the CBD and Marina Centre to accommodate the future growth of the city. Around 50 hectares of land in Marina South, immediately adjacent to the existing CBD, has been set aside for the expansion of the existing CBD. With gross plot ratios between 9.0 and 15.0, it could accommodate up to 6 million sqm of space when fully developed, almost twice the size of the existing CBD today. The New Downtown thus has the capacity to meet the demand for office space over the next 50 years (Singapore URA, 2002).

Kaohsiung Multi-Functional Commerce & Trade Park

As the most important industrial and port city of Taiwan, Kaohsiung has been facing radical restructuring of the traditional industrial sectors and the function of the port. The manufacturing-based industries kept moving out for more than a decade. The world ranking of the Kaohsiung Port has dropped from 1990's top 3 to 2002's top 5 as one of the world's busiest transshipment centers. Containerization is changing the infrastructure of the Kaohsiung Port and relocating the new port area to the south, which released a large-scale derelict port and industrial land near the existing city center. The changing industrial sectors and the regional competition among major Asian ports have forced the city to adjust its economic as well as physical urban structure. In 1995, a national urban policy responded to the situation, in which Kaohsiung was chosen to be the site of manufacturing and sea trans-shipment center as the Asia-Pacific Regional Operations Center (APROC). The previous port and industrial land along the waterfront was designated as a new city center namely the Kaohsiung Multi-Functional Commerce & Trade Park (KMFCT Park), which aims at redeveloping Kaohsiung's old port area into a hub with multiple functions of financial, commercial, global logistics, trans-shipment and other related services.

The KMFCT Park is composed of three major functional zones:

1) The Cultural & Leisure Zone: A 77 hectare old port area is to be redeveloped into a waterfront commercial and recreational zone, which will provide citizens with high quality public open space and help promote the city's tourism and commercial development.

2) Commercial & Trading Special Zone: For moving Kaohsiung from a traditionally industrial city to a global port city, a district of 210 hectares is planned as a financial and business district, including significant office and commercial development, international convention center, an international Expo Center and other facilities.

3) Warehousing & Trans-shipment Special Zone: This 300 hectare district is used as a center of product distribution, high-tech processing and manufacturing, which will stimulate international investment and promote domestic business development in Kaohsiung. As a center of re-export, the district undergoes a value-added process and provides a place to re-process, manufacture and re-export containers during the trans-shipment.

As a new city center, the port and industrial-based component remains one of the key generators of urban growth, where the goal of the KMFCT Park is to target attracting 40% of the three million trans-shipment containers of the Kaohsiung Port to operate at the new city district in the vicinity of Kaohsiung

Figure 2. The Aerial view of Marina South Model. (Source: Singapore URA)

Figure 3. Aerial View of the KMFCT Park Master Plan. (Source: Kaohsiung City Government, Arte Jean-Marie Charpentier)

City. Through the composition of the three functional zones, the KMFCT Park is expected to attract international and domestic investment to the city. Initiated by the City Government of Kaohsiung, the plan of new city center aims at transforming Kaohsiung into an advanced global port city of the 21st century in the Asia Pacific Rim.

TWO ASIAN PLANNING SYSTEMS

Singapore Planning System - the Three-Tiers Urban Planning and Design Control

In Singapore, the shaping of physical urban space is highly influenced by a top-down government-initiated system, which is composed of three tiers of planning and design control namely an island-wide conceptual plan, district-wide development guide plan, and the site specific urban design guidelines. As one of the most influential planning authorities, Singapore Urban Redevelopment Authority (URA) has incredible capacity in the preparation of planning policy, land use planning and urban design guidelines in different spatial scales. The overall planning concept of the whole island decides land use policy and development strategy in a broad perspective. The district-wide development guide plan gives planning parameters such as population growth, development area, land use, gross plot ratio, infrastructure and the framework of public open space. The specific urban design guideline in the so-called sale of site provided detailed design control covering gross floor area, the uses on the first story and other key stories, building height, setback and bulk control, which constitute the essential urban physical quality, urban form, streetscape, roofscape, pedestrian network and vehicular system for the specific land to be released by government.

Island-Wide Conceptual Plan

The upper tier of Singapore's planning system, the Concept Plan, comprises the strategic planning and land use policy with the long-term vision of the physical development of Singapore. There have been several revisions of the concept plans since 1971, 1991, and 2001 and recently a new plan is to be re-

viewed in 2005. In the 1991 Concept Plan, the idea of developing a new downtown at Marina Bay area was proposed. In the Concept Plan of 2001, the new blueprint projected a scenario of a 5.5 million population for the next 40 to 50 years (Singapore URA, 2001). Throughout these three concept plans over three decades, we observed how the national urban policy responded to the challenges and different situations based on limited natural resources and the scarcity of land.

The Concept Plan of 2001 includes initiatives to be flexible and responsive to the needs of businesses, to support value-added industries and to provide for the growth of Singapore into an international business hub. For the vision of new city living, the Concept Plan aims to create a more livable city, one where Singaporeans can live comfortably, with a wide choice of housing locations and housing types. The business section mentions that the vision is for Singapore to be an economically vibrant city, a city driven by cutting-edge technology, high value-added industries and services, a global financial centre with strong infrastructure. While for recreation, the plan aims for turning Singapore into a fun and exciting city by providing places for enjoyment (Singapore URA, 2001b). In this island-wide con-

Figure 4. Concept Plan 2001 of Singapore. (Source: Singapore URA)

ceptual plan, the New Downtown at the reclaimed land of Marina Bay is the key proposal for integrating the live, work and play components. It will help reinforce or enhance Singapore's "business competitiveness and strengthen Singapore's status as a global and financial international business hub" (Singapore URA, 1997). The Concept Plan 2001 captures the vision of Singapore in the new century. The broad directions set out in the plan will be translated into more detailed plans as part of the review of the Master Plan 2003 (Singapore URA, 2001).

District-Wide Development Guide Plan

The broad strategies and policies in the Concept Plan are realized in detailed planning parameters through Development Guide Plans (DGPs), a lower tier of the planning control system. DGPs are essentially statutory local plans that contain details such as land-use zones, development intensity, transportation networks, open space and recreational areas and conservation designations that guide land development in a demarcated area. Singapore is currently divided into 55 planning areas. For each of these areas, a DGP was prepared where the broad strategies contained in the Concept Plan were translated into operational details at the local level. As each DGP was completed, it became the reference for development control and provided guidelines to landowners and developers on the type of use to which their land could be applied (URA, 1991a).

The District-wide plan is also called the master plan, which is reviewed every five years, most recently in the Master Plan of 1998 and 2003. It is a comprehensive review of land use, plot ratio and building heights. In the case of the DGP at Marina South, the planning parameters such as site area, land use, gross plot ratio, gross floor area, uses on the first story, outdoor

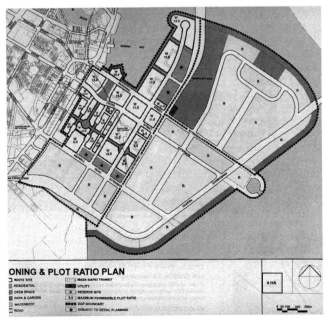

ONING & PLOT RATIO PLAN

Figure 5. Land Use Zoning and Plot Ratio, Marina South 1997. (Source: Singapore URA)

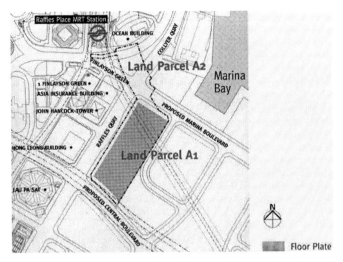

Figure 6. The map in Sale of Sites at Marina Boulevard, 2001. (Source: Singapore URA)

uses, building height and building setback are designated. The objectives of the master plan are specified as concepts such as a new leisure environment, all weather comfort, car-free pedestrian routes, and multi-means transportation systems.

Following the district-wide planning, more detailed design guidelines are sometimes implemented at certain strategic land parcels owned by the government, in which the planning authority URA usually invites tenders for the design and development of the specific site. The third tier design control is incorporated in a public-private development mechanism called "sale of site," in which some mandatory regulations and design guidelines are listed by URA. The successful tenders shall submit to URA and other authorities for their approval with full and complete plans, elevations and specifications of the development. Figure 6 shows an example of sale of site at the new downtown at Marina South. It is comprised by two parts namely Land Parcel A1 and Land Parcel A2. The proposed development is designated as the uses of commercial, residential and hotel mainly on parcel A1. In addition, the developer has to incorporate parcel A2 including a car park station and an underground pedestrian mall, which is traditionally a public space or facility (Singapore URA, 2001). The example shows how the relationship between public and private sectors are set through a particular development mechanism. The detailed urban design guidelines are clearly stated in the sale of site document through the land parcel plan, urban design conditions in the general plan and plans of key levels such as the basement, 1st story and 2nd story plans and other design guidelines, such as envelope control.

Kaohsiung Planning System – A Mixture of Traditional Zoning and Planning Permission

Compared with Singapore, Kaohsiung's governmental planning has relatively less control or influence on the formation of the physical urban environment, where different stakeholders of private sectors and informal sectors play significant roles in planning and development processes. The mechanism of planning decision-making of Kaohsiung has a similar three-tier structure, comprehensive development planning, urban land use plan and urban design review, which are comparable to the 3-tier planning system in Singapore. Recently, at the policy level, some social expectations and political agendas from the government and local community envision Kaohsiung to be an "Ocean Capital," "Cultural Kaohsiung" or "Southern New World." However, they are not well articulated to the three tiers of the planning system. For the policy and strategic planning of the whole city, there are varieties of plans including comprehensive development plans, economic and development strategies, urban landscape planning and urban design policy. Most of them rest on ideas only and lack tools of enforcement or specific practical guidelines. Although the comprehensive development plan of Kaohsiung is like the concept plan of Singapore in terms of the level of planning, its connection to the urban land use plan is not clear. At the second tier, the urban land use plan provides zoning and floor area ratio (plot ratio) based on blocks and districts, which is comparable to Singapore's district-based development guide plan. For the urban design control, Kaohsiung doesn't have the similar mechanism as Singapore's sale of site. The urban design control goes to a procedure of design review, which is closer to the system of discretionary permission in the UK.

Comprehensive Development Plan

The comprehensive development plan of Kaohsiung is a policy oriented strategic plan for urban growth and development strategies. It plays a key role in the facilitation of urban infrastructure and future development under governmental administration. Along with the other policy planning such as the plan to promote Kaohsiung to be the Asia-Pacific Regional Operations Center (APROC), it bears directly on the crucial task of creating a better living environment for Kaohsiung. It ensures the equitability of land development, which means that different regions have their fair share of development opportunities, fair allocation of resources, and fair slice of development profits, as well as bearing a fair portion of the costs. It emphasizes sustainable development across all sectors from urban development to building transportation infrastructure to nature conservation etc. The plan implements decision-making at the local level with the involvement and participation of key agencies and aims at adjusting the spatial structure of land and the making of a greater efficiency of land use.

Urban Land Use Plan

The second tier of the Kaohsiung planning system is the urban land use plan, which aims at providing land use, zoning and floor area ratio for the management of urban land develop-

ment. The urban land use plan is reviewed every five years and managed by the urban planning committee and supervised by an upper-level committee in central government. According to the Kaohsiung Urban Land Use Plan, the land use character of each parcel is defined by a few land use categories, namely residential, commercial, industrial, cultural, public space, utility, transportation uses etc. There are other sub-categories under each main land use, which provide detailed information on uses and intensity for guiding individual development.

For the KMFCT Park, the whole area is divided into three functional zones: The Cultural & Leisure Zone, Commercial & Trading Special Zone and Warehousing & Trans-shipment Special Zone have been subdivided into parcel systems with allowed land uses, intensity, infrastructure, public space and suggested potential development programs. Compared with the existing fine-grain urban blocks and districts, the parcelization within the three functional zones is much coarser in the KMFCT Park, which was obviously affected by the existing ownership situation. The coarse-grain parcelization also implies that the future development of the KMFCT is still very uncertain. It lacks clear urban visions as well as external forces to trigger the development.

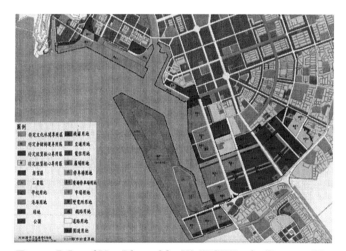

Figure 7. Land Use Plan of the KMFCT Park. (Source: The Bureau of Public Works, Kaohsiung City Government)

Urban Design Review

Compared with Singapore's development mechanism through the sale-of site system, the urban design control in Kaohsiung relies upon the mechanism of design review, which is closer to the planning system of discretionary permission in the UK. Under this system, the review procedure of permission is usually applied to planning, development, and construction processes. Under a similar mechanism, Kaohsiung's urban design control is conducted in the designated "special district" such as the KMFCT Park through the urban design review process carried are released on short term leases for temporary uses such as 'barbecue-steamboat coffee-shops', a pool hall, two bowling centers and a mix of small shops. For some strategic locations along the waterfront promontory area, some midterm programs such as commercial, entertainment and cultural facilities were recently initiated or have been envisioned for a period of 30 years. At the same time, a few parcels closer to the existing CBD areas are released for longer-term development programs such as office, high-rise urban housing and mixed-used development based on the lease period of 99 years. Through the mechanism of sale of site, the planning agency can execute regulations and guidelines and manage the long-term urban change according to urban policy and the market situation.

In Kaohsiung KMFCT Park, the ownership distribution is limited to a few major stakeholders like the Port Authority, the Ministry of Economic Affairs, military institutes, state-owned companies and Kaohsiung City because the land has been used mainly for industrial and port function. Within the 587 ha, almost 80% of the land is owned by the state or state-related enterprises and the remaining 20% of land parcels go to very few private enterprises. Most of the land in the KMFCT Park originally belonged to Qian-Zhen, Kaohsiung export processing zones, Middle-Island commercial port zone, and the commercial zones of Pong-Lai, Yan-Cheng, and Ling-Ya. The separation of land sovereignty, jurisdiction and the management of the land among city, port and other governmental authorities makes the direct operation of planning power difficult, which requires certain mechanisms of consensus building and integration among those stakeholders. Until 2002, the development of KMFCT Park has seen no significant progress except TaiSugar Logistics Park and Software Technology Park belonging to Kaohsiung export processing zones.

Regulations and Incentives

Although regulations and incentives play a key role of planning control in both Singapore and Kaohsiung, they are organized in a very different form and context. In Singapore, the regulatory enforcement of urban land use is clearly articulated with the upper-tier conceptual planning and the lower-level design guidelines through a 'sale of site' mechanism. The recently released sale of site of "White Site Development/ Financial and Business District" in 2001 and "Business and Financial Center (BFC) at Marina Bay" in 2004 are perfect examples to show how the governmental tools of regulation and incentive are implemented. To insure the feasibility and flexibility of the early development at Marina South, the 2001 White Site Development plan cited a new concept called "white zone," a new zone with the flexibility of mixed uses of commercial, hotel or residential, for attracting the master developer to achieve a well-integrated development that will meet all the needs of

out by the Kaohsiung Urban Design Review Committee. The committee examines the aspects of urban design quality, form control and urban landscape from the proposals within the special district. If there is any revision of the urban land use and development intensity, the plan has to be submitted to the upper-level Urban Planning Committee and get their approval, in which the Urban Design Review Committee can not authorize the urban land use changes. The dual mechanism shows that the Kaohsiung urban design control is only partially the system of discretionary permission like the UK. It also is subject to the typical urban land use and zoning system. Table 1 shows how complicated the review processes of urban design and land development are, which is juxtaposed with the control of the upper-tier urban land use plan.

GOVERNMENTAL TOOLS OF THE TWO ASIAN PLANNING MODELS

In Singapore and Kaohsiung, we have observed two governmental actions and responses to new economic challenges and global city competition through major urban interventions, the New Downtown in Singapore and the Multi-Functional Commerce and Trade Park in Kaohsiung in the 1990s. As one of the key driving forces, how does governmental planning help manage these urban changes? Upon the two very different urban scenarios, what are the planning mechanisms, planning systems and planning processes behind the scenes of urban transformation? Furthermore, what kind of planning tools could the government use for implementing the urban design and planning policies?

Schuster argued that there are five and only five tools that governments can use to take action for the shaping of the urban physical environment. These are ownership and operation, regulation, incentives and disincentives, enforcement of property rights and information. The five tools of governmental actions, however, are constrained in the world of action by politics, economics, and preexisting social relationships and institutional structures (Schuster & de Monchaux, 1997). As a temporary framework, the hypothetical concepts are applied here for the comparison of the two planning systems in Asia. It is a useful framework and we will argue later that the temporary framework of five tools is not sufficient for explaining the two Asian experiences.

Ownership, Direct Operation and Property Right

The most direct tool of governmental planning is ownership and operation, where the state can implement policy through direct provision by owning and operating resources (Schuster & de Monchaux, 1997). In the case of Singapore, the fact that more than 70% of the land belongs to the state shows that the government has the dominant ownership and direct operation over the future uses of the land. The land ownership in Kaohsiung is much more fragmented, decentralized and complicated. It can be observed from the fine-grain city fabric and the types of uses in the existing city.

In Singapore's Marina South, a reclaimed land mainly owned by the state, the government has the direct control and operation of when, how and what type of development should be implemented. At the early stage of development, some parcels

modern businesses. In 2004, the BFC project, the largest URA sale of site project after Suntec City was released on a 3.55 ha waterfront site together with adjoining 1.8 ha of subterranean space with the potential development capacity up to 438,000 sqm gross floor area (GFA). A minimum 60% of the GFA for offices is stipulated to ensure that the strategic objective of the BFC will be achieved. The remaining space can be put to other

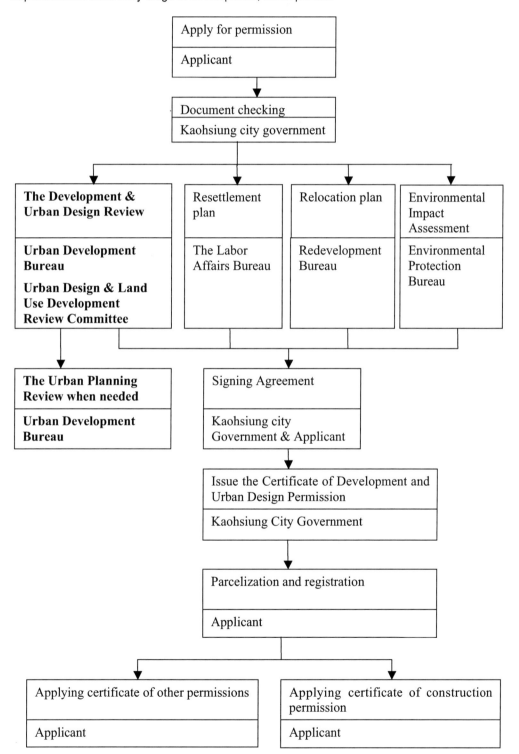

Table 1. The review procedure of development and urban design permission in Kaohsiung. (Source: Urban Development Bureau, Kaohsiung City Government)

commercial uses as well as complementary hotel, residential, entertainment and recreational uses (Singapore URA, 2004). Through the clear planning regulations and urban design guidelines, the plan still provides certain flexibility in land uses as a form of incentive for development of the specific site.

Without the single-track and systematic procedure of Singapore, the governmental tool of regulation and incentive in Kaohsiung appears to be more complicated but more negotiable through the design and development review procedure. In the example of the Kaohsiung World Trade Center project, we observed that the regulatory planning parameters are applied to a situation with multiple stakeholders, where government plays a role of both gate keeper and incentive provider through setting up a series of "reward regulations" for stimulating investment and development. In this case, the priority was set by city government for reviewing each development proposal through urban design review and development review for permission. The priority will go to those land owners, who have intentions to develop their land under the plan of Kaohsiung World Trade Center or to donate land for public uses. The mode of BOT (build-operate-transfer) is encouraged. A series of reward regulations was adopted for attracting investors and enterprises to participate the development of KMFCT Park. For example:

- After completion of development, the landlord who obtained the land for the first time and applies for a construction permit within one year of his registration will enjoy a 25% F.A.R. bonus of the planned volume. Otherwise, the F.A.R. bonus will be reduced 5% each year. By the fifth year, the landowner shall start his construction, or there will be no F.A.R. bonus and the landowner will have to reapply for it.

- For stimulating the initiation of development, the F.A.R. bonus application is based on a "first come, first served" basis with a limitation on the total amount. When the F.A.R. bonus has reached 115% of the total F.A.R. amount, no more bonuses will be given.

- The applicant who combines two or more parcels or blocks to one development site can apply the Transfer Development Right (TDR) mechanism to calculate his total development, and qualifies to apply the F.A.R. Bonus.

- When applying for a construction permit according to the F.A.R. reward regulations, the developer should conduct a traffic impact analysis and offer a proposal for solutions.

The criteria or the reward regulation is implemented based on a process of design and development reviews, in which the regulatory planning parameters are used as a form of incentive for stimulating the development.

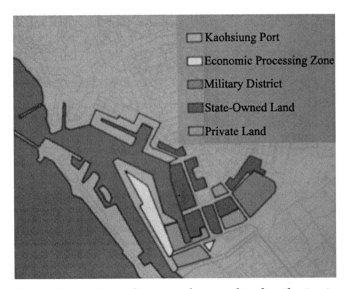

Figure 8. Land jurisdiction and ownership distribution in the KMFCT Park. (Source: The Bureau of Public Works, Kaohsiung City Government)

Information and Participation

Besides the governmental tools on ownership, property rights, regulations and incentives, the collection and delivery of planning information is another key aspect of governmental intervention to help shape the physical urban environment. The aspect of planning participation shows very different pictures in Singapore and Kaohsiung in terms of the mechanism of participation and the degree of involvement from citizens.

In Singapore, the information giving and consultation was usually done when a new concept plan, master plan or urban design plan was proposed. The planning authority URA usually exhibits the plans in URA Exhibition Hall or the community center to get feedback from the public. In the example of the New Downtown Plan at Marina Bay, the exhibition attracted more

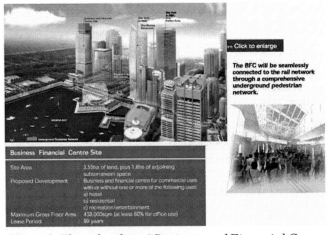

Figure 9. The sale of site "Business and Financial Center (BFC) at Marina Bay" 2004. (Source: Singapore URA)

Figure 10. The exhibition ceremony of City Center, 2003. (Source: Singapore URA)

Figure 11. Exhibition of Draft Concept Plan 2001. (Source: Singapore URA)

Figure 12. Symposium held by URA 2000. (Source: Singapore URA)

sues in 2000. Two issues were studied on balancing Singapore's scarce land resources among the competing land uses of housing, parks, industries, and how to retain identity in the context of the intensive use of land. Initiated by government, the two focus groups comprise professionals, interest groups, industrialists, businessmen, academics, grassroots organizations and students. Their proposals were formulated through interaction with various governmental agencies, site visits and a public forum with the public. Some of the recommendations from the focus groups were incorporated into the Draft Concept Plan 2001 (Singapore, URA 2001).

In Kaohsiung, the involvement of grassroots or citizen groups seems more active through creative opportunities and channels. The recently built mechanism of "community planner" and "community architect" encourage direct participation and communication in urban and community affairs and the creation of public spaces.

The idea of directly involving participants, citizens and the local community in the decision making process was introduced to Taiwan in the context of social and institutional change in the early 1990s. Community planners or architects are expected to play key roles in mediating different social interests and values among social and citizen groups. The community architect or planner is not only the professional planner or designer for the community space, but also the consensus builder of the community. The system of "community architect" and "community planner" was started in Kaohsiung in 2002 from the establishment of the first community architect's studio in Ling-Ya. It was initiated by the Kaohsiung City Government and the first "community architect" system was introduced here to encourage local architects to help improve the urban environment of Kaohsiung (Dialogue Architecture, 2002). Compared with other cities and counties in Taiwan, the quality of space making seems more emphasized in Kaohsiung and the evidence is shown in various urban and public architecture projects initiated by the new system recently.

than 12,000 visitors (including about 6,500 online visitors) in less than three weeks since the opening of the exhibition on June 26, 2003. The exhibition was prolonged to five weeks and had a total amount of 18,000 visitors. General interest from the public is high but the feedback mechanism shows a relatively passive way of participation.

In addition, public consultation was sometimes conducted through Focus Group discussions to obtain opinions from representatives of architectural, property and financial industry leaders. For example, the Minister of National Development launched the public consultation phase for the Concept Plan 2001 with two focus groups on land allocation and identity is-

Five governmental tools	The characters of the tools	Singapore	Kaohsiung
Ownership and operation	The state will do X	***	*
Regulation	You must (or must not) do X	***	**
Incentives /Disincentives	If you do X, the state will do Y	*	**
Establishment, allocation, and enforcement of property right	You have a right to do X, and the state will enforce that right	*	***
Information and participation	"You should do X," or "You need to know Y in order to do X."	**	***

*Table 2. The degree of effectiveness of the five governmental tools: ***Strong, **Medium, *Weak. (revised from Schuster & de Monchaux, 1997)*

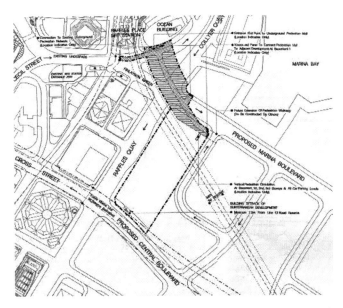

Figure 13a. Urban design guideline-envelope control. (Source: Singapore URA)

Figure 14. The framework of public open space. (Source: Urban Development Bureau, Kaohsiung City Government)

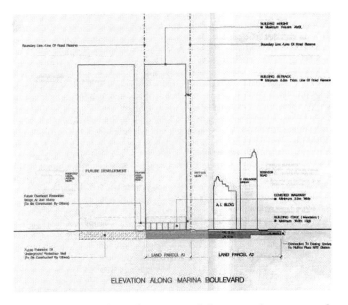

ELEVATION ALONG MARINA BOULEVARD

Figure 13b. Urban design guideline-envelope control. (Source: Singapore URA)

Design Guidelines

From Table 2, we have summarized the effectiveness of the five governmental tools based on the experiences of the Singapore and Kaohsiung planning systems. The evaluation of the degree of effectiveness of the different governmental tools is debatable, and needs to be verified through more evidence.

However, there is one key aspect that is missing in Schuster's proposition regarding the assessment of potential governmental tools. The design guidelines, a technical aspect of urban form and urban quality control, have significant influences on the shaping of the physical urban environment. Although they

are both related to the directional operation of government and the aspects of regulations, we have found some fundamental differences in the lower-tier urban design control between the two cities.

Singapore's design guidelines focus heavily on physical guidelines, which are implemented through the particular development mechanism of sale-of-site. At this level, URA provides more detailed guidelines from the location plan, site plan, land parcel plan to the urban design conditions plans such as the general plan, basement plan, 1st story plan, 2nd story plan and envelope control plan. So the guidelines range from urban form making to three-dimensional skyline control (Figure 13 & 14). It is a site specific guideline and the quality control of urban space is supported by a planning agency with a strong capacity for physical planning and urban design.

Kaohsiung's urban design control is relatively more flexible, general and policy oriented than Singapore's. Compared with the site-specific guidelines in Singapore, the design guidelines are conducted at a district-block level, which emphasizes more the general performance of the whole district and is not confined to how an individual site should perform in the specific site context. It appears on those designated special districts such as the KMFCT Park, where the urban design policy is proposed in the strategic planning, design competition or urban design master plan initiated by the Kaohsiung City Government. For some other districts where the master plan or detailed plan are still drafted as the traditional approach to land use planning, it is relatively unclear what the district-wide guidelines should be for controlling local environmental quality. Without the rigorous

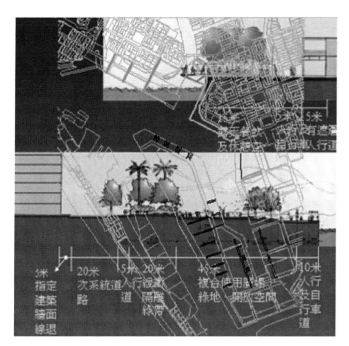

Figure 15. The guideline for public open space and landscape. (Source: Urban Development Bureau, Kaohsiung City Government)

urban design guideline as Singapore's sale-of-site mechanism, the urban design control in Kaohsiung relies upon the mechanism of urban design review.

CONCLUSION

The incredibly fast urban transformation of new city areas in Singapore's New Downtown and Kaohsiung's Multi-Functional Commerce & Trade Park are clear examples for analyzing the two distinctive Asian planning systems. They are also good examples for us to rethink the institutional bases and cultural implications behind urban changes. Within the three-tier control of the two Asian planning systems, we have observed a more articulated system all the way from concept plan, master plan down to the site specific urban design guidelines in Singapore, where another three-tier system, an uncertain urban planning policy, a relatively rigid urban land use plan and a review-based urban design control was formulated in Kaohsiung.

In the experiences of Singapore and Kaohsiung, we found that the mechanism of planning decisions and implementation are not usually made in a pure form as the five governmental tools, ownership and operation, regulation, incentive, property rights and information, proposed by Schuster and de Monchaux. They are sometimes performed as the hybrid of a few different tools or sometimes emphasize one particular aspect of planning tools with more delicate contents. To understand these two Asian models of planning decision making, we have made use of the five hypothetical categories as the preliminary framework for examining their differences and similarities. We

also argue that the five tools are not sufficient for explaining the Asian experiences. Some hybrid form of governmental tools such as the participatory oriented approach and the design review process in Kaohsiung and the delicate contents of urban design guidelines in Singapore have made the quality of urban design decision-making different in their particular urban contexts.

REFERENCES

Dialogue Architecture. 2002. Architecture & Political Ideology / Southern Dimensions –Kaohsiung. Dialogue Architecture+Design+Culture, Taipei: Meizhao Culture Enterprise Co. Ltd.

Kaohsiung BPW. 2003. The Briefing Of Design Of Xingguang Quay, Kaohsiung: The New Construction Department, Bureau of Public Works Kaohsiung City Government.

Kaohsiung BPW. 2003. Vision for Kaohsiung, Kaohsiung: The Bureau of Public Works Kaohsiung City Government.

Kaohsiung BPW. 2002. The Future Blueprint of Kaohsiung, Kaohsiung: The Bureau of Public Works Kaohsiung City Government.

Kaohsiung BPW. 2002. Remaking Kaohsiung in Asia: The Bureau of Public Works Kaohsiung City Government.

Kaohsiung BPW. 1999. Kaohsiung Maritime Trade Centre and Commerce Park Special District Urban Design Project, Kaohsiung: OMA Asia.

Kaohsiung BPW. 1999. Kaohsiung Harbor Maritime Trade Centre & Commerce Park, Kaohsiung: EDAW.

Kaohsiung BPW. 1999. City Concept Design, Kaohsiung: ARTE Jean-Marie Charpentier.

Kaohsiung BPW. 1998. The Planning Act for Kaohsiung Global Development Strategy, Kaohsiung: The Urban Development Department of Bureau of Public Works Kaohsiung City Government.

Kaohsiung BPW, Senhai International Construction Consultive Co. Ltd., Dinghan International Construction Consultive Co. Ltd.. 1995. Kaohsiung Multi-functional Commerce & Trade Park Comprehensive Plan and Rezoning, Kaohsiung: The Bureau of Public Works Kaohsiung City Government.

Kaohsiung City Government. 1999. Kaohsiung Waterfront 2020 Urban Design Symposium, Kaohsiung: Kaohsiung City Government.

Kaohsiung City Government. 1996. The Plan Of The Research On The Early Stage Of Developing Kaohsiung Into Asia-Pacific Regional Operations Center, Kaohsiung: Kaohsiung City Government.

Kaohsiung Harbor Bureau, M.O.T.C. 2003. Port of Kaohsiung 2003, Kaohsiung: Kaohsiung Harbor Bureau.

Lin Q R. 1995. Urban Design in Cities of Taiwan, Taipei: Chuangxing Press Co. Ltd.

Schuster, J M, de Monchaux J, Riley, C A. 1997. Preserving the Built Heritage: Tools for Implementation. Hanover, NH: University Press of New England.

Singapore URA. 2004. Business Financial Centre Site Released for Sale on Reserve List. Skyline, May/June, 2004, Singapore: Urban Redevelopment Authority.

Singapore URA. 2003. Downtown at Marina Bay, Singapore: Urban Redevelopment Authority.

Singapore URA. 2003. Ideas for a great city centre draw more than

18,000 visitors. Skyline. Singapore: Urban Redevelopment Authority.

Singapore URA. 2001a. Skylines: Draft Concept Plan 2001, Singapore: Urban Redevelopment Authority.

Singapore URA. 2001b. The Concept Plan 2001, Singapore: Urban Redevelopment Authority.

Singapore URA. 1997. Annual Report 1996/1997, Singapore: Urban Redevelopment Authority.

Singapore URA. 1996. New Downtown: Ideas for the City of Tomorrow, Singapore: Urban Redevelopment Authority.

Singapore URA. 1991. Living the Next Lap: Toward a Tropical City of Excellence, Singapore: Urban Redevelopment Authority.

Tan S. 1999. Home, Work, Play, Singapore: Urban Redevelopment Authority.

empowering communities

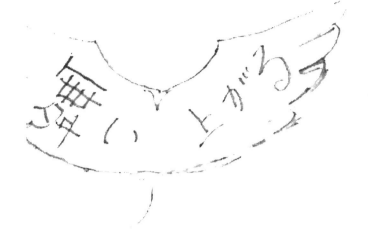

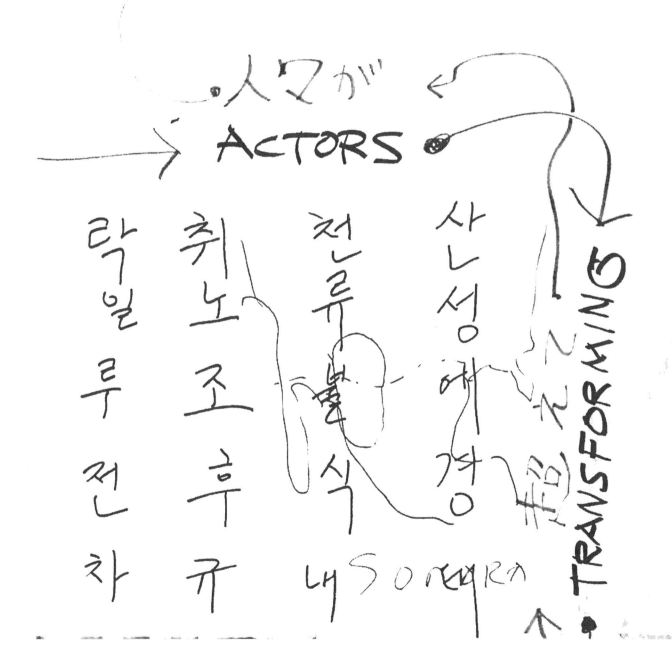

EMPOWERING COMMUNITIES THROUGH SEATTLE'S DEPARTMENT OF NEIGHBORHOODS[1]

Jim Diers

Local governments throughout the United States are facing a dual dilemma. Their resources are not keeping pace with increasingly complex social issues, especially when the federal and state governments are devolving more responsibilities than money to them. Voters are reluctant to approve additional resources because they feel a sense of alienation from their government at all levels.

The common response has been to "reinvent government" to be more like a business with a greater emphasis on "efficiency" and "customer service." Although it is true that government needs to improve its business practices, there is a danger inherent in treating citizens as customers. To the extent that government treats citizens only as customers, citizens think of themselves only as taxpayers and feel that much more alienated from their government.

This deep sense of alienation is often misdiagnosed as apathy. Statistics showing that fewer and fewer people are voting and are joining community organizations have led some to the conclusion that increasing numbers of citizens no longer care about their community or their government. This analysis, I believe, blames the victim. Citizens don't vote because they have seen little evidence that their votes matter. The 2000 presidential election only confirmed what so many people already suspected: their votes didn't count. Likewise, people hesitate to join community organizations because they are tired of attending meetings that lead to nothing but more meetings. Whether they are participating in a planning workshop or a discussion of bylaws, too many people have a hard time seeing a positive relationship between their civic involvement and the quality of their lives.

I am convinced that people still yearn for a sense of community and want to contribute to the greater good. They also want a voice in their government. What they are looking for has less to do with reinventing government than it does with rediscovering democracy. True democracy requires deeper involvement than going to the voting booth once a year; people need to be engaged in their communities and with their government on an ongoing basis. People will commit to such involvement to the extent that they see results.

I say this with confidence because of the high level of citizen engagement I witnessed in Seattle between 1988 and 2002. Tens of thousands of people participated in implementing more than 2,000 community self-help projects such as building new parks and playgrounds, renovating community facilities, recording oral histories, and creating public art. Thirty thousand people guided the development of 37 neighborhood plans. Scores of new ethnic organizations and neighborhood-based residential, business, arts, history, and environmental organizations were established. Five thousand people a year were involved in cultivating plots at 62 community gardens that they built themselves. Organizations celebrated an annual Neighbor Appreciation Day, and individuals delivered 18,000 greeting cards to caring neighbors. Many people with developmental disabilities and other formerly marginalized citizens participated in community life for the first time. These are some of the many activities that accounted for survey results showing that 43 percent of Seattle's adults regularly volunteered their time for the community and 62 percent participated in at least one neighborhood or community organization.

Civic engagement created additional resources for the public good. P-Patch community garden volunteers generated 10 tons of organic produce for food banks each year and maintain more than 17 acres of public space. Community members invested more than $30 million worth of their own cash, materials, and labor in completing over 2,000 projects that they initiated. Likewise, broad-based ownership of the 37 neighborhood plans led to voter approval of three ballot measures worth $470 million for library, community center, and park improvements recommended in the plans.

Perhaps more important than the financial and other material benefits of civic engagement are the social benefits of a stronger sense of community. No amount of public-safety spending can buy the kind of security that comes from neighbors watching out for one another. Similarly, neighbors supporting latchkey children or housebound seniors can provide a kind of personal care that social service agencies can't replicate.

There are other things that communities can do better than government. Community members have local knowledge and can provide a local perspective. At the same time, they think more holistically than government departments that tend to specialize in specific functions.

The community is often more innovative than the city bureaucracy and can constitute a powerful force for change. When the City of Seattle planned to build incinerators to deal with its garbage problem, the community demanded a recycling program instead. When electricity rates escalated after the City bought into a nuclear power project, the community pushed for a model conservation program. It was the community that introduced the Seattle Police Department to community policing and insisted on its implementation.

Likewise, the community has power where city government does not. The City couldn't persuade the Seattle School District to host community school programs, but the community did. Government couldn't evict a pornographer from the sole theater in Seattle's Columbia City neighborhood, but the community did.

None of this is meant to suggest that there is no role for government. While the community provides a local perspective, government must look citywide to ensure that neighborhoods are connected and that each is treated equitably. Community innovation needs to be balanced by a certain amount of government standards and regulations. My point is simply that cities work best when local government and the community are working as partners.

True partnership requires government to move beyond promoting citizen participation to facilitating community empowerment. Citizen participation implies government involving citizens in its own priorities through its own processes (such as public hearings and task forces) and programs (such as block watch and adopt-a-street). Community empowerment, on the other hand, means giving citizens the tools and resources they need to address their own priorities through their own organizations.

In 1988, the City of Seattle had long been known if seldom commended for its emphasis on process. That year, the City made a sea change toward community empowerment with the creation of a four-person Office of Neighborhoods. The office quickly grew into a department that, by 2002, had nearly 100 employees and a budget of $12 million a year. The Department of Neighborhoods differs from other City departments which are responsible for separate functions such as transportation, public safety, human services, or parks and recreation. Neighborhoods is the only department focused on the way citizens have organized themselves: by community. That unique focus enables the Department to decentralize and coordinate City services, to cultivate a greater sense of community and nurture broad-based community organizations, and to work in partnership with these organizations to improve neighborhoods by building on each one's special character.

Neighborhood Matching Fund

The Neighborhood Matching Fund has been surprisingly successful at what it set out to do: "build community," both physically and socially. Through the program, the City provides funding in exchange for the community's match of an equal value in cash, volunteer labor, or donated goods and services in support of citizen-initiated projects. From $150,000 in 1989, the program grew to $4.5 million by 2001, a year in which it

supported over 400 neighborhood-based projects. Not only are the projects transforming the physical appearance of the neighborhoods, they are building a stronger sense of community by involving thousands of people from all walks of life. The program has also yielded additional resources, numerous innovations, and new partnerships between communities and city government.

Over its first 13 years, the Neighborhood Matching Fund backed more than 2,000 projects. Community groups used the program to build new playgrounds at most city parks and public schools; create new parks; reforest open space; plant street trees; develop community gardens; restore streams and wetlands; create murals, banners, and sculpture; install kiosks; equip computer centers; renovate facilities; build traffic circles; pilot community school programs; document community histories; develop neighborhood plans; organize new groups; and much, very much more. These projects are visible in every neighborhood of Seattle.

In 1991, the Neighborhood Matching Fund was recognized by the Ford Foundation and Kennedy School of Government at Harvard as one of the 10 most innovative local government programs in the United States. The program has, in turn, fostered many innovations of its own. To name just a few, the Fund has been used to create Seattle's first wheelchair-accessible playground (Alki), drug-free zone (Garfield), community school (Powerful Schools), intergenerational oral history (African American community), use of murals to combat graffiti (Central Neighborhood Association), reforestation with native plants (College Street Ravine), reuse of rainwater (Cascade), "gray to green" conversion of asphalt to park (former Webster School), restoration of a wetland to drain a ballfield (Meadowbrook), and use of a troll to spark economic development (Fremont). The community, which initiated all of these projects, tends to be more creative than the bureaucracy.

In Seattle, the bureaucracy has learned over time to accept, if not wholeheartedly embrace, community innovations. That certainly wasn't true initially. When I first talked with the director of the Department of Parks and Recreation about the Neighborhood Matching Fund, her reaction was, "We don't want people messing with our parks." I bit my tongue for a change and listened. She had legitimate concerns. "What about liability for volunteer work? Who will enforce our department's standards? Where will our department find time to be involved in these projects? How will the improvements be maintained?"

We worked with Parks and other City departments to figure out how to make the program work for them. We found a carrier for liability insurance. We agreed not to fund any project unless it had been reviewed and approved by the appropriate departments. The Neighborhood Matching Fund pays for two positions in Parks and one in Transportation, providing guidance to the community and a liaison to other staff members in those departments. All project contracts include provisions for ongoing maintenance by the community, the appropriate department, or both.

Now Parks and Recreation is one of the Neighborhood Matching Fund's strongest advocates. Rather than saying no to community ideas that Parks can't afford, the Fund gives the department a way to meet the community half-way. If an idea has a lot of community support, that is an opportunity for Parks to work collaboratively with the community. If the community support doesn't materialize, Parks isn't seen as the obstacle. The Department of Parks and Recreation has developed many more positive relationships with communities as a result of the Matching Fund. Parks has also found that community members take care of the projects they create, often utilizing the department's Adopt-a-Park program. Seattle Transportation, the Arts Commission, Seattle Public Utilities, and the School District have had similar conversion experiences.

Of course, a big incentive for departmental participation is the additional resources. Besides the $23 million contributed by the Neighborhood Matching Fund between 1989 and 2001, the community has generated more than $30 million in match. Every dollar invested by the program in recent years has leveraged an average of $1.60 in community match.

A large portion of the match has come in the form of volunteer labor. At last count, over 700,000 volunteer hours had been contributed to projects. Many hours of skilled labor have also been donated. Together, these skilled and unskilled volunteers account for tens of thousands of people, many of whom have become involved in their community and with their local government for the first time.

The Neighborhood Matching Fund gives people an opportunity to get involved without necessarily going to meetings. Although meetings have been the traditional form of community involvement, many people are meeting-averse. Too often, meetings seem to result in nothing but more meetings. The Matching Fund enables people to make a short-term commitment in support of a time-limited project. They know their involvement is making a difference and they see results. In the process, they develop relationships that may lead to their participating in other projects or maybe even attending meetings. The Matching Fund has proven to be an effective tool for increasing the membership of existing community organizations.

The creation of new organizations is another result of Neighborhood Matching Fund projects. Many neighborhood arts, educational, environmental, and historical groups as well as ethnic organizations trace their origins to a Matching Fund project. There are now more ways than ever before to be involved in community life.

The Neighborhood Matching Fund empowers communities in other ways as well. Not only do citizens initiate, manage, and implement projects, it is community organizations that make the major funding decisions. In the first year, when there was $150,000 available, the money was divided equally among Seattle's 13 districts. Each district council was responsible for deciding which projects to fund with its $11,538. Some districts didn't have enough proposals to use all of the money while other districts had many more solid proposals than they could support.

The next year, neighborhood leaders decided to have only one citywide pot of money so that they could compare proposals across districts and fund those that demonstrated the greatest need and the most involvement, no matter their location. Each district council rated the applications from its district and appointed a representative to a Citywide Review Team that rated all of the applications. The combined district and citywide scores were used by the City Neighborhood Council to recommend which projects to fund.

That year, 1990, there was $1.5 million available to support projects requesting $2.3 million. The City Neighborhood Council members, however, recommended only $1.1 million in awards, because they thought that the remainder of the proposals were of insufficiently good quality. Can you imagine elected officials leaving money unallocated when they had constituents asking for it? But the citizen review process is not subject to politics, and for that reason it is highly respected by politicians (and by other funders who readily contribute to projects that have the Matching Fund seal of approval). Both the mayor and city council have consistently upheld the recommendations of the City Neighborhood Council. Not only does the citizen review process have great integrity, it has this additional benefit: with citizens making the recommendations, politicians don't get blamed for rejecting proposals; elected officials are identified with only the funded projects and can take their bows at the continuous stream of groundbreaking and ribbon-cutting ceremonies.

Community-Driven Planning

As a former community organizer, I hated neighborhood planning. Planning was too often the City's substitute for action. Plans came out of city hall with only token involvement of the community. Not surprisingly, the planners were the only ones who really understood or cared about the plans' vision and recommendations. With no constituency to implement them, the plans usually just sat on the shelf.

So when I was appointed director of the new Office of Neighborhoods, although I was expected to hire planners, I hired organizers instead. I wanted to make sure that all communities had a strong voice and could utilize the City's programs and services. It seemed to me that marginalized communities in particular would benefit more from organizers than from planners.

Yet planning was clearly called for by the Neighborhood Planning and Assistance Program that my office was charged with administering. With no planners on staff, I had to figure out how to do the planning. I turned to the only resource available, the Neighborhood Matching Fund. With the support of the City Neighborhood Council, we made planning an eligible use of the Matching Fund. The result was a very different, bottom-up approach to neighborhood planning. That model of planning differs from traditional planning in five major respects.

First, with the new model, it is the community rather than city government that initiates the planning process. When the City initiated plans, often the community was either uninterested or suspicious about the City's real motives: "What are they going to try to get past the community this time?" The community won't initiate a plan through the Neighborhood Matching Fund unless it is clear about exactly why a plan is needed. After all, planning is a lot of work and, if planning is not really needed, that energy could be better expended elsewhere.

Second, the new model lets the community define its own planning area. When the City developed plans, it often used census tracts to determine boundaries. The community instead defines the neighborhood by its own understanding of the neighborhood, usually in accordance with the boundaries identified in community council bylaws.

Third, the community identifies its own scope of work. City plans tended to focus on the function of the department that was doing the planning, typically land use or community development. When the community is in charge, community members plan for what is important to them, whether that is economic development, public safety, human services, recreation, open space, transportation, affordable housing, education, history, or arts and culture. Often, communities want to address all these elements with a comprehensive plan: communities tend to think more holistically than do City departments.

Fourth, the community can hire its own planner rather than ending up with whatever planner the City assigns them. They can look for a planner who works well with people in addition to having good technical skills. It makes an inestimable difference when a planner is accountable to the community.

Finally, with the new model, community members become much more involved in the planning process because they are required to come up with the match. Since it might prove difficult to conduct successful fundraisers for planners' salaries, the community's match usually consists of hundreds of volunteers. Community volunteers are active in every step of the process: submitting the application, hiring the planner,

drafting and conducting surveys, and developing the vision and recommendations. That means that people understand the plan and feel ownership of it. They hold the City accountable for implementing the plan and, moreover, they take responsibility for much of the implementation themselves.

Coincidentally, the first community that chose to develop a plan through the Neighborhood Matching Fund was Southeast Seattle, where I had worked as an organizer. Through discussions in their district council, all 12 community councils and business associations in this racially and economically diverse community decided to develop a joint plan. They formed a planning committee comprising one representative from each organization, and they selected SouthEast Effective Development (SEED), a local community development corporation, to serve as their consultant.

Although many plans for Southeast Seattle had been developed over the years, this would be the most inclusive planning effort to date. The planning committee members made sure that their respective stakeholder groups stayed well informed and actively engaged throughout the process. As part of the effort to broaden participation, the planning committee employed an innovative outreach strategy. Survey forms were distributed in the most racially diverse places in the community; namely, the schools. To increase the rate of return, the committee persuaded the local Darigold plant to promise a free ice cream cone for every survey completed. This outreach strategy cost little but netted nearly 1,500 completed surveys.

Not surprisingly, the resulting Southeast Seattle Action Plan had broad community support. When the plan was presented to city council in 1991, council chambers was packed with community representatives demanding that the plan be adopted; be adopted *and* implemented. The City agreed to prepare an annual progress report, and the mayor himself delivered it each year at a large community meeting.

The City followed through on all of the key plan recommendations. The small, deteriorating Rainier Community Center was demolished and replaced with the largest community center in Seattle. Millions of dollars were spent to repave the community's major arterials. Additional street and alley lighting was installed to enhance public safety. Priority went to the processing of permits in target areas along Rainier Avenue South, facilitating major new commercial development. The City purchased a vacant block near Rainier Avenue South and South Dearborn Street for intensive residential development, including co-housing and homes for first-time buyers.

Equally important, the community did its part to implement the plan. Much of the residential and commercial development was undertaken by SEED and other community-based organizations. Local businesses partnered with the City to improve the facades of their storefronts and the appearance of adjacent streets and sidewalks. With help from the Neighborhood Matching Fund, the community built playgrounds, painted murals, and planted street trees as recommended in their plan. The Southeast Seattle Action Plan is one important reason why more Matching Fund projects have been completed in Southeast Seattle than in any other part of the city.

Other neighborhoods soon followed Southeast Seattle's example. Queen Anne, the International District, Pike-Pine, Roosevelt, and North Beacon Hill developed their own comprehensive plans. Some communities initiated issue-specific plans targeting parking, traffic, public safety, historic resources, or business district revitalization. Other groups used the Neighborhood Matching Fund to create site-specific plans for new parks or playgrounds.

Lessons Learned

There are many routes to community empowerment, and each community needs to find its own way. My hope is that by sharing the lessons I have learned on my own journey, I can make it easier for others to find routes that work for them. Because these lessons are scattered throughout the book and some did not get included at all, I want to conclude by summarizing what I have learned about community, community organizing, community initiatives, and the role of government.

The first lesson I learned is that a neighborhood is not the same as a community. A neighborhood is a geographic area that people have in common while a community is a group of people who identify with and support one another. It is possible for a neighborhood to lack a strong sense of community and, conversely, it is possible for there to be a strong sense of community among people who don't share a neighborhood. A community can be defined by a common culture, language, or sexual orientation regardless of geography.

Strong communities are those that rely on their own resources, including the assets that each and every person possesses. As the Eritrean Association of Greater Seattle puts it, "Our mission is guided by our shared vision that each member, from the youngest to the most senior, has a need to be cared for and nurtured and at the same time each one has the ability and the responsibility to contribute back to the community."

Individual reciprocity is not sufficient, however. Communities are most powerful when they take collective action. The process of building that kind of power is called community organizing.

The key to community organizing is to start where the people are at. The more local the activity, the higher the percentage of people who will get involved. Starting where people are at, however, also means respecting their sense of community, whether or not it is tied to geography. It further entails building on existing networks. Most people are already organized and

cannot reasonably be expected to develop an entirely new set of relationships and find time for yet another organization.

Starting where people are at also involves identifying their interests. That does not mean promoting a cause and seeing who follows; that means listening. The organizer should be prepared to hear and understand interests that may differ from her or his own. If a common interest involves an issue, that issue should be framed in a way that is as immediate, as specific, and as achievable as possible. People get involved to the extent that they can have an impact on the things they care about. Community plans, projects, and social events are other good ways to bring people together. Whatever the approach, whatever the issue, it is best to think big and start small.

One good place to start is with community-initiated planning, which can have numerous advantages over planning conducted by institutions. Many more people are motivated to get involved. Local knowledge and values are incorporated. A more holistic approach is generally taken. And, the resulting plan is much more likely to be implemented. This assumes, of course, that the planning process is inclusive and that it is coordinated with neighboring plans.

Likewise, community self-help projects tend to have qualities that are missing in projects generated by institutions. Innovations are more likely to emanate from community efforts. Communities have a knack for converting a problem into an asset whether it is a graffiti-covered wall, vacant lot, abandoned building, dead tree, garden waste, fallen apples, discarded bicycles, wet ballfield, stagnant pond, broken pipe, or incessant rain. Communities design and build some of the best-loved public spaces which, in turn, build a stronger sense of community. A good example is community gardens, which are also a tremendous tool for conducting environmental education and feeding the hungry. If the community is involved in producing public art (and why else would it be called public?), the art will probably reflect the community's character and values and be integrated with the fabric of the neighborhood. People tend to respect and maintain community projects.

Community initiatives generally have a positive effect on the environment. While academicians struggle to define and measure sustainability, strong communities tend to practice sustainability whether or not they have ever heard of the term. In communities, people care for one another and the place they share. Just as they value heritage, communities are mindful of future generations. They are also more self-sufficient and less reliant on outside resources. Meeting present needs without jeopardizing future resources is not only a common definition of sustainability, but it is the goal of empowered communities.

Community school programs are one example of the creative use of resources that would otherwise go to waste. School facilities are typically underutilized much of the time, including evenings, weekends, and summers. Yet, school gymnasiums, libraries, computer centers, theaters, woodshops, kitchens, classrooms, playgrounds, and parking lots could be put to good use by the community. Neighbors with skills, knowledge, and time to share, meanwhile, are generally overlooked by the schools. By fully utilizing the resources of both communities and schools, community school programs can benefit students and neighbors alike.

Strong communities can also play a major role in crime prevention, but too many block watch programs focus on encouraging residents to install deadbolt locks and peer through their peepholes for suspicious behavior by outsiders. Real security comes from opening doors to community life. No amount of public safety spending can buy the kind of security that comes from neighbors caring and watching out for one another.

Community initiatives such as these are essential as local government revenues fail to keep pace with increasingly complex social and environmental issues. Government can be a catalyst for community initiatives but, to do so, it must first change some bad habits. Too many local governments treat citizens as nothing more than customers; citizens, in turn, think of themselves only as taxpayers; government resources, consequently, continue to decline. All local governments have citizen participation processes, but most of them are only a charade. As Daniel Kemmis wrote about public hearings, "the one element that is almost totally lacking is anything that might be characterized as 'public hearing'."

Government must learn to see neighborhoods not simply as places with great needs, but as communities with tremendous resources. Communities can do so much that government cannot and, working together, they can do even more that could not be done otherwise. For example, citizens are willing to tax themselves for projects and programs that their communities request. Government can tap these resources to the extent that it respects the wisdom of the community and acts more as a facilitator than as an expert.

ENDNOTES

[1] Excerpted from Neighbor Power: Building Community the Seattle Way. University of Washington Press. December, 2004.

Assessing the Depth and Breadth of Participation of Seattle's Neighborhood Planning Process

Hilda Blanco

ABSTRACT

Neighborhood planning is the closest practice we have to participatory democracy. As Dewey put, "Democracy begins at home, and its home is the neighborly community." Prompted by Washington State's Growth Management Act (1990), which required cities to prepare comprehensive plans to accommodate their growth allocations, the City of Seattle recently undertook (1995-2000) an extensive neighborhood planning process, recognized as a successful model for participatory neighborhood planning. The framework of the neighborhood planning process was the City's Comprehensive Plan (1994). Seattle's comprehensive plan adopted a strategy of concentrating new growth in a set of centers, from urban (e.g., Downtown), to industrial (e.g., Duwamish) to urban villages, to distressed neighborhoods. Seattle developed an innovative way of generating neighborhood buy in-it left it up the neighborhoods to organize themselves for planning, while providing them with guidelines, some technical assistance, and funds for hiring consultants (from $80-100,000 per urban village center). The City estimates that over 20,000 people participated in the neighborhood planning process that produced 38 neighborhood plans. Also, Seattle established a distinctive way of reviewing plans for incorporation into the comprehensive plan, and for implementing such plans (e.g., reorganization of city services, and incorporation of plan recommendations into the capital budget). This paper sets out the characteristics of the neighborhood planning process and examines the participatory aspects of the process, using the distinction developed by Berry, Portney, and Thomson (1993) that outlines various aspects of the breadth and the depth of participatory democracy. To assess the extent of participation along these two dimensions, this paper will rely on a review of city documents, and a set of structured interviews with planners (both public sector and consultants) that were active in the process, as well as neighborhood activists. It will conclude with exploratory findings on the breadth and depth of Seattle's neighborhood planning process.

5

citizen movements and design activism

The Development of the Environmental Movement and Open Space Planning and Design During the Democratic Period in Korea

Mintai Kim

ABSTRACT

During the last few decades, Korea experienced rapid economic growth and has achieved full democracy. Along with these changes, the successful introduction of the discipline and profession of landscape architecture and the subsequent creation of environmental NGOs all worked together to impact Korean society in positive ways. This paper examines literature and newspaper articles to document the changes in the environmental movement from the perspective of landscape architecture. The goal is to document and understand the phenomenon of the very active environmental movement there and draw from it lessons that might be useful for other countries.

INTRODUCTION

In the developing world the earliest stages of modernization typically concentrate almost solely on economic growth often at the expense of the environment. Over a relatively short period since the 1950s after the Korean War and ensuing decades, Korea achieved remarkably rapid economic growth. Fueled by this, Korea has undergone many socio-cultural changes. For decades, the predominant focus of the society was economic development. It generated national wealth but also generated environmental challenges.

Korea has gone through phases of compressed modernization. Compressed modernization refers to accommodation to drastic economic change, rapid adjustment to technology, rapid degradation of the natural and built environments, dramatic social and political change within short periods of time, and accelerated escalation of cross-cultural influences since the mid-twentieth century.

Concomitant to the period of economic development has been the process of democratization. People could not express their opinions publicly during the long lasting military regimes that ended in 1993. With full democracy the society became more open and the public began to voice demands for a better living environment. These demands are expressed in terms of the creation of many non-government organizations (NGOs),

at the center of which are environmental organizations. Compared to contemporary NGOs in other Asian countries these environmental organizations are very influential, moving (sometimes manipulating) public opinion and often blocking government development projects. They are in fact often criticized for being too biased toward the protection of environments and not allowing necessary development.

The discipline of landscape architecture was at the heart of the environmental movement in the 1990s and played a key role in educating people about the environment. It provided theoretical backing for the environmental movement from the study of ecology. The power movers in Korean environmental NGOs are said to be landscape architecture scholars.

The field of landscape architecture was introduced in the early 1970s. It matured during the 1980s and started to produce major design products such as the Olympic Park (1988). Many of the landscape designs promoted environmental protection and sustainable development. With the new open space development, people learned the value of natural resources. Local residents after seeing the ecologically sensitive developments in other areas asked the same in any development in their local jurisdictions. For any major design projects to be approved today, it seems every design must have some environmental or ecological themes or components for its justification.

PRE-1972

Traditional Korean landscape architecture cherished and protected the natural landscape and emphasized harmony between nature and its dwellers. Many of the traditional landscape architecture works, from such small-scale works as gardens to large places, employed ecological principles.

That tradition was discontinued during Japanese colonial rule from 1910 until 1945. The Japanese used the Korean peninsula as a stepping stone to invade China. The natural landscape and environment was devastated due to war preparations. When the colonial rule was over, mountains were bare without large trees or any sustainable vegetation. The outbreak of the Korean War five years later made the devastated landscape even worse. At the end of the war, Korea was in ruins.

As soon as the war was over, the first national priority was given to economic recovery and growth. Rapid economic growth produced massive environmental pollution and has led to environmental crisis. However, environmental problems were set aside except for nationwide re-forestation of the bare mountains.

1972 - 1982

This is still the period when economic development was predominant. The Korean economy grew rapidly and Koreans started to accumulate wealth. Systematic national land management and development was initiated in 1972 and as a result, in the ensuing three decades the quality of living improved significantly. The population grew from roughly 32 million to 48 million; urbanization from 50% to 86%; highway 3.1 times. The potable water supply from 35% to 85%; sewage treatment capacity from nothing to 66% in the late 1990s. However, along with this came the deterioration of the environment.

Dictatorial government suppressed any form of social-political movements including the environmental movement. The government considered the pollution issues as anti-government strife because they considered it to be an impediment against economic growth, and strongly oppressed and jailed environmental activists together with other political opponents. For this reason, the Korean environmental movement worked in tandem with political democratization movement.

1972 also marks the dawn of modern landscape architecture in Korea. The Korean Institute of Landscape Architecture was formed that year. Landscape architecture programs were established in two universities in 1973. Over the next decade, ten college-level programs were established.

Historic landscapes, such as historic gardens and palaces, were restored by landscape architects, national parks were established, national park related facilities were developed, and highway landscapes were constructed. Most of the works were government initiated and monopolized and carried out by the Landscape Architecture Corporation.

As can be expected in a young profession, the landscape designs and products, however, were a pre-mature imitation of western landscape design. The majority of educators were US educated and they were eager to apply what they learned directly to Korea without cultural considerations. Little attention was given to the environmental issues.

1982 - 1992

Once relative economic wealth was achieved in the 1980s, people's attention has moved to other issues, such as environment, education and social welfare. A strong public sense of urgency regarding the environment and the political freedom to voice that urgency grew.

In 1982, the first environmental NGO was established, Korean Research Institute of Environmental Problems in response to widespread pollution as a product of rapid industrialization. Other NGOs were formed soon after and they raised such environmental issues as nuclear waste, air pollution, golf courses and protection and reclamation of coastal wetlands. The movement was, however, limited still because ex-military president Roh ruled the country, although he was less oppressive compared to his predecessors. The environmental movement was considered a part of political movement because it was

mainly carried on by politically-charged students and religious people.

Landscape architecture started to mature. More landscape architecture programs, including graduate programs, were established. The depth and breadth of the profession grew to include ecological and environmental issues in education and in practice.

Major sporting events, such as Asian games (1986) and the Olympics (1988) brought huge number of projects to the profession. Sports facilities, Olympic village, and memorial parks were constructed. At the same time, new building projects as a result of rapid economic growth brought many new projects to landscape architects. Several arboretums were constructed. Former military bases were converted to public open spaces.

The sheer number of landscape architecture projects was remarkable and citizens started to notice the value and importance of the profession. Landscape architecture started to be recognized as a field with future. Getting into the landscape architecture programs in colleges became more and more competitive.

1992 - PRESENT

In the 1990s, Koreans saw democracy in full bloom. In 1995, local governments gained autonomy. Formerly appointed positions became elected positions. Politicians quickly learned the value and power of landscape architecture in gaining votes and presented many landscape architecture-related platforms. Since the advent of full participatory democracy, major open space projects have occupied central positions in the campaign platforms of the candidates for every mayoral race in Seoul.

Economic wealth, accompanying leisure, major sporting events and politicians demanded more from landscape architects. In the early 1990s, the field of landscape architecture started to actively participate in the environmental movement. Landscape architects were heavily involved in the initial stage of environmental movements.

Environmental Movement

By the 1990s, the environment became an essential issue in Korea society. The majority of Koreans expressed concerns about the environment. Hot issues, such as sustainability and conservation became the central issues and overrode economic development priorities. Responding to these concerns, in 1994 the Ministry of Environment was established initially to regulate pollution.

In 1992, the Korean Federation for Environmental Movement (KFEM) was formed, consolidating several independent environmental NGOs. It started to play a central role in the environmental movement. Many believe that the establishment of KFEM was the turning point in the Korean environmental movement. The number of environmental groups exploded. At present, 250 environmental groups exist and over 200 of them have been estimated to have been established since 1990. Korean environmental groups can be grouped into three different categories: 1) groups closely related to governmental policy and initiatives (e.g., Environmental Preservation Association, Council for Environmental Science, National Movement for Environmental Preservation); 2) Social organizations that participate actively in the environmental movement (Korean YMCA and YWCA, Consumer Association, Press Association); and 3) Independent environmental groups organized by intellectuals and scientists (Alliance of Environmental Movements, Society for Environment and Pollution) (Peritore, 1999).

These environmental groups began to wield enormous power. Along with other political/economic NGOs, these environmental NGOs strongly influenced elections as well as playing a central role in the political reform movement.

The first true democratic government of 1993 brought changes to the relationship between government and environmental organizations. Government started to consider NGOs as a partner and worked together. Issues have changed, too. Industrial pollution issues gave way to trash and landfill, vehicle emission, non-point source water pollution. Around 1995, the number of members in NGOs started to double and triple. The NGOs mounted several successful endeavors to protect the environment, including preventing a dam construction on the environmentally sensitive Dong River.

Socio-Political Change and Landscape Architecture

Behind all the changes were landscape architects. Environmental awareness among citizens also grew partially thanks to landscape architects advocating and promoting environmental awareness through their work.

Landscape architecture expanded and shifted its realm from design of golf courses, ski resorts, other types of resorts and theme parks to ecologically sensitive and sustainable design. It seems every landscape architecture project needs to have some ecological or environmental elements in it these days. Major parks tend to include environmental education centers.

A particularly remarkable phenomenon is the conversion and rebirth of such disliked facilities as sewage treatment plants, trash incinerating facilities, and garbage dumps to parks and environmental education venues.

Such national-level projects as Inchon International Airport, ambitiously constructed to become East Asian hub-airport and World Cup Park, rejuvenated the profession. The World Cup Park launched landscape architecture in South Korea into the forefront of urban environmental design.

World Cup Park. completed in 2002, is a massive environmental design effort which converted a 90-meter-high toxic landfill into a huge, multifaceted environmentally-friendly park and sporting facility.

The present administration of Seoul Metropolitan Government is well into a complex, large scale project to uncover and restore the historically important Chonggye river presently obscured by a double-decker freeway through densely settled downtown Seoul. The project is estimated to cost over $5 billion. The Seoul Metropolitan Government allocates approximately 10% of its annual budget for landscape architecture.

Through these highly visible projects, citizens became aware of the importance of the environment and the role landscape architects play. It was also said at one point that behind every important decision made by environmental organizations are landscape architects.

There exist almost 50 landscape architecture programs, approximately half the number of the programs in the United States. They all in one way or another emphasize ecologically sensitive and sustainable landscape architecture.

CONCLUSION

The trend of the environmental movement is changing from anti-pollution to ecological planning and sustainability. Participants changed from political movement leaders to public. Relationships between government and NGOs became favorable. The environmental movement became more participatory. It was all happening because the public was aware of environmental issues and was eagerly participating in the environmental movement.

The environmental movement in Korea was successful partially because of the discipline of landscape architecture. Landscape architecture educated the public about the importance of the environment. Because the field emphasized ecological and sustainable development early on, the field matured quickly, accumulated knowledge and was ready to influence and support the environmental movement.

REFERENCES

Chung, B. 1999. Korean Society's Modernization and Incongruity. Koreana. Spring 1999.

Kim, M and E. Addison. 2003. Imprinting Landscape Architecture on the Developing World: The Role of the Academic Discipline in the Parks of Seoul. *CELA conference.*

Korean Institute of Landscape Architecture. 2002. Korean Landscape Architecture: 1972-2002. (in Korean).

Korean Federation for Environmental Movement (KFEM) website. http://kfem.or.kr (visited on April 2004).

Peritore, N.P. 1999. Third World Environmentalism: Case Studies from the Global South. University Press of Florida.

CITIZEN TRAIN
How Direct Democracy, Participatory Design, and Pacific Rim Businesses are Creating a New Seattle Monorail

Kristina Hill

ABSTRACT

This case study presents a story of how local citizen organizers challenged institutional authority to create a 14-mile transit line using the initiative process, otherwise known as direct democracy. Second, it reviews the recent history of a single-purpose municipal government that was created by those citizens, which tried to stay "true to its grass-roots" using participatory techniques in planning and design. Construction on the monorail line is scheduled to begin in the fall of 2004. I will present the controversies and innovations that drove decisions during the last six years of this movement as lessons learned. The monorail movement in Seattle began in earnest in 1997, when a cab driver succeeded in getting an initiative on the city-wide ballot by collecting petition signatures outside coffeehouses. I have been a participant observer in this movement, as an appointed member of the monorail Board, which was once a "public development authority" within the City of Seattle's government, and is now a separate municipal authority known as the Seattle Popular Monorail Authority. A total of three successful citizen initiatives was required to create this Authority, and provide it with a budget of $1.6 billion USD funded solely through local taxes. Throughout this process of citizen initiatives, different methods were used to engage both supporters and affected residents to give input on design and planning decisions. Now that the monorail government authority exists, different methods are being used to maintain public involvement, while continuing some of the techniques that have worked well in the past. Websites and email have played important roles in this citizen movement as communication tools, as have sandwich signs, neighborhood-based meetings, and "publicity-stunt" events. I examine the three different phases of this movement to see which strategies were used during each, and to assess the different effects each of these had on helping the project advance towards construction and operations. I also present issues related to transit in the Pacific Rim, where national trends seem to heavily influence the type of transit technology that is selected in those countries. Seattle's transit choices reflect the mixed influences of the light rail industry in the US, particularly in its neighboring city, Portland, Oregon; the Canadian approach to transit used in Vancouver, BC; and the availability of Japanese urban transit examples, in ways that may be unique to the Pacific Rim. The citizen-driven nature of this transit effort seems to be unique to Seattle, and may offer useful lessons to its neighbors.

GENDER ISSUES IN COMMUNITY DEVELOPMENT

Alternative Movement Against the Kobe City Artery Project, Post-Hanshin-Awaji Earthquake

Satoko Asano

ABSTRACT

The purpose of this paper is to define the characteristics of women's activities, and that of gender hierarchy within community, and to consider strategies for gender-balanced community. As an example, I have used the case of the alternative movement against the post-Hanshin-Awaji earthquake artery project, Nishisuma District, Kobe City. This paper focuses on the activities of "the Housewives Group." After the Hanshin-Awaji earthquake, the Kobe City government decided to construct three traffic arteries in the Nishisuma District. A number of Resident Groups took swift action for an alternative plan to rebuild the community after the disaster, but negotiations with the city government broke down. It was too challenging to succeed with mass community organization and action because so many residents had been displaced and there were differing opinions amongst the groups' leaders. The Housewives Group, though they had no previous experience of community action, started their movement belatedly, in 1996. They first had to overcome Japanese patriarchal gender bias, which denied women the ability to speak with their own voice or to take political action. Despite the challenges, they succeeded in forming a community organization. In the year 2000, riding on the back of their actions in the late 90s, the residents established an ongoing research project. Despite their hard work, members continue to be suppressed and barred by the state of patriarchal social conditioning in Japan. They have been forced to channel their aims into subcontracted work in the community. However, in evaluating their new roles within the community, they are pleased to find new vigor in their lives, vigor and meaning, which differs from traditional gender role assignment. In conclusion, this case suggests the importance of empowering both men and women to practice equally within community, both localized and extended.

INTRODUCTION

In Japan, mainstream citizen participation has been increasing since the 1960s. A number of important laws were passed in the 1990s. For example, the "NPO Action Law" and the "Free Access to Information Law." In 1995, the Hanshin-Awaji earthquake showed that community development systems needed to be established. It is common knowledge that the earthquake caused severe damage over a large area. Public services ceased to operate, and a lot of communities couldn't cope with residents' needs. As a result, numerous volunteer organizations gathered to support and resurrect people's lives.

Kobe City is now one of the most advanced cities, in terms of citizen participation in Japan. In 1981, before the earthquake, Kobe City established the Machizukuri Municipal Bylaw. This states that the mayor can approve a community movement as a Machizukuri association, so long as it has residents' approval and funding support. It also requires deployment of planners or designers, and materialization. Kobe City is also famous for land development. During the modernization process, Kobe developed trading ports, and has been transferring earth and sand from the mountains to the bays since the 1950s. There were some conflicts between residents and the Kobe City government before the earthquake. You may be aware that the post-earthquake reconstruction process had enormous problems in terms of citizen participation.

Regarding the relationship between women and community development, it seems that some studies have emphasized the domestically focused gender role and characteristics of female-initiated community movements. Other studies have defined gender hierarchy in the community. Women are forced to engage in unpaid or low-wage work, particularly because

Figure 1. The suburbs are located in North, West and Tarumi ward, and the north of Suma ward.

Japan's government leaves welfare work to the community. It does not provide funding or support for social welfare. Japan is in 32nd place on the GEM index, though it holds 9th place on the HDI index, and 11th place on the GDI index.

Considering these contrary but interrelated characteristics of gender role and socio-political hierarchy, it is important to define the relationship between these characteristics from the viewpoint of gender dichotomy. What here follows is an example using the case of the Nishisuma District, post-Hanshin-Awaji earthquake, focusing on the actions of the Housewives Group.

NISHISUMA DISTRICT AND RECONSTRUCTION PLAN AFTER THE HANSHIN-AWAJI EARTHQUAKE: ARTERY PROJECTS

Nishisuma District is located southwest of Kobe City, in Hyogo Prefecture. Nishisuma was developed as a suburb before WWII and is a middle-class residential area. This area features low wooden houses and narrow streets which ambulances are unable to enter. There are also a few parks. The destructive effect of the earthquake was enormous, though fortunately fires did not break out.

The government's reconstruction plan comprised three traffic arteries: Suma-Tamon Road 36m wide (six lanes, including elevated lanes), Chuo Artery 27 to 36m wide, and Chimori Road 22m wide. These arteries now connect the inner area with the new town, and were passed by law, by 1968: prior

to citizen participation in municipal issues being approved. Residents are concerned about the environmental impact: air and noise pollution, the landscape, and their community lives.

COMMUNITY MOVEMENT AGAINST THE ARTERY PROJECTS

There are ten community groups in negotiations with the government concerning this artery project. Six groups belong to the Jichikai, which is the smallest unit of administrative organization in Japan. Four groups are non-administrative. One group acts for Machizukuri, which translates as community development. The other three groups are types of opposition to the artery projects. Before the earthquake, Nishisuma District was zoned into only three Jichikai. After the earthquake, one Jichikai was subdivided. From a gender perspective, the leaders of these community groups are all men, except for the Housewives Group.

The community movement process in Nishisuma can be divided into four periods.

Period One: Before the Earthquake

In 1992, the Kobe City government planned readjustment of town-lots in Nishisuma District, including plans for seven arteries. They also set up the "Nishisuma Machizukuri gathering" which was composed of Jichikai and other units of the administration (for example, the Women's Conference", and the "Elderly meeting"). In early 1994, the government made a proposal to set this gathering to the Nishisuma Machizukuri

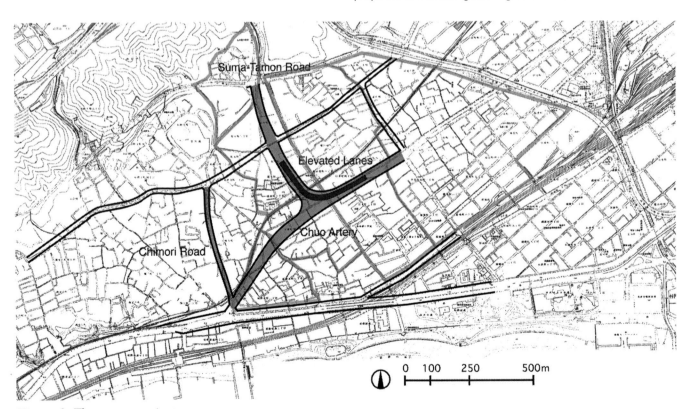

Figure 2. The artery projects.

association in order to actualize their plan, but some members opposed, and the gathering was dissolved. Some of the Jichikai were then reorganized to enable the government to withdraw the plan. However, in June of that same year, the government publicly announced the plan. Three Jichikai requested that the government reconsider. The government then set the council, excluding Nishisuma residents, and terminated the deliberation that December.

Period Two: Post Hanshin-Awaji Earthquake (17 January 1995. Winter)

The Kobe City government ultimately decided to construct only three of the seven previously proposed arteries. Then they altered the manner of the project from readjustment of town lots to buying–up the ownership of the lands and dwellings obstructing the construction areas. This determination resulted in the landowners losing their right to reconstruct buildings on their lots even though many of them had lost their houses by the earthquake. Furthermore, the government became able to negotiate only with the landowners.

Residents formed the "Nishisuma Machizukuri Conference", demanding that the government reconsider the artery project, and approach the city's reconstruction from a completely different angle. They collected more than 8,000 signatures, assessed the impact of potential air and noise pollution from the arteries, and tried to establish the Machizukuri association on the same network as the Jichikai. The government ignored their actions for two years.

This deadlocked situation stagnated community movement. Subsequently, the wider community was dealing with organizational issues; the residents had scattered and leaders' opinions clashed. By December, the Machizukuri Conference showed compromise regarding the artery proposals, and lost centripetal force within the community. On the other hand, some of the Jichikai were gradually reorganized, and the Housewives Group and the Meetings against the Artery Projects materialized in 1996.

Period Three: Negotiations Regarding Environmental Assessments by Six Jichikai

In December 1996, the Head of the Kobe Bar Association published the opinion that the government should carry out environmental assessments before constructing the arteries. The following year, six of the Jichikai published the same opinion, and requested that the government make their investigation plan available to view. Kobe City government evaded the request and claiming a "temporary step", they provocatively announced the upcoming schedule for the arteries' construction.

Following the announcement, the same six Jichikai opposed the planned schedule. The Housewives Group petitioned

residents' opinions and collected signatures to appeal to the City Assembly. By December 1997, they had collected more than 13,000 signatures, although it appeared that over the course of the year, people's attention to the issue had declined. The Meeting against the Artery Project formed The Network against the Artery Project. This new network's members consisted of people from community groups; it's purpose being to refer to the arbitration of environmental assessment. More than 2,500 residents applied for the arbitration on the same day that the Housewives Group appealed. The arbitration was accepted.

These networked community actions forced the government to release the investigation plan to the six Jichikai. The plan revealed that the government had no plans whatsoever for the welfare of environmental conservation. The six Jichikai published that the investigation plan was not solid enough to practice.

Period Four: Progress of Negotiations and Risk Factors

The arbitration committee recommended that the government execute an environmental assessment in conjunction with residents. The government agreed to cooperate. Additionally, the government suggested that one artery plan could be partially changed from four lanes to two lanes in the year 2000. However the two sides, government and residents, were still in dispute over the elevated road. The complexities and pressures both of the negotiations, and of all six Jichikai attempting to put forward a collective opinion, became so severe that it almost caused dissolution of all six groups.

THE ACTIVITIES OF THE HOUSEWIVES GROUP

The Housewives Group is a horizontal and loose network of women. The core comprises about fifteen women, all of whom are over the age of fifty. It was formed in March 1996. The founder said, "I participated in a community meeting as soon as I came back home in fall, after the earthquake. However this meeting concerned making an alternative reconstruction plan, which was amazingly just a readjustment of town lots. When I queried why they were merely considering a readjustment plan, the leaders became angry. I was then excluded from the discussion … It was not only housewives but also the elderly and displaced citizens who were not given voice to express their opinions. I was sure that housewives (women) were entitled to state their opinions. In any case, we need a network of women beyond the Jichikai area because the opinions of each Jichikai are different."

Step One: Group Work

It took seven months to form the organization in 1996. A monthly women-only meeting was held. They attempted to facilitate communication with each other on the back of their policy that everyone has the right to free speech. An average of ten to fifteen housewives participated at each meeting, though

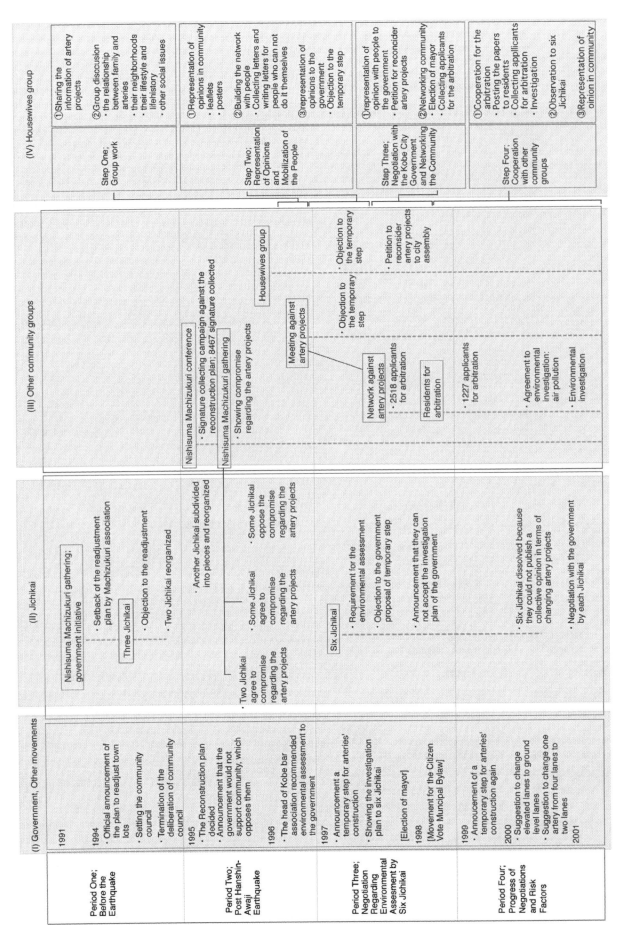

Figure 3. Community movement process in Nishisuma.

the total number was about thirty. They discussed the artery projects from a homemaker's point of view. It also gave them a forum to discuss their neighborhoods, their life histories, and other various social issues of concern. These other issues broached the environmental pollution of another region, and the impact of the United States' Naval Base in Okinawa. Through this process, they were able to more fully understand the impending influence of the artery projects, as well as the interests and viewpoints of their group's members.

Step Two: Representation of Opinions and Mobilization of the People

The Housewives Group succeeded in bringing the peoples' attention to the artery projects. They posted leaflets and simple pamphlets to each house in the area, and made large posters to represent their opinions and arrest the people's attention. The posters said such things as "Do you know about the highway artery project? We are very anxious about our health. Please consider this project and call us."

They then built a network of residents by publishing pamphlets of letters they wished to lobby. During this process they were also able to manage residents' post-earthquake needs. Following the destruction and havoc the tremor had caused, these women had become extremely sensitive to diversity and were weak subjects as people. When the first twenty-odd letters of the group were collected, it was found that the contents differed vastly. The group believed that various ideas and opinions must be represented, and so collected more letters. Following this action, they were then asked to write letters on behalf of citizens who were unable to do it for themselves, for example, aged people. Consequently, about two hundred letters were collected.

These actions made it clear that other community groups were unable to organize residents effectively, and were not allowing across-the-board freedom of speech. Some other groups questioned the right of the Housewives Group to act only through women's voices, and often criticized their actions.

Step Three: Negotiating with the Kobe City Government and Networking the Community

After the Kobe City government suggested the construction of the arteries as a "temporary step," the Housewives Group began to lobby and prepared to petition the city assembly. They made best use of the abundant network of residents, and collected more than 13,000 signatures in only three months. At the same time, they were asked to participate in the mayoral election campaign and in arbitration action with other community groups. They were accepted as part of the movement and contributed enormously.

Step Four: The Importance of Community Movement in regard to Gender Role Assignment Risks

As negotiations with the government through the arbitration and the six Jichikai advanced, the Housewives Group supported their actions. They did such things as posting leaflets, measuring air pollution, and observing meetings. For example, the number of applicants for additional application of arbitration was 1,227, and they rallied about 1,000. They came to play an important role in the community movement, but they couldn't decide on negotiation or publicity strategies as a stand-alone group. As a result of this situation, they were unable to prevent the dissolution of six Jichikai. In addition, they pointed out that they could not fully act as they wished without the cooperation of other groups. As a result, the number of participants to arbitration declined.

To summarize from a gender perspective, in regards to these alternative motions against the artery projects, we must divide the movements into two groups: community movements, and the Housewives Group's movements. Firstly, after the earthquake, men orchestrated alternative movements, and women were excluded, therefore finding it difficult to participate. Secondly, the Housewives Group organized citizens, making use of their network, and their instinctual sense of caring for families and the neighborhood. They contributed towards community actions during difficult times, and were accepted for their efforts. Thirdly, the Housewives group played the role of arousing people's attention, but they were excluded from negotiation decisions. This situation was due to vertical and impenetrable patriarchal conditioning within the movements, and society as a whole.

RECOGNITION AND EVALUATION OF THE HOUSEWIVES GROUP'S MEMBERS

I examined the recognition of gender stereotypes and the evaluation to community movement of the Housewives Group. I headed twelve members and analyzed with the KJ method.

Lifestyles and Recognition of Gender Stereotypes

All members of the group have almost finished raising their children, and don't have full time jobs. This enables them to spend a lot of time in community interaction and to have decent networking opportunities with residents. Many of the members highly value community, and as homemakers, they fear the impact of artery projects in relation to their families. On the other hand, prior to women's participation and action, many of the members believed that women were disempowered regarding anti-government actions. They also believed that the overarching patriarchal image of the housewife was "useless." Some women said that these social constructs stemmed from their social conditioning as children by Japan's gender-biased education system. One of the women interviewed stated, "My parents educated me to believe that the most important role for women was to be obedient to others, and never to talk back or disagree." Another said, "My parents said that women must be engaged in housekeeping and did not need higher education."

The Relationship between the Evaluation of the Movement and the Characteristics of The Housewives Group

Concerning the excellent results of the community movement, the Housewives Group members respected:

- To negotiate with the government, and to allow the government to approve the mediation of environmental assessment, thus altering part of the artery project.

- At the community level, the factors of negotiation are to organize large numbers of residents and to network community groups with each other.

- At the Housewives Group level, to acknowledge each members' point of view, and to then act collaboratively.

- At the family level, to be understood by family in terms of the relationship of family and community movement and to members' activities.

- At the members' personal level, to put forth their beliefs to others, including their family members, the other Housewives Group members, residents, community groups and the government.

They suggested that the primary factor for their success was their lifestyle, which included allowing time for activities and networking with residents, as well as their flexible behavior toward others. One member stated, "Men are stubborn to others, but women think a lot about each other. Our flexibility is an important factor in our approach to them." These characteristics of housewives are especially beneficial to community organization.

In addition, it is most significant that so many members admired their understanding of government and community so much. They said things like, "It was a special experience, my first in being given a chance to share my beliefs with others, to collect signatures and to participate in the demonstration march in front of the government offices. These kinds of actions are traditionally viewed as unladylike." And another, "When I looked down the townscape from the municipal assembly on the 24th floor of the government office building, I could understand how this architectural viewpoint gives the city planners increased power; so distant from our lives on the ground level." These comments suggest that they were previously quite estranged with the givens of the public spheres of government and community, but that they have since developed motivation to try and overcome their oppressed state in regard to the representation of women, and negotiation practices. The strong realism of participating in public movements and of being engaged in the public sphere, give them their incentive to act.

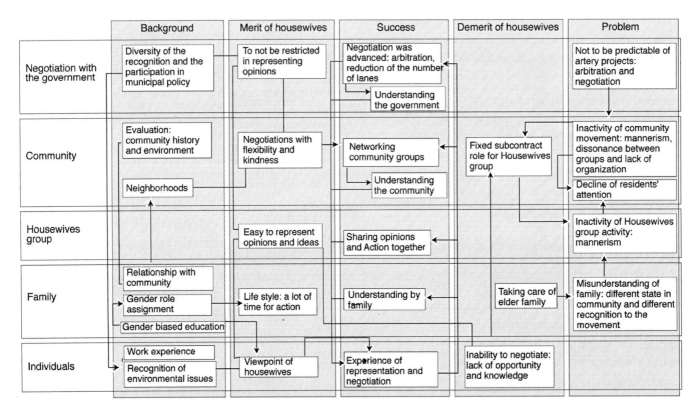

Figure 4. Recognition and evaluation of the housewives group members.

Regarding the problems concerning community movement, the Housewives Group indicated that:

- In negotiations with the government, they were far from optimistic about the arbitration and the reconstruction of community through partnership

- At the community level, that it is difficult to coordinate community groups and to rouse peoples' attention to arbitration because it takes such a long time, and community movements can become stereotyped.

- These situations are the same within the Housewives Group, but we cannot overlook that they regard it as a serious problem that they were forced to engage in fixed subcontract work and could not promote their own activity after their 1997 petition. They were anxious that they were unable to act as a mediator between residents and core members.

- At the family level, time management was hindered because they had to take care of elderly family members, causing difficulty in attending night meetings. They were also hindered by the misunderstandings of their family members.

- At a personal level, their sense of suppressed communication with people, other groups, and the government, coupled with their lack of knowledge about arbitration.

Some members related the subcontract work to gender discrimination issues. They stated that it is difficult for them to attain the power to negotiate, despite struggling to overcome the barriers. It is challenging to break the stereotypical view that "the housewife is not good at discussion," particularly in a country that did not receive the greater benefits of the late twentieth century feminist movement. "When some community design experts came to Nishisuma, I talked about some critical issues concerning community action. I thought it was a chance to state my opinion that each group should communicate with the other groups. However, after the meeting my viewpoint was rejected. They told me that I had to speak in the role of resident, and that the members of the Housewives Group must be stupid." This comment implies a contradiction that "residents" are reasonable but "women" are unreasonable. Some members did however sympathize with the gender role assignment. They felt distressed about representing their opinions in public, and took a passive, rather than active, role. "When I forwarded my opinions in some forums with members, I felt that I was not adaptable to such a type of ceremony. I would like to do subcontract work." "I feel fearful of my activity, stepping into the public sphere so much."

I once suggested to the Housewives Group that if they stop their subcontract work, other community groups would recognize their crucial role. However they feared that if they were to cease their subcontracted work, they might also lose the power of arbitration. They queried, "If the government were

to announce that, would they close the arbitration at the same time?" In gender studies it is said, "the gender hierarchy in emergency times stems from the every day."

CONCLUSION AND RECOMMENDATION

Conclusion: the Possibilities and Risks of Gender Dichotomy

This case defines the relationship between women's activities and gender dichotomy in Japan in two instances. Firstly, women act as women, devoting their lives to a domestic role and taking care of their families. They are able to use their time and residential networks, as well as satisfying the needs of residents so kindly and elaborately, through their actions. These characteristics are the catch returns of being so heavily engaged in the private sphere, and hence provide the possibility of female-led community development. They therefore need group work before they can represent their opinions in the public sphere. They must overcome their socially conditioned gender stereotypes.

Secondly, some men and women globally, including Japanese, have become accustomed to the vertical relationship of men and women in patriarchal society. Women have been separated from community movements, especially from the anti-government lobbies in Japan. They need to bring themselves out of the private sphere, and into the public, so that they can negotiate with the government and coordinate community groups. Even if women do participate with political actions, they suffer the risk of being subcontracted by men, either compulsorily or spontaneously. These characteristics reflect their lifestyles and gender-biased conditioning through education and the system as a whole. This causes problems within community organization and is the inevitable limit of gender dichotomy.

Recommendation: How to Support the Community Development of Gender Equality

I must emphasize that this is but one case concerning gender inequalities, and it reflects the characteristics of only one suburb. Most of the residents are middle-class, and the lives of men and women are separated. Most men work outside of their community, while the women stay in their homes. There are numerous types of community movements, which are promoted by both men and women in Japan. But it remains fact that women, especially middle-aged women, work in bad conditions and positions in their communities, even though they play such an invisible but crucial role.

I also make sure that the role assignment in community itself is not a problem. Both the negotiation with government and the organizing community are important. I point out that if people challenge taking on new roles in community, we must approve of and support them.

The Nishisuma case suggests that we must make a program to empower women. It implies that we need a revised sense of community, in which the two sexes work together harmoniously, respecting and supporting each other. Of course, to be effective in Japan, this program must be established as official practice. If this remains as a custom in community, experts or NPO / NGO staff must support them unofficially.

As experts, we can respect their lives and characteristics. We can encourage them to be proud of themselves and their role within the family, and to speak their opinions as women. If the need arises, we can talk in semi-private or semi-public spheres together. We can also recommend they read literature pertaining to other women's actions, or invite experts to talk about the role of women in community movements.

We can encourage them to overcome their weaknesses and to develop a new empowered role in the community. In the case of Nishisuma, these women value their new role and their insight into understanding government and their community. The reality of overcoming gender-biased obstacles drives them towards new challenges. We can suggest that they partake in new and unique actions, and give them advice on how to build networks with various groups beyond the localized area.

Finally, for those who suffer from gender hierarchy, or any other type of vertical hierarchy, we need to constructively criticize the conditions of community movement, whilst maintaining some of the characteristics of community. The privilege of outsiders is that they can either be severely shocked by the situation, or ignore the traditional practice of gender role assignment.

REFERENCES

Ueno, K. 2000. Machizukuri by Women. Gakugei publish.

Stall, S. 1997. Community Organizing or Organizing Community? Gender and the Crafts of Empowerment. A COMM-ORG Working Paper.

Grieve, M. and Bringham, R. 2001. Women as Catalysts for Social Change. American Planning Association.

Saito, N. 2000. From Surrounding to Center. Study of Douwa Problem.

6

shaping community futures

GATHER AT THE RIVER
Identification and Preservation of Local Culture

Patsy Eubanks Owens

ABSTRACT

This paper focuses on the search for community identity and vision through the development of a park master plan. Many residents of Knights Landing, a small, unincorporated community, and the designers saw the park planning process and the future park as an opportunity for uniting the sometimes divided community while also celebrating the rich history of the place. Participation strategies for this project included employing techniques to reach the Latino/a and Anglo populations as well as children and the elderly. The resulting concept for the park design, "Gather at the River: to remember our past, enjoy our present and build our future," lays the foundation for a community gathering place that will welcome everyone and celebrate the unique qualities of this place and its people.

THE COMMUNITY, THE CHALLENGE

Knights Landing is an unincorporated community of approximately 800 residents located in the Central Valley of California thirty minutes northwest of Sacramento. Adjacent to the Sacramento River, it is a diverse community rich in agricultural heritage. Comments from residents give a clear and accurate description of the community. (See Figure 1.) Understanding the history of this community is critical to understanding the discussions related to the creation of this community park. Much of the physical community was lost in floods and fires, but the memories and significance of these places is vital to the residents and is reflected in the park design.

The Patwin native-American tribe once lived along these riverbanks and were followed by Anglo settlers in the early and mid 1800s. Named after the ferry crossing established by William Knight, the town had a hotel and several warehouses by 1853. Spurred by bustling river traffic associated with agricultural production throughout the valley, the community continued to thrive between 1860 and 1890. Several floods in the following years washed away much of Knights Landing's progress. Subsequent flood control measures, levees, canals, weirs and bypasses, have aided to prevent future devastating floods (Walters and Anderson, 1992; Owens 1999).

How would you describe Knights Landing?

- Small town, nice people, nice community, friends.

- Falling apart; gone downhill.

- One big family; everyone watches over everyone else; Community cares for you.

- Fun, noisy, windy.

- 2 communities, divided Latino, white, small rural community, country town, poor, lots of tradition, lots of history, people know each other

- Not much for kids to do. We have to go out of town to Woodland. There aren't any organized sports except for the soccer. It's safe for kids, though.

- There are very rich people and very poor, and not many in-between. The town is small and rural. No services.

Figure 1. Community responses during interviews.

After suffering difficult economic times along with the rest of the country during the late 1920s and 1930s, Knights Landing was dealt a devastating blow when Front Street and its many businesses were destroyed by fire in 1938. The Front Street area was never rebuilt; businesses did not reopen or moved and much of Front Street disappeared under tons of rocks as the levees were created in 1947. The resulting levees cut the community off from the river both visually and physically. Although the river once played a significant commercial role for the community (the largest yield was over two tons daily of salmon), recreational fishing and boating are now the primary activity (Walters and Anderson, 1992).

Mexico has had strong ties throughout the years to this area from the original land grant to William Knight from the Mexican government to more recent family members moving to join their loved ones. Today, Knights Landing's population is predominately Hispanic and Anglos. The Anglo population tends to be older while the Latino/a residents are younger with children in the local school. In recent years, the Latino/a residents have led much of the efforts to improve the community and planning for the future.

At the invitation of community leaders in 1999, landscape architecture and community development students at the University of California, Davis worked with the residents to define goals for the community's future. In the following years, students in design studios have worked with the residents to work toward these goals. One goal, and the challenge that is the focus of this paper, was the development of a design master plan for a community park during a landscape architecture studio in the spring of 2001.[1] The park master plan was the backdrop for a much more difficult task of bringing diverse community members together to identify the qualities and characteristics of the community they want to preserve and showcase. In addition, there was the challenge of creating a place that was useful and meaningful to all residents, young and old, Anglo and Latino/a. As the only designed open space in the community, this centrally located park plays both a symbolic and tangible role in bringing the community together.

THE ISSUES, THE PLAYERS, THE APPROACH

Working within the time constraints of a 10-week quarter, the design process had to be efficient and effective. With community participation in the process a high priority, the approach undertaken was based on Hester's 12-step process (1985). To adapt the process to this particular community and project, steps were shortened or conducted simultaneously and information obtained by previous design studios was used, but the community-focused spirit of the process was retained. In developing the participation techniques, we also had to keep in mind that many community members were Spanish-speaking. All the materials we prepared and all meetings had to be bilingual.

The initial meetings with a few community leaders (teachers, a non-profit leader, and volunteers) gave the design team a strong indication that the park needed to be more than a pretty place to play and picnic. These leaders wanted a park that everyone in the community would be proud of and would use. They wanted a place that was made for them and not one that they could find anywhere else. The search for the community identity and vision for the park is the crux of this paper and the foundation for the park master plan.

Several techniques were used to gain a better understanding of the community, the desires of individuals and community groups, and their visions for the park. For the most part the techniques are ones that have been used numerous times before, but the combination of these techniques, their specific design, and their delivery provide lessons for an effective means of understanding a community's spirit and desires. The methods used are discussed here.

To gain a sense of how the residents perceived their community and their desires for the future park, we conducted a listening phase where we interviewed the "opinion leaders"[2] and placed suggestion boxes throughout the town. Thirty-one opinion leaders were interviewed; no one that wanted to be interviewed was turned away. Ten persons interviewed were non-Hispanic whites and twenty-one were Hispanic. Our list of opinion leaders included Water Board officials, members of the Citizen's Advisory Committee, Grafton Elementary school faculty and staff, religious leaders, long-time citizens, existing park users (the Soccer Club), and a cross-section of citizens from various demographic groups (young, old, Spanish-speaking, English-speaking). During each interview we asked

if there was someone else in the community that they thought we should talk to and then added that person to our list of interviewees. From the interviews we learned about how these residents feel about the community in general and the park in particular. Many of the sentiments we heard at our first meeting were repeated in these discussions. Residents wanted the new park to "meet the needs of all the community members."

During this same period, we also solicited input from the broader community. In an effort to ensure that everyone had an opportunity to voice their opinion in the early stages of the project, we placed suggestion boxes in several locations. We selected locations that received frequent use from various segments of the population -- the Community Center, the Senior Housing Facility, Mom's Diner (the only local restaurant), the Plug & Jug (a local convenience store), the Post Office, and the Grafton Elementary School Office. From these boxes, we received many suggestions regarding the park design: The respondents wanted to make sure the park was handicap accessible, existing vegetation was retained, and a large party area for celebrations was included.

While we were learning about what the citizens envisioned for the park, we also wanted to learn about the park itself and the surrounding community. We conducted a site analysis that included examining the existing vegetation, drainage, soils, views, history, ownership and uses. (The existing park included outdated and dangerous play equipment and minimal picnicking facilities. See Figure 2.) In conducting the site analysis, we were surprised to learn that most people did not know who owned the park property; there was uncertainty if it belonged to the School District, the water board or someone else. We discovered that the property is owned by the School District, but there is an agreement for maintenance to be conducted by the Water Board. In addition, the soccer field is maintained by the local soccer club. We also reviewed information obtained by the earlier group of university students. Several citizens led these students on a walking tour of the community during which they learned that the "missing" Knights Landing was important to the residents. Stories of the businesses that were once located along Front Street and childhood memories of the river were prevalent. This earlier group of students also conducted a photographic survey with the residents. Images of places such as those that are most special, most fun, least valued, and saddest were useful in understanding the community. In addition, the photographs of a place that "is" Knights Landing underscored the importance of the river and agriculture to the residents. (See Figure 3.)

After this initial phase of information gathering, we held a community meeting to share what we had learned and to enlist the community's help in verifying and further defining the goals

Figure 2. Outdated play equipment.

Figure 3. The Sacramento River.

Figure 4. Bilingual community workshop flyer.

for the park development. We designed the meeting to welcome everyone. Bilingual notices (Figure 4) were posted throughout the community and phone calls were placed to everyone that had been interviewed. The meeting day and time were selected to work with other community activities. In addition, several residents suggested we include a potluck dinner so that attendees could come immediately after work and bring their children. The potluck was an excellent idea because it gave a feeling of openness and camaraderie. Another important element of our workshop presentation was the inclusion of one of the students from the previous course. Community members often become discouraged when yet another group of students arrive to "study" them and give them a report or some pretty drawings. In an effort to show that we were continuing the work of the earlier students, not starting over, our translator for the evening was one of the previous students. A native-Spanish speaker from Mexico, this older student was well remembered from the earlier work.

The interviews and responses in the suggestion boxes had given us ideas for the types of things the residents wanted to see in the park, but they did not tell us how these elements should function or what they should look like. At the workshop, we had the attendees work in smaller groups and discuss the items they would most like to see in the future park. These discussions allowed them to describe how they would like

to use the park facilities and why they were important. For example, one item that had received mention in the interviews and the suggestion boxes were barbecue and picnic areas. Through the workshop discussions, we learned that they wanted places for not only small family gatherings, but also places the overall community or extended families could use for celebrations. In addition, the desire to ensure that everyone would use the park came out in several of the discussions. For example, the track discussions included comments that the older residents would prefer a walking trail with shaded seating areas to a track around the soccer field.

As discussed by Hester (1985), we wanted to involve residents in establishing the design concept or gestalt for the park design. We decided to begin these efforts by working with the elementary school children. We developed an interactive lesson plan on design and concept development and met with three classes of 3rd and 4th grade students. After discussing design, creativity and concepts, we had the students each develop their own "theme" or "big idea" for the park. Afterwards, the students worked with two of their friends to develop a concept and a model of the park illustrating their concept. (See Figure

Figure 5. Student concept-building workshop.

5.) Ideas generated by the students included: a rainforest in outer space, camping, rich river, and enchanted garden. These ideas reflected the students' desires for a design that was modern or futuristic and naturalistic. They wanted a park that had natural elements such as "a native garden in local riparian setting," "a fishing rock," and "trees and hills," but also "futuristic lights" and "space ship play structures."

Based upon all the information gathered in these workshops and interviews, we prepared several exhibits to be displayed at a community celebration. We developed three schematic designs showing location alternatives for park features, program element boards with design options for various features, and a working model. These displays allowed us to obtain input from residents who had not been involved in the process thus far and also to give them an opportunity to learn what was being discussed. The feedback was also useful in furthering the design decisions particularly in regard to the design style of specific elements. For example, celebration attendees placed dots next to the photographs of design elements that they liked best, therefore we learned that those responding liked the modern play structures more than the natural timber structures. This finding, and others, was in keeping with what we had heard from residents at our earlier workshop and from the elementary students.

The input of the community members through this process gave us a clear indication of some of the most important concepts they wanted incorporated in the park. Beyond the functional elements of the park, they wanted the park to be a place to bring the community together, a place to remember and celebrate the history of the area, a place to respect the agricultural and natural landscape, and a place to inspire residents to work toward a better future. Armed with the knowledge gained in all the previous steps, the landscape architecture students generated a long list of potential design concepts. Four of those concepts were developed into design plans: Common Ground - Higher Ground, Bridge with the Past, The River, and Together at the River. After internal critiques and professional review, the final design, "Gather at the River: to remember our past, enjoy our present, and build our future," was developed.

The resulting design was presented to the community at a well-attended meeting at the school. In addition to young, old, Anglo and Latino/a residents, the local Water Board, School Board, and the County Parks Department were all represented. As a first step to "transferring the ownership" of the park back to the community, we asked one of the teachers, and active park planning participant, Maria, to act as the meeting translator. As the design presentation proceeded, it became clear that Maria was embellishing the students' descriptions with ideas she had heard from fellow residents at the workshops. It was clear that she understood where the design ideas had been generated

and their underlying intent. The excitement and energy in the room increased with the presentation of each component of the design. As we were completing our presentation and were explaining that this master plan was the start of a process and not the end, we could see the community members begin taking the baton of responsibility. The discussion quickly turned to ideas for funding, materials or construction expertise. Following the meeting, community members formed an "action team" and have continued to work toward the realization of the park. Their concept of "Gather at the River: to remember our past, enjoy our present and build our future" lays the foundation for a design that will welcome the entire community and preserve their unique qualities.

LESSONS LEARNED

The park planning experience in Knights Landing provides lessons for others assisting communities with design or planning projects. These lessons are derived with the objective of increasing the effectiveness of the participation in regards to identifying and responding to community member concerns. The lessons are intended to be applicable to many participation methods and not limited to those we used.

Participation begins with individuals.

Communities typically have someone that others trust and that is an advocate for the project. This person is the door into the community, but should not be seen as the only connection to other community members. Other individuals with differing ideas are sure to be in the community and need to be sought out. Community members should be given an opportunity to speak out individually either through one-on-one interviews, surveys, suggestion boxes, comment cards or other means. Many people are not comfortable voicing a dissenting opinion in a public setting so opportunities need to be provided to allow for those opinions.

Beyond the active community leaders, the community "power holders" (in the Knights Landing case, the Water Board and School Board members) need to be brought into the process early.

Their participation in the early stages has a double-sided benefit – they hear what the residents are thinking and wanting, and they have an opportunity to explain requirements that the project will have to meet. Officials can be convinced of a project's merits and become welcome project allies when they hear the enthusiasm of community supporters. Before bringing these power holders into discussions with community members, however, it is important to gauge their willingness to work with the community. If they are not willing to work with the community, it is best if the residents first have an opportunity to generate and discuss ideas amongst themselves. In one instance at a meeting following community workshops, we had a county official rejecting every idea even before it could be fully articulated. Luckily the community members knew they had the support of others and did not discard ideas just because the official did not like them.

Asking obvious questions often reveals surprising answers.

When we conducted our site analysis of the town and park, we were able to note what we could see, but only through talking to the residents did we learn about what had once been and what they thought. We started by asking simple, open-ended questions such as describe Knights Landing. Instead of limiting their responses to a physical description, the residents told us about the social, economic, historic and cultural character of the community. In the earlier student project, residents were asked to photograph a variety of places in the community – places that were the most fun, the saddest, etc. These techniques provided a wealth of information and also started the community members looking at their home in a different way. In addition, obvious questions such as who will pay for it, who will take care of it, who will use it need to be answered. The answers can significantly influence the design.

Community members need to be asked to help with the project.

Volunteers are often relied upon in participatory design projects, but we found that asking people to help out (instead of waiting for them to come forward) had great benefits. Persons who might not otherwise be involved take an active role in the project, untapped leadership can be found, and the residents' sense of empowerment increases. The role of their involvement can take many forms. Residents can be asked to assist with the information gathering (Hester, 1999), presentations and other forms of dissemination, design generation, and construction. During one of our later construction parties, we spotted a Spanish-speaking woman who was working hard and was very comfortable with the tools. Through a bilingual community member, we asked her to take charge of one section of the planting and supervising others. She would never have proposed herself for this position, but was thrilled to be asked and did an excellent job. In some cultures volunteering is frowned upon because it looks as if the person thinks they are better than others (McGrew, 1998); they prefer to be asked to help. (For further discussion of cultural influences on participatory methods, see Owens, 2000 & 1997 and Daley, 1989.)

Previous work should be built upon, not repeated.

It is surprising, but not unusual, to learn that even the smallest, most out of the way community has been studied, mapped or "master planned." The information gleaned from previous efforts should be acknowledged, examined and used when

appropriate. Community members become very frustrated and discouraged when they feel like they are repeating a process that they have already completed. Although the information may have been gathered in a different manner or is in a different form than would currently be used, the design team needs to finds ways to verify and update the information without starting over. In the same vein, if new residents join a design process late, they need to have an opportunity to voice their opinions, but not to override decisions that have already been made. Those that have been involved in the project should be given the responsibility of explaining the information that has been gathered, the discussions that have taken place and the resulting decisions. Newcomers should be given an opportunity to raise questions and learn if those questions were answered in previous discussions.

Designers using community participation methods must "learn how to punt."

Unlike some design processes where the participation of residents is not needed, a participatory process requires that the designer have alternative means in place for involving community members. Community meetings are unpredictable; sometimes fewer persons than expected show up, sometimes more than expected. Alternative plans need to be thought through before the meeting – how to facilitate one large group versus several smaller ones, or how to have more groups than expected. Many other scenarios can also occur. What if, as we had happen in Knights Landing, a large group of children show up part way through the meeting? We had a contingency plan in place for a children's group, but had to make adjustments for the large number of young participants and their late start. Other surprises beyond the number of attendees also need to be addressed. In our attempt to have a poster display at the outdoor community gathering, we had to deal with strong winds. The posters had to be laid on the ground instead of being mounted vertically. Their reduced visibility had to be compensated for by asking attendees to come over and look at them.

Lastly, an important lesson to be taken from this project is that the designer needs to be the designer.

Designers know what questions need to be answered, the opportunities a project holds, and the range of possibilities for design. The community members in Knights Landing understood that they knew more than the designers about their community and about their desires for a park, but they also knew that the designers knew more about how to put it all together and could give them ideas and guidance. They needed the designers to take their desires and give them form. In addition, the designers were the facilitators that encouraged and directed the search for community identity that formed the foundation for the park's design. Without these broad-based community outreach efforts, it is likely that the design would have answered many of the functional desires of the involved community members, but the multi-generational and cultural spirit of the park's design and the overall community's dedication to its completion would not have materialized.

CONCLUSION

For a design to be responsive to a place and its people, the vision for the design needs to reflect that community. The designer must actively seek the involvement of diverse community members in identifying this vision. The participatory design process used in the Knights Landing project allowed us to reach many members of the community and to engage them in the discussions and decision making. Children, teens and elderly, as well as adults, were engaged in various stages of the design process. The involvement of Latino/a and Anglo community members was actively encouraged and supported. These diverse groups worked separately and together to understand their own desires for the park design and to develop a design that would be supportive of their collective vision. Other communities will have different residents, issues, and desires, but the lessons learned in Knights Landing will be helpful to designers assisting with their planning efforts.

ENDNOTES

[1] Construction documents were not prepared during this studio, but student involvement in the realization of the Knights Landing park continued afterwards. Several components of the master plan have been implemented including the design and installation of a playground, the siting and construction of the Knights Landing Family Resources Center (FRC) and the landscaping of the FRC entry.

[2] For our purposes opinion leaders were persons who represent a larger group in the community or who are in some way more involved with decision-making for the community.

REFERENCES

Daley, J. M., Applewhite, S.R., and Jorquez, J. 1989. Community Participation of the Elderly Chicano: A model. International Journal Aging and Human Development, 29(2), 135-150.

Hester, R. T. 1999. Refrain with a View. Places, 12(2), 12-25.

Hester, R. T. 1985. Landstyles and Lifescapes: 12 steps to community development. Landscape Architecture Magazine, Jan/Feb.

McGrew, S. 1998. Master' Thesis, Community Development Graduate Program, University of California, Davis.

Owens, P. E. 2000. That Same Ole Participation? Places, 13(1), 34-36.

Owens, P. E. 1999. Community-Building: Learning a Participatory Process. (A summary of Knights Landing goal setting). unpublished report.

Owens, P. E. 1997. Community Participation in a New Cultural Context. American Society of Landscape Architects: 1997 Annual Meeting Proceedings. Washington, D. C., 123-127.

Walters, S. and Anderson, T. 1992. Knights Landing: The River, The Land and the People. Woodland, CA: Yolo County Historical Society.

CRAFTING WESTPORT
How One Small Community Shaped Its Future

Douglas Kot and Deni Ruggeri[1]

ABSTRACT

This paper discusses the ongoing participatory design effort in the small coastal community of Westport, California since May 2003. It opens with background information about the identity of its people and places, followed by detailed discussion of methods and results used during the process of designing its new town center. While the Westport community is, in many ways, representative of others of similar size and location, its idiosyncrasies led to unique results with regard to both methodology used and design outcome. The evolving needs of the community and their changing opinions regarding the location, functional relationships and views were incorporated in a design that was carefully crafted, adjusted and calibrated throughout the process. Moreover, the effects of a highly identifiable physical environment on residents' perceptions of spatial form resulted in sophisticated design solutions. Additionally, the way of life in Westport defined the need for a flexible process that addressed the community's remoteness and limited resources.

THE COMMUNITY

Westport sits on the edge of California's Lost Coast—it is the northernmost town on Highway 1. Similar to its environment, Westport has always been a community of rugged individuals. It owes its history to the lumber industry, whose peak occurred by 1900, when it was the largest town on the north Mendocino

Figure 1. Postcard of Westport, California.

Coast. However, the rough coastline, strong winter storms and newly completed rail service to nearby Fort Bragg soon spelled the end of Westport's boom. The lack of economic pressure during the twentieth century left an intact village of historic New England saltbox houses. Today's full-time population of approximately 150 and service area of less than a thousand people fits easily into this one hundred year old setting.

Nowadays, a handful of commercial establishments provide limited employment opportunities. Most residents who work are engaged in informal agriculture or employed in the health care service sector in Fort Bragg. While they are aware of the village's limited resources, local residents wish for new economic development opportunities that could provide a few more jobs for locals and attract new families: goals that can only be achieved if new houses are built.

The physical geography of Westport is at the same time its most valuable asset and one of its greatest shortcomings. With no access other than California Highway 1, which winds along the coast, Westport has remained just beyond the reach of second-home real estate pressure. Its isolation has helped preserve its tight-knit community, confirming it as a place where residents all know each other and conflicts are resolved through an old-fashioned show of hands. In more than a few instances, Westport residents have shown a deep commitment to their community, coming together and setting aside conflicts in order to resolve problems the village has faced. They have succeeded in saving the Headlands from development, built a small school and church and have managed to build a water treatment facility: an ambitious undertaking for such a small community.

California coastal communities like Westport are at a crucial point in their history. The rising demand for vacation homes and real estate prices has led developers to smaller, more vulnerable communities for easier and more profitable real estate opportunities and brought San Francisco Bay Area tourists to increasingly remote coastal towns. It would appear to some that tourism and real estate may be the only economic prospect left for residents struggling to survive the shutdown of the last timber mill. Today, only half of Westport's housing stock is occupied year-round by permanent residents, many of whom are being forced to search for more affordable places to live. For those who remain, the challenge is to accommodate tourism without it dominating the local identity.

PROJECT BACKGROUND

The fear of tourism, gentrification and identity loss are common concerns for residents of small coastal towns like Westport. In the past, the residents have banded together and fought developers' attempts to turn the village into a second-home enclave of part time residents without roots in the place (McNally, 1987

Figure 2. Aerial Photo of with the "Pea Patch" boundaries highlighted. (Graphic: Westport Community Design Team)

and Hester, 1988, 1987). At this time, however they recognize the need for a community-wide vision to guide their future. As a result, they have chosen a democratic design process as an instrument to help them reclaim control over their own community and achieve the desired improvements.

The recent process of "Crafting Westport" originated when two long-time residents acquired the prime development site known as the "Pea Patch," a 45-acre parcel of land to the north and east of town. This land was scheduled for development of 10-15 trophy vacation homes that would have sprawled on four-acre parcels across the entire site. The two residents had a radically different vision. To make more than an exclusive second home subdivision, their intent was to preserve most of this land as open space and wildlife habitat, build a few houses, and donate the land for a Community Center. It became clear through the process that any development must be consistent with the character of the historic village while providing a balance of jobs and housing suitable to both the existing community and new families.

PROCESS

Westport's Citizen Participation followed the community development framework outlined in Randy Hester's "Planning Neighborhood Space for People" (1982) and "Community Design Primer" (1990). This method seemed particularly appropriate to the task of creating a design for new development and public facilities while at the same time working on a strategic vision for the future of the community. Moreover, the methodology had been previously applied in communities such as Manteo, NC and Caspar, CA, which are similar to Westport in size and location and had succeeded in helping those communities shape their future. Through Hester's Twelve Steps, residents were able to participate actively in the design of their neighborhood rather than having to accept the solutions envisioned by an outside professional. The "Crafting Westport" process employed the modification of the Twelve Steps outlined below.

Listening

The Westport Listening Process began in September 2003 and continued through April 2004. The list of potential interviewees was generated from the county of Mendocino record of property owners. This list was later reviewed and edited and cross-referenced against another list later provided by the clients. Approximately 120 person-hours were devoted to interviewing a large majority of full time residents and many of the second-home owners. In total, 54 personal interviews were conducted and two informal conversations occurred. Additionally, small group Listening occurred with members of the Parent's Club on 25 September 2003 and the Westport Village Society during their annual meeting on 7 November 2003.

Figure 3. Photo of Listening taking place on the headlands. (Photo: Jacque Armstrong)

The interview questions were developed and refined by the design team. The questions were designed to begin broadly and then focus on site-specific information. The first six questions were aimed at establishing what the quality of life in Westport is like. Questions seven through ten focused, more specifically, on Westport and the lives of the residents in more detail by asking them to describe their favorite locations for a variety of activities. The next questions were designed to address the future of Westport by asking about growth and change. Questions 18 through 23 focused further on the "Pea Patch" and potential uses for the site. The three final questions were open ended, allowing residents to add any further comments on Westport, the process, or the list of interviewees.

With the exception of a few contrasting views of what the future of the village should be, most residents showed support for the creation of a new Community Center and the need for new economic opportunity. The interviewees expressed the desire that new buildings be consistent with the Westport building tradition and that new housing units be affordable. Overall, the

Listening step provided the Westport Design Team with a clear set of goals for the future of the Pea patch and the overall community.

Feedback on the interviews from residents was favorable. Many residents commented that the "painless" interview allowed them to recall memories they had forgotten. Some residents felt there was some redundancy in the questions. This was particularly evident in the section regarding growth and change. During the development of the questions, the design team felt it was important to distinguish between these concepts. However, forcing our professional jargon on people did not lead to the expected result. During the interviews some residents used the concepts interchangeably, proving that the distinction between "growth" and "change" was not made clear to the residents.

Workshop

Given the remoteness of Westport, the Community Design Team's effort was grouped into a few weekend-long workshops during which the community was involved in the design process through a variety of activities and events. The first workshop took place on November 8, 2003 at the Westport Community Church and involved over 30 people, including old and new residents.

The workshop started with a verbal introduction that focused on answering questions with regard to the meaning of community participation and the extent of the residents' involvement in the design of a Community Center. The introduction was followed by a PowerPoint presentation summarizing the inventory findings and the Listening interview results. Later, the workshop's participants had the opportunity to review, confirm and rank the list of potential goals and compile a list of priorities for the village. This information, together with the results of the activity mapping, became the foundation of the programming exercise and walking tour that followed.

The programming exercise was the first crucial step towards design and development of a plan for the site. The Walking Tour allowed the Team to learn about patterns, sacred places and possible user conflicts that became an essential part of the development of a spectrum of plans and a final design.

Introducing the Community to Itself: The Data

This activity was intended to establish the dialogue between the residents and the design team. The presentation focused on, "What we (as outsiders) know about your community" and provided an opportunity for the residents to clarify misrepresentations. This was a particularly important step for the new residents of Westport that allowed them to actively participate in the workshop. Additionally, it created the desired dialogue between the facilitators and the residents as well as dialogue between old and new residents.

Question focus	Goals
Process Questions	Residents appreciated being included, but questioned their role in the process as the land is privately owned.
Westport Positives, Negatives and Potential Improvement Issues	Many residents described Westport as a "family" with some "dysfunction." Most saw Westport as a "paradise" defined by natural boundaries, but some cited need for new activities in town.
Community Center and School Questions	Those interviewed indicated strong support for a Community Center, yet the need for a new school was not clear from interviews.
Economic Development Opportunities	Creation of new jobs was seen as "key" to attracting new residents. Economic development must be consistent with the way of life and skill set of the residents.
New Housing and Development Issues	Preserving the character of town is the most important issue; most residents agreed that new housing could be a good thing if done properly.

Table 1. Interview Questions.

Confirming Goals

From the very beginning of our involvement in Westport, it was clear that a primary objective—in addition to designing a new Community Center—was the establishment of widely supported priorities for the community, which would guide the community's future actions. The goal setting exercise aimed at confirming the goals that the design team had gathered during the interviews, integrating them with those of the workshop's participants.

Using the Nominal Group Technique, or NGT, (Delbecq, Van de Ven, Gustafson, 1975) as a guide, participants in each of the teams were asked to answer the question: "Given the summary of the Listening and analysis presented to you, and your experience living in Westport, what do you feel is the most important action to take for the future of Westport?" Each group member listed five of the most important actions for the community and

presented them to the rest of the group. With the facilitator's guidance, the groups discussed each person's goals, voted on the five most important, and recorded them on a large sheet of paper. At the end of the process all groups convened and voted on the most crucial goals by placing a colored dot next to those they considered priorities. The exercise resulted in a list of sixteen goals that were posted on the walls as reminders to all participants. The evolution of these goals from the Listening through the Goal Confirming stage is shown below.

A large number of votes went to support a new Community Center and to preserve the architectural character of the village. Consistent with the findings of the interview process, the workshop goals fit into three broad categories: preserving the character of town, creating a stable economy, and building new community facilities.

In general, the goals were clearly articulated—perhaps, because of the structure of the question, which asked the residents to use a noun and a verb in their responses. The use of the NGT as a goal setting exercise was very successful. Using highly structured exercises during the group workshops allowed the facilitators to lead the small groups in a professional manner and immediately established their process expertise, which put the residents at ease and allowed for increased cooperation.

Activity Mapping

During the second part of the workshop residents were asked to "draw events, places and things that may be part of the town's collective memory and to map Westport's "sacred structure." In particular, we asked residents to focus their attention on daily activity patterns, community rituals, public events, and special places within the community. Through this exercise, new information about the idiosyncrasies and unique aspects of the community was gathered. Most importantly, this was the first step that revealed the pace of life in the village.

The exercise's implicit goal was to increase people's sensitivity to the nuances and unique aspects of their community that constituted its "sacred structure" and learn more about spatial factors in these places. Through this process, the residents communicated their activity patterns to the team, which highlighted the important aspects of the community that "could inspire the form of the design" (Hester, 1982, p. 150). Through this exercise the residents of Westport articulated that lingering in the landscape is an important part of their life.

In general, the residents cited and sketched many activities associated with the existing centers of town. In particular, "newsing" at the Store and post office or just hanging out on the deck to the south of the Store to drink and relax after work were mentioned as the most important of their daily activity patterns. The events associated with holiday activities were

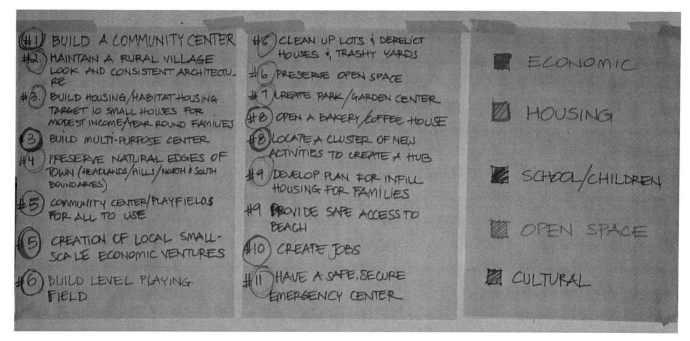

Figure 4. Goals following the Confirming Goals workshop. (Photo: Douglas Kot)

listed by many of the exercise participants, but according to the sketches, they occur in a variety of locations around town. The current patterns of activity included the use of the "Pea Patch" for special events and soccer practice as well as a view-shed north from town. The front porches were often listed as a key component of the social space of the town and as places where neighbors interact with one another.

Additionally, the relationship with nature was a common thread in the mapping of daily activities. Residents cited the views to the ocean and the hills as defining elements of the town. People engaged nature in a variety of ways—from relaxing on their porch, gardening and watching wildlife, to active recreation like walking around town, stopping to view the ocean and the wild-life, hiking and fishing. An example of Westport's relationship with its surroundings was made evident when the interviewees shared that they hike across a plank to sit on "Bridge Rock," just off the Headlands, when they need to be alone.

From a methodological standpoint, the Activity Mapping exercise yielded mixed results. The exercise was successful in that residents were asked to think about their activities in depth in order to increase their awareness of the subtleties of the town. However, this application should have been presented as guided fantasy/self-hypnosis/visualization, rather than a drawing exercise. The guided fantasy has a better likelihood of success in this application because it begins with the participants visualizing themselves in their daily activities. The results yield a composition of ideas rather than a composed drawing. In Westport, the residents had a difficult time communicating these issues graphically for fear of being judged based on their drawing skills rather than the content.

Program for the Pea Patch

This activity used interactive game techniques to develop a program for the "Pea Patch" and the school site. The goal for this exercise was to involve participants in developing a program that could be used to measure the design alternatives similar to Hester's (1982, p. 153) "conceptual yardstick."

In order to accomplish both goals, the game used figure-ground maps and a series of cutouts representing possible building types, sizes, and acreage. Each participant was asked the question: "What activities do you most want to do that you can't currently in Westport?" Participants listed the activities on index cards and started to locate cutouts on the maps identifying the locations where they imagined the activities would occur. The individual designs were shared with group members and ultimately assembled into a plan for the team. The teams were asked to name their design and present it to the larger audience.

The Programming Workshop resulted in a clear design proposal for each group. The spatial aspects of the exercise seemed to be well embraced by the participants. Despite our initial skepticism, the method used was clearly understood by the members of the community. Notwithstanding the excellent results, a few changes could have dramatically improved the exercise. Firstly, the number of cutouts was limited and did not provide participants with a variety of typologies and sizes. Moreover, no specific cutouts for recreation space were available, leading some of the community members to believe they could fit a soccer field into a site much smaller than necessary. A few facilitators used different colors to distinguish each person's activity and cutouts, leading to plans that were easier to inter-

Figure 5. Photo of a resident sketching activity setting. (Photo: Douglas Kot)

Figure 6. Photo of a facilitator during the programming exercise. (Photo: Douglas Kot)

Figure 7. Photo of a facilitator during the walking tour. (Photo: Randy Hester)

pret and more revealing of possible conflicts between uses and locations. This should have been standardized in advance and would have allowed easier comparisons between the plans.

The Community Introduces Itself: The Walking Tour

On the following day, a walking tour began by looking at the site and then moved to the larger context of the town. The main goal was to re-present the information from the Listening step and its results in a spatial forum. Additional goals included:

- Looking for design opportunities experientially, rather than conceptually.

- Mapping activity patterns of the residents and discussing wind, sun, topographic and other environmental influences on the patterns.

- Soliciting stories related to particular places.

- Gathering feedback that could inform the design of the village center.

The tour touched upon most of the town's "sacred places" as well as a number of other controversial sites. The act of simply walking around the village allowed residents and members of the design team to experience phenomenologically the sacred places they had previously sketched and discussed. This process revealed spatial details and nuances that may have gone unnoticed, or issues they may have otherwise been uncomfortable talking about.

The walking tour was successful because it covered dynamic aspects of living in Westport. Highlights of the tour pointed out the particular way in which people interact with their neighbors, and also allowed the residents to share their beloved views of the landscape. The participants were able to test the site programming decisions developed on the previous day against the complexity of the topography of the proposed site. Further, it called attention to some of the complex design typologies that exist in the town, such as the tradition of leaving half of the lot width open from buildings or other structures that may obstruct views, the importance of views at the end of main streets, and Westport's unique habit of parking on the perimeter of a lot.

From a practical standpoint, the reliance on a script made the walking tour seem (in the words of one resident) "scientific" and allowed community members to develop trust in the process to begin talking freely. However, for some residents the questions seemed to be too structured, giving them the wrong impression that they were not allowed to talk about issues unless included in the script. Once participants warmed up, and got used to the method used, most of them shared their opinions and the questions became almost unnecessary. Because of its size and way of life, the script was too organized for the Westport community, which values informal conversation over structured dialogue.

The Alternative Plans

The design process began in January 2004 as the final studio for the Master's of Landscape Architecture students at Berkeley who were engaged in the project to develop a new town plan for Westport. The studio was directed by Randy Hester and consisted of nine students, two of whom had participated in the interview process in 2003. For the other students, the first exposure to Westport involved reading reports summarizing the natural conditions, architectural heritage, and the interview results, and then visiting Westport for extended periods of time.

The first task consisted of the development of a master plan for the town. In their own design process each student was encouraged to begin thinking about economic development strategies in addition to the physical plan. It was tacitly agreed

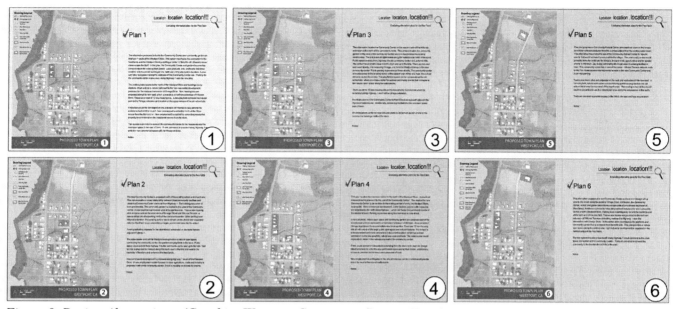

Figure 9. Design Alternatives. (Graphic: Westport Community Design Team)

that any development should be consistent with the previously set goals, program, unique character and skill set of the existing town. The students interpreted this in different ways that led to a variety of alternatives.

The students' designs were synthesized into six alternatives that featured different locations for the Community Center. The alternative plans balanced two distinct design strategies: the ritual town center (separating the Community Center from daily life), and the everyday town center (those that located the new Community Center nearest existing centers). In general, the plans kept new development concentrated near the town on the previously disturbed part of the site, which served two purposes: first, to maintain the edges of the existing town, and second, to preserve a maximum amount of open space. The plans were presented to the town during a meeting held at the Westport church on April 10, 2004. Residents provided feedback on the presentations and had a lively discussion on each person's favorite plan. Comments and suggestions from residents that were unable to attend the meeting were incorporated through a mail-in survey.

The discussion and survey data were analyzed to determine a direction for the final plan. Through the data, the residents expressed their priorities to the design team, which included:

- The Community Center should to be close to the Store and Post Office.

- The new houses should be organized around a central open space.

- The new construction should maintain the town's character.

- The town's edges should be preserved.

- The Community Center should accommodate ritual and everyday uses.

- The future school must have safe access.

These newly refined priorities were mapped over the alternatives to determine how the plans would be modified into the

Figure 9. Activity mapping sketch. (Drawing: Westport Resident, Joe Bernard)

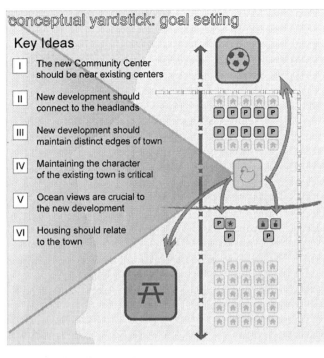

Drawing Legend

P	★		禾	🏠	⚽		
Parking	Store	Comm. Center	Head-lands	Housing	Play Field	Church	School

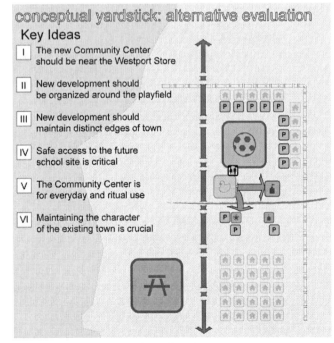

Figure 10. Conceptual Yardstick.

final design. While key components of the priorities carried through all the steps, seeing the concepts displayed graphically allowed the residents to better articulate their spatial needs.

Final Design

The final design relied on the previous steps to establish the needs of the residents, the character of town, the community's way of life and the unique ecology of the place. The plan locates the new town center to the north of the Westport Store relying on the strength of the existing town center. It became clear from observing the residents' that the maximum distance between the Store and the new Community Center should be equal to the distance from the Store to the church. This distance represents the threshold between walking and driving for most residents in the community. In the plan evaluation the residents wanted to enhance the water drainage immediately to the north of the Store. By combining the desire for enhancement with the need to be close to the Store an opportunity for a community garden is present, which greatly satisfied the residents.

The main organizational element of the final design is the play-field, which is buffered to the south by the community garden and framed to the north and east by new houses. On the west side of the common, new commercial development is extended to the north of the Community Center, which will provide a buffer between the recreation space and the busy road. The common is to become the backyard for the community, where the adults can watch the children safely play. In much the same way that Westport maximizes other resources, and because the common is to function as both the "everyday" and the "ritual" center, it was important to plan for flexible use of the space. The perimeter of the space is envisioned to be spectator space during soccer practice as well as parking for the town barbecues.

DISCUSSION: "CRAFTING WESTPORT"

Designing a building, an entire neighborhood, or any other part of a village or city's landscape through the participation of its users requires an iterative process and various degrees of users' involvement and intensity. Unlike traditional planning efforts, where the designer's experience and intuition are given first priority in determining the outcome, a participatory process builds upon the values and needs of a community. These needs are incorporated using methods and techniques that are applied in different ways throughout the process in order to achieve the best possible result (Hester 1990). It is through such reiteration that residents are able to refine the design and adjust it to their changing needs. Because of this constant refinement, results are lasting, valued by all residents, and inspire a stronger sense of ownership. Such a process resembles the work of a craftsperson, constantly refining his/her piece until the right balance between the original intention and the uniqueness of the raw material is achieved and translated into a beautiful form.

Figure 11. Final Plan. (Graphic: Westport Community Design Team)

The Westport Design Team has borrowed this concept and adopted it for the "Crafting Westport" process. We feel that it most accurately represents what we learned from our experience in Westport. Our effort was a slow and careful, iterative process, in which users' needs, values, and local wisdom were heard, analyzed, discussed, and incorporated into the design for the new village center. Rather than problems that needed to be solved, the idiosyncrasies of the community helped us adjust the process and became instrumental to its successful outcome. The evaluation criteria were refined throughout the process—sweeping ocean views lost significance to the importance of the Westport Store. The desire for a central green space aligned with the programmatic need for active recreation to become the town common in the final plan. This main organizing element is both a component of the design and part of the existing community—it represents the village way of life and allows for smaller residential lots consistent with the existing by providing a hierarchy of open space.

Westport's Spatial Literacy

Kevin Lynch (1960), Amos Rapoport (1977), and most recently Yi-Fu Tuan (1990) have written about the important role that the environment plays in the development of a strong sense of identity. The Design Team had the opportunity to experience this concept first-hand in Westport, where they became aware of the existence of a symbiotic relationship between the place and its people. This assumption was confirmed by the results of the Listening, which stressed the importance to preserve the steep hillside and its wildlife from being developed and confirmed that the Headlands and the beaches are sacred places. Rather than a background to its residents' lives, Westport's environment was a fundamental component of their identity. Framed by water and woods the community exists on a narrow shelf on the edge of the land. By preserving the town's character, residents seemed to claim the sacredness of their own identity.

The unique symbiosis between people and place led to another idiosyncrasy. The residents' daily interaction with a surrounding environment that was highly "legible" led to design sophistication—an ability to synthesize, visualize, and resolve highly complicated design problems. On many occasions, residents clearly described their landscape in terms of districts. Ideas ("the Headlands, the flats, or the slope"), easily identifiable edges ("the forest to the east, the rugged coast to the west"), and landmarks ("bridge rock, the cardboard sliding hill,") translated into designs that displayed many of the characteristics of highly "imageable" environments (Lynch, 1960). Throughout the process, residents clearly understood the importance of preserving the village's block structure, density, and edge and pushed for "new urbanist" design solutions, displaying an instinctual understanding of complex urban design issues. Similarly, during a later phase in the process when they were asked to choose among varied plan options for the Community Center, the residents of Westport privileged values such as the preservation of open space, a clearly defined village edge, and a tight fabric of smaller lots.

The view from the inside

Throughout the participation process, the design team gained gradual understanding of the Westport way of life, which informed our process, our evaluation tools, and the final design. Hester (1982, 1990), Tuan (1990), and Gans (1962) talk about a "view from the inside" which describes differences in perception between outsiders and insiders of a community. As the Design Team became more familiar with the way of life in Westport, we noted that the participants' words never changed, but our understanding of their meaning evolved. As a result, the "conceptual yardstick" (Hester, 1982) used to evaluate the project changed, leading to a better-informed process and place-appropriate design. Additionally, our early misconceptions regarding the importance of views and other organizational elements were clarified.

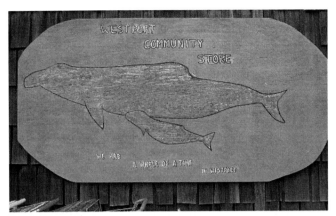

Figure 12. "We had a whale of a time in Westport." (Photo: Douglas Kot)

At the early stages of Listening and Confirming Goals it was clear that the residents thought that landscape views were important organizers of the community. As the design process began, the alternatives sought to provide equal views from all the new houses and a community center with sweeping panoramas to the white water, rocks and sea. The community confirmed our understanding of this important issue, but when voting for alternatives, the plans that oriented views to the town common took precedent over ones with more dramatic views of the ocean. We speculate that the view issue is more nuanced to the community, because the community is surrounded by scenic beauty and if they desire a view they walk to the edge to find it. In contrast, the outsiders—including second home owners, tourists and the Design Team seemed to be most impressed by the sweeping white water views to the Pacific Ocean and assumed the new houses and Community Center should look upon them.

Our original evaluation criteria included strong connections to the existing town centers including the Store, church/school, and Headlands. We also believed that the new housing should compactly adjoin the existing town and that the community center would be physically located in the center for everyday use, or it should be on the edge for the ritual events. Further, it was clear that the community desired a large open space for recreation and community gatherings, but that the current field functioned well for these events. In reality, however, the residents believed that traffic along Highway 1 was too much to force a physical connection to the Headlands. Therefore, the new development was organized around a central town common that could be used for the ritual and the everyday events.

CONCLUSION

"Crafting Westport" served the community on many levels through both process and design. The residents have created a plan that is spatially compact in order to preserve open space for wildlife habitat and the character of the town. The process has revealed the fine balance between housing, employment,

and community needed for life in Westport, while the final design has emphasized the residents' needs for affordable housing and childcare over those of tourists.

The story of Westport is about iterative dialogue between designers and residents. It is also about adapting methods to build upon–rather than react to–the idiosyncrasies of a place. A key component of the "Crafting Westport" process was reflecting on what we thought was important as designers, but did not prove to be important to the community. This reflection allowed us to transform the design criteria to integrate the residents' spatial literacy and inherent knowledge of their community and resulted in a community development project, in the true sense of the word.

ENDNOTES

[1] Douglas Kot and Deni Ruggeri are equal authors of this article.

REFERENCES

Delbecq, A., Van De Ven, A.H., and Gustafson, D.H. 1975. Group Techniques for Program Planning: A Guide to Nominal Group and Delphi Processes. Glenview, IL: Scott, Foreman and Co.

Gans, H. J. 1962. The Urban Villagers: Group and Class in the Life of Italian Americans. Glencoe: Free Press.

Hester, R. 1990. Community Design Primer. Mendocino, CA: Ridge Times Press.

----. Planning Neighborhood Design for People. 1982. Stroudsburg, PA: Hutchinson Ross.

----. The Landscape Occupies Us: a Portrait of a Small Town. 1987. Places, 4 (4).

Hester, R. et al. 1988. We'd like to tell you...a child's-eye view of Westport, CA. Small Town, 4 (4)

Lynch, K. 1960. The Image of the City. Cambridge, MA: The MIT Press.

McNally, M. 1987. Projects on the Ridges? Ridge Review, 6 (4)

Rapoport, A. 1977. Human Aspects of Urban Form. Elmsford, NY: Pergamon.

Tuan, Y-F. 1990. Topophilia. A Study of Environmental Perception, Attitudes, and Values. New York: Columbia University Press.

ESTABLISHING COMMUNITY ENTERPRISE IN KINOSAKI

Soshi Higuchi, Haruhiko Goto and Nobuyuki Sekiguchi

Figure 1. Townscape of Kinosaki. (Photo: Goto Laboratory)

ABSTRACT

This paper examines a case of community design movements in Kinosaki town, a hot spring resort in Japan. Citizens' initiative in community design is needed because of a coming municipal merger problem in the year 2005, a huge change and reorganization of local authority boundaries on a nationwide scale. Kinosaki is characteristic for having zaisanku, which owns and manages hot springs as a profitable communal asset. Family business people like traditional-styled innkeepers are involved in community design centered on tourism promotion. Participatory community design workshops have been undertaken for listing the projects for community design for the next 100 years. The process of listing the projects itself is also the process of creating new shape to the local governance. There is controversy over establishing a new organization such as a community enterprise as one of the main actors to carry out the projects. It is necessary to create new organizations by citizens' initiative, on the basis of existing organizations.

INTRODUCTION

Japan faces a huge change in the system of governance in the near future. There are approximately 3,100 municipalities now in Japan, but some of them will be merged together in a few years. The Japan Government's policy is to decrease the number of municipalities to 1,000. It is said that the actual number will be somewhere around 2,000. Municipal mergers have happened a couple of times in the modern history of Japan. Several effects are expected as a result of municipal merger. One is promotion of efficiency in public service and finance. Another is improvement to public service and residents' convenience, and so on. The largest reason, however, is to deal with financial deficits in the central government's and local municipalities' budgets.

On the other hand, there is the fear that it becomes difficult to offer pubic service corresponding to the detailed characteristics of each area with limited human and financial resources. In this situation, the role of citizens' initiative in community design becomes more important. It is necessary to organize citizens' groups and create good relationships with new municipalities in order to enforce local governance. It goes without saying that the existing citizens' network and movement are important when organizing new groups and citizens' initiatives.

As a report of the collaboration work with our laboratory at Waseda University, this paper examines the recent case of *Kinosaki* town, a hot springs resort with 4,300 residents and approximately a million annual visitors, in Hyogo prefecture. The town also is expected to be annexed into one city with five neighboring municipalities so as to hold approximately 90,000 residents next year. There is a beautiful townscape with seven public hot springs buildings, traditional-styled inns, a river with trees along it.

CITIZENS' INITIATIVE IN KINOSAKI

Kinosaki has a unique governance system. There used to be four villages in the old *Kinosaki* region. When those four were merged into one town, *Yushima* village, which owned the source of the hot springs, established the quasi-local authority (*zaisanku* in Japanese). The aim of *zaisanku* council is to manage the public hot springs. The council composed of 11 selected residents from *Yushima* has decision rights as to any reform of the hot springs. There is another council in an old village unit to manage communal assets other than the town council.

A secretariat of *zaisanku*, which is called the Department of Hot Springs, is set up in the Kinosaki municipality to actually manage the public hot springs. Salaries of employees in the Department are paid not by the Kinosaki municipality, but by *zaisanku*. Reforms of hot springs are also done from the budget of *zaisanku*. Zaisanku is financially blessed because of entrance fees to the hot springs.

Promotion of the hot springs resort itself is done mainly by the local Tourist Board. The Tourist Board is mainly organized by local business people such as traditional-styled innkeepers. They plan and carry out events, sometimes clean the river, and are involved in many other activities. The Kinosaki municipality gives some financial aid to the Tourist Board for tourism promotion. Tourism promotion is an important factor of town

Figure 2. "Community Design Drama"-the third workshop. (Photo: Goto Laboratory)

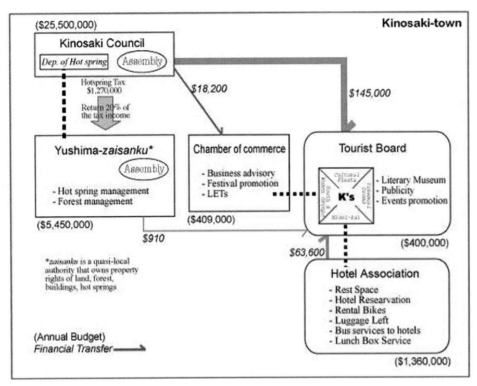

Figure 3. Relationship of the current organization before the merger.

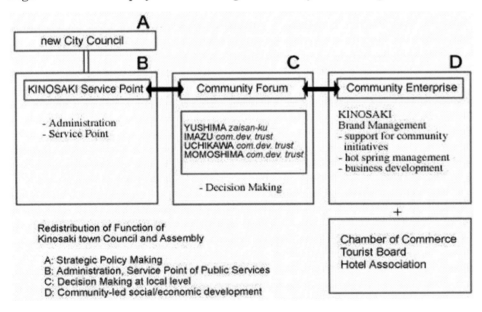

Figure 4. Redistribution of self-autonomy function.

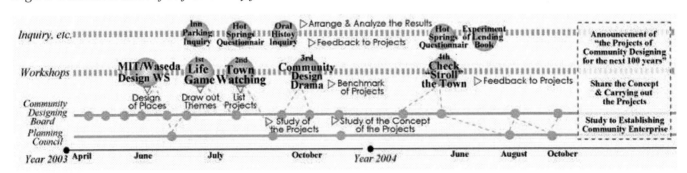

Figure 5. Flow of community design.

development in *Kinosaki* because many residents run tourism related businesses.

It is a concern that the newly merged City Council might decrease the budget for town design in *Kinosaki*, and also financial aid to the current Tourist Board. To handle the case, the Community Design Board was established last April. The Board has been working on listing the projects of community design for the current town area covering the next 100 years with our laboratory. The Community Design Board consists mainly of local young people, some of whom run traditional inns. Ten meetings were held last year, some of which members of our laboratory attended.

PARTICIPATORY COMMUNITY DESIGN WORKSHOPS

Participatory community design workshops have been held since last April, three last year and one this year. The results of those workshops have been reflected in the projects of community design. Our laboratory had also held a joint design workshop by graduate students of Massachusetts Institute of Technology and Waseda University in June of last year. At the workshop, some residents and members of the Community Design Board had an opportunity to have discussions with students.

The first workshop was called "Community Design Life Game," where residents answered questions concerning problems in the town, assuming that if they are to spend a lifetime of 100

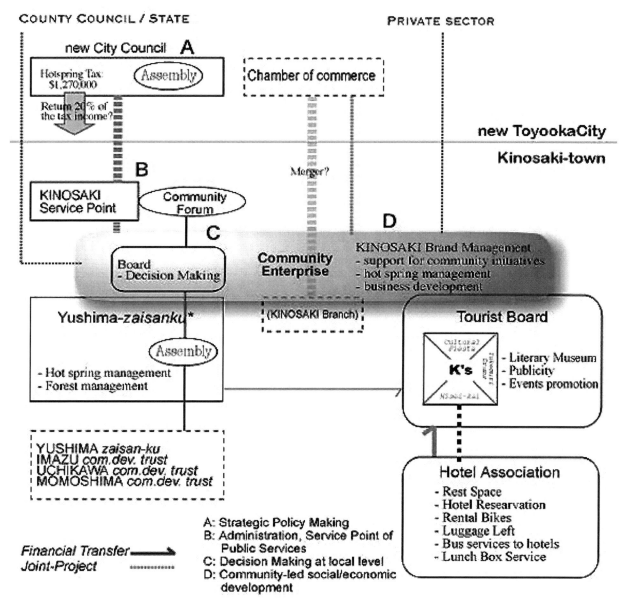

Figure 6. Relationship of new organizations after the merger.

years in the town. Discussions were made after the game. The aim of this workshop was to discuss themes of community design in *Kinosaki*. Six themes were drawn out: welfare, education, transportation, nature, events, and townscape. At the second workshop, "Town Watching," participants were divided into six groups of residents and students to find actual sites relating to themes drawn out from the first workshop. Walks were followed by discussions so as to recognize problems and to share future images of the town. The first two were held in July of last year.

In the third workshop, "Community Design Drama," students and residents participated in playacting. The drama had two simple scenarios, each showing possible future with or without the community enterprise. Dramas were done to share further understanding on predicted situations after the municipal merger and the composition of the enterprise. In the discussion, a lot of detailed questions came out as to the establishment of the enterprise. Even though the workshop itself could not enhance participants' morale to establish the enterprise this time, it was a precious opportunity for residents to discuss the situation after the municipal merger and the enterprise. After the workshop, the chairman of the Community Design Board mentioned the demand of community brand management, which would encourage residents to establish community enterprise.

Finally, three workshops were held last June. Students of Goto Laboratory discussed a concept of the projects of community design and proposed the theme "stroll." This concept was admitted in the Community Design Board and the Monitoring Board. The aim of workshops this time was to examine the concept. Accordingly, one workshop involved walking around the natural areas surrounding the town, another workshop involved following written signs in town. The final one was to walk around the town to check for various signs. The workshops were planned based on feedbacks from the previous ones.

The process of listing the projects of community design itself is also the process of creating a new shape of local governance. Residents' spontaneous movements to hold workshops for their own community activities were seen. Such spontaneous movements can happen without the help of outsiders like our laboratory.

ESTABLISHING COMMUNITY ENTERPRISE

As one of the main actors of the community design projects, there is a controversy regarding whether to establish a new organization like community enterprise. The existing Tourist Board and Chamber of Commerce can be a driving force in a community enterprise since the members are so actively involved in community design. A planning sector with wide and long-term vision is needed in a community enterprise since

the current activities are tourism-oriented. New organizations are expected to be involved in town management including brand management of the resort *Kinosaki*, which the current associations are not handling.

Reorganizing the current Chamber of Commerce into TMO (Town Management Organization) is considered to be another option. As a set menu of planning in Japan, it is required for a central commercialized area to establish a TMO. Although it is known that most TMOs do not function well because of lack of management know-how and financial problems. A TMO is able to get financial aid from the Japanese government menu. New organizations like community enterprise can become TMOs. In either the case of new organizations or the current association, residents' spontaneous movements are important for local governance.

Considering the process of management and decision making of important communal assets, *zaisanku* will remain and function as it has. However, there is a controversy to establish a Community Forum to discuss community problems for enough pubic service after the merger. It is very important for the new organizations to create equal partnership with the new city municipality. In doing so, municipal mergers can be a good opportunity for creating local governance.

CONCLUSION

Residents cannot rely on the local municipality after municipal mergers in terms of rich public service and financial support. Residents are needed to do what they can do by themselves. Residents in *Kinosaki* have had local initiatives in tourism promotion. After the Town Municipality leaves the town, stronger local initiatives in other fields will be important. Through the participatory workshops, other fields of community design have been experienced. It is expected that more spontaneous movements will emerge to carry out the projects by residents. It goes without saying that new projects should be added one by one according to residents' movements. Community enterprise is expected to support such movements by the residents.

REFERENCES

Goto, H., Murakami, K., and Yoshida, M. 2003. In Search of a Shape of New Governance, Quarterly Magazine *Machizukuri*. Gagugei Press.

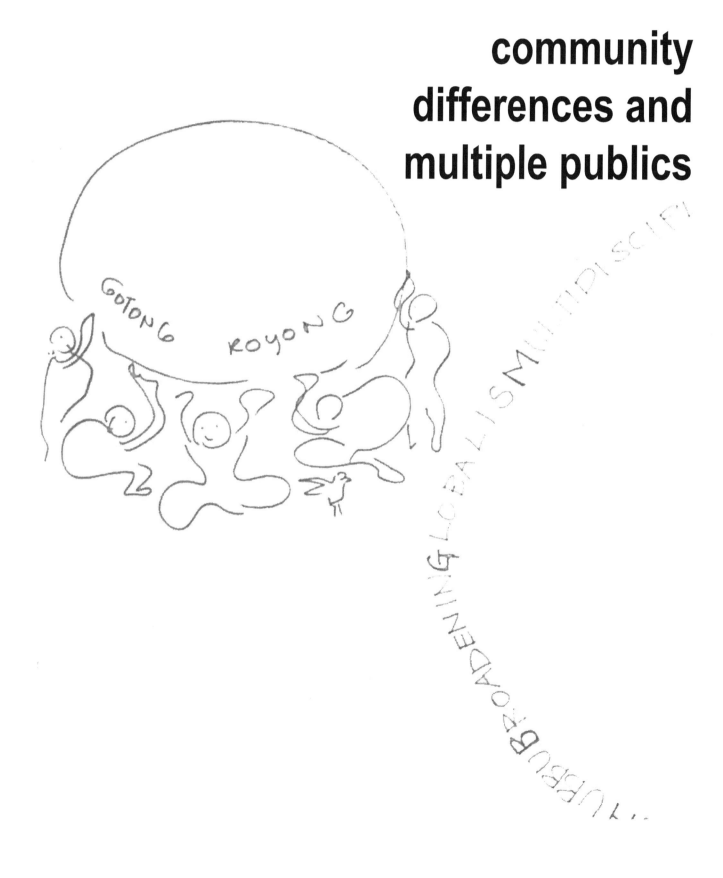

7

community differences and multiple publics

MULTIPLE PUBLICS, URBAN DESIGN AND THE RIGHT TO THE CITY
Assessing Participation in the Plaza del Colibrí

Michael Rios

ABSTRACT

Contributions from cultural and feminist studies raise fundamental issues about contemporary culture as expressed between different social groups and epistemological problems associated with universal claims about the public sphere. At the heart of these critiques is the interrogation of relationships between subject and object, and distinctions between diverse forms of knowledge. However, lacking is a related account of the design profession and the normative relationships that exists between experts and non-experts, professionals and clients. This paper introduces some of these recent debates as a critique of conventional approaches to participation in the design of the public realm. Using the case study of a renovated transit hub, I introduce the term multiple publics to highlight the value of inclusiveness in urban open space projects. In doing so, I argue for strategies that begin with difference as a starting point in the design of public space.

INTRODUCTION

Despite the existence of a variety of methods and techniques associated with citizen participation, the design of the public realm is often tailored to the tastes and preferences of cultural, economic, and professional elites. This often results in projects that do not meet the needs of the poorest and most marginalized citizens. As such, public space can be viewed as a material expression of 'actually existing democracy' (Mitchell, 2003). However, as citizen participation in the design of public landscapes increases in importance, how are different voices expressed and what is the role of planning and design professionals in an increasing pluralistic and global culture?

This paper introduces some of these recent theoretical debates as a way to problematize conventional and functionalist approaches to participation in the design and production of the public realm. A case study of a renovated transit hub in San Francisco is presented that involved a range of stakeholders including advocates for universal accessibility, the homeless,

youth, older adults, and artists in a gentrifying Latino neighborhood.[1] The existence of overlapping jurisdictions also required the collaboration of several government agencies at the local and regional levels. After introducing contributions from other fields, I identify the limits of the current model of citizen participation that often emphasizes manufactured consensus and conflict avoidance. The case study is then presented as an illustration of an alternative model of citizen participation in the design of urban open spaces.

SITUATED KNOWLEDGE, THIRD SPACE, AND THE RIGHT TO THE CITY

Feminist and cultural theory raise fundamental issues about contemporary culture as expressed between different social groups and the epistemological problems associated with universal claims about the public sphere. In some of the discussion on the topic there has been a spatial turn, both metaphorically and materially, that introduces concepts such as situated, hybrid, in-between, and third spaces to describe the social and cultural condition of marginalized groups (Haraway, 1988; Bhabha, 1994; Soja, 1996). Rather than viewing culture as a fixed object or dependent on relationships that privilege dominant groups, some argue that identities can not be assigned pre-given traits, but rather are mutable and fluid processes of negotiation; performative rather than fixed (Bhabha, 1994). Similarly, the term third space has been used by others to disrupt dualistic epistemologies such as space and time, real and imagined geographies (Pile, 1994; Soja, 1996). In material terms, third spaces are produced by processes that move beyond forms of knowledge which divide the world into dualistic, binary relationships (Johnston, Gregory, Pratt, and Watts, 2000).

More recently, geographer Don Mitchell draws on Henri Lefebvre's 'right to the city' to discuss the struggle over social justice (2002). Mitchell argues that such a right is dependent upon public space—how it is produced, who can make claims for its use, and ultimately as an expression of a truly democratic society. He critiques (neo)liberal urban reforms which increasingly seek 'order' as a purposeful strategy to police who has the right to inhabit public space. In opposition to the commodification and securitization of the public realm, Mitchell calls for continued struggles over public space as a fundamental right that is a defining characteristic of citizenship. An essential part of Mitchell's argument is the multiplicity of the public realm and the importance of different (political) identities in the appropriation and production of public space. It is the right to the city and the existence of multiple publics which serve as the basis to critique the current model of citizen participation in the design and creation of public spaces.

THE LIMITS OF THE CURRENT PARTICIPATORY MODEL

The exclusionary practice of citizen participation

Public participation has been an important mechanism for social groups to influence the making of public space. Emerging from the civil rights movement as a response to the lack of public involvement in decision-making, participatory planning and design has been the primary means for responding to the pressing needs of marginalized populations. As a result, many methods and techniques have been developed intended to involve different groups in decision-making.[2] However, despite these efforts the design profession is silent when it comes to recognizing its complicity in promoting an exclusionary public realm. While attempts are made to seek input from the public, it is often the case that genuine public discussion is limited.

Many of the methods and techniques used in participatory process are now used as a form of placation to manufacture consensus rather than a means to enter into a meaningful dialogue about conflicts and differences between a range of participants, professionals, and other stakeholders in public processes (Lake, 1994). This often bounds the discussion of public concerns and priorities to certain social groups over others. As a result, public participation has become a highly bureaucratic, standardized and disingenuous process.[3] These issues raise concern about contemporary citizen participation which assumes a universal and neutral framework for decision-making. From this perspective, a value system that privileges rational discourse over conflict and difference can be viewed as a form of oppression (Sandercock, 2000). By taking on an increasingly narrowed scope and by focusing primarily on the binary interaction between professionals and clients, public and private sectors, the dominant participatory model has overlooked the broader issues of identity, representation, and agency within the broader political and cultural economy. Together, these inadequacies have greatly limited the effectiveness and legitimacy of participatory approaches and the role of design professionals. Approaching public process from a position of neutrality, design professionals often overlook their own inherent biases and how these values contribute to promoting a universal and totalizing public realm.

Multiple publics

The concept of multiple publics provides an analytical concept from which to begin to theorize the possibilities for an alternative practice of urban design. To begin with, it questions the idea of a singular, liberal, public realm which purports to be the forum where all citizens come together to discuss matters of common interest and concern. In critiquing Habermas's conception of the public sphere, Nancy Fraser (1990) observes that "we can no longer assume that the bourgeois conception of the public sphere was simply an unrealized utopian ideal; it was also a masculinist ideological notion that functioned to legitimate an emergent form of class rule" (1990: p. 204). Fraser proposes the creation of 'subaltern publics' comprised of different social groups with their own unique claims and epistemology. To Fraser "the idea of an egalitarian, multi-cultural society only makes sense if we suppose a plurality of public arenas in which groups with diverse values and rhetorics participate. By definition, such a society must contain a multiplicity of publics" (p. 212). Fraser's 'subaltern publics' draws consistent parallels with other feminist scholars which argue the importance of social difference in public decision-making (Young, 1990, 2000). Heterogeneity and multiplicity in the public sphere presupposes openness to social difference as a starting point for discussions concerning the public.[4] However, discourses concerning citizen participation within the design and planning professions primarily center on consensus and agreement. Conflict is to be avoided and clear boundaries are drawn between participants and professional facilitators. Rarely do professionals question the boundedness, both of problem statement and physical extent, of public projects.

To move beyond these limitations, arguments are being made for rights-based models of planning and design that begin with cultural and social difference (Sandercock, 1998, 2000; Mitchell, 2002). However, some might ask, is it possible to overcome social differences to identify commonality among multiple publics? As the following case study illustrates, participatory process that emphasize social group differences can achieve this goal, and in doing so, also facilitates dialogue about larger, global issues (Friedmann, 1987; Miller and Eleveld, 2000). In practical terms, such outcomes can enable policy reform and the changing of institutional procedures that involve the public in democratic decision-making.

CASE STUDY: PLAZA DEL COLIBRÍ

The Re-making of the Mission District

The Mission District is home to about 60,000 residents, or 8% of San Francisco's population (U.S. Census, 2000). It is easily accessible to downtown and includes several major transportation hubs including Bay Area Rapid Transit and multiple bus lines. Mission Street is the main corridor running north and south through the district, which intersects with 16th Street, a major transfer point for regional and citywide transit. The Mission is also the cultural center for the larger Bay Area Latino population, and is the historical location for immigrant arrivals including an influx of Latino immigrants after 1950. However, by the mid to late 1990's, there was a sense among long-time Bay Area residents that the social landscape was changing. People were less empathetic to the acute social problems of the Mission including homelessness, drugs, and gang violence (Solnit, 2000). For a variety of cultural and economic reasons, the neighborhood had become a desirable

Figure 1. A homeless man lies on the plaza while police officers stand in the background watching a parade go by. (Source: Michael Rios)

location for residence and night life. Proximity to downtown, accessibility to transportation, a pleasant micro-climate, and an abundance of warehouse spaces attracted outside investment from individual builders and real estate agents alike.

It is against this backdrop that a group of non-profit organizations and local activists began a discussion about recent transformations of the Mission District and how a Bay Area Rapid Transit (BART) station located at the corner of 16th and Mission Streets became a magnet for displaced and homeless populations. Some residents believed this was the cause of drug dealing and other illicit activity on the station's plaza, and that part of the problem was attributable to the design and layout of the BART plaza.

Engaging Difference

Beginning in 1996, a series of community meetings and workshops were held to address community-wide concern about the declining conditions at 16th and Mission Streets.[5] Among the original participants were non-profit organizations,

Figure 2. Three-dimensional models were used to facilitate small group discussion and enable workshops participants to develop design and programmatic ideas for the plaza. (Source: Michael Rios)

social service providers, police officers, residents, and public agency representatives. To broaden the outreach to low income and non-represented groups, a series of focus group meetings were held with hotel tenants, the physically and mentally challenged, artists, senior citizens, and local youth. The purpose of these meetings was to identify issues particular to these groups and to encourage participation in subsequent community meetings. These groups confirmed the wider concern about the deteriorating conditions of the transit plazas surrounding the station and a desire to see this open space improved. From these meetings emerged particular concerns as experienced by these different groups as well as a list of solutions for improving the station. Based on this vital information, further site assessment, and subsequent workshops inclusive of focus group participants, a series of design principles were established to respond to site conditions and the multiplicity of groups actually using the plazas, albeit for different reasons. Three principles guided the design: increasing accessibility and choices, improving visibility and connectivity, and encouraging a diverse range of activities and people on the plazas.

Legitimizing difference

One of the outcomes of the focus groups was the ability to openly discuss issues not directly tied to the project. Many hotel tenants identified police harassment as a major safety concern. Advocates for universal accessibility were able to identify specific issues particular to the visually and hearing impaired as well as individuals using wheelchairs, such as poor sight lines and head-high hazards. For local artists, many were troubled about the growing gentrification in the neighborhood, its effect on the community's identity, and the lack of public places to express dissent.

Acknowledging special needs of different plaza users, the conversation broadened to include a multitude of identities and interests. As one of the project team volunteers noted, "there was an understanding that there were different publics and that conversation had to happen early on between the different publics." With each subsequent workshop, interest from the neighborhood grew. The local newspaper began promoting the project and encouraging people to participate (New Mission News, 1998). Many were pleased that Mission Housing, a community-based organization, led the project. In addition to organizing the initial focus group meetings, Mission Housing reached out to a significant Latino community which comprised the Mission District. Special attention was given to encouraging participation from this group and included bi-lingual translations and providing daycare at meetings and workshops. Urban Ecology, the initial planning consultant representing urban design, land use and transportation interests also aided in outreach efforts. The organization conducted surveys during different times of the day and week to gain an understanding how the space was used by transit riders.

There was general agreement that the plaza was going to be an inclusive space. A design team volunteer and resident of the Mission noted that "because of who the lead partners were in this particular process, they were able to turn out a wider range of folks– the more marginalized folks who use the plaza or live nearby in residential hotels." Revealing to many was how this urban open served a vital function for many living in the neighborhood:

> One of the things for instance that came out, one of the aspects of SRO's (single room occupancy hotels), is that people who live in SRO's are not allowed to have people in their rooms and they have no living room or community facilities, so they have no place to go other than their room. So I think the plaza is in fact a place where people can be comfortable and hang out and visit and just watch the parade that goes by and goes on there 24 hours a day.

The responsiveness of public agency officials and staff was a surprise for community members, and in many ways, agency representatives were viewed as equal participants in the process. In the course of the project, the agencies increasingly served in roles unfamiliar to them– that of advocate and facilitator– despite that the project was being managed by several non-profit organizations. "In a way the agencies are not the public, but they are a public in this conversation," as one participant noted. This sentiment was confirmed by an agency representative: "Institutionally, we were doing something we've never done before… we had no control over who was going to be designing the thing or how it was going to go forward, so we were forging new territory." This initially provided a challenge to many of the agencies which had not worked collaboratively with one another:

> You step into a setting where nobody is in charge…you got the regional agency and the other guys and everybody

kind of coming on with their own perspective you're bound to run into some…. At least lack of clarity and that can generate conflict. It can generate conflict also in terms of internal agency priorities.

However, despite these hurdles the different agencies were able to move forward, and in the end, embraced community participation as a vital aspect in realizing the project to its completion.

While the outcome of the process helped to solidify support for the project, it also validated regional efforts to support neighborhood transit improvements in the urban core. As a recipient of funds from a newly funded transit enhancement program of the Metropolitan Transportation Commission (MTC), the project helped to serve as a demonstration of a successful community participation process and was used as a model for subsequent projects funded under the program. Plaza del Colibrí was also the first completed project under the program and served as one agency representative noted "a major poster child" for transportation sales tax re-authorization in the region. Funding for MTC's transportation program, which started with less than $12 million in 1998, has increased to over $50 million and includes funding for community planning, capital projects, and transit-related housing (MTC, 2004). The project also served to change many policies and procedures of the participating agencies. "The fact that this project was in essence designed by the public was something really new for BART," commented one of the BART Board Directors. "It began a process of reinventing the way we plan and think of our existing stations (and) has really transformed the organization of BART."

Materializing difference

What started out as a minor transportation improvement became a viable public open space to serve different users. To create a new image for the plaza, the project team conscientiously sought out the involvement of local artists.

Figure 3. The symbol of the hummingbird is culturally significant for immigrants and migrant workers. (Source: Michael Rios)

Figure 4. Colorful papel picado was chosen as a detail for railing surrounding the BART entry. (Source: Michael Rios)

Using symbols and colors familiar to the predominately Latino and immigrant population, local artists helped to re-imagine the space to be culturally relevant to the community. For example, hummingbirds, which are featured in the detailing of new handrail panels and a community board, migrate between Mexico, the United States, and Canada. They also symbolize migrant workers which speaks to the history of Mission District as the home to many Irish, Latino, and more recently, Asian immigrants.[6] Additional features included the use of vibrant colors for the railing panels which were designed to mimic *papel picado*, or paper cutting, which is used for neighborhood festivals, celebrations and special occasions.

An assessment of the improvements after the year the plaza was formally dedicated, indicates that most, if not all, design criterion have been met.[7] In addition to the well-integrated public art, the completed plaza addresses many functional aspects as well. This included improving visibility and accessibility, and encouraging a diverse range of activities and people on the plaza. Sight lines have dramatically improved to allow visibility across the plaza, and seating now accommodates a range of plaza users including residents, the homeless, youth, seniors and transit users. The usable space has been increased, eliminating pedestrian conflicts and providing ample space for a bus waiting area. Lighting has also been improved to address safety concerns and the use of the plaza at night.

Problems, real and perceived

A considerable amount of energy has gone into thinking about how to activate the plazas with different uses. Many, including the project team members, felt that the implementation of programmatic elements has been the most disappointing aspect of the project. Several local art groups were invited to assume responsibility for programming rotating art exhibits in the plaza space. A community arts board was designed and equipped to provide space for this function. However, as one of the individuals managing the project confessed, "there was really no art association that would step forward to play the

Figure 6. The inclusion of vending is intended to activate the plaza space. On opening day, local organizations were encouraged to sell food and other items for their own fundraising purposes. (Source: Michael Rios)

institutional role that was expected. They all sort of thought there were deep pockets and they should just get paid to show up for things." In another instance, participants wanted to ensure that the space could also accommodate an outdoor market. Specific equipment was installed for such purposes including water taps, electrical outlets, phone jacks, as well as a secure space for storage and. However, institutional barriers and rigid permit requirements of both BART and the City of San Francisco, has prevented vendors from using the plazas to date. Some feel that the space is ready to receive these uses and it is only a matter of time before these and other programmatic issues will be addressed. The fact that the process allowed these ideas to be discussed and considered, down to equipping the plaza with water and electricity, should not be overlooked. In 2003, the project was recognized with a San Francisco Beautiful award, the only transportation project in the city to win this award.

DISCUSSION

Despite the increasing importance of citizen participation in urban design projects, this case study illustrates the complexity of participation in diverse settings. In an increasingly pluralistic society, approaches to community participation in the design of public landscapes need to be equally plural. In the case of

Figure 5. The redesign of the plaza increases visibility, increases the usable square footage of the plaza surface, and provides for a range of seating choices. (Source: Michael Rios)

Figure 7. Plaza del Colibrí serves a variety of uses and users including a space for gathering and relaxation. (Source: Michael Rios)

Plaza del Colibrí, defining the public in terms of its multiplicity enabled a range of diverse interests and actors to find successful solutions that satisfy both individual group and collective goals. In addition to physical changes that responded to participant goals, the process also yielded changes to institutional procedures and served as a demonstration project which informed regional transportation policy leading to increased funding for such projects.

Transit stations represent a significant component of the public realm, both in terms of the amount of people that use public transit as well as the level of resources invested in related infrastructure. Despite trends toward privatization and consumption, transit stations serve a vital public function, that of providing mobility to all citizens. As such, spaces of mobility can also be viewed as places of struggle, resistance, and hopefully democracy, in an era when the public realm is quickly disappearing.

As public space is being transformed into privatized enclaves for consumption on one hand and made more 'secure' by government regimes on the other, a critical form of urban design practice is urgently needed. As this case study illustrates, engaging difference in the planning and design of urban open space can advance the goal of democracy, not only in terms of participation but also in terms of the production of meaning for different social groups.

Another important issue that this case study raises is the changing roles of different actors from the public and non-profit sectors. It would appear that historical state functions such as planning and implementation are being transferred to governance networks that blend elements of civil society and the state. More studies are needed to explore this changing relationship and the consideration of these actors as equal participants in constituting 'an actually existing' public realm. In the end, are we not all citizens struggling to create democratic spaces?

ENDNOTES

[1] A longitudinal case study was undertaken that included pre-design site observations and an exit survey in 1996. Subsequent site observations of the completed project and semi-structured interviews with key informants were undertaken in May, 2004.

[2] See Sanoff, 2000.

[3] For a similar critique of citizen participation, see Hou and Rios, 2003.

[4] For a discussion on the topic of "difference", See Miller and Eleveld, 2000. The authors argue that "having differences" implies continuation of dialogue, as opposed to "being different" which implies essential characteristics that "prevent communication and cooperation" (2000: p. 89).

[5] In total, the participatory process involved close to ten community workshops and presentations over the span of five years. A community advisory committee was created during the implementation phase,

representing individuals and organizations from throughout the neighborhood.

[6] This is described in detail from a program handed out during the dedication of the plaza on May 17, 2003.

[7] An on-site assessment and observations of plaza use was conducted between May 10-13, 2004.

REFERENCES

Bhabha, H. K. 1994. The Location of Culture. New York and London: Routledge.

Fraser, N. 1992. Rethinking the Public Sphere: A Contribution to the Critique of Actually Existing Democracy. In Barker, F., Hulme, P. and Iverson, M. (Eds.), Postmodernism and the Rereading of Modernity. New York: Manchester University Press.

Friedmann, J. 1987. Planning in the Public Domain: From Knowledge to Action. Princeton, N.J.: Princeton University Press.

Haraway, D. 1988. Situated Knowledges: The Science Question in Feminism and the Privilege of Partial Perspective. Feminist Studies, 14(3): 575-599.

Hou, J. and Rios, M. 2003. Community-driven Placemaking: The Social Practice of Participatory Design in the Making of Union Point Park. Journal of Architectural Education. Vol. 57: Number 1, September: 19-27.

Johnston, R. J., Gregory, D., Pratt, G., & Watts, M. (Eds.). 2000. The Dictionary of Human Geography (Fourth ed.).

Lake, R. W. 1994. Negotiating Local Autonomy. Political Geography, 13(5): 423-442.

Metropolitan Transportation Commission. (2004) Transportation for Livable Communities, http://www.mtc.ca.gov/projects/livable_ communities/ [July 2004]

Mitchell, D. 2003. The Right to the City: Social Justice and the Fight for Public Space. New York and London: The Guilford Press.

Miller, G. D., & Eleveld, M. R. (2000). On "Having Differences" and "Being Different": From Dialogue of Difference to the Private Language of Indifference. In S. F. Steiner & H. M. Krank & P. McLaren & R. E. Bahruth (Eds.), Freirean Pedagogy, Praxis, and Possibilities (Vol. 19). New York and London: Falmer Press.

Miller, V. November 1997. Neighborhood takes aim at the 16th St. "Nightmare Plaza". New Mission News.

Pile, S. 1994. Masculanism, the Use of Dualistic Epistemologies and Third Spaces. Antipode, 26(3): 255-277.

Sandercock, L. 1998. Towards Cosmopolis: Planning for Multicultural Cities. West Sussex, England: John Wiley and Sons.

Sandercock, L. 2000. Cities of (In)Difference and the Challenge for Planning. DISP 140: 7-15.

Sanoff, H. 2000. Community Participation Methods in Design and Planning. New York: John Wily and Sons, Inc.

Soja, E. W. 1996. Thirdspace. Cambridge and Oxford: Blackwell Publishers.

Solnit, R. 2000. Hollow City: The Siege of San Francisco and the Crisis of American Urbanism. London, New York: Verso.

Young, I. M. 1990. Justice and the Politics of Difference. Princeton, N.J.: Princeton University Press.

Young, I. M. 2000. Inclusion and Democracy. Oxford and New York: Oxford University Press.

NEGOTIATING COMMUNITY DIFFERENCES
Comparing International District and Kogane

Jeffrey Hou and Isami Kinoshita

ABSTRACT

This article examines the challenge of negotiating community differences in the cases of two historic communities undergoing changes and redevelopment—the International District in Seattle and the Kogane District in Matsudo, Japan. Based on findings from participant observations and interviews, the article examines how the fragmentation of local communities presents both challenges for planning and opportunities for rethinking the practice of participation. The article argues that the challenges for participatory planning in fragmented communities lie not only in understanding and articulating the community differences but also in generating creative ways for meaningful interactions and negotiation of competing visions, interests, and values. The experiences and outcomes in International District and Kogane both suggest the importance of informal processes. Without the limitations imposed by institutional processes and formal participatory mechanisms, informal activities and social events can often produce unexpected and significant results. They allow planners and community organizers to navigate political and cultural nuances in negotiating community differences.

INTRODUCTION

The practice of participation in community planning is currently faced with the challenges of community change. Specifically, the fragmentation and continuing social and political changes present a profound contrast with the traditional notion and norms of 'community.' While the concepts of 'community' and 'community building' continue to dominate the discourse of participatory planning, the notion of unitary community no longer applies to the fast-changing social conditions in cities today. To examine this dilemma and its implications for participatory practice, this article compares two recent cases of participatory community planning in the context of fragmented communities—the International District in Seattle and the Kogane District in Matsudo, Japan. In both cases, the planning processes were confronted with the challenge of engaging fragmented communities through participation. Through a comparison of these two cases, the article examines how the fragmentation of local communities presents both challenges for planning and opportunities for rethinking the practice of participation.

The findings for this study are based on the authors' extended contact and involvement in the respective neighborhoods and planning processes.[1] Through participant observations and interviews with key stakeholders, we explore ways in which participatory planning in different contexts can engage multiple constituents while allowing for negotiation of internal differences. Through a discussion of the cases, we are interested in identifying possible models of participatory planning that recognize the internal cultural, political and social differences within the 'communities.' In particular, we are interested in the fluidity of community process that extends beyond the institutional process and formal settings. Finally, as the U.S. model of participatory planning has often dominated the discourses of community participation in general, we are interested in potential insights into alternative models and methods of participatory planning practice that emerge from and address the needs of specific cultural contexts.

COMMUNITY DIFFERENCES

In recent years, critiques of 'community' have become a focal point in political science and planning theories concerning social movement and contemporary social conditions. To many, the idea of community can be both a discursive and mobilizing instrument to engage in the politics of difference, as well as a concept that reinforces uniformity within a social or cultural group. For example, Sandercock (1998: 191) argues that the myth, or narrative, of community operates to produce defensive exclusionary behavior by describing who was here first, who really belongs. Young (1990: 227) further argues that the ideal of community denies and represses social difference, and that the polity cannot be thought of as a unity in which all participants share a common experience and common values. Tonkiss (2003, 299) also argues that a notion of community, most pointedly, can both enfold forms of diversity in the city and outline pockets of relative homogeneity along class, ethnic or cultural lines. In the context of these discussions, 'community' can become both an instrument and an obstacle in the local planning process.

Recent critiques of participatory planning have also centered on the challenge in coping with differences among the participants and stakeholders in terms of values, motives, and world views. The challenges often reside in the interests of seeing the community as unified (Baum 1994; Umemoto 2001; Lane 2003). The difficulties include overcoming diverse communication styles, cultural nuances, and group politics (de Souza Briggs 1998; Umemoto 2001). More specifically, Umemoto (2001) articulates the challenges to participatory planning as including

Figure 1. King Street, heart of Chinatown, International District. (Jeffrey Hou)

Figure 2. Summer festival organized by community business association. (Jeffrey Hou)

Figure 3. Danny Woo Community Garden, created in the midst of community activism in the 1970s. (Jeffrey Hou)

communicating across culture-based epistemologies, soliciting voices of multiple publics, and working with communities where cultural background of residents is different from one's own. The understanding of community differences therefore has direct implications for the practice of participatory planning. The ability of negotiating differences becomes an important question and agenda for the practice of participation.

CASES: INTERNATIONAL DISTRICT AND KOGANE

International District, Seattle

Seattle's International District has often been touted as a uniquely historic and multi-ethnic neighborhood resulting from successive waves of immigration. Since the late 1880s, Chinatown and Nihonmachi (Japantown) have existed side by side as Seattle became the hub of Asian immigration in the Pacific Northwest region of the United States (Chin 2001). The Chinese and Japanese immigrants were followed by Filipinos who began to arrive in Seattle starting in the early 1930s, mainly as seasonal laborers migrating between Alaska and Seattle. Starting in the 1920s, a significant African American community also resided in the District adding to the ethnic diversity of local residents. During World War II, the district suffered a major blow as Japanese American residents were sent to the internment camps. Only few returned to live in the District after war. Although the Chinese American community experienced increased levels of economic and social mobility during and after the War, many Chinese have left the district to seek housing outside in the neighboring areas, as the hotels and family association buildings were unfit for families to live in (Chin 2001, 73). By the 1960s, the District became primarily a community of poor and aging bachelors living in substandard single resident occupancy hotels.

Facing the blighted conditions of the neighborhood on one hand and encroaching development on the other, community activism began to emerge in the district that coincided with a Pan-Asian American movement in the 1960s and 1970s. The battle against the nearby construction of a large sports stadium, the King Dome, brought together activists from diverse ethnic backgrounds. While the King Dome was eventually built, many activists stayed to form new community-based organizations that provide housing and other social services to local residents, particularly the low-income elderly. In addition, the City agreed to establish a historic district to protect the historic and ethnic character of the neighborhood. Today, while community activism still thrives among the social service organizations, the district is faced with continued challenges. New developments continue to threaten the character and identity of the neighborhood. The presence of vacant and dilapidated buildings continues to dominate the image of the area. Finally, a new Vietnamese business area has been formed just outside the historic core of the district bringing tensions to the boundary and identity of the 'community.'

While the pan-ethnic movement has been successful in obtaining government resources and gaining recognition for local Asian communities, it has also become a source of contention within the district. Specifically, persistent tensions have existed between social service organizations and the traditional community and family associations. The division often along ideological, political, and sometimes ethnic lines also influenced their positions toward various issues in the district. For example, on the parking issue, the social service organizations generally favor public transportation that would better serve the district's low-income residents, while merchants strongly favor expansion of parking capacity to attract customers who visit the district by cars. On housing development, the social service organizations advocate for more affordable and mixed-income housing in the district, while private landowners and merchants generally favor market-rate housing to spur economic development in the area.

Debates concerning the official name of the district highlight another persistent tension in the district. Many in the Chinese community prefer the name 'Chinatown' or 'Chinatown-International District.' For the social service organizations, the name "International District," implies a more inclusive acknowledgement of the ethnic diversity in the district. The disagreement also reflects a profound and significant divide over the different definitions and perceptions of 'community' in the District. While the social service organizations focus on the needs of the local residents regardless of their cultural background, others have emphasized the business interests and see the district as the center of specific ethnic communities. These conflicts and tensions present a major challenge in local planning as exemplified in a recent attempt to create an urban design master plan for the district.

Kogane District, Matsudo

The Kogane district in Matsudo City was a former post town in the Edo age (1603—1864). Located on the historic Mito Kaido, it served as one of many resting stops for travelers between Edo (now Tokyo) and Mito. In addition to its location and primary function, family clans played an important role in the development of the area and continued to be influential in the district's affairs. The grandeur and prominence of the former family temples in the area testify to the power and influence of the clans. Today, however, while historic landmarks such as Tozenji Temple and Hondoji Temple remain prominent in Kogane, the historical townscape has become increasingly unrecognizable as a result of urban development since the late 19th Century. In 1896, a railway from Tokyo divided the town into north and south. During the 1960s, widespread housing estate developments in the greater Tokyo region resulted in

Figure 4. Redevelopment project at Kitakogane Station as viewed from the historic shopping street. (Jeffrey Hou)

demographic and physical transformation of the area. In the 1990s, a high-rise redevelopment project around the local train station led to the latest change in the neighborhood, as supermarkets and department stores attracted business away from the local shops along the historic main street. To address the decline of local businesses and historic character, a group of local merchants, schoolteachers, outside professionals, and younger-generation residents from the clan families began to organize activities in hopes of revitalizing the historic neighborhood.

Similar to the International District, the 'community' in Kogane is also divided in many ways. One such division is directly reflected in the physical separation as a result of the railroad. The separation has led to the differential developments in north and south. While urbanization has drastically transformed the spatial character of the South, the North has remained largely rural with landowners depending on incomes from real estate and farming. In recent years, the separation is further reinforced by the mammoth redevelopment project near the train station. Besides the north-south divide, the population in Kogane is also divided socially and politically among ranks of traditional clan families and recent residents, with the clan families having greater prestige and influence in the district despite their smaller number. In recent years, with growing development of housing estates in the area, newcomers have become the majority in the district. However, this demographic shift has not been reflected in the leadership and political process in the district.[2]

The longtime residents and newcomers often differ in degrees of involvement and attachment to the neighborhood. The

Figure 5. (Left) Community meeting in the International District. (Jeffrey Hou) Figure 6. (Right) Participatory workshop in the International District. (Jeffrey Hou)

Figure 7. Children's neighborhood exploratory tour. (Isami Kinoshita)

former often express their pride of local history, whereas the latter are generally disinterested in the neighborhood and local affairs. However, the sense of attachment among the longtime residents appears to be more connected to their family history rather than the collective identity. While the traditional clans enjoy a highly regarded status in the district, the traditional hierarchy has become an obstacle to the process of community development. On one hand, the newcomers have been excluded from local decision-making. On the other hand, within the local leadership, the competing interests and conflicts often between the different clan families also prevented different stakeholders from working together.

Figure 8. Schoolchildren examining the work of the Chiba-UW collaborative studio. (Jeffrey Hou)

PARTICIPATION IN THE FACE OF DIFFERENCES

Politics of Multiethnic Community

How do the planning processes in International District and Kogane cope with the internal differences within the communities?

Figure 9. Temporary community cafe to encourage social interaction.

In the face of new construction as well as the need for economic revitalization and physical improvement, a recent effort has been taken in the International District to develop an urban design master plan. Led by Inter*Im Community Development Association (ICDA), a long-time local housing and community advocacy group, the project would produce plans for streetscape and open space improvement, as well as a review of current land use and preservation guidelines. The planning process followed a characteristically bottom-up approach in Seattle involving community process and participation of local stakeholders. However, this process was stalled at the very beginning as other community groups challenged the role of IDCA in representing the community and leading the project. The dispute was eventually resolved in part by including a large number of community representatives on the project's steering committee. However, once the project started, another disagreement emerged over the name of the district itself. The lack of agreement on the name again stalled the planning process for months before members of the steering committee agreed to hold a special meeting to settle on an official name for the project. During the meeting, an agreement was reached

Figure 10. Construction of the Pocket Park.

Figure 11. Opening ceremony.

Figure 12. Mural created by local schoolchildren.

to recognize the multiple communities within the district and to rename the project '*Chinatown, Japantown, Little Saigon – International District Urban Design Plan.*'

As a result of delay caused by persistent conflicts and arguments, the final planning document did little more than reaffirm the unique cultural and physical characteristics of the district and included a list of general recommendations for improvement. Nevertheless, while the result was disappointing to several committee members, many also acknowledged the very process itself as a positive outcome of the project. To many, the planning process was the first time that representatives from opposing groups in the district could sit together to work on a project. The stakes of the project forced many participants to communicate with each other who would otherwise have no opportunity to speak with each other. Several participants acknowledged that the project became more about 'community building' rather than producing a plan. This positive outcome is evident in the fact that several members of the committee have stayed involved and currently continue to work together on the implementation phase of the project.

Social Events and Activities

The grassroots process in Kogane took a radically different path compared to the International District. Rather than having a clear planning agenda or a road map and as a response to the rigid local planning process, the group of shop owners, schoolteachers and local organizers began with several outreach activities that included neighborhood exploratory tours for children and an "Art Flea Market" to engage other local merchants. These activities helped awaken interests among many local residents. For example, the responses from the children have in turn encouraged their parents, mostly newcomers, to discover the neighborhood. A citizen group was formed following the activities. Named "Bikimae Club," the group includes several younger-generation landowners, primary school teachers, and professionals.

In addition to working with local merchants and school children, the citizen group also enlisted help from faculty and students at nearby Chiba University. Starting in 2001, classes from Chiba University conducted systematic studies of the district's resources and characteristics. In 2003, the Chiba faculty and students engaged in a collaborative design studio with their counterparts at the University of Washington in Seattle.[3] The

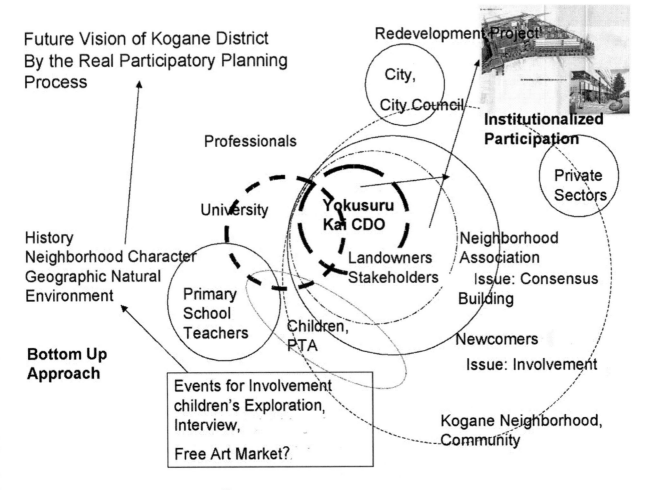

Figure 13. Community process in Kogane.

studio brought students and faculty from both universities to develop proposals for neighborhood improvement. The works of the students were displayed at vacant storefronts and sidewalks, and were presented at a neighborhood symposium organized by the Bikimae Club. The exhibit and symposium generated further interest among the residents. Inspired by the students' proposal, one landowner offered part of his private garden to create a community café and pocket park, open to the public. The pocket park was completed in the following year as a design-build project undertaken by the students at Chiba University.

Another important outcome of the community building process was the move to establish a new neighborhood organization in the district. After five years of involvement in neighborhood activities, several landowners decided to form a new association to carry out larger community development projects and to involve more stakeholders. At the district level, through personal networks among several landowners, the new association '*Kogane wo Yokusuru Kai* (Association for Better Kogane)' has been effective in involving other community leaders and merchant organizations. While the process in Kogane has not led to formal planning outcomes, the small-scale activities initiated by citizen organizations have animated communication and interactions among local residents and raised their awareness of the issues and history of the district. The activities serve as an important first step toward formulating future visions for the district and contribute to capacity building among the local citizens.

REFLECTONS: INFORMAL PROCESSES IN NEGOTIATING COMMUNITY DIFFERENCES

Despite the remarkable differences in planning contexts and participatory approaches, the experiences and outcomes in the International District and Kogane both suggest the importance of informal processes in addressing and negotiating internal differences within the respective communities. The most meaningful and transformative part of the participatory process in both cases has occurred outside the institutional process, including informal communication and social events. In the International District, while planning process produces little substantive results, many participants view the rare interactions, including efforts to communicate outside formal meetings, as constructive in eventually creating a working relationship among the opposing stakeholders despite their differences. In Kogane, the outreach activities created a process that bridged different groups and stakeholders in the district, including merchants, landowners, long-time residents, and newcomers. Specifically, the activities involving school children transcended the perceived boundaries between the different groups. Through the exploratory tours and dialogues, what used to be family heritage became a shared history. In both International District

Figure 14. (Left) Creating a community at the Community Pub – "Yu Shin." (Isami Kinoshita) Figure 15. (Right) Pub visit by the Chiba Prefecture Governor (left). (Isami Kinoshita)

and Kogane, the informal processes have been particularly important in addressing the political and cultural nuances in the respective contexts. It allowed for creation of new meaning and understanding in the community.

The cases of International District and Kogane exemplify the nature of political and cultural differences within rapidly changing urban communities. The politics of difference are not just a phenomenon of contemporary social movement but a reality that permeates through different sectors of society. The presence of differences presents particular problems for participatory planning as it challenges both the notion of homogenous and unified 'community' and the limited repertoire of institutional consensus building process. The comparison of the participatory planning experiences here is therefore significant in providing insights on how participatory planning can work with internal differences and fragmentation in urban communities and continue to be a legitimate, useful, and empowering planning practice. As evident in International District and Kogane, participatory planning process should recognize community differences as the inevitable characteristics of democratic society. However, the challenges for participatory planning in these contexts lie not only in understanding and articulating these differences but also in generating creative ways for meaningful interactions and negotiation of competing visions, interests, values, and cultural differences. The tools and mechanisms of negotiation should not be limited to institutional processes and formal mechanisms as commonly found in literature and practice. Instead, informal activities and social events can often produce unexpected and significant results and are a necessary step for navigating through community differences.

ENDNOTES

[1] In the International District, participant observations were made throughout the planning process, in community meetings, workshops, and informal contacts with individuals in the community. In addition, semi-structured interviews were conducted with key neighborhood stakeholders and organizational participants in the local planning process. The research is part of a jointly funded project supported by the Royalty Research Funds at University of Washington. The co-

investigators of the project include Daniel Abramson, Gail Dubrow, Jeffrey Hou, and Lynne Manzo, with assistance from Amy Tanner. In the case of Kogane, action research has been conducted through involvement in the process of the community enhancement activities since 1998. Observations of the community activities were conducted at meetings of local citizen groups. Interviews with the residents were also made in different phases of activities.

[2] In Japan, *Chonai Kai* (Neighborhood Association) has the responsibility of managing a neighborhood. It plays a quasi-governmental role as virtually the smallest unit of local municipal administration. In Kogane, the board membership of Chonai Kai has been composed of the traditional clan families. Newcomers on the other hand have been excluded from participating in the association.

[3] The studio was jointly developed and conducted by the authors, along with Professor Sawako Ono at Chiba University. More information about the studio is available at http://www.caup.washington.edu/larch/chiba.htm.

REFERENCES

Baum, H. 1994. Community and Consensus: Reality and Fantasy in Planning. *Journal of Planning Education and Research*, 13: 251-262.

Bollens, S. A. 2002. Urban Planning and Intergroup Conflict: Confronting a Fractured Public Interest. *Journal of the American Planning Association*, Winter 2002, 68 (1): 22-42.

Chin, D. 2001. Seattle's International District: The Making of a Pan-Asian American Community. *Seattle: International Examiner Press*.

de Souza Briggs, X. 1998. Doing Democracy Up-Close: Culture, Power, and Communication in Community Building. *Journal of Planning Education and Research*, 18: 1-13.

Hou, J. and A. Tanner. 2002. Constructed Identities and Contested Space in Seattle's Chinatown-International District. Groundworks: CELA 2004 Conference Proceedings. Council of Educators in Landscape Architecture. SUNY, Syracuse, New York. September 25-27, 2002.

Lane, M. B. 2003. Participation, Decentralization and Civil Society: Indigenous Rights and Democracy in Environmental Planning. *Journal of Planning Education and Research*, 22: 360-373.

Sandercock, L. 1998. *Toward Cosmopolis: Planning for Multicultural Cities*. Chichester, NY: John Wiley & Sons.

Tonkiss, F. 2003. The Ethics of Indifference: Community and Solitude in the City. *International Journal of Cultural Studies*, 6(3): 297-311.

Umemmoto, K. 2001. Walking in Another's Shoes: Epistemological Challenges in Participatory Planning. *Journal of Planning Education and Research*, 21: 17-31.

Young, I. M. 1990. Justice and the Politics of Difference. Princeton, NJ: Princeton University Press.

PARTICIPATORY DESIGN, THE SPIRT OF PLACE, AND THE PITFALLS OF PROFESSIONALISM Evaluation of the Town Center Design Process in Caspar, California

Carey Knecht

ABSTRACT

This case study evaluates the citizen participation process used in the design of a town center for Caspar, California, a five-hundred person community on California's Mendocino County coast. This essay considers participatory design as a method for bridging the difference between the local and the global, between the world view of residents – who often have a rooted, particular perspective that stems from and contributes to the local sense of place – and landscape designers – who often live elsewhere and tend to have a more detached, abstract perspective. Participatory techniques that widened, and that narrowed, this divide are identified.

BACKGROUND

Caspar is a small coastal community in California's Mendocino County, approximately 160 miles north of San Francisco. The town sits in a relatively uninhabited fifteen-mile stretch between Mendocino and Fort Bragg. The town lies on a coastal plain overlooking the Pacific Ocean, at the base of the forested hills of Jackson Experimental State Forest. It straddles Highway One, the artery carrying car travel and development through the North Coast corridor. Currently, approximately 500 people live within the informal borders of the unincorporated town.

The town site of Caspar originated as the center of the Caspar Lumber Company's operations, which began milling lumber in 1861. In 1997, after four decades of dormancy, the Company's 300 acres were offered for sale.[1] Faced with the possibility of having 80% of the town's open space developed as a resort or suburb, concerned citizens formed the Caspar Community, a non-profit organization devoted to "consensual self-determination" (Caspar, 2003). In the self-governance system they initiated, residents hold quarterly meetings in which they make decisions using an informal consensus method. Any resident willing to commit the necessary time can join the non-profit's Board of Directors, and for important decisions, this leadership group does significant outreach to those who do not attend community meetings. These inclusive methods have earned the Caspar Community county recognition as a de facto local government.

In 1998, Caspar residents worked with faculty and students from the University of California, Berkeley, to form a long-range vision for the town's development. This process, led by Professor Randolph Hester, has been guided by a 12-step method of community participation (Hester, 1984). Students in Hester's 1998 landscape architecture studio design class led residents in creating a phased plan for the town's development. Following this plan, residents first protected the town's most sacred place – the ocean overlook known as the Caspar Headlands – by raising money to have it made a state park. They then turned to priority two: creating a community center in an old school located at the intersection of two key roads. In February 2002, they purchased the school building and contacted Hester to help them design the surrounding property.

TOWN CENTER DESIGN PROCESS

On September 8, 2002, Professor Hester directed a community visioning charrette, assisted by a group of graduate students, including myself. After this charrette, I began acting as the project manager and, under Hester's guidance, did a large portion of the work to translate citizen desires into a Town Center design.

The Town Center design emerged through an iterative process of design and community feedback. This process included seven steps (primary actors listed in parentheses): 1) individual visioning in a guided exercise (approximately seventy residents at an initial charrette), 2) sharing individual ideas and choosing priorities, in small groups led by Berkeley graduate students, then presenting the priorities to all charrette attendees (residents attending the charrette), 3) integrating the small group priorities to define the site program and goals (Berkeley team), 4) brainstorming four initial Town Center designs (Berkeley team), 5) giving feedback on the initial designs (residents on the Caspar Community Board), 6) integrating the Board's comments into one design and presenting this to residents (Berkeley team), and 7) providing feedback on the final design (residents).

After the design priorities were compiled from the small group lists in step 3 (above), several people from the Berkeley group brainstormed four possible Town Center designs. The preliminary designs share certain elements, such as a building to block the cold north wind, but otherwise have different organizing structures – a village green encircled by a road, an internal Main Street to bring commercial activity closer to the existing school building, sequentially larger green spaces

opening from the school building toward the Headlands, or a new creek to carry stormwater across the site. The plans have approximately the same commercial square footage but different numbers of housing units.

We sent the preliminary designs to the Board for their feedback. Despite our adherence to community generated program elements (e.g., a firehouse) and our attempt to produce desired qualities (e.g., "intergenerational"), the Board's responses to initial designs were lukewarm (e.g., "we weren't wild about any one of the plans;" "we all had reservations of some aspects shared by all the plans"). They rated each design and drew suggested changes to each design on cellophane overlays.

The design team compared the Board's suggested changes to the four designs, looking for patterns. We incorporated changes that they consistently repeated in the final design: buildings should not block views to the southwest and east, parking and circulation should wrap around the outside of the site, and drainage should be unobtrusive. They desired that certain required commercial space be off-site, and that a maximum of four housing units be built. However, their central complaint was not immediately clear to us. They suggested changes to the plans' details, but for three of four plans, even those they preferred, they removed or minimized key elements without commenting on the overarching structure. For example, they removed the street from the "Main Street Plan" without rejecting the idea of a shopping promenade. We did eventually realize that the Board usually suggested buildings be smaller, fewer, and scattered more irregularly. We came to understand that whereas we tended to cluster buildings to enclose open space, their suggestions often arrayed active spaces like beads on a necklace.

In the visioning charrette, participants had drawn their "most loved" town center and listed its essential characteristics to incorporate in Caspar. To understand whether the lukewarm response had been because designers missed a particular guiding spirit, the design team re-examined the individual visions, with careful attention to residents' design precedents and to what attributes of those places residents valued. Anything that seemed new or unfamiliar in the visions was noted, as something possibly excluded from the design. These unfamiliar concepts revealed three clusters of missing elements: rural looseness; spaces defined by people and ritual rather than built form; and a spiritual reverence for nature.

Incorporating these changes, the Berkeley team drew a single design and presented it to approximately fifty residents. To show the spirit of the town center, particularly the previously missing elements, the final design had a number of small scenes showing people cloud-watching, jumping into a pile of hay, and sitting around a campfire circle. We suggested this final design be implemented in phases. The presentation emphasized four aspects of the design: ecological site factors, changes between the preliminary and final designs, activity scenes in the final design, and a phasing sequence in which the final design could be built over time as funding opportunities and community needs arose.

The response was overwhelmingly positive. When asked to "please state your favorite thing, or one thing you would change," no one opposed the overall design, and only four people chose to make a suggestion (e.g., that the property have a caretaker). Seven of forty attendees particularly appreciated the process (e.g., "I'm amazed with the discussion and how everyone contributed to come up with the plan"). The written survey yielded similar results. The community seemed to feel that designers had faithfully translated their desires into a design.

DISCUSSION

In short, we began with four initial designs that were not well-liked and ended with a final design that was much more positively received. Which techniques caused this gap in understanding to arise, and which helped restore communication?

Three aspects of the process appear to have fostered or perpetuated misunderstanding. First, details which would communicate desired attributes did not survive the small group prioritization of goals. Residents and/or group leaders often collected the group members' detail-rich suggestions under a detail-free heading. The residents in my group collected several items, including "suncatchers and refractors and things that wave in the wind to highlight the presence of nature and awaken your senses," and summarized the group as "environmental sustainability." Such abstract language allowed significant leeway for designer (mis)interpretation, particularly since designers studied the group summaries instead of the brainstorm lists before designing. An improvement to this method would be to ask groups not only to prioritize their goals but also to "please select one or two concrete details that demonstrate what each of your most important goals might look like." Alternatively, when compiling the small group goals, the compiler could review the brainstorm lists and provide both goals and supporting examples to designers.

The second technique that may have widened the resident/designer gap was that the Berkeley student team brainstormed preliminary designs in Berkeley without community members present. As designers sought to spatialize goals such as "environmentally sustainable" and "intergenerational," physical and social details from our studies or from Berkeley's urban environment were more mentally available than the Caspar environment. Instead, we could have brainstormed initial designs while still in Caspar. Since this was not possible, we could have attempted to regress to the mindset we had

when in Caspar through photos and other methods. To help people remember Caspar clearly, while we were in Caspar, I could have asked everyone to draw sketches, gather small plant or soil samples, take photos, or keep a journal of their personal reactions to the place. If people individually chose what to record about the physical setting, they would be more likely to remember not only the setting, but the feelings the setting evoked. By reviewing these reminders, the Berkeley team would be vividly recalling Caspar's particularities when designing, instead of Berkeley's. Of course, the details that are important to students will not be the same as those important to residents, so this strategy should be combined with strategies that remind students of the residents' priorities.

Finally, a focus on form and professional-looking graphics probably inhibited communication about the initial proposals. Board members responded to details in the scenes, such as the placement of buildings. But the most important details – people and their activities – were not drawn in the preliminary landscape plans. Thus, as noted above, their comments on details did not tell us whether they preferred a shopping promenade or a village green. They objected to the main street, but because people were not shown walking on a boardwalk from store to store, the Board did not comment on the overall concept. Although their feedback was still crucial and quite helpful, detailed scenes of people shopping or lounging on a green would have made our central questions clearer and given us the answers we needed.

Fortunately, four other aspects of the process seem to have assisted communication and restored local desires and vision. First, structuring the initial charrette around three different modes of expression – drawing, writing, and talking – meant that a person comfortable in any of these modes could communicate their individual vision. Second, since the visioning session led residents through a long (10-15 minute) guided imagery exercise, it solicited some responses that were quite imaginative and artistic. Impressionistic drawings and poetic descriptions were especially valuable in helping us find a spirit to guide the Town Center design. Third, asking the Board to review initial designs and draw suggested changes provided crucial corrections on physical elements' size and placement. Finally, citizen comments suggest that the phasing diagram and the phasing story told in the presentation were quite important. The plan seemed uniquely suited to the community since we explicitly recommended they adapt it to suit their needs and resources over time.

THEORY & CONCLUSIONS

Participatory design has been promoted partially for its ability to overcome race, class, and gender divisions (e.g., Umemoto, 2001). This study shows that even when designers and residents share many demographic characteristics and personal values (e.g., environmental sustainability), and even when designers are attempting to follow citizen-generated criteria, significant gaps in understanding can arise. In this case, the gap seems to be the pervasive difference between the local and the global – between the rooted, particular perspective of residents and the more detached, abstract perspective of designers.

This local/global duality is at the core of large bodies of theory, including place and placemaking (Tuan, 1977; Bruner, 2001), and bioregion and re-inhabitation (Berg & Dasmann, 1978; Snyder, 1995; Thayer, 2003). Most definitions of "place" begin with the five senses – sight, sense, taste, touch, and smell. Kevin Lynch explains "the sense of a region" as "what one can see, how it feels underfoot, the smell of the air, the sounds of bells and motorcycles, how patterns of these sensations make up the quality of places, and how that quality affects our immediate well-being, our actions, our feelings, and our understandings" (1976). These small sensory impressions combine and create an overall identity for a place. Theoretical literature often claims that a "place" is a space imbued with meaning, so that places are "embedded in the everyday world around us and easily accessible, but at the same time are distinct from that world" (Jackson, 1994). Its meaning comes from three sources: biophysical properties, social and political processes, and a sociocultural interpretive framework (Cheng et al, 2003). The concept of "place" emphasizes how quirky, particular, and extraordinary aspects of a location combine to make a unique impression.

The concept of "bioregion" is similar to the concept of "place." Bioregions are not simply "geographic areas having common characteristics of soil, watershed, climate, native plants and animals," but also "a cultural idea… (A bioregion is) a geographic terrain and a terrain of consciousness" (Berg & Dasmann, 1978). Bioregionalism differs from place theory in its greater emphasis on ecological factors, but the two concepts overlap greatly (e.g., Hough, 1995). Like "place," "bioregion," emphasizes individual sensory experience, focuses on interactions between nature and culture, and celebrates local peculiarities. The opposite of place and bioregion, "placelessness," is not just the existence of "look-alike landscapes," but also that "behind these lies a deep-seated attitude that attends to the common and average characteristics of man and place" (Relph, 1976: 79).

Advocates of both places and bioregions recommend actively strengthening the uniqueness of places by placemaking or reinhabitation. Reinhabitation refers to settling in a particular place, considering oneself a permanent member of local human and non-human communities, accepting its ecological limits, and working to repair the social and environmental fabric of a lifeplace (Berg & Dasmann, 1978; Snyder, 1995; Thayer, 2003). Caspar residents seem to have begun this process of reinhabitation. They have formed a self-governance organization and through this organization, they work for a greater balance between their human community and aspects of local ecology. For example, they host an annual Gorse Festival to have a celebration while promoting the removal of this aggressive thorny shrub through work sessions and information sharing. One resident even ferments "gorse wine." Activities like this, which strengthen local culture and ecosystems such that they begin to co-evolve, are the essence of reinhabitation or placemaking.

With Caspar residents working to reinhabit their particular locale, does this mean that the initial communication gap between residents and designers was between place and placelessness, between place-promoters and place-obliterators? Could designers be missionaries of a global monoculture? Some writers charge that the current academic environment perpetuates a culture of "rootless professors," whose greatest allegiance is "to the boundless world of books and ideas and eternal truths" at the expense of geographic membership (Zencey, 1996: 15; see also W. Jackson, 1994). After studying the codes of ethics in landscape architecture professional organizations, Bob Scarfo concluded that "the landscape architect's knowledge and abstract language… cannot subjectively convey the inhabitants' values. Nor can it produce contextually meaningful landscape forms" (1987: 687).

More benignly, the communication gap may just have been a cultural gap between Place A and Place B. The design team might be sympathetic to place-related thinking and even have allegiance to a certain place, but to a different place than the location of the design project. This is certainly possible. My life in Berkeley is different from life in Caspar in almost all sensory, social, and cultural details. For example, the background noise in my life is traffic, not ocean surf or seals barking. I buy basic groceries as I walk home, but Caspar inhabitants have to drive seven miles on the highway. During the day, I see many more people; during the night, they see many more stars. When residents jokingly refer to my "urban aesthetic," they are suggesting that these many details combine to make my design preferences different from theirs.

This second possible gap, between Place A and Place B, is likely to be present frequently, since few landscape architects limit their work to their immediate residence. But this second gap may frequently combine with or trigger the first gap mentioned, between place and placelessness. Even designers sympathetic to place-specific thinking may shift into a more universal, abstract mode of thinking when asked to understand a new spatial context and offer services to its residents.

The risk is that this universal, abstract mode of thinking would drown out local influences. To counteract this, designers should become aware of when abstract or outside influences are loudest and then be more deliberate about listening. In the Caspar case study, four types of universal influence or detachment were most important. First, our lack of personal relations made it possible for us to disregard the impact of the design on single individuals when local residents could not. Second, we knew and invoked a wide palette of design shapes and precedents, many of which were slightly exotic, like Italy's Piazza San Marco, or abstract, like the Golden Nautilus. Third, since we participate in a professional design culture, academic knowledge and trends shape our priorities. In Caspar, one preliminary design emphasized stormwater management. Though important in Caspar, we focused on stormwater primarily because of Berkeley faculty members' strengths, and because of increasing concern with stormwater pollution in the San Francisco Bay. Fourth, our preconceived design-related norms of right and wrong influence our designs. In Caspar, we repeatedly pressed for raising the density of the town center. I still think more housing would help Caspar achieve its goals. But my commitment to high density originated in the San Francisco Bay Area, where rapid population growth is devouring Central Valley habitat and farms. I can't say I weighed the issues in Caspar with a fully open mind.

Of course, these four differences between designers and residents form the core of the design profession's strengths as much as its weaknesses. As designers, we are paid for possessing these same attributes: personal disattachment, wide knowledge of possible designs, time-evolved and current design skills and judgments, and awareness of design decisions' broader social and environmental impacts. The forms, ideas, and values we bring can cross-pollinate local ideas to create excellent new solutions. It allows designers to serve as educators. Designers can even accelerate widely-desired social change if they provide compelling design options that are particularly socially or environmentally responsible (Hester, 1995). Participatory design provides the method for maintaining our profession's strengths while not obliterating or obscuring a place's uniqueness.

Without deliberate effort, design can be a top-down process that ultimately promotes homogeneity. However, participatory techniques can help designers honor the specificity of local ecology and culture. To avoid communication pitfalls, designers should be particularly aware of shifts from details to abstractions. Ideally, residents should navigate designers to the level of abstract principles and then back again to details. Techniques that promote a holistic understanding of the place through artistic methods are also especially helpful. Special care should be taken when dealing with social relationships, design precedents, academic trends, and normative judgments, because these are areas where a cosmopolitan or detached perspective is most likely to override or drown out local influences. Participatory design can serve as a method for bridging differences between "the local and the global;" between the world view of residents – whose views come from and contribute to the local sense of place – and landscape designers – who often live elsewhere and tend to be somewhat cosmopolitan due to their training and professional frame of reference. As placemaking and reinhabitation efforts increasingly counter placelessness, designers should teach themselves to assist communities trying to "become native to [their] place" (Wes Jackson, 1994).

ENDNOTES

[1] The Caspar Lumber Company's acreage had previously been sold to the Caspar Cattle Company (CCC), owned by a long-time resident who wanted to prevent harmful development. But was the first time the land truly might have been purchased by a developer was when the CCC could no longer hold the land and put it up for sale in 1997.

REFERENCES

Berg, P., and Dasmann, R. 1978. Reinhabiting a Separate Country. San Francisco: Planet Drum Foundation.

Berg, P. 2002. Bioregionalism. Available at: http://csf.colorado.edu/bioregional/2002/msg00029.html. Retrieved 1/26/04.

Caspar Community. 2003. Available at: http://casparcommons.org/. Retrieved 5/5/03.

Bruner Foundation, Inc. & Werner, R. 2001. Placemaking for Change: 2001 Rudy Bruner Award for Urban Excellence. Cambridge, Massachusetts: Bruner Foundation.

Cheng, A. S., Kruger, L. E., Daniels, S.E. 2003. Place as an integrating concept in natural resource politics: Propositions for a social science research agenda. Society and Natural Resources 16: 87-104.

Hester, R. Jr. 1984. Planning Neighborhood Space with People. 2nd ed. New York: Van Nostrand Reinhold Co.

Hester, R. 1995. Life, liberty, and the pursuit of sustainable happiness. Places 9: 4-17.

Hough, M. 1995. Out of Place: Restoring Identity to the Regional Landscape. New Haven: Yale University Press.

Jackson, J. B. 1994. A Sense of Place, A Sense of Time. New Haven: Yale University Press.

Jackson, W. 1994. Becoming Native to this Place. Louisville: University of Kentucky Press.

Relph, E. 1976. Place and Placelessness. London: Pion.

Scarfo, B. 1987. Stewardship: The Profession's Grand Delusion. Landscape Architecture 77:46-51.

Snyder, G. 1995. A Place in Space. Washington DC: Counterpoint.

Thayer, R. 2003. LifePlace: Bioregional Thought and Practice. Berkeley: University of California Press.

Tuan, Y-F. 1977. Space and Place: The Perspective of Experience. Minneapolis: Minnesota Press.

Umemoto, K. 2001. Walking in Another's Shoes: Epistemological Challenges in Participatory Planning. Journal of Planning Education and Research 21: 17-31.

まちづくり

いなの

たましい

べんりなことばず

わけもわからず

どこもかしこも

INTEGRATED SLUM REDEVELOPMENT WITH A HEART
Mojosongo, Solo, Central Java, Indonesia

Antonio Ishmael Risianto

ABSTRACT

This paper briefly covers a "Community Planning" experience in "redeveloping" slum/squatter areas in Indonesia. "Community Planning" here is part of the overall community participation process which also includes community actions and implementation. This paper attempts to show that "Community Planning & Participation" were the key factor in making this project a reasonable success. It is an attempt to also show (especially to the Local Government) that so often they have taken the simplistic path by just evicting these slum/squatter communities by force. Yet it does not really solve the problem.[1] This paper briefly discusses the interlink/interface of a "holistic approach," the integration and coordination of activities of the various key players (Stakeholders) in this "urban game" under this "community dynamic planning" and implementation process. It discusses the supporting means as well as the problem faced in enabling this slum/underdeveloped district to change to become a "normal" settlement as pockets "for the low income" to be able to also live in cities - being part of the total mutual symbiotic Urban Fabric of the overall City Plan.[2]

INTRODUCTION: THE CONTEXT/PROBLEM

This case study was conducted in one of the urban fringe areas (of about 200 Hectares) that were rapidly (but haphazardly)

Figure 1. The existing slum and squatters.

Figure 2. No jobs. Survival?

growing as an Urbanized Settlement.[3] These fringe areas, as is often also the case in many poor underdeveloped countries (in Asia, Africa, and Latin America), were one of the poorest districts in the City. Most were the result of the pressure of mass urbanization phenomena of masses who were all searching and struggling for their survival. So how can we redevelop these underdeveloped areas in a more humane way for its citizens = "A City for All?"

The slum/squatter redevelopment efforts were done through several interlinking and integrated "problem solving development packages." These were all done though the "Community Planning" approach.

- Community self-rearranging squatter's land, voluntary self "informal housing" (shacks) demolition, and collective rebuilding new homes.

- Resettlement to a new "Community Based Housing" development (a special program where the community can become their own Developer) to make ways to logistically enable the existing squatters' land to be re-developed.

- Re-arranging existing riverbank slum settlement, based on an "Eco Village Model." Community internally re-ordering their physical environment, rearranging legal but hazardous "informal housing" all to "opening up" the way of the large World Bank's anti-flood river normalization project.

Figure 3. *The frequent slum evictions against the urban poor.*

Figure 4. The garbage in the river.

- Maintaining and improving the existing as well as creating new "(poor) peoples' economic centers."

- Improving the natural ecosystem along the over-polluted and flooded waterway zones, through resettling "pig farming" and introducing "appropriate technologies" for a collective/ ecological soy bean cake production operation.

- River Clean-Up program, including Community Garbage Management through Recycling and Composting Eco Station program and building Community Latrines.

- Improving the "settlement infrastructure" in providing special pedestrian and "only motor cycle accesses," through community alley paving and bamboo bridge building program.

The fringe area of this low-income settlement (called "Kampung") consists of a combination of sporadic still semi rural settlements, with pockets of very dense (legal) "slum" and (illegal) "squatter" settlements. The attention of the project focused on the most critical slum and squatter settlements at the crossing of the main inter-regional road, traditional market, all along the riverbanks, and along the edges of the creeks and even settlement encroaching the cemeteries.

A tertiary river branch passes through this "Kampung" which are so heavily polluted by rampant unorganized pig farming and the combination of un-ecological "Soya bean" production. On top of this, the lack of latrines and the rampant flooding caused by direct garbage dumping practices clogging waterways creates an unbearable foul smell in the whole environment for a livable human settlement - A water polluting source to the main river that covers a great area all through the southern end of the region. The uncontrolled growth of the squatter settlement started clogging the major regional circulation link from the *Center Business District* (CBD) to the more formal residential districts at the northern outskirts of the city. This then caused a city circulation "bottleneck."

The World Bank was then involved with a City & Regional Development Program (SSUDP) and placed this district as a priority zone to be "managed" for improving the overall city/ region. This included the objective to "prevent wild" settlement growth and open up "new urban land" for supporting the City's shortage of low-income housing. World Bank then set a major "Urban INFRASTRUCTURE" investment program, consisting of the building of roads, normalizing the city river with a citywide levy building program that also covers this district. Nevertheless, for more than 2 years after the levy project was approved and planned, it had faced a "dead lock" situation because of its inability to clear the needed river bank's "land" for its construction.

That this "conventional infrastructure engineering" project was unable to start was its failure to place the importance of the "Social Factor" in the total development package. A proposal was then re-introduced to consider the "PEOPLE's PARTICIPATION" which got underway after we were asked to lead support this assignment.

THE OBJECTIVE: THE 'MPE' FACTOR

For simplicity, a way to see the "objective" is to see this effort as a "three-pronged focus" that was considered and implemented in this assignment as a whole and inseparable from what we believe can solve the slum/squatter redevelopment problem in a more sustainable way:

a. The "M": "Meta Development"

An objective and effort that was often not so well "concerned" in conventional large "engineering based" projects was "the Mental & Social" development in the form of "trust," "willingness," "inner cooperation," care, the mental frame, and "social togetherness" in solving problems. These are so gravely important in city development *where public resources are scarce* (common situation in most underdeveloped governments.) Other forms of this "Meta Development" are called "Human Capital Development," the sense of belonging, the culture, the self enablement, the participatory energies . . . the willingness, the preparedness, the want to organize themselves ("community strengthening" or often called "organizing the unorganized" or "formalizing the informal sector") . . . or basically "Giving a Heart."

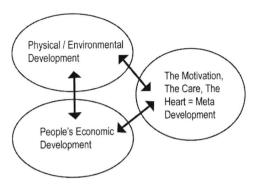

Figure 5. MPE Factor.

Figure 6. Community planning at night.

b. The "P": Physical/Environmental Development

The development of the appropriate "Physical and Environmental development," especially the support for basic infrastructure services (minimal water, sewerage, electrical access) will be key as a catalyst to trigger community participatory energies.[4] This includes the development of public/community space and environmentally friendly infrastructures.

c. The "E": (Poor) "People's Economy" Development

This considers the underlying reasons of why the squatter settlers/low income population is there in the first place: looking for jobs/income to survive.

Solving with only the physical infrastructure and housing development alone does not seem to solve the underlying problem. The target Community cannot survive with just housing, riverbank levies, roads, and public toilets alone. They were basically there for "jobs/income" to survive without guarding this resource the sustainability to survive will fall apart. The low income will eventually be forced to move out.

Both physical development and "people's economy"/self-supporting jobs/income, requires "mental energy" as a "bonding chemistry." This is often the 'missing factor" in the total "development system."

This is the "MPE " objective/focus that we have learned and followed by an interlinking/interface "Community Planning and Implementation" process.

The (Community Planning/Participatory Development) Process

The process was a continuous link of working together between four main Actors/Stake Holders, namely, in this case: the target community (the poor, the squatters, the existing local inhabitants); the local city Government, the Community Facilitators, and the World Bank. Each of these "Development Actors" has basically their own unique resources needed *"to be mixed for attaining feasible solutions."*

The process basically was, what is often named a "Symphonic Planning and Negotiation Process" among the various main Development Actors, each supporting the intricate and dynamic situation under a strategic, psychological and political sensitive game of constant changes, and negotiation/lobby process and all focused on the development of the aforementioned three-pronged MPE objectives.

Simplifying the Process (still rather complex looking) can be seen in the following diagram:

The parts of this Community Planning process are not really "phases" but all passing more a dynamic process and often incrementally just grow, refined and mixed to constant mobilization of enabling resources to gear towards concrete/real actions (whatever it is) . . . often called the "Dynamic Urban Planning" process.

a. The Understanding of the General Context: The role of the "External Development Analyst"

Looking at the Macro and Micro view. Seeing the problems from the external view based on the Science and the state of the art of Regional and Urban Planning "Knowledge," Urban Management, and often practicing "Appropriate Technology" (AT). With this base, initially developing "Cards of Strategic Local Development Assumptions" of different possible problem solving development alternatives, possibilities, and preparing assumed scenarios.

b. The Community Entry Strategy and Learning "the local knowledge"

Entering the community is one of the critical points of this "Building Block of Trust." "The Student Entry" seems the best method so far, as "Students" are usually seen by the community as neutral, pure, free from "hidden interest" and "still learning." *"Just try not to act so smart but humble, "more human," and that they are all just 'learning together from each other' to solve local problems."*

c. The Initial Confirmation of These Strategic Development Assumptions

This is done through informal "raps"/dialogs with the locals, that might surprise us for its outcome. The "External Party's" perceptions of problems and assumed solutions might be so totally different/inappropriate. Often views and values were mixed with the discoveries of unrealistic to " ordinary external logic," like hidden history of "local politics" or even mystical beliefs or even " non- modern values" (like cost).

These Refined "Cards of Strategic *Development Assumptions*" will then be the basis tools for the more focused Community Planning Action Plans.

With this information, the Community Facilitator can then conduct an array of meetings (even meeting to set meetings) towards these "Community Planning Sessions" often called "Community Discussion Together" sessions.) Usually starting with the Community Leaders then with large groups of representation and then smaller groups with different interest focus to solve problems.

The Community Planning Sessions were often prepared through the Community Facilitators gaming simulation exercises: especially of note were the preparation methods/strategy (and "tricks) to guard against the "Santa Claus Syndrome"/the "Begging Syndrome" and the "Demanding Syndrome." Instead the overall Community Planning were with the strategy to shift: "Who NEEDS Who." Or the game where the *"COMMUNITY NEEDS the Government"* instead of the "Government Needs the Community." These strategies are very often the vital approach to enable to solve the problem.

Each specific CASE (Sub case/problems) then have its own "urban game play" to meet its own particular context and idiosyncrasies

Some Samples of These VITAL "LOCAL COMMUNITY RESOURCES"

- *Willingness in sharing resources, trading, shifting resources (especially on land or place) in rebuilding/rearranging, reordering the slums.*

- *The willingness to resettle to another location.*

- *Willingness to self – demolish their own informal housing that are necessary for the rebuilding slums or being in the way of the infrastructure construction zone.*

- *The willingness to shift or improve jobs if it is inappropriate, polluting, or inefficient or causing negative inter business competitions.*

- *Willingness to guard against " new" illegal squatters.*

- *Willingness to protect and manage rivers and waterways zones from direct garbage dumping.*

- *Willingness to temporarily stay at temporal accommodation while the construction of redevelopment is underway.*

The overall process of "Community Planning" were interfaced with the so-called "COMMUNITY MICRO ACTION" packages. The Community will only participate when they see the efforts benefit them. If the Community Planning is "No (real concrete) action, Talks only" (NATO), the whole process will die. Deliberate MICRO ACTION Packages are then necessary in the Building Blocks of the total Development. It often starts small and continues to significant community actions, such as demolishing 150 homes by themselves.

Some Samples of Micro Community Actions

1. Community Based Garbage Management: "Recycling and compost Eco Station." Compost and Flower Pots for additional Income Generation.

2. Collective Soya bean waste treatment plant. Assisting local "people's industry" (Bird Cage production and marketing support.)

3. Community Paving (muddy) Alleys program via the community Paving block machine Tool Loan program.

4. Multi-purpose block making as a community business.

5. Building community collective Bathroom.

6. Community Measuring Land Together as part of the self-rearranging settlements process. Community land surveying together in and for land sharing together.

7. The total Re-building process for NEW HOUSING Resettlement Development through the Community Based Housing Scheme (Tri Use Loan Program: Land –Construction – Income Generating) a scheme where the Target Low Income Community will be their own Real Estate Developer.

Figure 7. Self-help housing.

Figure 8. Block making machine triggering community energy.

8. Worker's Housing Quarters Consolidation: Demolishing their own homes, moving houses, even re-partitioning "row labor quarters" to make things fit. Self-Help Rebuilding infill housing with Micro loan, block machine tool loan program.

9. Cleaning the River Together: "Gotong Royong"

A legend: Clean River Program

A Goddess prosperity being cursed and captured as a Dragon in the bottom of the deepest spot of this polluted river. Only if the Community can release her from captivity by cleaning the river, the spell can be freed to raise the Goddess to the surface.... then back to the "Golden Age."

10. Re-building an existing legal riverbank slum settlement, based on an "Eco Village Model." Community internal rearranging of the physical environment, rearranging legal but hazardous "informal housing" and "opening up" the way of the large World Bank's anti-flood river normalization project.

11. Rebuilding the Slum (West Bank Housing through Land Consolidation and Tri Use Loan Program).

12. Developing "People's Economic Street Hawker Center" from the income generating Loan Program mix.

13. Filling the Center with a Heart: Active people enabling improving local Art and Dances as a Community Income generating business. Music and local dance performance traditional food cooking (via local competition).

14. Preparing for an indigenous street fair tourism destination event (unfinished program).

All these Problem Solving Community Actions were like a WEB and slowly reinforcing itself to become a stronger and a more sustainable rebuild of the new "settlement."

All these cases were based on the "Participatory Community Design" approach, not only following Architectural or City Planning Design, but also its relation to designing the legal Land Re-certification, Area Management by the Users themselves.

Figure 9. Envisioned Housing.

Figure 10. The physical result.

CONCLUSION

There are no specific conclusions to note, but more of an experience learned.

This case study was an ongoing project. Even though it has been selected as UNDP's Best Practices and selected by the Ministry of Human Settlement as a main sample for national slum redevelopment programs, it still has a long way to go, with lots of problems – bureaucracy, politics, ego feuds, and corruption. Some examples of Community Planning Design deviation include: the designed "low-income housing" without clothes-drying facilities, the cancellation for urban "community gardening" micro project along the river bank, the change of having the traditional people's market become a "low income super market," and car access entering the low income neighborhood, all contributing to a danger of marginalization.

One of the worst of these problems was a "political, bureaucratic delay." A long awaited and promised disbursement of a housing loan forced group of the community to live in pig pens as their "temporary housing" for almost a year!

I hope, we can learn from each other, while making new friends in this "Pacific Rim" conference. The hope for all of us to support each other to make our efforts and work easier, especially in convincing the various City Managers/Executing Governments, Policy formulators, and also International Development Institutions, that "Community Planning" should not be an "experiment" any more but a "Common Practice" in urban (even rural) management of making our cities/environment a better and sustainable place to live (including the poor in most underdeveloped countries).

Especially directed to large International Development Agencies (a.o., WB, ADB, JBIG, etc.), I hope they can be more adaptive to this process and more able to support the "Community Planning" approach in the overall Development strategy — to realize the underlying missions/existence/purpose in "poverty alleviation/sustainable development."

Especially now, there is a need to rethink the larger Macro/Global Development issues that are a more apparent cause of mass unemployment, mass rural-urban migration, and mass environmental depletion all over the globe. These are often issues 'above the clouds' beyond comprehension (including for me) where 'below' on the ground, the poor are struggling with their lives, a day-to-day survival.

When the poor have nowhere to go and become a growing mass in despair, caused by these intangible and negative global forces, there tends to become a hidden push to terrorism. We can't just ignore this and pretend the global poor don't exist.

ENDNOTES

[1] It was indicated that mass evicted squatters usually just move to another place to squat to survive. A never-ending "solution?"

[2] Especially appropriate and logistically needed if the City's majority population is low income.

[3] One of a medium size city in, Solo, Central Java (Population of about 500.000 people in 1997).

[4] Review a "Guided Land Development Method" (GLD) which is also,

a preventive land and urban development program from unplanned growth that requires "Community Planning" as a key factor for its implementation.

Antonio Risianto is Team Leader SSUDP Mojosongo Development Consultants: To add, this assignment was in large part done by a very dedicated team of friends and unforgettable student volunteers. Among others, Mr. Rossario, Mr. Yamto, Mr. Bahrul, Mr. Adir, Mr. Bagyo, Mr. Widi, Andi Sul, Ambo and Andi Siswanto (Pt Wiswahkarman) and lots of advice / support from Mr. Suhadi (ex World Bank), Sri Probo (USAID), Parwoto (World Bank), George Soraya (World Bank), Mr. Tjahyono Rahardjo (Univ. Sugiopranoto), Tonny S. (from the Local Provincial Government), Prof. Hassan Poerbo (ITB), Thanks to Prof. R. Geothert, MIT, Prof. Chris Alexander / Prof. Sara Ishikawa, teaching me "the magic of Pattern Language" at UC Berkeley, Prof. Richard Meier: Urban Game Simulation, at UC Berkeley, who all are leaders and have struggled for this "Community Planning/Participation approach together. Without them, Mojosongo wouldn't even have a chance to be redeveloped.

Figure 11. The center becoming a market: modernization?

SOCIAL ORGANIZATION IN THE SERVICE OF IMPROVING LIVING STANDARDS
The Valle del Yaqui Project

Sergio Palleroni

ABSTRACT

The Yaqui of the Valle del Yaqui (Valley of the Yaqui) in the Sonoran Desert, in the State of Sonora Mexico, are one of the more culturally isolated groups in all of Mexico. Living in the midst of one of the economic "boom" states of the country, and only a few hours drive from the US states of Arizona and California, their economic and social situation nonetheless has deteriorated as a consequence of the economic growth of the surrounding region. Deprived of their traditional hunter/gatherer migratory patterns by the growth of large scale agriculture for the US marketplace, the Yaqui Indians have, for the most part, seen their standard of living and their social situation dramatically deteriorate. In response, a highly innovative Sonora wide public / private initiative has emerged, that, though founded to provide appropriate housing to the Yaqui, is also addressing their economic and social situation. PROVAY, the Comite de Promocion Social del Valle del Yaqui (the Committee for the Promotion of the Social Development of the Valley of the Yaqui), has created a populist campaign of the Yaqui, and non-Yaqui population, with collaboration from business, industry, and social organizations working in the valley. Using models developed in Asia of community-based social banks, and some of the most innovative technologies currently being proposed for strawbale building, the project has been able to help the Yaqui build their own economic and social capacity while attracting significant international funding (e.g. Inter-American Bank) that is acting in service of the projects priorities. This paper will explore, from the perspective of the foundation and development work, the ways in which this model was implemented and has successfully allowed the Yaqui to maintain their cultural/social values while developing their capacity to survive in this region that is rapidly transforming economically and socially.

PRACTICAL NPO ACTIVITIES CORRESPONDING TO THE SOCIAL AND DEMOGRAPHIC CHANGE IN A SUBURBAN COMMUNITY

Yuko Hamasaki

ABSTRACT

The fundamental factors for cultivating well-being in a changing suburban community will be discussed through NPO "Egao" ('Egao' means 'a smiling face' in Japanese) which was established in a typical residential town in Japan. Some proactive residents who have lived in this town since 1965 established the NPO Egao after continuous participatory activities to improve their community. An old terrace house that used to be used by small neighborhood shops was converted into an NPO office. The main functions are the private day service center for the elderly, the child support center with a library, and the culture center. The characteristic points are; 1) Informal support for the elderly to compensate for the lack of institutional public services for the elderly who wish to live at home. NPO Egao supports the caregivers as well as the elderly through counseling, and offers opportunities for children or spouses to accompany their elderly family members. 2) A well-coordinated network with Takurosho (a community-based multi-functional facility for people with dementia) helps to provide effective care for the first stage of dementia. 3) Recently, there are increasing cases in which old parents who have lived alone in rural areas are invited to live in their child's home, or nearby. However, many of these newcomers experience transfer-shock. In these cases, NPO Egao functions as a mediator to introduce them to new friends in the community. 4) The library provides lending services and a reading class for small children and lectures for parents. 5) NPO Egao is carrying out informal and flexible services that aim to accomplish community building instead of a conventional welfare service. Nowadays, social problems range from care for the elderly to family relations. The practical activities of NPO Egao and the findings from them present the potential for a community solution.

INTRODUCTION

Needless to say, one of the biggest social problems in Japan is the unbalanced population ratio resulting from the combination of the rapidly increasing number of senior citizens and the decreasing number of youth. The field of welfare study is expanding widely and deeply with growing complicated problems influenced by recession, or family problems such as domestic violence, child abuse, etc. From this background, many specialists point out the importance of neighborhood relationship or community power for problem solving.

On the other hand, recently many volunteer groups have established NPOs (Non-Profit Organizations) for the purpose of compensating for insufficient public services, or developing community-based activities according to their missions. It may be true that NPO is expected to be a new force for the solution of community problems, which are one reflection of social circumstances.

In this paper, we discuss the case study of an NPO, "Egao," that was established by neighborhood volunteers to accomplish their mission: the cultivation of well-being in their suburban community. The mission statement of NPO Egao is, "We will carry out neighborhood building (Machizukuri) in the aim of establishing a community in which all residents, from the elderly down, will be able to live affluent lives and feel relieved. We will contribute to the improvement of the social well-being of the community as a whole. In order to accomplish this goal, we will implement various projects concerning welfare and culture for all residents, including children and the elderly, through collaborative work and mutual understanding."

This writer is a member of the board of directors for NPO Egao and has worked with these residents for 8 years as a researcher, as well as a volunteer. In this paper, various aspects of NPO Egao are described with the insight obtained through real experience as a co-worker, and at the same time analyzed objectively from the standpoint of a researcher.

CHARACTERISTICS OF THE RESIDENTS

NPO "Egao" was established in 2000 after 35 years of continuous participatory activities aimed at the improvement of the quality of life in neighborhoods. The direct motivation was the desire to build a nursing home complex in their neighborhood, though their attempts to do so failed. However, their concept of community care remained strong, and eventually became NPO "Egao." The town called Nagazumi was developed as the first suburban residential town in Fukuoka. From the cultural point of view, it is famous as the birthplace of the nationwide theatrical circle "Kodomo-gekijyo," which provides cultural richness and a healthy spirit to children.

The core members of NPO Egao have always been pro-active about building a better community. Their attitude is summarized by the fact that they transferred their instinctive desires into social actions. Those 39 years are divided into 3 periods according to the character of their activities, following their life stage and social background.

This analysis is summarized in the diagram below.

Period	1965-1980s	1985-1990s	2000-2004
Life stage	Childcare	Caregivers of parents	Aging themselves
Object	Theatrical circle	Nursing facilities	NPO
Concern	Education	Social assets	Informal service
Product	Human network	Common values	Social capital

THE DISTINCTIVE POINTS OF NPO "EGAO"

When we examine the intermediary role of NPO Egao from an analytical point of view, they connect two different (sometimes opposite) characters of objects.

A) Formal - Informal

In general, one of the most important functions of an NPO is filling the void between the public and private sectors to accomplish a purpose. Among welfare systems, this model is more realistic than most others. Although well-being should exist primarily in people's minds, we see many gaps between needs and welfare services. The service system works on the basis of contracts in both the public and private sectors, which produces a frame of limitations. On the other hand, users' needs in their daily lives have no borders and cover a wide range. When we face this reality, we see that NPOs can play an important role in providing various services in a flexible manner, and responding to each need.

In Japan, after implementing the long-term care insurance system, the situation of care for the elderly has dramatically changed. This new system has many useful aspects. However, there exist some problems, such as potentially prohibitive costs for low-income people, limitations and regulations concerning home-helpers' work, and the inadequacy of dementia certification, etc.

The fact that NPO Egao offers informal services for people with dementia, and is coordinated with the formal special service of Takurosho, which is a community-based multi-functional facility for dementia, is especially practical.

For example, one couple moved to Nagazumi from an island to live near their daughter's family. The husband had dementia and the wife had been suffering from the burden of caring for him. The problems become heavier because they had no acquaintances in the community. The daughter consulted with the staff, and NPO Egao worked to make links to the community for the couple. According to the formal service system, only the client may use the service, whereas, in this case, both the client and the caregiver started to attend the informal day service. The flexibility and hospitality of allowing caregivers to come along is a characteristic aspect of the day service provided by "Egao," a private service managed by volunteers. After a while, the husband started to use the Takurosho's special day care, his condition remarkably improved. As the couple became familiar with the community, the wife gradually became more optimistic about her own life. In other words, community-care networking between formal and informal services produced therapeutic results for people with dementia and improved the couple's quality of life.

B) Family - Facility (home care - institutional care)

Most people want to live out their lives at home. However, the accomplishment of this desire is not easy for several reasons, such as limitations of caregivers or family relations. In Nagazumi, there are two kinds of facilities, which are well coordinated with NPO Egao to support families. One is a nursing home complex with assisted-living and the other is Takurosho.

For example, one user of NPO Egao, a 98 year-old lady who lives in assisted-living, is a very independent person. When the woman's daughter learned of her mother's cancer, she wanted her mother to maintain the same conditions as long as possible. So, the NPO Egao staff coordinated a conference meeting with two facilities and families. As a result, the lady was allowed to live in the same assisted-living situation. In similar cases, most elderly people leave assisted-living and move to a hospital. In addition, nowadays she uses the NPO Egao day service with the support of her daughter. Also, Takurosho accepts the role of assisting NPO Egao and providing help in emergencies. Concerning those people who want to stay at home or in assisted-living in the same community, NPO Egao and Takurosho consult with their families about a supportive care system.

C) Newcomers - Old neighborhoods

Fukuoka is the most urbanized city in Kyushu, and the center of business, local politics, merchandise, education and culture. Many of the younger generations from peripheral rural towns have established new families in Fukuoka. As a result, old parents have had to stay by themselves. Recently, we have observed the phenomenon of those elderly people moving to Fukuoka to live nearby their children and families. However, it is very difficult for the older generation to become accustomed to urban life. In addition, they cannot be optimistic about making new friends in the town. Although the community center provides cultural circles for the old to encourage social activities, newcomers often hesitate to get involved in established associations. Sometimes this transfer shock causes another family problems. In order to solve these problems, NPO Egao welcomes newcomers in their day services and connects them to the old members of the neighborhood. Once the newcomers feel the friendship of people from the same generation, they increase in vitality and establish new lives little by little. NPO Egao, based on the community and open to everybody, is able to fulfill this intermediary role.

D) Children - Elderly

One of the unique intergenerational programs at NPO Egao is the combination of a cooking class for children and eating together with the elderly. In this case, the teachers are elderly people who are healthy and active, while those who are over 80 years old and need more care are guests. Children learn how to cook traditional Japanese meals, which their mothers no longer cook, and also experience hospitality. As most families are nuclear families, children often do not have a chance to communicate with the older generation. This event is a very worthwhile experience for the children. On the other hand, the elderly people feel the happiness of social activities with children. At the same time, they are satisfied by the perception that they are included in the neighborhood activities.

The story telling parties for the elderly are popular among the participants. Although this is not a collaborative intergenerational activity, the idea comes from a unique organization targeted at both children and the elderly. Usually, story telling is common for small children who cannot read well. The old whose poor eyesight inhibits their reading pleasure are also comfortable listening to stories. One excellent aspect of story telling for the elderly is that they can share their feelings on the stories with friends in the circle.

A STUDY OF NPO EGAO IN TERMS OF STRENGTHENING THE FABRIC OF THE COMMUNITY

The following are the explanations of Figure 1.[1]

NPO Egao is an important organization for strengthening the community fabric, which will create a new community context. Although NPO Egao is a newborn organization, the indigenous neighborhood has made it a resident-driven, active body. When we examine the meaning of NPO Egao in the community from an historical point of view, the following observations are seen in terms of social background, function of buildings and demographic change.

When people moved to the new suburb, Nagazumi, from surrounding areas, they were mostly nuclear families (typically composed of parents and 2 children). Most of the homeowners

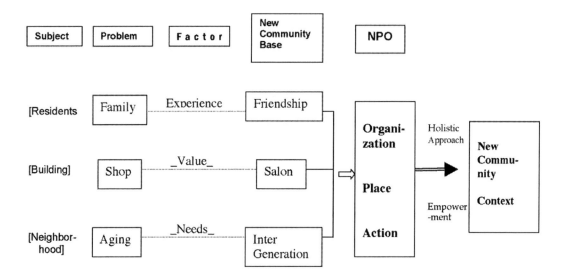

Figure 1. Diagram of relations and the flow to make components of NPO and future development.

were white-collar, salaried workers. Their children graduated from university and they did not return to the community after obtaining jobs. Only the old parents stayed in the community, and the parent-child tie has become weaker. As a result, friendship became more important than family relations for making safety networks for themselves.

NPO Egao's building is an old two-story terrace house composed of 3 parts. The first floor of it used to be used as a meat shop, cheap sweets and drinks shop and a barbershop. When supermarkets opened new stores in the community, these small shops experienced difficulties with management. After the shops closed they were just empty buildings for a while. The owner has a good understanding of the NPO's mission and lends it to them for cheap rent. Now, the first floor is a day service center and a community restaurant, and the second floor is a library for children and a culture room.

In order to see the building's change of function in regard to people's sense of value, we may refer to the fact that in general people recently prefer "mental satisfaction" to "possession of goods." When shops occupied the building, money and goods were the subject of exchange. Now, mutual communication and human contact are the main contents of the activities. The community restaurant sells meals and drinks, but people come there first to communicate with other customers, and second to eat. In this way it is a kind of salon for social exchange.

As mentioned before, when the Nagazumi community started, the residents were of similar family composition, and the average homeowner's age was from 35 to 45. Now, 39 years later, most of them are over 70 years old.

In order to empower these elderly groups, as well as the community itself, NPO Egao is making efforts to provide opportunities for intergenerational activities. Formal welfare services are officially only for the older generation. However, NPO recognizes intergenerational needs. In other words, the older generation should be included in the whole community as an independent group. From this approach, they get energy through exchanging their feelings among other generations, and then they find well-being from inside themselves.

Other important activities connecting different generations are held in the Egao library. Elementary school children may drop in at the library on their way home every Wednesday to read or borrow books. Small children under 6-years-old come with their mothers and join the story telling class. Also, there is a class for mothers to learn the techniques of story telling. Children and mothers meet in these occasions and gradually make friends.

According to the above study, the new community base is composed of friends (friendship), salon (mutual communication) and intergenerational activities.

NPO Egao provides "organization," "place" and "action" for future development. NPO Egao stemmed from the volunteer-work of residents, and the staff is organizing many activities to develop friendship and collaborative works in the community. This organizational role covers not only activities within the NPO but also in the Nagazumi community as a whole.

"Place" is a key factor for expanding good relationships in the neighborhood. In this case, "place" does not only mean physical space. People accumulate experiences and emotional memories of the "place," and it can foster the mutual trust, the sharing of common values and happiness through face-to-face interaction.

In the case of evaluating NPO Egao from the viewpoint of the establishing process, it can be said that it is basically the product of many years of social action. They continue to take further actions to solve occurring problems and to implement their mission.

Nowadays in Japan, many NPOs work as welfare offices for long-term insurance systems for the elderly, while NPO Egao implements distinct programs aiming at community building, and focusing on all generations' needs. These actions create momentum among the residents that will lead to community solutions.

When NPO Egao develops social actions, it takes a holistic approach to solving community problems. The fact that each phase is built on collaborative work reinforces the fabric of community context. In other words, it is an empowerment process.

In light of all the processes mentioned above, it follows that a new community context will be produced.

CONCLUSION

Through the case study of NPO Egao, the following characteristic points have been identified as important factors for the cultivation of environmental well-being in changing suburban communities.

• Start from awareness

Problems often exist behind small aspects of daily life. The question is whether or not people are aware of the fact that small problems often arise from deeper problems. The staff of NPO Egao have sharp observant eyes. Starting from awareness, the second point is how to interpret private matters as a part of the community's problems. As NPO Egao is a kind of community salon, there are lots of opportunities for information exchange. Even through simple chatting or gossip, sometimes realistic problems can be discovered.

• Holistic and open approach

Social problems have various complicated aspects. In order to reach the fundamental issue, the approach should be holistic. One of the catch-phrases of NPO Egao is "we are open for everyone." This describes their attitude of approach to the neighborhood as well as their hospitality.

• Solve the problem step by step

When we face problems, a superficial understanding will result in failure. In the staff meetings of NPO Egao, we discuss problems in detail and exchange opinions from diversified viewpoints. The solution process goes step by step, and takes time. Social problems concerning care for the elderly often relate to family problems. Understanding the background crucial for solving the problems requires detailed consideration.

• Accumulate experiences

Through continuous activities to achieve their aspirations, the staff has realized the value of social action. Events are accumulated as experience, as well as community assets. The realization that they could overcome the problems at hand becomes their confidence, and generates the energy to take a step forward. Starting from the theatrical circle activities for children, all experiences have been accumulated and added to the practices of NPO Egao.

• Evaluate in terms of people's minds

When it is time to make decisions the priority of the criteria becomes a key factor. One common understanding of NPO Egao is that the most important criterion should be in people's minds. How the people concerned accept the matter should be discussed both at the first and last phases of decision-making.

NPO Egao exists in the midst of continuous social change in the neighborhood. It always pays attention to the community assets and the characteristic background of Nagazumi. Their activities are woven into the community context and strengthen the human network.

In the future, there might be some unexpected social problem in the community. Even in that case, the five points mentioned above will be applicable, possibly with some modification. Each case will add to the unique growth and evolution of NPO Egao.

I would like to extend this study as a researcher as well as a practitioner of community building among residents.

ENDNOTES

[1] Notes to Figure 2: 1) In order to analyze the changing process, the residents, building and neighborhoods are placed as subjects in this study. 2) Social problems have occurred in the field of family relations (Family), commercial environment (Shop), and population composition Aging. 3) In the process of establishing NPO, residents have been influenced by some factors, such as their experience, a sense of value and social needs.

TOP-DOWN OR BOTTOM-UP PARTICIPATION?
Exploring the Nexus of Power, Culture and Revitalization in a Public Housing Community

Lynne C. Manzo

ABSTRACT

Since 1993, public housing authorities across the country have been involved in efforts to revitalize over 100,000 units of public housing through a competitive grants program called HOPE VI (Housing Opportunities for People Everywhere). This program, administered by the US Department of Housing and Urban Development (HUD), was created to "eradicate severely distressed public housing."[1] Essentially, the goal of the program is to replace dilapidated housing with new units, and to disperse pockets of poverty by creating mixed-income communities. This requires the demolition of existing on-site housing, the development of a new master plan and the construction of a new housing development. Because of the intention to create a mixed-income community, this also means a net loss of public housing units on site. Notably, HUD has also mandated that the redevelopment of HOPE VI communities involve the participation of current residents and the broader community in which the site is situated. While this is an important requirement, it creates a tension between exclusion and inclusion, as residents are involuntarily displaced, yet their input is sought through the master planning and relocation process. This paper focuses on a particular HOPE VI site on the southwestern edge of Seattle, Washington in order to understand the unique dynamics of a community in transition, specifically those related to power, culture and participation. This site, known as Park Lake Homes, is comprised of 569 units that house an extraordinarily diverse population. There are over 35 different languages spoken by residents, although Cambodian, Vietnamese, Somali and Arabic predominate. Many residents are refugees from their home countries. The fact that the community is so ethnically diverse, and composed of public housing residents who are among the poorest and most vulnerable of American households,[2] only adds to the complexity of the dynamics within this community. Through observations of a series of public meetings and community design workshops, as well as interviews with residents, the early phase of the redevelopment process is examined to ascertain the extent and nature of participation, and to shed light on residents' experiences and opinions of the process. In doing so, this research will compare efforts to garner participation in the redevelopment process with people's lived experiences. Implications for empowerment, cross-cultural communication and what constitutes positive community change will also be addressed.

ENDNOTES

[1] United States Department of Housing and Urban Development. (Oct. 21, 2003). Notice of Funding Availability for Revitalization of Severely Distressed Public Housing.

[2] Housing Research Foundation (2001).

9

ARTivism

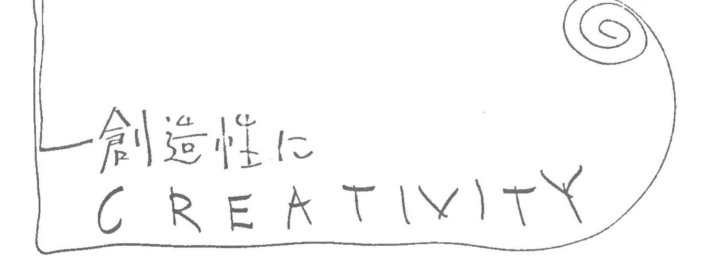

創造性に
CREATIVITY

IDENTITY POLITICS AND COMMUNITY ARTIVISM
A Strategic Arts Project of Cultural Landscape Conservation at Treasure Hill, Taipei

Min Jay Kang

ABSTRACT

Artivism is a conscious combination of art and activism, and is adopted to demonstrate a more radical approach and value-loaded attitude to engage in social-spatial issues through arts projects. Artivism is also an intentional attempt to bring about the community and environmental concerns and collaborate with the participant subjects to precipitate the transformation of certain social meaning. In the case of the Treasure Hill settlement in Taipei, a series of planned community artivists projects (GAPP, Global Artivists Participation Projects) were strategically initiated to confront difficult urban planning and cultural landscape conservation issues. This paper will review the processes and outcomes of GAPP from both the project director's insider perspective and from the community's evaluation of how individual daily-lives in a pre-modern, pre-planned setting are inevitably influenced by waves of artivists movement. From rags to tags, from squatter movement to institutionalized artists-in-residency program, will Treasure Hill evolve into an obsolescent urban settlement of organic nature or a progressive urban planning model of creative sustainability? This paper will not only be a case study on artivism, but also an interface of more dynamic discussions on an on-going process of landscape conservation which will eventually affect the future of many residents of a marginal, heterogeneous community.

THE FLUIDITY OF PLACE IDENTITY

Place identity refers to two different but interrelated concepts. It reflects certain distinguishable, self-manifested idiosyncrasies of a place in terms of its spatial form; yet it also implies how cultural subjects identify with a particular place through daily practices or committed discourses. The recognizable spatial features connect directly with the collective memory and the cognitive maps of the cultural subjects; while their identifications with a place further inscribe meanings to and reinforce personal attachments with the cultural landscapes and spatial narratives of the place. The place-bound identity varies in scales: it can be as expansive as a country (which is oftentimes imagined), or as intimate as a store (a gay bookstore is a reincarnation of a social subgroup's collective identifications and a corner grocery store may represent a locus of tacit identifications of a neighborhood). It can strengthen the internal cohesion of a finite area or converge the intercommunication network of a dispersive social community into a symbolic place as a substantial support of identity politics (Calhoun, 1994; Pile &Thrift, 1995; Keith & Pile, 1993).

The significance of place identity of the local is stressed in many theories and discourses of planning, architecture, human geography, and landscape studies, especially those which follow the phenomenological approaches (Relph, 1976; Seamon, 1979; Warf, 1986) and Heidegger's philosophy of place and dwelling (*domus*) (Norberg-Schulz, 1988). Place identity, accordingly, is expected to counter the place-annihilating forces of industrial modernism and the transnational flow of capitalism. The processes of rapid urbanization and homogenizing globalization are criticized as unyielding threats to the meaningful local and its associated values, while place identity indicates a type of resistance against such threats through conscious community empowerment, re-established grassroots confidence, and conservation of the vernacular authenticity.

The Heideggerian discourses of place identity meet serious backfire from the post-structuralist dialectics on differences, complexity, urbanity, and mimesis (Jacobs, 2002; Jameson, 1994; Girard, 1995). Heidegger's personal association with the Nazi identity and place aesthetics exposes a moral doctrine veiled under the façade of strong place identity, which is also exclusive, defensive, anachronistically nostalgic, and static (Leach, 2002). On the other hand, the romanticized images of the vernacular can be quickly subsumed by the post-modern kitsch and the culture industry to manipulate a sense of historical and local legitimacy (Ellin, 1995). Place identity sometimes becomes a cultural tool of capitalist leisure consumption, penduluming between its original strategic position of resistance and a new recreational potential of middle-class aesthetics. The uprising community empowerment voices echo the political call of place identity, yet the pervasive flow of tourism easily offsets the grassroots struggle for autonomy and, in the milieu of complex urbanity, the emphasis on a community's common consensus can lead to a bumptious tribalism if the concomitant individual differences and diversity of urban living are overlooked. The city, in a crude way, challenges exactly the necessity of place identity since the anonymous freedom of individual citizens (therefore, dissolving identity rather than forging identity) is regarded as an indispensable urban psyche.

The argument of identity through consumption and mimesis, instead of articulate place narrative and meaning interpretation, augments another debatable dimension to the discourse of place identity. The studies of mass culture, urban culture, and cult, heavily influenced by the Baudrillardian analysis of consumption and not restrained by the Marxist moralistic ideologies, confront different realities of identity tempered by cultural propaganda, image anesthetics, media network, internet communication, gender politics, material desire and fetishism (Baudrillard, 1994; Butler, 1997). These types of identity induced by mimesis and image industry weaken the bond of place identity, but re-affirm the positive draw of a global city (still an identifiable 'place'). Magnified by the critical issues of identity politics and the ambiguous sense of constantly changing urban reality, place identity no longer serves the static purpose of dichotomizing place from placelessness (of modern urban landscape); rather, it's a dynamic and shifting concept which contextualizes cultural subjects' physical/psychological experiences and imagination with particular places.

The recognizable traits of place identity often symbolize collective rootedness; however, the internal nuances within bounded cultural subjects or between sub-divided places, or certain individuals' up-root/rootless intentions in a cultural group, perform subtler patterns of distinction among the identified commonness. *Differences* and *others* thereby mirror the frailty of place identity from a critical distance (Nancy, 1991). For example, a marginal squatter settlement of heterogeneous minorities located at the edge of a city, disempowered and chaotic at first glance, exhibits an unapologetic defiance against the place identity of the city as a whole as well as against the concept of an allied community. Such a place of disregard can simply be itself or be turned into a place of resistance. Yet, resistance itself does not necessarily lead to an organized community or a better place identity since, essentially, the squatter settlement has never been the outcome of a conscious plan or act. It is thus debatable that fostering place identity in a place like this should aspire to upgrading its organic charm or maintaining its critical stance.

Castells (1997) suggests to divide the form of identity into three categories: *legitimizing identity* forged by dominant social institutions; *resistance identity* fending from an oppressed position to counter the domination logic; and *project identity* - through which cultural subjects re-establish their social position to strive for a reform of social structure. Place identity operates across all three types, but is more critical of the ideological manipulation of *legitimizing identity* and of the reactionary tribalism of *resistance identity*. Place identity is doubtless territorial, but it goes further to summon "a progressive sense of place" (as a repudiation to a nostalgic sense of place, Massey, 1993) with an emphasis on the formation of subjects and project identity. However correct and appealing it seems,

a place-project identity still appears elusive and jargonized if not realized in reality. As an agent to activate this concept, community artivism comes to the fore.

THE POLEMICS OF COMMUNITY ARTIVISM

Artivism is a conscious combination of art and activism, and is adopted to demonstrate a more radical approach and value-loaded attitude to engage in social-spatial issues through art projects. *Artivism* is also an intentional attempt to bring about the community and environmental concerns and collaborate with the participant subjects to precipitate the transformation of certain social meaning. Artivism, from this regard, seems to be a creative and constructive tool to serve the social purposes of activism or to build place identity from the bottom up. Yet artivism is also self-reflexive and disinclined to take things for granted. The place-specific artivism project can, therefore, problematize the legitimacy of punctuating fixed place identity and initiate a critical dialogue between art, activism, place, community, and cultural subjects.

The polemics of involving direct community participation in the process of making public art seem particularly acute while art confronting the organic (or unorganized) grassroots community. Whether art uses the community as the backdrop or as indispensable subjects; or whether community participation enhances or diminishes the autonomy of art often triggers vehement debates on both sides of community empowerment and public art; and the skeptics might as well question the necessity of art in a perceived mundane community on such a basis. Yet the effect of art in strengthening community identity and inducing creative social transformation is relatively palpable, compared with public discussions and calculated actions. Art, if not deliberately offensive, can also be liberating and fun to motivate a greater variety of community members who are otherwise perceived apathetic and voiceless by the power representatives. Community is, after all, not an undifferentiated mass of people; and art should not be expected to simply tend the need of an institutionalized whole.

Art can take many forms; while the aesthetic quality, refined craftsmanship, and creative expressions of art are commonly appreciated, the other aspects of art (particularly modern art) its independent nature, unrestrained freedom, personal opinions, and critical thinking, to name a few are understated, controversial, or even considered defiant and detrimental to a coherent society. The liberal spirit of art does not follow traditional values and morals stereotypically associated with grassroots communities. The outsider artists sometimes set back a necessary distance from the community to secure a broader perspective while representing the community through their works. The double-edged blade of art in a community thus cuts both sides: it is a creative force to inspire, and in the meanwhile, an aggressive intervention to disturb the daily-life patterns of an ordinary community.

Comparing with general public art or installing art in a community, the concept of community artivism focuses less on artists and artworks than the community itself. The implication of activism also indicates that the involved community is, to some degree, in certain condition of needing advocacy support and direct mobilization. Community artivism inevitably turns strategic from this perspective. It is then crucial to specify issues arising from that certain condition and the characteristics of the particular community (*rural* or *urban* community, urban *fenced* community or urban *fringe* community, *historical* community or *squatter* settlement) to measure the best-fit actions/projects for the community be it linked to landscape conservation or community empowerment or environmental protest. With this understanding, community artivism has to construct an action scenario and a local narrative from within; thus, even critical or controversial art projects can hardly disrespect the community in the name of art. But still, the place-bound community artivism needs to further explore the possible solutions for the following questions:

- How does community artivism, acting *in situ* to given social and landscape values, reinforce the autonomous creativity of collective and independent cultural subjects without relegating the creative processes to condescending services for the functional need of the community?

- How can an outsider's keen observation and perceptive sensitivity of human-environment relations be transformed into creative forms of representation that also includes the experiences and stories of the implicated community?

- Can artivism become a myth-making tool to help community individuals identify with their living environment and endow meaning to the associated landscape through creative processes?

- How does artivism translate community stories and landscape narratives into sensible forms, and how do such forms manifest community qualities as well as its internal heterogeneity?

- Can artivism deal with the fear and desire of the community individuals as well as the community psyche as a whole?

- How can artivism be transcended from reactionary purposes to creative initiatives for place identity?

The Power of Place Studio at UCLA demonstrated an exemplary mechanism of initiative community artivism through the public history workshop, which gathered narrative materials from community participatory story-telling process for an inventive art project (Hayden, 1995). It not only represented the subaltern life-force of urban plebeians via the interpretations of paintings, books, and sculptures; but also transformed a line of cold wall in a commercial area into a moving profile of an Afro-American woman's life history. For the community residents who had participated in the workshop or simply passed by, reading the completed art project was like looking back at themselves and the ordinary scenes of their everyday lives etched into the realm of art. Through the reflexive gaze of art, the power of identity brought forth a brand-new and progressive sense of place.

THE 2003 TREASURE HILL GAPP (GLOBAL ARTIVISTS PARTICIPATION PROJECTS)

To further elaborate on the relationship between community artivism and place identity, the 2003 GAPP at the Treasure Hill settlement, located in a zoned-parkland of Taipei City, contributed first-hand observations and experiences to the related discourses with a wide range of community actions and art projects. Originally initiated to confront difficult urban planning and cultural landscape conservation issues of the riverside squatter village, the 2003 GAPP witnessed the creative power of art as well as the heightened tension between the community and art.[1] When the highly political and calculated tactics of conservation persuaded the city government to recognize the settlement's artistic potentials for public good and the original squatters as an integral part of the unique and artistic milieu, the settlement became officially perceived as an artists-in-residency setting for struggling poor artists. Yet the residency status of the squatters was far from secure. It would have to go through extremely uncertain and long processes of rezoning and historical heritage review to make the squatter residency and their self-help buildings legal, and it was hardly an easy task to persuade both the urban planning committee and historical heritage committee that conservation of this cultural landscape and the community did not diminish the public value of Treasure Hill's existing land use as a public park.

To argue the legitimacy of replacing the green park with an artistic village was controversial, to advocate a social welfare program within the artistic village to preserve the social network of the Treasure Hill community was an even more challenging idea. But first of all, Treasure Hill had to be seen and its value appreciated by the general public to precipitate the necessary legal procedure of rezoning. One of the tacit missions for the 2003 GAPP, therefore, was to raise Treasure Hill's publicity and public support through an art program. But the medium exposure also caused disturbing consequences in the community's low-key lifestyle. Art was never a familiar term at Treasure Hill before, however, the "artless" community was obliged to participate in art projects or to make contact with art in their daily routines during the 2003 GAPP to boost the opportunity of being exempt from the green bulldozers of the Park and Recreation Department. Art might be a ticket to permanent residency, practically speaking.

Yet the close encounter with art, for the community participants, did have some unexpected effects inspired or perturbed, but more than activism's political purposes or an exchange of participation for residency on their relationship with the city, the community, the environment, and themselves. Even though the overall plan for GAPP attempted to attenuate the impact of high-concept and avant-garde art on the extant community and to get as much participation from the community as possible, the insistence of maintaining the artivists' autonomy did leave indelible traces on the community and the fragile landscape. In a way, the Treasure Hill community would never be able to return to its innocent age of being an organic settlement at large once its land ownership was reclaimed by the government and zoned for park use in an urban system. The crisis of being institutionalized was impending, and it was only a matter of *how* it would be managed in the future. Art programs stood out as one of many options.

From rags to tags, from squatter movement to an institutionalized artists-in-residency program, will Treasure Hill become an obsolescent urban settlement of organic nature or a progressive urban planning model of creative sustainability? The following description of the 2003 GAPP is based on a project director's subjective perspective, and represents only a portion of the entire programmed event. Meanwhile, a far more complicated planning process for the conservation and restoration of the Treasure Hill settlement and its adjacent landscape, thanks to the direct feedback from the GAPP experiment, is trying to lay out a feasible management program for the Treasure Hill Co-living Artsville.[2] Perhaps, it's not art itself but the intensity of art implemented within a short span of time that really affects the squatter community, and that evaluation should not be overlooked.

THE OTHER HOME-LAND THEME

Before there was GAPP, the Treasure Hill New Discovery Film Festival programmed in the 2002 Taipei International Arts Festival had put Treasure Hill on the city's art map. The community was thereafter transformed from the setting for multiple filming locations into the scene for cinema arts happenings. The Treasure Hill Family Cinema Club, informally organized by graduate students at National Taiwan University Graduate Institute of Building and Planning and community members, screens popular and alternative films - from propagandist military films to art-house documentary films - every Wednesday at the re-painted white wall of a defunct building left blank after the large-scale demolition in 2001. The Club has tacitly become a new community tradition, simply by showing films at regular hours at a ruins-turned-plaza to draw

residents out of their living rooms to gather for a weekly event at a new public arena.

The 2003 GAPP further expanded the collaboration experiment between the community and the artivists by ushering in artists and activists from all over the world to initiate creative artivist programs related to landscape and settlement conservation. The 2003 overarching theme was designated "the Other Home-Land" a dialectic between the social and cultural others and their transitional shelters into the alternative homeland, as well as a reflection of the collective identity of many immigrants in the community from different eras and native lands - inviting global artivists to probe into the historical roots, marginal status, current reality, ecological aspects, and subconscious psyche of the Treasure Hill settlement.

The lineup for the 2003 GAPP included: the multi-dimensionsional landscape art project *Organic Layer Taipei*, the collaborative lomography project *Asia 108 and the Street Gallery of Treasure Hill Flood Images*, the *Ethnography and Choreography Film Festival* at the Treasure Hill outdoor cinema plaza, the 3-week 3-group environmental theatre and workshop series *Happening*, the field experimental actions and international forum of *Ecological Homeland and Micro-climate Architecture*, the subtle *Garden Portraits* project, the international *Creative Sustainability and Self-help Center* participatory workshops and forum, the domestic *Artists-in-Residency Program* and *the Treasure Hill Tea +Photo*, and the paper-pulp based landscape art project *Blue River*. The interested artivists came from Finland, Japan, Germany, Spain, the US, Indonesia, Singapore, Malaysia, and other regions of Taiwan to participate in the experimental event. Unfortunately due to the constraints of time, budget, resources, and artivists' own schedules, very few of them could stay more than a month to really blend in or establish long-term relationships with the community. Their proposals and actions had to rely on the second-hand descriptions of Treasure Hill and their brief observations and perceptions about the site. However, they all seemed to find inspiration in the uncommon setting and context of Treasure Hill which, unlike a planned artistic village composed only of artists, was blunt, honest, real, unpretentious, and socially critical. Some of the invited proposals were targeted toward community needs or planning purposes in other words, their artivist goals and expected outcomes were clear at the outset. Those projects will not be discussed in detail in this paper, though they are not less interesting or creative. The following chosen projects are relatively more ambiguous in setting objectives and open to artistic interpretation. Their scrupulous moves between artistic imagination and community activism became dynamic and unpredictable processes in exploring the meaning of place identity in the most unlikely place.

THE *ORGANIC LAYER TAIPEI* PROJECT

The Finnish architect-landscape artist Marco Casagrande proposed an artistic concept "the attic" for his project at Treasure Hill based on his keen observation, sensitive intuition, and personal social-ecological concern. The attic, excluded from specific use types in the Western dwelling unit, is a special space which takes in many less used yet not to be discarded objects of the family. The attic space does not follow any architectural order, and may not be considered necessary for a house. Yet some afternoons, one crawls up in the attic, withdraws a photo album from ten years ago in a corner and opens a diary from five years ago at that corner, memories well up as each page turns, then she realizes that the attic is the indispensable subconscious and soul of a house.[3] Casagrande argues that Treasure Hill is the Attic of Taipei edged out from the city's land-use plan. He found a used military belt and a family photo album in an abandoned house, and the memento stimulated a personal scale of association that connected his own memories with Treasure Hill's idiosyncratic social context. He thereby conducted a series of artivist projects to converse with Taipei's subconscious.

Casagrande and the participant students first put on black jumpsuits (costumes used for the underground city workers in Fritz Lang's classic film *Metropolis*) to dig out a huge amount of garbage to search for traces of community memories on one hand, while on the other hand, to directly help the community clean up the living environment. The deserted objects were displayed on the grassy lawn like a free flea market after general classification, and very soon many of them were picked up again by different community residents. Casagrande then applied some of the remnant materials for props and lighting to develop a nocturnal environmental theatre based on his concept of the attic. Treasure Hill in the daytime was so much taken for granted, but at night when the fire lit up, the subconscious of the city began to manifest itself through a mysterious and surreal unfolding.

Casagrande and 30 torch-holders dressed in black stood at various dark corners on the ruins façade (de)constructed by the bulldozers which demolished 38 riverfront dwelling units in 2001. Each empty window frame was lit up by flickering fire, altogether reflecting a bizarre yet tangible dreamscape. Casagrande disappeared into a dim chamber for a few minutes, and then came out through fire as a veteran running from the threat of war. His costume, symbolizing local veteran's casual dress code, came directly from the discarded materials cleaned out of the memory lane earlier. He sat on a broken chair for a while and took a sip of alcohol; then all of a sudden, he gushed out flame from his mouth like an anguished beast. Right above him, torches of fire descending from the top of the hill created a zigzag route which re-connected the upper-level dwellings with

the ground. That was the "flow of consciousness" meandering through different chambers of memory, and would be the pattern of a future stairway to be constructed in the second mode of the artivist project.

When the fire gradually faded, the bright spot-lights illuminated a series of larger-than-life photo portraits hanging on some of the remnant building walls images of the original residents who were cast out when their houses gave way to the claws of the "green bulldozers." At the beginning of the theatre, the first torch was lit by the 78-year-old neighborhood chief lady; the still-burning flame came back to her when the performance was over. She did not seem to understand what the theatre all meant, but she was affected as many community neighbors were mesmerized and claimed that Treasure Hill had never been more spectacular.

The second mode of the project conducted by Casagrande lasted 10 days. Extremely hard labor by the "underground city workers in black" and local residents removed many truck-loads of garbage; finished a series of stairways, platforms, and a bamboo bridge, connecting the community route with used construction materials; cultivated more than 20 plats of vegetable garden; constructed a view deck and a garden tool space under the trees; diverted slope drainage into a made-over ecological pond; and built an organic-form shelter out of bamboo stems for a future farmers' market. These impressive works were not only the outcome of an artist conception, but also evidence of what the community used to be and was to become, made possible by intensive collaboration between the artivist team and the community.

Casagrande and the collaborative team also completed four sets of "book-stop" made out of used steel scaffold, containing soil, native plants, photo albums, mementos, and swings to carry local residents. At the end of the second mode project, more than 100 community residents and participants, dressed in black "Who Cares Wins" T-shirts, pushed the wheeled book-stops from Treasure Hill to the "independent book-store streets" of the nearby Gong-guan area for a themed parade entitled "Transporting the Fire, Delivering the Books." Each resident and every story at Treasure Hill was regarded as a dust-sealed book, and when the book was re-opened and the light in the attic re-kindled, the city would be re-reading the 'brewed' scenario of the overlooked settlement. The community's grand march into the city brought in new energy and new perspective from the very margin. It was a bold claim to request the city to look straight at Treasure Hill, as well as a reflexive attempt to help the Treasure Hill community re-visualize themselves via the others' gaze.

The parade was itself a street theatre. The underground city workers in black jumpsuits put on white masks and red wide-brimmed leaf hats, carrying tall red banners and banging pots and basins along the way. AM radio tunes and buzz, often pressed to the ears of the senile veterans in the community when they paced around the neighborhood, was amplified through a loud speaker and accompanied by impromptu tenor saxophone to set the parade's eccentric and jazzy tone. Many curious bystanders and passersby were so overwhelmed that they couldn't but follow the pied piper to march on.

The parade stopped at a used bookstore to purchase used books and left a Treasure Hill native plant at the store corner. The native plant was also planted at the entrance corners of many idiosyncratic coffee shops along the route, where their street-front windows were showcasing images of Treasure Hill taken by a group of Asian artists (Asian 108) and some community residents in the manner of a street gallery. The parade marched on to Jing-jing gay bookstore to present the book-stop, the bookstore owner raised their pink triangular flag to gesture a grand welcome and recited a radical paragraph from a manifesto book that most represented the spirit of the independent bookstore. The Treasure Hill community purchased the book and placed it in the book-stop as an enthusiastic support for the gay community.

The parade continued onward to the feminist bookstore, the leftist underground bookstore, the Taiwanese-culture themed bookstore, and the Mainland-Chinese literary publication based bookstore to present book-stops and purchase books. Each owner of the independent bookstores personally picked the most significant book of the store to recite out loud in front of the street crowd and put it in the book-stop, then the parade team replied with the most energetic cheer and scream. The "Transporting the Fire, Delivering the Books" parade was not only a declaration of squatter settlement conservation, but also an unexpected meeting of Taipei's different social groups and communities and a warm exchange of their cultural emotions. They expressed their individual identities and dignities through the art form of an action theatre on the public streets, and they treasured each others' voices of differences. The encounter was brief, yet the meaning was extraordinary - as art critique Wang Moe-Lin put it, the parade was a leftist re-writing of the city map charted by a dynamic flow of citizens at the margin.

Marco Casagrande's Organic Layer Taipei project at Treasure Hill attracted extensive medium attentions and gained explicit governmental support. For the very first time, the Bureau of Cultural Affairs of the Taipei City Government agreed in public that the illegal squatter residents were an integral part of the settlement conservation when the commissioner of the Bureau had a direct conversation with Casagrande. The conversation content was published in the China Times, a major newspaper in Taiwan, which cheered up the community and the planning crew's morale. Many community residents expressed to Casagrande and the participant students their hospitality and

friendship, regardless of the language barrier. But Casagrande's progressive move and zealous artivist actions were not without controversy.

For a project this ambitious and of this magnitude, the 2-week span of planning and implementation was less challenging than problematic. Other than the few key persons, most participants were not able to fathom the meaning of the project, let alone the community residents. Some people were touched and inspired by Casagrande's actions (a carpenter resident living close to the constructed stairway later self-built a step garden on the ruins façade, to be described later), but some residents were annoyed that their daily lives were affected by the project. Some critiques even questioned, did Casagrande see the Treasure Hill community as only the provisional actors or the subject of his artivist performance? Did the entire event fulfill the artivist's own artwork or the community need? Casagrande was audacious to touch on the issue of community psyche despite the expectation for him to mobilize and organize a marginal society toward common goals through artivism. But what could be the consensus on the public interest of Treasure Hill, and how long might it take to reach that goal? The past social actions and protests focused on the imminent crisis of community banishment, but once the crisis was changed into opportunities, can the community come up with a new vision without knowing itself? Casagrande interpreted the meaning with such an intense empathy, but how far was that from the truth of the community?

THE GARDEN PORTRAITS PROJECT

Quite on the contrary to Casagrande's eye-opening and theatrical approach, the artivist project Garden Portraits, proposed by community activists Jeremy Liu and Hiroko Kikuchi, kept a very low profile. They were invited to engage in creative programming of the vegetable garden cultivated by a few community individuals since the previous Organic Layer installation, but they were also aware that their project schedule at Treasure Hill was constrained and their understanding of the community and its complex situation was largely from second-hand reports and mail. Other than giving practical advice about community garden management, they decided to initiate an art project based on their temporal, personal, and intimate interactions with the cultural subjects to indirectly encourage informal discussion and conversation about the vegetable garden.

The "publicness" of the vegetable garden had become a critical issue in the community since, for the first time, the behavior of growing vegetables in the open land of Treasure Hill was deemed legitimate under the guise of the Organic Layer Taipei project, yet formally sharing the produce for public profit was still a novel concept for the squatter residents whose petty illegal farming by the river bank used to cater for private purposes only. However, to grow vegetables on open lots and to work directly on the land had been recognized as one of the most significant living patterns of the Treasure Hill community. The challenge for Liu and Kikuchi was to bring more residents to the garden and to further raise their interest in participation and establish a mechanism in management through an art project; obviously it was not a mission that could be completed in less than 10 days.

Without any strong intention to push gardening and public discourse, Liu and Kikuchi proposed a simple and workable scheme: taking portraits of the Treasure Hill residents among the lushest garden area. Before the shooting actually happened, they tried to talk with as many families as possible about their stories, perceptions, needs, and their willingness to take part in the garden portrait project with the help of a few students who had been doing a social survey for a long time. Without the student intermediaries and their previous meticulous social study, these artivists could hardly win the community's trust and carry out their project in such a short time. Upon agreement, Liu and Kikuchi would ask each individual or family to bring something particularly meaningful or valuable to be included in the portraits, be it a favorite vegetable, possession, homeland folklore, or human being.

Through translation, Liu and Kikuchi got to sit down and chat with different individuals and families in their own living rooms. The informal interviews led to a variety of story telling, soon many agreed to come to the garden and take the portrait photo, notwithstanding that some of them did not even grow anything in the garden yet. A newly wedded couple came to the green spot in their formal wedding attire, happily holding each other; the neighborhood chief lady came with her gardening partner, proudly presenting their new crop; an earnest painter with a learning difficulty took his loving single mother by the arm, shyly smiling at the camera; one veteran showed up with his old pal dog in his arms, grinning like a naughty child; each face, indeed, told a story. Altogether, 17 portraits were taken at the same position then nicely framed in a bright red color. These portraits were given back to the participant residents by the artivists as something to remember and talk about; in other words, the artwork disappeared into the residents' living rooms once they were finished.

This was exactly Liu and Kikuchi's intent returning the subjectivity of creative art back to community individuals and diminishing the role of an outsider artist. The exhibition space of this particular work would be the community itself, and an avid art appreciator would have to visit all these families and talk with them to understand the full spectrum and depth of this art project. Liu and Kikuchi argue that, "this project is about bringing the garden to the homes as a balance for the interest in getting the people to the garden. It is the beginning of a

"dialogue of space" between the home and the garden." Before the portraits forever retreated to the walls of 17 private rooms, Liu and Kikuchi invited all of the photographed to present their portraits in a public forum which was the only public viewing of the complete work. These residents sincerely expressed their feelings and perceptions about the Garden Portraits project and the vegetable garden itself. Even though it was a long way from the discourse about the management of a public organic garden, almost every attendant of the forum was deeply affected by the heart-felt presentations and stories of the portrayed.

The Garden Portraits was an artivist project with an open end. It was meant to be the beginning of a real portrait studio project, continuing to take pictures and document the life stories and changes of the community (the concept was somewhat resumed later by Yeh Wei-li's Treasure Hill Tea + Photo). Liu and Kikuchi's conscious act of hiding their artist status (it also reflected the post-structurist idea of "decentering the subject," Smith, 2001) in order to shift the focus on the subjectivity of the residents did reveal a great respect for the Treasure Hill community and carefully reserved a limited outsider's distance in interpreting the community. Yet their humble approach also provoked serious questions about artivism and artwork: when the artwork virtually disappears, do the artists further help empower the subjectivity for the community or simply declare the death of their own subjectivity? Do the artists thereby promise a continuous commitment to the community or retreat from the scene and sever their relationship with the community since they will not have to be responsible for their work (there is virtually no artwork)? Does "artwork" have to be the original sin of artivism because the artist's role of reinforcing the creative self through her/his works is somehow condemned?

Perhaps the conscious retreat of the artistic self exposed the structural problem of a conscientious artivist's short-term commitment through a project commission. It is an honest as well as strategic and paradoxical reflection on the reality that the outsiders cannot blend into the community in a short span of time to represent the community's needs and desires. Even if they move in to acquire a quasi-insider status, is their stay perceived as legitimate to motivate certain community actions? Is it possible that, in some way, an artivist's role is to conduct a genuine and sincere *dialogue* with the community based on her/his in-depth understanding and empathy for the community, no matter how long she/he can commit to the community? It is definitely not appropriate to re-write the community with the artist's personal signature, but it is also not necessary to give up one's artistic signature and difference in the face of the much-too-generic term of community.

HAPPENING - THE TREASURE HILL ENVIRONMENTAL THEATRE SERIES

"The Fire in the Attic" performance by Marco Casagrande and the workers in black transformed Treasure Hill's ruins façade into a theatrical space which, according to some local theatre critics, could be Taipei's most outstanding stage. In fact, the idiosyncratic ambiance and spatial tension of the Treasure Hill community a living squatter escaping the control of modern urban planning, unwilling to succumb to specific elite aesthetics, and interweaving its organic texture with the surrounding natural environment preset an intriguing context for the critical contemporary fringe theatre and environmental theatre. Under the GAPP framework, "Happening: the Treasure Hill Environmental Theatre Series" aimed to delve into the collective consciousness and personal experiences of the settlement via re-interpreted spatial scenario and body performances, as well as to extend the social and environmental dimensions of theatrical art by adapting to Treasure Hill's critical alternative space.

The first Happening performance was not in the original program. A visiting Indonesian behavior performing artist Yoyo Yogasmana who happened to be undertaking a Muslim Lebaran ritual in Taipei, decided to perform the ritual at the Family Cinema Club plaza with the Sun-Son Theatre, a drum-based theatre group about to start its artist-in-residency status at Treasure Hill for the Happening series. The Lebaran ritual was mesmerizing and exotic. Its religious themes about catharsis, redemption, and forgiveness, crossing cultural and language barriers, resonated effectively with the onlookers' perceptions through the performers' movements and expressions. Many community residents came unprepared to be transported to a fantastic dreamland, yet touched by a sensible religious mood, they appreciated the ritual with curiosity and respect. Hence, when Yogasmana invited participation from the audience, all attendants felt more than willing, or even competed to join the performance.

Despite the wind chill, Yogasmana soaked and fluttered himself in the cold water in an abandoned bathtub, while Sun-Son Theatre's mystical chanting echoed around the plaza. He came out of the water under the floodlight, standing motionless for a long while like a traumatized man with a soul redeemed. Then he sat down with the Theatre performers around a circle of petals, gradually swaying their bodies into waves of circular motion and humming their inner voices into a hypnotizing rhythm. Even if the performance had been rehearsed, there were dynamic moments of improvisation when the onlookers were engulfed in the ritual. Some Treasure Hill residents were asked to spread flower petals on Yogasmana to cleanse his spirit, they did that with honor and deep respect as if they were saints baptizing a disciple. The air was charged with a shared belief beyond the dogma of religion. The dramatic finale evolved from a gentle quest for forgiveness when Yogasmana held an onlooker's hands and vibrated with the hopping sound of drums, then the onlooker moved to his side to shake the second onlooker's hands. As the drumming went on, every onlooker stood up and gave her/his hands to Yogasmana and the growing line of hands for each other's forgiveness. The drumming got louder and more passionate, shaking hands started to go with dancing feet. Without any instructions, everyone in the plaza was holding hands and dancing wild! It was magical and liberating. And it happened in the most unlikely corner of a secular city.

It seemed that at that particular moment, whether it was Muslim or Catholicism or Buddhism it did not really matter; yet, rarely had any community in Taipei or Taiwan been granted an opportunity to witness a religious ritual or theatrical performance of such a "difference" and thereby to expand the scope of inter-cultural experiences. The Lebaran ritual was certainly not related to Treasure Hill's everyday life or the community's perceptual domain on the surface. It was exactly this unfamiliarity that evoked an overwhelming sense of curiosity and excitement out of the ordinary. This impromptu performance did not treat the audience as passive or receptive objects as many fixed-frame theatres did, and it elicited immediate and enthusiastic participation without specific narrative formation or meaning exploration. In a sense, it trusted that human feelings shared common ground and transcended political and social estrangement. It did not seek for a complete understanding of meaning or storyline, but called for a primitive resonance from the heart. The Lebaran ritual and the following theatre series did not cater to the community needs or routine expectations (but did a Taiwanese or Chinese opera serve better purposes at the heterogeneous Treasure Hill community? And if it did, based on what conjectures?), it accentuated the community's acceptance and appreciation for "otherness."

The Sun-Son Theatre started a week-long drumming workshop following Yogasmana's performance the next evening. Surprisingly, quite a few elderly residents came with their grandchildren to learn hand-drum playing. Since drumming required less musical technique with tunes and chords, the workshop participants picked up certain fun rhythms to jam with one another soon after the instructor demonstrated basic steps and orchestrated layers of playing. Even though some of the drummers occasionally missed the beat, it did not sound bad once individual drumming was wrapped within the collective funky rhythm. It was simply fun since no beat was a wrong beat. Very often, the theatre members would start a bonfire in the lawn plaza adjacent to the bamboo grove and tempt workshop drummers and onlookers to dance to the fire-and-drums. Strange at first glance, yet it was also refreshing to watch the Treasure Hill elderly residents playing drums with professional drummers while women and children danced intoxicatedly by the bonfire a lighter and brighter side of the community stereotypically associated with a sedate state and an aging image.

In the meanwhile, the Sun-Son Theatre set up another mask workshop to teach paper-mache mask making at the community terrace lawn. Waste paper and newspaper were transformed into a variety of artistic masks with the help of simple technique and touches of creativity, and the outcomes would later become props and ornaments for the weekend performance. Again, some enthusiastic participants from the community showed up every day to make art, mixed occasionally with cynical and skeptical looks from the passersby. But there was one particular comment from an old handicapped veteran, after he observed the mask workshop for a few days, that surprised the planning team most. He said, "if I did not join the army in my youth, I would have strived to be an artist." His statement indicated a psychological desire never made clear in the previous social survey and interviews, but unexpectedly revealed during the workshop. This episode was meaningful and encouraging for the GAPP experiment. If artivism could inspire certain individuals to bring out or recollect their creative sides, it might be able to discover new creative powers of the community overlooked by formulated community empowerment process.

Another intriguing comment was gently expressed during the bonfire dance by a woman who had been living at Treasure Hill for more than 30 years. She was then wrapped up in the wild drumming and fire dance taking place in the lawn plaza where a group of older male residents usually sat around the bamboo grove chatting, and she said, "It's good to be able to come down here and watch performances. I rarely set foot on this lawn after the grocery store was gone. Those old men sit under the bamboo all the time, and if not for the dance, I would not come down to the lawn." Her comment was mild but sarcastic if compared with the description of the highly-adored pattern of "a group of local senior citizens sitting under the bamboo trees chatting." Indeed, in a marginal community like Treasure Hill, subtle issues of gendered spaces were rarely exposed under the criticism of political-economy and zoning injustice in general. Cherishable spatial patterns of an organic settlement were well documented at Treasure Hill, but the previous comment critically pinpointed that some of those patterns might also be romanticized and shield the unquestioned power relations within. The critical distance of artivism did not intend to undermine the living patterns of Treasure Hill, but to further look into the taken-for-granted realities under the commonness of community.

The eventual performance by the Sun-Son Theatre drew a huge crowd to Treasure Hill, many of them heard of the place for the first time. The series of performance adapted many

unlikely corners for different scenarios the frame of a broken window, the relics of a torn down building basement, the strip in front of a line of blank walls, the steps leading to an old family barbershop, the terrace lawn, the outdoor cinema plaza, to name a few, - the ingenious uses of peculiar environment and spaces shed new light on Treasure Hill, as if untold stories were hidden at every corner of the community. Constrained by an extremely low budget, the theatre group summoned many professional volunteer performers to interpret Treasure Hill through their improvised or contextualized theatre. The audience had to follow the performers around the community spaces and stand right in the settings. Boundaries between the real, the unreal, and the surreal sometimes dissolved when the theatrical stages and the living environment were both deconstructed and re-constructed by each dramatic turn. The performances seemed to disclose modern human conditions and vulnerability more than the stories of Treasure Hill.

Quirky, mysterious, and awe-striking, the theatre combined dances, poetry-reading, aboriginal chanting, drumming, and role-playing to conduct physical dialogues with the varied environments. It was not easy to eliminate the image of a tethered man cocooning in the ruins window or of a woman in a 10-meter-long red veil dragging herself inch by inch uphill. And when she disappeared into the woods on the terrace lawn, along came a couple of half-naked celestial beings and a Flamenco dancer charging the melancholy night air with a heart-wrenching dance. The bonfire drumming and dance, accompanied by Yoyo Yogasmana's bizarre body-roping ritual, culminated the evening performances and unleashed the emotions of the enthralled audience. Many Treasure Hill residents and families who attended the drumming and mask workshop, some even in costume, exhibited high spirit and wild instinct for dancing. The fire glowed, and nobody seemed to care if they ever fathomed the meaning of the environmental theatre.

The Sun-Son Theatre workshops and performances were, predictably, received with controversies. And the community reality was, there was always only a small portion of the entire population motivated enough to join the public events, especially when these events had no direct relations with their private interests or pleas for their understanding. Complaints about the drum noise and the intense activities whispered behind the workshops and performances, even though very few came forward to the organizers. Skeptics were not convinced that the exogenous arts program could do much to the community when the fireworks died out, not to mention that the fireworks themselves might be seen as disturbances rather than celebration of the community life. It was always a legitimate question to ask if high art could actually represent the best interests or the needs of the community and if the 'fireworks' type of arts program could help the community further establish its own identity. But such a question was also a much-too-easy one if it did not further distinguish whether the community was an appropriate site for a reinforced identity or on the contrary, for dissolving identities; or, whether we should look beyond the need-base to differentiate the nuances of the community psyche. We could go on to question the discrimination between traditional cultural events and an arts program, and if the latter could, given a longer time span of sedimentation, be absorbed into the former. Could the community events be liberating, free, and fun (if not offensive and intrusive) rather than meaningful, purposeful, and appealing to the majority? Would there be alternatives in constructing the community narrative other than telling comprehensible stories - for instance, poetry grounded on perceptual experiences?

The Taidong Theatre and the Parliament Theatre two burgeoning fringe theatre groups tried different approaches for the Happening series at Treasure Hill. The Taidong Theatre chose a specific theme "Where do I come from?" to reflect the community characteristics of Treasure Hill and structure their scenario thereafter. They meant to do some interviews with local residents about their backgrounds and life stories, vis-à-vis their own immigrant experiences. Instead, they established a broadcast workshop and gave the community residents vocal training to tell stories through an expressive medium. It was a creative and fun approach as well as an effective tool for the few participants to manipulate drama through their voices.

The Parliament Theatre moved into one of the squatter houses to make close contact with the residents everyday. They attempted to arrange a few potluck dinners with the community and to participate in the garden farming in hopes that their theatre piece could develop out of real community life.

But perhaps the previous Sun-Son Theatre and Marco Casagrande's dynamic projects ate up too much community energy, these two theatres both had difficult times involving resident participation even though their theatre subjects addressed more community issues. The week-long residency also did not allow these two less experienced groups to get acquainted with the community and work out their own rehearsal schedules. Reactions to their workshops and performances were tepid, but ironically, complaints were hardly heard. Many residents were not even aware of their existence. The Taidong Theatre finally got to perform with a few residents at the lawn plaza, asking again and again that fundamental "where do I come from?" question; but the Parliament's performances, following a disinterested potluck party, were largely self-serving without calling much community attention. Considering their original project ambitions, the disappointment of their performances cut even deeper than the controversies about the previous theatre. For a play involving the community's internal narratives by the exogenous group or individuals, it

took serious interaction and strategies to make things work; otherwise, the duration of residency had to last much longer than a week.

THE ARTIST-IN-RESIDENCY PROGRAM AND THE TREASURE HILL TEA + PHOTO

The last phase of GAPP called for proposals from domestic artivists who, once chosen, would acquire a two-month artivist-in-residence status to adapt an abandoned housing unit at Treasure Hill and make art on a grant basis. Altogether seven artivist individuals and partners were selected by a committee, who was informed about Treasure Hill's situation and history, to carry out their independent projects. These proposals, ranging from photography studios, sound projects, installations, and recycled object composition, reflected the diverse backgrounds of the artists as well as their interpretations of the community and its adjacent environment. The cultural subjects of Treasure Hill were not particularly emphasized, but subtly implicated as an indispensable part of their projects. The living squatter community located at the edge of the city became a source of creative and critical inspiration for these young artists. Yet unfamiliar with its complicated zoning problems, none of them attempted to challenge the state machine or to initiate another social movement; instead, they chose to humbly engage in more personal and poetic conversations with the site and the people. Unlike the Environmental Theatre series, they didn't induce direct resident participation through specific workshops either; in a sense, they were more like an ad-hoc artist team neighboring the Treasure Hill community making art projects about their neighborhood.

These creative and temporary residents caught the community's attention when they moved in, and their behavior was also monitored by certain moral standards. The Treasure Hill community was not particularly conservative compared with other parts of the city, but the original residents were always cautious about reckless misdemeanors and sabotage. The first lesson for any artist-in-residency at Treasure Hill would be that the artist does not have privilege over the community and that the daily-life patterns of the community do not have to adapt to any artist's personal will unless consent is given. Throughout this artist-in-residency program, the tacit understanding was mostly respected except for a few incidents which magnified certain individuals' anarchistic conduct into unnecessary tension between the program and the community. Due to such unpleasant experiences, the community might take more drastic measures to write down a community charter to regulate themselves and the future newcomers if a part of Treasure Hill were gradually transformed into an artist sector.

However, their artwork and projects did not cause too many raised eyebrows despite that some were walking on a thin line between being provocative and inspirational. *The Sounds from the Landscape* project employed many hi-fi microphones hidden at various corners all over Treasure Hill, then installed inside a line of tubing beside the trail of the lawn plaza. A passerby could easily hear sounds of a dog-barking, insect-chirping, cooking, mahjong-playing, or even talking and fighting through the speaker tubes. It was a surprising slice of Treasure Hill's mundane reality never before documented, but it could also be interpreted as a breach of privacy. *Me and the Minute of Being with Myself* project asked any volunteer to enter a disturbing, Duchamp-ish room to be absolutely solitary, then push the shutter of an aperture camera for a minute-long exposure. The artist was curious about how one was thinking at that singular minute, which would be written down or drawn out in a notebook by the experimental subject. Some weeks later, the front chamber of the house was filled with intimate self-portraits and documents. Fear and desire abounded in the strange room. It was more about human and community ego than the community stories.

Among all artist-in-residency works at Treasure Hill, one particular project stood out as the most noteworthy. The *Treasure Hill Tea + Photo* (THTP) project by Yeh Wei-li and Liu He-rang started with a simple concept to establish a humble teahouse in the community, open and free to all who passed through. And behind the teahouse, a professional portrait studio would take pictures for those who came in to drink tea and share stories. Yeh and Liu brought many books and portfolios to the teahouse, along with some re-assembled and manufactured objects that they found in the community, and ingeniously rearranged the setting to make the living room into a library-gallery type of space. They intentionally avoided aggressive and manipulated interactions with the community residents in hopes that passersby might step into their semi-public yet highly intimate teahouse by accident or as if they were just visiting a neighbor on some casual evening. In a way, they wanted art and community life to collide in the most relaxed way around the least expected corner.

Yeh and Liu's low-key attitude did not open the door wide enough to receive an impressive influx from the community, but many students and outside visitors came frequently to chat with artists and take portraits. They made prints of the portraits for the visitors and exhibited some of them on the wall of the living room. Once in a while, their immediate neighbors would show up and the planning crew would bring some local residents to take pictures. Yeh and Liu picked a few excellent portraits and enlarged them into light boxes, one of which was of his next-door neighbor. But at the end of their project term, portraits of the Treasure Hill residents were comparatively fewer than those of the outsiders. Yeh believed that they needed more time to develop the project.

So when the rest of the artists moved out after the final open-house exhibition, Yeh and Liu resumed their teahouse photo studio and further expanded it to another dwelling unit to include a dark room and a carpentry workspace. Gradually more local residents' portraits showed up on the wall, quietly replacing the outsiders' slots. Yeh decided to actually move into Treasure Hill and become a local resident. He committed at least two years to reinforce his collaboration basis with the community and to lead a life of making art in the community at his personal expenses. His project would come to fruition if a photography facility and resource center could be established to offer classes and lectures to the public.

Yeh's commitment to the community was not for his personal benefit or reputation. He acknowledged that the real subjects for his work were the local residents, but their participation would no doubt augment the social meaning of his or any artist's work. He observed that, in a letter to the mayor of the city, "…the social fabric that makes up Treasure Hill is a rich source of inspiration, history, and sustenance for artists to draw from. The oral histories passed down through exchanges with the residents here contextualize and deepen the experience and understanding of being in Treasure Hill. For without the voices and lives of these living residents, Treasure Hill would be but an empty shell of crudely constructed rubble." Yeh was actually writing to request that the city not dislocate the residents even if the squatter buildings were preserved. His statement, along with letters from many other artivists and scholars who had come to experience Treasure Hill or work there and shared the same stance, played a vital role in persuading the city government to recognize the community residents as an integral part of the future artist village.

The formal surface of the THTP project displayed faces of all walks of life, who happened to show up at a particular time in Treasure Hill. Yeh argued that, "through our differences in histories, backgrounds, languages, class and education, life experiences that are shared and told and retold ultimately give clues to where and who we are." He expressed a humanistic, understanding, and unassuming value for his ongoing project and dialogue with the community, and that was in many ways more significant than a condescending approach of token participation.

GAPP REPERCUSSIONS A SEMI-CONCLUSION:

GAPP was at first consciously developed as a strategic tool for cultural landscape conservation at Treasure Hill. It was meant to turn a pre-determined, somewhat dogmatic and unilaterally wishful idea of implementing an artist village in a grassroots squatter community into a conservation tactic as well as a contextualized program to explore the social outreach of liberal arts. The original intention of GAPP, admittedly, questioned arts' autonomy and did not see art for art sake.

Artivism was derived from and at the same time antithetic of art. Artivism's punctuating activism challenged art for not being serviceable to more meaningful social purposes, and this critique might just subvert art's understated essence the use of being useless. Artivism is affiliated to the Frankfurt School's "negative aesthetics" (Adorno, 1984; Marcuse, 1978), but not yet built up on a firm aesthetic ground. It's more of an activist proposal than a manifesto of aesthetic movement. Adorno's argument of social meaning within the autonomy of art is a long contemplation on the nature of art as well as a critique of high-culture aesthetics being dominated by the institutional powers. But the fine balance between social critique and autonomy of art needs to be learned through practice. Casagrande's attic concept for Treasure Hill (and his associated actions) was artistic and exotic, but it did capture the spirit of the place more precisely than many previous social jargons. Then we can examine where the autonomy of art lies (if there indeed is) and if it achieves the intensity of social critique in this case.

There were a few episodes of GAPP emerging after the flamboyant events were cooled down and most artivists were gone, invoking the creative subjects out of the subordinate society of Treasure Hill. These episodes surfaced among the ripples of GAPP, but were not programmed to happen accordingly. Some were always there or already there but had hardly been noticed or looked at squarely. Some were indeed inspired by the artivists' projects. Mr. Lee, a self-taught carpenter living right behind the stair path conceived and built by Marco Casagrande's artivist team, began to follow the steps after the *Organic Layer* project was officially over. He constructed another stairway going down from his personal window to the main path with better recycled materials and better craftsmanship, then he cleaned another garbage dump into a look-out patio. Gradually he added a small garden, a line of plant-filled pipe fence, a few ingenious built-in seats, a couple of driftwood handrails, a billboard, and so on. And his construction is still growing. The community and the live-in planning crew got to know him more and more because he always mentioned that his cultivation was for the public and not to privatize any more land and he did improve the quality of the environment at the fuzzy edge of Casagrande's artivist project. He has turned himself into another artivist without being crowned with a laurel.

Lin Mu-shan had a measles attack during his childhood, and he remained like an innocent boy ever since. He had problems articulating language or learning at school, but he had an enthusiasm for painting. He lived with his mother quietly at the upper level of the Treasure Hill settlement after his father and brother passed away, and he started to take painting lessons at the Eden Welfare Foundation. Very few neighbors in the community knew his talent till the last stage of GAPP when Yeh Wei-li opened his Treasure Hill Tea + Photo next door to Mu-

shan's home. Mu-shan hung out at the teahouse photo studio oftentimes with a strong sense of curiosity and enthusiasm, and he communicated with the photographer in a special way. Yeh took portraits for him and enlarged one of them into one of the most conspicuous light-box artworks of the studio. In the meantime, Mu-shan's paintings were chosen for an exhibit in a prominent city gallery and used for the promotion poster. Yeh shot a series of Mu-shan's paintings to be used in an upcoming book (all the copyright income will go to Mu-shan's family), Mu-shan helped Yeh paint his studio walls and ceiling. And soon Yeh will invite Mu-shan to paint in his studio when his learning term at Eden Foundation is over. Mu-shan became more and more visible in the community, and he even designed the logo for Treasure Hill when the international Creative Sustainability Self-help Center project initiated a collaborative mural artwork at the entrance of the community. Mu-shan's instructor at Eden Foundation wrote a letter to the project office about his growing confidence. His new paintings and exhibitions are occasionally the topic of neighborhood conversations. To say the least, a new set of micro social relations is evolving and restructuring. The artivists are now simply community neighbors, and the old neighbors have become real creative artists.

Mr. Ding, after participating in many different projects and events, began to voice that the Treasure Hill community should come up with their own artwork. He joined the photography session with young Asian designers to take pictures of Treasure Hill for the Street Gallery exhibition, and his work impressed and surprised everyone. Then he proposed a marvelous idea during a performance meeting recording a CD of native-land folklore representing different immigrant histories of Treasure Hill where one could easily capture dialects and accents from a variety of Mainland China provinces, Southeast Asia, and other regions of Taiwan. His proposal was almost realized when two musicians/sound artists from the artists-in residency program volunteered to help. But the lack of budget and adequate equipment postponed it. Mr. Ding was not frustrated, and built a decorated archway at the fork of two alleys near where he lived entitled "Gazebo for the Other Homeland" on one side and "Residence of Befriending Neighbors" on the other. Under the archway was a corner of literature with poems and aspiring words selected by him. With the onward push from GAPP, he seemed to gain the stamina and legitimacy for what desired to do.

If ever Mr. Ding's folklore assemblage CD can be recorded, we will also be expecting Mrs. Chu's fabulous Huang-mei tune, Mr. Feng's heart-breaking harmonica, Mr. Lee's traditional erhu fiddle, the big family of the neighborhood chief lady doing theatrical, and many more local voices. With creative powers from different individuals with distinguished characteristics and histories, the Treasure Hill community is undergoing a transformational process that might transcend a localized resistance identity into a place-project identity. There are always higher priorities of problems to be solved rezoning details, landscape conservation, community livelihood, building restoration, continuous aging, and so forth, and the community is not yet firmly organized to reach any consensus in the wake of GAPP. But somehow from the few identified individuals, the disempowered squatter community cannot be merely perceived as a collective lump of dependent minorities waiting for care-takers. Art may not do much of practical use value to improve their income, but the creative power which art unleashes from the community infuses a breath of fresh air and new possibilities to a squatter nearly sentenced to a penalty of eternal demise.

ENDNOTES

[1] The Treasure-Hill settlement is a fringe urban village characterized by its intimate physical relations with the Guan-Yin Hill and the Hsin-Dian River and conservation of the treasure-hill settlement has confronted the rationale of modernist planning in Taipei which prioritizes urban function as a whole rather than collective memories of the few. Stigmatized by some urban discourses as the tumor of a pro-growth city, the informal and pre-modern appearance of the settlement is not only reminiscent of the tight spatial fabric of the city's organic past, but also houses the everyday life of many immigrants and families of different periods of urbanization, many of whom are elderly veterans and members of the disempowered social underclass.

On one hand, the Treasure-Hill settlement is condemned as an urban squatter area whose residents maintain their basic subsistence on piecemeal self-help mode; yet on the other hand, it is ironically romanticized as a hill-side village setting which bears the potential of an artistic community. Either viewpoint cannot depict the situation of the settlement today. Ever since the declaration of a future park according to the city's physical plan in the 1990s, the Treasure-Hill settlement was overcast in a gloomy shroud of insecurity.

[2] After the planning responsibility for the Treasure Hill Settlement was transferred from the Department of Park and Recreation to the Bureau of Cultural Affairs, the cultural imagination faced the challenge of programming a "planned" village out of an "ordinary" settlement by piecemeal evolution.

OURs (the Organization of Urban Re-s) is now commissioned by the Bureau of Cultural Affairs to undertake the planning task as well as the 2003 GAPP, and for the time being, the new program intends to propose a "co-living commune" which will incorporate the original residential units as "welfare homeland an alternative social housing," a youth hostel, an ecological learning field, and an artist-in-residences program. All the residents of the new village will share the facilities of a co-kitchen, a co-dining room, a bakery, a café, waterfront organic gardens and farms, a co-op neighborhood self-help center, and various workshops for recycled-material-based arts and creative theatres, darkroom, etc. Restoration of the physical structures will call for the help of International Workcamp, and all the labor put to the care of the community can be transferred as a substitute for rent or meals.

[3] The attic concept appears also in the phenomenological study of Gaston Bachelard's *the Poetics of Space.*

REFERENCES

Adorno, T. 1984. Aesthetic Theory. C. Lenhardt tr., G. Adorno and R. Tiedemann eds, London: Routledge & K. Paul.

Bachelard, G. 1957. The Poetics of Space. Presses Universitaires de France.

Baudrillard, J. 1994. Simulacra and Simulation. Tr. S. Galser. Ann Arbor: University of Michigan Press.

Butler, J. 1997. Excitable Speech: A Politics of the Performative. N.Y.: Routledge.

Calhoun, C. ed., 1994. Social Theory and the Politics of Identity. Oxford: Balckwell.

Castells, M. 1997. The Information Age: Economy, Society, and Culture Vo. II The Power of Identity. Oxford: Blackwell.

Ellin, N. 1995. Postmodern Urbanism. Cambridge: Blackwell.

Girard, C. 1995. The Politics of Complexity in Architecture, in Journal of Philosophy and the Visual Arts no. 6.

Hayden, D. 1995. The Power of Place: Urban Landscapes as Public History. Cambridge and London: The MIT Press.

Jacobs, S. 2002. Shreds of Boring Postcards: Towards a Posturban Aesthetics of the Generic and the Everyday, in Post, Ex, Sub, Dis, Urban Fragmentations and Constructions. ed. [GUST], 010 Publishers, Rotterdam.

Jameson, F. 1994. The Seeds of Time. N.Y.: Columbia University Press.

Keith, M. and Pile, S. 1993. Place and the Politics of Identity. London and N.Y.: Routledge.

Leach, N. 2002. The Dark Side of the Domus, in What Is Architecture. ed. A. Ballantyne. London and N.Y.: Routledge.

Marcuse, H. 1978. The Aesthetic Dimension: Toward a Critique of Marxist Aesthetics. Boston: Beacon Press.

Massey, D. 1993. Power Geometry and a Progressive Sense of Place, in J. Bird, et al. eds, Mapping the Futures: Local Cultures, Global Change. London and N.Y.: Routledge.

Nancy, J-L. 1991. The Inoperative Community. ed. P. Corner. Minneapolis: University of Minnesota Press.

Norberg-Schulz, C. 1988. Architecture: Meaning and Place Selected Essays. N.Y.: Rizzoli International Publications.

OURs (Organization of Urban Re-s). 2004. The Treasure Hill Co-living Artsville Planning Report, commissioned by the Bureau of Cultural Affairs, Taipei City Government.

Pile, S. and Thrift, N. Eds., 1995, Mapping the Subject: Geographies of Cultural Transformation. London: Routledge.

Relph, E. 1976. Place and Placelessness. London: Pion.

Seamon, D. 1979. A Geography of the Life-world. London: Croom Helm; N.Y.: St. Martin's Press.

Smith, P. 2001. Cultural Theory: An Introduction. Cambridge: Blackwell.

Warf, B. 1986. Ideology, Everyday Life and Emancipatory Phenomenology. Antipode 18: 268-83.

COMMUNITY DESIGN PROCESS TO REGAIN PEOPLE'S EXPRESSION
The Case of the Collabortative Art Project at "Izumi no Ie"

Naoki Kimura, Masato Dohi, Sanae Sugita and Shutaro Koyama

ABSTRACT

This paper reviews the collaborative art project conducted at a welfare facility called "Izumi no Ie" in Setagaya, Tokyo. Focusing on the 8-month process and its results, we will describe how the participatory program should be designed and how the designers should play their roles. Izumi no Ie is a home and workplace for people with physical disabilities. Approximately 60 people are working and 40 of them are also living in this facility. Many of them have lived here for a long time (as many as 19 years on average) with little contact with the local community. The facilities of Izumi no Ie, which were built 40 years ago, are also old. We conducted a series of collaborative art workshops from May to December 2003, and designed the common spaces at Izumi no Ie. Our workshop team mainly consists of university students at Tokyo Institute of Technology. In addition to design the spaces that brought light to the old facilities, we aimed to encourage the people to show their individuality and self-expression, through the process of changing their living spaces with our team. Our workshop team discussed what kind of program would be necessary and how we should play our roles to achieve our objectives. In the process of design the mural, canopy, and the garden, we learned that we needed a participatory design process in which people's creative power is recognized. We also realized how we could inspire people to change through the process of space design.

INTRODUCTION

This paper reviews the collaborative art project conducted at a welfare facility called Izumi no Ie in Setagaya, Tokyo. This project, in collaboration with the facility staff and residents, allowed us to rediscover the power of the community design process. Focusing on the 8-month process and its results, we will describe how the participatory program should be designed and how the designers should play their roles.

Izumi no Ie is a home and workplace for people with physical disabilities. It was built in 1964 as a social welfare facility in Setagaya, Tokyo. As of March 2003, 65 of the residents are working and 47 of them are living in the same building. The five-story reinforced concrete building was built 40 years ago and looks very old. Although it does not have enough facilities, there is no hope of rebuilding it for budgetary reasons. The primary activity in the residents' daily lives at Izumi no Ie is to work as subcontractors and to meet the product delivery deadlines. Many of them have lived there for a long time (as many as 19 years on average) with little contact with the local community.

At the pre-workshop meeting, one of the staff at Izumi no Ie pointed out the problems within the institution. The facility lacks living spaces, and is not ideal for respecting privacy. What is of more concern is that the people who have been isolated from society for a long time may have lost their independence and self-respect. In addition, Izumi no Ie is expected to close or to be scaled down for budgetary reasons. As a consequence, the people will have to become independent from the institution.

In this Collaborative Art Project, we planned to design the common spaces at Izumi no Ie through a collaboration with the residents. Our workshop team mainly consisted of university students at Tokyo Institute of Technology. In addition to designing spaces that brought light to the old facilities, we aimed to encourage the people to show their individuality and self-expression through the process of changing their living spaces with us.

PARTICIPATION PROCESS

We started the workshop program in May 2003. By January 2004, we had completed 2 terms of the workshop program. Through the 8-month program, we conducted 9 workshops for discussion and design, and 8 days for painting on the facilities.

The Term 1 Workshops: Planning Process

In the first and second workshop programs, we gathered the residents' wishes and talked about what we are going to change. During the first program, we took a tour around Izumi no Ie with the 10 residents (assigned by the facility) and discussed how they wished to change the spaces. At the beginning, participants didn't talk much about their ideas. But after going on the tour with us, they started to talk about their wishes towards the living spaces, particularly when they sat around the sketch plan of Izumi no Ie that we had prepared. We were able to gather many ideas that would bring light to the old facilities.

The ideas were suggested for various parts of the facilities. Voting took place during the second workshop program, and the courtyard was selected as the stage for our artwork. The courtyard was surrounded by buildings and a corridor. Traditionally, it has been used as a storage space or a path, and did not attract residents' attention. But it has been located in a visible area from their workroom, living room or bedrooms. People wanted to change this place into a common garden which they can see and spend time in. We decided to make the building wall, storehouse, and the corridor our art canvas.

The Term 1 Workshops: Design Process

From the third program, we started to draft the design of artwork to be painted on the facilities. The residents and our team had discussed the rough image of the design earlier, but how to actually produce the design was still a big issue. Our workshop team conducted various brainstorming discussions about the program. How can we bring out the residents' self-expression in such a limited time? What kind of collaborative work can we share with the residents? How can we draft the design with people who are not familiar with art production? As a result of the discussions, we decided to ask all the participants to draw a picture on a sketchbook and to create a collaborative collage using everybody's picture. We handed out sketchbooks to the residents, including those who had not participated in the workshops before. Two weeks later, many design sketches, which revealed people's individuality, were collected.

Ever since the collage workshop started, people who had been solely engaged in the everyday facility activities, began to join our project. Participants drew collage designs, combining all the residents' pictures and concepts as important elements for the collaborative product. Going through these processes, we finished drawing the design plans for the murals, corridor, and roof.

The Term 1 Workshops: Painting

After the completion of the design process, we worked in the courtyard to paint. During this painting stage, more and more residents came out and joined to help with the walls and roof. We washed the walls, drew drafts on the walls, and painted the murals. We also painted on the tiles and flowerpots. On the transparent corridor roof, we used colored film instead of paint. We completed the artwork in a week.

The Term 2 Workshops

The Term 2 workshops were conducted from October to June. As a result of the discussion with the residents, we continued to work in the courtyard. People expressed additional interest in having some space for rest, as well. In these series of workshops, we not only continued painting the artwork but also focused on creating a useful common garden with a new wooden deck and benches.

By that time, our workshop team and residents had built a relationship that allowed discussions at an equal level. At times, we had ambitious debates about the design plan. At other times, residents even supported us when we needed some help. Members of the original construction team offered their special skills for laying concrete and paving when we built a wooden deck and a slope.

By the end of this process, the residents' courtyard was surrounded by various pieces of artwork and people were able to see them from the new deck space.

PARTICIPATION PROGRAM

It was the third and fourth workshop programs that stimulated the hottest discussion among the team members. The main concern was how we should create the design of murals and other artwork. At our program design meeting, ideas such as the following came up: a) elect the best design among those made by several groups, b) the workshop team will let people draw sketches and make a collage, or c) let people draw sketches and make a collage together. If we wanted to guarantee the realization of the design, it would be less risky to let the people select a collage drawn and made by the workshop team. But in order to respect the purpose of our project, to encourage people to regain their self-expression, we need to put the act of designing into the hands of the residents. In this case, there is a risk that the creation of the design will not be completed with such limited time. Our concerns were whether they would be able to draw their own images of art or not and how we could make a collage design together.

Finally after numerous discussions, we chose to stick to our original purpose and let people draw and make a collage together, despite the anticipated risk. As a result, the residents drew what they wanted to express, beyond our expectation. Although the collaboration was not easy, we were able to make the collage together successfully. People showed their self-expression, as a result of our ultimate choice based on our trust in the people's creative power.

WHAT CHANGED THE PEOPLE?

The collaborative work didn't necessarily start with the residents' approval at the beginning of this project.

Including the first 10 participants who were assigned by the facility, most of the people at Izumi no Ie felt uncomfortable with the project that would disturb the order of their daily lives and tasks within the institution. Very few people responded positively to our initial invitation and there were even voices of opposition at the beginning. But that changed little by little as the workshops moved forward. After two or three workshops, the first 10 participants began to express their opinions actively. Also, people who had been engaged in their daily work began to come and see our work. Some people temporarily stopped their work to join us. The design process was challenging and interesting for us, too. After the collaborative design process, many residents and our team built a relationship that allowed discussions at an equal level. As a result, about half of the residents joined our project of their own accord.

Not all residents at Izumi no Ie participated in this community design process and regained their self-expression. However, we have discovered that a program that is carefully structured based on our trust in people's creative power can bring out people's independence and self-expression. In such programs, we need to work with people on equal terms and to enjoy it.

Through this experience, our workshop team members have changed, as well. Most of the students had no experience working with people with disabilities before this project. At first, we had concerns and questions about how we could work together and what we should support. However, as we proceeded with our project that relied on people's independence and self-expression, our support transformed into an equal relationship with the residents. People taught us the meaning of an equal process.

FEATURES OF COLLABORATIVE DESIGN

In the design process, we put the act of design into the hands of the residents and not only enjoyed the creation of space but also shared an aesthetic value. As a result of this process, all the artwork drawn in the courtyard revealed all the participants' personalities (refer to Figures 5-7). The design that had been drawn by multiple people, so called amateur designers, offers features different from those of works drawn by one talented artist. Our participants' design has a collaborative rhythm, in which each piece intertwines together.

We also realized that we need some level of design skills to produce the plan that contains various senses of values. That is, to find elements of excellent designs made by people, to lead people in sharing the aesthetic senses, and to find an answer that allows various aesthetic values to exist together.

For example, among the design group for the mural on the building, while some residents wanted to draw in bright colors, others preferred quiet tones. As a compromise, both bright and quite colored parts were arranged within the mural. Also when the corridor group was drawing the collage by trial and error, features of each plan had to be respected while deciding the design.

DIFFICULTY OF CONTINUAL IMPLEMENTATION

Originally, this project did not start with full approval from Izumi no Ie. In order to implement a successful community design process within a social welfare facility that is run under its existing operations and structure, it is imperative that we have facility staff who share the same passion to change the situation of the facility. Our art project was realized thanks to the support from some members of the staff. But there is always the risk of termination if the facility's position changes. If those staff cannot stand by our side due to any internal reasons, it would be very difficult to work in the facility. Between the first and second terms, we had this particular problem ourselves, but we managed to resume the project, as a result of intense discussions with the staff of Izumi no Ie. This problem will be inherent in such a project that tries to change the existing values and system, which we will continue to face in the future.

CONCLUSION

Community designers can choose from various communication styles. When we select the most open group process without fear of risks, people start to express themselves. When we put the act of design into the hands of the people, we can create designs that allow each aesthetic sense of the people to intertwine together.

It would be too soon to say that Izumi no Ie has changed in only the eight months of our project period. We learned the difficulty of sustaining our collaborative project within an institution run by its own existing system and structure. But this project convinced us that the people, who have been isolated from society for a long time, can regain their own expression and enjoy the creation of new space through adequate community design processes.

INVOLVING COMMUNITY IN THE CREATION OF GATHERING PLACES

Milenko Matanovic

ABSTRACT

The Community Gathering Places program helps realize a vision of healthy and vibrant communities where people take responsibility for creating meaningful, art-filled environments that foster respect and safety among neighbors, nurture young people, integrate beauty and encourage citizenship.

INTRODUCTION

Since it incorporated in 1986, Pomegranate Center experimented with moving art out of the conventional "art" environment of studios, galleries and museums and into the street, the workplace, and the market square. We wanted to demonstrate how artists can work outside the narrowly defined world of art and actively involve ourselves in building better communities. From the beginning, Pomegranate Center has dedicated itself to linking art with social and environmental issues. We strive to connect justice with beauty—concepts that often exist in parallel universes. When we bring them together, the result is greater social vitality.

Pomegranate Center has committed itself to link concerns and disciplines that often exist in separate mindsets. We believe that the complex problems facing contemporary communities can not be solved from any single perspective. Economy, environment, education, the arts, urban design, civic involvement, ethics–these must function together in a coherent system. To promote one interest category at the expense of the others is to do little more than move a problem, and its pain, to a different part of the community. The question is not whether economics is more important than the environment, or education more than the arts, etc. They are all important. The challenge is see their interrelationship and get them working together.

Pomegranate Center's philosophy has been founded on the conviction that the real potential of a community lies in the spaces between interests, disciplines and ideologies. Creation of physical gathering places emerged as a specific and concrete strategy to practice this more holistic philosophy.

WHAT IS A GATHERING PLACE?

A gathering place is a space for the entire community—what used to be called the commons. It usually occupies an important central location. It is designed to accommodate private and quiet enjoyment for individuals, small gatherings, and community celebrations. Its purpose is to serve all people, from toddlers to old-timers, and everyone in between. For these reasons gathering places must accommodate a spectrum of features: seating in quiet places for reading books or eating lunch, tables for card games or chess, a tot-lot with an adjacent shelter where parents can visit and supervise, as well as an amphitheatre for performances, weddings, and other forms of community events. Gathering places work best when surrounded by stores, coffee houses, restaurants, bus stops, banks, or schools. The more reasons people have to visit a gathering space, the more successful it becomes.

THE NEED

Our work responds to the steady decline of community life we have experienced over the last half century. Because of the rapid change in our society, modern communities are faced with a range of complex issues including sprawl, traffic congestion, environmental degradation, loss of pride and civic identity, and decreased participation in the kind of activities that increase local vitality. Many people have come to feel that the democratic concept of community itself is no longer useful, and that individuals must fend for themselves by exploiting personal advantage. Where it exists this condition has created a society of people confused about their responsibilities as neighbors and citizens. This leads to social fragmentation, ideological polarization, and the inability for the individual to see one's place in the larger world. This creeping ghettoization may one day have us all living in gated communities where the need to engage with the differences of others has been erased from our lives and the lives of our children. To us, this dark scenario cries out for alternatives. A healthy community attempts to turn diverse points of view into gifts that give rise to mutually beneficial cultural and economic relationships. These differences give a community local character and flavor—an identity that builds a sense of belonging and pride.

We recognize that the physical environments of our cities, towns and neighborhoods reflect our psychology and that to find creative solutions we must map both our material and mental landscapes. Well-designed places encourage participation, trust, and a sense of safety. They help us feel at home in the neighborhood. Poorly designed places, conversely, promote isolation, fear of neighbors, and social dis-ease. At Pomegranate Center we work to influence the way our society thinks about communities by connecting the outer and inner realities. Our work, therefore, is both practical and educational. It bridges the hands-on construction of gathering places and public artworks with the ongoing exploration of ideas that make communities healthful and neighbors responsible.

WORKING PHILOSOPHY

- Art belongs in everyday life.

- A community's physical design shapes social and civic behavior.

- Successful gathering places rise from the setting—nature and culture determine their shape and character

- Densities must increase to prevent further sprawl. As they do, gathering places serve an essential purpose as "community living rooms." They serve as incubators of community life.

- Through inclusive, decisive, honest, grass roots involvement differences between people become gifts.

- Involvement increases pride, ownership and stewardship.

- Community problems can be solved only by crossing professional, ideological, cultural and political boundaries.

- Human beings are a part of the natural environment and not apart from it. We should treat nature as we wish to be treated.

- Something gratifying can always be done right now on behalf of longer range ideas and visions.

- A sense of humor is a survival tool.

- An "early success" project is vital in generating ongoing community participation and support.

We at Pomegranate Center believe that well designed, livable cities preserve open land by encouraging people to live in town. Suburban sprawl creates environmental impact far beyond merely the land occupied by homes and businesses. We are reaching the point at which these impacts destroy the very amenities that people seek in suburban living. In response, communities are beginning to encourage—and, in some cases, mandate—higher density development. Amenities such as gathering places are one of the keys to making increased densities work.

POMEGRANATE CENTER SEVEN-FOLD MODEL

Pomegranate Center's Gathering Places model has seven aspects, each aspect representing an important goal. Our aim is that each project solves more than one problem at the same time. We've been testing this model in many diverse settings since 1991. Hardly any of our projects embodies all aspects of the model. Still, in each project we try to implement as many aspects of this model as is possible.

Figure 1. Design Workshop, Terrace Hill, Redmond, WA.

1. Full involvement of community members in all phases of the process, from conception through construction and stewardship.

No one understands a place like its own residents. Before the design phase begins, we listen to the community's needs and desires and discuss what a gathering place should look like, its use, and its values. This process, and the information it generates, forms the foundation for the project: not only does it provide the vision, but in the process we learn about the talent that resides among the community members: some are good craftspeople or know construction, others have design ideas or know of a source of materials we can use, and others still want to prepare food for the work parties. The design takes into account all these factors. Once we have finalized the design, we invite the community—old and young—to participate in the construction phase. When the project is built, we work with the community to develop events that make use of the gathering place and organize an adopt-the-gathering-place group for clean-ups and basic maintenance. We also encourage the entire community to regroup for annual upgrading of the gathering place.

This participatory process offers an extraordinary opportunity to explore important lessons of citizenship and democratic principles, helping people become better prepared for responsible and constructive involvement in society. This is especially relevant because we often do projects with many recent immigrants from countries with little or no participatory experience. Our process provides excellent opportunities for learning teamwork and leadership skills. Indirectly, participants can learn the importance of a democracy: the power of a commonly-shared vision; increased communication, crossing traditional cultural and ethnic lines; marketable skills in construction, arts, and crafts; valued ideas that directly influence and shape the created result. As often as we can we involve youth. For example, we involved over thirty children peeling wood logs that were used to construct mail-box shelters, tables and benches, street lights and a kiosk at Springwood Apartments in Kent, WA. Some of the children were born in Ukraine and were taught this skill during their upbringing. These young people turned into leaders, teaching adults what they knew. We've seen similar emergence of unexpected leadership in many projects.

2. Site-responsive design.

Design must arise from the land, and we try to design gathering places so they appear as if they have always been there. To achieve this timeless quality, we try to acquire the knowledge of the site. Prior to designing, we study the site:

- Where does the sun rise and set? How does the sun move across the sky during the seasons?

- Where do we find summer shade or a warm spot in the winter?

- What landmarks should not be touched: special rocks, trees and other plants, animal trails, etc.

- What materials could be used in the design?

- How do animals (if any) live in this space?

- How does the wind move?

- Does any noise reach the site?

- Where does water drain?

- What are the site's textures—colors, plants, earth forms, human creations?

We discourage any design work until these questions are answered.

3. Continuous process.

We try to compact the entire process into as short a period as is possible under different conditions. The goal is to compress the process so that people who work with us can see their ideas taking shape. This is hard to accomplish in existing systems where the regulations make processes very long

Figure 2. Friendship Park, Vladivostok, Russia.

and convoluted, so much so that those who participate at the early stage rarely have endurance to see it through to the end. We've been involved with projects in Mexico, Russia and China where the entire project was designed and constructed in 10 days to 5 weeks. In our model, the same core group of leaders is involved from the initial concept, through design and construction, to eventual programming of the gathering place as well as its stewardship and maintenance. This provides for continuity and a well-earned pride and ownership.

4. Generous use of hand-made elements that bring art, character and uniqueness into an increasingly prefabricated world.

Our projects are filled with details that celebrate human history and the environment. We take into account volunteers who may have little or no artistic or construction experience. Our designs lean toward organic forms. This is in part the result of artistic sensibility. In part it is because it is easier for volunteers to participate in the creation of such forms. In a straight wall, every misplaced stone or brick would show. In a curved wall, on the other hand, mistakes become a part of a character—an expression of the creative force of various people and their sensibilities.

Before there were architects and planners, people were quite capable of building villages and towns that are full of visual mastery, anchored in the knowledge of the place, and extremely smart in the use of local materials. There should be a place in contemporary life for such common sense creations, and we think that community gathering places offer a way to practice everyday art.

5. Design for all generations and many purposes.

A gathering places should be designed with quiet spots for contemplation, areas for play, places for encounters with friends, and areas such as amphitheaters for performances and celebrations. They should be designed for children eager to run and explore, and there should be warm spots where seniors can people watch.

Gathering place is where social encounters happen freely and unexpectedly, contributing to a stronger sense of community,

Figure 3. Strawbale wall at Esperanza Gathering Place, Mattawa, WA.

better relations among neighbors, reduced vandalism and crime, increased safety for children, renewed volunteerism and stewardship, and more everyday beauty.

6. Use of environmentally sustainable practices.

As often as possible, we use salvaged materials from the site or reuse of vintage or environment-friendly materials. We used straw-bale construction, shelters made of small diameter timber that currently have little commercial use, walls using rocks found at the site or salvaged copper, cobblestones and bricks, green roofs, etc. We try to use non-toxic stains and paints.

7. Sacred space.

Medieval cathedrals were ambitious undertakings that involved the entire community in creating a lasting monument of their common faith. Now, in our time, such singular expression does not fit our modern diverse world. However, people need a place

Figure 4. Friendship Park, San Diego, CA.

where the sacred can exist, and gathering places have the potential of creating a metaphor for common life and replicate, in a much humbler way, the cathedral-building experience. In 1994, James Hubbell and I led a team of Russian, American and Mexican architecture students in the creation of the Pearl Amphitheater in Vladivostok, Russia. During the initial week, one of the Russian students mentioned that it was strange to be in the same room with Americans, people portrayed as their enemies. Another student suggested that our proposed park's design should address this historic tension. Then another student suggested that we should design how this tension can be resolved. Yes, said another, we should think of a pearl that starts with irritation and ends in something beautiful. This conversation created a spiritual base that lead to the eventual design of the gathering place.

Figure 5. Volunteers stain kiosk at Pickering Farm Community Teaching Garden, Issaquah, WA.

TRACK RECORD

Since its inception, Pomegranate Center has used its skills in service to many diverse projects:

- Eleven gathering places;

- Three friendship parks in far-east Russia, China, and the United States;

- Several community-based plans for parks, trails, and other amenities;

- Numerous public art projects;

Figure 6. Kelkari Amphitheater, Issaquah, WA.

Figure 7. Terrace Hill bus shelter, Redmond, WA.

Figure 8. Salishan Gathering Place, Tacoma, WA.

- Advising municipalities, developers and communities how to integrate social, environmental and design issues (including Chattanooga, Tennessee; Kamenice, Czech Republic; Guan Han, China; Pattonsburg, Virginia; Issaquah, WA; Burien, WA; Calgary, Canada; Ottawa, Canada, etc.)

- Three performing art festivals and live performance series (over 50 performances);

- Four curriculum programs linking youth with community;

- A creek day-lighting project;

- A teaching garden demonstrating environmentally sound practices;

- Interdisciplinary design workshops focused on sustainable design;

- Numerous lectures and workshops instructing others about Pomegranate Center's philosophy and community-building methods

- Publications (Watershed Waltz; Evergreen Builders' Guide) and various articles

PROCESS

Every project is different. The following outline is to serve only as an indicator for how the process may work. Depending on the situation, proposed steps may be changed, eliminated or added.

Step 1. Project Committee Formation

Assemble a group of dedicated, diverse, and positive individuals to facilitate the project.

Step 2: Project Committee Ground Work

Team members set basic ground rules, attend training workshop, review the neighborhood data—population trends, demographics, etc., acquire baseline neighborhood information, review and refine project timeline, research and form outreach partnerships, and fine tune the project plan.

Step 3: Outreach

Neighborhood Workshop I: engage as many neighbors as possible to identify what assets already exist, identify future needs, and create a menu of ideas for improvements.

Step 4: Initial concepts

Internal Pomegranate Center workshop I: develop design concepts based on the Neighborhood Workshop I ideas.

Step 5: Neighborhood Approval

Neighborhood Workshop II: review, critique and approve design concepts

Step 6: Develop project timeline, budget, outreach materials

Step 7: Finalize design

Internal Pomegranate Center workshop II: develop specific designs; secure permits (if needed)

Step 8: Neighborhood celebration:

Share the project to involve more people

Step 9: Secure support:

Grants, donations, corporate support, in-kind support of materials, volunteer pledges, equipment, tools, and skills

Step 10: Fabrication and construction:

A series of participatory hands-on workshops

Step 11: Develop stewardship strategies:

Examples: Adopt a park, regular events, etc.

Step 12: Grand celebration:

Opening ceremony, recognition, plaques galore, etc.

Step 13: Improved Practices

The Committee assembles project evaluations from all involved, conducts a reflection workshop to extract lessons learned, writes an improved practice summary, develops a report and conducts a post-project survey.

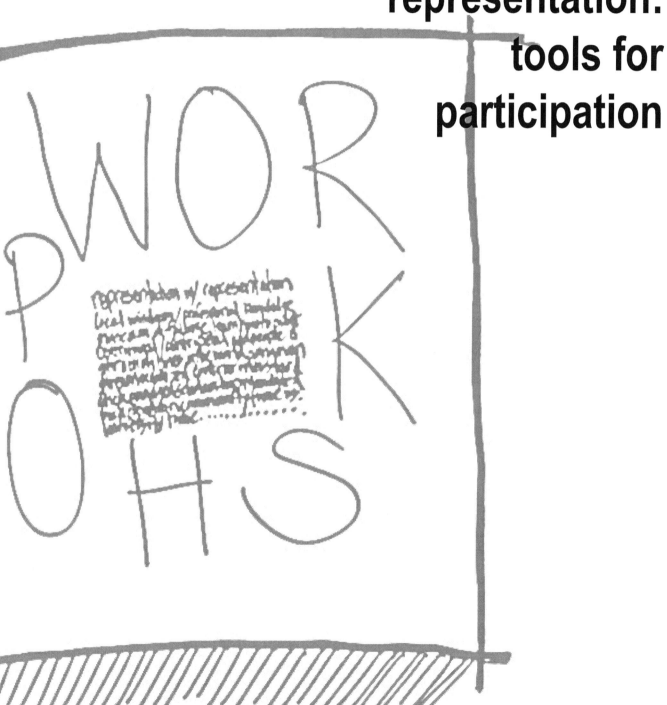

power and representation: tools for participation

DEMOCRATIC DRAWING
Techniques for Participatory Design

Randolph Hester[1]

ABSTRACT

This is a reflective paper that examines techniques community designers use in creating places with people. One of the difficult tasks community designers perform is exchanging complex ideas, science, and technical information with diverse publics. Even more difficult is listening to and then drawing values and ideas of others. More difficult still is to synthesize and draw designs for imagined environments collaboratively. Although drawing is a key part of professional design education, these nonverbal communication problems challenge every community designer. Drawing with the public is immeasurably more complex than the communication techniques learned for traditional architectural or planning practices. So what techniques are used for creating collaboratively? A review of community design projects from the proceedings of the Democratic Design in the Pacific Rim conferences reveals numerous improvisations in shared drawing. These "representative representations" might be categorized as follows: 1) representing people, 2) exchanging professional knowledge and local wisdom spatially, 3) coauthoring design, 4) empowering people to "represent" themselves, and 5) visualizing deep values: community, stewardship, fairness and distinctive place. The intent here is not to compare techniques across cultures, although observations will be made about drawing skills that seem particular to certain social contexts. The goal, rather, is to uncover and highlight spatial representation techniques that seem to be particularly effective in overcoming the difficulties of transactive design especially of actual form making. The most used nonverbal techniques include recording social ecology patterns (11 out of 101) and building sense of community through workdays and walking tours (10 out of 101). Most used of all techniques is the workshop. Three fourths of all the articles (75 out of 101) mention workshops without describing non-verbal methods, content or design outcome. The workshop seems to be the participatory "black box" through which community designers are as inarticulate as traditional designers are about creative form making. Surprisingly few articles (5 out of 101) describe methods in which design is coauthored, passing representation of form and space back and forth between community and designer.

INTRODUCTION

Some years ago I was challenged by a colleague to describe precisely how participatory designers draw and otherwise communicate with communities differently than other designers do with their traditional clients. He implied that we are no different. We use presentation drawings and models like any other designer. Then he suggested that community designers talk more and aren't as skilled at nonverbal communication.

My unprepared response went something like this. In a democracy, the design of the landscape depends on the representation of the public. This public representation, I called it "representative representation," forces inventive drawing. Drawing against or for others is substantially different than drawing with or by others. We, as community designers, draw with the community and frequently they do the drawing. Then I cited drawing on your feet and designing upside down, two techniques I often employ, that suggest that participatory design requires special drawing skills.

In reality, I wasn't this articulate, but the idea of representative representation led to more thoughtful reflection. "Representation" refers to our governing process and is the basis of representative democracy, as in the American slogan, "No taxation without representation!" which rallied sentiment for the Revolutionary War against England. For designers, representation also refers to the drawings that make an image or likeness of the place we are creating. When combined this creates a community design slogan "No representation without representation." In English, "representational" has a particular meaning of being realistic or lifelike instead of abstract. But often architectural graphics are misrepresentational. They are intentionally used to persuade by providing an idealized, misleading picture of what the place would be. Participatory drawing can be distinguished from traditional architectural representation by considering these various definitions.

Figure 1. No representation without representation.[2]

By "representative representation" I refer to the way drawing is used to communicate with communities as honestly and realistically as possible through grass roots democracy in direct "face-to-face" exchanges to design the landscape. The communication is about exchange of spatial information, not persuasion. This communication is often nonverbal because the picture is less ambiguous than the spoken word. Typically this is accomplished through graphic simulations of ideas, choices and plans for the landscapes we are designing with community members. In participatory work, drawing is used to collectively visualize, communicate and design.

"Drawing" is used here to include the representation of the landscape by designers and community members through a broad range of media from sketching, painting and collage to modeling by hand or machine. "Drawing" is also used as any way to visualize precisely and correctly places being designed. This would include stories turned into pictures, looking at photographs or visiting nearby precedents, all of which "draw" an image into the mind's eye of the collective group. Drawing is used in community design for a great variety of purposes such as understanding a place, communicating the detailed dimensions or essence of a space, exchanging spatial, philosophical or programmatic ideas and imagining choices for changing a place. Drawing is used throughout the entire design process, from beginning steps like active listening, to final steps like post construction evaluation. Obviously only a few of these represent the landscape in a literal and figurative way, but all are essential to the participatory design process.

METHOD

I focused attention on the techniques participatory designers use that distinguish us from other architects, landscape architects and city designers. I did a content analysis of the proceedings from the conferences on Democratic Design in the Pacific Rim, a group who practices only participatory design. I read every article and studied all graphics for specific reference to nonverbal techniques used to honestly and precisely design collaboratively. I reviewed articles from each year the group has met. There are 87 papers in the proceedings. I also analyzed the handouts and notes from field study presentations, four in Japan, seven in Taiwan and three in Hong Kong. This gave a total of 101 papers that I analyzed.

I found five domains of skill especially critical to democratic landscape design. In this paper I will briefly describe each of the following:

- Representing People

- Exchanging Professional Knowledge and Local Wisdom Spatially

- Coauthoring Design

- Empowering People to Represent Themselves.

- Visualizing Deep Values: Community, Stewardship, Fairness and Distinctive Place

I kept a rough numerical tally of techniques as I analyzed the articles and graphics and I'll report those. I'll also draw case examples from the proceedings to illustrate the techniques. In a few cases I'll rely on methods from my own work.

Some generalizations should be made at the outset. Descriptions of spatially explicit democratic design techniques were found in about a third of the articles. There were far more descriptions of verbal techniques such as listening, interviews, surveys and story telling than how that information informed design. In most articles workshops are referenced without description of the content or how that content is explicated in spatial or experiential terms. Similarly, goals like building social capital, networks and local identity describe intents with little explanation about methods for achieving them.

On the other hand, the articles and graphics that are explicit about techniques that communicate and lead to appropriate design offer informative examples of how representative representation is and can be distinguished in ways that truly matter. I highlight these in the following descriptions.

REPRESENTING PEOPLE

The lifting of martial law and increasing democratization in Taiwan, natural disasters, government secrecy in Japan and China and the civil rights movement and related urban renewal and freeway battles in the United States made designers aware that we did not have the skills to adequately represent people in the design process. In the worst cases many people were ignored altogether, represented as objects in Cartesian space, or depicted as standardized normative everyman. Most painfully, minorities, the poor, the elderly or the slightly deviant were not represented at all. The recognition of this problem led to a concerted research effort to understand and portray human perception, cognition and response to both the urban and wild landscape. Sociologists and environmental psychologists built a substantial body of research that could be applied to design. In retrospect, it seems that the research findings that are expressed in visual and spatial terms are most used by designers; less imageable research, no matter how important, remains unused. It is often left to the community designer to figure out how to transform nonspatial research on cultural rituals and economic variations into a form suitable for designing places. In other cases, designers must do project-specific investigations to record idiosyncratic desires and patterns of behavior. In some few cases designers try to picture the deeper substance of everyday life and the whole of dwelling as a means to represent and design appropriately for people. In representing people, four methods are most

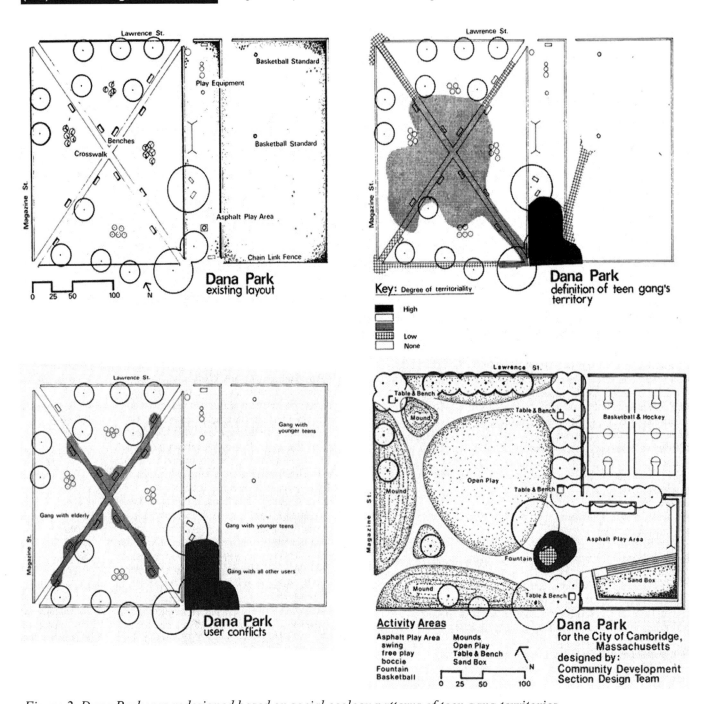

Figure 2. Dana Park was redesigned based on social ecology patterns of teen gang territories.

described in the participatory literature. I expected these to be found in the content analysis of democratic designers in the Pacific Rim: Making Research Spatial, Environmental Justice Maps, Recording Social Ecology Patterns, and Picturing Everyday Life.

Making Research Spatial

Increasingly there is published research available on human environment interactions that can be applied to design. *With People in Mind* by Rachel and Stephen Kaplan and Robert Ryan comes immediately to mind because it provides social research findings and explains the design implications. But most social

research requires "translating" before it is useful for designers. It is not clear how much of this research is being used by the democratic designers in the Pacific Rim. Only five of the 101 articles reviewed mention using pre-existing research, typically site specific census data and historic information. As one exception, Mark Francis describes using his extensive review of recorded trends in park design as a foil for the design of Central Park in Davis, California. He expressly wanted the park to be more of a social center for diverse and divergent groups than most parks provide. The result is an unusual combination of settings from a farmers market and youth center to native gardens and a central valley beach.

Figure 3. The Iraralay Demonstration House was inspired by daily life patterns but accommodates modern needs.

I was surprised at how few cases discussed the use of existing research to represent people. Do we really ignore already published research and rely almost exclusively on firsthand observation and narratives?

Environmental Justice Maps

Frequently powerless people have difficulty or lack the resources to represent themselves. In cases of extreme oppression, community designers may map relative deprivation that calls attention to injustices of distribution, access and exclusion. For example, park lands are frequently concentrated in affluent neighborhoods, a situation that is simply accepted until dramatically visualized with maps, graphs and diagrams, usually the work of community designers. Environmental justice maps focusing on availability of park lands, concentration of toxic sites, relative housing quality, access to natural open space or other environmental factors can often spur action among officials embarrassed by a previously invisible reality.

Although making invisible injustices visible is an important part of community design history, there were no explicit uses of environmental justice maps in the cases presented in the proceedings.

Recording Social Ecology Patterns

Behavior and social ecology mapping based on careful firsthand observation can create patterned visualizations of human activity not unlike soils maps or vegetative mosaics. These geometries suggest design solutions. In 1968 we discovered the utility of territorial mapping when we created maps of the turf that the Dana Park gang in Cambridge, Massachusetts defended. We did this by participant observation, hanging out with the gang for several months, mapping the territory they most often occupied and from which they excluded others. These maps explained, in spatial terms, conflicts with and crimes against other users, and ultimately was the primary piece of analysis that inspired a new park design that solved the turf wars.

Among the democratic designers recording social ecology patterns is the most frequently employed nonverbal spatial communication tool. It is described as central in ten of the 101 articles over a range of settings: the use of creeks, parks and neighborhoods in Northern California; an urban wilderness park, Elephant Mountain, in Taipei, everyday patterns of life of poor women in Taiwan; and new immigrants, the aging and youth in Hong Kong. In one particularly complete description, the design of the Iraralay Demonstration House on Orchid Island was generated from patterns of everyday life. These patterns were discovered by the designers only after hours spent observing what the Iraralay people did around their houses and village. The resulting house form, although thoroughly "modern" in many aspects, is obviously inspired by traditional ways of dwelling and retains every essential activity from ancestral worship centered on the Tomok, to chatting with friends on the sesdepan. The front yard provides working space and a direct connection to the harbor and ocean beyond. The house itself is three houses in one to provide seasonal comfort just as traditional homes did. This is the most extensive systematic patterning reported, and the building form that resulted reflects the authenticity and depth of the observation. It is a stunning building, unique to its place and people.

Picturing Everyday Life Whole

The careful, systematic recording by a participant observer uncovers patterns of sociopetality, idiosyncratic behavior and social interactions prompted by environmental stimuli, but this seems to be too mechanical for some Pacific Rim designers. They are searching for methods to capture more wholistically everyday life. I discovered the value of this when doing the town plan for Haleiwa, Hawaii. My son and I used our time off to sketch with water colors at important spots frequented by locals like Matsumoto's Shave Ice and The Ice House. Through painting common scenes we saw for the first time the recurring pattern of social centering at the interface of indoor and outdoor space tempered by changing sun patterns.

The habit of lingering in the cool of such places defined the essence of everyday life there. In all of our previous systematic behavior mapping we hadn't noticed this sociopetal pattern that was unconsciously designed in the vernacular landscape. We employed the pattern to create more such successful places.

More experimental approaches are reported in the design of the spatial scenarios the National Taiwan University group used to design the shop house reconstruction in Kuo-hsin township after the earthquake. The design team tried to get the homeowners to tell them their own stories, to narrate their everyday lives in space. Eventually the designers were able to transform the stories into the language of space, providing residents pictures of how their lives might be in new houses.

The memory interviews used in the design of the Quaker Retirement Community in Sandy Springs, Maryland, may have likewise given a qualitative picture of everyday life. This method certainly enhanced empathy.

Jackie Kwok and Michael Siu describe another innovative way to picture everyday life. Immigrant women were given cameras and asked to take pictures and then discuss their everyday activities and settings. This allowed each woman to clearly express her evaluative comments about her living environment, her image of self and family and her everyday life rhythm.

I could identify only these few examples and I have read considerably between the lines, but I am interested to know if this desire to capture more wholistically everyday life is generating new approaches. Additional information about techniques that more qualitatively describe the gestalt of everyday life rather than separated patterns would be valuable. I would be particularly interested in knowing if these qualitative gestalts of everyday life are most useful when combined with quantitative pattern languages.

EXCHANGING PROFESSIONAL KNOWLEDGE AND LOCAL WISDOM SPATIALLY

For several years the Pacific Rim Conferences sponsored lively debate about the role of professional knowledge and native wisdom. From this John Liu concluded that good results are usually attributable to a fully engaged interaction between the professional and the people. How does this interaction occur? What methods do community designers and community members use to exchange, accumulate and synthesize knowledge and wisdom?

Once the designer can comfortably work with community groups, he or she understandably wants more from them. Teaching lay people elementary professional spatial thinking can produce significant public design benefits. All people can map and draw, some quite well. But like beginning students, they need to be assisted in observing the landscape carefully, thinking complexly about a place of which they only know fragments, imagining nontraditional resources that are so familiar they don't see or value them, using precise and sometimes faraway precedents, accounting for natural changes in the landscape, generating holistic spatial concepts and evaluating plans.

And in turn, lay people want more from us. They and we benefit from what they teach us. Community members know their own idiosyncratic needs better than we do, therefore, they need to inform any program. They often know details of the culture and ecology from years of dwelling in a place that professionals are likely to miss. In some cases there resides a deep and compelling local wisdom that provides time-honored precedents, gestalts, and ways to do things. Here I will highlight some of the techniques useful in the exchange of local and professional knowledge and wisdom. I will concentrate on techniques that explain how the exchange occurs.

Imagining Unseen Resources

In all poor communities, and most comfortable ones, successful development is dependent on discovering some previously unrecognized resource to capitalize the project. This process has been labeled finding fish heads, a waste product that can be turned into a benefit. Community designers often draw the fish heads diagram and have community members seek out local, undiscovered resources. They may photograph, sketch or simply list them. But often these resources are taken for

Figure 4. Painting uncovered the interface of the indoors and the outdoors, sun and shade, wind and calm essential to seeing everyday life in Haleiwa wholistically.

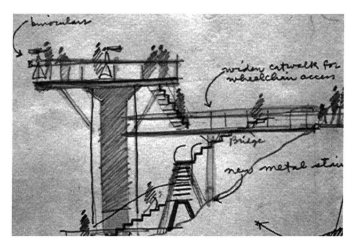 

Figure 5. A quick sketch showing its reuse saved the Nike Missile Tower from demolition and turned it into a wildlife observation deck.

granted or viewed negatively; in those cases the designer must map and sketch the resources before they are acknowledged. In the design of San Vicente Mountain Park in the Santa Monica mountains in California, our design team recognized the remnants of an old Nike missile base as a resource that, if restored, would be useful and, if recycled, reduce cost. To local citizens the remaining tower was a safety hazard, the concertina wire fences inappropriate in a park and the concrete bunkers eyesores. They insisted the military remnants be removed. During a design workshop, quick sketches showed how the tower could be transformed into a wildlife observation deck, the concertina wire lined walkways into interpretive trails, and bunkers into benches. After additional research the military concept was deployed in full as the design gestalt with support of residents, most of whom had seen the hazards anew through the quick sketches. The recycled military artifacts provided a special place, capturing the past while reusing the missile relics to satisfy changed values for nature study, picnics and mountain biking.

In the proceedings are several cases where discovering unknown resources was essential to the successful design. In the case of the various Kyoto Hiroba, a city official with the design team inventoried used equipment and materials in the city storeyards. He then made these resources available to neighborhood groups. Recycled play equipment, granite curbs and other materials, which could not otherwise have been afforded, became available for use in the parks. The community groups often used these recycled materials in their local Hiroba. In another case in Matsu, Professors Liu and Hsia gave lectures about how the dilapidated buildings could be repaired, not just for historic preservation, but also as a local economic development strategy. This contributed to the recovery of many of the culturally significant stone and wood structures in which the third conference was held. This seems a particularly important role for the sensitive outside expert in community development.

Additional techniques to discover unseen resources include Lessons from Poverty, Small and Large, Rare and Commonplace, Conscious Nonconsumption and Dirty Enough to be Happy. These are all described in the Hong Kong proceedings.

Thinking Complexly

Community problems are embedded in complex systems that require systematic, cross-sectoral thinking. Drawing the relationships of all the components necessary to make a successful project can get designers and community to think holistically and sometimes outside the box of both narrow interests and narrow disciplines. A diagram stimulates the organized brain; a diagrammatic cartoon provokes thinking outside the normal. The synetics methods for making the familiar strange and the strange familiar can often help stimulate complex thinking.

In the case of a riverfront revitalization project in Mount Vernon, Washington, one middle-aged resident told us, "The river is not a part of me anymore." Others told us not to worry because the service clubs would implement the plan. We made cartoons of a broken heart with his words and the river plan with "the Service clubs will do it" as a caption. These were shown as a slide in a community meeting. This was the most powerful drawing done during the whole design process. It called personal attention to the community's disassociation from the river and the hopelessness of a river revitalization unless attitudes changed. The city intended to spend little money on improvements, and most people expected volunteers to do all the work. The river caused flood damage, was a dumping ground, and separated good and bad districts of the city. No one seemed to care about it. So why, we wondered, did people want to do anything to revitalize it? The cartoons prompted residents to begin thinking about the problem more holistically and realistically, and most concluded the river had such a bad reputation among adults that they didn't really expect it to be

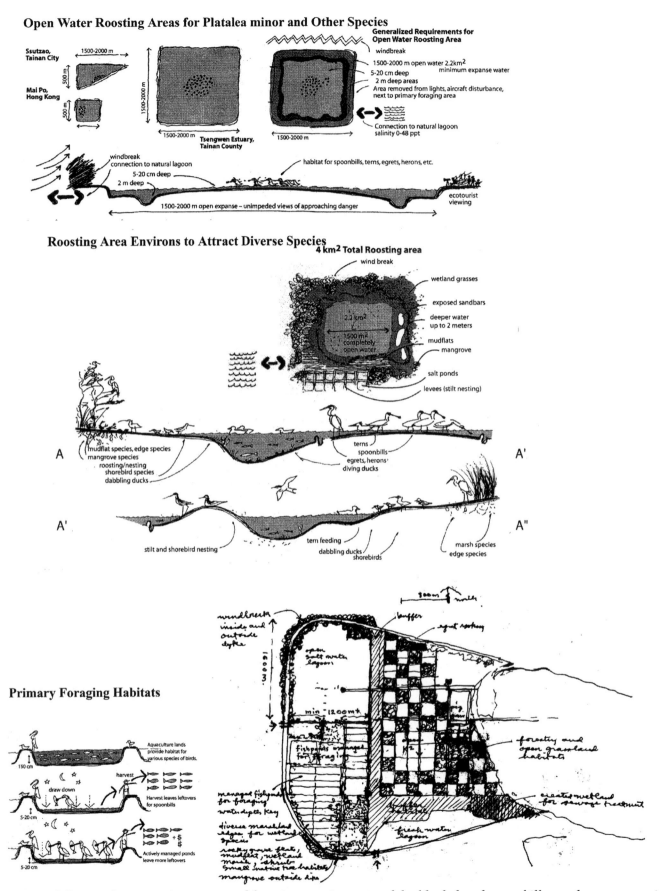

Figure 6. Research on roosting areas and foraging requirements of the black-faced spoonbill was drawn as precise spatial geometries to design villages to provide local jobs in bird watching and ecotourism.

revitalized. By thinking about the project more complexly and deeply, the community wisely abandoned the idea of doing a grand revitalization. They undertook small projects that service clubs and other volunteers could implement.

Two cases of such serious, interwoven thinking projects are described in the proceedings. One is the urban design work for Central Street of Ma-Kung City on the P'eng-hu Islands. Yu Chao-Ching describes a holistic approach that attempts to address community rehabilitation considering a complex web of legal and institutional problems, zoning contradictions, conflicting goals of land speculation and historic preservation, uncompetitive businesses and a degraded environment. For over ten years the designers learned and helped residents understand the complexity. By 1998 the group had developed a comprehensive plan to address the full range of entangled problems.

In a similarly multifaceted problem the Kyoto University team working on the Yoshino River attempted to help the community understand the intricate relationships between attachment to the river, flooding and single-species plantation forestry. Because these cases attempted to address extremely difficult problems by complex thinking, it would be especially informative to have updates on their progress. It would also be useful to see how other community designers come to understand and help communicate complexity through graphic means.

Making Science Spatial

One of the unique contributions that designers often make to community design is to translate conservation biology and wildlife habitat research into spatial patterns. At the simplest level this involves activity-mapping the territories of wild species, similar to recording human ecology patterns. We did this to determine the impact of habitat loss and the need for core areas and corridors in order to preserve the cougar population in the Santa Monica mountains. At a slightly more complex level, it involves understanding spatial relationships between multiple natural species like the cougar, coyote and quail. Human activities further complicate the relationships producing island and edge impacts, triggering rescue effects and changing species compositions. The fact that ecosystems are dynamic and evolving, as is the scientific knowledge, makes local wisdom especially important. Often local cultural patterns of resource use have been created over centuries to keep a balance with some essential species. Sometimes this wisdom is overrun or lost. Other times it is surpassed by science. As with social research on human behavior, urban ecological research almost always needs to be synthesized conceptually and spatially. In creating Big Wild in Los Angeles, we worked with citizens and scientists to draw research (much of which seems counter-intuitive due to the intricate food webs and habitat relationships) in forms useful to land use planning

and design. The drawing of the island effects on wildlife of the proposed Reseda to the Sea Highway was central to the creation of Big Wild in Los Angeles and the eventual abandonment of the freeway. Beyond these, visualizations of wildlife, natural processes like the relationship between coefficient of runoff and flooding, hungry water and erosion, or nutrient cycles remain mysteries until clearly diagrammed. By accurately portraying such complex science with citizens they develop the basis for ecologically sound stewardship activities like ecotourism, habitat restoration, species reintroduction, storm water management and urban vegetation enhancement.

In the proceedings there are numerous descriptions of community efforts to accurately draw natural science findings. Jeff Hou and Marcia McNally point out the joint work of local and international scientists, local fishermen and designers to create a picture of the spatial needs of the black-faced spoonbill. Each knew different parts of the habitat niche puzzle. Most scientists didn't realize the spoonbills roosted during the day and foraged widely at night, but local fishermen did, and international spoonbill expert Malcolm Coulter knew how far, up to 30 kilometers. As more research was done, more precise spatial geometries were drawn for use in the design of villages to attract economic development based on bird watching.

Similar efforts are described by the Kyoto University team in their work with the Vision 21 Committee. They listened to the deliberations of the 12 experts who were trying to determine the best approach to preserve or recreate the ecological systems of the Yoshino River. The Kyoto Team then synthesized the complex and often contradictory science and drew this for the experts and residents to better understand. This work is particularly complex due to the dramatically dynamic nature of the river system, the scientific findings, politics and social values about the river. Scott McCreary describes similar complexity in the Ecuador ARCO oil exploration debate and the use of an independent scientific review process to reconcile industry claims and local knowledge.

One of the most difficult aspects of landscape to visualize is natural change over time, whether it is river dynamics, old-field succession or park vandalism. The exercise of drawing the expanding shadow from a maturing tree, or drawing what a place was like a century ago and will be like a century from now, can create the most essential visual dialogue. In Castle Rock, Washington, which was partly destroyed by the eruption of Mount Saint Helens, we worked with long-time residents to recreate large pastel drawings of what the Cowlitz River had been like in town before the eruption, immediately after, ten years after, and what it might look like in the future. At the time it was a dead wasteland of gray pumice and debris 50 feet high in places. Previously it had been a maturing riverine ecology teeming with wildlife. When the drawings were shown at a community meeting, one woman looked at the lifeless present and said, "The birds don't sing here anymore." The audience hushed, many cried. It was no overstated metaphor. Songbirds disappeared when the habitat was washed away and buried by the debris flow. The future drawing gave hope but only after the catharsis from the set of evolutionary drawings spread throughout the city. Understanding the evolutionary, changing nature of the landscape via drawings is seldom so dramatic, but always useful.

Getting a Gestalt

Both citizens and designers are better partners in design when they are deeply rather than superficially engaged in the problem solving. One of the most critical aspects of deep involvement is getting a gestalt, the most essential image that cannot be derived simply from the sum of its complex parts. Ricardo Legoretta recently told me that for him getting the most essential idea is 95% of the design. It is not additive or even qualitative, and certainly not easy to draw, even for the most accomplished designers. To get a gestalt, community and designers have to move beyond polite superficial thinking, to probe and exchange core ideas and visualize the most profound synthesis of the situation. This is often done via a combination of sketching, collage, poetry, sense of the meeting, and free association following rigorous analysis. In Manteo, North Carolina, the mayor expressed the concept of, "Come sit on our front porch, let us tell you of the dreams we keep," after he had analyzed a number of collages expressing what citizens considered the gestalt. The front porch gestalt was so to the point that it provided both metaphorical and literal inspiration for the community plan.

In the proceedings there is the report of a poem written by a resident of the Sandy Spring Friends House with the telling line, "...bring color to another's life." This gestalt reshaped the circle and inspired the design. In another case, Endoh Yasuhiro describes the shared balconies at M-Court as representing the spirit of the co-housing, the merging of space and living, an approach he uses to capture the essential life pattern in architectural form.

Generalizations Versus the Experience of Precise Place

Often in public landscape design there is a rush to judgment based on a generalization without careful consideration of the place itself. Community leaders sometimes make decisions without ever visiting a site, relying instead on stereotypical images of the place. John Liu notes that, "People often only voice wants not grounded in place." Participatory exercises that require careful observation and discriminating looking can transform generalizations into space-specific problems that can be addressed by design. In the case of Runyon Canyon Park in Hollywood, most residents stated that they never went to the canyon because they feared for their safety. There was

building momentum to fence the whole park and remove the vegetation or sell parts of the park for private development. We made a map of Fearful Places in the park by asking residents to note exact spots where they were afraid and why. On walking tours they showed us precise locations. The resulting Fearful Places map showed only a few specific places of security concerns. Residents feared homeless people along narrow, enclosed walkways. In 99% of the canyon, residents felt completely safe. The map focused attention on the trouble spots, stopped the sale of public land and prevented wholesale and indiscriminate vegetation removal. The few trouble spots were designed to provide greater visibility. Homeless people agreed to locate to less traveled spots. The nagging fear was addressed with specificity.

Similar exchanges are noted in the proceedings. In the case of Densha Hiroba in Kyoto, a general fear that they would miss scheduled extracurricular activities prevented some school-aged children from using the local park. The designers addressed the vague but prevalent worry by locating a large clock readily visible to all park users. Similarly, the spatial scenarios led the designers of the shop houses in Kuo-hsin township to conclude that the most important part of a household design project lies in its specificity. Vague, nonspatial desires had to be concretized in real space and time for success.

Scored walking tours are the technique most often used to encourage the experience of precise locations and to dispel overblown generalizations. Several articles highlight the need for the designer and community members to experience the place together and to have spontaneous exchanges based on the sensual qualities in the real place. This is frequently accomplished by carefully scripted interpretation and dialogue about prearranged topics at particular sites. Such scored walks were used in the planning of Central Park in Davis. Others mention community exploring trips, walking and boat tours and watching tours. In most of these it is not clear exactly how the event influences the design per se.

COAUTHORING DESIGN

Through participatory design we learned that the built landscape could be enriched by transactive processes, but designers and involved citizens needed mutual empathy and a common language in order to design together. I am not discussing programming or analysis, but the actual event of making form as a group. To do this, designers had to learn to walk in the shoes of users and vice versa; we had to communicate clearly without jargon. Users and designers had to learn a shared language of everyday landscape in order to coauthor design. Representing people's activity patterns and critical needs described above is essential for programs and in some cases inspires design, but here I am interested in the precise techniques we use to do form-making with people.

Yu Chao-Ching states the value of seeing reality instead of impression in designing collaboratively. He recalls that, "During the process of participation, we made every participant 'see' the objects that we were going to discuss." He continues, "We used 'seeing' instead of 'impression' or 'imagination.'" He concludes that, "The more participants visualized, the more impressions and exciting imaginations they could recall" and "the precise visualization gave continuity between the past, present and future" making "results clear and concrete."

The language most useful to me is the drawing which, when thoughtfully done, is less ambiguous than spoken words, especially given culture, class and gender language differences. Equally useful for others are particular types of models, maps and texts. In the proceedings there are almost no descriptions of the particular methods we use to actually design with other people. I will describe techniques I know well in hopes of stimulating others to write explicitly about methods most useful to them in making form collaboratively.

Designing Upside Down

Once, sitting in a community meeting, I realized I was drawing upside down so that community members could more readily read the ideas we were generating. With practice, I got better at it. It is a useful skill and of symbolic import. I notice now that whenever I write upside down it changes the collaborative dynamic because the group is alerted to how serious we must be about communicating via a precise shared nonverbal language. We have to be sure we are understanding each other, even if it takes longer than normal.

And we have to be attentive to the various languages participants use. During the design of a new community center in Yountville, California several distinct languages were essential to the design. One mother always studied our drawings carefully but said little in the meetings; she would take the drawings home and write us letters describing how she would imagine using the spaces we proposed and suggesting detailed ways to improve the design. Her written language was spatial prose, insightful and precise. Her comments were narratives but always concluded with pointed design changes. She would describe how she imagined using the proposed library with her young children then admonish, "Move the computer area next to the little kid's reading space so I can supervise and work at the same time." The city manager's language was the capital improvements budget spreadsheet, architecturally graphic, but hardly spatial. Our measured drawings evolved from sketches, usually in plan and section. This was the most expressly visual language. Each of us had to metaphorically and literally write upside down in order to communicate effectively in coauthoring the design. The design workshops took more time communicating in so many "languages," but over time participants began to use each other's means of

expression. Spreadsheet and story telling became integrated into upside down sections.

Sketching What Others Say

Related to this is the skill of sketching what another person says. This requires aggressive listening. The designer not only listens but also sketches while listening, trying to give form to the idea a community member is expressing verbally. The resulting sketch tests whether two or more people are visualizing the same thing and often becomes the medium of exchange, a way to elaborate or create new designs. In some cases the sketch completely replaces verbal communication. I noticed this for some years working with contractors before I understood its power as a means of designing what people say. In the construction of Marvin Braude Park in Los Angeles, we were rebuilding a part of the Santa Monica mountains scarred by a failed freeway with thousands of cubic yards of mud slide soil. Although our layout and grading plans provided general direction, most of the detailed design, including earth form and rock placement, was done in the field. The dirt contractor and I quickly learned that words and even flags did not produce the desired results. I resorted to sketching what he said, starting by directing the grading to landmarks via sketches oftentimes as the bulldozer followed. Sometimes he would take my sketchbook and redraw the most likely outcome of a slope stabilization or drainage way. He would point out that I drew beautifully but inaccurately. He, in contrast, drew crudely but in precise bulldozer language. We soon began sketching the next day's, and even week's, work in perspective triangulated to existing points of reference, in some cases miles away. Eventually we made almost all decisions about pathways and overlooks by perspective sketch, using the formal working drawings less and less.

In the proceedings John Liu describes a dramatic moment that changed the design for the Ilan Theatre. In one meeting with local performing artists, someone made the suggestion that the proposed theater would be much better if it weren't separated from the vital street performances that occurred all over the surrounding downtown. Some felt that performances in the theater should begin as parades through the streets leading to an oversized front doorway and down a street-sized aisle directly to the stage. While performers talked about this, Liu sketched. He made a reasonably scaled drawing showing the shape and size of the entry sequence. The sketch became the focus of the conversation, allowing the group to elaborate and expand on the initial idea and discard unworkable aspects. The sketches provided a reality check for the much less precise verbiage. Often nonspatial narrative is so ambiguous that everyone is understanding a spoken word in completely different, often mutually exclusive, ways. Liu's drawing turned the words into agreed upon form.

Drawing On Your Feet

Sketching is a convenient communication between two people or a small group; it is much more difficult but equally useful to sketch with large groups of citizens. I have observed Daniel Iocafano and Yoshiharu Asanoumi drawing their ideas on butcher paper almost as fast as a hundred residents generated them. They can listen, think and draw on their feet faster than most people think on their feet. This is a critical skill in democratic design. Iocafano and Asanoumi train people to do this. With practice I have learned to listen, draw, exchange and even paint explicitly enough to use the quick painting not to just record ideas, but to design with public groups, but it is difficult for me. When we did the plan for Parque Natural in South Central Los Angeles, we did almost all the design work on big tables under a tent on the then-derelict site. I drew most of the organizing principles as community members and design team discussed critical issues. The form of the main design features, including a community center and zocalo, recreated arroyo and wetland, nature passeo and meadow, were coauthored by interactive sketching. Details of the architecture, including the dimensions of the columns needed to create social spaces at entries, lighting for the meeting room and materials of floor pavers, were negotiated by quick painting. Idea. Sketch. "Do you mean this?" "No, more diffused light." Sketch. "Like this?" "Yes, that's better." This transparency of design elicited creative exchanges.

The contentious issue of fencing was resolved most innovatively through the sketch process. I did one drawing on my feet that was particularly important. Due to gang warfare and general safety concerns, residents listed park rangers and fencing at the top of the list in creating the program for the park. Staff and some community leaders were opposed to fencing largely because they assumed it would be unwelcoming chain link. Residents insisted. During one debate, I remembered an exquisite ironwork fence I had seen in Spain. I had taken

the time to sketch it when I was there and remembered its essence. As people argued, I sketched it, rather poorly, from memory. "What about doing a fence something like this?," I asked. In the group were employees of the numerous metal fabrication industries in the neighborhood, one of whom responded, "We can make that." Another moved closer and said in Spanish that it couldn't be made as I drew it. I couldn't understand him, but that didn't matter because he was already correcting my drawing with an easier-to-manufacture detail. Over the next few design workshops the sketching resolved successive issues of liability, city standards, costs and details. The design evolved from my fuzzy, abstract memory, through a background of misunderstood words, to a metal wetland with marsh reeds forming vertical fencing and native egrets creating gates. No doubt my rough drawing of the fence quickly and big enough to share changed the contentious verbal sparring into collective creativity, but I wasn't truly drawing on my feet like others did. I drew in my sketchbook measuring only about one foot by one and a half feet. It is difficult for me to draw clearly on huge sheets of butcher paper in front of a lot of people.

The Big Map

I only have some of the skills needed to draw on my feet. To draw effectively on one's feet requires not just the capacity to call up and sketch imagery from remembered precedents, but also the graphic skill to quickly draw more complex ideas and to do so in front of large groups of people.

In the proceedings, Yu Chao-Ching describes a method he uses called the Talking Big Map. The Talking Big Map, typically for the entire community at a scale that fills a whole wall top to bottom, becomes the medium of visualized conversation. On it people or Yu record varying opinions about settings in the community. I recently observed Yu and Huang Chien-Hsiu leading a workshop in Hualien using such a Talking Big Map. The map filled the room and obviously had been used before.

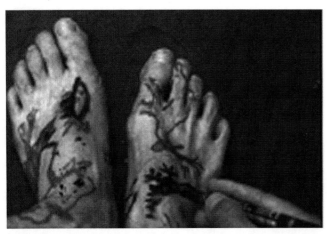 

Figure 7. Drawing on your feet and sketching upside down are non-verbal communication skills particular to community designers.

Figure 8. Most of the major design elements and details were drawn in community meetings, using precedents recalled by the landscape architect and often revised by a resident with construction expertise.

People knew where their homes were. The day I observed, it was the focus of discussion about improvements along the old rail line, district by district. As Huang elicited comments, Yu drew the ideas people had directly on an overlay. He drew quickly and clearly, pausing only for clarification. After several hours they had recorded dozens of proposals for each district. The Talking Big Map provided a collective memory of the ideas generated that day, but it also seemed that the Talking Big Map provided a focus and memory chamber for the entire planning process week after week.

The single text used by Scott McCreary provides a similar, although nonspatial collective memory and focus. Surprisingly for a group of designers, there are few spatially explicit collaborative design techniques precisely described in the proceedings. It would be particularly instructive for other participatory designers to describe in detail methods they use for coauthoring form making.

Figure 9. Yu Chao-Ching and Huang Chien Hsiu use the Talking Big Map and Model to assist the community in designing the abandoned railroad right of way in Hualien.

EMPOWERING PEOPLE TO REPRESENT THEMSELVES

If used collaboratively, or if transferred to the community, most of the previously discussed drawing techniques provide residents new skills and more control over community life and place. A few techniques particularly empower. Three of the following four are discussed in the proceedings: Envisioning Unity, Power Maps, Citizen Science and Making Choices.

Envisioning Unity

Participation shows people the power of working together, verifying the saying, "United we stand, divided we fall." How is this unity and its authority made explicit? The cases indicate that community designers use particular methods to increase community unity. Numerous cases, including Menlo Park, SAVE, Hsiang-Ching Bao Village and Bao-Zan-Yan squatter settlement, employ newsletters to communicate, build a sense of community and encourage collective action. The Talking Big Map discussed previously creates a shared visual experience that serves as a collective unified memory, heightens a sense of community and helps even disjointed groups imagine that they could come together with the confidence to achieve a common goal. These are explicit graphic methods for building power through unity.

Other techniques are less explicit and direct. Every community workshop that concludes with a sense of shared purpose likely provides a subtle image of collective power. And certainly street protests and other collective actions that produce even small victories provide concrete evidence of the power of unity. The massive sleep-in in Taipei streets, Snails Without Shells, provides the most dramatic example of this in the proceedings. That image is so evocative of the power of unified action that it adorns many community design offices as a poster child of empowerment.

Power Maps

Although control of community events is sometimes readily apparent, there are almost always complex and unseen power relationships that determine the successful outcomes of community plans. Drawing a power map can make clear what is known and unknown about local control, and can spur

necessary action to determine key hidden authority, formal and informal. Power maps, when complete, look like food webs and, like food webs, they almost always lead incrementally to powerful forces. Discovering those powerful forces is essential to local empowerment in order to identify enemies of local control, parties who benefit directly and indirectly from local exploitation, and groups both inside and outside the community that manipulate local insecurities and factionalism for their gain. Mere knowledge of these alliances is empowering in order to expose and fight parties that would undermine any grass roots improvements and to strengthen and form alliances of mutual empowerment.

There were several cases where designers stated that they consciously sought an understanding of power relationships. The spatial scenarios after the Taiwan earthquake revealed that women who spent most of the time at home always deferred to older men to decide the arrangement of the house in spite of the men seldom being at home. Other cases note power plays determining design outcomes, but I could find no mention in the proceedings of power maps being made to explicitly visualize power relationships.

Citizen Science

Volunteers increasingly are involved in scientific monitoring of the environment and landscape change. The Nature Mapping Program in Washington State trains volunteers to identify wildlife species and to use maps to record locations of wildlife sightings. Fifty thousand volunteers participate to create a database of wildlife concentrations that supplements professional studies. These are used in land use planning decisions. Similarly, the Cornell Laboratory of Ornithology and the Audubon Society involve 42,000 participants in the Great Backyard Bird Count. The Keeping Track Program, which trains citizens to track and map wildlife, and revises local land use plans accordingly, recently intervened in a local planning decision to reverse a local general plan proposal to locate housing in wooded areas rather than in more visually sensitive open spaces. The Keeping Track data showed the import of the forest areas for wildlife, leading to a reprioritization of habitat ecology over scenic beauty. In none of these cases is a community designer an important participant, but many

Figure 10. Community workshops in Setagaya engendered a sense of shared purpose that carried over to create locally controlled neighborhood places.

Figure 11. Citizen Scientists in Korea monitor changes in wetland productivity, vegetation and bird habitat as a result of the 40,000 hectare Saemangeum dike project which many people fear will lead to multiple local extinctions and the loss of thousands of jobs in fishing industries.

other professionals are. They train volunteers to do their own research using science and volunteer mapping to inform local decision-making.

There are a few cases in the proceedings of such citizen scientist activities. It appears that community people did some mapping in and around Nishinari Park to develop solutions acceptable to the residents and homeless. In another case, Berkeley residents sometimes do their own research about playground equipment, but these are seemingly coincidental to the process compared to citizen science activities reported elsewhere.

Making Choices: Maps and Models

Drawings and other concrete representations that give people realistic choices empower. Visual preference tests and simulations provide communities with clear alternatives. To be successful drawings must be easily read, compared and evaluated. Designer's favorites must be drawn no more beautifully than other choices.

In the proceedings there are numerous examples of drawings and models being used to provide the basis for making choices. "Before" and "after" drawings are noted in the Hsin Kan case. Moveable model parts allowed youth to create their own plans for Union Point Park and then critically evaluate the best solutions. Two- and three-dimensional models were used in planning and evaluating Wanchai and Luen Fat Street Parks. In the most imaginative case, a full-scale model of the proposed creek plan allowed residents to design alternatives in precise detail for Kitazawagawa, a stream in Setagaya. The final plan, in which residents rejected a typical engineering solution for the creation of a complex stream with multiple, carefully orchestrated wildlife habitats, was built at real life size in a local school yard to make last minute adjustments in the plan before approval and construction.

This case points out an important aspect of making choices and evaluating plans for social suitability before they are built. Residents can readily do this using methods previously described in representing people—most notably drawing activity and social ecology patterns, and in the Setagaya case, by walking through the simulation. The difference is that the potential users have to imagine (rather than observe) how they

and others will use a space. The resulting evaluation can often correct design flaws before construction preventing costly mistakes, saving money and enhancing social suitability.

Designers and residents involved in participatory design learn the power of the drawing in many of its dimensions. We learn and relearn that you can draw almost anything—an idea, a place or an action—and that by drawing it you visualize it, grasp it, and can understand it better. Drawing an unseen thing—whether it is a map of environmental injustices or barriers to civicness, a diagram of the political power structure or concepts of naturalness, or perspective sketches of various preferred settings for a picnic or watching shooting stars—makes that unseen thing known, visible. That empowers people with the ability to grasp the thing and change it.

VISUALIZING DEEP VALUES: COMMUNITY, STEWARDSHIP, FAIRNESS AND DISTINCTIVE PLACE

Participatory design is accurately viewed as a populist endeavor, advocating that local people, the users, know what is best for them. This user needs approach is a consumer, demand driven model that is producing many of the problems community designers seek to remedy. Meeting short-term needs and wants frequently results in exclusivity, injustice, and a material culture opposed to fundamental values held by community designers.

Community designers as a group are dissatisfied with and seek to change this status quo. For example, they are much more concerned about and work to overcome environmental

Figure 12. Workshops, workdays and walking tours are frequently used to provide shared imagery for design, shared community activity, and sensual experience of the place being considered.

injustices than most other people in their society. Likewise, they worry more about the increase in privatization of community resources, diminishment of sense of community, destruction of ecosystems and biological diversity, and loss of distinctive cultures and places to homogenized, global styles. Most people, John Liu observes, tend too easily to adopt external images and values as their own.

To address these problems and nurture societies with deeply held values regarding community, ecological stewardship, environmental justice and distinctive places, community designers use methods to help people visualize this alternative and slightly idealistic world. In the proceedings three distinct techniques for this are offered—community building, mapping sacred landscapes and recalling through imagination and hypnosis values rooted in place.

Building Community Experientially

In order to overcome what seems to be a misplaced emphasis on individual freedom and an associated loss of community responsibility, participatory designers seek to build a sense of community while undertaking projects that build the physical community. Workshops, workdays and walking tours create both shared imagery for design and shared community activity. The simple act of walking around their community to look at paving materials provided a collective experience and the discovery of a precedent for the paving of Yachimun Street in Naha, Okinawa. This tour resulted in community agreement on a stone-paved path based on traditional coral stone pavers. Similarly, Endoh takes participants to co-housing projects to look at precedents and to build group solidarity. The joy of collective action guides the projects in Setagaya. Street parties and nature walks similarly build community and help residents rediscover the enchantment of nature, the unique sensual quality of their community and the pleasure of the company of others. These activities create the atmosphere for fireflies, funerals and old photographs to influence values and plans for the future of community.

These techniques typically utilize no graphic simulation; rather they depend upon the direct experience of the physicality of culture and landscape. Smells, sounds and touch replace drawings. They make sense of community truly sensual. The technique to build community experientially is the second most mentioned method among the cases from the Democratic Designers in the Pacific Rim.

Mapping Sacred Landscapes

In societies increasingly disassociated from natural phenomena and place, recording sacred places provides an antidote to environmental anomie. Sacred places represent deep values, often counter to superficial wants and needs. The sacred place exercise begins by asking people to individually list the places

they most value in their city, then in small groups visit, map and record those places with photographs or sketches. This typically heightens awareness of subconscious attachments to and dependence upon the landscape. The results can be used directly in the community design process as we did in Manteo, North Carolina. In another case recorded elsewhere, the United States Environmental Protection Agency realized that the sacred landscapes mapping could encourage better land management, and in 1997 undertook a demonstration project in Pennsylvania, Maryland and Virginia to assist communities in the identification and visualization of sacred places. The goal of the project is to reverse status quo land neglect and stimulate local stewardship in an effort to improve water quality miles away in the Chesapeake Bay.

In the proceedings are similar techniques like Yu's Community Identity System, which concretized community values in Peng-hu and framing special places with red picture frames in Setagaya. These and other similar projects to identify sacred places typify efforts to make Machizukuri actualize values. All of these related techniques call up and make concrete profound values, many counter to prevalent consumer demands.

Recalling Values in Place Through Imagination and Hypnosis

Although most people don't have precedents of great places from years of architectural history courses, most do have a storehouse of personal experiences that provide qualitative and quantitative measures of good environments. Many of these personally experienced places embody values contrary to the status quo and useful in public design for a more caring society. But people generally have a hard time recalling these precedents explicitly enough to use them in design. Self-hypnosis, or guided fantasy, can help people recall and draw their favorite street, square or landscape in such detail to inform design. Drawings done after a hypnotic visualization are amazingly clear in dimension and in more ephemeral aspects like light quality. These drawings help people to revisualize values embedded in place and create nurturing, supportive designs. These remembered places allow us to be much more critical and realistic about how big a site is, what fits, what doesn't, when a site is too crowded and the impact of a low tree canopy versus a tall canopy. The informed design discussions that result could never happen without the detail of precedents visualized and drawn. This is particularly useful in determining what people mean by "natural," a key concept for landscape design and one that has many abstract interpretations. Drawings make the abstract value concrete enough to guide design.

In the proceedings I describe our early experiment with hypnosis at the Harvard Law Child Care Center, which produced answers contradictory to those given in a previous

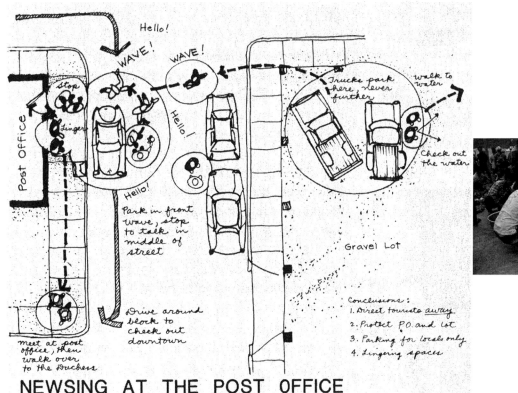

Figure 13. The two most used nonverbal, spatial techniques are the recording of social ecology and building community experientially.

questionnaire. Endoh notes that talks about earliest childhood memories lead to materialization of value laden spaces like the mudroom (doma), veranda (engawa) and fireplace (irori). These spaces traditionally enhanced the most meaningful contacts between people and other people and between people and nature. In one case the description of a remembered irori led a young child to say, "Dad, I wish I could live in a house with a fireplace like this." Endoh is able to incorporate these most profound settings into co-housing, creating places that become purveyors of humanizing values. Endoh is the most articulate of community designers in this regard. His designs speak of soft boundaries or ecotones rather than hard divisions or strict edges. These soft boundaries encourage exploration just as the "participation process cultivates in residents a sensitivity to what really matters" in life, rich human relationships and "wild nature, birds singing and the shadow of the moon up in the sky." All of these are attempts to make places grounded in intense values to overcome mundane, profane and alienating places. There are also attempts to articulate dreams in the case of the Kyoto hiroba, and to encourage empathy in the case of the Emotional Landscape Models used in the design of the Sandy Spring, Maryland retirement community. In other cases, as Richard Meier stated, they also attempt to draw out of people their most heroic insights and find ways to implement them. All are counter to the prevailing dominant culture. It would be particularly useful to know exactly how Endoh and others

draw out these value laden memories and imaginations and transform them into nonverbal visualizations and design form. Are some approaches more effective at cultivating sensitivity to rich relationships, to wild nature, to heroic empathic acts, to stewardship of people and place?

CONCLUSIONS

For me this review rekindles the promise of the ongoing exchange of Democratic Designers in the Pacific Rim. On a personal level, it reminds me of how much I have learned from other's participatory approaches and democratic design methods and how much insight I have gained into my own work by comparing it to and being challenged by others.

Normative and Experimental Techniques

On a more academic level, this review indicates that there are both normative techniques for drawing representationally as well as experimental techniques. The norm, expressed in the techniques most reported, indicates that this group of democratic designers relies on workshops and verbal exchanges. In about three quarters of the articles there is reference to a workshop without description of the content or how the content is explicated in spatial or experiential terms. There are almost as many references to workshop and/or community meeting as all spatially explicit techniques combined. This has been the norm in the United States for several decades where community decisions most depend on nominal group process as the technique of choice.

Among the most-used nonverbal, spatial techniques are the recording of social ecology patterns and building community experientially. Other methods mentioned frequently in the proceedings are techniques to envision the power of unity, to make science spatial and to capture the experience of precise places. Consider briefly what each of these indicates. Social ecology patterns is a traditional technique of social designers. It is easy, although time consuming to do, and it produces spatially explicit data about social nuance, the sum of which likely explains its extensive use among participatory designers.

The use of techniques that emphasize experiencing the place collectively seems to be increasing. Workdays and walking tours are fun, require physical exertion, provide hands-on learning, heighten sensual pleasure of places, build community, and stimulate imagination and creative problem solving based on the sense and reality of a place. All of these explain why participatory designers are using these phenomenological methods more.

The frequent use of techniques to emphasize the experience of a precise location corroborates this trend among participatory designers to turn abstract, often vague wants, needs and knowledge into place-specific design actions. These methods suggest an increased attention to design that not only meets programmatic needs but also is based on an intense experience of the life enriching qualities unique to each place and culture.

Community designers have long been committed to empowerment of people so it follows that many methods help people visualize the empowering aspects of unified action. The key here is the use of drawing in the broad sense to create an image of their collective power. Participatory designers work on increasingly difficult issues, technically and scientifically. Often these issues are so complex that no one understands them very well, not scientists themselves and certainly not designers and communities of lay people. It makes sense that drawing is being used to comprehend these complex problems and their spatial consequences.

Some of these most employed techniques are also among the more experimental. This may be explained in part because these techniques are most interesting to us right now. Among the experimental techniques are making science spatial and transforming generalizations into the experience of precise locations. There are conscious inventive efforts to ground design in the sensual experience of place and to tap into deeper values, not just superficial wants. Other experiments with map size (the Big Map), turning narrative into explicit space (spatial scenarios) and picturing everyday life whole (memory interviews) offer promising results.

Even in the use of traditional social ecology mapping there are innovations that suggest a shift in community design intent. Recording social ecology provided patterns of behavior, extremely useful but isolated from intention, attitudes and experience. Some of the cases combine behavior mapping with narrative to give a more holistic picture of everyday life. There seems to be a concerted effort to overcome modern abstraction and post-modern deconstruction of life space and to design it whole, to capture its sensual and experiential nuance. This represents an emphasis on social suitability based on imagination, meaning and values in addition to behavior, justice, and distribution of goods.

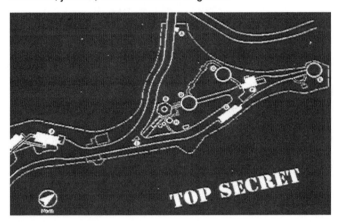

Figure 14. Is the workshop the mysterious black box of collective creativity or can community designers explicate the top secrets of its success by carefully articulating favored procedures?

Figure 15. Is socially transformative design disguised in conservative aesthetics while conservative social agendas experiment with superficially radical aesthetics?[3]

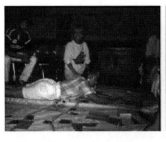

Figure 16. What techniques can most usefully engage communities in designing, not just programming, the future environments which they will inhabit?

Nonverbal Design and the Black Box

Return, for a moment, to the finding that community design relies most on verbal techniques like workshops rather than drawing and other nonverbal spatial representation. In all of the articles only one-third explicitly describe the use of spatial representation. Even fewer describe techniques leading directly to design, and almost none describe the built outcome.

I found only five out of 101 articles that describe techniques for coauthoring design in which spatial representation passed back and forth between community and designer. Many of the techniques mentioned create the program and lead up to design (recording social ecology patterns and making science spatial, for example) and some may even produce design decision-making (making choices with maps and models), but few describe collaborative form making.

This review might easily conclude that participatory design has a black box, the workshop, that is more democratic but equally elusive as the black box of traditional designers. To overcome this we need to be much more explicit in describing our methods and how they lead to or do not lead to action and outcomes, including designed and built landscapes. It would be especially informative to have in-depth descriptions of techniques that are spatially and experientially explicit and that capture and reshape place values.

The challenge of my colleague lingers. Do community designers shy from spatial explicitness? Are community designers more dependent on verbal communication and less skilled at spatially and experientially explicit communication? Or are our nonverbal techniques simply different and possibly superior when intensely and personally grounded in the place and culture?

Participatory Methods and Radical Design in Conventional Clothing

In a related topic of debate this review leaves little doubt that participatory design methods are more process oriented and less product oriented than other design approaches, products like building sense of community and empowerment

notwithstanding. But contrary to the often thought and sometimes spoken claim of elitist designers, there is scant evidence that the built design resulting from participatory processes is inferior. From this review the participatory design products seem unusually carefully crafted and reasonably low maintenance in addition to being well used and socially suitable. They are often figurative rather than abstract. There is loving attention to detail. There is no conceptual art nor is there deconstructed futurism. There does seem to be a comfortable, even conventional aesthetic in most participatory projects.

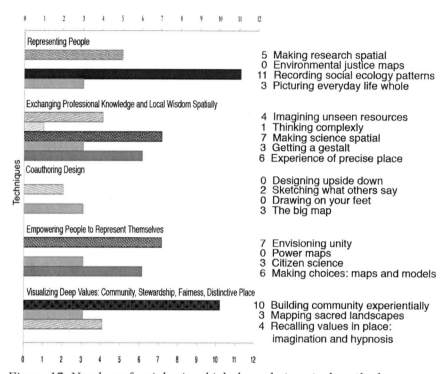

Figure 17. Number of articles in which the technique is described.

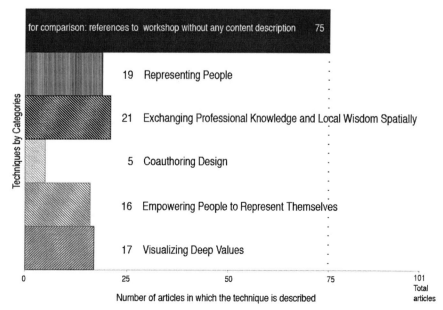

Figure 18. Number of case studies employing techniques by category in proceedings of Democratic Designers in the Pacific Rim (1999-2002).

Is socially transformative design disguised in conservative aesthetics while conservative social agendas experiment with superficially radical aesthetics? Does this directly result from the participatory process or certain participatory methods?

Skills Particular to Participatory Design

Participatory efforts share most drawing techniques with other designers. Careful observation, using research, developing concepts, and making choices are part of most design procedures.

Many representational techniques, like environmental justice maps, imagining unseen resources, envisioning unity, thinking complexly and building community experientially, may, on occasion, be shared with community organizing and development. There are also drawing methods that are likely the near exclusive domain of participatory design. Recording social ecology patterns, picturing everyday life whole, exchanging generalization for precise locations, designing upside down, mapping sacred landscapes and recalling values in place seem to be particular to participatory design.

Almost all of the drawing techniques discussed have special relevance to participatory design. What most distinguishes all these methods of drawing is the specific ways they are used in participatory contexts. They help designers express what other people think is important. They create a common language so complex publics can work together to make their own habitation. They nurture and inform civic debate. They include the excluded and they make democratic design from the bottom up. These differences in drawing are profound.

ENDNOTES

[1] Graphics provided by Randy Hester and Jeffrey Hou.

[2] From The Bostonians Playing Excise-Man, 1774. print attributed to P. Dawe.

[3] From Rural Studio: Samuel Mockbee and An Architecture of Decency by Andrea Oppenheimer Dean and Timothy Hursley.

DRAWING THE LINES IN THE WORLD AS COMMUNITY DESIGNERS

Masato Dohi

ABSTRACT

This article examines the issue of spatial form and social process. It puts forward ideas on the potential of 'nature' to show spatial borders and systems even in urban areas, and argues that we should read this potential to develop new city or urban form. To continue and deepen this argument, I will relate my thoughts on design process and try to connect with city or urban planning. Four cases of those I have experienced are chosen here to explore the design process: the case of King Estate Park, Oakland C.A., Suma-ward Kobe Japan, Narai Park Aichi Japan and Izumi settlement Tokyo, Japan. Each case will not be described as a whole. Instead, the focus will be on the most critical step of practice to consider what community design has created around space and society. Through this exploration, I hope to show that community design relies on and derives from some 'natures of human character' even when our project's objective is not nature preservation or rehabilitation. After all, using this 'nature of human character', community design could realize a vital space in people's relationship on site. However, how can we organize these sites on an urban scale? This question was a main theme of my presentation at the Hong Kong conference in 2002. I will trace briefly the idea that I have presented on natural systems and spatial-social form. At last, the connection between a well-managed design process and urban scale planning will be explored. The fractal concept will be introduced. With this concept, topics on form and process, design and planning or function and nature will be reconsidered.

WE DRAW LINES

We draw the lines. By drawing the lines, we imagine good space. We try to draw meaningful lines so that the space can be precious for people. This is why we need citizen participation. It is only through this process that lines have meaning and begin to live. If we do well, lines with rich meaning begin to create space, which gives meaning to people and to which people give meaning. At this moment lines we drew manifest themselves in space and society. Community designers draw the lines on paper, card, and wall or even on foot; all of these are to draw lines in space and society, and it happens only when these lines are meaningful.

I would like to examine the meaning of the lines we draw and the meaning of drawing the lines, particularly in this severe time and world. First I will consider the meaning of lines drawn in community design by reflecting my own experiences. Then I will connect it to the hypothesis that I presented at the Hong Kong conference, 2002. Second, I will look at the meaning of drawing the lines of community design in this world. This is an attempt to clarify the opponent lines and to establish our strategy.

WHAT COMMUNITY DESIGN TAUGHT ME: LINES WITH MEANING

I would like to trace four scenes from my community design experiences to reflect on what community design teaches me. I will not describe the whole process of each project but just address the essence of community design. Though the projects I choose are not ecology or nature oriented, there are aspects of nature in the designs done with people and community.

King Estate Park Design Project

From 1993-1994, I engaged in the park design project with the students of University of California, Berkeley and Randy Hester in Oakland, California. This community had about 4000 residents. The park site is 39 ha. and located in the center of this community on the hill. It was the first community design project for me and was very enjoyable, but I won't tell these stories here because you already know. It is the last phase of drawing out the final design proposal for the park that I would like to show. After geographic analysis and community input, three students including myself each drew a park design. Though the elements used for the park design were almost the same, each design became quite different. We had meetings to discuss the idea and basis of each design to determine a final proposal to the community. Each designer explained how he or she recognized the community input and expressed them in spatial form. We could agree on many parts except two points of design— placing a path on the ridge of the hill and planting tree on the top of the hill. Discussion went in circles and seemed endless. While we prompted people to reach some consensus, it was absolutely difficult to realize the consensus among designers who have strong

Figure 1. *King Estate Park Location.*

Figure 2. *King Estate Park Workshop.*

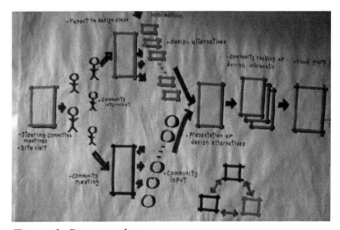

Figure 3. *Process plan.*

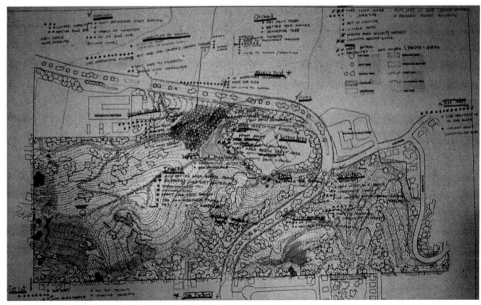

Figure 4. *Residents' opinion feedback.*

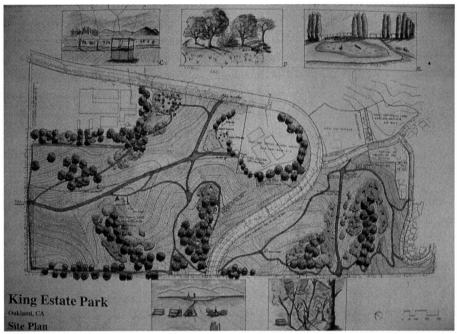

Figure 5. Preliminary plan.

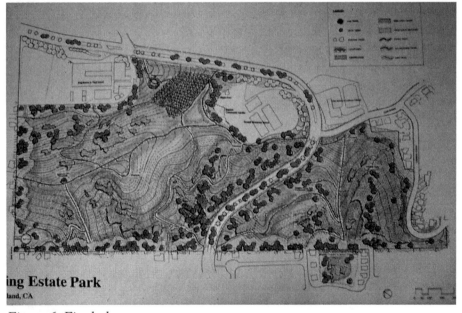

Figure 6. Final plan.

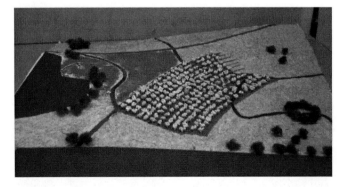

Figure 7. Image model.

orientation to ones' own design. Even after one month of tough argument, the designers could not reach consensus. We finally asked the community to 'tell us more'. In this case, one solution was chosen over the other, and designers accepted this result with much frustration. I had believed as a designer that my design proposal was most honest to community input and also most beautiful, so I could not understand why community people wanted an oak tree on the top of hill.

Other designers and I unwillingly redrew the park design according to the community's wishes. I compared this final design with my previous design to console myself. At this moment I suddenly understood how the final design, which combined three designers' concepts and the community's opinion, was rich and fertile with meanings. While I still could see clear rhythm, unified codes and right zoning from my previous design, the final design looked disordered at a glance. But once I imagined that I was walking on the site designed as in the final design, I could find livable and joyful space. I should just accept this new design. How can we come to understand the beauty generated from encounters with other people's value, the beauty not of minimalism but 'maximalism'? This was, for me, a point to rethink what designers should do in the world.

Secret Road of Everyday Life: Sakuragi-cho, Kobe City

Space has social contexts behind its spatial form in community. I would like to show a secret road in this sense. Sakuragi-cho is located in a lovely residential area developed as a villa zone about 100 years ago. Over 1000 residents within 370 households live in this community. Sakuragi-cho also had been hit and damaged deeply by the earthquake of 1995. Kobe City authority had decided to put several new, vast roadways in this area just after the earthquake as a recovery project, and one of these roads will cut this community in two. 30m in width and over 10m in height, the road will bridge over the existing railway. People in this community had to get over calamity and

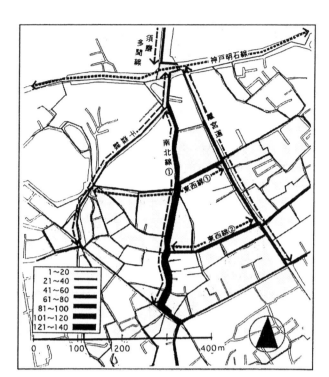

Figure 8. *Streets used by walkers.*

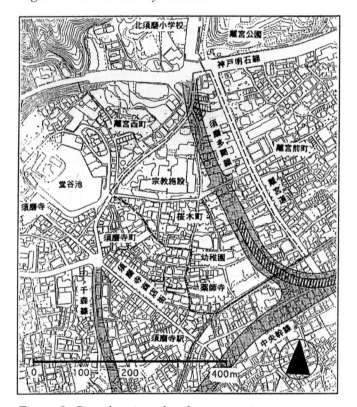

Figure 9. *City planning plan for restoration.*

at the same time fight against this stupid roadway plan. We, the community design team of Kyoto University, have acted with this community.

Among the many things and events we have done with community, I will show the simple research for use of the existing street (1998). We have asked community members

Figure 10. To see the height of the road.

to trace the streets they use every day, and overlaid them. What we can read in the result map is that the main street of this community is not Rikyu-michi (imperial villa street), which is straight and has sidewalks. The narrow and meandering street running next to Rikyu-michi is the main street for this community. I think it is difficult for outsiders to know this simple fact, including designers. But if one can ask residents in an adequate way, they will tell us these kinds of things that are natural for them.

Though this main street is a secret street, every community member knows it as an important part of his or her daily life. It is like a path created by creatures in the forest. If you have rambled in the forest with a person who knows the forest well, you understand how many things this person can see. These things cannot be seen nor even exist, when people who do not know try to find them. Can designers discover many things in the forest created through peoples' lives? I suspect designers or planners have seen these forests just like vacant lots in many cases. As the forestland has been developed without method, developments today are being carried out in the forest of people's daily lives without method.

The main street of Sakuragi-cho is a stage of community life. On this sunny, comfortable stage, people are walking and talking and kids are running through. People love this street in their life. The new roadway cannot be loved because of its form and use are out of scale. People cannot give and accumulate the meanings to this road. They are struggling against this road because it will bring noise, vibration and air pollution. But it may be said that they are also against the appearance of space to which they cannot give meanings.

Narai Park, Okazaki city, Aichi Prefecture

In this case of a park design project, I will examine how peoples' thoughts are connected to spatial form and how spatial form limits peoples' thought. Narai Park is located in a residential area of Okazaki city, Nagoya Prefecture, With an area of about 1.3 ha., the park was closed for 4 years for construction of an underground reservoir. Before reopening, residents of this area gathered and created new park designs with a community designer, and they proposed their plan to the city government in 2000. The city accepted their park design proposal.

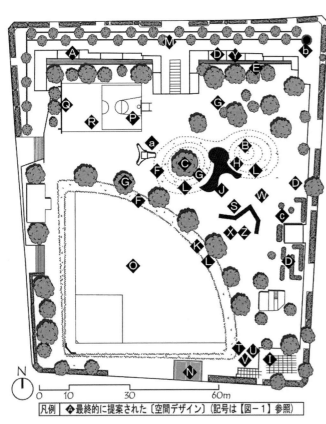

凡例 ◆最終的に提案された〔空間デザイン〕（記号は【図－1】参照）

Figure 11. Residents' plan.

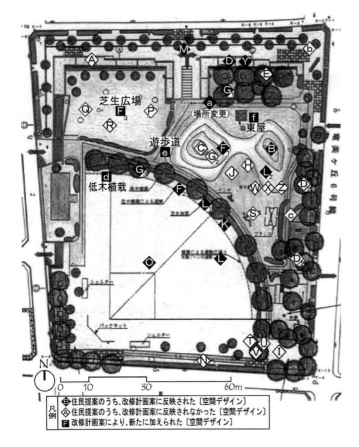

凡例
◆住民提案のうち、改修計画案に反映された〔空間デザイン〕
◇住民提案のうち、改修計画案に反映されなかった〔空間デザイン〕
◆改修計画案により、新たに加えられた〔空間デザイン〕

Figure 12. City park bureau's plan.

Figure 13. Work-shop scene.

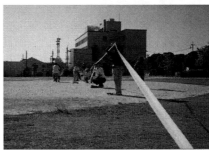

Figure 14. Checking the form of the mound.

Participatory process to reach design at Okazaki Park followed basic steps of community design. People expressed their own needs using colloquial language first, and imagining the spatial apparatus that meets their needs, then they moved to spatial language. Finally they studied how these spatial languages should be spelled out under the site conditions; and then they design. Community designer Yutaka Amano who led this park project pointed out in his article that spatial apparatus designed by residents for Okazaki Park covers every facility observed in parks designed by specialists. And he succeeds in showing design elements that can be seen in the park designed by residents. Residents imagine spatial design apart from the function. This means that their needs range in plural functions, and that they connect their needs directly to spatial design without reduction into function. When they encounter the difficulties to put several functions in a spatial design, they trace back their discussion that lead to such design, and overcome their difficulties in managing the way of use. In the case of the park project, each design detail for this park has discussions and stories behind it. One can trace the peoples' thought from design details.

On the other hand, the latter phase of this case shows the other character of spatial design. The city authority accepted the residents' proposal and revised the plan for the park. However, the plan revised by the city park bureau looks similar to the residents' plan, but the facilities constructed are very different. Biotope, basketball hoop, gated ball field, recycling post, little open-air library, tiny theater and athletic facilities were deleted and grass field, arbor, planting and alley were added. I do not think city officials had some particular bias. They might just cut the facilities that seem difficult to maintain and added general things found in common parks. The officials, who have not been at the meetings to design the park, could not notice that there were diverse discussions and processes behind each design detail on the residents' plan.

But what really is surprising is that the residents who participated at the meeting could not notice the difference of these two plans. During the meeting, the discussion was around the plan proposed by the city officer. They never went back to the plan designed by themselves. I think this shows peoples' ability to realize and criticize the space is weak compared with that of designing it. In other words, people tend to easily accept the alteration of their every day circumstances or the imposed design. Or it may be said that human beings can adapt to environmental change even when we can now change our environment extensively.

Izumi-no-ie (Fountain House) Art Project, Setagaya Ward, Tokyo

As presented in Mr. Kimura's in this proceedings, we are engaging in an Art Project at the institution for disabled persons with its residents. I will not go into detail except to mention just one instance when we discussed the goal and risk. The goal of this art project is to encourage the residents to express themselves through creative activities. After nearly 20 years of living in the same room separated from society, they have a difficulty to speak out.

Figure 15. Kit for collage.

Figure 16. Art work.

Figure 17. Art work.

The risk of project management is mainly from its tight schedule. We anticipate showing the results for first step in a very short time. When we decided on the final design for wall and roof painting, we altercated among staff about the workshop program. We had three plans for this stage: (1) We propose several designs for residents to vote on; (2) Residents individually design and we collage them; and (3) Residents do the collage themselves. After heated discussions, of course we have chosen (3) to pursue the goal but risking the project management. I think there should be some steps we cannot control completely in the participatory process. And I believe that peoples' creativity would be expressed at this moment. The joy of creation cannot be generated under complete control. But we know that when this moment comes, it is sometimes difficult to leave creativity to participants because creativity is the soul of a designer. Tight schedules become an excuse for not trusting peoples' creativity in this case and surely there are many other excuses for this. But we should reach for the aesthetic of collaboration. And it can be realized only when we trust peoples' creativity. If people describe their own worlds to each other, as a result, the design which has every detail filled with every persons' world appears. Residents of Izumi have expressed their worlds on their walls and roofs eloquently after decades of silence.

LINES WITH MEANING

In the following, I will sum up my characteristics of community design.

Community design is work in which many persons' imaginary worlds are laid out and expressed in space. In many sites, people have laid out their worlds and accumulated the meanings through their lives. Though people show high ability to create the space and to give the meanings, sometimes they hardly perceive a change in the space and a deprivation of the accumulated meanings. So designers must be very sensitive to touch their space and meanings. Designs in which many peoples' worlds are imposed on each other, is frequently dominated by designers who are educated as specialists, and it is often difficult to reach consensus among the designers. But

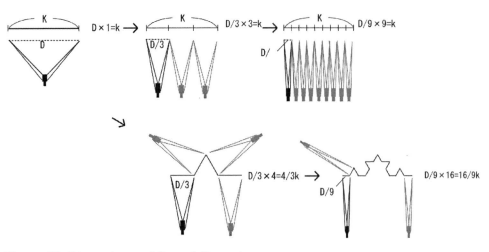

Figure 18. Dimension and fractal dimension.

only through this difficult process, designers can express their own values of beauty, not just make the people's desires realized in the space. One's expression would be best realized through crashing against the others' expression and amalgamating with each other. Designers are not an exception. To practice this process, we need to take risks in project management. We should trust the people's ability to express their own world and to take on these steps. Community design, which does not take on this process, would never be able to make the peoples' world expressed in space. This kind of participatory design is not honest with people and even for space.

With this process and character, though design may lose clear rhythm and order at a glance, it will express diverse worlds. Each design detail will be connected to each story, and each story will link to each person's life and value. The more you zoom in these design details, the more you find diverse background.

Once you recognize these stories in details and zooming out again, you will find rhythm and order that seem lost before, with complex relationships. When the essence of collaborative work is expressed in space, it will not be recognizable at a glance. But later on, the complex and diverse worlds will be revealed in multiple ways.

I believe the practice and space of community design, creating a diverse and complex world, could be analogized with the natural world. Through people's sincere and creative communication, stories linked to each line we draw and the combination of these stories can appear as if the nature has created the lines itself.

I suppose that this phenomenon is derived from the community's character. Because a community is the lifestyle of human beings created by 'nature', the lines community designers try to draw become the lines of 'nature'. People's ability to imagine, collaborate and express their own world, which we should trust, is also created by nature. People use this ability to line their own world in space and society before the modern era. This line is always moving as it has born, lived and died. Our lines in design and planning should trace and emphasize this community moving line both spatially and socially.

Fractal Lines: Community Design and Planning

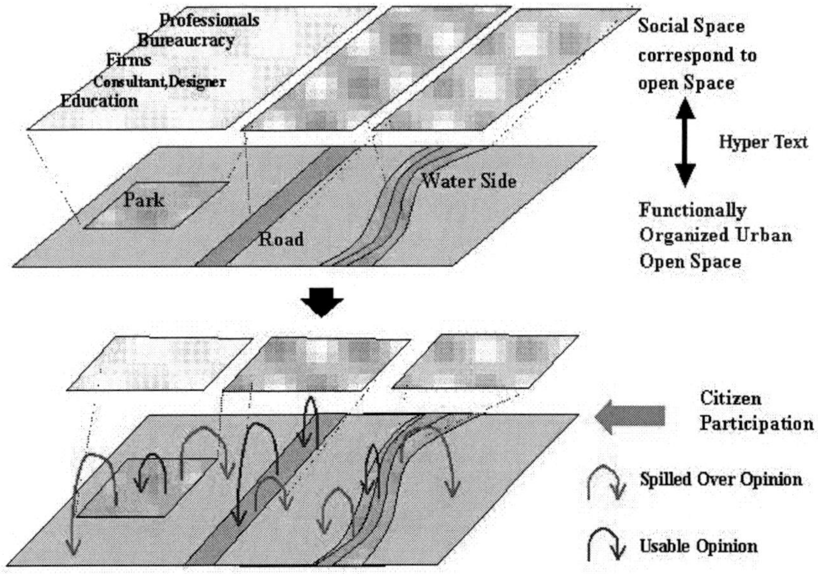

I have presented the potential of lines created by nature, showing the case of the river basin at the Hong Kong meeting. I discussed that river basin which is obviously a physical space created through natural process, can also be a social space through participatory process. The underlying problem is that the meaningful lines we draw for the community do not seem meaningful at the level of urban planning. There are already many lines dedicated just for some functions in both space and society. At the Hong Kong meeting, I intended to look for a strategy to overcome this gap. I also mentioned that a lot of useful opinions or ideas have been abandoned just because they were unsuitable to the projects. It could be called a 'participatory spill-over'– spatially spilled over from the site and socially spilled over from bureaucratic branch. This phenomenon shows not only a social loss

Figure 19. Functional structure of space and society (top). Spillover of participation (bottom).

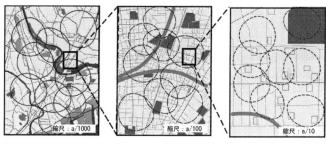

Figure 20. Fractal sphere of tiny creature.

but also less meaningful spatial and social organization. We need to tackle against this organization to make our lines livable and meaningful without limits. And again, the way of spatial organization observed in nature could be one of the clues to establish the strategies to reach our goal.

Here, I would like to borrow the mathematical concept of 'fractal' to progress this thought, particularly in thinking and connecting the relationship between design and planning. It is said that natural form can be approximated through fractal mathematics. The repetition of similar form with regular rule seems to be the point. According to this theory, there should be diverse solutions according to the scale. In other words, it is impossible to determine the form or line statically. If one zooms in on a detail, the information quantities become bigger. Think about a river basin. Comparing 1:10000 and 1:1000-scale plan, the latter should have more information. This does not mean that 1:10000 is wrong, and 1:1000 is correct. Let us think 1:1 scale. Even with this scale, a watershed line could not be determined a priori because of winds, trees or something on the ground. But each drop of rain should flow on one side or the other. It means there is watershed line certainly, but it cannot be decided prior to the flow. Watershed line always exists, but it is always moving. To draw this kind of line in nature, we need to approximate.

This character of fractal line looks very similar to a community boundary line. In this case, instead of raindrops, people's perceptions would be an important factor to determine the line, and it is undoubtedly moving in their lives. The difference between watershed and community boundaries is that whether they embody meanings or not, a human being has the ability to find and generate meanings in nature. So the fractal line of nature becomes a fractal line of meanings for people's lives and societies. This is why the lines we draw in and with community can become fractal lines.

If we advance this analogy of fractal dimension of spatial design, it will enrich the spatial scales that designers are used to. At the same time, it will liberate spatial design from mere spatial manipulation.

I believe this would be one of the answers to the question 'how we can show community design as design theory and form',

which we have been looking for since the first conference at Berkeley. This is the meaning of the lines we draw in the community.

The Meaning of Drawing Lines

I would like now to think beyond the above proposal about the design of community design, the meaning of drawing the lines, through the following reflections.

Nature shows complex systems. It can be observed as a whole like the Gaia hypothesis and also in a tiny creature or cell. Entirety consists of parts, and every part reflects the entirety. Every partial system depends on other partial systems and as a whole they create the entire system. Each part keeps moving to become a system, giving and getting the things from outside one's system. It might be called 'Auto-poiesis' system in sociology. The boundary line is moving and cannot be specified as static because it is always determined by the system itself. I think this line expressed in space can be explained as a fractal line.

This thought brings me immediately to another question. If community is generated by the nature of human beings and is a partial system, how would it be connected to other communities, or other kinds of social associations or nations?

I know that entirety is reflected in even one community, so it can be said that when we engage in community work we handle the entirety. I know this philosophical background is one of the most important principles for community design. On this principle, we do not have to fight against community persons about national policies or other issues not concerning the community directly. We just need to think and act for the community with the community members. So in this way, the question brought to me could be retreated from our strategy or be essentially different from community design. Though it might be right, I do not want to agree with this point of view. First, it seems like architects' withdrawal from urban design or withdrawing urban issue from architecture itself during the 1970's. If community designers focus their job only inside the community, who would think about and act on urban issues or world issues? One should begin to seek the way to realize environmental justice in the city and in the world. Second, limiting our job in the community seems dishonest to the line we draw in the community. Or it could be said that if we limit our role in a community, we will not be able to draw the line of community as 'nature'.

I think we need to face to the new situation around community design. We should consider the communities' characteristics apart from nature. All of us know that often cities, nations or even the world have been organized and composed regardless of nature. As I have written at the Saitama conference in 1999 and at the Hong Kong conference in 2002, I believe the first formulation of the modern city is function. The function for the production and reproduction of goods has led to the transformation of the modern city. City or nation is organized to follow function spatially and socially. There are many rigid and static lines drawn to follow function through space and society, even in every community. Compared with those spatial or social lines of function, the line of community is very weak and subtle. It is because that community has an ambiguous role in this functional structure of city or nation, at least in Japan. When we begin to think the relationship between community and community, city, nation, world, the existing functional structure should be considered.

I suppose that there are other kinds of lines through community and other systems. Every nation and city tends to create some identity. This may not be bad, but sometimes the identity given by the outside authority draws the lines in community and among them. For example, during the Second World War, Japanese communities have worked as bases of totalitarianism. There was a line that fenced people in a community to watch each other and created ethnic myth.

We can think of other kinds of segregating lines that tend to divide the people like gender, homelessness, disability or other issues. These lines also exist in communities and between communities, cities and nations. They can be ugly. I think this is also the evidence of community's natural character. But once these lines rage outside of community throughout a nation, we, at least Japanese community designers, do not have any strategies or tools to deal with them. Along with functional lines, these cultural lines also constitute nations and the world. The former tends to eliminate any meanings, and later one fills the vanity hole of meaninglessness with false meanings.

We know how to fight against these lines in our field – the community. But meaningless lines and false meanings are still drawn and growing even stronger in the world today. I believe that the meaning of drawing lines in a community as community designers is to fight against and overcome these meaningless lines in order to create environmental justice in the world.

I WOULD LIKE TO KNOW

I do not know yet what new strategies should be established to overcome the obstacles we are facing. Using our skills to draw meaningful lines like nature, how could we connect communities with each other or should we make 'bigger community' with communities? I think I have grasped the meaning of the lines we draw, and I am wondering how this meaning could extend to the world.

MAKING THE INVISIBILITY OF THE URBAN COLLECTIVE MEMORIES VISIBLE
Participatory Design Process as a Form Making Urban Landscape and the Positioning of the Participatory Designer

Annie Yung-Teen Chiu

ABSTRACT

In an urban development project in Taipei, a new shopping mall is proposed on an old paper mill site, yet the residues of the unresolved labor/capitalist conflict continued and the design of the park became a symbolic battle for urban cultural production—a series of questions followed: who has the right to interpret the workers' past? Can illusive collective memories of individual groups be made concrete in a Taipei urban landscape through a culturing process such as participatory design? The answers were looked for in a series of participatory workshops where various constituencies came and participated in the design of the Labor Cultural Park. While paper mill workers have stories, even written text of the autobiography, the task of transforming the written and verbal text into visual text, to convince the city that workers' past can be represented in the design of the park, presents a challenge for participatory designers. Images of the park, plan and model would be completed and compared side by side with the landscape designer hired by the developer in the planning meeting. In the labor participatory design workshop, labor workers and students went through some definitive processes: listening, sharing, returning to the site, mock-up and making the model. The workshop became a process of searching, exchanging ideas, producing designs, and finally transforming voices of wound/trauma into landscape. The participatory design process became a setting which empowered those involved. This paper ends with a series of questions on the role and positioning of design in the urban social movement. Is participatory design a form of strategy or final concretization of collective memories? Ultimately, as design professionals, how do we maintain our subjectivity, searching for new answers through design problems and at the same time igniting the engine for social change.

THE SEARCH FOR COLLECTIVE URBAN MEMORIES, EVEN IN THE SHOPPING MALL

As the rise of the consumer oriented lifestyle permeates our everyday life of urban living through various media, the forces of capitalism and culture seem to concretize into spatial culture forms, such as cafés, bookstores and flagship boutiques. They are all housed in a new building type—the shopping mall in the global city. Echoed by Rem Koolhaas, who maintained that shopping is the prevailing urban experience in today's urban environment, the newly generated building type, the mall, would also invade airports and museums, railroad stations and schools (2002). In other words, it is not just the commercial space being commodified, there seems to be little differentiation between public and commercial space. The dominating "barcode" landscape has become the everyday urban scene of Taipei, supporting it through a capitalist world economy through the branding of public space. Through the capitalistic logic of commodification and homogeneity of brandscape, the shopping mall as a building type and phenomena of 'mallification' have become the archetype of the capitalistic city and common logic in planning the Asian city. As the center of the financial and cultural capital, malling the city gave Taipei the look of a first world city: from the unveiling of the tallest building in the world, to the exotic arcade street, the spectacles of the shopping mall have also represented the image of urban progress which parallels the appearance of the global city, confirming the status of the internationalization of Taipei.

From the financial center to cultures of urban upper-middle class lifestyles, the shopping mall is the microcosm of urban living, through the manifestation of urban leisure in the space of private economy. Ultimately, the appearance of the publicness is only the appearance of consumption space. Ironically, the civility can only be expressed as simulacrums of prop display – expressed through the reinforcement of images of family values, individual lifestyle choice, or the metropolitan identity, which operates as a façade to serve the economy of global-capital and local corporate capital—this is best theorized by the figure based on Mike Douglass' framework in which the civil society, state and private economy are the key triangulation in the formation of the public sphere of Pacific Asia. In the case of Taipei, the strong emphasis of the private economy, with strong support by the state, as well as the local government seems to support the construction of consumption space. Civil society is greatly off balance, not to mention the obsolete inquiry of the public sphere in the urban environment. Yet the seamless cooperation between capital and culture has formulated a web of culturing of late logic of capitalism in which the opportunity to seek the public sphere in urban space became available, reachable through the spatial cultural form of globalized consumption space, only in appearance.

Appearance of Public Space and Disappearance of Public Idea

Public space in shopping malls, with names like square, park, plaza has been widely used in all the open spaces of the Taipei shopping malls. Similar to the Prada flagship boutique in New York, Rem Koolhaas has noted the concept of the public plaza as site of the public forum where one can sit and communicate. His anti-flagship boutique is to combine shopping with public space for more cultural pursuits. 'Public space' has become a display of the sight of civil society and has been internalized into an architectural concept and standardized forms. This is what John Hannigan regarded as 'pseudo public space' or 'virtual privatization of the public.' In this paper, I would argue that the planning phase where public voices can be heard through different constituencies, is where public space and ideas can be generated. The urban design phase is crucial, contested terrain for designers, where public debate regarding how urban public design spaces should be negotiated even at the design level. Through one empirical case of the mills into mall in Taipei, the role the participatory design process played, "reenact and recreate the past," and at the same time allow the representational mode for the labor workers who otherwise lost a voice in the private development project, could speak and participate in the culture of design. This happens during the planning of the shopping mall in which the stories regarding Taipei's urban past are sought after, discovered and represented.

Searching And Making Collective Memories Visible In Urban Design And Planning Process

"...the past is a social construction mainly, shaped by the concerns for the present."

"collective memory was rooted in concrete social experience and associated with spatial and temporal frameworks. Memories were recalled by time periods, by recollecting the places visited and by situating ideas or images in patterns of thought belonging to specific social groups. Memory was essentially social—based on lived experience—the activity of recollection must be based on spatial reconstruction."

Halbwachs on Collective Memories

According to sociologist Halbwach who defined collective memories to be "selective, socially constructed, contained spatiality—a society's memory is reconstruction of past" (Halbwachs, 1992; p 33). This means the reality of the past would sharply differ from the working class construction of reality which would differ from those of their middle-class counterparts. The different versions of the storyline about the paper mills through different agents, instead of the developer's version through presentational drawings of the architect or landscape architect, was and should be public process—the urban design phase ultimately is the field of play for defining the civic spaces. Presentation can thus become media of visions and tools of interpretation where memories can be discovered and the past can be reenacted, recreated and challenged. Thus even shopping malls can be voiced by various constituencies. In this particular case, the worker collectively rejects the plan of the architect's proposal as an ideological 'happy ever after image' of the circular disk, instead, intending to propose a different vision of their past through their collective memories. Yet such memories are chaotic, though order is there.

The participation workshop which served as a coming together of the workers to recreate the past through imaginative reenactment that would otherwise slowly disappear in the haze of time. Through the organization of the participatory workshop: from chaotic fragment storytelling, diverse points of view, to final return to the mills for site visits and clarification and design choice. What is envisioned is the future of the public/civic space in the supposed commodified dominated urban development.

From Site of Production to Sight of Consumption- Transformation of Taipei Society: A case of Shi-Lin Paper Mill to Sunshine Mall

"The story is one of the oldest forms of communication. It does not aim at transmitting the pure in-itself or even (as information does) but anchors the event in the life of the person reporting, in order to pass it on as experience to those listening." ("Uber einige Movie bei Baudelaire," I. p. 611)

From here on, I will use the tone of storytelling to narrate the formation and process of this collaboration, which is still on-going; in no way am I presenting an objective point of view, but take a different route in search of public and alternative positioning of design.

This is a classic story of the conflict between labor and capital.

On the last day of the paper mills, no information about their future was told. They found out they were laid-off, the day before the factory closed, they never knew that they would not be able to return to the place where they worked for 30 years.

In November of 2001, the smokestack was taken down; this contradicted the earlier decision made in the land use changes from industrial use to commercial use where three historical elements are to be kept, namely: the brick wall, the smokestack and the CEO circular-shaped room as part of the urban planning negotiation with the Taipei City planning department in exchange for more benefits. After the first planning phase passed, however, the developer took down the smokestack for safety reasons.

Yet it is clearly in violation of the planning committee's draft order. The destruction of the smokestack symbolizes something different for different people who are involved: for the ex-laborers, it meant *"losing an old friend."*

Insurgent Space—Demonstration in front of Taipei City Hall

The union demonstrated in front of Taipei City Hall in February 2002, which was the first time for many of the these workers. The ex-laborers became actors in a play, acting out the importance of the smokestack and the inhumanity of the Shi-Lin paper mills. The Shi-lin paper union was not a political union. It previously functioned as an organization for leisure events for the workers in the mills, and was responsible for staging the dramatic play for the planning ordinance violation of the paper mills (now called the Sunshine Development). In front of the city hall, the workers were protecting something ephemeral such as their memories, on the future site of shopping mall.

By acting out *publicly*, it is significant that people are acting out what is hidden in the planning process, ordinances which are never followed, laws that could be easily tampered with. At the same time, the act illustrated that the private development project in Taipei should have public and transparent processes which allow public participation. Stepping in the unfamiliar territory, by fighting for the resurrection of the smokestack has brought them into the Taipei urban planning process. *"We want the smokestacks to be put back up, just for memory,"* one worker sighed.

There were scarcely any pictures or documents, so with help from the Labor Bureau, and partners, they used the only things they had left—their memories of the past, and began to tell stories of the factory, from the event which described their working conditions, to the production, and reproduction process, in order to testify that their memories of the place are just as legitimate as the boss' version. It was clear that to go beyond protest, they needed to interpret their labor cultural park on their own.

In the Name of the Public

Time and time again, in the public hearings of the shopping mall redevelopment project, they fought standard practice by showing photos of job related injuries, in trying to establish their legitimacy and getting their voice heard to tell different versions about the mills. They were literally pushed aside in the urban redevelopment project.

The Sunshine Real Estate Redevelopment has already been in the planning process for at least 8 years. Time was spent on transforming the land use from the industrial site to the commercial use—the usual capitalistic logic where the consumption value outweighs the production value of the site. There seems to be an oversight that allows private development to beat the complete disposal of the real estate developer's fantasy. Specifically, the fate of public space donated in exchange for zoning variance nevertheless remains in private interest. Behind closed doors, the donation to the city, often becomes a formality or acts as meat on the bargaining table between the city and developers.

The urban design plan for the shopping mall went through various schemes, from high rise design by a Japanese architect which would totally destroy the existing factory to a finalized scheme headed by an American designer who just completed the infamous *Shin-tien-di* (The New World, a redevelopment project which successfully combined a traditional Shanghai colonial stone house and a new outdoor shopping center.) The architect, Ben Woods, after seeing an old photograph of the mills, decided to keep all the "old stuff" and even reinvented the old scheme to be the major design concept of the shopping mall.

Architect's Version of the Past—One Conceptual Idea

By March 2003, the final conceptual scheme of the shopping mall went into the planning phase – not only was the old brick wall kept, but the smokestack was also to be rebuilt as the symbol of the industrial era of Taipei City, represented in the mall.

In March, Ben Woods came up with a design scheme he referred to as the reinterpretation of *tradition, modernity and nature* by breaking down the development neatly into three pieces. Dissatisfied with the traditional shopping mall of the inward orientated circulation and viewpoints, he wanted to recreate the experience of strolling in the night market where wondering and seeing is part of the shopping experience. The site was divided into three parts: traditional is the old part of paper mills, including the resurrection of the smoke stack; brick wall, and seismic sounded old structures as the traditional ambiance; and the modern, a seven storey shopping mall was to mimic the industrial look by using new material to interpret the industrial look of today, and finally the community park symbolizing nature would tie the whole project together. While in three distinct pieces, the architect tried to create physical as well as visual penetration in which there is always opportunity to see from one place to the other. The idea of looking outward was important, where there are opportunities to view the past in nature and the chance to stand in front of the modern factory and turn around to see "tradition".

Participatory Design in Urban Planning Process—Allow Different Narratives or Interpret Stories About the Urban Past

After the "tradition, modernity and nature" scheme finally went through the planning phase, it was important that the union come up with an alternative plan for the Labor Park. After the rejection of the conceptual park design provided by the designer, the participation workshops were organized as a forum to tell stories and to listen to the stories. The rejected scheme was essentially a disk-like shape which symbolized the "union between labor and capital," engraved with "we are all family" for the labor memorial aspects by working with the paper mills workers. Collaborating with university architecture students, the workers, with the help of students, envisioned the future of the park as well as the recollection of past memories of the mills, involving activities, such as returning to the mills to make the mock up of the missing object, like the smokestack or the water reservoir. The spatial history of the mills was constructed.

Public Histories: The Life Story of the Young Girl

In the essay "Claiming Women's History in the Urban Landscape," Dolores Hayden demonstrates a powerful case in which "the stories of diverse working women can be inscribed in public space, as a way of creating a public, political culture which carries the American city into the future" and that "in the stories of the working women can lie the history of urban space and its public meanings" (Hayden, 1995; 354, 369).

I went into the workers' oral history workshop conducted by the Labor Bureau and the Union, and heard a most amazing story from the paper mill's sixty year-old female worker. Prior to this I was conducting a design studio investigating the Shi-lin paper mills. It was on the verge of being just another hypothetical shopping mall space design.

It is really not what she said, but how she said it that moved me, for I have read the book compiled from the oral story and came only to 'get more information.' Apparently shy in front of the public, she knew specific information like, the date she started working in the factory, the date and events when she left her job—the story of the paper mill is also the life story of a girl's life. I think I was haunted by her specific details, as to the dates, places and events and most importantly her pain and happiness as she won prizes for the best worker. Both her physical pain from the job, and the betrayals for her 30 years of loyalty to the company were expressed not through words of hatred, but rather a melancholic tone of comprehension of her life in the factory. The one anecdote told regards her role as a working mom, in which she describes the guardroom as a place away from the public-ness and separate from the outsider. The guardroom is also the earlier form of the breast-feeding room. The story provides dimensions which are more than spatial, but involve the complexity of history, gender, and the life of the blue collar working class. It was the first time the factory space of the past came to life, through narration of the spatial story.

Figure 1. One of the first sessions, the workers divided into groups and discussed their working environment. Some tried to sketch what they remembered about the space.

Figure 2. Workers returning to the paper mills, for the first time since the layoff, and begin to mock-up the scale of the reservoir, with red tape.

Proposing Alternatives: on the Other Side of the Table

During the participatory design workshop, an invitation was extended to the landscape architect who was to design the Labor Park, in order to listen to ex-paper mill workers' side of story. In one of the earlier workshops, the groups were divided into three: production, reproduction (leisure) and labor injury—things that workers specifically want to be remembered by. The information out of that workshop was formulated into the program of the park. Yet after three hours of brainstorming sessions, rather than jotting down the information and asking questions to clarify the story, the architect later complained and continued to speak as the 'professional' as to what a park has to be like without listening to their side of story.

"They are just telling a whole bunch of stories, it is just a park."—landscape architect

"They are not the only workers; these are just opinions of the few."—ex-owner and representative of the paper mills

The designer, who supposedly has the instinct and insight of translating abstract feelings into forms, did not realize the stories are the irreplaceable design theme and the possible channel into the past had he listened. During the workshop, in the most efficient manner, the landscape designer promptly provided solutions for the park, after 'listening to the story.' He came up with the design guidelines, in sketches and verbal descriptions:

The pathway is straight which represents the rationality of the factory.

The use of material on the pavement would use all materials from the site.

The light represents fire.

The chair was set up so workers can sit down and think about their past.

Landscape and flowers represent feeling and hardship.

There was no contest as to who has the capacity to imagine the future of the urban landscape. The spatial history *is* there, but no one *is listening.*

Positioning and Roles: A Possible Alternative Role of Cultural Making

Even in urban social movements, mostly in the protest phase, designers are often absent or design skills are hidden, since designers' have long been trained in the making of a product, rather than making culture, since the product is often to provide services to capitalists. From this experience, I view participatory design as strategic as well as a force for the concrete design of the urban future, the latter is equally empowering, compared to the legislative theater and the like. If the desire to create places

Figure 3. Workers came to studio, describing in detail the assembly line and at the same time, listening to some of the schematic design idea presented by students.

can be a core value, the motive for urban social movements can move beyond the discursive and return to the real space-this in turn would allow insurgent space to become civic spaces or spaces of civility. As a strategy to gain momentum to participate for urban futures, to show voices of the workers can be heard in the planning process, information which would not have been acquired through the conventional design process, since most information and sources are often secondary and biased, are being re-examined in the process of the workshop. The difference between the conventional designer and participatory designer is related to the question of why we design and whom we should design for. Skill at representation has long been at the core of professional education, through mastering traditional representation media such as drawings, and now computer animation, and video imaging. These tools are utilized only so the war can be fought against the construction of a capitalistic city and maybe at times the game can be won. Professional design competition seems to be limited to the mastery of the tools and chooses to leave the subjectivity of what they represent to the client. Conventional designers seem to leave the positioning outside of the profession. The limitation of the design profession, limited by capitalistic operation, by division of labor, by taste dictated through class, has made "a park for the next generation" almost impossible. Appearing only in the real estate advertisement, the future vision of the park had not been a major concern of the labor union. Instead, the worker surprised us all by showing how their memories are to be represented and how their experience can become the blueprint for the future park in which people would one day stroll and experience their memories. Meanwhile, to make change, and alter the status quo is the major concern of the union leadership—which views the participation as a strategy, a negotiation process, the right to interpret their culture in challenging the status quo which would also slow down the process to ask for more—from symbolic to the material form of the urban landscape.

The participation workshop is not only the site of urban negotiation, but a possible site where healing, remembering, and forgetting, where human conditions are searched for and revealed. Throughout the process, the workers have transformed the most negative comments regarding their unjust treatment, to finally focusing their energy on remembering the past, and the road to envisioning the future is a concrete and optimistic one, at least for moments in the workshop.

Meanwhile the developers have also initiated a similar participation workshop by inviting different groups of the workers to discuss what they want, and it is operated more to offset the legitimacy of this workshop. The pseudo, but formally recorded workshop, is easily detected since the question-answer format is only to serve the interest of the developer. While participation workshops can be a formality or political

strategy, the process of searching, perhaps for democracy, for social justice, or collective memories can only be examined in the minutes of the workshop.

While in the participation workshop, everyone enters with specific goals and ideological assumptions, but at the end, their positions have shifted. In the end, workers begin speaking eloquently about the design of the future park, not as information or opinion providers, but how they can experience the space through the students' schemes, as to how design can be improved. At times, it was not clear who was the professor, who the students, and who the workers.

Union workers have played different roles in city design, from passive to active: from the labor movement in staging the protest of the insurgent space to participating in the participatory design session in order to produce real civic space. The workshop is significant in that the attempt to create change through representation, provide possible light in the new possible role of design in urban process and finding new meanings in the role of design as a plausible tool for urban change, both materially and symbolically.

Participatory design process can be both a process of collaboration and contestation. Any urban public space is an opportunity to search for urban meanings: whose memories are to be stored, and how can participatory designers facilitate such voices, especially the weak ones? Participatory design workshops provide the chance to tell the story and turn the story into representation that people can continue to imagine. While design often plays the role of cosmetic effect, which masks the capitalistic scheme of commodifying space; as a tool, it is time to serve something else—in representing people's values and interpreting what is civil society to illuminate the city's unspoken or unseen so it becomes visible, audible and meaningful for us all.

REFERENCES

Douglass, M. 2003. Local City, Capital City or World City? Civil Society, the Post-Developmental State and the Globalization of Urban Space in Pacific Asia International Workshop on Capital Cities in Asia Pacific: Primacy and Diversity. Academia Sinica, Taipei, 19th and 20th of December.

Hannigan, J., 1998. Fantasy City-Pleasure and Profit in the Postmodern Metropolis.

Halbwachs, M. 1992. On Collective Memory. University of Chicago.

Hayden, D. 1995. The Power of Place: Urban Landscapes as Public History, MIT Press.

Zukin, S. 1991. Landscape of Power: From Detroit to Disneyworld, University of California Press.

Zukin, S. 1995. The Cultures of Cities. Blackwell.

Zukin, S. 1998. Urban Lifestyles: Diversity and Standardization in Spaces of Consumption. Urban Studies, 35 (5-6): 825-889.

nature(s) of place

Flood and Frog
change
us a lot.

OPENING A PRIVATE GARDEN TO THE PUBLIC THROUGH AN INTERMEDIARY
The Case of Rikugien Garden in Tokyo in the 18th Century

Sawako Ono

ABSTRACT

This paper deals with Rikugien garden in terms of opening private space to the public. Rikugien was the garden of the lower residence of the Yanagisawa clan, a daimyo family, in the city of Edo (now Tokyo). When Nobutoki Yanagisawa lived at the lower residence in the 18th century, he accepted visitors to the garden regardless of their status, occupation, age, gender or place of residence. Visitors without any connection to Nobutoki asked for permission to visit the garden through an intermediary. Those who worked for him in the lower residence acted as intermediaries. It is meaningful that various people visited the garden of a daimyo residence at a time when social classes were strictly separated in many aspects of life and daimyo residences usually shut their doors to outsiders. In this case, the garden provided an opportunity to open the daimyo residence to outsiders and introduce them inside. Also, the intermediary made anonymous outsiders identifiable individuals who in turn gained a sense of connection with the place.

INTRODUCTION

The feudal lords, or *daimyo*, in the Edo period (1600-1868) were given three residences, upper, middle and lower, as their living quarters during their attendance in the city of Edo every two years by government request.

The upper residence was located in the center of the city, near Edo castle, while the middle and lower residences were usually on the outskirts of the city. The clan head lived at the upper residence, which also served as a center of the clan administration. The retired clan head and their heirs used the middle residence as their living quarters, which also acted as a place of refuge in case the upper residence was destroyed by fire. The lower residence was used, depending on its location, as storage warehouses for supplies from the home province, hunting lodges or villas for the clan head.

Rikugien was the garden of the lower residence of the Yanagisawa clan that governed the fief of Kohriyama near Kyoto. The garden was founded when Yoshiyasu Yanagisawa (1658-1714), Shogun Tsunayoshi's grand chamberlain, was granted the site in Komagome for his lower residence. He spent seven years building a garden for the lower residence, from 1695 to 1702. The garden was a typical *daimyo* garden and known as one of the finest gardens in the city. Many scenes were arranged around a central pond to suggest noted scenic spots. In this garden, visitors enjoyed various vistas as they proceeded along garden paths by the waterside, in the woods and on the grass-covered knolls. The garden was so splendid that the Shogun himself visited it several times.

Nobutoki Yanagisawa (1724-1792), Yoshiyasu's grandson, lived in this lower residence after his retirement in 1773. He recorded his daily life there in his journal, "*Enyu-nikki*" or "Journal of Feast and Pleasure" (Yangisawa, 1773-92). According to this journal, the garden gave him many pleasures. He strolled in the garden almost every day with his attendants and sometimes with his

Figure 1. Garden of the Yamato Koriyama clan's lower residence (plan of the Rikugien garden). (Edotokyo Museum Collection)

wife. He often spent many hours taking care of the plants. Gathering garden products, such as edible greens, chestnuts, and mushrooms, was another of his pleasures. Nobutoki was a man of wide interests and his garden served as a place where he could enjoy them. He composed haiku and was one of the leading members of the haiku party at that time. He often invited his companions for a haiku gathering in his garden. He also loved kabuki so much that he directed performances with a script written by himself to be performed on a stage built in the garden.

He also showed his garden to many people. For him, the garden was "a place to show," as well as a place to enjoy natural features. Various people, for example, samurai, townsfolk, farmers, priests, women, and children, visited the garden. Some had a connection with Nobutoki, such as his retainers and their family, relatives of his servants, and his acquaintances, while others did not. Those who had no connection with the Yanagisawa clan asked for Nobutoki's permission to visit the garden through an intermediary. Nobutoki accepted visitors to the garden almost all year round (Table 1).[2] The number of visitors who did not have any connection with him began to increase as the area around the lower residence gained popularity as a suburban recreational spot.

We will see how *daimyo* gardens came to be opened to the public by examining the descriptions in Nobutoki's journal.

VISITORS

According to Table 2, most of the garden visitors in 1779 had some kind of connection with Nobutoki. He showed his garden occasionally to clansmen who visited the lower residence on business. He also showed them the garden as they accompanied the clan head on his way to and from their province. It was also a custom of the Wakayama clan to give permission to their clansmen to visit the garden of their upper residence as they accompanied the lord from their province. The upper-residence garden of the Wakayama clan was well known for its magnificence. Therefore, clans that had a garden worthy of a visit showed their garden to fellow clansmen from the province. This served as a reward for their service in Edo, and also demonstrated the power of their clan. When his married daughter and sons or his acquaintances visited him, Nobutoki sometimes showed the garden to their attendants. This also was a reward for them, and to his children's attendants, a demonstration of his power. These examples indicate that a garden was attractive even for the lower classes, such that looking at it was regarded as a reward.

In addition to Nobutoki's clansmen, the families and relatives of his retainers or servants who worked at the lower residence, his haiku and kabuki companions and his acquaintances also visited the garden. Among such visitors were his retainers' wives, his aunt, mother-in-law and distant relatives, the family doctor's sister-in-law, the gardener's niece, haiku companions and their friends, and a kabuki actor and his household. Those who occasionally visited the lower residence on business also saw the garden. For example, a man from a tofu restaurant in Asakusa, which Nobutoki patronized, visited the garden when he came to pay the season's greetings. His companions also came to look at the garden and often brought their families or acquaintances. Nobutoki sometimes met them and gave tours himself, or treated them to sweets in the garden.

	Jan.	*	Feb.	Mar.	Apr.	May	*	Jun.	Jul.	*	Aug.	Sep.	Oct.	Nov.	Dec.	*	Total
1773						4		3			3	1	4				15
1774	2			4	2			1			1	1	2				13
1775			2	4	7	4		1	1		2	9	3	4	2	1	39
1776	1		6	6	3	1		2	1			3	3	1	1		27
1777	1		4	12	5	2		1	10			3	3	2	1		44
1778			4	8	3				1	1	5	6	5	2	2		37
1779	3		5	12	4	3		2	5		3	2	8	1	1		49
1780	1		5	25	13	7		3	12		6	10	47+	3	1		134
1781	2		7	8	18	12	7	3	6		3	11	20	1			98
1782	1		5	29	20	7		8	4		8	9	32	1			124
1783	3		5	16	41	19		12	3		6	6	29	5	2		147
1784	1	7	3	47	10	3		9	9		7	10	13	2	1		122

	* : leap year																
	47+ : 47 and many others																

Table 1. Number of visiting parties.

After 1780, the number of visitors to the garden increased. In particular, the increase in the number of outsiders was considerable. They varied in social status, occupation, gender and age: a high official of the Bakufu and his wife, members of other clans, merchants and their families, doctors, farmers, priests, and nuns, for example. Most of them lived in the city, however, some came from outside of Edo.

Some examples of such visitors in 1783 are as follows. First, there are many samurai. In March, Nobutoki accepted two clansmen from the Tsu clan and five from the Doi clan. In April, besides members of other clans, a police sergeant, two foot soldiers of the Bakufu, a female family member of one of the Shogun's vassals accompanied by retainers, and a doctor visited the garden. Two clansmen from the Todo clan accompanied by a nun, six women, four children and a servant came to see the garden in May, and a firewatcher in June. The wife of the former lord of the Matsue clan appeared with attendants in October.

Townsfolk visit the garden too. Most of them came from downtown where many wealthy merchants and wholesale dealers lived, and from the lower residence neighborhood where small shopkeepers, samurai and farmers lived. Among those who came from downtown were a party of four women, merchant parties, clerks and one of their customers, and a merchant family. Three girls accompanied with their mothers and attendants came to an

| | those directly related to Nobutoki | | | | outsider | | | | |
	Vassals & their families	Servant's families	Friends	Unspecified	Samurai	Towns-folk	Farmers	Mixed	Others
1779									
Jan.	●	●	●						
Feb.	●●	●●	●						
Mar.	●●●	●●	●●●●	●●					●
Apr.	●	●	●					●	
May			●●						
Jun.		●●							
Jul.	●●	●●	●						
Aug.	●●●								
Sep.			●	●					
Oct.	●	●●●	●●●●						
Nov.			●						
Dec.			●						
1780									
Jan.									●
Feb.	●●●	●	●						
Mar.	●●●● ●●●●	●●●	●●●●	●	●●●●	●●●●		●	
Apr.	●●●● ●●●●		●●●			●		●	
May	●●	●●	●●						●
Jun.	●●		●						
Jul.	●●	●	●●●●	●●●	●		●		
Aug.	●●	●●	●						●
Sep.	●●	●	●●●	●●					●●
Oct.	●●●● ●●●● ●●●● ●	●●●●	●●●● ●●●● ●●●	●●	●●●● ● ●	●●●● ●●●● ●			●●●
Nov.			●		●			●	
Dec.			●						
1783									
Jan.	●		●	●					
Feb.		●	●●		●	●			
Mar.	●●●●	●●●	●	●	●●●	●●		●	●
Apr.	●●●● ●●	●	●●	●	●●●● ●●●● ●●●● ●	●●●● ●●●● ●●●● ●●●●		●	●
May	●●●● ●	●	●●	●	●●●● ●	●●	●		●●
Jun.	●●●●	●	●		●	●●●	●		●
Jul.	●●				●				
Aug.	●		●●●	●					●
Sep.	●●				●●●	●			
Oct.	●●●● ●●●	●●●	●●●● ●●●● ●		●●●	●●●● ●			●●
Nov.	●●		●		●	●			
Dec.	●	●							

Table 2. List of visitors.

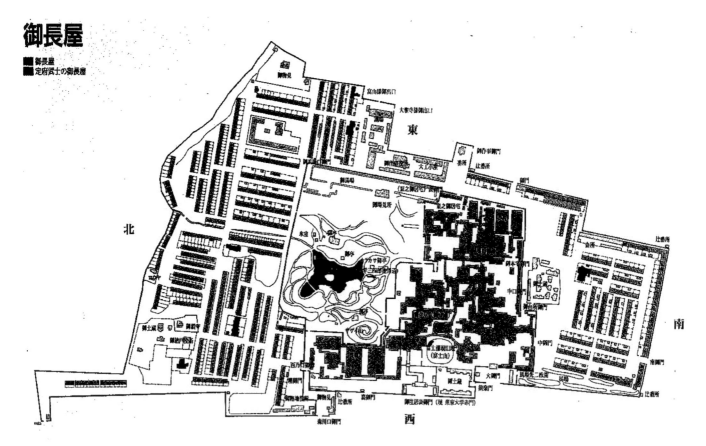

御長屋

■ 御長屋
■ 定府武士の御長屋

Figure 2. Upper residence of the Kaga Clan.

interview for jobs in June. The daughters of wealthy merchants worked at daimyo residences at that time. After the interview, they asked to visit the garden. They took advantage of this opportunity to view it. This indicates two things: the garden was attractive to many people and they could ask to visit the garden without reserve.

Among those from the neighborhood, there was a merchant's household, a party of three women who visited Nobutoki's servant, and two parties of neighborhood residents. The neighborhood residents visited the garden every year on the same day, the 8th of April. We will discuss this matter later. Besides samurai and townsfolk, there were priests, doctors and a few wealthy farmers among the visitors in this year.

Many visitors came in groups, such as business companions, a household or community people. The number of people in a group often exceeded ten people, including children and servants. A wholesale ornamental hairpin dealer's household from Nihonbashi included six women, four or five men and three children accompanied by their family physician. There were also visitors who come alone. Once, a tailor from the neighborhood came by himself.

Nobutoki recorded each visitor's name in his journal. Therefore, he knew who had come to see his garden. He sometimes watched visitors enjoying his garden from his room or from behind a garden hedge, and delivered sweets or wine and snacks as a compliment to particular visitors.

It seems that the number of the visitors increased as the district near the lower residence became increasingly popular as a suburban recreational spot. There were many attractions such as shrines and temples, a noted flower-viewing spot, and other scenic locations along the small river at the spot. Many fashionable restaurants sprang up along the river during this time. Furthermore, many gardeners lived near the lower residence and their own gardens attracted people, especially in the chrysanthemum season. Some visitors to the garden stopped by when they came for a pleasure walk in this district. Rikugien must have been one of the attractions in the district.

INTERMEDIARIES

Outsiders asked for Nobutoki's permission to visit the garden through an intermediary. Those who worked for him in the lower residence, for example, retainers, maids, manservants, and gardeners, acted as intermediaries. Nobutoki's entries in his journal, "by request of," "accompanied by" or "guided by" indicate the presence of an intermediary.

Examples of retainers and servants acting as intermediaries in 1780, as written in Nobutoki's journal, are as follows.

- By request of Matsumoto, court ladies of the Tatebe clan visited the garden (Mar. 12).

- Accompanied by Mizoguchi and Gensuke, a constable who is their drum instructor (Mar. 17).

- By request of Wasuke, two women and a girl (May 20).

- Accompanied by Shoetsu, three vassals of the Shogun (Oct. 20).

- Guided by Beigyo, a doctor of the Doi clan (Nov. 3).

- Guided by Shimoyama, two priests and a samurai (Nov. 5).

Matsumoto, Mizoguchi and Shimoyama are retainers who worked at the lower residence. Beigyo is a retainer who managed Nobutoki's haiku affairs. Wasuke is a manservant and Shoetsu is the personal physician. In these examples, we can see that regardless of their status or post, they brought various visitors. Mizoguchi and Gensuke invited their drum instructor. Beigyo seems to bring his haiku companion. Samurai and townsfolk at that time kept company with others beyond their status through mutual interests. Such connections worked well for the intermediary. On the other hand, Matsumoto made his request to Nobutoki because his sister-in-law had a position as a lady's maid of the Tatebe clan. Kinship was a very effective connection for requesting permission for a visit. Nobutoki recorded many examples in his journal, such as "Two vassals of the Echigo clan, distant relations of Kuramochi, came and were shown the garden (July, 7)" and "showed the garden to two women, distant relatives of Yamamoto (Aug. 20)."

Townsfolk acted as intermediaries as well. In March of 1780, Sei Suzukiya accompanied eight women from her neighborhood. We do not know who she is, other than that she regularly came to the lower residence on some engagement. Like her, townsfolk who regularly came to the lower residence on business or for other reasons often acted as intermediaries. For example, Fushimiya accompanied several groups. On October 9th, 1782, he accompanied a small party consisting of two merchants, a doctor (probably), and a woman, and again on the 25th of the same month, a party of their families. Two more families joined in this party. They were twenty-three in number, including children. We can conjecture that having heard of the splendid sights of Rikugien, the first visitors' family members, and the additional two families, wanted to visit the garden and asked Fushimiya again to gain permission for a visit. Fushimiya also accompanied three parties to the garden in 1783: eight merchants in March, six women in April and five rice dealers in June. His connection to the lower residence must have been well known among his acquaintances and they often asked him to act as an intermediary.

Saburobee Nagai and his attendants visited the garden on the 6th of March in 1784. In this case, a former maid of a court lady of Nobutoki's household requested to visit the garden. Two weeks after his visit, Nagai's wife wrote a letter to the court lady requesting permission for his acquaintances. They visited the garden led by Saburobee the very afternoon that Nobutoki accepted her request. This suggests that Saburobee's wife had a connection with the former maid, by way of whom she was introduced to the court lady. Some connections were formed between them upon her husband's visit to the garden. She subsequently used this new connection for later requests. Thus a range of visitors spread among various people.

Seibee, the gardener, also brought many people to the garden. He lived in the lower residence neighborhood. He came to work in the garden of the lower residence when he was requested to do so. We already saw that his niece visited the garden. She had come to visit him from a village near the lower residence. Seibee also brought neighborhood residents to the garden several times in spring. Furthermore, in October 1780, he took his wife and her companions, and again his neighborhood residents to the garden to see newly planted chrysanthemum beds. In October of the next year, a party of a townsman and five women from his neighborhood visited the garden through Seibee's intermediation. He also accompanied several parties from downtown, a household of a guard of Edo castle and vassals of other clans. One of them was a party of a young lord of the Dhotsu clan. Seibee's other clients were probably vassals of the Shogun, other *daimyo*, and wealthy merchants downtown, who asked him to act as an intermediary to visit Rikugien.

It seems that most requests were made beforehand. However, as we saw in the case of Saburobee Nagai, permission could be given on short notice. There is other evidence indicating that the garden could be visited relatively freely. Once, as Nobutoki strolled in the garden with his wife, a retainer came to inform him that two of his clansmen were asking to see the garden. He immediately allowed them entry. Another time, a townsperson came to see the garden. Upon seeing Nobutoki, he hid himself, but Nobutoki made his retainer give him a tour of the garden.

Not everyone's request was accepted. He refused a request made through his son on the excuse that he refused many other requests. However, judging by the description in his journal, anyone who wanted to see the garden probably was able to visit it if he/she found someone who worked for Nobutoki in the lower residence. Visitors made the most of even the remotest connection to the intermediary to visit the garden.

Daimyo residences were usually closed to outsiders. The lower residence in Komagome was enclosed within walls with gates, a moat and bamboo bushes in the same way as other *daimyo* residences were. That they accepted garden visitors regardless of status, occupation, age, gender or place of residence

凡例
▦大名屋敷地
□旗本御家人屋敷地
▦寺社地
■幕府用地
□町地
▦田畑・土手

Figure 3. Zoning by status.

indicates that the garden provided an opportunity to open up the *daimyo* residence to outsiders through intermediaries.

BACKGROUND TO OPENING THE GARDEN

Evidence of a Good Lord

During the Edo period, it was considered that a good feudal lord should share pleasures with his people. Showing his garden was regarded as remarkable evidence of a good lord. In "*Seizan Iji*" or "The Deeds of Nishiyama," a record of Mitsukuni Tokugawa, the clan head of Mito, it is written that Mitsukuni showed his garden to anyone who asked to look at it even if his social status was low (Yoshinaga, 1938). Hence there were visitors picnicking with food and drink in the garden all year. Mitsukuni was known as a good lord, and this episode is recorded as one piece of evidence that he was a benevolent lord.

It was desirable for a good lord to show his garden to his people. This notion probably affected the case of Rikugien, too. However, we can assume that there were other factors in the case of Rikugien. They are to be discussed in the following.

Appreciating Elegance and Tastefulness in a Garden

Visiting a private garden through an intermediary seemed to be common at the time. Nobutoki himself tried to visit gardens that were noted for chrysanthemum beds. In October 1783, he sent his retainer to the retainer's haiku companion living in the lower residence of the Fukuyama clan to ask to visit chrysanthemum beds there, but his request was not granted. Again in October 1784, as he took a stroll near his residence, he sent his attendant to a daimyo residence to request a viewing of the chrysanthemum beds in their garden but was again refused. However, he had visited these chrysanthemum beds several years previously. These incidents indicate that people freely asked to visit a garden although compliance depended on the convenience of the owner.

An Edo guidebook listed a peony garden as a favorable outing spot. It says, "Because it is a private garden, it cannot be entered without permission. Ask to view the garden at the back door" (Kusakihanagoyomi, et al.). On the basis of this description, we can assume that there was a widespread understanding that if anyone asked to visit someone's garden, the request would usually be granted.

In the cases described above, people asked to visit a garden because of the beauty of the flowers in the garden. Appreciating the beauty of a garden was regarded to be elegant and tasteful. Moreover, this was considered outside the standard constraints of ordinary life. People who had a sense of the elegant and tasteful were well thought of and they associated with each other regardless of social status or position. Therefore, ordinary rules of society, such as the distinction between a privately owned garden and public space, may not have been applicable when elegance and taste were the issue. It was considered that gardens should be open to all who appreciated its beauty.

Nobutoki's status as a retired lord might have made it easier for him to accept various visitors in his garden. Being free from the ordinary rules of living, he was free to enjoy the life of the elegant and tasteful. The name of his journal, "Journal of Feast and Pleasure," expresses his stance on his life in the lower residence.

To Lend/Borrow a Garden

Nobutoki often lent his garden to his companions. On March 5, 1779, he wrote in his journal, "At about three o'clock in the afternoon, Kikudo, Nunozawa and others with children came. I lent the garden. They enjoyed themselves at the teahouse and left in the evening." Kikudo is a haiku instructor and Nobutoki's haiku companion. On April 16 of the same year, he wrote, "Shoetsu, his brother-in-law, several samurai and two or three townsfolk came to see the garden. I lent the teahouse there." Shoetsu is his personal physician, as we saw earlier. Besides these episodes, in 1781, one of his sons borrowed the garden, and in 1782 he lent it to his retainers to enjoy it freely.

The following example shows that the "lending/borrowing of gardens" was frequent among those familiar with each other. In March 1840, a widow of one of the Shogun's vassals recorded in her journal that her household, including children, visited a garden of the lower residence of another vassal of the Shogun (Nikki, 1978). He was her distant relative and often invited them to visit the garden. They spent all day there kite flying, herb gathering, and eating and drinking while the owner remained at the upper residence.

The incidents described above suggest that there was a generally accepted idea that gardens were, to some extent, common property, even if they were shared only among those who were closely related.

Event of Buddha's Birthday

On the 8th of April, people in Edo celebrated Buddha's birthday. In the lower residence, Buddha's birthday festival was held at a monastery in the garden. On this occasion, Nobutoki opened his garden to his clansmen's families. Nobutoki wrote in his journal in 1775, "because of Buddha's birthday festival, showed the garden to clansmen's families." On the same day, he also wrote, "This is the day when Dentsu-in, Goji-in and so on open their gardens on the event of Buddha's birthday." Therefore, he himself visited, with his sons, the gardens of temples near his residence that were open for the day. Several guidebooks on Edo mention this event as "opening mountain" (Saito). Therefore, at that time, in Edo, it was customary for temples to open their gardens to the public on Buddha's birthday.

We do not know the origin of this event. However, in some rural areas in Japan, there is a custom that women climb a mountain near their village to gather wild azalea branches. The date of this event is usually the 8th of April. This custom is considered to be an agricultural ritual announcing the start of farmwork.

From 1782, on the request of Seibee, the gardener, neighborhood residents also came to see the garden. People in Edo might have visited gardens instead of climbing a mountain. The agricultural ritual must be changed to a Buddhist festival. However, to prove this hypothesis, we must examine the connection between the garden and the mountain in Japanese culture.

CONCLUSION

Rikugien, a garden of the lower residence of the Yanagisawa clan, accepted visitors without distinction of status or position when Nobutoki Yanagisawa lived there after his retirement. Outsiders who had no connection with Nobutoki asked for his permission through an intermediary. Those who worked at the lower residence acted as intermediaries.

This was a way to open privately owned gardens to the public when social classes were strictly separated in many aspects of life, and *daimyo* residences shut their doors to outsiders. The garden provided an opportunity to open the *daimyo* residence to outsiders. This made it possible to provide a place where various people were able to gather without distinction of rank. Opening the garden to outsiders through intermediaries made anonymous outsiders identifiable individuals who appreciated the beauty of the garden and gained a sense of connection with the place.

REFERENCES

Edotokyo Museum. Sankin kotai. Tokyo.

Iseki, T., Nikki or Journal. 1. 1978. Tokyo: Benseisha, 102-106.

Kusakihanagoyomi Koto Junran Shiji Yukanroku. In Mitamura, E. (ed.), Edo Nenjugyoji, Tokyo: Chukobunko.

Ono, S. 2000. "Garden Visit" at the Anei-Tenmei Era in Rikugien, Journal of The Japanese Institute of Landscape Architecture, 63(5): 361-366.

Saito, G. Toto Saigiki 2, Tokyo: Heibonsha.

Yanagisawa, N. 1773-1792. Enyu-nikki or Journal of Feast and Pleasure, In Geinoshi kenkyukai (ed.), 1977, Nihon Shominbunka Shiryo Shusei, 13, Tokyo: Sanichi shobo.

Yoshinaga, Y. 1938. Korakuen Zakko, Zoen Kenkyu, 25, 11-12.

BUILDING A MULTICULTURAL LEARNING COMMUNITY THROUGH THE NATURE OF PLACE

Julie Johnson

ABSTRACT

Children's experiences of place, and their participation in shaping it, may serve as inspiring references for more ecologically designed future communities. This paper addresses the context of school as a significant, yet often neglected, social and ecological community in the lives of children, and explores the potentials of nature and participatory design to foster the development of a multicultural learning community. A review of research and theory on children's learning potentials in nature and in school landscapes, and on participatory design with children, is provided and used to reflect on a Seattle, Washington, elementary school as a case study for such a community.

INTRODUCTION

As planners and designers, we envision how communities may change, and advocate certain values, processes or outcomes. To achieve a more sustainable future, I believe we need to examine children's experiences of community, and explore how their experiences may provide awareness, understanding, and motivation to work together as-and in-community. Kevin Lynch noted, "In childhood we form deep attachments to the location in which we grew up and carry the image of this place with us for the remainder of our lives" (Lynch, 1984:825). Children's experiences of their place, and their participation in shaping it, may serve as inspiring references for creating more ecologically designed communities.

In the United States, public schools exemplify the increasing cultural diversity that holds new challenges and opportunities for community design and planning. What better place to begin participatory design processes, than where diverse groups share a common purpose and place? At school, children, families, teachers, and others form a learning community. Children spend much of their waking hours in this context, developing meaningful relationships and critical understandings that inform their cognitive, social, physical, and emotional development. Multicultural understandings can be fostered through informal individual interactions, as well as through

Figure 1. A common image of an urban school landscape, where asphalt abounds. (Photo: University of Washington Department of Landscape Architecture teacher workshop)

curriculum and other activities that foster the development of the school as a dynamic, living community.

Yet as a place to build community, all too often school landscapes are asphalt expanses with token entry plantings. What lessons do such impoverished environments convey, how do children participate in these places, and what does this suggest for our collective future? A review of recent research sheds light on the importance of nature in childhood, the development of ecological literacy, and the role of school landscapes in children's learning. Referencing this research, as well as theory on children's participation in design, this paper examines a Seattle, Washington, school as a case study for building a multicultural learning community through the nature of place.

LEARNING IN NATURE

Childhood Values

Our contemporary society makes children's experiences in nature increasingly less common, as access to natural environments becomes more difficult and time is spent in other contexts. However, a growing body of research and theory on children's relationships with nature illuminates the powerful role nature plays in their development (e.g., Cobb, Carson, Moore, Kahn, Kahn and Kellert, Nabhan and Trimble). Nature affords children open-ended experiences and personal narratives that enrich the body, mind and spirit in lasting ways. Clare Cooper-Marcus has found that many college students, when asked to describe a favorite childhood place, "recall a wild or leftover place, a place that was never specifically 'designed'" (Cooper-Marcus, 1986: 124).

Children's experiences in nature are needed not only for their personal development, but also for their understandings of and commitment to care for their local ecology—their ecological literacy. In his articulation of this concept, David Orr states that "ecological literacy is driven by the sense of wonder, the sheer delight in being alive in a beautiful, mysterious, bountiful world" (Orr, 1992: 86) and this begins in childhood. Orr outlines three

Figure 2. Children's sensory-rich experiences in nature afford personal narratives of place. (Photo: Julie Johnson)

common features to developing ecological literacy: childhood experiences in nature, a role model who serves as a mentor in nature, and critical texts that inform and inspire (Orr, 1992: 88). Schools seem an ideal context for such a construction of ecological literacy.

The Nature of Schools

Yet in many cases, school landscapes provide other lessons. A landmark study of what children read from their school landscapes reveals the importance of nature. As part of its study, the British organization Learning Through Landscapes conducted interviews and tours with children to identify how they interpreted school landscape elements, and the impacts of schoolyard design on their behavior and attitudes. The results illustrated that the landscape provides a "Hidden Curriculum," one that "affected children's attitudes and behaviour, not only in relation to the grounds or whilst children were using them, but in terms of the school as a whole" (Titman, 1994: 55). Children interpreted extensive paved areas as dangerous, ugly and boring places. They often noted the paving "was all their school could afford and read from this that the tarmac was a measure of the worth of the school and of themselves as a part of it" (Titman, 1994: 33). Not surprisingly, children attributed positive values to natural elements, and such elements inspired creative play. Among these elements' attributes, trees were recognized and valued as living things to play on and protect, ponds were a source of living creatures to discover, bushes that afforded hiding places became treasured retreats, and flowers that were planted by the children elicited pride and caring.

In their book, Natural Learning: The Life History of an Environmental Schoolyard (1997), Robin Moore and Herb Wong provide a vivid testimony to the learning potentials of nature in school, where children participated in making and sustaining a habitat-rich landscape. They describe how teaching and learning occurred in the schoolyard through an integration of three domains of education: formal education of lessons; informal education gained through daily experiences, particularly play; and nonformal education characterized by resource people facilitating learning outside a classroom context (Moore and Wong, 1997: 195-6). The schoolyard became a community gathering space, where parents and neighbors used and helped care for it. This place offered rich interactions and meanings that remained with children, as follow-up interviews in subsequent years revealed (Moore and Wong, 1997: 186-9).

In recent years, innovative programs and models across the United States have begun transforming school landscapes.[1] Gardens, habitat creation or restoration, and cultural or interpretive elements replace formerly neglected space. These efforts often grow through creative partnerships and broad goals that engage and catalyze a diverse community. The schoolyards may assume new meanings as a sensory-rich outdoor classroom, a dynamic place for play and discovery, and a treasured space for community life and learning.

Connecting schoolyards with a larger open space network allows opportunities for children to explore, understand, and care for ecological systems more fully. Educator David Sobel has articulated a developmentally appropriate framework for environmental education with children. Sobel proposes: "In early childhood, activities should center on enhancing the developmental tendency toward empathy with the natural world; in middle childhood, exploration should take precedence; and in early adolescence social action should assume a more central role" (Sobel, 1996: 12). This strategy could flourish in an open space system that extends from just outside the school to varied places that afford a spectrum of natural and cultural features.

PARTICIPATORY DESIGN WITH CHILDREN

Theory and approaches for undertaking democratic participatory processes with children have received increasing attention in recent years. The work of Roger Hart, Robin Moore and Herb Wong, Bruce Race and Carolyn Torma, and others present the values and approaches of such processes with children and youth. Building from Sherry Arnstein's metaphoric ladder of levels of participation, Hart (1992, 1997) articulates a ladder for children's participation. The lowest rungs of manipulation, decoration, and tokenism represent non-participatory approaches. Higher levels offer more authentic roles for children in the extent and authority of their participation. Hart notes that children's choice in participating is an essential principle.

Specific to the context of schools, Moore and Wong (1997) offer critical insights on participatory processes with children. They trace ways in which children engaged in design phases, including site assessment and design workshops. Through such activities as planting and caring for plants, designing and building a giant compass and sundial, and observing creatures that began to inhabit the site, the transformation process became the source of multidisciplinary studies as well as creative play.

As a model of participatory design, the development of the environmental schoolyard described by Moore and Wong could not have been achieved without multiple constituents

and supporters worked alongside with children. They include college students and specialists from the UC Berkeley and organizations such as Audubon and the Oakland Museum—as well as family members and teachers. Additionally, the site's offerings as a community space engaged families and others in the life of the space. In these varied venues, mutual learning opportunities were afforded among all members of this robust community.

SEATTLE CASE STUDY: DEARBORN PARK ELEMENTARY

A Seattle school serves as an informative case study to consider the potentials and challenges of fostering a multicultural learning community through participatory design of its landscape. Located in the heart of an inner city neighborhood, approximately 95% of Dearborn Park Elementary students are ethnic minorities (Jensen, 2003: B1). The school's surroundings are unique, with an adjacent City park, forested ravine, protected wetland, and power line easement. Yet the school building suggests little connection with this context, featuring an inward-focused plan and ribbon windows placed far above a child's or adult's view.

In the mid-1990s, a convergence of opportunities opened the doors to learning in the landscape. The school started an "International Garden" featuring plants from the schoolchildren's cultures. The principal saw potentials of the landscape supporting newly adopted inquiry-based science curriculum and visualized the school's focus becoming environmental education. The City's Parks and Recreation Department was working with the Trust for Public Land (TPL) to acquire a wooded parcel adjacent to its park, which TPL recognized for environmental education and stewardship connections. A partnership of people from various organizations came together to identify learning opportunities, including Washington Forest Protection Association who provided teacher training and curriculum. The succeeding principal, Evelyn Fairchild, worked with the partnership and her school to advance this vision, and it has become a growing reality.

Transformation of the forest got underway on Earth Day 1996, as teachers, students, TPL and Parks staff, and other volunteers removed debris and invasive plants. These restoration efforts continued, with each class adopting a portion of the forest. A path was re-created, and a bridge across the ravine was built as part of a loop trail.

In 1997, a masterplan was developed through a participatory process that engaged students, teachers, school staff, community members and other organizations. The design team held a sequence of workshop meetings with adults. Design activities with children occurred as part of their studies, which were supported by the principal and teachers. Student groups undertook analysis and programming exercises in the landscape with applications to their curricula. The designers explained their goals and undertook design workshops with each grade, in which students built models of their design ideas. The completed masterplan drawings of varied gardens, restoration areas, and interpretive elements and spaces were posted at the school for classes to review.[2]

The masterplan identified improvements to existing outdoor learning spaces and identified new opportunities for learning, much of which has been implemented through further design, grants, partnerships, and student participation. The International Garden plots evolve, as the school's Service Learning Coordinator coordinated edible plantings this year, and an incoming first grade teacher plans to use the garden with her class (Shenberger, 2004). Native plant and butterfly gardens identified at the front of the school have been planted. Formal gateways to both the wetland and forest have been built and incorporate children's art illuminating features and qualities of these spaces. The wetland area is now accessible with a platform, interpretive tile signs, and an amphitheatre-like gathering space with log benches.

In early 1997, I was inspired by the children's robust understandings of the forest when visiting a fifth grade class with a colleague. Graphs of measurements taken in the forest were posted on the wall, and samples of poetry written by students while in the forest were shared. When the teacher asked who would like to give us a tour of the forest, a flurry of hands went up. Our tour revealed the guides' enthusiastic knowledge of the life of the forest and their sense of ownership in it. They pointed out native plants, and one noted how he identified a fern after finding it in a library book. As we walked along, they picked up litter on the trail. One expressed dismay at waste in the ravine, noting that its intermittent stream goes into Lake Washington and thus so would the waste—a potent insight of the ravine's ecological context.

Today, teacher Janice Hunt's fifth graders continue learning and teaching in the forest. Students learn to work together while they study plants and ethnobotany, measure areas, remove invasive plant species, plant, write, and lead tours (Hunt, 2004). They give tours to visitors as well as students in each of the school's grades, sharing their insights of this place. Naturalists from organizations such as Starflower Foundation and Seattle's Earthcorps work with the fifth graders. The ethnically diverse Earthcorps staff work with student groups as they survey and study forest plots, identify and tag native plants, remove invasive plant species, and research what should be planted in their plots. The students present their planting ideas to Earthcorps, and learn how to plant as they restore their plots. Students wrote about the plants and developed a CD.

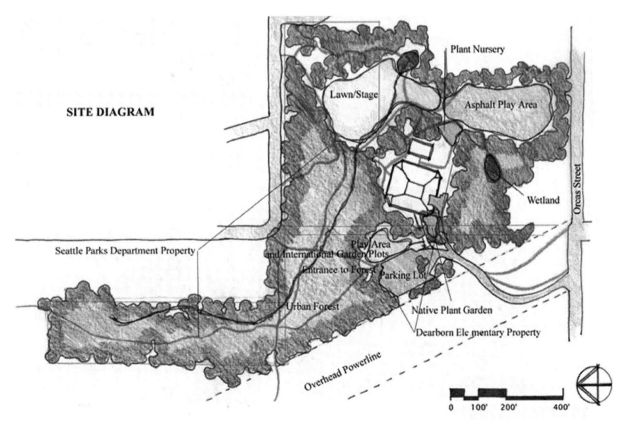

SITE DIAGRAM

Figure 3. Dearborn Park Elementary School's surroundings include forest areas, a wetland, city park, and power line easement. (Diagram by Anna Tamura, adapted from Allworth Design Group Site Improvements and Woodland Restoration plan, 1998)

In addition to restoration efforts, creative expressions reveal students' personal connections with the forest. Hunt takes the class out at times throughout the year for reflective writing; the students choose a place to sit and write poetry, stories, and reflections. She asks them to name the space they choose. Hunt recalls that two girls named their spot "dreaming place" and another student, who chose a stump, named it "Bob" (Hunt, 2004). Students have painted rocks for the entry that depict plant and animal life of the forest, and this past year the students designed a mosaic project with Earthcorps, which will be mounted near the forest entry this fall.

The wetland also has become a powerful place of learning and community-building. Fifth grade teacher Rebecca Clark works with students in wetland restoration efforts, where they learn to work in groups as well as in this place. Audubon Society has worked with the class. Interpretive signs, a bat house, and piles of dead English Ivy give testament to the students' participation in stewarding this sensitive environment. Like the class studying the forest, these students share their firsthand knowledge as wetland guides. Clark uses the wetland as a curricular context and a place for less formal learning. She brings the students to the wetland at times for lunch and for its calming influence (Clark, 2004).

The school's goal of the environment as an integral focus for learning is being fulfilled, and it is recognized as a model and resource. Earth Day Events held here include various organizations and attract classes from other schools. Student guides interpret the forest and wetland areas on Earth Day and on other days when visitors come calling. In considering potential challenges and improvements, the principal and staff I interviewed see opportunities (Clark, Fairchild, Hunt, Shenberger, 2004). These include design features, such as more permanent interpretive signs in areas and benches for gathering in the forest, as well as means of facilitating student learning with more volunteer mentors. Another challenge lies ahead, as planning is underway for the school's renovation, and the relocation of facilities may impact outdoor learning areas.

REFLECTIONS

Several factors seem to contribute to Dearborn Park Elementary's development as a multicultural learning community, including its diverse landscape context and design, creative partnerships, committed leadership, dedicated teachers, and participatory design approaches. Children's learning experiences in this landscape are a model of participatory design and multiple learning approaches that seem to build community and may foster their ecological literacy. Students work collaboratively in studying, designing, and improving their landscape, and share their insights with others. Teacher Janice Hunt has "noticed students showing more pride in themselves and their

Figure 4. A sign marks a recently planted area along the forest trail at Dearborn Park Elementary School. (Photo: Julie Johnson)

Figure 5. Dearborn Park Elementary School's wetland entry features children's tiles. The amphitheatre-like sitting space and an interpretive sign are behind. (Photo: Julie Johnson)

school"(Jensen, 2003: B5). There is little evidence of vandalism on the site, and student-made signs call attention to the special qualities of this place.

Like the Berkeley school featured in Moore and Wong's *Natural Learning* (1997), participatory design is central to the students' learning in their landscape at Dearborn Park Elementary, although primarily through formal education. The masterplanning process engaged diverse constituents, including children, through analysis, programming and design activities. Children's participation seems to fit middle rungs of Hart's ladder of participation, where children are consulted and informed of decisions, yet their actions are prescribed and they do not play an active role in decision-making.

In realizing the masterplan, classes undertake design and development of site restoration and interpretive elements. Fifth grade students' work on forest plots suggests a high level of participation, in reference to Hart's ladder, as they choose a plot and undertake a process of analysis, planting design and restoration. They research to develop their proposals and present their ideas for review. Similarly, students using the wetland for learning become well versed in the plants of this environment and what is needed to restore it. As guides of their respective settings, students share their knowledge and values to the members of their own school community and of the larger community who visit. While these curricular-based activities may not offer genuine choice in participation, other opportunities for informal and nonformal education could be developed (per the Berkeley school) and enrich children's choices and types of participation.

It is interesting to note that each of Orr's three features for developing ecological literacy are found in this school. Students' hands-on and extensive experiences enable them to know and care for their landscape. Their teachers and others, such as members of Earthcorps or Audubon, mentor these experiences, and older students mentor younger ones. Texts provide insights, as children study topics such as plants appropriate to their forest plots. Research is needed to examine if and how students' experiences are indeed fostering their ecological literacy, and if this endures over time.

Other factors could strengthen ecological learning and community design, including a more extensive, integrated open space system. Like other Seattle schools, Principal Fairchild notes that fifth graders raise salmon and release them at a creek distant from the school. She identifies a long-term goal to release the salmon at their wetland's creek (Fairchild, 2004). Daylighting this creek as an open space link to Lake Washington would enable rich opportunities for exploration and social action identified in Sobel's environmental education framework for middle childhood and early adolescence.

Another factor that could enrich this community is greater parent and neighborhood involvement, which the Berkeley school's success drew from (Moore and Wong, 1997). Principal Fairchild notes that a school PTA formed this spring (Fairchild, 2004)—an important step in building the school's community and resources. Informally, people visit and enjoy this site, and they are welcomed. A "welcome" rock painted by fifth graders at the forest entrance indicates both the connection students have to this place, and an invitation for its community to grow:

The Children's Forest consists of 2.6 acres of deciduous forest whose trees range from 50-100 years old. Once a pioneer town, the forest is now used for environmental education for students in the local Beacon Hill schools. Students are helping to restore the forest to a more natural state. As you walk through you may notice restoration efforts like planting pots, invasive plant species removal and trail renovation. Notice the smells and sights of wildlife and plant life that will surround you on your hike through your forest.

Figure 6. A gate and interpretive rocks, including a "welcome" rock, mark the entrance to the Children's Forest at Dearborn Park Elementary. (Photo: Julie Johnson)

In an increasingly urban world, opportunities to "notice the smells and sights of wildlife and plant life" need to be part of a child's daily life. This case study illustrates how the development of an ecologically designed school landscape can support learning and foster community. While this school's physical context may be somewhat unique, it offers insights into the values of creating and restoring nature on and near schoolgrounds. In transforming existing schoolgrounds, or locating new schools within an open space system, strategies are needed to make ecological design a reality through participatory design, policies, and programs that enrich children's experiences and engage them as vital members of their community. They then, may carry the lessons of this place forward, as a model for building the future.

ENDNOTES

[1] Programs for school gardens and habitat exist through national organizations, such as the National Wildlife Federation's Schoolyard Habitat Program. Two notable examples of citywide programs for schoolground transformation are the Boston Schoolyard Initiative, which involves a partnership of foundations with the City of Boston, and Seattle's Grey to Green Program, involving city departments, school district, and community members. Dearborn Park Elementary School, described in this paper, received Grey to Green Program funds for its wetland restoration and boardwalk. Two Berkeley, California, schoolyard projects are well documented as inspiring models, occurring at different times: the schoolyard described by Moore and Wong begun in the early 1970s, and the Edible Schoolyard begun in the mid 1990s.

[2] A more extensive discussion of the development of Dearborn Park Elementary School's landscape planning and design is presented in Design for Learning: Values, Qualities and Processes of Enriching School Landscapes by the author of this paper.

REFERENCES

Carson, Rachel. 1956. The Sense of Wonder. New York, NY: Harper & Row, Publishers.

Clark, Rebecca. 2004. Interview with author. June 16.

Cobb, Edith. 1977. The Ecology of Imagination in Childhood. New York: Columbia University Press.

Cooper-Marcus, Clare. 1986. "Design as if People Mattered." in Van der Ryn, Sim and Peter Calthorpe. Sustainable Communities A New Design Synthesis for Cities, Suburbs and Towns. San Francisco, CA: Sierra Club Books, p. 124.

Fairchild, Evelyn. 2004. Interview with author. June 16.

Hart, Roger A. 1997. Children's Participation: The Theory and Practice of Involving Young Citizens in Community Development and Environmental Care. London: Earthscan.

Hart, Roger A. 1992. Children's Participation: From Tokenism to Citizenship. Florence, Italy: UNICEF International Child Development Centre.

Hunt, Janice. 2004. Interview with author. June 16.

Jensen, J.J. 2003. "Dearborn Park turns nature into classroom: Seattle school's surroundings are perfect teacher." The Seattle Times. March 2: B1, B5.

Johnson, Julie M. 2000. "Design for Learning: Values, Qualities and Processes of Enriching School Landscapes" Landscape Architecture Technical Information Series (LATIS) issue. Washington, DC: American Society of Landscape Architects, http://www.asla.org/latis1/LATIS-cover.htm

Kahn, Peter H. Jr. 1999. The Human Relationship With Nature: Development and Culture. Cambridge, MA: MIT Press.

Kahn, Peter H. Jr. and Stephen R. Kellert, eds. 2002. Children and Nature: Psychological, Sociocultural, and Evolutionary Investigations. Cambridge, MA: MIT Press.

Lynch, Kevin. 1984. "Coming Home: The Urban Environment After Nuclear War." in Banerjee, Tridib and Michael Southworth, editors. 1990. City Sense and City Design: Writings and Practice of Kevin Lynch. Cambridge, MA: The MIT Press, p. 825.

Moore, Robin C. 1986. Childhood's Domain: Play and Place in Child Development. Dover, NH: Croom Helm, Ltd.

Moore, Robin C. and Wong, Herb H. 1997. Natural Learning: The Life History of an Environmental Schoolyard. Berkeley, CA: MIG.

Nabhan, Gary Paul and Stephen Trimble. 1994. The Geography of Childhood: Why Children Need Wild Places. Boston, MA: Beacon Press.

Orr, David W. 1992. Ecological Literacy: Education and the Transition to a Postmodern World. Albany, NY: State University of New York Press.

Race, Bruce, AICP, AIA and Carolyn Torma. 1998. Youth Planning Charrettes: A Manual for Planners, Teachers, and Youth Advocates. Chicago, IL: American Planning Association.

Shenberger, Maureen. 2004. Interview with author. June 16.

Sobel, David. 1996. Beyond Ecophobia Reclaiming the Heart in Nature Education. Great Barrington, MA: The Orion Society and the Myrin Institute.

Titman, Wendy. 1994. Special Places; Special People The Hidden Curriculum of School Grounds. Surrey, Great Britain: WWF UK/ Learning through Landscapes.

FROM EARTHWORM TO POCKET MONSTER
Childhood Experience of Nearby Nature and Adult Environmental Behavior Over Time in Taipei Min-Quan Elementary School Neighborhood

I-Chun Kuo

ABSTRACT

There is some agreement that childhood experiences of nature are important for humans to develop environmental knowledge and values. There are, however, few longitudinal and even fewer studies focusing on the relationship between children's experiences of nearby nature and their environmental behavior as adults. In this research, a questionnaire was designed to ask four different age groups about their childhood experiences of nearby nature and their current environmental behavior. The four groups each spent their elementary school years in the same Taipei, Taiwan neighborhood at different time periods (1970's, 1980's, 1990's, 2000's) when the character and availability of nearby nature changed rapidly as agricultural villages transformed into urban neighborhoods. For example, those who were children during the 1970's had access to an open channel stream; the 1980's group experienced a partially culverted stream which was completely culverted in the 1990's. The youngest group experienced a new artificially created watercourse above the original creek location during the 2000's. The research findings show that the children's experience of nature declined from the 1970's to 1990's and increased again between the 1990's and 2000's as the places where children played changed. The results also show that an increase in the children's experiences of nearby nature translated into increased participation in environment – related activities as adults. This paper will present a case for why environmental planners/designers; science educators and parents should revalue the importance of nearby nature in creating neighborhoods for rich experiences with nature.

INTRODUCTION

What is the relation between children, nature and animals? Whether cruelty as in pulling apart worms and

222

fish or in the kindness of helping an injured bird, the bond connecting animals and children is something mysterious. Developmental psychologists have conducted research on children-animal relationships and found that animals provide children imagination and joy as well as nonverbal language communication (Melson, 2002). Moreover, from a human ecology standpoint, children themselves are part of the animal world (Cobb, 1969). Veterinarian studies have concluded that childhood experience with pets help develop one's concern and empathy for animals and nature (Serpell, 1980.) Natural resource researchers found that most wildlife-oriented activities occur in the home range (U.S. Fish and Wildlife Service, 1980.) Landscape architecture and environmental psychology studies also found that nearby nature affects people's preference and satisfaction with their homes (Kaplan, 1985). Children-animal relationship research, however, emphasizes laboratory and home based animals while children's relation with those wild animals that live in our environment as our neighbors are not studied, especially in urban residential areas. Further, urban ecological studies debate the size and ecological function of the urban green spaces. Other studies conclude further merits of urban nature for the urban physical-chemical environment without considering human relationships with the environment. There are, as observed, few studies focusing on the relationship between children's experience of nearby nature and their environmental behavior as adults.

Technology has animated nature. Our animal stories have changed from the *Aesop's Fables* to *Finding Nemo,* a fantastic animal world using 3-D animation. Our culture's source of biological knowledge has changed from direct experience through everyday life to secondary fiber optics. Even the knowledge itself has widened and deepened its scope from visible to invisible nature. In Taiwan, children are facing more and more pressure to learn, although the educational system has changed many times *for them*. In the late 1990's there was an educational reform called "Native Education" when the importance of environmental education was emphasized, and local culture and ecology were prioritized. However, everyday experience with nature for urban children is very limited when trying to follow the everyday assignments and tests of environmental education. Parents feel more frustrated than thankful given the very limited natural resources in their everyday urban environment. To create educational opportunities, people are focusing on intensive educational sites with strong experiential/educational intensity rather than everyday experience with nearby nature. Here, a general mistake people make is that the single events are emphasized and the cumulative effects are neglected. On one hand, people are worried about children's formal education. On the other hand, adults are so busy that they ignore their immediate environmental changes and their impacts on children's education.

Given all the complexity of cultural and environmental change, do our little *Homo sapiens* today play with plastics instead of chasing after grass hoppers, putting beetles in the pencil boxes and following ants trails? Is there some affinity between children and animals, basic but significant, that does not change with time and technology?

It is our responsibility as landscape architects and environmental planners that if urban residential nature is important for children, then we should create and protect it.

BACKGROUND

In 1949, the United Nations Counselor Group was invited to develop seven regional plans in Taiwan. At that time, new planning concepts such as compact housing, residential neighborhood unit, new town plan and zoning were introduced due to the influence of these popular ideas in the United States and Europe. In order to resolve problems of housing deficiency in the old city center, the Taipei City Government started a land rezoning plan to develop a new community in the Development Restriction Area covered with rice fields, farms and grassland near Taipei Airport. Today the population of Min-Sheng community is 82,025 and its area is 29,846 km^2.

The Min-Quan Elementary School Neighborhood is a part of the Min Sheng community. Most of the children who grew up in the neighborhood were students at the Min-Quan Elementary School, and shared the experience of environmental change over time in the nearby places. The history of the neighborhood environment has not been documented before, however, some childhood spatial elements are mentioned in people's casual conversation, such as "the big ditch" in the neighborhood. Tables 1 and 2 are some examples of the environmental changes.

METHODS

Research Questions

- If the natural environment in neighborhoods changes over time, does the childhood experience of nature change, too?

- Did nature in the neighborhood once educate children? Does it today?

- Do childhood experiences of nature in the neighborhood affect people's environmental behavior as they become adults?

Questionnaire Design

People were asked to fill out a questionnaire with eight questions. Table 3 shows how the questions are asked in the questionnaire with respect to research questions. The mean age and number of questionnaires are listed in Table 4.

Period / Map	Description	Period / Map	Description
1910's	• Pin-Pu Plane Tribe • Keelung River flood plane • Three houses near the neighborhood creek • Farms, wetland and grassland (until 1967, less than 15% area was developed)	Pre 1970's[1]	• Natural, possibly agricultural use (Fu-Min Drainage) • Surrounded by paddy fields • There were only three households along the creek during the 1920', and less than 15 in the 1940's during the Japanese Colonial Period.
1970's	• First concrete embankment of the Keelung River was built in 1970 • Community was newly developed: "The United Village" "Public Services Housing" "The United Village (II)"	1980's	• Concrete channelized • Water quality was getting worse due to waste inputs. • Flooding after typhoons (rains) • A child's accident happened
1980's	• Taipei Airport was built • Chun-Shan National High way went across the river • More development in the community "Min-Ren Building", "Shin-Kong Building" and "Jien-Chen Garden Luxurious Building"	1990's	• The channel was covered and the water flew underground in a culverted form, serving as a run-off collection channel. • Some equipment and lawn on the surface.
1990's	• Min Quan East Road built • Fu-Yuan Street widened • Neighborhood creek culverted • Keelung River "straightened" • Riverside Park designed	2000's	• A new "ecopark" was designed and complemented exhibiting ecosystem of Taipei Basin. • Aquatic species introduced and wetland constructed • High biodiversity • Some people set their turtles free in the pond • Some egrets and night herons forage here
2000's	• Clear boundary between the neighborhood and a larger nature-the Keelung River • No more neighborhood vacant lots • Neighborhood ecological education park constructed		

Table 2. Environmental change of the neighborhood creek.

Table 1. Environmental comparison of the neighborhood surrounding area.

Research Question	Questionnaire
If the natural environment in neighborhoods changes over time, does the childhood experience of nature change, too?	(Q #1) Think about your childhood, what did you do when you were not in class? (What place? Talk about this place. What did you do there? How many times a week?) (Q #3) In your neighborhood, were there natural places you could play? (What place? Discuss this place. What were you doing? How many times a week?) (Q #4) Please circle your childhood experiences in your neighborhood. (Q #7) Please circle the animals you touched in your childhood.
Did nature in the neighborhood once educate children? Does it today?	(Q #5) Please put a star on the childhood experiences of nearby nature that made you interested in natural science. (Q #6) What kind of plants and animals were in your neighborhood when you were a child? (Q #7) Please circle the animals you touched in your childhood.
Do childhood experiences of nature in the neighborhood affect people's environmental behavior as they become adults?	(Q #4) Please circle your childhood experiences in your neighborhood. (Q #8) Please circle the environmental behaviors you actually do now.

Table 3. Research questions and questions in the questionnaire.

	Mean Age	Childhood	Number of Questionnaires
Group 1	38	1970's	25
Group 2	28	1980's	31
Group 3	18	1990's	26
Group 4	10	2000's	28

Table 4. Questionnaire distribution.

FINDINGS

The findings show that children experienced less and less nature in the neighborhood since the 1970's when the neighborhood was developing. Diverse natural environments in the neighborhood for children to play in the 1970's turned into vacant lots in the 1980's where children enjoyed playing with nature. In the 1990's parks were almost the only places in the neighborhood for children's nature play. In the 2000's children enjoy well-designed ecoparks with high biodiversity and nature features in the neighborhood, however, childrens' daily lives are much more regulated than before. Figures 1-3 are main findings of the research.

Surprise: Gender Matters!

Although the differences between boys and girls were not asked in the research questions, there are interesting differences in the findings. The first interesting finding is from the multiple choices where people circle their childhood experience of nearby nature. Experiences related to "kill" and "sympathy" was chosen for comparison in Table 6.

The results show that there is no significant difference between boys and girls in "general kill."[2] However, boys are especially good at "unusual kill"[3] – 22% had ever pulled butterfly's wings off and 31% cut off ant's legs. The mortality of "unknown creatures" is as high as cockroaches, which is something people *must kill* in Taiwan.[4] The results show that girls show more sympathy to living creatures than boys do.

Animal Species Girls and Boys Touch

11 out of the 15 species boys touch more than girls do are Arthropods. Among the species the girls touch more, 7 out of 21 are mammals and 2 are birds and only 4 Arthropod species. Other interesting findings are that girls touch tadpoles and boys touch more frogs; girls touch more snails and boys touch slugs; girls touch mosquitoes while boys touch cockroaches. The strangest finding is that girls touch snakes more than boys do.

DISCUSSION

From the 1990's and through the 2000's, despite a decreased amount of natural environment, decreased travel frequency and the number of nature visits of children compared to the previous twenty years, the number of visited natural sites, number of species and CNNED increased. An increased experiential diversity per travel event implies a higher experiential intensity for the children in the 2000's. How does it happen?

A cue helps interpreting the result. In the 1990's the environmental movement started in Taiwan. Environmental issues such as a more prevalent concern for the nature, animal rights and quality of life were reestablished and highlighted. In

Period/Photo	Description
1970's[1]	• "The little frog" was one of the earliest TV cartoon in the 1970's. •Adventure stories of a brave frog •Japanese cartoon.
1980's	• "Xiao-mi-fong" –the Japanese cartoon of adventures of a little honey bee who was looking for his mother • It was a story about adventure and friendship in the nature. •The cartoon was played on TV everyday.
1990's	•The pocket monsters, also created by Japanese artists, are magical creatures living in boxes. Children could have them in their pockets. •The pocket monsters are kids' weapons, helpers and friends. •There are over 100 species of pocket monsters. Many of them are based on real animals/plants and many are imagined.
2000's	•Pocket Monsters still popular in the 2000's because they are always evolving and getting more and more powerful. •The scenarios are mostly in urban environment.

Table 5. Change of the animal cartoons. Media played an important role in childhood after the 1980's. The animal cartoons, which changed from real animals to imagined ones reflect different contemporary concept of animals.

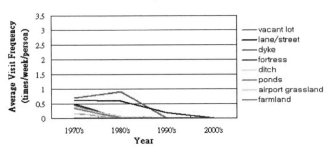

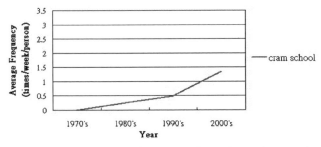

Figure 1. Places children go after class change from 1970's to 2000's.

the neighborhood, a well-designed ecological park was built in 1999 that provided children intensive experience of nature in a limited area. Although not as wide and wild as the natural places of the 1970's and 1980's, the park in the 2000's provides rich experiences of children's everyday play with nature.

People who grew up in the 1970's who have the highest experiential diversity show the lowest linear correlation between childhood experience and adult behavior. Why? One can find some points (people) are off the trend among the 40-year-old adults (children in 1970's) and several 28-year-old adults (children in 1980's). And these are people who had richer experience in their childhood but show lower environmental activities participation.

Some reasons were given by themselves written in the questionnaire, such as "in order to make a living, I can't take care of other things..." which follows Maslow's theory of "hierarchy of needs" that "people will not have concerns about higher-level environmental concerns if their basic needs for food, shelter and physical security are barely met.[5] "Other

Children in the 1970's

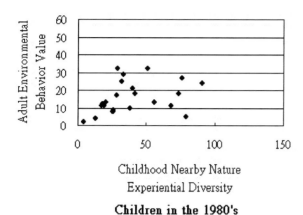

Children in the 1980's

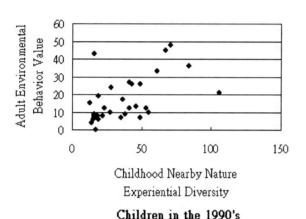

Children in the 1990's

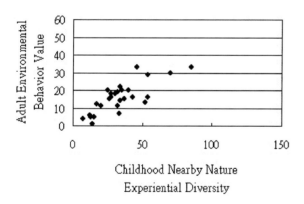

Figure 2. Distribution of childhood nearby nature experiential diversity and adult environmental behavior illustrate their correlation.

possible reasons may be due to the life-stage of 40-year-adults, where their focus of life is different from the other two, such as family, children, house...etc. For 28-year-old adults, since most of them are still single, they can probably afford to be more environmentally active than people in their 40's. For 28-year-old adults, however, influence from the childhood is less than the 18-year-adults due to pressure from jobs and financial constraints, as a respondent states: "in order to buy a house, my everyday life is about making money...I miss those

Important Places for Nature Play

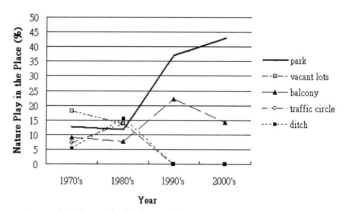

Figure 3. This graph shows the percentage of nature play that happened in the parks, vacant lots, balcony, traffic circle and the ditch. Importance of parks dramatically increased since the 1980's when places other than parks for nature play gradually disappeared.

		%Boys (n=54)	%Girls (n=57)
General Kill			
	Kill Termites	35	33
	Kill Cockroaches	59	63
	Kill Spiders	28	28
	Kill Unknown Creatures	57	56
Unusual Kill			
	Pull off Butterfly's Wings	22	7
	Cut off Ant's Legs	31	23
Sympathy			
	Stop Others from Killing	20	32
	Put Injured Creatures in Safer Places	24	28

Table 6. Gender differences in the way children relate to insects.

naïve childhood days..." The other reason is from education; during 1990's environmental movement, 28-year-old adults today were in high school, and were educated to be more environmentally conscious. 18-year-old adults, although less environmentally active, have the highest linear correlation between the childhood experience of nearby nature and adult environmental behavior. The results imply the importance of socio-economic status of individuals and both social and environmental education. Following the results we can predict that when the 18-year-old adults grow older, influences from their childhood experience of nearby nature may as well be diluted.

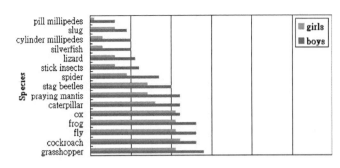

Figure 4. Animal species boys touch more than girls do.

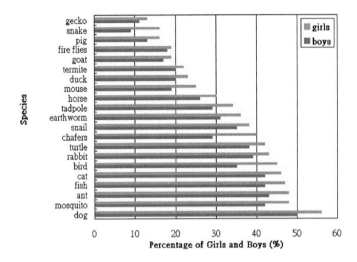

Figure 5. Animal species girls touch more than boys do.

CONCLUSION

1. Nearby nature in the studied neighborhood changed with time and this change altered generations of children's everyday experience of nature from the 1970's until the 2000's.

The research showed that many experiences of nature were lost with the disappearance of the natural environment (streams, vacant lots, grassland and so forth). The diversity of children's experiences of nature declined between the 1970's and 1990's (from 39 to 33) but increased again after the 1990's (from 33 to 40) following the pattern of environmental change. Based on the data analysis, the thesis concludes that childhood experience of nearby nature and the direct contacts with the animal species evolve with the neighborhood environment. A neighborhood environment with diverse natural features supports diverse experiences of nature.

2. Children's life style including experience of nature changed from exploratory experiences to more controlled and regulated ones over time between the 1970's and the 2000's.

Based on the research data, children's nature visits declined steadily from the 1970's (0.73 times per day) to the 2000's (0.25 times per day). One can conclude that children in the 2000's do

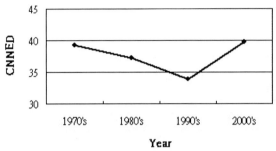

Figure 6. Childhood experience of nearby nature.

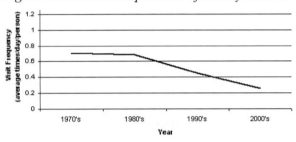

Figure 7. Children's nature visit after classes.

not go outdoors often and seldom explore their neighborhood environment as much as their parents' generation did. Both social and environmental reasons contribute to this result. Children of the 2000's return home or go to the cram schools directly after school, and have fewer choices of nearby natural environments to build their own knowledge and experiences.

3. Neighborhood environmental change influences how children define "nearby" and their childhood territory.

How near is regarded as "nearby" depends a lot on the accessibility of those natural locations. In the Min-Quan Elementary School neighborhood, the higher dyke and the widened roads were main elements as cutters of the children's natural territory.

4. Children's natural territory shrank over time following the steps of development. Public parks are the last pieces of land for children to experience nature in the 2000's in the studied neighborhood.

The research showed that children in the 1970's and 1980's grew up with more diverse nearby nature; children in the 1990's enjoyed the least amount of nearby nature in the built out neighborhood (16 nearby natural places in the 1970's; 13 in the 1980's; 7 in the 1990's and 11 in the 2000's.); children in the 2000's have more designed nearby nature in the parks (43% nature play). Importance of the parks in providing good environments for children to experience nature was proved in this research. It is believed that this is a common fact for many developed urban residential areas.

5. Neighborhood environmental alterations change wildlife habitat in the neighborhood.

Following the disappearance of waters and bare soil grounds in the 1970's and 1980's, many wildlife species disappeared as well. Mudfish and snakes, which indicate higher biological diversity disappeared after the 1970's. Biological indicators of open water such as dragonflies and mosquito fish disappeared after the 1980's. Domestic species, urban adaptive species and invasive species became much more abundant after the 1980's and had become part of children's experience of nature.

6. Neighborhood environmental change affects wildlife habitat and therefore the educational opportunities as well.

People who grew up in the 1970's and the 1980's showed more familiarity with a wider range of animals (remembered biological diversity: 3.62 and 3.71) than the younger age group (remembered biological diversity: 2.86). Children in the 2000's used inclusive natural categories which could be an implication of insufficient exposure to nature.

7. In highly urban neighborhoods, designed "ecoparks" make natural environments available for children to enrich their experiences with nature.

Children today demonstrate a higher degree of experience of nearby nature given smaller and fewer nearby natural environments compared with the past. One can conclude that a well-designed ecological park compensates as an excellent alternative experience of nature.

8. Childhood experience of nearby nature could be a determinant of adult environmental behavior.

This paper is an exploratory research finding a positive statistical relationship between childhood experiences of nearby nature and adult environmental behavior, which provides some empirical support for a link between the two phenomena. Assuming the respondents have accurate memories of childhood and answered the questionnaire without extreme biases, the result of this survey tends to confirm the existence of a link between childhood experience of nearby nature and adult environmental behavior.

9. Life stages and hierarchy of needs affects the influence childhood experience of nearby nature has on adult environmental behavior.

Some cases showed that even growing up with rich experiences with nature, socio-economic constraint would play a part in a person's environmental behavior. The research confirms psychologist Maslow's "hierarchy of needs" theory and helps us more deeply understand relationships between childhood experience of nature and adult environmental behavior.

ENDNOTES

* Travel is calculated from places children go after class except the homes.

** Frequency of children's nature visit is the sum of frequency of natural visit people answered in the questionnaire.

[1] The photo representing pre-1970's environment was not taken at the actual site since no on-site picture was found. However, the environmental characteristics were similar.

[2] This is a general term based on the observation that people generally kill some creatures that are pests or just unlovely—the reason varies.

[3] This is from the observation that children sometimes torture living creatures to death for some reason.

[4] It is believed that most of the people in Taiwan, both man and woman hate cockroaches, a species makes people scream, cry and kill, according to my own observations.

[5] Peter H. Kahn, jr. "Bayous and Jungle Rivers: Cross-Cultural Perspectives on Children's Environmental Moral Reseasoning". In Herbert D. Saltzstein (Ed) Culture as a Context for Moral Development: New Perspectives on the Particular and the Universal. SF: Jossy-Bass Publishers. 1997. p.27.

REFERENCES

Bronfenbrenner, U. 1979. The Ecology of Human Development: Experiments by Nature and Design. Harvard University Press.

Carr, S. and Lynch, K. Where Learning Happens. In P. Shepard and D. Mckinley (Eds) The Subversive Science: essays towards an ecology of man. Boston: Houghton Mifflin.

Chou, S-H. 1998. Methods and Materials of Children's Experience of Natural Science. Taipei: Psychology Press.

Chu, R. L. 1993. The Study of Urban Image in Ming Sheng Community.

Clay, G. 1969. Remembered Landscapes. In P. Shepard and D. Mckinley (Eds) The Subversive Science: Essays Towards an Ecology of Man. Boston: Houghton Mifflin.

Cobb, E. 1969. The Ecology of Imagination in Childhood. In P. Shepard and D. Mckinley (Eds) The Subversive Science: Essays Towards an Ecology of Man. Boston: Houghton Mifflin.

Cohen, E. 1994. Animals in Medieval Perceptions: The Image of the Ubiquitous Other. In Animals and Human Society. Aubrey Manning and James Serpell (Eds).

Cronon, William. 1995. "The Trouble with Wilderness; or Getting Back to the Wrong Nature." In Uncommon Ground: Toward Reinventing Nature, ed. William Cronon, 69-90. NY: W.W. Norton & Company.

Darley, J., Glucksberg, S., & Kinchla R. 1994. Psychology. N.J. : L. Erlbaum Associates

Groth, Paul. 1997. Frameworks for Cultural Landscape Study. In Understanding Ordinary Landscapes, ed. Paul Groth and Todd W. Bressi, 1-21. New Haven: Yale University Press.

Hart, Roger. 1979. Children's Experience of Nature. NY: Irvington Publishers, INC.

Hester, Randolph. 1979. "A Womb with a View: How Spatial Nostalgia Affects the Designer." Landscape Architecture. September.

Hester, R. T. and McNally, M. J., et al. 1988. We'd like to tell you... Children's Views of Life in Westport, California. Landscape Architecture. Jan-Feb.

Inagaki, K. Hatano, G. 2002. Young Children's Naïve Thinking About The Biological World. Psychology Press.

Kahn, P. H., Jr. 1997. Bayous and Jungle Rivers: Cross-Cultural Perspectives on Children's Envirowmental Moral Reasoning. In Herbert D. Saltzstein (Ed) Culture as a Context for Moral

Development: New Perspectives on the Particular and Universal. SF: Jossey-Bass Publishers.

Kaplan, R. and Kaplan, S. 1989. The Experience of Nature: A Psychological Perspective. Cambridge University Press.

Kleinsinger, S. B. Learning Through Play: Science A Practical Guide for Teaching Young Children.

Landau, D. Stump, S. 1994. Living with Wildlife: How to Enjoy, Cope with, and Protect North America's Wild Creatures Around Your Home and Theirs. SF: Sierra Club Books. California Center for Wildlife.

Lennard, H. L., Crowhurst L., and Suzanne H. 2000. The Forgotten Child: Cities for the Well-Being of Children. Carmel, Calif.: International Making Cities Livable Council.

Lynch, K. 1977. (Ed.) Growing Up in Cities. The MIT Press.

Magurran, A. E. 1988. Ecological Diversity and Its Measurement. NJ: Princeton University Press.

Manning, A. Serpell, J. (Eds). 1994. Animals and Human Society. London: Routledge.

Marcus, C. C. 1979. Environmental Autobiography. Berkeley: Institute of Urban & Regional Development, University of California.

Mead, M. 1977. "Children Culture, and Edith Cobb." In Children, Nature and the Urban Environment: Proceedings of a Symposium-Fair. USDA Forest Service General Technical Report. NE-30.

Melson, G. F. 2001.Why the Wild Things Are: Animals in the Lives of Children. Harvard University Press.

Moore, R. C. 1986. Childhood's Domain. London: Dover, N. H: Croom Helm.

Nabhan, T. 1994. The Geography of Childhood. Boston: Beacon Press.

Orr, D. W. 1992. Ecological Literacy. Albany: State University of New York Press.

Pearce, J. C. 1985. Magical Child Matures. NY: Dutton.

Piaget, J. 1969. (English Translation). The Child's Conception of Time. NY: Basic Books, INC.

Southworth, M. 1970. An Urban Service for Children Based on Analysis of Cambridgeport Boys' Conception and Use of the City. MIT Dissertation.

Serpell, J. 1986. In the Company of Animals: A Study of Human-Animal Relationships. UK: Basil Blackwell Ltd.

Spenser, B. and Spenser, M. 1989. The Child in the Physical Environment. John Wiley & Sons Ltd.

Tuan, Y-F. 1974. Topophilia and Environment. In Topophilia: A Study of Environmental Perception, Attitudes and Values. NY: Columbia University Press.

Tuan, Y-F. 1977. Experience and Appreciation. In Children, Nature and the Urban Environment: Proceedings of a Symposium-Fair. USDA Forest Service General Technical Report. NE-30.

Vessel, M. F. and Wong, H. H. 1987. Natural History of Vacant Lots. California Natural History Guide No. 50. CA: University of California Press.

Wohlwill, J. F. 1983. The Concept of Nature: A Psychologist's View. In Behavior and the Natural Environment, ed. NY: Plenem Press.

A POST-OCCUPANCY EVALUATION OF LOW-INCOME HOUSING
Do User's Values and Preferences Overlap with Sustainable Development Principles?

Amy Dryden

ABSTRACT

The objective of this study is to determine how user preferences for outdoor space support or undermine sustainable site design. The study examines how these preferences can inform site planning and offer guidelines for sustainable development. Sustainability, a cultural and ecological process, is advanced through professionally and industry derived guidelines primarily informed by ecological function. Yet, it is user needs and values that create socially sustainable places. Therefore to successfully address both ecological and social parameters of sustainability, user preferences need to be understood. Understanding user preferences is particularly important when advancing sustainable design in a non-market based system like affordable housing. Through a post occupancy evaluation (POE) survey this study explores user needs and preferences of private and public outdoor space (parking, open space and building typology) in two affordable homeownership housing developments in Oakland, California. The survey included an owner given tour of private and neighborhood outdoor space, prioritization of the outdoor spaces and making spatial trade-offs. The survey results showed a strong preference for private yard space, privacy and boundaries. These preferences need to be reconciled with the communally based approach of sustainable site design. Additionally, users desired more paved surfaces to make spaces usable. As spaces are paved over the volume of runoff increases beyond original design intentions, counter to sustainable goals. Common areas are highly valued for the large outdoor area, although rarely used by adults and often by children. Satisfying the ideals of privacy and boundaries as well as including suitable amenities can increase the frequency of use. This analysis produces an alternative perspective as well as a set of sustainable site design guidelines, which better respond to user's needs, specifically addressing both green site design and social sustainability. Within this context designers and architects can consider the ecological and social factors of sustainable site design more critically.

INTRODUCTION

Sustainability has been the mantra to combat sprawl since the nineteen-nineties. From broad global agendas to theoretical frameworks, sustainability has made its way into the legislation of some cities as well as into the offices of professional designers and planners. These frameworks and ideologies have prompted submission of written proposals and guidelines of physical form from the building industry and professionals to advance sustainability as a practice. Sustainability requires that development be altered from conventional practices, and that those alterations must be usefully debated within the context and influence of the given social and ecological environments. With a continual increase in building, particularly residential, it is critical that developments are well planned in order to improve the quality of the environment and the satisfaction of the users.

Continued progress in building science, technology, and operations provides resources for designers, developers and planners to create and require more ecological environments. Industry defined ecological checklists provide development standards to increase densities, conserve land, natural resources and energy, which may or may not be conducive to the human environment in which it is being created. The human use of space is critical in determining the success of the design particularly because sustainable design emphasizes communal aspects of space, consequentially reducing private space.

Environmental goals should not be abandoned for social preferences. Rather ecological design must incorporate social aspects. Spaces not grounded in social understanding can fall back on ecological geometries and be confused as good design. Though site design will influence social behavior, the manipulation of space to induce ecologically informed behavior of people may be an over-estimation since cultural context plays such a strong role. A truly sustainable

site incorporates both environmental values and user values to sustain community and individuals.

This study evaluates the relationships between sustainable site design guidelines and residents' preferences and values regarding outdoor space. These needs and preferences are explored through a post occupancy evaluation survey in two affordable homeownership housing developments in Oakland, California. The survey focuses on three aspects of residential site design: open space, permeable surface/parking and the building footprint. These facets represent the types of spaces most affected by sustainable site design guidelines. These priorities are compared to a composite list of ecologically derived guidelines to understand the overlap of the ecological and social ideals. This will inform a set of sustainable site development characteristics and dilemmas, for designers and planners to consider.

	105th	Jingletown
Comparable Conditions		
resident profile	30-80% median income	80% median income
homeownership	first time	first time
cost of home	$117,000	$98,000-$129,000
number of units	40	53
communal open space	yes	yes
square footage of home	1080-1180	900-1424
Variable Conditions		
density	12 d.u./acre	23 d.u./acre
development type	single family	townhouses
development profile	4-3 bdrm	32-2 bdrm, expand to 4
	15 - 3 bdrm, expand to 4	9-3 bdrm, expand to 5
	21 - 4 bdrm, expand to 5	5 - 3 bdrm with office
construction type	new	new
parking conditions	2 spot tandem driveway	2 spot tandem driveway
	auto and pedestrian street	shared parking lot
		auto pedestrian court
Ecological Conditions		
infill property	no	yes
increased density of area	yes	yes
attached housing	no	yes
drought tolerant landscaping*	yes	yes
near transit	no	yes
stormwater treatment	no	no

* this was called for in plans but not necessarily planted.

Table 1. A comparison of the characteristics of the Jingletown and 105th Avenue Developments.

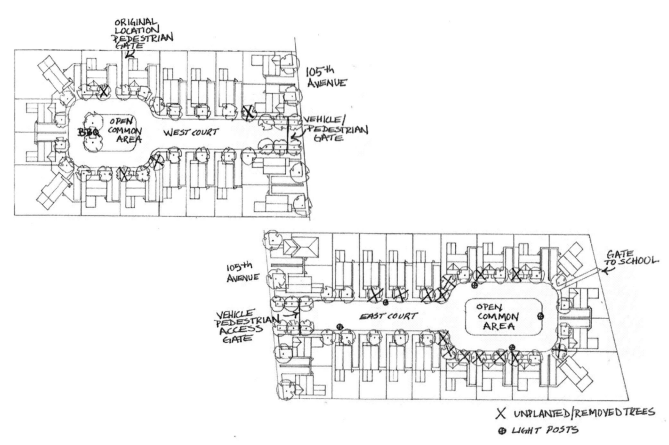

Figure 1. The East and West Court plan of the 105th Avenue development.

My hypothesis is this: if the values regarding outdoor places (yard space, neighborhood space and parking) of low-income homeowners are understood, then the site design can be acceptably and thoughtfully altered to include ecological design guidelines. This is particularly critical because much of sustainable design focuses on a reduction of private space and an expansion of communal space. Additionally, low-income homeownership does not operate in a market driven system. My expectation is that communal space although valued is less valued than private space. If this is true then it has design implications on sustainable site design guidelines.

STUDY SITES

After a review of several developments in the city of Oakland, CA, two developments were chosen for this study. The 105th Avenue project in East Oakland developed by East Bay Habitat for Humanity, a volunteer based affiliate of a national organization, and the Jingletown Villas in the Fruitvale District developed by Oakland Community Housing Inc. (OCHI), a community based homeownership and rental developer, met the criteria. Several factors were considered and determined to be consistent across the two developments, including jurisdiction, square footage, low-income, rate of homeownership, site layout, age of stock and housing price (See Table 1). The projects have a comparable number of total units, only the density and

therefore housing typology vary. Each development has its own history of design and development, which influenced the respective final designs.

EAST BAY HABITAT FOR HUMANITY AND THE 105TH AVENUE SITE

East Bay Habitat for Humanity was formed in 1988 as an independent affiliate of Habitat for Humanity International, a Christian-based, non-profit, affordable housing developer. Their mission is to create homeownership opportunities for low-income families by building decent, affordable houses and to enhance neighborhoods by working with homeowners and the community. East Bay Habitat serves families in Alameda and West Contra Costa Counties whose income is 30% - 80% of the median income (low and very low) as defined by the US Department of Housing and Urban Development.

The homes, built primarily with volunteer labor, are sold to low-income families with no monetary down payment required and a zero interest mortgage. Families are required to invest 500 sweat equity hours as a down payment for the land and the house with a thirty-year mortgage. Because East Bay Habitat is the developer as well as the lending institution, the mortgage payments accrued from completed homes are used to fund future projects. In 1999, with volunteer labor, homeowner sweat equity and private funding, East Bay Habitat completed the 40 single-family homes project on 105th Avenue.

Design of the East and West Court

The East and West Courts on 105th Avenue are two private streets located in the Sobrante Park neighborhood within walking distance of a middle and an elementary school, several churches, a corner store and a newly built charter school. Other commercial facilities are as little as 2 miles away. The development consists of two cul de sac streets with 18 and 22 two-story single-family homes. Each cul de sac has an automatic vehicle gate and two locked pedestrian gates. The building setbacks are 10 feet on the main roadway; this minimum setback was determined by the designer. A 5-foot setback was used for the houses at the back of the court because of the reduced foot and vehicular traffic. An access gate was placed at the rear of the lot for pedestrian access to the middle school located behind the development. The Homeowner's Association maintains the private street and common space (See Figure 1).

The development has 12 dwelling units/acre on the 3.4 acre site consisting of three and four bedroom with two exceptions- one five and one six bedroom. Private yards are fenced along the back and side yards with an access gate on both sides of each house. The 25-foot long driveways are all privately owned with additional parking in the street. Parking is restricted at the cul de sac to allow for emergency vehicle access.

The paved surfaces make up approximately 50% of the site including buildings (20% of that 50%) and driveways and the street (30% of the 50%). The common green open space makes up 9% of the entire development while private yards account for 41% of the total open space (See Figures 2 and 3). Each house was to have a tree planted in the front yard unless removed by the resident or never planted in some cases.

Design Intent

Design intent was influenced by the design process, which included three public workshops, city requirements, East Bay Habitat for Humanity and their budget constraints, the volunteer architects, the city, and the immediate community. The developers felt it essential to get the community's input due to their familiarity with the neighborhood; the development would be a new part of their community. The workshops with the neighbors were the most influential force in the design process. They were clear about what they wanted to see in their neighborhood and what they expected to work.

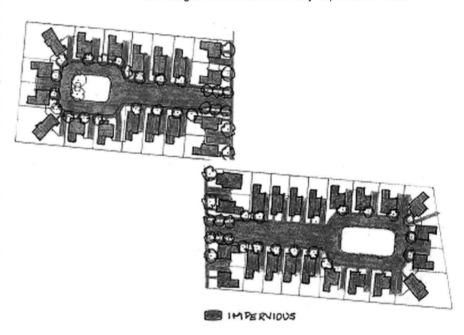

IMPERVIOUS

Figure 2. These diagrams represent the impervious area of the site.

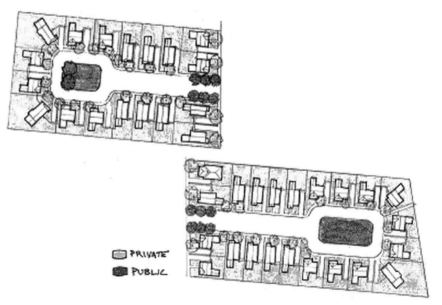

PRIVATE

PUBLIC

Figure 3. These diagrams illustrate the majority of the open space of development is on private property.

The neighbors presented a strong voice against some of the initial design decisions including collective parking, attached clustered housing, kids' play space separated from the vehicles and a communal open space that interfaced with the neighborhood. The neighbors conveyed that people needed their own private space to supervise. They were concerned that semi public areas such as a common parking area would not be well used if becoming public to the neighborhood. In their experience, common areas with ambiguous ownership were not well supervised. The neighborhood believed private fenced property would be the most successful design for the neighborhood.

Prospective homeowners were not necessarily choosing the neighbors or the neighborhood; they were choosing affordability and the opportunity to have a house. With such diversity amongst people with a broad range of lifestyles, privacy is essential.

OCHI AND JINGLETOWN

Oakland Community Housing (OCHI) was formed as a private non-profit housing development corporation in 1973 to serve residents whose homes were demolished by City Center Redevelopment. Beginning as a collaborative effort of a grassroots community-based coalition, their goal is to make a positive impact on people's lives by producing and managing quality affordable housing, including rental and home ownership units. As a developer and property manager OCHI provides services for the residents such as after-school programs, counseling, community computer resources and onsite daycare.

OCHI, working with the City of Oakland, was the developer and manager for the Jingletown Villas development, which included an equity share program for first time homebuyers who make 80% of the median income, was completed in 1997. Despite the layers of regulations through HUD and the city, Jingletown was highly recognized for good design. HUD and National Partners of Homeownership selected the development as a model for responding to community needs and innovative construction. Additionally, the development received the 1997 Pacific Coast Builders Golden Nugget Award for Best Affordable Attached Housing.

Design

Mike Pyatok of Pyatok Architects was the architect who worked with OCHI along with 60 people from the surrounding neighborhood to design the development and select the building typologies. Jingletown is comprised 53 townhouses on three parallel private streets off of a residential street in the Fruitvale District of Oakland. The development is within walking distance of an elementary school and a shopping area. It is within 3/4 mile of the Fruitvale BART. The neighborhood is tucked in between the major roadways of 12th Street, 29th Avenue, the 880 freeway and an on/off ramp for the 880 freeway. There are approximately 18 units to a pedestrian court, which is similar to the total units on each cul de sac at 105th Avenue. The building typologies mimic the surrounding architecture to integrate with the single-family character of the neighborhood housing stock (See Figure 4).

The 20-foot wide auto-pedestrian courts were designed with colored concrete, bollards and rolled curbs identifying the multi-use roadway creating a more pedestrian friendly environment than the conventional asphalt road. The entrance on each of the courts is not gated, however there are private property postings at the sidewalk. Individual houses with 5-8 foot setbacks have private fenced front and back yards as well as 15-foot long private driveways or designated parking spaces. The houses are grouped in clusters of 8 and 10 dwelling units around a smaller common area, complemented by the larger area at

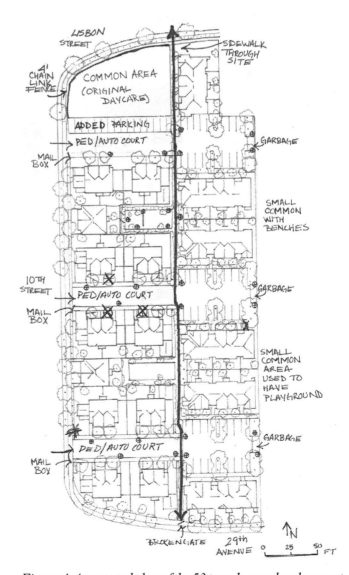

Figure 4. Annotated plan of the 53 townhouse development of Jingletown Villas.

the north end of the property. A central walkway runs through the development for easy pedestrian access to the school and shopping area. The access at 29th Avenue is gated. The 53 townhouses at 23 dwelling units /acre on this 2.3 acre site were designed to accommodate lower income and allow for lower mortgages and stretch subsidies.

Seventy percent of the site is covered, 38% of which is buildings, and driveways and the street make up the remaining percentage. The remaining open space is divided between 19% common green open space and 21% private (See Figure 5 and 6).

Design Intent

Pyatok had several design intents for the development including providing visual and physical access to the animal shelter park area which was not permissible, pedestrian access through the site via a north/south sidewalk integrating the development with the community, grass play in the common areas and hard surface play the pedestrian/ auto courts and clustering houses

to back up to small landscaped areas. The houses with low backyard fences allowed residents to be in their backyards and easily supervise the common area. The original intent was to build a community center and daycare on the north end of the site. Without the funds available, the community serendipitously received a larger open space with a short 4-foot chain link fence, which marks the main corner between the neighborhood and the development.

The only ecological practice utilized by both developments was to increase the local density. This is often the driving force for affordable housing because increased densities result in lower costs.

PRACTICABILITY OF SUSTAINABILITY

Through efforts to encourage sustainability and make it more accessible, not-for-profit organizations, developers and designers have worked to create physical conceptions of this ideology. Sustainability concepts such as minimizing environmental impacts, conserving natural resources, encouraging superior building design to enhance health, safety and well being of the residents, providing durable, low maintenance dwellings and making optimum use of existing infrastructure, were integrated into planning doctrine through aspects of land use planning and site design. Focusing on

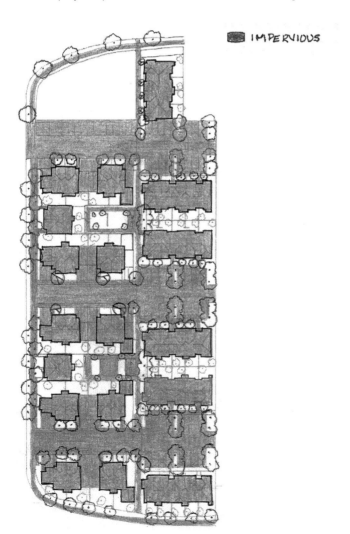

Figure 5. This diagram represents the 70% impermeable surfaces of the Jingletown development.

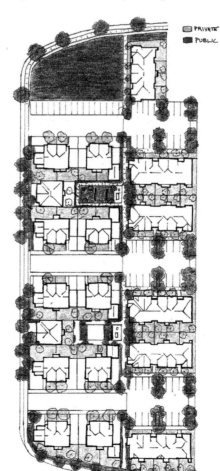

Figure 6. In Jingletown the open space is relatively equally distributed between public and private property.

environmentally sensitive development, designers and planners were encouraged to address the construction practices, life-cycle costs of building materials and dismantling operations: the cradle to grave approach.

In the Bay Area alone, there are several sources of guidelines for sustainable commercial and residential development addressing these aspects of building design. Organizations range from regional coalitions, including the Bay Area Alliance for Sustainable Development, to county waste managements such as Alameda Waste County Management Association to municipal offices like the San Francisco Mayor's Office of Housing. These guidelines are often broken down into four main categories: site and building design, resource conservation, energy and water efficiency, health and safety. These goals are realized through several aspects of site design including impermeable surfaces, housing typology, land use, landscaping and open space and the preservation of natural resources.

1. Impervious surfaces include roofs / buildings and paved ground surfaces for streets, sidewalks and driveways are deemed unsustainable both in energy intensive production of the material and the effects on the hydrologic cycle and the micro-climate. A reduction in paved area reduces consumption of nonrenewable energy used in production and the material itself, and decrease total volume and pollutant level of stormwater and ambient temperature.

2. Land use and land use patterns affect every aspect of sustainable design. Conventional land use patterns increase automobile use, land development and infrastructure costs. Infill development and mixed use utilizes vacant parcels and existing infrastructure increasing density and population in urban areas in proximity to amenities while providing an alternative to driving, thus reducing travel needs and creating a more pedestrian friendly community. These ideologies are reflected in New Urbanism.

3. Landscaping (and preserving natural resources) has an ecological impact as well as social while providing a functional space. In California, traditional landscaping irrigation consumes 40-60% of the residential water use. Trees and other vegetation reduce water runoff, decrease the impacts of the heat island effect and provide an appealing aesthetic. Using plants appropriate for the climatic conditions lessens the burden on municipal water supplies creating a positive regional impact.

The community components of ecologically informed spaces such as public spaces and shared lots cannot be integrated into design without understanding the needs of the community. For example, LEED provides guidelines that address sustainability issues including increased densities to reduce land consumption, prevent sprawl and provide green spaces for community gatherings. Yet, the characteristics of open space are not addressed to achieve the LEED rating for density; instead, the existence of common green space is generalized as beneficial to the community. In another case, it has been illustrated that people are less concerned with the housing type and more concerned with parking security, privacy and yards. There is less of a focus on façade than user needs. If needs are sacrificed or disregarded then the community building touted design has impeded community.

Social sustainability, which considers quality of life issues, requires the inclusion of the explicit and implicit needs of the users, both individually and as a community, into the design plan. Development patterns can either inhibit or contribute to the establishment of strong communities and neighborhoods. Therefore awareness of the relationship between human behavior and the built environment is paramount. With this in mind, Corbett and Corbett, through their work in developing Village Homes state "the key to sustainable development lies in having planners and engineers understand and work with nature and human nature rather than habitually trying to overcome them."

Designers have addressed, investigated, experimented with and reviewed how these social factors are manifested in physical design. Based on the previously discussed literature the following qualitative characteristics would promote successful environments for the individual as well as the community: Common open space; Pedestrian access; Privacy- balance of public and private; Shared space including parking, mailboxes, courts for chance encounters; Vegetation and trees; Integration into the neighborhood both by design and physical access; Diverse housing; Activism in the neighborhood; Knowing ones neighbors and Participating in civic affairs.

For a place to be sustainable (and successful), it must respond to the human use and the function of the space. Philosophically, development practices need to be altered to sustain our population, yet the alterations must be developed within the context of the human environment. To understand the human component and user satisfaction, residential developments (in this case) must be surveyed.

A post occupancy evaluation ties the concepts of social sustainability, ecological design and trade-offs together for analysis.

METHODOLOGY

A POE strives to establish how a particular built environment satisfies its user's needs and perceptions, hence how it facilitates and/or deters human activities. In evaluating design decisions and environments, questions like what was the intended use versus the actual use?, what is the comfort level of the people? and what spaces are important for function or value? are asked. By understanding the effects buildings have on their users and occupants, designers can minimize problems and maximize benefits for future designs to address user needs.

In light of the research, I chose to use the POE survey as my method of eliciting information to understand user's preferences and values for outdoor areas in residential developments. A three-part survey instrument, conducted in person, was developed to fulfill this goal of understanding values and needs, as well as the trade-offs users would be willing to make. A multiple method approach, triangulation of measurement, was used to enhance the credibility of the results thus producing a richer data set. The total population sampled was 93 households. I was able to survey 50% (20) of the 105th Avenue development and 38% (18) of the Jingletown development, resulting in a total of 38 surveyed households. The total sample is considerable but likely is not large enough to make a statistically significant comparison between the two developments. Every effort was made to solicit every homeowner in each development, including several follow-up visits if a homeowner was not at home. One survey was conducted in Cantonese and three in Spanish. The survey was voluntary and I offered no compensation.

In the first section of the survey, residents were asked to give me a tour of their private outdoor spaces and the neighborhood outdoor space. "Neighborhood" was defined as the development. This ethnographic approach was developed primarily to provoke the residents to think about how these spaces are used, by whom and when while they were looking at the space. It was my belief that this would produce a more "honest" response and description of the spaces, as well as trigger recollection of the uses of the space in question. It is also my assumption that this recent discussion would allow individuals to make better judgments about the trade-offs offered in the third part of the survey.

The second section was a prioritization exercise. Residents were asked to prioritize six spatial categories: Yard Space, Available Space, Vegetation, Neighborhood Space, Boundaries and Privacy. This was followed by a prioritization of three to four site design elements under each of the spatial categories.

The trade-off portion of the survey was developed to understand resident's values and what they would be willing to compromise if two elements they valued were in direct competition with each other. The three categories for the trade-off questions are based on three aspects of site design: open space, building type and parking. It is my assessment based on the reviewed sustainable guideline list that these aspects are often the most manipulated to create a "sustainable design." For this reason it is necessary to understand where people are willing to make sacrifices.

Behavioral observational studies were completed over multiple days of the week and hours of the day in September through December to ensure that various uses were captured. As I would walk through the development, I would note who was outside, behavioral traces and physical conditions of homes i.e. clotheslines or hoses in front yards.

To evaluate the overlap between ecological and social aspects of design, I chose to use a composite list in order to ascertain the most complete list of sustainable elements from various sources including Alameda County Waste Management, LEED, New Jersey Sustainable Site Design, Environmental Building News and the previously discussed literature. The guidelines are discussed in terms of community and site issues. The resources include sections on material selection, site selection, lighting, plumbing and construction practices. Although, these are all critical areas of sustainability, only those specifically related to residential site design issues were included in this list, addressing:

Community Design Issues: to provide a context which would facilitate a cohesive community.

Stormwater Management: to increase natural evaporation, infiltration and transpiration while increasing permeability. There should be no net increase in rate and quantity of runoff.

Site layout and selection: to decrease land consumption, utilize existing infrastructure including transportation and stormwater, as well as provide open space.

Landscaping to Reduce Heat Island: to decrease the radiant heat from material of low reflectivity which increases the ambient air temperature (resulting in an increased need for air-conditioning).

Water Efficiency: to reduce overall water consumption and utilize climate resources.

Energy and Atmosphere: to reduce energy consumption and utilize natural resources.

INTERSECTION OF ECOLOGICAL AND SOCIAL ASPECTS OF DESIGN

Can these ecological guidelines coexist with the user preference? The answers are "yes," "no" and "maybe."

Yes: The ecological guidelines do not conflict with the conditions stipulated by the user preferences.

No: The ecological guidelines conflict with the conditions stipulated by the user preferences and the two cannot coexist without radical compromise.

Maybe: This is essentially a conditional yes. The ecological guidelines can be implemented but only with a bias towards the user preferences as guidelines for design. Without the homeowner buy in the design would not be successful.

By comparing the data conclusions to the sustainable site design guidelines previously outlined the consistencies and inconsistencies can be identified. The results of the data present architects and designers with sets of dilemmas. There are three examples of the data presented here addressing the public and private concept, parking and open space. The findings and the implications will illustrate the spatial tradeoffs.

Public and Private Concept

The idea of public versus private space is not new. Not surprisingly, there is a strong preference for private spaces, boundaries and general privacy. Ecological design parameters strive to economize land use and decrease square footage to reduce the overall impervious area, increase building efficiency and promote community. These efforts can impinge on privacy, private space and boundaries needed for successful utilization of outdoor spaces.

In both the ranking of the spatial concepts and the site design elements, the private spaces were the most important (See Tables 2 and 3). For example, under neighborhood space which included common space for kids, parking on the street, physically separated houses and community gardens: physically separated houses was the most important use of neighborhood space. The fenced in backyard was the most important type of personal yard space. Interestingly, there is a higher preference in Jingletown where the density is higher.

Connecting to the neighborhood and designing for pedestrian and bicycle access, though good in theory, are incompatible with the user preferences, particularly in depressed neighborhoods where the need for security is higher. These two conditions require a design that integrates the site into the neighborhood through a physical connection. As a result of the design intent, both developments have been affected by access by the neighborhood through the site and have sought alternative solutions. For example, there must be a minimum boundary between semi public and private and a clear strong boundary between public and semi-public/private because design creates the perception of public or private which in turn affects behavior.

At 105th, one pedestrian gate was eliminated at installation by both the neighborhood and the residents and a gate through to the school was welded shut eliminating its function. At Jingletown, the residents are designing out this intentional condition by placing gates across the publicly designed sidewalks. The public access directly conflicts with the gradations of public to private. The design intent was to have public access adjacent to semi private areas, which lead to private yards with 4-foot fences and an open entryway (See

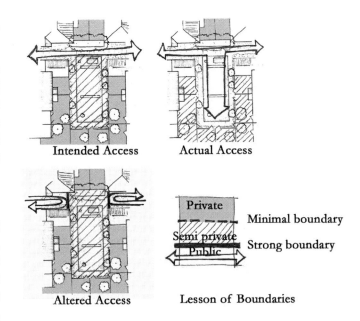

Intended Access · Actual Access · Altered Access · Lesson of Boundaries

Figure 7. The intended connection to the neighborhood had unintended consequences which led the community to seek a solution requiring strong boundaries between public and semi-private.

Figure 8. Seventeen of twenty families surveyed use their porch regularly. This regular activity creates places for a casual interaction and surveillance in the public space.

Figure 7). The result was public access to common areas, transforming private yards to public. The residents' solution was to eliminate through traffic by installing locked gates across the "public" sidewalk. Previously, they had all extended the 4-foot backyard fences to 6-7 feet and installed gates between the backyard and common space. These actions restored intended safety and use of the semi public and private areas. This conflicts with the original intent of integration and creating a more cumbersome utilization of common space as well as reducing intended sunlight and ventilation of homes and supervision of the common areas.

Successful use of space and development of community requires a priority for privacy. If a development is private, including a private street, then public access through the site is inconsistent with the residents' understanding of their ownership and maintenance of the development. Juxtaposing a public access way next to a private common area for the development invites a violation of privacy and a misuse of space.

Parking

User's value parking both on the street and off street while designers would like to reduce parking to increase density and use of public transit, reduce impervious areas and promote alternative behavior. Providing adequate parking is a highly contentious issue because designers and users may define adequate differently. Having enough parking, both private and street, is highly valued by residents and if possible they are willing to create more to fit needs.

The driveway – a flexible flat space- can support 14 different activities. It is second in the frequency of activities, which take place there- it is not just for a car. It is more important than larger backyards and outdoor storage areas. This is not to say that driveways are the only option.

66% of the residents would be willing to park in a common lot, whereas 33% said they would never give up their driveway. This tells me there is some flexibility in the design but the definition of adequate is not consistent between users and designers.

In the case of Jingletown the development originally had 1.4 parking spaces per unit. By eliminating visitor parking and renting the spaces to residents it has been raised to 1.7 and paving the north end of the site to create even more parking is under consideration.

Parking is reduced when developments are built in proximity to transit and designed for more pedestrian and bicycle

	Combined		105th		Jingletown	
Yard Space	**156**	228*	**96**	120*	**58**	108*
private backyard	**65**	152	**65**	60	**68**	54
front yard	50		50		45	
front porch / stoop	46		46		31	
having side yards	39		39		34	
Privacy	**146**	228	**77**	102	**72**	108
visual privacy from street	**120**	152	**63**	60	**59**	
protection from noisy street	99		44		51	
visual privacy from neighbors	82		50		37	
protection from hearing neighbors	67		43		33	
Boundaries	**132**	228	**66**	120	**66**	54
between adjacent houses	**85**	152	**50**	60	**38**	
between common and private space	75		34		43	
between street and house	68		36		27	
Available Space	**123**	228	**77**	120	**46**	108
parking in your own driveway	**92**	152	**46**	60	**45**	54
outdoor storage area	75		44		33	
larger yards	60		30		29	
Neighborhood Space	**103**	228	**61**	120	**46**	108
physically separated houses	**110**	152	**56**	60	**52**	54
common areas for kids	105		60		45	
parking on the street	98		53		46	
community garden	67		31		37	
Vegetation	**99**	228	**55**	120	**39**	108
plants / gardens in front yard	**120**	152	**62**	60	**57**	54
trees near house / window	101		53		44	
trees in neighborhood	95		47		46	
plants / gardens in neighbor's yard	67		38		36	

*represents highest possible score of Importance Index

Table 2. A table was created from the ranking section to understand the cumulative importance of each of the spatial concepts and site design elements.

access and mixed use. The ultimate ecological goal to reduce impermeable surfaces conflicts with parking needs of users. Incorporating permeable paving is the technological solution that does not conflict with conventional design and user preferences, in theory. Economics, aesthetics and product performance influence whether or not this is a viable solution. Under these circumstances, I think it is critical to understand this relationship to ensure a more ecological design- not a less ecological design once we are gone.

In my thesis, I have laid out some approaches that are both compatible, like tandem driveways, and less compatible, like car share programs, with the survey results. For this population, access to transit and higher density are not resulting in alternative behavior but alternative design. In an effort to provide more ecological development, do designers fulfill the will of users and provide more parking than required by code as the profession looks to reduce required parking spaces? Or should design and ecological goals dictate the form of parking? With the complexity of variables, it is essential to consider and weigh the particular social and ecological values. Mitigation of the less desirable characteristics of parking may be the best approach.

Open Space

While open space is valued, it must be modified by the word "private," either for the resident or for the development. Without this security, places like fronts of houses, backyards and common areas remain unused. While, designers and developers look to maximize open space, minimize built form for density and storm water management, residents are paving their backyards to make them usable.

Private backyards was the most important space with the highest intensity and diversity of use of backyard- 79% said it was the most important on the lot where paved surfaces are valued for use. Some residents named it the most important in the neighborhood.

Front porches not patios are used more than front yards. The front porch is social space where 90% of the 105th residents sit on the front porch everyday where as only 33% of Jingletown residents ever use the front yard or front patio. In minimizing street widths to provide possibilities for social interaction and reduce impervious area while increasing density, it is essential that buffers be maintained. Without the buffers of an acceptable setback or an elevated porch, the front will be less inhabited, negating possibilities of social interaction. Too narrow a frontage forces residents to the back negating social intercourse, yet the feel of a narrower street has been shown to be more appealing to residents. The ecological goals of narrowing street width and decreasing setbacks which reduce resident's boundaries can be successfully achieved knowing

that the front yard functions as a boundary and an aesthetic and the porch functions as a boundary and social space. The design should include just enough front yard to plant something, an elevated porch to create privacy and boundary and a social arena for casual interaction, achieving both ecological, social and community goals.

Conceptually, decreasing impermeable areas and increasing open space are complementary goals. Several conditions make these two parallel ideas less compatible. First, unplanned paved areas produce unplanned increases in volumes of runoff. In the tour, 85% of the residents have either paved their yard or are planning to pave their backyard. The typically small spaces of the backyard are valuable for the diversity of activities, which can occur on the paved surface. Second, built out spaces are used actively. The active use of porches makes them a more appealing community benefiting design than front yards.

Because green open space is so appealing aesthetically and ecologically, it is critical that its design is thoughtfully developed within user parameters to prevent green deserts or future non-ecological modifications. With the diverse possibilities of site layout, the level of activity should inform the size of different areas to satisfy use and increase casual interaction (See Figure 9). The designer is again faced with the dilemma of creating paved surfaces, which users desire more for usable space. The actual use of space can allow the designer to manage the

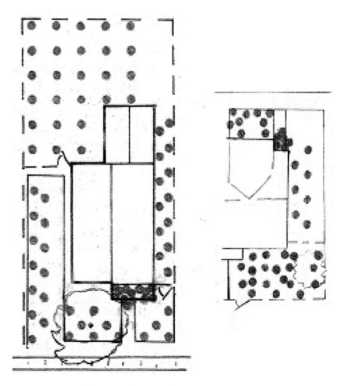

Figure 9. The number of activities is proportionally similar for each site. This data in conjunction with the types of activities can be used as a guide to determine which spaces to minimize and maximize.

site layout to accommodate user preferences and ecological goals and mitigate increased built areas.

An observation: The Design and Alteration

The 105th Avenue development, which was of the least design risk is also the least altered. On the other hand, Jingletown residents are altering the site in fundamental ways that do not align with the designer's intent or the ecological guidelines. The parking that was reduced is being increased. Second, the intentional accessibility through the site, which reduced the privacy, security and usability of the interior common areas has been eliminated. Third, the backyard fences designed for supervision and connection to the common space and light and ventilation to homes have been altered for privacy by raising the fence height and installing gates.

How do alternative development practices become acceptable and unaltered? Architects and designers can use this data to think about site design more critically in its physical form.

The results and discussion presented here provide a better understanding of this relationship in order to consider site design more critically. The ability to address the intersection of user preferences and sustainable development guidelines fall into three categories, First, technological solutions such as pervious concrete, fulfill ecological demands without explicitly requiring alternative behavior or living conditions or site design. Second, education of ecological and financial benefits can result in a voluntary adoption of ecological alternatives. Third,

subtle spatial solutions responding to the users needs can result in both a socially and ecologically responsible design.

These possibilities and conditions present a set of dilemmas to design professionals, which we are required to address in order to complete a successful design. As professionals looking to create more sustainable developments- which are by definition environmentally and socially responsible, our understanding of these possibilities and conditions will allow site designs to be altered in a thoughtful manner in order to accommodate sustainable goals. By anticipating the needs of the end user by social and economic demographics, we can avoid future alterations of the site that would be sustainably and ecologically detrimental.

Additionally, affordable housing does not function in a market demand condition, which typically allows for a best fit of buyer to home. This makes it more critical to understand the social implications of design. This also raises the issue of different income levels. A complimentary extension of this research would be to survey middle-income development where there is a market demand condition. It would be effective to understand the possibilities in these developments as well. Additional research based on the survey instrument should include more detailed questions, which have explicit ecological goals. This would include a deeper understanding of the three ways I found to address this intersection: technological, educational and spatial solutions.

	Combined		105th		Jingletown	
Personal yard space	total activities	total number of mentions	total activities	total number of mentions	total activities	total number of mentions
backyard	29	261	25	119	19	101
front porch	17	94	13	46	6	16
driveway	14	97	12	45	6	33
front yard	13	89	11	35	8	34
side yards	6	39	6	23	na	na
fence / edge	5	49	3	4	5	10
Neighborhood space						
street	12	90	6	28	5	11
sidewalk	10	89	9	38	8	45
neighbor's front yard	9	71	11	53	10	47
common area	9	69	6	34	6	31
small common area	8	57	na	na	8	37
edge / gate to neighborhood	5	51	11	53	10	47
neighbor's driveway	5	47	5	9	4	16
neighbor's porches	4	30	4	14	1	1

Table 3. Additionally, I compiled the number of activities and frequency from the tour section of the survey.

**participatory
environmentalism**

Breath 是我对花
感觉 在之流中身
is the unbearable
in the mainstream

Mainstream + Dam
=
FLOOD

(主流受阻成灾)

THE IMPORTANCE OF BEING ENGAGED
The Role of Community Participation in Urban Creek Stewardship

Victoria Chanse and Chia-Ning Yang

ABSTRACT

The 20th century witnessed a change in how the stewardship of urban nature is practiced: from a top-down, distant, centralized, professionals-leading regime to a local, participatory, grassroots movement. Focusing on urban creeks in the San Francisco Bay Area, this paper proposes to further this movement by combining volunteerism with spontaneous use. Through examining research on these two modes of engaging people, we hypothesize that volunteerism and spontaneous use together create a participatory culture of urban nature stewardship

INTRODUCTION

Today, volunteers play a key role in urban nature stewardship in the US.[1] In 2003, roughly 1.1 million people volunteered through environmental organizations on stewardship activities. The rapid development in environmental volunteering is demonstrated by the Environmental Protection Agency water monitoring program group list which jumped from 44 groups in 24 states in 1988 (Riley, 1998) to 832 groups in 50 states in 2003 (EPA, 2003). These figures signify how, in urban areas, the environmental movement is shifting from wilderness preservation or developmental controls to a local, participatory form of environmentalism where citizens no longer depend solely on government agencies or professionals to take care of the "natural environment." The transformation is ongoing, and in light of its significant implication to our sustainable future, it deserves articulation.

This paper proposes to advance this transformation by combining two ways of engaging people which were treated separately or even viewed as contradictory in prior studies: volunteerism and spontaneous use.[2] We will first give a brief review of the evolution of urban nature stewardship in the past century. Focusing on the urban creek movement, the sector that attracts much attention in the San Francisco Bay Area, we will then examine the benefits and constraints of both volunteerism and spontaneous use, and how they complement each other. By juxtaposing these two modes, we can obtain important clues on how urban creek stewardship programs successfully engage people in a broad, participatory way.

THE EMERGENCE OF PARTICIPATORY URBAN NATURE STEWARDSHIP

To articulate the characteristics of current urban nature stewardship, it is necessary to briefly review how this stewardship evolved in the United States. This review follows the important events in the professions concerning the planning and design of urban nature, for the obvious reason that until two decades ago, landscape architects, city planners, environmental planners and engineers were completely entrusted to shape and maintain urban nature (Table 1).

The early beginnings of stewardship in urbanized areas came in the form of shared agrarian and public places. A unique characteristic of cities in the United States is that they were developed at the zenith of the Industrial Revolution. Unlike British and European cities where large royal hunting preserves and estates became available for public parks during the nineteenth century, open spaces were wrested from the private land market for industrial and housing development in cities in the United States. The Colonial Commons, such as the Boston Commons, emerged from the resolve of early proprietors and inhabitants to retain suitable lands for the town's agrarian and civic purposes (Platt, 1994). Commons therefore form the prototype of urban nature stewardship in the United States.

Landscape architecture is probably the first profession with the spirit of urban nature stewardship (Scarfo, 1988). The urban park movement in the late 19th century regarded parks as the public land for public good. Although social control has always been part of the agenda (Rosenzweig, 1983), landscape architects assumed the role of the paternalistic land steward with the power to determine the aesthetic presentation and beneficial use of these public lands. For example, Frederick Law Olmsted's goal for Central Park was to create a pseudo-rural countryside: "to supply the hundreds of thousands of tired workers, who have no opportunity to spend their summers in the country…" (Platt, 1994: 23).

From the 1890s, the modern movement left an unmistakable footprint in city planning and engineering. Two influential schemes, Ebenezer Howard's Garden City and Le Corbusier's Radiant City, resulted not from observing how real cities work but from the Utopian imagination of a few, introduced open space systems that dictated for at least half a century how citizens would interact with nearby nature. Although the Garden City ideal promoted the communal control and ownership of open land in perpetuity (Hall, 1997: 93), in practice this translated into large expanses of open space commonly lacking in definition or function which soon wooed criticism for destroying city fabric and creating placelessness (Jacobs, 1960; Relph, 1976).

Period		Effects on urban nature				Spirit of urban nature steward-ship
		Landscape Archi-tecture	City Planning	Environmental Planning	Grass-root move-ment	
1760-1850	Industrial Revo-lution	Loss of urban nature (except Colonial Commons)				Prototype: urban nature put as public trust
1850-1900	Urban park movement	Olmstedian parks				Professional as patriarchal steward
1890-1930	Progressive Era	Reform parks (organized play, social programs)	Modern move-ment (Garden City, Radiant City; working with engi-neers to obliterate creeks)	Scientific re-source manage-ment	Roadside beauti-fication	Professional betrayal of public trust
1930-1965	New Deal and Post-war Era	Modern move-ment, recreational facilities		Regional planning movement "land ethic"		Emergence of ecology-based stewardship
1965-1980	Environmental preservation	Experimental parks	Suburbanization	Wilderness preservation, environmental regulations	Community gar-dens, neighbor-hood parks	(Ecological deter-minism applied on remote nature)
1980s-	Urban nature restoration		Urban revitaliza-tion, new urban-ism	Open space preservation and restoration	Urban forests, urban streams	Participa-tory urban nature stewardship

Table 1. The evolution of urban nature stewardship.

Parallel to this development was the wholesale transformation of urban streams through over-simplified modern techniques of flood control and erosion control. Planning and engineering measures to channelize and culvert urban creeks led to flooding, erosion, and a physical and emotional disconnect from nature. Modernism thus signified the era of professional betrayal of urban nature stewardship, while the actions of the authoritative "stewards" backfired against people's real needs to experience nearby nature.

The planning and design of urban nature in the Progressive Era (1890s-1920s) emphasized an industrial model of rationalized processes and standardized production, with a central motto of "efficiency" (Cranz, 1989). Parks and playgrounds focused on organized activity and design standards that were to be copied by public agencies regardless of locality (Mozingo, 2000). Resource management also partook of the spirit of the era, stressing scientific decision-making and the prevention of waste. However, stewardship in this era heeded little to humanitarian needs of urban nature, such as its aesthetic, recreational or educational values.

The New Deal and the ensued post-war period generally extended the rationale of the previous era regarding urban nature "stewardship." In landscape architecture, modernist forms propagated through the design of suburban expansion and urban renewal projects (Hester 1983). Park design became a repetitive provision of recreation facilities (Cranz,

1989). In the emerging field of environmental planning, however, professionals found new ground in which to manifest stewardship by setting aside wilderness areas far from the reach of urban dwellers. In the regional planning movement, sustainability informed by ecology was first injected into the notion of stewardship.

Aldo Leopold's "land ethic" (1949) conceived of the land not as property but as a community of all creatures that dwell upon it. He explicitly argued that land is in the people's trust, and that human beings should assume land stewardship for the health of human and nonhuman creatures. Stewardship hereupon took up a broadened sense distinct from the traditional anthropocentric view. Consequently, in planning practices, stewardship meant land acquisition and regulation through government intervention.

Following the post-war development and energy crisis, the 1960s and 1970s was characterized by the nationwide protest against large-scale construction projects. The federal government passed a spate of environmental laws such as the Endangered Species Act, the Clean Air Act, and the Clean Water Act. Parallel with this development was the establishment of the ecological planning framework by Ian McHarg. Here, the professionals were concerned with rural—not urban—lands, with wilderness preservation rather than the creation of something, and with management more than design (Lynch, 1980). As a result of this passive ecological determinism and the wholesale middle-class flight from the inner city, urban nature was largely neglected, with the exception that grass-roots efforts in some neighborhood parks and community gardens heralded the emergence of participatory stewardship.

CONTEMPORARY URBAN NATURE STEWARDSHIP

Since the 1980s, the environmental movement has taken a different direction, namely the restoration of urban nature.[3] Grassroots efforts to restoration can be traced to community gardens as part of a grassroots reaction to limited activities and community control over public parks. The urban forest movement in the 1970s and 1980s involved organized groups to plant street trees to improve the environment in inner cities. This movement was then followed by the urban streams movement to reclaim the creeks as community amenity (Riley, 1998).

Community advocacy for urban nature restoration is regarded as antithetical to the old preservation scheme in various ways. Jordan (2000) argued that environmentalism after the 1960s generally failed to conserve nature in our crowded and increasingly democratic world. Preservation provides an extremely limited repertoire of ways to contact nature and results in a kind of "elitism." He declared that with restoration rather than preservation as a model, "millions of people will spend more time creating intimate wild places in their own neighborhoods and less time visiting—and consuming—nature in remote wilderness areas" (ibid.: 33). Instead of biological sustainability that prescribes a plot extensive enough to remain viable by itself, Nassauer (1997) presented the notion of "cultural sustainability"—the survival of a system dependent on human care. She asserted that for urban nature to achieve sustainability, stewardship on a widely shared basis is imperative.

In pursuit of this movement to form a culture of human care, we will focus on urban creeks and examine two distinct modes of creek interaction: volunteerism and spontaneous use.

VOLUNTEERISM IN URBAN CREEK STEWARDSHIP

Many creek groups in the San Francisco Bay Area emerged around the 1980s when citizens fought against Army Corps of Engineer's large-scale public projects to culvert and channelize creeks for flood control or commercial developments. Today, volunteers play multiple important roles in stewarding urban creeks. They monitor water quality, plant vegetation, remove non-natives, monitor in-stream habitat, sample aquatic insects, promote watershed education, and keep an eye on the creek daily. Through these local creek stewardship programs, volunteerism has generated three types of outcomes.

Individual benefits

According to surveys investigating the psychological benefits of volunteering in stewardship programs, Grese et al. (2000) found that the first and foremost item given was the satisfaction that it "helps the environment." Such satisfaction was linked to the feelings of self-respect and peace of mind. In other words, just as the urge to interact with the environment, helping it is also an innate urge to many. The growth of grassroots stewardship programs can be accounted for by the opportunities they provide for many to fulfill this urge or responsibility toward the nearby environment.

Volunteers also considered "learning new things" and "doing something tangible" important personal benefits. Most Friends of Creek groups provide get-your-hands-dirty activities such as planting willows or transplanting seedlings in the nursery that volunteers, adults or kids, really seem to enjoy. In effect, the hands-on activities achieve similar benefits as recreation to the individuals. Farrell's (2003) study revealed that 84% of the volunteers participating in the stewardship program of the Golden Gate National Park perceive their experience to be recreational, although their initial motivations for volunteering were for conservation or other "duty-based" reasons. As a result, volunteerism enhances individual knowledge, responsibility and control of the creek, and could be purely "fun" at the same time.

Enhancing access and ecological health

Many grass-root groups recognize the importance of enhancing community awareness through improving visual and physical access to creeks. For example, Friends of Five Creeks had a volunteer architect design a bridge along the Ohlone Greenway; Friends of Baxter Creek also took on a Gateway project to build a trail that connects the creek to regional trail systems. More likely, access points were created for the practical convenience for the stewardship activities and spontaneous uses. Stewardship programs usually start from claiming and transforming abandoned lots next to the creek or informal accesses by bridges.

Although the scientific studies documenting the measurable success or failure of volunteer efforts are few in number since some of these projects are still young, evidence suggests that these volunteer efforts do enhance local ecological health. For example, through intensive planting and vegetation management efforts, plant cover and species diversity along Sausal Creek in Dimond Canyon did improve (Chanse and Herron 2003). This is especially significant since approximately 86% of the plant species at the local and regional levels in the Sausal Creek watershed are endangered or listed.

Fulfilling legal requirements

Local water agencies have good reasons to welcome and encourage these grass-root stewardship activities, since the amount of tasks in watershed management is simply beyond the scope of most city staff. Currently only 37% of the nation's streams are monitored by government agencies for water quality control purpose (Riley, 1998). With professionals pitching in to develop bio-monitoring measures that can be easily adapted by the volunteers (e.g., Resh et al., 1996), stewardship programs are not only beneficial to the individuals and communities, but have evolved into a task force to have crucial work done.

Challenges of Urban Creek Stewardship Programs

Yet urban creek stewardship programs also confront a number of difficulties, such as funding and the skepticism of science and engineering professionals. However, what we want to emphasize here is a most basic difficulty: people's lack of interest. In restoration, the commonly enumerated "high goals" of conceptual values (water purification, habitat enhancement, native vegetation, etc.) better reach those who already appreciate such values, and therefore tend to limit the strata of participation. In the San Francisco Bay Area, as exuberant as the creek stewardship programs are, they concentrate at the upper to middle class neighborhoods.

Envision, then, promoting restoration by focusing on spontaneous use in urban creeks: "so your kids can catch crawdads in the creek, you can hear frogs from your house, you can pick berries there, you can sit down by it, dangle your feet in the creek while looking at the pretty birds and listening to the gurgle of water-it's all free service for you and your family..." it is possible to deliver the image of a "restored creek" to a much broader audience. If environmental stewardship is to go grass-roots, urban creek stewardship programs need to get down to the very basics of experiences in daily life.

In many ways, the evolution of urban nature stewardship into a participatory and democratic form re-connects people to the creeks and their local ecological system. Through such programs, neighborhood and school groups gradually take charge of the creek from government agencies, making urban creeks visually and physically accessible, and practically maintain the ecological capacity of the creek for daily contacts. In other words, consciously or unconsciously, volunteerism sustains the social and physical environments necessary for spontaneous, every-day urban creek experiences. By adding spontaneous use into the mission of stewardship programs, we can further avoid the rigid, heavy-duty impression and elite image of ecological restoration. The success of the Friends of Sausal Creek in involving the residents owes no small part to its strategies to encourage hands-on contact and casual

access to the creek. In contrast, the controversy in Chicago prairie restoration stems to a large degree from failing to involve nearby residents who use the place spontaneously and from regarding restoration as a task that can only be accomplished by highly trained volunteers (Helford, 2000).

SPONTANEOUS USE IN URBAN CREEK STEWARDSHIP

Environmental stewards (mostly professionals but sometimes volunteers) tend to regard spontaneous use at urban creeks a threat to their efforts, as witnessed by the fences or impenetrable "vegetation buffers" established around restoration projects. True, spontaneous use can cause impacts such as vegetation damage, incidental animal kills, soil erosion, organic pollution by baits, turbidity and disturbance of fish by active in-stream uses, trash resulting in animal deaths or injuries, etc. Yet all too often "human impacts" are indiscriminatingly attributed to activities of disparate scales before unbiased research is conducted on the actual level of impacts.

There is evidence indicating that activities such as catching frogs, skipping rocks, listening to water or swimming, are in fact implicitly linked to the development of urban creek stewardship. Ecological research has confirmed that the frequent disturbance of nearby nature through conscious or unconscious human

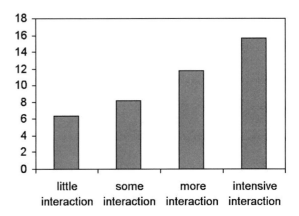

Figure 1. Effects of creek interaction (above) and use frequency (below) on creek commitment. (Mean Oral Commitment Points were generated from survey data).

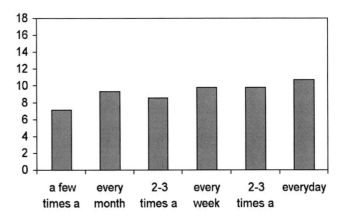

activities can benefit the eco-systems. Satoyama (backyard-mountain) research in Japan and coppicewoods research in the UK both documented how coppicing, collecting nuts, picking fruits, harvesting bamboo shoots, etc. prevent over-dense stands and create unique and extremely diverse habitats that would not have existed otherwise (Tadashi, 2002; Buckley, 1992).

Furthermore, the Marsh Creek survey project (Yang, 2004) revealed the following:

1. Adult users with higher creek interaction levels commit themselves more to creek enhancement efforts, since such uses provide more memorable experiences and therefore enhance users' value of the creek. Compared to the content of use, frequency of use has much weaker effect on stewardship (Figure 1).

2. Adults who allow their kids to play in the creek also possess a higher value and commitment for the creek.

3. Kids who play spontaneously at the creek demonstrated much richer knowledge (including habitat features) on their creek drawings compared to kids who do not play at the creek.

Field observation also found that spontaneous uses at urban creeks might well be regarded as management schemes (Yang, 2004). For example, one section on the Marsh Creek floodplain was featured by a diverse dirt path system maintained by frequent trample and wear. These narrow paths cut through the slope and floodplain and lead to various points of the waters edge (Figure 2). Very possibly some of them provided in-cuts during floods and created a thin secondary flow that attracted tadpoles and fry fish to gather (Figure 3). Similarly, kills happening to crayfish and bullfrogs help to check the population of exotics; junk collecting helps to reduce trash; trampling maintains barren lands that are important for marginal communities and animal passage.

To avoid the potential harm by spontaneous uses, sharing knowledge and responsibility with users through participatory process, particularly through volunteerism, is the only sound strategy. Children are often eager and capable to contribute to community affairs but discouraged to do so (Hart, 1997), so involving them in restoration activities such as plantings and monitoring water quality and habitat quality would be a way to allow children to contribute. In addition to the popular programs that employ children's help to scoop migrating fish over barriers or protect bird nests, catchers can learn to differentiate the native, exotic, and invasive species that harm biodiversity; they can become the primary predators of invasive exotics. Environmental actions responding to habitat management goals can become an integral part of the school curriculum. Through these actions, daily life can again

Figure 2. The dirt path system developed on the floodplain of Marsh Creek between Balfour Bridge and Valley Green Footbridge.

be connected with the pulse of the biotic world. The bottom line is that spontaneous users do not interact with the stream because they want to harm; they do so out of innate affinity. By educating children about how to be stewards, we have their gleeful cooperation; excluding them, we invite objections and doom a future constituency and eco-literacy.

CONCLUSION

The past two centuries illustrated the process of nature drifting away from the city as well as people's daily experiences. Industrialization and urbanization empowered planners, designers and engineers to little by little eliminate, eradicate, and sanitize nature from cities. Evolving from counting on professionals as patriarchal stewards and experiencing the professional betrayal of public trust and ecological determinism that forsakes urban nature for countryside, at the end of the 20th century we finally saw the burgeoning of a more democratic and participatory form of urban nature stewardship. Institutions, neighborhood groups and individuals increasingly use stewardship programs as a way to address environmental deterioration and community anomie through developing a shared sense of ownership. This participatory stewardship creates a new type of public space that is not based solely

Figure 3. The secondary flow was possibly created by a dirt path.

on use; it teaches residents about the ecology of a place and engenders a sense of shared connection to a place.

This paper examines how two ways of engaging people: volunteerism and spontaneous use can together create a culture of participatory stewardship. As two distinct modes of creek use, they also supplement each other: Spontaneous use cultivates volunteerism while volunteerism sustains the environment for spontaneous use ecologically and socially; volunteerism instills knowledge, responsibility and control that check spontaneous use from exerting harm, spontaneous use discovers new values, conceptions and ways of interaction that prevent volunteerism from getting rigid.

By inviting volunteers to experience hands-on contact with water, wildlife and loose parts (i.e. spontaneous play) in the stream environment, we obscure the division between stewards and users, producers and consumers with practical benefits. Incorporated with volunteerism, spontaneous use constantly refreshes the knowledge base and avoids rigid indoctrination of ecology. It also deepens creek attachment instead of depending solely on those who already possess the attachment; and volunteering simply becomes more fun and less a "worthy but boring cause." Together they motivate a healthy human-stream relationship and evolve a culture of urban creek stewardship.

ENDNOTES

[1] By urban nature stewardship, we mean "the duty to protect or use wisely urban nature as public trust."

[2] By spontaneous use, we mean "a mode of nature interaction resulting from innate tendency."

[3] Restoration here is broadly defined as "intentional human practices to actively create or manage areas for their desired natural qualities," a definition modified from Gobster and Hull's work (2000, p.11).

REFERENCES

Buckley, G. P. 1992. Ecology and Management of Coppice Woodlands. London: Routledge.

Chanse, V. & Herron, C. 2003. Along Sausal Creek: An Assessment of the Vegetation, Habitat, and Morphology of An Adopted Urban Creek. Research paper for LA227, Department of Landscape Architecture and Environmental Planning, University of California at Berkeley.

Cranz, G. 1989. The politics of park design: a history of urban parks in America. Cambridge: MIT Press.

Farrell, S. D. 2003. "The Recreational Value of Community-Based Stewardship within the Field of Ecological Restoration." in Recreation. San Francisco: San Francisco State University, 199.

Grese, R. E., Kaplan, R., Ryan, R. L. and Buxton, J. 2000. Psychological Benefits of Volunteering in Stewardship Programs. In Paul H. Gobster and R. Bruce Hull, eds. Restoring Nature. Washington D.C.: Island Press.

Hall, P. 1996. Cities of Tomorrow: An Intellectual History of Urban Planning and Design in the Twentieth Century. Blackwell Publishers: Oxford, UK

Hart, R. 1997. Children's Participation: The Theory and Practice of Involving Young Citizens in Community Development and Environmental Care. London: Earthscan.

Helford, R. M. 2000. Constructing Nature as Constructing Science: Expertise, Activist Science, and Public Conflict in the Chicago Wilderness. In Paul H. Gobster and R. Bruce Hull, eds. Restoring Nature. Washington D.C.: Island Press.

Jacobs, J. 1961. The Death and Life of Great American Cities. New York: Random House.

Jordan, W. R. III. 2000. Restoration, Community, and Wilderness. In Paul H. Gobster and R. Bruce Hull, eds. Restoring Nature. Washington D.C.: Island Press.

Leopold, A. 1949. A Sand County Almanac: Sketches Here and There. New York: Oxford University Press.

Lynch, K. 1980. Managing the Sense of a Region. Cambridge, MA: MIT Press.

Mozingo, L. A. 2000. A Century of Neighborhood Parks: Presumptions and Proposals. In Does the Neighborhood Landscape Matter?: a conference held at the University of California Berkeley Department of Landscape Architecture and Environmental Planning, October 19-22, 2000. Berkeley.

Nassauer, J. I. 1997. Placing Nature. Washington D.C.: Island Press.

Platt, R. H. 1994. From Commons to Commons: Evolving Concepts of Open Space in North American Cities. In R. H. Platt, R. A. Rowntree, and P. C. Muick, eds. The Ecological City. Amherst: University of Massachusetts Press.

Relph, E. 1976. Place and Placelessness. London: Pion.

Resh, V. H. Myers, M. J., and Hannaford, M. J. 1996. Macroinvertebrates as Biotic Indicators of Environmental Quality. In Methods in Stream Ecology, F. R. Hauer and G. A. Lamberti, eds. San Diego: Academic Press, 647-665.

Riley, A. L. 1998. Restoring Streams in Cities: A Guide for Planners, Policymakers, and Citizens. Washington, D.C.: Island Press.

Rosenzweig, R. 1983. Eight Hours for What We Will: Workers and Leisure in an Industrial City, 1870-1920. New York: Cambridge University Press.

Scarfo, B. 1988. Stewardship and the Profession of Landscape Architecture. Landscape Journal 7: 1, 60-68.

Tadashi, I. 2002. The History of Human and Satoyama. Tokyo: Shin-Shisaku-Sha.

Yang, C. N. 2004. Inviting Spontaneous Use into Urban Streams. Doctoral Dissertation. University of California, Berkeley.

Community Participation and Creek Restoration in the East Bay of San Francisco

Louise A. Mozingo

ABSTRACT

The creeks of the upper East Bay of San Francisco have been the location of two decades of precedent setting creek restoration activities. This discussion will review the essential role of both citizen activism and NGOs in the advent of a restoration approach to creek management. Beginning with small pilot projects to "daylight" a culverted creek and spray paint signs on street drain inlets, participation in the restoration of the East Bay creeks has evolved into a complex layering of participants. This involves government agencies, three essential umbrella NGOs– Waterways Restoration Institute, the Urban Creeks Council and the Aquatic Outreach Institute, and local grassroots groups organized around individual creeks – the "Friends of" groups (i.e. Friends of San Leandro Creek). The discussion will focus on role of the "Friends of" groups in restoration advocacy and accomplishment and will present ongoing issues of inclusiveness and ecological effectiveness in citizen initiated creek restoration.

CREEK RESTORATION

Although the science of creek restoration has been widely researched and debated, less inquiry has been directed to the essential role that NGOs and citizen activism has played in both the evolution of creek restoration and its implementation. The East San Francisco Bay, the "East Bay," has been for the last twenty five years an "innovation hearth" for creek restoration. In large part this has been the result of the commitment and expertise of several key activists and grassroots community support of the restoration idea. This paper discusses the relationship between creek restoration in the East Bay, NGOs, and grassroots citizen's groups as they have grown together.

Community involvement in East Bay creeks began in the 1970s with citizens groups, from Boy Scout troops to creative artists, cleaning up the trash in open creeks in their neighborhoods. (Schwartz, 2000, 4; Waldman, 1993, 3) Then, in the 1980s a series of catalyzing events took place around East Bay creeks.

The City of Berkeley daylighted a short stretch of Strawberry Creek. Carol Schemmerling, Commissioner of Berkeley Parks

and Recreation, had been inspired by an article of Bay Area historian Grey Brechin on the possibilities of daylighting creeks in Sonoma County north of San Francisco (Schemmerling, 2003). Doug Wolfe, a landscape architect for the City of Berkeley, proposed that a short culverted stretch of Strawberry Creek crossing a new neighborhood park in Berkeley then culverted, be opened or "daylit." As a first step in proposing the unprecedented idea, Wolfe named the new open space Strawberry Creek Park. As he later reported, this "lead to the question 'Where is this creek?' My answer was that it was 'Twenty feet down and waiting'" (Wolfe, 1994, 2). Controversial in the extreme, Wolfe found political support from Carol Schemmerling, and David Brower, founder of Friends of the Earth, and a city council member. With vocal citizen support at public meetings the radical concept prevailed. The notion that a reopened creek could be an asset rather than a hazard proved to be a lasting inspiration (Schemmerling; Wolfe, 2-3).

Also in Berkeley, a small but telling community education act took place on city streets. With the success of Strawberry Creek Park, Carol Schemmerling wanted the location of the underground drainage systems and their connection to visible waters made obvious in the city landscape. Environmental activist Richard Register designed a stenciled sign for storm drain inlets along the streets of Berkeley announcing "Drains to Bay." (Estuary Online, 1997) As a resident of Berkeley later recalled: "I was puzzled and then excited by the frog symbol on a storm drain announcing the presence of Derby Creek under my street. Eventually I came to accept that there was a real creek down there hidden away from view by the asphalt, houses, and lawns of Derby Street. And it was kind of thrilling to think of that bit of nature literally under my backyard" (Strain, 1995). Versions of this now exist all over the country.

The flood control project for Wildcat Creek in the north East Bay generated significant local attention. By the early 1980s, a twenty year history of flood control proposals, some quite innovative, had culminated in a bare bones proposal for a trapezoidal channel without vegetation to deal with flooding along Wildcat Creek, a stream running through a primarily African American low income neighborhood. Motivated local residents, committed environmental science advocates (particularly Ann Riley who went on to found the NGO Waterways Restoration Institute), and the newly formed NGO the Urban Creeks Council (Carol Schemmerling was on the Board) fought the traditional engineering solution and achieved a plan that dealt with flooding but also included restoration, water quality improvement, recreational trails, environmental education, and community outreach. The completed plan was generated not only from science but from community needs for aesthetics, open space, and job training. Residents and environmental advocates were at the table with engineers and government officials. Foundation funding provided community residents with an expert, Phillip Williams a hydrologic engineer, to critique and counter proposed plans. The process, though arduous by all accounts, resulted in a significantly different conception of the purposes of a flood control project. (Riley, 1989; Riley, 2001; Darlington, 1984)

The Wildcat Creek project, according to Phillip Williams, "changed everything." (Williams 2003, personal communication) It established restoration as an integral part of flood control management and demonstrated the importance of community involvement in restoration efforts. By the late 1980s, community groups interested in their local creeks began meeting as "Friends" groups (i.e., Friends of Cordinices Creek). These groups are the base advocates for community creek restoration in the East Bay, and became models for other groups regionally and then nationally.

By 1991, United States federal legislation required that local agencies that managed urban runoff provide programs to improve water quality. The Aquatic Outreach Institute began in 1987 as the education department of the San Francisco Estuary Institute an NGO that monitored water quality in the San Francisco Bay. By the early 1990s it received funds from a consortium of county and state agencies to increase community understanding of the impacts of urban runoff on water pollution and the importance of creeks and watersheds in local ecology in the East Bay. It has an extensive program to train teachers in creek oriented education for elementary, junior high, and high school kids. (Aquatic Outreach Institute, 2003)

Along with the Waterways Restoration Institute and the Urban Creeks Council, the Aquatic Outreach Institute is a third NGO supporting local efforts at creek restoration in the East Bay. As they have evolved they have divided tasks in support of local restoration efforts. The Waterways Restoration Institute provides environmental science support and evaluation of creek restoration efforts. The Urban Creeks Council focuses on restoration implementation at the local level, such as daylighting and revegetation, and manages job training crews of at risk youth (the East Bay Conservation Corps) and volunteer labor (Urban Creeks Council, 2002). The Aquatic Outreach Institute focuses on education, publishing a newsletter *Creeks Speak* the "Voice of East Bay Citizens for Creek Restoration" which connects all the local "Friends" groups. They also foster the establishment of local Friends groups as non-profits, able to apply for funding and organize advocacy (Aquatic Outreach Institute).

I watched the evolution of a local Friends group form with the support of AOI–the Friends of San Leandro Creek. In 1993 a few people began meeting who had an interest in the San Leandro Creek. With AOI they completed some initial projects. They designed a logo of a rainbow trout, first designated as a species in San Leandro Creek. They used this logo as the

marker for signs delineating the watershed boundary of the creek in the City of San Leandro. AOI wrote and published a booklet on the history of the Creek for wide distribution in the city. AOI helped establish a mailing list to announce regular meetings. And finally AOI assisted the organization in filing the necessary legal documentation to establish themselves as a tax exempt NGO eligible for funding from local, state, and federal sources. Since their establishment as a non-profit in 1995 they hold regular monthly meetings to organize a variety of creek related activities such as an annual clean up of the creek before the rainy season, an annual "Watershed Festival," and advocacy for project funding. The projects the Friends of San Leandro Creek undertook were: a public access park along the creek that included native plant restoration, a public art project, a small restoration project by a junior high school, and an under construction environmental education center along the creek.

In general, the Friends groups are able to broadly promulgate watershed awareness and creek restoration through key roles and activities in the East Bay. From the beginning, Friends groups organized creek clean-ups, now part of a state wide "Coastal Clean-up Day" that takes place before the rainy season. Clean-ups often draw many people who are not regular members of the friends groups. They reach out to other civic organizations, and in the process, make a very wide public aware of the importance and potential of urban creeks.

Very importantly, Friends groups are identifiable political entities. They can turn out in force for public meetings and encounters with politicians. Flood control agencies, the Army Corps of Engineers (who in the U.S. are responsible for many waterways and flood control projects), city public works departments, and open space agencies all have to deal with the Friends groups on projects that concern creeks, above or below ground.

The Friends groups provide an extraordinary source of volunteer labor in restoration activities. Much restoration work is very labor intensive and requires hand work. The Friends provide the labor to remove exotic species, plant natives, maintain restoration areas, build trails for public access, and build and run native plant nurseries. Many restoration projects would not be established nor survive without volunteer labor. Water quality monitoring in creeks is also a major volunteer activity of the Friends groups, alerting appropriate agencies in case of deterioration and demonstrating improvements.

Friends groups also imagine and conceive projects that are very locally responsive, often creative, that are not in the realm of "official" restoration activities. They expand awareness by just showing up at community events with the frequency and enthusiasm that an agency or even NGO representative could not.

Some issues exist, however, in focusing restoration efforts at the Friends level.

Using some GIS analysis of census tract data and the location of "befriended" creeks, on average the income levels around befriended creeks is $8-10,000 higher than those that are not befriended. Creeks that are more culverted are less likely to be befriended. Low income areas tended to have more creeks that are culverted than ones that are still daylighted. This emphasizes the issue that the Friends groups tend to draw from the more privileged residents of the East Bay and hence many, though by no means all, restoration efforts are concentrated in more privileged neighborhoods.[1]

At a grassroots level "restoration" can be many things that would not stand the test of an environmental scientist. For example, the Friends of San Leandro Creek removed exotic species and replanted the short stretch of the bank with redwoods–native to many creeks in Northern California but not this one. Hence the redwoods are as exotic as eucalyptus in this location and not self sustaining. Getting the right mix of enthusiasm and restoration science at the grassroots level can be a challenge. My colleague Matt Kondolf, a fluvial geomorphologist who studies stream restoration, fears that many restoration projects are more "gardens" than restoration.

Most of the restoration projects that have taken place in the East Bay in the last twenty years are non-contiguous projects of less than 500 feet in length. While often an object of great enthusiasm among local residents, from an environmental science point of view tough questions need to be asked as to how these projects really build healthy, self-sustaining ecological systems. In a recent study of the daylighting of a 250 foot section of Baxter Creek in the east Bay City of El Cerrito notes that the biological metrics of a restored urban stream are "an order of magnitude lower than those found in non-urban streams in coastal California." (Purcell, Frieidrich and Resh, 2002, 692-3) The hope is that these small projects will add up to larger, robust systems, but this has to be seen as a very long term goal.

Nonetheless, what has emerged in the East Bay in the last twenty years is a mutually supportive relationship between advocacy NGOs with expert staff and very grassroots citizens groups both working towards creek restoration. Together they constitute a powerful force of change in the way government agencies on the local, state and federal levels approach the management of water resources in urbanized areas. In the process they have changed the mindset of the wider public to understand the importance of the urbanized hydrologic systems. Alameda County, one of the two counties that cover the East Bay, reported that a series of surveys showed that in 1991-92 very few residents knew that urban runoff flowed to the San Francisco Bay; by 1994 70% of residents understood the relationship between stormwater flows and the Bay, by 1999 the figure was up to an astounding 85%. (Schwartz, 6) The base of this kind of "watershed awareness" lies in the "Friends" groups that now cover much of the urbanized watershed of the East Bay.

ENDNOTES

[1] The author would like to thank Jeff King for his assistance in this GIS analysis.

REFERENCES

Aquatic Outreach Institute. 2003. http://www.aoinstitute.org/aoi/about. Accessed 13 November 2003.

Darlington, D. 1984. Trouble on Wildcat Creek. Express. 6:33 (1 June 1984). 1,15-19, 21-22.

Purcell, A., Frieidrich, C. and Resh, V. An Assessment of a Small Urban Stream Project in Northern California. Restoration Ecology. 10:4. 685-694.

Riley, A. L. 1989. Overcoming Federal Water Policies: the Wildcat-San Pablo Creeks Case. Environment. 31:10. 12-31.

Riley, A. L. 2001. Wildcat Creek Restoration Project: A Case Study In Adaptive Management. presented at California Habitat and Floodplain Conference, March 12-14, Sacramento, CA.

Schemmerling, C. 2003. Personal Interview. by Katie Standke 17 October 2003.

Schwartz, S. 2000. A meandering history of Bay Area creek restoration. Sierra Club Yodeler. 63:7 (July). 4-6.

Strain, M. 1995. Verna Jigour Lecture. ADPSR Bulletin. Jan/Feb/Mar 1995. http://www.adpsr-norcal.org/menu/News/Bulletin. Accessed 13 November 2003.

Urban Creeks Council of California. 2002. http://www.urbancreeks.org. Accessed 15 April 2003.

Hands-on Action Proposals to Enhance the Traditional Daiju Weir on the Yoshino River and Leverage Citizen Power

Satoko Asano, Aaron Isgar, Shuichi Murakami, Tamesuke Nagahashi, Yuichi Sato, and Koichiro Yasuba

ABSTRACT

Since 2001, we have participated in the process of developing alternatives for watershed management for the Yoshino River in Tokushima, Japan. The Japanese central government seeks to replace a 250-year old traditional rock weir on the river with a big movable-gate dam. A citizen anti-dam movement known as Mina-no-Kai (Everyone's Group) has so far succeeded in preventing construction of the new dam. After winning a citizen referendum against the dam three years ago, the citizen activists have been supporting a study of two issues – how to increase upriver soil water retention capacity by revitalizing neglected watershed forests, and how to preserve the traditional weir. They asked 12 scholars from different disciplines to participate in this research effort known as Vision 21. We have been assisting this expert panel as facilitators and have simultaneously conducted our own research. Since the Hong Kong Pacific Rim Conference, we have conducted site analysis around the old weir through observation mapping of human activity on the weir and interview surveys with local residents who live around the weir. These two research approaches have allowed us to not only understand the diversity of both activities and the physical characteristics of the weir, but also to understand the relationships between these activities and spaces. In fact, the diversity of spaces sustains activities that are dependent on the relationships between spaces as well. In this paper, we suggest some points that should be considered before undertaking any changes to the weir and propose hands-on projects that would stimulate citizen use and understanding of the weir. We also consider the meaning of hands-on projects in the context of the anti-dam movement.

CONTEXT OF OUR 8 CONSIDERATIONS AND HANDS-ON PLANS FOR THE DAIJU WEIR

In order to stimulate the long-term involvement of individual citizens in the improvement and care of Daiju Weir, we propose tangible hands-on projects based on our study of its uses and spaces in this paper. First, however, we need to review the current political atmosphere surrounding Daiju Weir, because it will influence the outcome of all future projects.

Political background – Defeat in Tokushima Governor and City Mayoral Elections

After victories in the anti-dam citizens' referendum, the Tokushima City Council elections, the mayoral election, and finally the September 2002 Tokushima Prefectural Governor election, most citizens opposed to a big dam were optimistic and a sense developed that the Daiju Weir issue had been resolved. However, the new Tokushima Governor, who was backed strongly by the citizen activists, was unable to make tangible progress in assuring that the Daiju Weir would not be replaced with a movable-gate dam. While citizens who want to preserve the Daiju Weir as it is have been losing hope, the prefectural assembly has been active in promoting creation of the movable-gate dam. Furthermore, the mayor who was re-elected promising to oppose any kind of dam construction, including a movable-gate dam quit his post a year early in January 2004 and ran for election to the national House of Councilors in July as a representative of the ruling LDP party that supports construction of a movable-gate dam. Meanwhile in April, Masayoshi Himeno, the leader of Mina-no-Kai and the efforts to protect the Daiju Weir, also lost in a run for mayor. The political gains made by the energetic citizen movement in Tokushima up to September 2002 appear to have been erased. On the other hand, both the new governor and the newly elected mayor thought it necessary to declare publicly their opposition to a movable-gate dam and their support of preservation of the Daiju Weir. The new governor and mayor will have to deal with the friction between the popular desire to preserve the Daiju Weir and the forces that support the movable-gate dam. Still, the worries of the citizen activists are not small.

The citizens who have led the movement to preserve the Daiju Weir and find an alternative to creating a movable-gate dam have rediscovered and publicized the weir's attractions. At this point, their efforts to gain control over the destiny of the weir have been stopped at the ballot box, bringing them to a new starting point from which they must pursue tangible results on a smaller scale.

Proposals of the Vision 21 Expert Panel

In March 2004, the Tokushima City-sponsored Vision 21 report was published. The main topics are refurbishment proposals for the Daiju Weir and results of experiments testing the feasibility of a "green dam" that would reduce flood rates by increasing soil water retention.

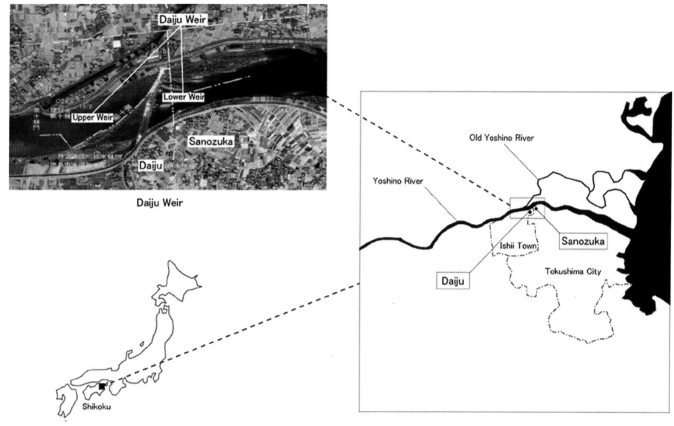

Figure 1. Location of Daiju Weir.

Three proposals were made for Daiju Weir refurbishment.

- Repair Proposal: ¥2.2 billion (repair of problem spots on the upper and lower weir, fish ladder improvements)

- Partial Renovation Proposal: ¥5.2 billion (renovation of the lower weir on the left (north) bank side, replace concrete on upper weir with 'aoishi' (blue) stones, fish ladder improvements)

- Compete Renovation Proposal: ¥7.2 billion (all of proposal 2 with the addition of right (south) bank side renovation, weir height reduction)

For the citizens, however, all three plans exceed their expectations in terms of both implementation costs and the degree of proposed changes.

According to the green dam research results, (1) the 24,000 metric tons of flood water estimated by the Ministry of Land, Infrastructure and Transport (MLIT), the number that is used as justification for building a movable-gate dam, is too large, and (2) the flood control function of forests could be improved through proper maintenance, including thinning, so that even the official number of 24,000 tons could be reduced by 20 ~ 30%. However, the actual action plan calls for thinning 60,000 ha, at a cost of ¥15 billion over 10 years.

These plans may seem expensive, but, considering the construction and 10 year running costs of a movable-gate dam of hundreds of billions of yen, the value and importance of the Daiju Weir Preservation Proposals and green dam plans presented in the Vision 21 Report are relatively economical.

Furthermore, even with the new mayor, the Vision 21 proposals have been made official directives of Tokushima City and will be raised with the national and prefectural governments. The chance of developing a large-scale public process has increased. However, realization of these proposals will require cooperation from the national and prefecture governments, so it probably will not be easy for individual citizens to become involved. In addition, for most citizens the spatial and temporal scales of the Vision 21 proposals may seem too large to feel a connection to.

RESULTS OF USE OBSERVATION MAPPING AND INTERVIEW SURVEYS

Overview of our research results

We found that the Daiju Weir is used for a variety of activities directly and indirectly on a regular basis, including fishing and shellfish hunting, water-play, walking, and social activity. In addition, in waterside classroom programs children play in the water, swim, observe wildlife and birds, boat, fish, and gather and eat algae and wild grasses. Events, including weddings, concerts, and candle light illuminations have also been held on the weir.

	Activity	Summer	Fall	Winter	Spring	Total
Activities associated with water	fishing	42	31	4	60	137
	catching fish, crab, shrimp or shellfish by net, trap or hand	22	6	7	4	39
	swimming, bathing, water–play	29	1	0	38	68
	washing with flowing water	4	2	1	0	7
	drawing water to tank, pail, or bottle	0	3	0	0	3
	canoeing	0	0	0	3	3
	observing bottom of river, turning over stones	15	13	19	51	98
	throwing stones in the water	0	4	0	1	5
Activities associated with scenery	viewing	27	39	25	95	186
	taking photos or videos	12	14	5	36	67
Activities associated with riparian environment	mowing	0	1	0	0	1
	exploring bush or sandbar	0	0	0	3	3
Activities associated with rights	keeping watch on poaching	0	0	0	4	4
Activities associated with communication	chatting	8	6	5	101	120
	taking care of children	14	1	1	17	33
	meeting	3	4	8	10	25
Other activities	walking	44	26	20	22	112
	taking care of dog	6	8	5	10	29
	exercising	0	0	2	0	2
	resting	4	4	10	2	20
	reading	2	0	0	2	4
	writing poetry	0	0	0	1	1
	making a phone call	0	0	0	1	1
	playing	0	9	0	0	9
	peeing	1	0	0	2	3
	eating	7	4	0	0	11
	littering	0	0	1	0	1
	parking bicycle	0	2	1	0	3

Table 1. Classification and frequency of activities observed on the Daiju Weir.

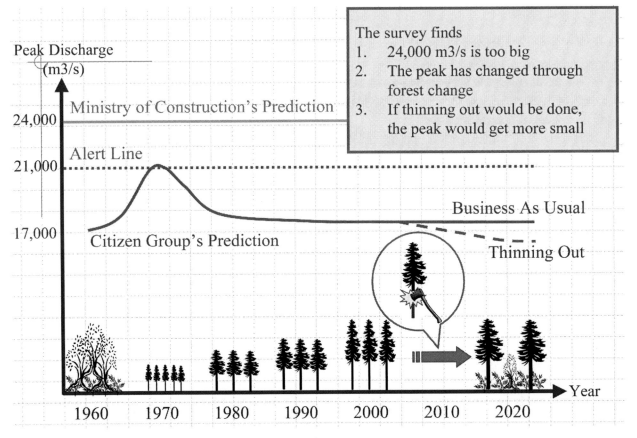

Figure 2. Vision 21 Report: Green Dam Survey Conclusion.

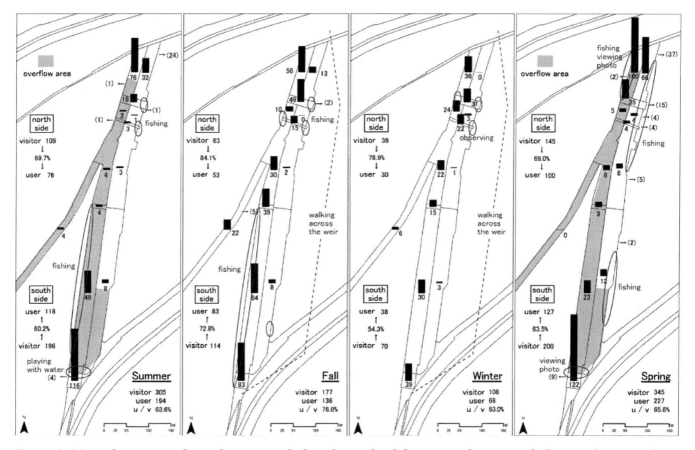

Figure 3. Maps showing numbers of visitors including those who did not enter the weir and of users who entered and used the weir.

We found 4 clear spatial use characteristics through our use observation research and analysis of the Daiju Weir on the Yoshino River.

- Through the accumulation of many years of patchwork repairs, the weir has become a mosaic structure of various types of interconnected spaces.

- With changes in the season and the amount of water flowing over the weir, even more variety of spaces is created within that mosaic structure.

On-site observations were executed on one week day and one weekend day in each season.

The weir is subdivided into 12 plots according to the difference of the spatial features. The numbers of those who used these plots are shown by bar charts and digits under them. Digits in parentheses show the numbers of those who moved from the plots to the adjacent water areas. Areas where typical activities were observed are shown by ovals.

- Each space that results from the combination of weir overflow condition and weir spatial structure has its own types of uses that correspond to the characteristics of the space.

- The low water embankment, the sand bars, the shallows and other areas near the weir, which change with the water level,

are connected spaces that also allow for a variety of uses and activities.

The tangible hands-on activities pursued by local people were even more diverse up to 30 years ago. Community groups conducted maintenance (weir mending, grass burning), and individuals used the weir area as a source of livelihood (cattle grazing, fishing, ferrying, trade, riverbed gravel dredging). In 1965, though, all management of the river was put under national jurisdiction, and all such uses became "illegal activities" and have mostly disappeared since.[1]

Eight Considerations for the Daiju Weir

Based on what we learned during our research, we are making eight suggestions about issues that should be considered in order to preserve the good points of the Daiju Weir before any physical changes are implemented.

1) Access to the weir from both banks

At present, about 60% of the people who visit Daiju Weir go onto the weir itself. Among these people are not only fishers and others with clear purposes, but also many people who come for the view, to walk and to observe the weir and its surroundings.

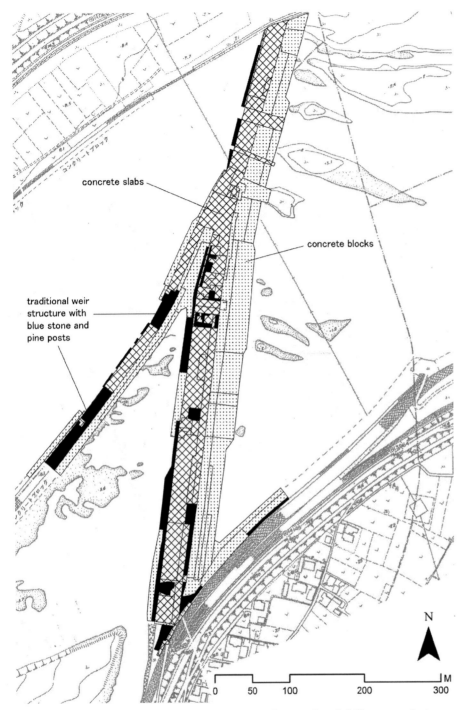

concrete slabs

concrete blocks

traditional weir structure with blue stone and pine posts

N

```
            ┌─────┬─────┬─────────────┬─────────────┐ M
            0     50    100           200           300
```

Figure 4: Patchworks of the Daiju Weir as the result of different techniques and materials of repairs.

2) Ease of movement

Several aspects of the weir make it easy to walk on. The maximum level change is 0.5 m at the fish ladders, but elsewhere there are few abrupt level changes. Flat or slightly sloped broad slabs connect most of the length of the weir with few bumps or gaps, and it is easy to see how to get to most other parts of the weir from a distance.

The reinforcing concrete blocks, however, depending on size and shape, can either provide paths or block a person's progress to parts of the weir. Sand has accumulated between the 1-ton concrete hexapod (6-legged) blocks over time making it possible for people to move across them (Figure 6). In contrast the 2-ton hexapod concrete blocks have not accumulated sand and have significant gaps that make passage difficult. In some places, they are so high that they even block the view (Figure 7). In contrast, the tops of some tetrapod concrete blocks and square concrete blocks are set close to the water level, effectively creating stepping stones and allowing passage across the water (Figure 8).

When water is overflowing, the weir becomes very slippery, making walking across sloped faces of the slabs difficult. At these times the level concrete framework for the slabs is important as a relatively easy to walk path, even when it is wet (Figure 9).

3) Water proximity

Various aspects of the weir structure make it easier for people to get closer to the water, including the water that comes right up to the top of the weir, the gentle slope to the edge of the water, and the reinforcing concrete blocks that reduce the depth of the water in places.

4) Access from the weir into the water

In addition to the proximity of the water, other aspects that make it easy to actually enter the water area include the proximity of the water, the gentle slope, and the presence of reinforcing concrete blocks and water breaking rocks. From spring through

Out on the weir, which is about 1 kilometer across, people can stand in the middle of a large river with water all around and encompassing mountains in the distance. This unique open space allows visitors to experience dynamic aspects of nature within the city limits. Considering the rapid disappearance of such spaces as rural areas around cities become urbanized, maintenance of access for people who want to walk, take in the view and otherwise enjoy the scenery should be considered carefully before implementing any spatial reforms.

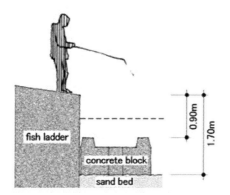

The side walls of fish ladders are frequently used for fishing. The concrete blocks placed for supporting the ladders are used as steps by people moving for those who move from the ladders to the sandbanks.

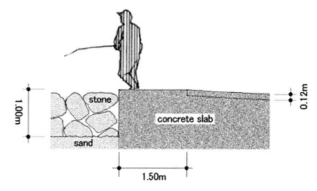

The flat and wide edges of concrete slabs function as circulation systems, which enable people to move across the weir and approach to water.

There are shallows where people swim, bathe or catch fishes on the downstream sides of the weir. Concrete blocks placed to support the old structure are flat on their tops, so they are used as paths to the shallows where people swim, play in the water and fish or as spaces for resting and watching children playing in the shallows. They also function as habitat where fish, shrimp and crabs can rest.

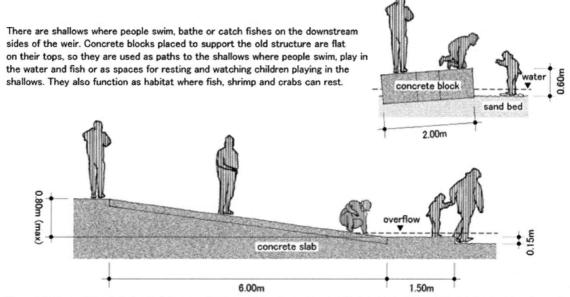

The gentle slope of the concrete slabs gives people access to shallow water flowing over the weir. Not only are passive activities such as viewing and touching the water possible, but children also actively play in the flow and slide down the slab in it.

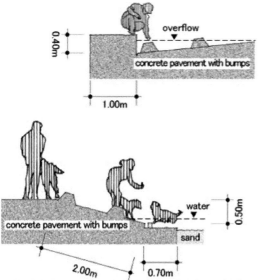

Irregular flows of water are caused by the sunken concrete pavement. People use these flows for washing.

Dogs wade through the gentle slopes of concrete pavements.

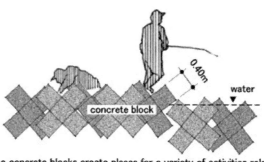

Even the concrete blocks create places for a variety of activities related to water. Sand and stones accumulate between the smallest blocks, allowing people to walk on them. Some people spend the entire day catching eels and crabs between these blocks.

Figure 5. Detail sections of the weir, describing the delicate relationships between activities and spaces.

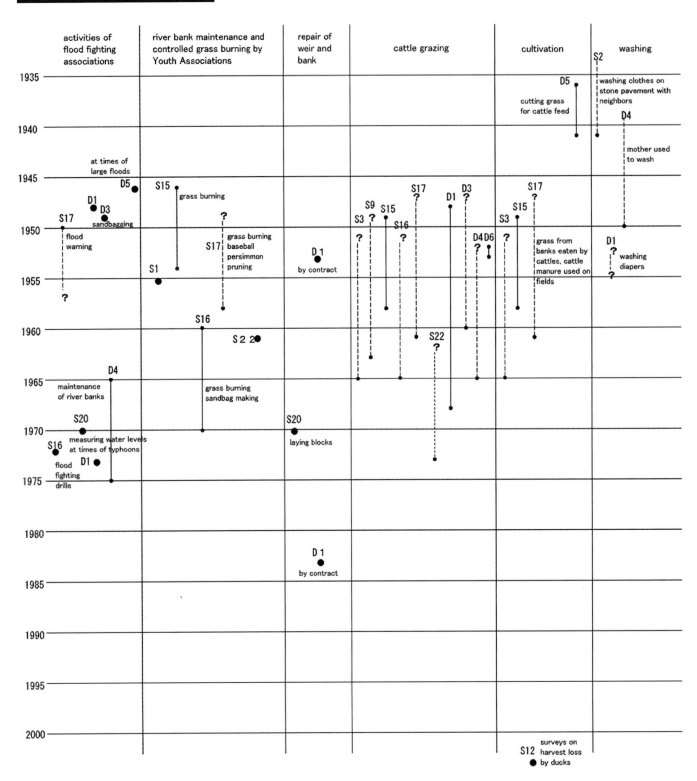

Figure 6. Activities of maintenance and livelihood by local people around the weir area.

Figure 7. 1-ton concrete blocks.

Figure 8. 2-ton concrete blocks.

Figure 9. Stepping stones of concrete blocks.

Figure 10. Walking path of the level concrete framework.

summer in particular, the shallows on the left bank downriver side have a high rate of water-play and shellfish hunting, while the lower weir downriver square concrete blocks, tetrapod concrete blocks, fish ladder side walls and the concrete blocks just below these, provide entry points and footholds in the water. Underwater observation using snorkeling gear and other activities involving direct water contact are abundant in warm weather and interaction with the water is also important for the previously mentioned waterside classrooms and other events.

5) Relation to surrounding spaces

The various uses of the weir are made possible through the support of the surrounding spaces. For example, fishers usually choose spots on the weir because of the proximity to adjacent water areas. Different types of fishing occur in the freshwater above the dam, in the downriver right bank deep tidal water area, and in the shallows of the downriver left bank. Water-play and shellfish hunting are not limited to just the weir itself, but occur often up and down river. Furthermore, activities such as taking in the view and photography, include the wide water surface and the river sandbars, reed patches and other surrounding spaces, not to mention the mountains and the sky that complete the visible environment. If these surrounding spaces change, we expect that the use of the weir will be influenced.

6) Animal and plant life

Fishing, shellfish gathering, underwater observation and similar activities are frequent, and the presence of aquatic organisms is one important factor in many uses, for example, during water-play. People catch and gather a variety of fish and shellfish, including trout, black bass, perch, mullet, goby, eels, crabs, crawfish and clams. Although relatively infrequent, we also observed activities related to non-aquatic life, such as bird watching, insect collecting and wild grass gathering. Changes to the natural habitat of the weir area would affect these uses.

As mentioned above, the approachability of the water and the relationships of the weir to the surrounding spaces are very important in making such activities possible here. In addition, the gaps between concrete blocks and flood breaks are important in allowing for some types of fishing and hunting crabs and crawfish.

7) The appeals and the danger of the weir when it overflows

In our research we found that water overflowing the top of the weir created one of the most immediate opportunities for users to touch the river water, but we must also mention the danger posed by strong flows. When a drowning occurred in August 2003, according to the MLIT public record of the nearby Daiju Sluice, the water level was only 20 cm higher than at the time of our May observations.

8) The value of processes

The Daiju Weir is a space that has developed over a long time. The traditional weir-building technique used aoishi stones fixed in place by vertical pine posts, while modern techniques used a variety of shapes of concrete, including both slabs poured on site and pre-manufactured units, to make patchwork repairs. Finally, erosion, accumulation and water flow are among the natural processes that have shaped the Daiju Weir. In this research, however, we were unable to identify a sense of historical value regarding the dam among visitors. In fact, our observations revealed that the upper weir, where the aoishi stones and pine posts used in the traditional techniques are still visible, was used infrequently. Access to this area is not obvious and probably not well known among users.

PROPOSALS FOR HANDS-ON PROJECTS

Value of hands-on projects

In order to implement the large-scale process of reevaluating plans to convert the Daiju Weir into a movable-gate dam, first individual citizens need to participate in small-scale processes that allow them to feel their personal and collective strengths and realize results through their own efforts. Given the current situation, small-scale processes with hands-on efforts that produce tangible results should increase confidence and experience and lay the groundwork to make approaching larger challenges possible.

Furthermore, on the spatial scale, at present, the largest reform proposed for Daiju Weir is the MLIT plan for a movable-gate dam. However, the Vision 21 Committee is proposing to reduce the height of the top of the weir by 1 meter to increase the amount of water flowing over the weir and increase the amount of fish swimming upstream. Though smaller in scale, this plan would also lead to significant changes to the rich mosaic space structure that allows for the current diversity of uses. Recreating a place that affords such variety would be difficult even using what we learned in this research. Accordingly, before implementing spatial reform of the current weir, thorough consideration should be given to the formation processes and elements that make each space, as well as to the intricate relationships between the spatial forms and their uses.

In addition, we must look at how past spatial formation processes have been transformed in the present. The majority of use now is for leisure activities. We observed few activities related to occupational fishing, farming or other livelihoods and we saw no instance of repairs or other activities directly related to the spatial formation process. Changes in local relationships to the river must be made clear, including the transformation of maintenance practices, in order to develop a new form for future maintenance.

Hands-on project details

Based on our eight considerations for the Daiju Weir, we are proposing some hands-on projects that could realize tangible results through the cooperation of local people. Our goal for these projects is, in addition to increasing the appeal of Daiju Weir and allowing more people to enjoy it, invigorating the activity of the people who live in the area around the weir, the citizen activist group that seeks to preserve it and the people of the towns upriver who are also concerned about the Yoshino River.

These proposals are meant to provide food for thought for the local residents and activist citizens who could accept them, reject them, or use them as starting points for developing their own plans. We hope that, at least, these projects will encourage proactive discussions about the future of the Daiju Weir. If there is interest, we may facilitate the organization of workshops to develop citizen ideas about the weir.

1) Promote upriver forest management and use the thinned wood materials to build simple structures using traditional techniques at the Daiju Weir to promote access.

Using wood from thinned forests upriver, build and place handrails, slopes, steps and decks, so that even when water overflowing the weir is high, visitors will still be able to enter the weir space and enjoy the scenery, the flow of water and wildlife observation. The wood structures should be connected without the use of nails, so that during floods they break apart and do not hinder water flow. Ropes would connect the parts so that they would not wash away. In addition to providing access, this project would recreate traditional river structure techniques.

In the same manner, thinned wood materials would be used to make footholds and handrails in large gaps between the 2-ton concrete blocks and elsewhere. In some places, the space between the 2-ton concrete blocks should be filled with gravel or sand. This would also improve habitat for aquatic organisms. At present the gaps between the 1-ton concrete blocks have accumulated gravel and sand naturally providing egg-laying places for *ayu* trout.

2) Create a map that shows the highlights, history and recreation spots of the Daiju Weir.

Create a map that shows the easiest routes and provides advice about walking on the weir, the best locations for water-play, fishing, underwater observation and other activities, as well as dangerous spots, with variations dependent on the level of weir overflow. This map should be put on an information board made from upriver thinned wood and could also be provided as a pamphlet for weir visitors.

3) Eco-tours to understand and appreciate the history and attractions of Daiju Weir

The fact that access to the upper weir is limited suggests that there is potential value in creating new sightseeing programs such as eco-tours that promote understanding and interest in the Daiju Weir. The citizen activist group and local residents could organize visiting the upper weir where aoishi stones and pine posts are used in the traditional weir-making technique. Visits could be made on foot when the weir is not overflowing, and by boat when the water level is high. In addition, the few surviving rock weir engineers could be asked to teach the weir building technique. Tour participants could do actual upper weir mending and, as is a traditional custom in Japan, write or inscribe their names on the undersides of the rocks to further enhance and record their personal connections to the weir.

4) The taste of the Yoshino River

A community restaurant operated in partnership between the citizen activist group, local residents and the fishing coop could serve fish and shellfish caught in the water around the Daiju Weir. Dishes could include *somen* noodles in *sanabori* broth, trout rice porridge, clam soup, deep fried crawfish, vinegared *ugui* fish and grilled eel. This community restaurant could begin by running for special events or seasonally. We imagine that dining on the water, literally and figuratively, would be quite popular. This idea enjoys significant precedence in Japan, where the custom of putting dining porches over waterways to provide relief from the summer heat goes back centuries.

5) Vegetation management at Daiju Weir

Some plants growing on the weir, such as the *akame* willow and wild roses, actually damage the stone structure with their roots. In the past, flooding often removed these plants, but at present, most flooding has been suppressed, so it is necessary to clear these plants by artificial means. In theory, this is now the responsibility of the national government, but, in fact, the only vegetation management to be conducted in years was by concerned citizens who undertook clandestine midnight tree removal. If the government would legally entrust vegetation management to local residents and the citizen activist group, weir preservation could become a partnership between the national government and locals and other concerned citizens.

CONCLUSION

With these proposals we have completed one stage of our research. Conducting further use observation and space research on similar river structures could be valuable for allowing comparison with the results of this research. Not only would such a comparison be academically interesting, it would also provide additional feedback to the groups and individuals concerned with the future of the Daiju Weir. Ultimately, the fate of this place, which has become a focal point in the battle against environmental degradation in Japan, depends largely on them.

Long-term preservation of the Daiju Weir will require changes in the policies of the national government, so continued political activism and pressure are necessary to continue to postpone the creation of a movable-gate dam. Lack of immediate large-scale successes, however, could be offset by small-scale hands-on projects with tangible results that would maximize the effectiveness of the collective strength of the citizens. These results could energize not only local residents and activists, but also upriver citizens who are concerned about the possibility of new dams in their neighborhoods.

The complex mosaic of spaces of the Daiju Weir that allows a great variety of activities is the result of centuries of natural and human processes. Understanding and promotion of the continued evolution of these processes on the local level is a key to saving this unique natural and artificial place for future generations.

ENDNOTES

[1] For example, at times of flood, repair of leaks in the embankment was the responsibility of the local flood prevention organization (membership overlapped with the youth group). Area people organized themselves, and conducted regular maintenance of the embankments and management of the river. Furthermore, local people, who benefited from the opportunity to earn extra cash for their labor, also handled weir mending.

13

community
design
pedagogies

DELIBERATIVE EDUCATION/ COMMUNICATIVE PLANNING
Social Learning for Community, Environment and Planning

Dennis Ryan and Christopher Campbell

All academic fields are challenged by contemporary urban change including globalization, social polarization, rampant consumer capitalism and diminution of nature and place. In response, the university is called to move to a new paradigm of engagement where learning is simultaneously acting in the world and where the scholarship of teaching is valued equally with scholarship of research. The AAHE subdivides this model into 3 areas - engaged pedagogy, community based research, and collaborative practice – but all are fundamentally about educational practices that address real world problems and create involved and committed citizens. Engagement is a familiar concept in the design and planning disciplines and it is a term often associated with the studio and applied learning dimensions of education in these fields. But too often the educational experience is limited to one to more episodes of community – connectedness to provide hands-on learning and insights. Yet good planning and design is fundamentally a transdisciplinary and dialogical praxis. It calls for close listening and social learning across a range of related disciplines, vivid participation and critical consciousness, trust, creativity and innovation, and thoroughly reflective practice. This is best learned in an educational context equally interdisciplinary, collaborative, and dialogic. Traditional contexts in design and planning education often teach the principles for engagement and participation – and then foster their application in work with the community. But the context itself is neither richly trans-disciplinary nor collaborative in its practices. In other words, what we teach is often not reflected in how we construct our teaching and learning environments. We say one thing and do or live quite another. Community and Environmental Planning (CEP), an award-winning, University of Washington interdisciplinary program is an experiment in undergraduate education and a practicum in democracy and planning itself. CEP manifests John Dewey's dictum: "Education is not preparation for life. Education is life itself." In CEP, education is lived, not taken nor received. It is something actively made - fully struggled with and accomplished in community with others. In CEP, education is deliberative and planning is a verb. In this paper we describe CEP's deliberative principles and associated practices including 1) building and using social capital and the reflective practice of we, 2) making teaching/learning public and connected in the world, 3) constructing a hegemony of optimism and self-directed learning, and 4) citizenship and community as CEP verbs.

ENGAGING CHANGING COMMUNITIES IN THE COMMUNITY DESIGN STUDIO

Nancy Rottle

ABSTRACT

This paper describes two recent Community Design studios at the University of Washington which engaged communities to help solve importunate problems. Based upon student and instructor evaluation and reflection, the paper presents pedagogical strengths and weaknesses of the studios and outlines the potential contributions of design service learning to communities in need. It proposes a set of guiding heuristics to optimize the community design experience for students and sponsoring communities within the context of engaged scholarship.

INTRODUCTION

Communities in the Western United States constantly face new pressures brought to bear by rapidly changing economic, environmental and demographic forces. Through interacting with communities to address pressing problems, students and faculty in the design studio can explore contemporary issues, practice participatory design and planning techniques, and provide services otherwise unavailable to unempowered populations. This paper describes two graduate landscape architecture studio courses that employed participatory methods in solving community design challenges. In the first, a small Alaskan community faced an impending influx of "big box" stores in their town center; in the second, a Western Washington agricultural town hoped to forestall sprawl threatening to destroy surrounding rich farmland, while simultaneously revitalizing their traditional business district. Lessons from both courses may inform the conception and organization of such studios and influence their success from the students', communities' and faculties' perspectives.

TWO CASES

The Case of Homer, Alaska

The influx of large-store retail–"big box" stores–in small towns is causing rapid change in downtown cores across America and affecting community economies, environments and identities. The citizens of Homer, Alaska, faced with the prospect of a big-box store locating in an undeveloped center of their town, asked the Department of Landscape Architecture, University of Washington for assistance. They sought research on

outcomes in similar towns to inform their decisions on store size limitations, and design solutions that envisioned a new town center applying various store size caps and incorporating civic uses. Issues included impacts on existing businesses in the town of 5000, citizen attachment to the forested town center site as a result of five years of dreaming and ad-hoc use, the town's reliance upon scenic and fishing-based tourism, a desire for a strong pedestrian-oriented town center, and lack of a planning tradition or official planning department. A $10,000 grant covered our travel costs and printing of design posters and summary documents.

After reviewing literature on big-box stores in town centers and on small town planning and design, the class traveled to Alaska to conduct site and town analyses and to meet with town leaders, agency personnel, and concerned citizens. The students facilitated two workshop-oriented open houses, one for business owners and another for citizens at large. Information sessions and meetings during the week-long site visit were arranged and advertised by our primary contact in Homer, giving students a broad yet in-depth window into governmental structure, issues and constituency groups. Free time was used for our site and town analyses, including a day to explore the dramatic coastal landscape that draws tourists to its scenic and recreational opportunities.

With Homer's qualities, issues and opportunities understood, the class worked together to conduct case study research on how twelve similar towns in western North America had treated impending invasions of large-store retail, analyzed common outcome patterns from the case studies, and synthesized a set of planning tools that towns could use to prohibit, control or produce mitigation benefits from big-box stores. As a class, we worked as a collaborative "think tank" to conduct, synthesize and present the case study research, and to develop a design approach that would also serve as a research process.

Figure 1. Students designed two workshops with the Homer community to solicit ideas on town center improvements and opinions on large retail stores.

Figure 2. Six teams tested inclusion of large retail stores of varying square footages—20k, 40k and 66k–in a new town center. The six alternatives were compiled in a summary booklet.

Six small student teams then developed alternative designs to test how well stores of designated sizes could be integrated with civic facilities, housing and open space on the hillside, 30-acre town center site. Each team worked with a given size of a 20k, 40k, or 66k square foot (sf) store, all considered by the Homer city council as a potential size cap in the central business district. A team returned to Homer near the end of the term to present results of the case study research in the form of a "design toolbox," and to show the six alternatives, given in PowerPoint presentations in two community meetings. The case studies were collated in a binder and on CD and given to the City, and the six design alternatives with accompanying implementation guidelines were compiled in a full-color 11" x 17" booklet, with ten copies given to Homer. Several of the students' designs were featured in a local newspaper article.

Informed by our work, the town's debate on potential retail store size cap enlarged, with an ultimate decision by the city council to invoke a 20,000 sf limit in the central business district, and a 35,000 sf limit in a district on the commercial edge. Perhaps more important, citizens became aware of planning tools available to them and the City expanded the small planning staff into a full department. A project proponent summarized our influence, "Not a City meeting goes by where a "term" [from the student work] isn't used, a "vision" isn't referenced, or the action of one of the towns from the 'case studies' isn't discussed." A town center planning committee formed, using the students' designs as a basis for their work. The students received an Honor Award from the American Planning Association/ Planning Association of Washington, and a Merit Award from the Washington Society of Landscape Architects. Additionally, two students were inspired to conceive and complete thesis projects in Homer.

The Case of Burlington, Washington

A common development pattern is for towns to develop large retail on their edges, usurping valuable farmlands and draining

economic energy from their downtown cores. The town of Burlington, Washington is located in the Skagit Valley, one of the richest agricultural areas of the Pacific Northwest, and less than a two hour drive from Seattle. With its location adjacent to Interstate-5 and a connecting state highway, Burlington has grown a large number of outlet malls and large wholesale and retail stores on its edge, despite its population of only 7500. Farmers on the town's outskirts have begun to request annexation in order to develop their lands, while the downtown's main street is struggling to survive. Efforts to preserve Skagit Valley farmland have been active for the last decade, and Burlington's urban edge is seen as an important containment to irreversible erosion of the valley's critical agricultural mass.

Our Community Design studio was asked to explore how the town's center might be revitalized through a transfer of development rights (TDR) program through which developers could purchase development rights from farmlands—thereby preserving those lands in perpetuity while compensating the owners–and apply them to a downtown core "TDR receiving area" to allow increased housing and commercial density in the designated district. Our charge was to work at three scales: 1) to create an open space infrastructure to ensure a high quality of living in the compact town, 2) to develop alternative scenarios for the 70-block town core and main retail street, and 3) to design individual projects that demonstrated how higher density and commercial use could enhance the town's livability and sustainability.

Similar to the Homer studio, we began with a shared review of relevant literature, and students developed precedent studies of open space systems, medium-density housing types, and small town revitalization projects. These were presented to the class, and where possible we visited the projects during a field day. Though the distance presented somewhat of an obstacle, each student made at least three visits to Burlington for town, district and site inventory and analysis. We asked the city's planner, our sponsor, to assist with setting up three sessions with citizens: an early open house to hear their concerns and ideas and learn about the community and context; a mid-way workshop to engage them in designing alternatives for denser massing for the downtown core; and a final presentation of and dialogue about the students' plans and designs. Town planning staff also attended our mid-term and final reviews. The town funded the studio with $5000 to cover van transportation costs, student time to create and maintain a website and to produce a color booklet of the students' designs and accompanying recommendations at the three scales, and printing of the booklets given to the client. The class worked as a whole to develop the Open Space Plan, in groups of four to develop downtown core plans, and individually or in groups of two to design their proposed housing or commercial area projects.

Learning from Small Towns

Community Character, Vitality and Large Retail
Case Studies for Homer, Alaska

There's no place like Homer...

Many of the communities studied have similar characteristics to Homer.

Location: at "the end of the road"

Growth: significant population growth experienced in the past few decades

Economic base: economies centered around tourism, fishing, art, and local businesses

Nature: natural surroundings considered to be vital community assets

Community: an active community that seeks economic growth which will not infringe on "quality of life"

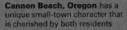

Ashland, Oregon is an historic town that is attracting new residents and is a popular tourist destination. The town has strict zoning ordinances, design guidelines and a retail size cap of 45,000 square feet, which together have been effective in preserving the town's character and economic health. No "big

box" retail exists within the city limits, though large chain stores are within seven miles.

Bainbridge Island, Washington has maintained its small town character by restricting retail size within designated zones (5000 and 14,400 in certain zones), promoting a **mixed-use, walkable downtown** through permit requirements and design guidelines, and limiting formula fast food restaurants. In the downtown core, **parking is limited to the side or back of buildings, or on the street.** Large stores are allowed in one zone, and must comply with **detailed design guidelines.**

Bozeman, Montana has several large retail stores but now limits retail size to 75,000 square feet unless the retailer pays large **impact fees.** Design and site development standards apply to buildings over 40,000 square feet, aimed at **breaking up façades** and addressing **responsibility for empty boxes.** Impact fees are used to develop the downtown core and to improve low-income housing.

Cannon Beach, Oregon has a unique small-town character that is cherished by both residents

and tourists. Its geographic setting, small lot size, **design guidelines, zoning ordinances** and **design review process for specific zones** have kept retail establishments small and preserved the community character. Some businesses may have been lost to large commercial stores in adjacent towns.

Fairview Village, Oregon is a new town that is interested in large retail to serve as **anchors** in the town center. The town has been designed with a clearly defined **civic and retail center,**

a variety of **housing types,** and **pedestrian access** to jobs, schools and shopping. One new 133,000 square foot store, which complied with **maximum parking spaces, architectural standards,** and **restoration of wetlands,** is possibly attracting smaller businesses to the area.

Gig Harbor, Washington has used strict zoning, detailed design guidelines and design review, and size caps of 35,000 to preserve

Case-Study Town Comparisons
listed roughly from less restrictive to more restrictive

TOWN	Population	Size Caps	Big Box (miles)**	Zoning	Design Guidelines	Architectural Standards	Design Review
Soldotna, AK	4,200	none	■				
Ketchikan, AK	8,000	none	■	■			
Steamboat Springs, CO	9,815	none -> 50k	■	■			
Bozeman, MT	32,000	75k	■	■	■		■
Nelson, BC Canada	9,300	none	■		■		■
Taos, NM	4,065	80k	■	■	■		
Fairview Village, OR	850	none	■	■	■	■	
Gig Harbor, WA	6,500	35k	■	■	■	■	■
Port Townsend, WA	8,400	75k -> 40k		■	■	■	■
Bainbridge Island, WA	20,000	5–14k*	■	■	■		■
Ashland, OR	20,000	45k*	(7)	■	■	■	■
Cannon Beach, OR	1,600	none	(7)	■	■		■

*In the most restrictive zone
**Although some towns have no large retail, residents can drive the distance shown to reach a big-box store.

Department of Landscape Architecture
Community Design Studio 503
University of Washington,
348 Gould Hall, Box 355734
Seattle, Washington 98195-5734
tel (206) 543-9240

Figure 3. The class researched twelve small towns to learn the outcomes of their treatment of large retail stores. The

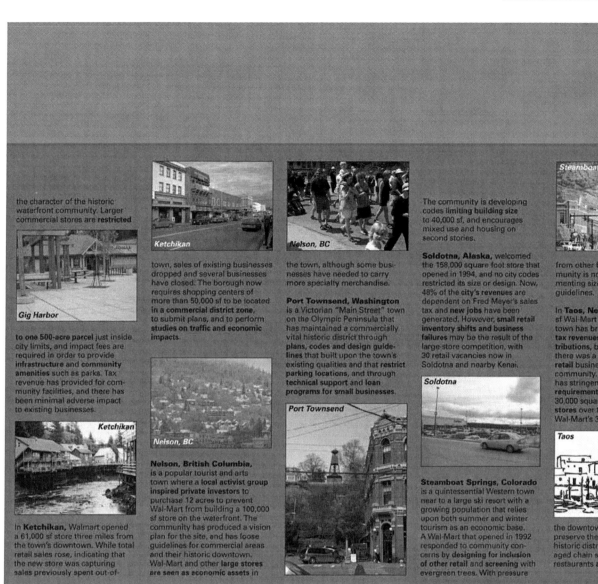

the character of the historic waterfront community. Larger commercial stores are **restricted**

Gig Harbor

to one 500-acre parcel just inside city limits, and impact fees are required in order to provide **infrastructure** and **community amenities** such as parks. Tax revenue has provided for community facilities, and there has been minimal adverse impact to existing businesses.

Ketchikan

In **Ketchikan**, Walmart opened a 61,000 sf store three miles from the town's downtown. While total retail sales rose, indicating that the new store was capturing sales previously spent out-of-

Ketchikan

town, sales of existing businesses dropped and several businesses have closed. The borough now requires shopping centers of more than 50,000 sf to be located **in a commercial district zone**, to submit plans, and to perform **studies on traffic and economic impacts**.

Nelson, BC

Nelson, British Columbia, is a popular tourist and arts town where a **local activist group inspired private investors** to purchase 12 acres to prevent Wal-Mart from building a 100,000 sf store on the waterfront. The community has produced a vision plan for the site, and has loose guidelines for commercial areas and their historic downtown. Wal-Mart and other **large stores are seen as economic assets** in

Nelson, BC

the town, although some businesses have needed to carry more specialty merchandise.

Port Townsend, Washington is a Victorian "Main Street" town on the Olympic Peninsula that has maintained a commercially vital historic district through **plans, codes and design guidelines** that built upon the town's existing qualities and that **restrict parking locations**, and through **technical support and loan programs for small businesses**.

Port Townsend

Steamboat Springs, Colorado is a quintessential Western town near to a large ski resort with a growing population that relies upon both summer and winter tourism as an economic base. A Wal-Mart that opened in 1992 responded to community concerns by **designing for inclusion** of other retail and screening with evergreen trees. With pressure

The community is developing codes limiting **building size** to 40,000 sf, and encourages mixed use and housing on second stories.

Soldotna, Alaska, welcomed the 158,000 square foot store that opened in 1994, and no city codes restricted its size or design. Now, 48% of the **city's revenues** are dependent on Fred Meyer's sales tax and **new jobs** have been generated. However, **small retail inventory shifts and business failures** may be the result of the large-store competition, with 30 retail vacancies now in Soldotna and nearby Kenai.

Soldotna

Steamboat Springs

from other franchises, the community is now considering implementing size caps and design guidelines.

In **Taos, New Mexico** a 75,000 sf Wal-Mart on the outskirts of town has brought substantial **tax revenues** and **community contributions**, but in the first 11 years there was a 30-60% **loss of small retail** businesses in this arts community. As a result, the town has stringent **architectural requirements** on stores over 30,000 square feet, and **bans new stores** over 80,000 square feet. Wal-Mart's 3-mile distance from

Taos

the downtown has helped to preserve the character of the historic district, but has encouraged chain stores and fast food restaurants at the town gateway.

Lessons learned

Physical characteristics of box stores can be controlled through size caps, locational restrictions, design guidelines and an effective review process, architectural and site plan standards, restrictions on parking and signage, limits on certain types of establishments, requirements for screening, and stipulations on how empty failed stores must be treated. A combination of these mechanisms is usually required to make "big box" stores match small town character.

Economic impacts to towns can be mitigated by requiring impact fees, at construction and at regular intervals, to pay for infrastructure, security and fire services, and public amenities such as parks and pedestrian walkways. In addition, sales tax revenues often bring monies into the town coffers. However, impacts to small retail with similar products appear inevitable unless population growth or tourism is sufficient to offset business lost to the larger stores.

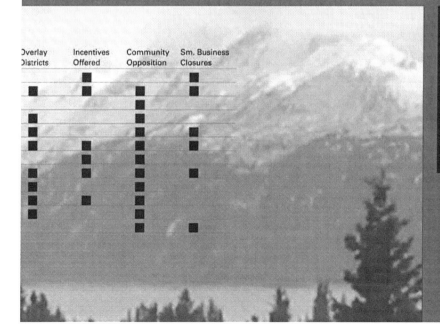

Overlay Districts	Incentives Offered	Community Opposition	Sm. Business Closures
	■	■	■
■		■	
■		■	
■		■	■
■	■	■	
■	■	■	■
■	■	■	
■		■	
■		■	
		■	■

This poster supplements the binder: "Learning From Small Towns: Community Character, Vitality and Large Scale Retail," a collection of case studies provided for Homer, Alaska by the Community Design Graduate Studio of the University of Washington Department of Landscape Architecture. For further detail on the case studies and analysis comparison, please refer to the case-study binder and associated documents.

case studies were compiled in a booklet and summarized on a poster (above). (Poster design by Laura Davis)

Burlington has since formed a citizen's task force to forge consensus on farmland preservation goals, who recently recommended that the town maintain a tight urban growth boundary rather than enlarging its city limits. The City will hire a knowledgeable consultant to further study feasibility and requirements to implement the TDR program. The City continues to heavily use the booklets of the students' designs, our model of the downtown core is on permanent display, and the planning department has fully adopted our Open Space proposal as their standing plan. Burlington's planner has been very satisfied with the studio outcomes, saying, "We could never have gotten to square one without your work. It's elevated our vision of our own community. We're now conscious of our potential, and we have higher expectations of the town's future."

EVALUATION AND REFLECTION

Do Community Design studios equally serve communities in need and the students who are paying tuition to take the courses? Should this "engaged learning" model be continued in schools of landscape architecture, and how can it be conceived to optimally serve both educational and service objectives? To answer these questions, I asked students in both studios to complete surveys asking about the benefits and drawbacks of the service-learning studio, and analyzed both the surveys and our standard open-ended course evaluation responses for thematic clues to strengths, weaknesses and possible improvements on the courses. For the Homer studio, nine surveys completed eight months after the course provided the majority of responses, while for Burlington, eleven responses from the end-of-term course evaluations and three completed surveys were the primary information source. Continued contact with the project sponsors, my own participation in community planning, and reflections on the design studios inform my conclusions about the advantages and disadvantages to the communities and the lessons for the instructor's dual role of professor and project manager.

Advantages for Communities

"Engaged" or public scholarship, when directly involving community members in the inventory, planning and design process and in contemplating students' research, planning proposals and designs, can offer the following benefits to communities:

- The experience helps residents learn about, become interested in, and appreciate the real places in which they

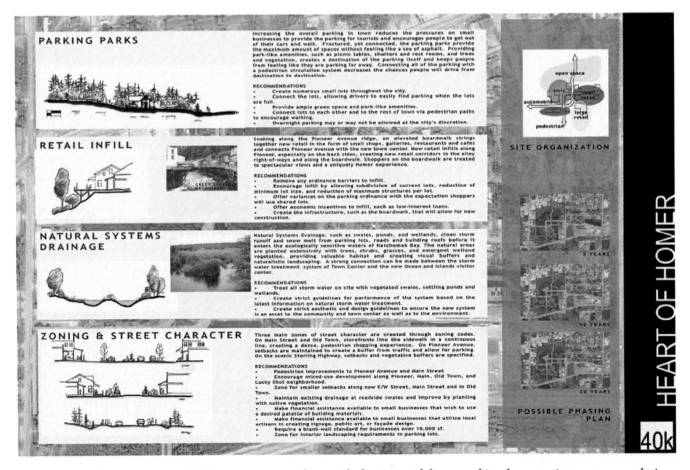

Figure 4. Each team annotated their town center plans with design guidelines and implementation recommendations.

live. The process can perhaps help to develop a new way of seeing—often experienced by students of landscape architecture—and an environmental literacy that is transferred to new situations.

- Participation in planning can empower citizens to take control of the destiny of their own communities, enabling them to counter the prevalent forces of global and national commerce. Participants can develop confidence by learning how other communities have coped with problems, through education about environmental and social issues, awareness of the tools available to them, and practice in engaging problems and trying on solutions.

- When residents actively participate in planning endeavors, they may be more motivated to support and advocate for the plan outcome and implementation.

- The design studio can give communities viewpoints, awarenesses, and tools they might not realize they need. For example the studio can take a broad overview and create a framework for the planning context (such as our open space plan for Burlington).

- Student explorations can help communities feel the edges of what they will consider, and perhaps push them further than would otherwise be possible. Because the work is not binding, students can explore options without generating polarization; because the work is not threatening, citizens may be more open to new solutions.

- The sheer work force in numbers, expertise, and intensity of a design studio can provide a project not otherwise possible within the budgets of small towns.

- The development of preliminary alternatives and visions by students can significantly advance the community participation process, which, while necessary, can be at times be unpleasantly contentious and overwhelming, requiring more time commitment than the common citizen can spare.

Limitations of the Studio Work

No disadvantages from our work have emerged, but it is important to recognize that the Community Design studio does not necessarily offer the same benefits as an adequately funded professional firm. For example, the short-term involvement of a single studio project doesn't provide follow-through with community projects, which typically require a time frame longer than an academic term. This situation could partly be remedied by a longer-term grant and consistency of an instructor's teaching assignment. Funding for development into a master's thesis can also provide more depth and catalyze the community to keep a project going.

In addition to the limitations of less professional experience, some students may be more interested in developing their own ideas instead of responding to the realities of a particular situation. The usefulness of the design alternatives are typically greatest in stimulating broad thinking on the part of the participating community and for preliminary fund-raising, rather than providing specific design options that are further developed into built projects.

Students' Views: Advantages

Both studios were rated highly by the students. They appreciated the problem sets and the solution approaches taken, and felt intellectually challenged. One student stated: "There was a real need for the work and that made it all the more challenging and educational." In the surveys and evaluations, positive responses common to both studios were:

- The opportunity to work on a real project, to serve real needs, and to encounter the kinds of problems and specific issues that are confronting communities today, incorporating political, social and ecological considerations.

- The opportunity to facilitate community design processes, to develop comfort and expertise with that role.

- The opportunity to interact with real people and receive response to their work from diverse perspectives.

- Most students cited the case studies (Homer) and precedent case study/field visit (Burlington) as valuable, though in both studios at least one student questioned the value of the time required to develop finished products.

The variation in the problem-sets and approaches for each studio stimulated differences in the student responses as well. Students frequently cited the value of learning about planning tools in the research process for Homer, whereas the design process was mentioned as a strength in the Burlington studio, which had a greater design and urban form focus at multiple scales. While some of the Burlington group questioned the value of every exercise, others saw the usefulness of them and appreciated the careful sequencing of projects that laid the foundation for final design. One student in the Alaska group also appreciated the opportunity to experience a different part of the world.

Students' Views: Disadvantages

While the realness of the problem and the involvement with the community were appreciated, common drawbacks cited by both groups were:

- The work load demands of the studio.

- The internal pressure to quickly absorb information and perform to professional standards.

Figure 5. Students built a model of Burlington's downtown core, which was used at the second community workshop to envision new densities and massing.

Figure 6. Students encouraged community teams to build their visions of Burlington's downtown, using wooden blocks, sugar cubes and clay.

- Lack of time for site analysis and for design exploration and development.

- Design solution restraint in response to a real situation.

- The difficulty of integrating the community's timing and research requests with the academic schedule and interests of the students.

The latter three were primarily cited by the Homer group. One student commented, "The time frame given by our clients versus our quarter schedule resulted in some stressful crunch times," and another noted "Bold thinking about community planning were limited by honest evaluation of the economic needs and practices of the community."

As mentioned above, some students felt too much time was spent on the case studies, particularly in the Homer group, in lieu of more time made available for design. Several in this group suggested that the literature review and research component be offered as a parallel or preliminary course

with additional credits. Some felt we needed more time with the Homer community. Because students saw the immediate potential impact of our work on the community, two wished an economic analysis had been available to inform their design scenarios and recommendations. Some felt the design production of a publication that documented their work was yet another burden.

From students working in Burlington, the most commonly cited problem was in relation to the small group composition and dynamics, or the relationship between the group and individual projects in light of the time constraint. However some also cited the value of learning to work in groups.

Several students saw that the perceived drawbacks also provided valuable learning experience; this kind of comment was especially prevalent in the surveys, which asked students to evaluate the balance between positives and negatives. Despite the disadvantages, all respondents to the Homer surveys felt the benefits outweighed or balanced the drawbacks. One student in the Burlington studio summarized that "The benefits outweigh the drawbacks infinitely. I think real world scenarios are much more helpful to our learning process."

Challenges for the Dual Role of Professor-Project Manager

From my own experience, I've found that teaching a studio that engages the community in order to solve their importunate problems presents significant additional challenges for the faculty involved. The instructor wears two hats, performing dual roles of professor and project manager. As professor, one needs to ensure that the students are gaining the essential theoretical understandings, learning about resources and existing solution prototypes, and practicing the complement of skills that will enable them to feel confident in planning and designing with and for communities. Translating a real problem into a course that brings essential learning about the complexities of planning and designing for communities but that feels manageable for the students within the constraint of a 10-week academic term– during which students are taking other courses and often have jobs–is a delicate act. Because the real issues may not emerge until the community is known well through site analyses and meetings, crafting an appropriate progression of applicable skill and knowledge-building exercises throughout the course without wasting students' time is especially challenging.

In addition, in the role of "project manager," one needs to ensure that the community is being served and that the agreed-upon products are completed and delivered. This role is a full time job in itself–making sure the work fits the (sometimes shifting) problem, that there are adequate resources, information, skills and processes for the students' work to be responsive to the problem and community, and that the work

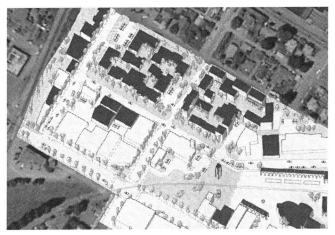

INTERWEAVING PATHS AND PLACES
CREATING A GREEN COMMUNITY BY LAYERING THE GREEN RING, GREEN LOOPS, AND GREEN SPINES
Opportunities: movement paths (variable speed options), sequential experience, ease of access, wildlife habitat

REGIONAL OPEN SPACE OPPORTUNITIES
CONNECTING COMMUNITIES
Burlington • Mount Vernon • Sedro-Woolley
Opportunities, combining existing and proposed open space,
using green paths to connect communities,
and creating open space destinations

Figure 7. The studio developed a "green infrastructure" open space plan to afford livability in the compact town. Burlington has adopted the plan.

Figure 8. Student proposals for increased density include a "Mercado District" (above), conversion of warehouses to live-work housing, cottage housing, neo-traditional neighborhoods, mixed-use residential and commercial development, and an eco-commercial district. Team plans for the core area and individual design projects were annotated and documented in summary booklets given to Burlington.

is presented to the community and documented in formats that are ultimately useful. The interplay between the community's and the academic schedule is yet another layer requiring tight management, since the academic schedule is inflexible; even a week lost during the quarter can have a significant impact on students' ability to address problems, affecting student learning and satisfaction and the depth of the products delivered.

The instructor is expected to provide background expertise for the studio, to equip the students to address community issues. However, because the concerns of communities vary widely, and problems can be contemporary issues with innovative approaches, the instructor may be developing areas of scholarly expertise through the engaged studio. While such

opportunities have valuable benefits, the instructor may need to research the issues and resources and may not always have the specific expertise to guide the work in the most time-efficient way (for example, I knew very little about big-box stores or their control by communities before the Homer studio). This adds another time requirement to the instruction. To acknowledge this level of expenditure and potential learning, universities are beginning to recognize the "engaged scholarship" that results from courses that double as public service. (Rottle 2004, Rice 2003, Ward 2003, Huber 2000).

HEURISTICS FOR THE COMMUNITY DESIGN STUDIO

From my experience with the Community Design and other studios involving community participation to solve real problems, and drawing from literature on engaged scholarship, I offer the following heuristics for university-community partnerships in the design studio:

- Define the problem clearly. Meet with the community sponsor and become familiar with the community and issues. This may require funding for a scoping trip if the project is remote. Narrow the problem set to feasibly fit the given academic term.

- Clarify expectations for product, process and schedule with the sponsor. The "scope of work" is a familiar format for most professionals, which can specify the number of meetings, the deliverables, and priority needs of the academic schedule. It should also note the expectations of the sponsor, and the specific time requirements of the academic term.

- Anticipate critical pieces of information needed from the sponsor or community, e.g. GIS files, aerial photographs, previous studies and planning documents. Advise the sponsor to hire consultants or consider a joint studio with another department if missing expertise or analysis is critical to solving the defined problem.

- Ensure there is a committed and available project manager from the sponsor/client group, who will be immediately responsive to requests for information, serve as liaison to the planning agency, and organize community meetings.

- Procure funding for a student RA to assist with tasks outside of normal studio teaching responsibilities, e.g. preliminary research of relevant literature and case studies, assistance with organizing and documenting community workshops, final documentation and publication of student work, creation and maintenance of a course website, and assistance with media translation and software use.

- Anticipate the expertise and resource familiarity faculty need to develop in order to guide students (e.g. big box issues, TDR, housing design, transportation systems). Allow time and possibly funding for this research.

- Clarify expectations to students regarding the level of design the studio will involve; if it focuses on a planning scale and requires time for community involvement, that these objectives may reduce opportunities for individual design iterations, but that it is a necessary trade-off given the time frame.

- Approach the studio as a scholarly endeavor. In the curriculum include the scholarly practices of: clear goals and problem definition; preparation through literature review and research; appropriate methods; assessment of results; effective presentation of the results; and reflective critique by the students, community and faculty (Rottle 2004, Ward 2003, Huber 2000, Glassick et al. 1997).

- Organize the curriculum to flexibly accommodate the amount of student time the Community Design studio can require. This may include adding a research seminar that accompanies or precedes the studio, or a two-term studio. While small communities typically don't have the resources to "purchase" an extra course in the curriculum, funding may help to offset departmental costs of creating an additional course.

CONCLUSION

As citizens become aware of their potential roles in community shaping, and realize the useful services that landscape architecture students and faculty can provide, the demand for such involvement will increase. Successful and satisfying community-university partnerships will cultivate the ground for further professional landscape architectural work of helping towns and cities to envision themselves and to realize their visions. The Community Design studio can therefore be a catalyst for enlarging the profession of landscape architecture, while preparing students to fill these expanding professional and civic roles. Practiced expertise in teaching such courses can optimize the experience for both students and communities, and help to gain support in the Academy and a place in the curriculum for the engaged Community Design studio.

Through the Community Design studio, we can perhaps also restore faith that the landscape architecture profession can make a difference in the quality of places citizens share, in small towns as well as major cities. I recently received an e-mail from a practicing landscape architect from the US state of Colorado, who had seen our Homer project course website and had decided to move to Alaska to pursue his profession there. He wrote, "I just want to thank you and your students for restoring my vision and enthusiasm for Planning and Landscape Architecture. It was nice to read what others are doing with their lives and to know that some people are living alternatively to the commuter-computer jobs so prevalent around here." He just may find some important work and a willing community in Homer.

REFERENCES

Glassick, C.E., Huber, M. T., and Maeroff, G. I. 1997. Scholarship Assessed: Evaluation of the Professoriate. San Francisco: Jossey-Bass.

Huber, M. T. 2000. Evaluating Outreach: Scholarship Assessed's Approach [online]. Pennsylvania: Penn State University. Available from: http://www.outreach.psu.edu/News/Pubs/Monograph/eval.html. Accessed January 2004.

Rice, R. E. 2003. Rethinking Scholarship and New Practice: A Central AAHE Priority [online]. Washington, D. C.: American Association for Higher Education. Available from: http://www.aahe.org/specialreports/part4/htm. Accessed August 2003.

Rottle, N.D. 2004. Universal in the Local: Practising the Scholarship of Engagement. Landscape Review, A Journal of Landscape Architecture, 9 (2), in press.

Ward, K. 2003. Faculty Service Roles and the Scholarship of Engagement. ASHE-ERIC Higher Education Report 29 (5). San Francisco: Jossey-Bass.

Recreating Community in Cancer Support Centers, Foster Homes and Developing Colonias Through the Hands-On Participation of a Design/Build Teaching Model

Daniel Winterbottom

INTRODUCTION

Scholars have suggested that future professionals, and by inference landscape architects, must think beyond the "box" to address the complexity of issues in the future, and that education must adapt to provide the critical skills needed (Boyer 1990). Design/build challenges students to think and work creatively in the tight frameworks of a ten- week quarter. Many design studio teaching models have linked design and community participation, but few have connected design, community participation and construction as cohesively as the design/build studio model (Winterbottom, 1999, 2002, 2003). Students interact with differing communities, diverse in age, ethnic background, income and needs. They accept multiple, overlapping roles, and are taught skills including community outreach, facilitation, design, cross cultural communication and information gathering, and project management. Students are encouraged to consider the ethical, functional, cultural and technical design implications as they deepen their awareness of whose needs are being overtly addressed, find appropriate solutions and build creative, responsive projects.

THE MODEL

Developed in 1995, the design/build studio at the University of Washington is offered as a ten week BLA (Bachelor of Landscape Architecture) capstone studio with an average class size of sixteen students. The students conduct material/systems research and site analysis in week one. Weeks two through four are devoted to participatory community design/construction documentation, and the remaining six weeks allotted to construction. A revolving student team manages the project and most decisions are made by majority vote. Twelve projects have been completed to date, all of which employed a participatory community design process to promote exchange, understanding and clarity. Eight projects focus on sustainable design, and four center on the healing and therapeutic value of gardens. Partnerships have been developed with the Seattle Public Schools, neighborhood councils, community centers, a cancer support facility, a major urban hospital, a foster home for children with AIDS and a state facility for the severely disabled. Funding has come from public grants, targeted funds from a college endowment, public levies and fundraising drives. Projects are chosen for their content and for the client's willingness to engage in community participation. Relationships grow across racial, class and economic barriers, challenging prejudices and assumptions. The skills of listening, empathizing, and mediating are practiced, common ground established, and the building process evolves with a deeper purpose and sense of partnership.

Exchanges abroad offer multiple facets of challenge and reward. Student perceptions are expanded through visits to the local residences, participation in traditional ceremonies and the daily exploration of the indigenous architecture, food, music, markets and festivals. The built component is the most tangible result of the design/build model, but clearly the educational outreach, cultural exchange, community understanding and shared endeavor are of equal importance.

CASE STUDIES

Lavandaria Santa Ursula, Communidad Santa Ursula, Mexico, 1998 is a small colonia of recent immigrants who have come from impoverished towns throughout Mexico. With no municipal utilities, the women routinely hike four-miles to wash clothes. The physical hardships and frigid water compromise their health, and the barranca (ravine) an important ecological corridor linking federal parks and ethno botanical reserves, is degraded by pollutants. We partnered with a non-profit advocacy group and the community to create a public lavanderia utilizing harvested rainwater. The primary goals were to engage the students and the community in cross-cultural learning, to use sustainable solutions, and develop replicable sustainable models.

The Process

This project grew from explorations with sustainable design and community process begun in Seattle, WA that were adapted for this unique culture and environment. Several assumptions were challenged and the design process evolved. For example, because foreign males were discouraged to engage in discussions with the women of the village, the female students took sole responsibility for soliciting their input, often using sign language (Eubanks Owens, Winter 2000). To curb resentment among the men who didn't perceive any direct benefit from the project, three local maestros (builders) were employed to share their knowledge of traditional building. To promote understanding of the project, a community forum was used to describe and discuss the value and fragility of the riparian corridor, the value of ecological design and the benefits of relocating the clothes washing activities.

We initially met with the women at the stream, discussed the project and observed the important social interactions occurring there. We visited traditional lavandarias studying their forms and spatial relationships. Once designs were developed, community reviews were held and the designers responded to comments. Community solicitation continued throughout the project and often during construction. Because the village has different groups of indigenous people with unique symbolic beliefs, we drew perspectives of the built project, asked the participants to color the drawings and discussed them until consensus was achieved. Other elements include a stone cooking stove built for traditional festivities and an adventure play area to engage the children as their mothers work. A plaza, the traditional community space, was integrated into the design, expanding its use as civic space for all.

The Outcomes

One significant result was the empowerment of the women of Santa Ursula, who had a major role in the process, and were most impacted by the project. The new plaza is the main social center for the growing village and the men, feeling their needs be considered, became more engaged as it took shape. By building and testing non-traditional technologies such as the roof configuration and the use of ferro-concrete, the community has accepted these new forms and methods. This is critical for future replication in other communities where there may be resistance to unfamiliar technologies. The outreach and open discussions enabled community members to better understand the connection between their local situation and global issues of resource use/abuse and environmental impact, laying a stewardship for their environment as they expand the community.

Incarnation Children's Center, New York City, N.Y., 2000 is a foster home for children infected with HIV/AIDS. Incarnation houses approximately twenty-four children whose parents/ care providers are deceased or unable to provide safe home environments. Many residents suffer from physical and psychological disabilities including autism, depression, loss of motor coordination and mobility. Once diagnosed with AIDS, the patient's identity is reconfigured and defined by the debilitating effects of the illness. The children receive both medical and therapeutic care, counseling and education. The design/build studio was invited to collaborate with the incarnation community to create a 6000 SF. healing garden.

The Process

Restricted by a five-week time frame and the difficulty of communicating with the children, due to their cognitive

disabilities, age and availability, a method was developed to solicit the residents, staff and administrators input. A volunteer coordinator was trained via phone in methods for surveying and participatory brainstorming/programming, and this component was administered prior to our arrival. The survey was circulated to staff and administrators to assess their needs, ideas and concerns and what aspects and programmatic elements they felt were important. The children expressed their dreams, needs and concerns during brainstorming sessions and these were notated. Upon arrival the studio team joined the Incarnation staff to discuss the effects of AIDS and resident's needs and to review the survey/discussion results. In a second session, initial concepts were developed with the staff and administrators. Five schematic designs were created, then reviewed by staff and volunteers and synthesized into a final preferred plan. Residents met with students to review the design, and modifications were made to incorporate their responses.

The Outcomes

In this project, the preliminary data collection and survey results and ensuing discussions and interactions laid the foundation for responsive design. The experience of working with this community was a new one for members of the design team. While the lack of our initial participation delayed bonding with the residents, it did stimulate project focus within the community prior to our arrival.

Relationships between students and residents and staff developed, most powerfully, during construction. As the design was transformed into built form, the children started using the components and even the most skeptical were galvanized. Spontaneous interchanges and specifically a discussion on grief and dying led by the executive director helped the design students overcome their identification of primary differences and gain a deeper understanding of life with AIDS. Many of the elements including a karaoke stage, wheelchair water feature, resident flower boxes, porch swing, and the grass rolling mound responded directly to the needs of residents and staff. In post occupancy visits, residents' engagement continues to be very high.

A primary benefit of the design/build model is the ability to reflect, reconsider and change the design as the project is being built. As a laboratory, elements can be placed and tested, reviewed with the community and changed where appropriate. For example, shortly after a wheel chair accessible sand box was set in place, the physical therapist brought out a wheel chair to test the height, illustrating that lowering the box a few inches would be ideal, and the legs were modified in situ.

Our intention in this project was to create an outdoor "home" for the residents, many of whom suffered from feelings of isolation and alienation. The stigma of the disease restricted opportunities to play in the public parks and many expressed a need for play activities within the building site. Residents wanted to invite friends and engage in "normal" activities. As a counterpoint to the building with its small, often crowded spaces, the gardens provide residents with a place to wander, find solitude or participate in interactive activities depending on their mood and abilities.

Participation in the construction had an unexpected benefit as the resulting physical exercise improved muscle development. The crossing of racial, class and cultural boundaries, was for many of the participating students the most profound learning experience.

Cancer Lifeline, Seattle, WA. 2000, a nationally recognized support facility offers those affected by cancer a range of services including nutrition, physical therapy and healing art classes, counseling services and research library. Programs are designed to decrease stress and the sense of isolation that come with a cancer diagnosis. Over 8000 participants are served annually.

In 2000 we were invited to collaborate with Cancer Lifeline participants to create three healing gardens on the roof of their new facility. Their mission statement asserted that "The gardens will restore a sense of order, safety, and privacy for those dealing with the chaos induced by this illness. The act of gardening produces a peaceful, effortless concentration that increases our capacity to rest. It creates more outward perceptions rather than inward self-consciousness, a valuable balance to the uneasiness of illness."

The Process

Prior to our involvement Cancer Lifeline convened a focus group to forward the following goals for the gardens.

- Create spaces that invite cancer patients to be, rather than do.

- A haven that expresses the power and order of nature and encourages introspection, self-expression and creativity.

- A place of tranquility, energy and meditation.

- Stimulation of the senses, exudes a caring touch, attracts animals.

- Incorporation of color therapy, herbalism, and aromatherapy.

- A place for relaxation and visualization.

Building upon the focus group's effort and prior to the studio's involvement, Professor Anne Kearny, an environmental psychologist, administered a survey and mapping exercise.

The survey, with open ended and scaled responses, was distributed to the 26 participants. The first set of questions addressed participants' perceptions and desires for the gardens, and included questions such as: How do you imagine using the spaces? What role should the gardens play in the center? What benefits will be provided? The second set, using a scaled index, asked what types of activities would one do when mentally fatigued? The final section asked if there are other things you do or places you go when you feel a need to restore, heal or refresh yourself. This data offered a psychological and emotional baseline to be used in the post occupancy study and also provided data of desired uses, role of the gardens and preferences for types of places.

In the cognitive mapping exercise, the participants were asked to:

- Write the characteristics most important to you personally. Take from the list by the focus group or add others.

- Once comfortable with your collection, organize them into groups or categories based on how you think they fit together.

- Label each category with a word or phrase that describes why you grouped these characteristics together.

These groups were then compared to each other and sorted to discern which characteristics were most frequently mentioned. Some of the most important characteristics include:

- Places to sit (91%)

- Scent/smells/aromatic plants (70%)

- Peaceful (65%)

- Water features (65%)

- Places to socialize in small groups (57%)

To conceptualize the gardens, the groups created by the participants were then combined into similar associations, resulting in four groups that formed the basis for the three designs.

- General Characteristics

- Social/Activity Garden

- Sensory Garden

- Meditation Garden

A general discussion with staff, administrators, participants (users of the services) and students was held on the first day of the studio and the effects of cancer were described, the results of the cognitive mapping were presented, and discussed, and visions for the gardens were explored. The attendees were divided into teams, each gathering in one of the three garden spaces where they developed conceptual plans. The students then further developed the concepts and produced three schematic designs for each space. Three were presented to the design advisory committee, and their comments informed the final designs.

The Outcomes

The cognitive mapping/participatory design process directly informed the three distinct gardens, each reflecting the desires and needs of the participants. The gardens have become a focal point at Cancer Lifeline. Through shared stewardship they enhance bonds among participants and function as retreats for solitude and intimate exchanges. The gardens define Cancer Lifeline as a place of regeneration and spirituality. It is a safe homelike environment that nurtures those searching for self-identity, hope and connection and those adapting into the culture of cancer. One participant, who resides in public housing, spends most of her days in the gardens, which for her have become a home away from home.

In contrast to Incarnation and Santa Ursula, few of these participants because of their physical condition, were engaged in the construction. Instead, they observed the process, giving input throughout the project.

CONCLUSIONS

As designers, working with a diverse range of communities, it has become clear that the term multi-culturalism must be used in its broadest context and that culture must be seen as not only an ethnic or racial definition, as important as those are, but also culture can be defined by a change of circumstance such as an illness leading to dramatic changes in self identity and perception, from both within and without. As these case studies illustrate, productive community participation requires flexibility and when used in design/build projects, many parameters including time frame, language, cognitive disabilities and health of the participants influence what type of participation might be most productive.

The design/build model presented in this paper, has, through outreach, inclusion, and engagement, empowered those displaced by poverty or confronting a terminal illnesses and enabled them to reestablish a deeper sense of community.

REFERENCES

Boyer, E. Scholarship Reconsidered. The Carnegie Foundation for the Advancement of Teaching.

Forsyth, L. and McGirr. 1999. Inside the Service Learning Studio in Urban Design Landscape. Landscape Journal, 18, (3): 166-178.

Thompson, W. 1998. Educating Las. Landscape Architecture Magazine, October: 100-145.

Winterbottom, D. 2003. Building to Learn, Part II. Landscape Architecture Magazine, April: 72-118.

Winterbottom, D. 1999. Una Lavandaria Promotes Sustainability. Designer/builder, October: 28-30

Winterbottom, D. 2002. Building as a Model for Learning. Landscape Journal, 21 (1): 201-213.

Winterbottom, D. and Smith, L. 1996. LARC 332, Landscape Construction Student Research Projects. University of Washington.

TO INSPIRE STUDENTS IN PARTICIPATORY COMMUNITY DESIGN
A Case Study from Ohnogawa Greenway Rehabilitation Proposal

Koichi Kobayashi[1]

ABSTRACT

The purpose of this paper is to cover and examine the following:

- **To illustrate how a community based design proposal was employed to inspire students in participatory community design**

- **To present how community based design could be utilized as an advocacy proposal**

- **To test how a short charrette type instruction could be employed to introduce students on planning and design process**

- **To validate the author's intuition in the profession and education in cross cultural situations**

INTRODUCTION

The project site was the Ohno River Greenway (3 km), located in Nishiyodogawa District of the Northwest sector of Osaka City with 6 million people. The client, Aozora Foundation was established in 1996 after a litigation settlement with a number of manufacturing industries in the District. Litigation was on environmental pollution (air, water and noise), and was widely publicized as Nishiyodogawa Public Pollution Litigation. Activities of the foundation cover: research and implementation on machizukuri (town planning/building), communication and information exchange on public pollution and environmental education. As a part of Machizukuri, the foundation had produced a proposal titled "Environmental Rehabilitation Plan of Nishiyodogawa District, 2000." Residents together with the foundation had produced inventories of the existing resources and problems and potentials of the District to support the plan through a wide public participation process.

Ohno River once was a free flowing canal used for transportation, fishing and recreation, still remembered by residents. It was covered and the site was converted to a bicycle road. After 30 years of installation, it is now called as Ohno River Greenway,

heavily used by residents for commuting and recreation. Lately, because of the green mass it provides, it had attracted infill high density residential development along the greenway, indicating its economic as well as environmental value. The rehabilitation of Ohno River Greenway was a major part of the plan to reintroduce native habitat and improve amenities. Time had been rapidly approaching in thinking of renovation of this valued treasure. The Greenway shows overgrowth of vegetation and wear and tear, and a new consciousness of the residents on environment exhibits a great need for adaptation of design and implementation plan.

An intensive two-week period was used by students assisted by instructors going through existing available resources of the site, meeting and working with the client and residents to produce a number of design proposals so that it could be used as an advocacy tool in future discussion with the owner and manager of the Greenway: Osaka City Public Works.

The project awaits the next step involving a preparation of an official design plan and presentation to public agency for discussion and adaptation. Students had an invaluable experience through this project and learned the importance of communication with the public and clients and also among design team members.

A design studio was organized to be their first design project for a period of two weeks with the following purposes:

- To illustrate how a community based design proposal was employed to inspire students in participatory community design

- To present how community based design could be utilized as an advocacy proposal

- To test how a short charrette type instruction could be employed to introduce students on planning and design process

- To validate author's intuition in the profession and education in cross cultural situation

AWAJI LANDSCAPE AND HORTICULTURAL ACADEMY (ALPHA)

Awaji Landscape and Horticulture Academy was established in 1998 and started its instruction in core courses in 1999. ALPHA currently is a part of the newly established Hyogo Prefectural University. ALPHA admits students with a minimum of a bachelor's degree for its core program.

In introducing ALPHA, the academy states the following:

Founded on man's love, respect and sense of awe towards life on Earth, Awaji Landscape Planning & Horticulture Academy (ALPHA) was established with the aim of pursuing a special discipline of landscape planning and horticulture. This discipline will be able to help shape regional culture and preserve natural environments by focusing on plant life as the ideal medium for bringing man and nature towards a closer relationship. ALPHA provides students with an educational research environment conducive to propagating new ideas, from conception to practical work, and with the facility to draw on the knowledge and wisdom inherited from others. The Academy also aims to disseminate its ideas to the world as a whole, to foster new leaders and to create an information resource that contributes to society. Both teachers and students within ALPHA share a great mission to nurture a foundation that incorporates the realities of modern industries occupying great areas of land while regaining and promoting landscapes and environments that allow human life and culture to better coexist with real nature. It is for these reasons that our education is considered as an actual study and to be of great historical significance.

It is a modern discipline aiming to restore the prominence of inter-relating fields, originally viewed as 'life space' studies, such as social living, civil engineering, architecture, landscape gardening, and industry. It also seeks to position community planning as a form of cultural activity that revisits the importance of our nature and regional culture without any priority for economic issues. There were many great achievements within science, technology and economics in the 20th century, a number unlike any other period in history. However, at the same time, we neglected our environment in pursuit of security and abandoned the richness of living together with the nature around us.

DESIGN STUDIO AND PROJECT

Purpose and Schedule

My teaching was primarily aimed at introducing planning and design process (process of inventory, analysis and synthesis) in a short period of time, forcing students to make decisions and move on and recycle back as needed.

The second priority of my teaching was to inspire students in participatory community design through a studio project assignment. The third priority was to expose students in English instruction given by visiting faculty from abroad.

The studio project was designed to be for two weeks with the following schedule:

May 8: Introduction of teaching staff, participating students and the project. Forming of six student studio groups.

May 10: Visiting the project site and interviewing the client/user group.

May 14-15: Consulting with Kobayashi. Students were encouraged to discuss about what their group wanted to do.

May 16: Presenting the Inventory and Analysis phase of the project. Students were advised to use as many visuals as possible. Keeping the objective of the project to renew and rehabilitate the project site in mind, students were requested to present how they saw, perceived, felt, heard and smelled.

May 20: Presenting each group's proposal. This presentation was exhibited on one sheet of 60cm x 90cm covering the entire process. Each team had ten minutes to present and five minutes for question and answer.

Date to be Determined: At the beginning of the project no schedule was included for presenting to the client due to a limited time frame. A number of students volunteered to make a presentation to the client group six months after.

Students

Thirty students from the first and second year initially signed up for the project and twenty-eight completed it. One third of the initial group was second year students.

The majority of the first year students came to ALPHA from no design nor planning background, which ranged from agriculture, law, literature, and political science. Only a few of them had a previous degree in art, environmental design and architecture. Graduates from ALPHA to date entered into a variety of professional areas including public agencies in planning and design, private design firms, non profit community organizations, contractors and material suppliers/manufacturers.

Project

The purpose of the project is to produce idea proposals for rehabilitation and renewal of the Ohno River Walkway in Nishiyodogawa Ward of Osaka City to a client group, Aozora Foundation of Nishiyodogawa.

The Client

Aozora Foundation was established in 1966 after a lengthy civil litigation and settlement process with a number of public agencies and private manufacturing industries. Litigation was on public environmental pollution on land, water, air and noise.

Aozora Foundation was established based on a settlement fund of 30 million yen. Three major purposes of the Foundation are:

- to undertake research work on rehabilitation of polluted areas and community planning for these areas,

- to publish and exchange information on experience from public pollution and community planning, and

- to assist in environmental education and implementation activities.

To summarize, the Foundation states: it is an organization actively engaged in Machizukuri (community planning and design) based on experiences from public pollution and also to assist others in such activities. As a part of Machizukuri, the Foundation produced a proposal entitled "Environmental Rehabilitation Plan of Nishiyodogawa Ward 2000" in 1998. Residents together with the Foundation produced inventories of existing resources, problems and potentials of the Ward in order to support the proposal through a wide public participation process.

EVALUATION AND CONCLUSION

At the conclusion of the project, evaluation of the program was requested from participating students. The following list a number of responses:

- It was a very concentrated program but too short.

- Too much time was spent in group dynamics- trying to understand group members.

Figure 3. Plan 2, welcome mascot "Harry" and willow tunnel.

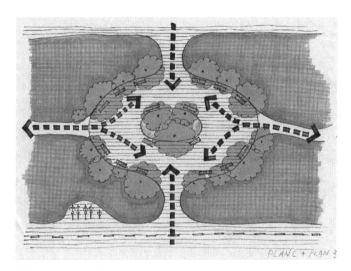

Figure 1. Work of team one.

Figure 2. Work of team one, Plan 1.

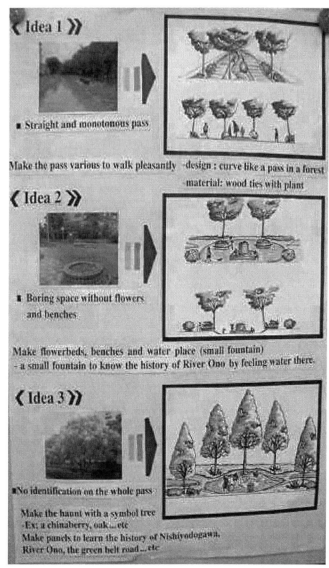

Figure 4. Work of team four.

279

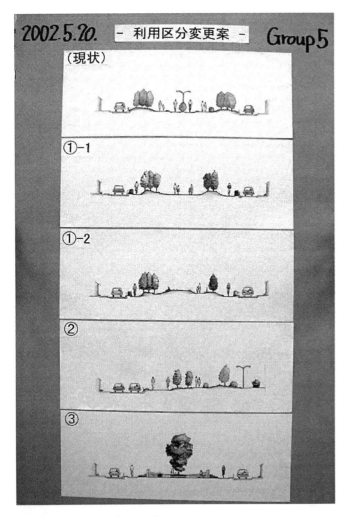

Figure 5. Work of team five.

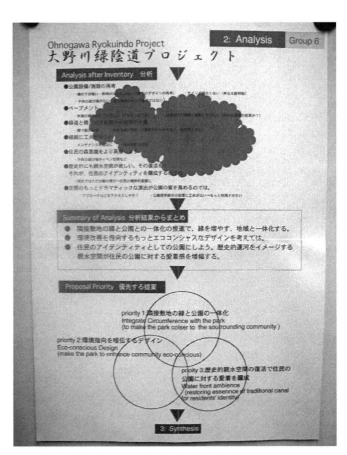

Figure 7. Team six analysis.

Figure 6. Team six inventory.

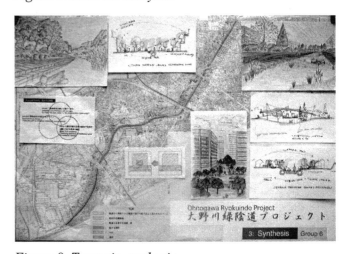

Figure 8. Team six synthesis.

- Instruction in English was hard.

- It is difficult to say that I acquired a sense in planning process.

- It is good that we try to communicate visually.

- It is good that we worked as a group collaboratively.

- We learned it is hard to transform ideas into physical form.

- It was a good experience working as a group and finishing it in time.

- It was the very first practical course/project that I undertook at this school.

- It was good that I was forced to make a decision in a positive way.

- We felt inadequate in presenting ideas.

- I got an inspiration from Ohnogawa Greenway Project to further my study.

Most of the evaluation and comments expressed were on the overall course offering and not directly on the studio project. It is not clear whether students were inspired in future participatory community design judging from their evaluation comments at this publication time.[2] One of the reasons for this may be that I did not directly ask whether they were inspired or not through the project. It may be too soon for the students to understand and perceive impact from this project. I contacted one of the participating students after two years of the program and received a very positive response on this question.

ENDNOTES

[1] The author was a visiting faculty from USA at the Awaji Landscape and Horticultural Academy (ALPHA), Japan during the spring of 2002. The author has over 30 years of professional and educational experience in the USA, Canada and Japan. Students with a variety of backgrounds had just started their program at ALPHA. A design studio was organized to be their first design project for a two-week period.

[2] I am happy to learn that the project itself may be continued with students participating from Kobe University under Professor Shiozaki's guidance. Professor Shiozaki is one of the Board Directors of the Aozora Foundation.

14

community and youth roundtable

Bridging Brandir

Landscape Liason

Action Aetheti

Crafting Crossing

Kung-Fu Kick-i

Believe Buyosp

Opportunity Optim

(e) Xpert (e) Xchang

COMMUNITY/YOUTH DEVELOPMENT
Exploring the Nexus Through Youth Leadership in Community Planning

Jonathan London

ABSTRACT

It is a deceptively simple formula: "youth contributing to communities <-> communities supporting youth." The mutual and inter-generational interdependence is appealing: so why is this vision a dream, largely deferred if not outright denied, in most communities? Why has the realization that youth and community development are inextricably linked – that youth are essential partners in community building, and that community building can provide developmental opportunities for youth – not been enough to make linking the two common practice? We contend that what is needed to move this realization into reality are concrete models of practice in which youth can play leadership roles in addressing community issues, and communities can learn to align themselves to better support their youth. While some excellent models of practice do exist, Youth In Focus seeks to contribute a method of Youth-led Research, Evaluation, and Planning (Youth REP) as a unique and powerful resource for those seeking to link community and youth development. Youth In Focus is a non-profit intermediary training organization that supports youth to apply their knowledge to improving the institutions and communities that affect their lives. We argue that Youth REP offers an approach that can contribute to the fulfillment of all of the following in Table 1.

Youth In Focus has implemented a number of projects with a community/youth development emphasis. Now, we seek to deepen our practice by enhancing our curriculum with new participatory planning and design training methods – developed to guide urban and rural youth of color, immigrant youth, and other under-represented youth as they apply their knowledge to revisioning and revitalizing their communities.

This paper will introduce Youth In Focus' Youth REP pedagogical model, present one case study (a youth-led neighborhood assessment to guide redevelopment

Community/ Youth Development Principle	Youth REP Supports and Opportunities
Open community dialogue with youth	Proactive forums for youth-adult partnerships based on youth-produced research/ evaluation/planning of community issues.
Perception of youth as resources and allies by adults	Youth offer data-backed analysis and recommendations and energy to help the community address common challenges.
Youth development opportunities rooted in community	Exploring community issues is the context and the content of the projects. Youth research the underlying issues of their specific project topics.
Opportunities for social action.	Youth engage in community building through "entry point" of research/ evaluation/planning.
Increase youth leadership capacity	Youth develop critical thinking, communication and analysis skills, as well as collaboration, conflict resolution, and team-work capacities.

Table 1. Community/Youth development principles.

approaches in the South of Market in San Francisco), and explore a series of questions relating to the further development of a community/ youth development training method. These questions include:

- What are the fundamental skills, areas of knowledge, and experiences needed for youth to play meaningful and powerful roles in community planning and design?

- (To what extent) Do these learning goals vary from participatory planning training for adults?

- What are the most promising methods of developing these planning capacities with youth?

- (To what extent) Do these methods vary from participatory planning training for adults?

This presentation seeks to both present the ideas and work of Youth In Focus, and engage in a teaching/learning dialogue to improve the conceptual understandings and practical methods of community/youth development.

YOUTH IN THE FRAGMENTED SOCIETY

Isami Kinoshita

ABSTRACT

Recently in Japan, the crimes caused by youth have been highlighted in the newspapers. Their lack of enough experience with human and nature contact might be one of the reasons for their violence. In the town planning system, places for youth to meet has not been given enough consideration. Commercial spots, such as amusement centers, game centers, convenience stores, etc. have become the places for youth to be. Semiotic theory analyzing commercial society might be fit mostly to youth activities in cities, as the example of cognitive maps of youth shows. There are many temptations in amusement centers that involve youth with drugs, sexual commercialism and violence. Furthermore, information technology has changed the style of communication between youth, as we have seen recently with the shocking news in which a 12-year old girl killed her friend at school, because of a disagreement in an internet chatroom. On the other hand, data from several international comparative studies about youth consciousness show the pessimistic Japanese youth consciousness concerning social matters and hope for the future. The nexus of youth participation in community planning is very important for re-structuring the relationship between youth and community. Youth have the ability to analyze community issues and make plans for problem solving. Youth leadership might contribute to community capacity building. Even though there are still large criticisms regarding children and youth participation, such as "even adults had not taken part in the community, not to speak of children and youth," some cases show the potential for youth and children to involve adults in their action research programs in their community and encourage their participation in community development.

CAN WE OVERCOME OUR MODERN HABITS OF TEACHING, LEARNING AND DESIGNING?

Elijah Mirochnik

ABSTRACT

Two of my projects with children, one in the early 1980s and the other in 2004, will lead to a comparison between the shift that I have made from a modern to a postmodern enactment of teaching and learning. In the earlier project, I initiated an educational model that brought together planners, politicians and public school children in Portland, Oregon. An air-inflated geodesic dome constructed by public school children displayed their visions of a "kid-friendly downtown." Their drawings became the data source that planners used to initiate policy and development incentives geared toward incorporating spaces and activities for children within the Portland downtown. In a recent project, I worked with a fourth grade teacher and children in a Washington, D.C. public school. Children created an air-inflated "body bubble," as part of a science unit that intentionally challenged the modern paradigm of scientific objectivity. Activities that enabled children to talk about, write about, and create art about their bodies in the first person "I" voices, were woven into their science curriculum. My recent work with children attempts to engage children in a process of transgression from the modern. In the case presented, transgression from a scientific vocabulary that privileges mind over body, and higher objective knowledge over second-class personal and artistic knowledge. In my presentation I will explore how the writings of Richard Rorty have helped me reinvent myself as a teacher through the use of a transgressive vocabulary that challenges old notions about knowledge, teaching and learning. I will explore how the fictional languages of the arts and the personal languages of autobiography.

REFLECTION IN ACTION
Freirian Praxis in the Northern Cheyenne Youth Restoration Art Project (R.A.P.)

Michael Rios

ABSTRACT

The construction of youth identity is a double-edged sword. Increasing media demonization of youth is coupled with the fact that youth represent the most actively targeted group of consumers in the marketplace. These social constructions fail to provide a space for youth to articulate their diverse fears, desires, and identities. In the case of youth on the Northern Cheyenne Reservation in the United States, this lack of agency is complicated by stereotypical dictations of "native" identity and the lack of specific Northern Cheyenne references in mainstream culture. In short, Northern Cheyenne youth are doubly exiled. The Northern Cheyenne Youth Restoration Art Project (RAP), a new community arts and design program in Lame Deer, Montana, is a response to the contemporary condition of Northern Cheyenne youth. The aim of Youth RAP is to bring art back into the spaces of everyday life as a guiding force for future generations. Youth RAP centers on a unique transcultural collaboration between local youth, a Northern Cheyenne artist, and university faculty and students. While there has been an upsurge of service learning in landscape architecture schools in recent years, few examples exist that extend beyond the confines of university campuses or the limitations of academic priorities and agendas. This paper presents the case of Youth RAP to illustrate the use of community-based design and art as a vehicle to explore issues of identity, landscape, and civic engagement, while designing and constructing communal spaces on the Northern Cheyenne reservation. As such, the case presents a place- and identity-based approach that integrates learning and service in a community setting. Paulo Freire's concept of praxis is introduced to describe a model of design pedagogy that is participatory in nature, and requires mutual engagement, collaboration, and reflection. YouthRAP works to transcend traditional modes of education and recognizes that knowledge occurs and develops in an arena of negotiation. As knowledge born out of collaboration and mutual engagement, this project functions on multiple levels:

- Social: an art-based approach provides a vehicle of agency for Northern Cheyenne youth to communicate their world to others.

- Cultural: this process-driven project illustrates the fallacious stereotypes of native people by revealing the rich complexity of hybrid and transcultural identities.

- Educational: design-build projects are both a material product and a site of discourse between native and non-native epistemologies, youth and adult realms.

15

outside-in/
inside-out:
bridging
professional
expertise and
local knowledge
in an era of
globalization

Evaluating
Native Wis
Democracy
Outside-in/
Husbandry

Sometimes
Artivism
Networks

→ L · I · N · E

OUTSIDE-IN/INSIDE-OUT
Bridging Professional Expertise and Local Knowledge in an Era of Globalization

Shenglin Chang and Tianxin Zhang

ABSTRACT

Professional planners and designers often face the predicament of planning for people and for contexts foreign to their own. They must deal with issues in cross-cultural values and perspectives. They must be able to communicate in languages other than their own. They must live and work in alien environments. In an increasingly globalizing world, this phenomenon is ever more apparent and critical. At the same time, more than ever before, people are traveling to new and alien places seeking recreation, excitement and alternative life experiences. The increasing pace of interaction between the local and the outsider exposes a wide range of issues concerning culture and development. For example, when we speak of local distinctiveness, is it distinctiveness as defined by the local, or is it as seen by the outsider? For the planners, is distinctiveness a conceptual construct applied to the local context, or is it to be discovered from the inside-out? To examine these emerging cross-cultural issues in the field of community planning and design, this panel discusses three separate cases: a sustainable forest management case in Lijiang, China, an eco-tourism development case on Matzu Island, Taiwan, and a case of community design and planning in the multi-cultural community of West Hyattsville, Maryland (USA). In their different socio-cultural settings and program contexts, these projects involve a wide range of local knowledge that local insiders are familiar with, and professional technologies that are introduced by outside experts. Together, the case studies examine the common issues of cross-cultural perspectives in community design that includes:

• How do we (professionals) understand the problems that local people face when they have to deal with unfamiliar and foreign environments?

• How do we (professionals) set goals and objectives when we help people face the above problems?

• How do we (professionals) engage people (participation) in making plans and designs for future environments that will help to resolve problems that people face?

Panel Participants (reversed alphabetical order): Tianxin Zhang (Beijing University, China), Yamamura Takayoshi (Kyoto Saga University Of Arts, Japan), Jonathan London (Youth in Focus, USA), John K.C. Liu (National Taiwan University, Taiwan), Margarita Hill (University of Maryland, USA), Aijun He (Tokyo University, Japan), Shenglin Chang (University of Maryland, USA)

INCREASING WALKABILITY IN WEST HYATTSVILLE
A Case of Cross-Cultural Participation in Community Design and Planning

Margarita Hill

ABSTRACT

Various public agencies in Maryland are pursuing community design and planning strategies that promote new urban patterns that are described by a plethora of buzz phrases: "Walkable Communities," "Livable Communities," "New Urbanism Neighborhoods," etc. In some part, this is a response to local advocacy planning and changing demographic patterns that call for the development of communities with compact, affordable, mixed-use housing, with comfortable pedestrian access to employment, retail and regional transit centers and with improved recreational facilities and schools. In an attempt to put together new planning strategies to address these concerns, stakeholders in the process face many challenges. One of these challenges is the growth of new immigrant and multi-cultural populations within certain local communities. More than ten municipalities within Prince George's County have populations where more than 25% of residents are foreign born. In West Hyattsville, nearly 30% of the population is foreign born with half of those community residents having arrived within the last 10 years. In addition, these communities are becoming increasingly diverse from a cultural perspective. In West Hyattsville, we see a population characterized as 25% White, 55% African American, 3% Asian, and 16% Hispanic. In addition, 10% of residents described themselves as multi-racial (a mix of two or more races). This multi-cultural context requires different methods of democratic process and produces many challenges in promoting community participation. This paper will describe the participatory community design and planning approach utilized in creating a plan for a more walkable community in West Hyattsville and discusses the issues that arose in the process. It will address the questions raised in the panel description and thus generate a discussion about how we understand, engage and plan for multi-cultural and new immigrant populations.

INTRODUCTION

Many communities across the U.S. are looking for ways to redesign their urban structure to make walking and bicycling a normal part of everyday life. The Center for Disease Control (CDC) calls these places "Active Community Environments," or "Healthy Communities" and is promoting active living through community design as a way to combat increased levels of obesity, diabetes, heart disease and stress in children, teens and adults. In the U.S., the incidence of overweight adults increased from 47% in 1976 to 61% in 1999 but in children and adolescents the prevalence of obesity doubled in the same period. In the last 25 years, in particular, Americans have become more sedentary as our communities have been predominantly designed around the automobile. Many communities do not provide safe, convenient access for a pedestrian, which is essential to creating more livable communities. Furthermore, they often lack: alternative transportation facilities, land use planning that promotes compact development, convenient links to schools and public facilities, adequate provision of recreation, parks and trails, and programs to address community safety and crime prevention. However, these are all important components of walkable communities.

Various public agencies in Maryland are pursuing community design and planning strategies that promote new urban patterns that are described by a plethora of buzz phrases: "Walkable Communities," "Livable Communities," "Smart Growth Neighborhoods," "New Urbanism Neighborhoods," "Pedestrian Pockets," "Sustainable Communities." In some part, this is a response to local advocacy planning and changing demographic patterns that call for the development of communities with compact, affordable, mixed-use housing, with comfortable pedestrian access to employment, retail and regional transit centers and with improved recreational facilities and schools. In an attempt to put together new planning strategies to address these concerns, stakeholders in the process face many challenges.

THE WEST HYATTSVILLE COMMUNITY

The West Hyattsville community extends over Wards 4 and 5 of the City of Hyattsville. It is poised for significant change since it has been recently designated as one of the county's TODZs (Transit Oriented Development Zone). It is located within the Capital Beltway about 2 miles outside Washington, D.C. and 2.5 miles from the University of Maryland's College Park Campus. As part of a strategic TOD planning program of Prince George's County, West Hyattsville is envisioned as the county's first mixed-use, transit village development. Prince George's County officials desire this type of development to eventually be extended to all 14 Metrorail stations in the county. The County is promoting Transit Oriented Development as one that includes, "compatible moderate to higher density development, located within an easy walk of a major transit stop, generally with a mix of residential, employment and shopping opportunities, designed for pedestrians without excluding the auto" (Parsons-Brinckerhoff, et. al, 2003).

Within the community of West Hyattsville, a 60-acre site of under-developed land exists adjacent to the West Hyattsville Metrorail Station. The city was interested in development options for this land, which lies within a community in need of larger revitalization efforts. The City's strategy was based on the hope that innovative development of this parcel would "jump start" revitalization efforts that would later extend to other parts of the community. The site lies within a community with a unique set of opportunities and constraints. One of the most significant opportunities is its location adjacent to the floodplain and creek alignments of the Northwest Branch of the Anacostia River and Sligo Creek that includes a public park network and various sports and natural recreation features. This location prompted community leaders to envision a mixed-use TOD model focused around a Riverwalk, similar to the community-led model in Naperville, IL. Other opportunities include a local commitment to "smart growth" and a history of public participation in community affairs (Murphy, 2003). However, the site is surrounded by underutilized commercial areas with marginal uses, run-down or vacant buildings, a perception that the area is plagued by crime, and various aging mid-rise housing developments creating a public image that has generated many obstacles for reinvestment in the community. Furthermore, the community's streetscapes are very auto-oriented, engineered so that traffic can quickly pass through the area and thus not supportive of local businesses nor pedestrians.

While the challenges presented by disinvestment and image problems have affected the city's ability to attract middle and upper income families to West Hyattsville, many others have been attracted by its affordability, the diversity of the population and a sense of community that often brings people together to solve problems or explore issues. A few demographic descriptors are noteworthy in understanding some of the community revitalization challenges for West Hyattsville, a community where almost half of the residents are renters, not homeowners. Family median income is $45,355, well below the State average, more than 10% of families do not own an automobile and more than 20% take public transportation to work.[1]

In West Hyattsville, nearly 30% of the population is foreign born with half of those community residents having arrived to the USA within the last 10 years. In looking at race as an indicator of cultural diversity in West Hyattsville, we see a population characterized as 25% White, 55% African American, 3% Asian, and 16% Hispanic. In addition, 10% of residents described themselves as multi-racial, a mix of two or more races. In establishing participatory process, language barriers can present unique challenges. Almost 27% of residents do not speak English in the home with 17% speaking Spanish and 13% reporting they do not speak English "very well" (U.S. Bureau of the Census, 2000). [2]

COMMUNITY DESIGN PROCESS

The University of Maryland, through the Community Design Studio of the Landscape Architecture Program, was asked to assist the City of Hyattsville by preparing a plan to outline strategies to create a more livable, walkable community and to generate ideas for the development of a Riverwalk and mixed-use TOD on the 60 acre-site. The project approach included the following phases: Case Study Research, Community Analysis, Participatory Community Design Workshops, Design Recommendations, Report Preparation (Hill, 2003), and a final presentation to the community.

Phase One: Case Study Research - Development of an Educational Product focused on "Livable, Walkable Communities"

Students conducted research on model communities where walking and bicycling is a normal part of everyday life. The first phase of the project outlined what "model" communities could look like and lessons that can be drawn from them. The focus was a comprehensive one that included: alternative transportation facilities, land use planning and compact development, links to schools and public facilities, provision of recreation, parks and trails, and issues of safety and crime prevention. The case study research phase provided education and inspiration to both students in the community design studio class and community stakeholders that participated in the community workshops. The six students in the class presented the results of their research in an educational session that was part of the community workshop on March 15, 2003.

Phase Two: Analysis of Existing Conditions - Community Inventory, Analysis

This phase included the development of a series of maps, community analysis, community audits and studies that identified existing conditions within the community and outlined the opportunities and constraints that these present. Students conducted inventory and analysis of existing conditions in the community and produced the following products:

1. G.I.S. Maps that show existing community infrastructure within the larger Hyattsville community.

2. Community Studies within West Hyattsville including:

- a survey of community residents to reflect community preferences and prioritize community design issues

- interviews with community "key informants" (community leaders, government officials, local police, religious leaders, etc.)

- an assessment of walkability as related to open space, recreation and the design of the existing streetscape environment.

Phase Three: Participatory Community Workshops

A community charrette was organized to gain input and provide design and planning education to community members on the topic of increasing walkability in West Hyattsville. During this workshop students presented the results of their case study research and the identification of opportunities and constraints that arose from the analysis of existing conditions. With the help of two professional landscape architects, Dr. Shenglin Chang and Ms. Renee Bartnick that facilitated the input from community members, participants shared ideas for increasing livability and walkability in West Hyattsville.

Phase Four: Development of a series of design recommendations for major "Windows of Opportunity"

In this phase, students provided a series of drawings and sketches that demonstrated the potential for re-design that exists in order to make West Hyattsville a more walkable, livable community. The specific sites that were the focus of these design recommendations are those that were identified by the workshop participants as being particularly important to increasing walkability and livability in Hyattsville. With only six students in the class, we outlined six project areas and prepared community revitalization strategies for each of these.

PRIORITIES IDENTIFIED THROUGH COMMUNITY PARTICIPATION PROCESS

Results of Interviews and Community Survey

A survey of residents, business owners, and community leaders was conducted in order to identify community needs and preferences. The survey was translated into Spanish and distributed in both languages throughout the community. More detailed interviews were conducted with local officials, business owners, and community leaders to gain additional insight. Ultimately more than seventy-five interviews and surveys were completed, and the following is a summary of the major findings.

The residents of Hyattsville voiced a number of concerns about their community including safety and crime issues, inadequate public amenities, and the lack of a strong and positive community identity. When asked, "Which aspects of Hyattsville do you find least appealing?" the community mentioned excessive crime, poor land use, too much traffic, and a lack of commercial amenities. The community also voiced concerns about the

existing lack of pedestrian amenities, a lack of housing options and job opportunities, visual blight, and out-dated parks.

During the surveys and interviews, the lack of a strong community identity was stated as a recurring issue. The community image is not well represented in the existing conditions along U. S. Route 1, Queens Chapel Road, Hamilton Street, as well as several other major circulation routes. The most common suggestions of how to improve the image and identity of the community were: revitalizing vacant lots, preserving and enhancing the historical core of houses, decreasing apartment buildings and increasing condominium communities, and offering incentives for residential and commercial owners to enhance their properties.

The community also expressed the need for inviting commercial spaces and improved transportation options. Lack of commercial amenities was the fourth most popular response among those surveyed or interviewed when asked what is least appealing about Hyattsville. One community re-design goal stated by the community was the need to establish Hyattsville as a destination point, not just a place that you drive through on

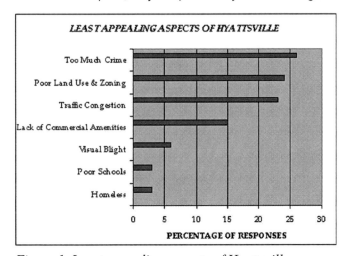

Figure 1. Least appealing aspects of Hyattsville.

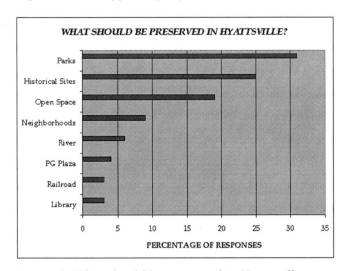

Figure 2. What should be preserved in Hyattsville.

your way to somewhere else. It was suggested that this could be accomplished by increasing commercial establishments, particularly retail stores, restaurants, and entertainment spots. Increasing public transportation options was also recommended as a strategy to alleviate traffic congestion. More specific suggestions included improved local bus and shuttle service, improved sidewalks, bus stops & benches.

In order to make Hyattsville a safer place to live and work, the community suggested revitalizing vacant lots and run-down properties. They also identified the need to increase the activity and visibility of the police, especially in isolated areas and parks. Some of the community voiced the need to establish a responsive and active local government. The community would like to see improved communication between city administration and the public, increased funding for youth and senior programs, and a more entrepreneurial spirit in local government.

When asked what spaces in Hyattsville were most valuable to the community, the most popular answers were the parks, open spaces and local historical sites. Seventy-five percent of those surveyed or interviewed named these places as sites to be preserved.

When asked to rate community amenities such as schools, parks, and shopping establishments, respondents voiced satisfaction with amenities such as schools and libraries, the post office, parks, and transit services. Amenities that are in need of improvement include entertainment establishments, restaurants, pedestrian amenities, and job opportunities.

Through the surveying and interviewing process, the community was asked to identify what services were lacking in Hyattsville, as well as suggestions as to what the local government could do to improve the community. The services people identified to be most lacking included commercial amenities and adequate crime prevention, representing over forty percent of all responses. Other services that respondents would like to see include: more public transportation options, traffic calming, community services, recreational centers, affordable housing, and improved parks. Respondents felt that the most important thing that government could do to improve Hyattsville was to increase crime prevention efforts.

While the primary mode of transportation for half of the respondents is the car, over 25% mentioned community problems related to traffic congestion. Increasing the number and variety of transportation options available would reduce the number of vehicles on the road and make Hyattsville more inviting to pedestrians. Widening sidewalks, improving lighting, and enhancing landscaping would create a more inviting pedestrian zone, and enhancing crosswalks and incorporating traffic calming devices would make it a safer place.

Various community residents mentioned that reducing visual blight should start with the revitalization of vacant lots. This would increase activity throughout the community and create

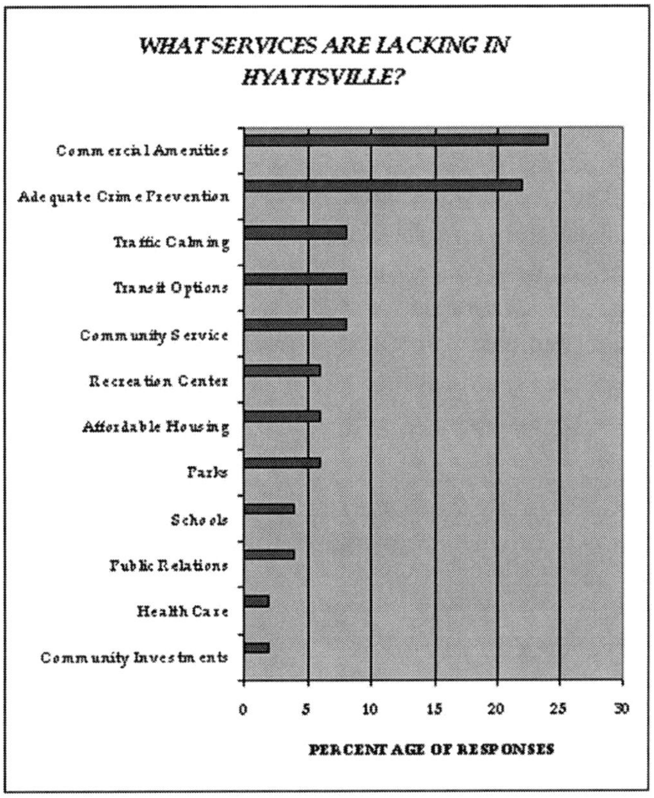

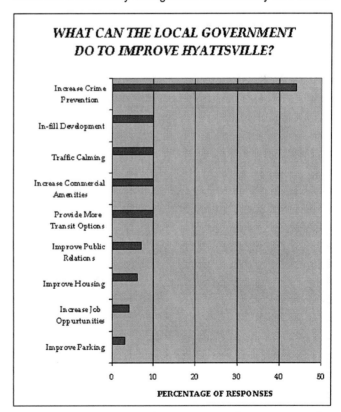

Figure 3. What services are lacking in Hyattsville.

Figure 4. What can local government do to improve the community.

more high-use spaces. Others mentioned the impact of large, unsightly parking lots. A number of respondents also mentioned problems associated with underused parks that needed updating.

Results of Community Workshop

A community workshop was conducted with local residents and community leaders with a series of exercises that assisted them in envisioning ideas for a revitalized, more walkable West Hyattsville. This workshop occurred on March 15, 2003 at the Hyattsville Municipal Building where over 20 community stakeholders participated.

Students made a presentation on the characteristics of an "active community environment," which included case studies from successful mixed-use and pedestrian friendly communities. Students presented the results of the survey and interviews with Hyattsville area residents and key informants. Students also presented opportunities and constraints that resulted from their community-wide inventory and analysis. This analysis focused on the public spaces within West Hyattsville, especially the streetscape environment and open space networks. After the students' presentation, a question and answer period followed with current and former mayors, council members and residents.

Following the question and answer period, attendees of the workshop were divided into two focus groups. Both groups were provided with large-format maps of the project area and markers. A group facilitator led the discussion and kept each team on task. The first exercise was to establish goals concerning West Hyattsville's revitalization. As group members made comments and suggestions, one or two people translated the comments into graphical form on the map. Next, objectives were established. These objectives described how the community's goals would be achieved. In these two exercises, participants could choose from a range of goals and objectives that had been mentioned in the survey and interview phase, or they could outline them and others and prioritize them. The last exercise was the discussion of design strategies. Here, participants were asked for specific design ideas and indicated where in the project area these ideas should be carried out.

While discussions were lively and different opinions were raised in regard to desired densities, the following goals were identified as being most important to achieve in terms of community revitalization of West Hyattsville:

- Focus on the pedestrian instead of the car

- Provide more active community centers and playgrounds

- Develop local transit to provide transport from Metro to home/shopping

- Develop reforestation program for Northwest Branch of Anacostia River

- Encourage more diversity of land uses and less chain stores

In the discussion of community design suggestions to improve the physical environment of West Hyattsville, a number of specific elements were identified as priorities:

- New bike trails, pedestrian trails, crosswalks, sidewalks, medians, traffic calming and landscape improvements at specific points identified by the participants

- Reforestation and native tree plantings

- Increased density and mix of uses close to Metro with pedestrian promenade

- Active public green spaces, "sensory gardens," restorative planting

- Infill development to minimize impact of large parking lots

- Community gateway

At the conclusion of the workshop, students were able to take suggestions from the community and synthesize them with their own design skills as they entered the design phase of the West Hyattsville revitalization project. The input from the workshops, surveys and interviews were incorporated into design strategies for six areas of West Hyattsville that were identified by workshop participants as having the most potential for improvement or transformation. They were: Prince George's Plaza, Queens Chapel Road Streetscape, Hamilton Street Infill Development and Streetscape, West Hyattsville Riverwalk Proposal, and the West Hyattsville Town Center. During the design phase, various community leaders were invited to the studio to comment on the design work in process, a presentation of student's design ideas was scheduled three weeks before the final community presentation so that students would get feedback before their design ideas were finalized. This formal critique session included jurors from the professional community, as well as, other landscape architecture faculty, and community representatives.

REFLECTIONS ON PARTICIPATORY PROCESS

In order to understand, engage and plan for a population that is culturally different from the planning and design team, our intent was to structure a participatory process that involves the community in a range of settings with multiple methodologies and across the various stages of the project. In this way, our goal was to engage as many perspectives as possible within a limited time frame. Since the demographic research pointed to potential language barriers, we were prepared to work in two languages: English and Spanish. Since personal conflicts limit people's participation in workshops, we attempted multiple methods of engagement and communication including

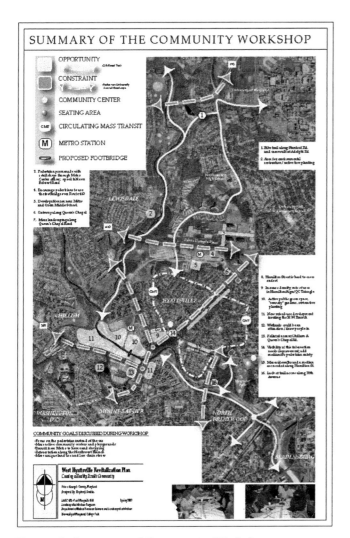

Figure 5. Summary of Community Workshop.

e-mail, phone, visits to workplaces, places of worship, places frequented in the community (grocery stores, popular restaurants, laundry, library, etc.).

In a community design setting that creates a partnership between communities and the university, a number of challenges are introduced into the participatory planning and design process. While partners share the ultimate goal of generating planning and design strategies that are sensitive to unique cultural and environmental opportunities and constraints of the community, participation goals differ across different stakeholder interests. Students are attempting to increase their learning and professional development skills. They value learning methods that allow them to gain insights that are outside of their understanding, in particular, when they come from different cultural and socio-economic experiences. Faculty are experimenting with different models, pushing the boundaries of what we know, and looking for better teaching and planning methods. Community members have an inherent interest in having a voice in the development process, making sure their specific needs are met. Some political or community

leaders may have an interest in the participatory process only to meet the legislated mandate for it, others may be trying to get support for specific ideas that are part of their political agenda, while others are negotiating with different interest groups in their community to understand where the larger community consensus exists.

Another challenge that is part of this university-community participatory model is rooted in the question of how do we nurture a commitment to service and civic engagement in the context of design and planning education. Inherent in the process is reflection on a range of civic issues including: social justice, environmental justice, social change, community voice (Who decides what the "common good" is), democratized access to information, and the redefined relationship between the "professional" and the community stakeholder as a reciprocal process of exchange of information and resources. Students are given the opportunity to engage with multiple players in local problem solving exercises. This allows students to hear and consider the voices of their fellow classmates and of their fellow citizens as part of the design and planning process and allows them to directly experience how this shapes the development of the physical landscape in addressing community issues. It allows the development of specific skills and competencies related to the landscape architecture discipline that are rooted in a service model (intellectual skills, participation skills, action-research skills, design & planning skills, communication skills) but that establish a reciprocal process where all the participants are both learners and teachers.

In a reciprocal educational model, the process flows in multiple directions, engaging multiple players: students, professors, professionals, community members, and government representatives. Students, acting as the professional team, learn from community members as they engage them in interviews, surveys, and by working with them during the community workshops and in their design process. They also become educators as they share what they have learned through their community analysis and case study research with community members. The interim design critiques are designed to include community residents and professional designers. This event becomes a learning tool, not only for the students, but also for the community members who hear a critique of the students' design approaches from a professional perspective. The dialogue allows community members to be exposed to a process of design inquiry that is different from the one they experience in talking to other community members. In some ways, this becomes another educational tool that may be helpful in future evaluations of design and planning proposals in their community.

CONCLUSIONS

While the cross-cultural community participation model for

design and planning outlined here in this paper, has many benefits for all of the stakeholders in the process it also has many challenges.

One benefit is the enhancement of students' personal growth and professional development that occurs while developing a commitment to service and civic engagement. In this regard, I believe the university can play an active role in civic renewal by engaging students in their communities and encouraging them to think critically about the importance of civil society and their roles as citizens in the democratic process. This is particularly relevant for landscape architecture students who will one day interface with the public as design and planning professionals. This experience can foster a sense of civic responsibility in landscape architecture students, so that they not only become prepared for professional careers but they are able to channel their knowledge and skills to promote the "common good" and to help solve public problems by engaging diverse partnerships.

There are obvious benefits to the community partners who benefit from a range of planning and design services. Sometimes these services assist communities in achieving physical change in their communities. Other times the process becomes an important fund-raising tool to support revitalization efforts; and other times the process is an important part of the community dialogue that occurs to focus community priorities and identifies issues that need further work and collaboration. The dissemination efforts related to this work help illustrate to the larger, local community the potential role that the university can play as a partner in civil society efforts. These partnerships not only provide much needed design and planning service to communities but also fulfill the university's interest in inquiry, innovation, education and service.

However, there are many challenges that occur when planning and design services are structured as part of the university teaching environment. One of the challenges is presented by the limited time frame of the studio environment. Sometimes the studio ends while there are continuing needs to refine the planning and design process for the community partner. Other challenges are presented by the struggle of the student professional planning team as they strive to overcome stereotypes presented by their preconceptions of underprivileged communities especially as they have been portrayed through the local media. There is also the constant balancing act that occurs as the instructor struggles to introduce students to a range of skills (GIS, community analysis, demographics, participatory process, design) while providing community service and relating to the client needs that are inherent in that relationship.

ENDNOTES

[1] The City of Hyattsville is characterized by 48.9% renter occupied housing units and 51.1 owner occupied. In Hyattsville 21.1% take public transportation to work and 13.4% do not own a car. This compared to the county statistics where 11.9% take public transportation to work and 10.5% do not own a car. In the neighboring, more affluent Montgomery County, only 7.5% of households do not own a car. Median income for households in the State of Maryland is $52,868 while in Prince George's County it is $55,256. This is in contrast to the median income in Montgomery County, which is $71,551. (U.S. Bureau of the Census. 2000).

REFERENCES

Hill, M., ed. 2003. West Hyattsville Revitalization Plan: Creating a Walkable and Livable Community. Landscape Architecture Technical Report No. 10. College Park, MD: University of Maryland Dept. of Natural Resource Sciences and Landscape Architecture.

Murphy, E. 2003. Community Legacy Final Application. Hyattsville, MD: City of Hyattsville. On-line at: (http://publicspaceforum.org/ hyattsvilleplan/process/ index.shtml).

Parsons-Brinckerhoff, Ehrenkrantz, Eckstut and Kuhn Architects and Bay Area Economics. 2003. West Hyattsville Transit-Oriented Development (TOD) Program and Alternative Concepts Plan. Upper Marlboro, MD: Maryland National Capital Park and Planning Commission of Prince George's County.

U.S. Bureau of the Census. 2000. (http://www.census.gov/census2000/. html).

MATZU PARTICIPATORY DESIGN STUDIO
How Does the Outside Professional Gain Understanding of the Inside Story in the Local Community?

John K-C. Liu, Hsing-rong Liu and Shenglin Chang

ABSTRACT

Matzu Islands, named after the goddess Matzu, are a minor archipelago of 19 islands and islets in the Taiwan Strait administered as Matzu County by Taiwan government. In 2003, the nine-thousand permanent residents mostly reside in the five major islands: Peikan, Nankan, Tungyin, Tungchuan, and Sichuan. Due to the geographical location, 8 miles off the coast of mainland China in Taiwan Strait, Matzu Islands, as well as Chinmen Islands, had been known as the most important military sites for Taiwanese troops who carried on the Chiang Kai-shek's impossible mission of re-conquest of Mainland China after the 1949 Chinese Civil War. During the Cold War years, soldier and military related outsiders contributed to large numbers of temporary population that fostered a versatile local economy for Matzu Islands. In the late 1990s, the hostile relationship between China and Taiwan gradually transformed into a business-first attitude, because many Taiwanese business owners have transplanted their companies, shops, and factories to China since the late 1980s. In the dawn of the 21st Century, the Taiwanese government withdrew the majority of the troops in Matzu Islands, and initiated the so-called "small three links," that allow trade, mail and people to cross the small stretch of water between Taiwan's Chinmen and Matzu counties and China's Fujian Province. This friendly action between the China and Taiwan governments has dramatically impacted Matzu Islands' military-based economy. Large numbers of troop outsiders departed from Matzu Islands, while many secret military sites were left abandoned. The total population, therefore, dropped noticeably from 17,088 in 1971, to 8,773 in 2003. Under this circumstance, in 2002, the Matzu County government sought outside expertise to transform its local economy from military based one into an eco-tourism one. In this paper we will use the case of Matzu in Taiwan to illustrate some of the issues that we are concerned with. In the case of Matzu, we have continued to refine our participatory approach to planning in response to some of the questions raised above. Many of the complications, contradictions, and dilemmas in cross-cultural communication and cross-boundary planning are apparent in tourism planning. In this paper we focus on three general questions to be answered, hopefully to generate a discussion and cross analysis with other similar case studies. We re-state these questions:

1) How do we understand the problems that people face when they have to deal with unfamiliar and foreign environments?

2) How do we set goals and objectives when we help people face the above problems?

3) How do we engage people (participation) in making plans and designs for future environments that will help to resolve problems that people face?

> *The task of the humanist is not just to occupy a position or place, nor simply to belong somewhere, but rather to be both insider and outsider to the circulating ideas and values that are at issue in our society or the society of the other. –Said, 2004, 76*

BACKGROUND

In the Fall of 2003, the Ministry of Education in Taiwan commissioned the Graduate Institute of Building and Planning at the National Taiwan University (NTU) to conduct a research project aimed at reforming the existing design studio curriculum at professional schools of design in Taiwan. This research effort is a part of a larger project to understand the nature and substance of "Creative Learning." Thus, within the general scope of Creative Learning, we identified two main issues of "creativity" and "participation." With these two issues in mind, we solicited four other schools of design besides NTU to collaborate on this research. They are Tamkang University, Chung Yuan University, Hua-fang University, and Shi-jien University.

A professor at each university conducted a studio course within the standard design curriculum. Students ranged from first-year undergraduates to first and second year graduates. They included students within the mainstream professional design majors of planning, architecture, landscape architecture and interior design. But they also included students from other disciplines, mainly at NTU, such as sociology, history, geography, etc.

The physical context for this design exercise is set in Matzu, which consists of five small islands off the China Mainland near the city of Fuzhou. Each team from the five schools is assigned to one of the five islands, and a town or a village is selected as the site for conducting the participatory design. The studios took place during the Spring semester of 2004.

To date, the teams have completed the work for the year and have separately prepared final reports. A final dialogue and exchange of experiences have been conducted with the aim of extracting common features in dealing with the issues of "creativity" and "participation," as well as identifying differences and divergent views about methods and processes. A review and evaluation of this project is being prepared for the Ministry of Education separately and apart from this discussion.

In this paper, we focus exclusively on the work of the NTU studio that involved six graduate students on the island of Dong-ju. For the writing of this paper, we rely heavily on students' records and notes as basic information on what actually took place. The instructors of the course, John K.C. Liu and Hsing-rong Liu, while knowledgeable and with previous working experience on this island, only participated one time each on site with the students. The third author of this piece, Shenglin Chang, visited the island during the summer of 2003, and is sensitive to the environmental and social issues on the island. In part two she provides an independent review view of the issues that we tried to deal with.

The Working Group

The core of the outside professional group, in this case, is the six-member student team. Their status and respective background disciplines are as follows:

• Li Yen-ru, female, 2nd year grad, geography
• Wang Chi-fang, female, 1st year grad, landscape architecture
• Huang Chun-hui, female, 1st year grad, architecture
• Deng Jia-ling, female, 2nd year grad, sociology
• Zuo Xiang-ju, male, 2nd year grad, civil engineering
• Xu Wen-juan, female, 1st year grad, history/journalism

When they first signed up for the studio class, their understanding of the course was primarily on using a real community context to study how to conduct a participatory design process. Their understanding of what is participatory design was based on some previous experience and on limited knowledge regarding community design and participation received through reading and lectures.

Besides the six students, there are several other students from the third year class who had worked on the island on another project last summer. They were interested enough to continue their involvement in this project serving as friendly and helpful elder students who would provide necessary assistance and introduction to the community.

In order for the group to work as a team, several sessions were conducted to introduce the team to the environment, the community, the design task, as well as possible methods of working together. The students were made to be aware that they have to share and work together based on each person's professional strengths, and to help cover each other's weaknesses. They further understood that, once in the community, they had to develop ways and means of involving the community residents in not only providing information, but also in the actual participation of the planning and design work.

The Assignment

There are three steps to the assignment as given to the students:

Step 1: Together with the residents of the island, develop a description of the local distinctiveness of place. This is phrased in terms such as unique qualities, specificity, special features, etc. The distinctiveness may be related to space, but it may also involve qualities that are non-physical. But we aim to focus on those qualities that come about as the result of people-environment interaction. Going into the community, the outside group had to figure out a way to involve the local residents in identifying these qualities.

Step 2: Determine, again with the input of the community, what is of real concern to the community, whether it's a problem waiting to be resolved, or a collective aspiration to do something in the community. Again, we leave the question open-ended as to whether it is a space problem or not, as long as it is an authentic/real problem that exists in the community.

Step 3: Develop a method for involving the residents in actually participating in finding the most appropriate answer to the problem as identified. And then carry it out. The result should be a plan, a design, or an actual action, which originates in the distinctive qualities of the place, extends to an understanding of a real problem, and then is resolved by a participatory design process.

The group then proceeded to outline a 16-week work plan in accordance with the above assignment.

THE COMMUNITY

Unlike the two main islands, (north) Bei-gan and (south) Nan-gan, which have more people, more villages, and more commerce, and unlike Dong-yin further to the north with its own connection to the mainland, the two islands of (east) Dong-ju and (west) Xi-ju are the most remote and least accessible of the islands in Matzu. As such, people here are even more placid and resigned, accepting whatever changes that might occur and going about their daily routines, making necessary adjustments without fanfare.

Thus, when the soldiers began to leave a few years ago, with the receding cold war between Taiwan and Mainland China, the local population began to dwindle as well since a large part of the local economy is based on serving the needs of the military.

Thirty years ago, there were several thousand residents and over ten thousand soldiers. But today, there are just a few hundred people left and less than two thousand soldiers. During the past several decades, peoples' livelihoods have already changed from harvesting one of the richest fishing grounds on the East Asia coast to that of providing services to the soldiers stationed on these islands after World War II. For the residents of Matzu, fishing is associated with their parents and grandparents, with stories told and history recorded. What took their place were barbershops and laundry stores, public bathhouses and video game parlors, grocery stores and Internet cafes.

At the height of military build-up, soldiers outnumbered local residents by ten to one. Business was thriving, and the work was much easier with greater economic return. During this period, real wealth was accumulated reflected in one of the highest personal savings rates in Taiwan, in a high real-estate ownership rate, and in the large percentage of young people now living in Taiwan.

With the rapid decline of military personnel, however, people must contemplate the future. True, some have already packed up and followed their young and their real-estate holdings to Taiwan or to the Mainland, but many have remained. Even with just a few soldiers lingering around, video-game parlors and barbershops are still in business. Particularly on the island of Dong-ju, the pace remains steady and calm, unhurried and somewhat oblivious. Old people continue to chat their hot afternoon away on favorite breezy spots, while a few kids still endlessly run around the alley ways with gusto. Underneath, people are asking the inevitable questions: stay or not stay, Taiwan or Mainland, country or city. Of course these questions seem perennial not only to Matzu, but to Taiwan as a whole. Yet, here on the remotest of these remote islands, such concerns reflect a brewing anxiety about one's essential connection to place. And it may be here that we as outsiders can best grasp the meaning of local distinctiveness through the resolution of this anxious contemplation of the future.

The Environment as Setting

Dong-ju is a small island, about 2 1/2 km long and 1 1/2 km wide. Similar to the other islands of Matzu, Dong-ju is a rocky outcropping among the many islands that dot the East China Sea close to the coast of the Mainland. There is scarce vegetation on the rocky surface, and it was not until the soldiers came fifty years ago that wind-breaker trees were planted to provide a green cover to the barren hills. Because of the rocky formation of the islands, there are many small coves which give dramatic views along the coast. The island of Dong-ju is the southern most of the Matzu islands. It is less steep than the other islands and has a gentle valley in the middle. Partly because of this land formation, a village settlement called Da-

ping, formed in the valley next to a gradually sloping valley which became the farming plots for the village residents. This form of settlement is unique among the islands as all other villages are fishing settlements along a cove on the coast.

Da-ping plays a very crucial role in defining the character of Dong-ju island. There are two other villages on Dong-ju, one is the northern village of Fu-jeng which sits facing a crescent tidal beach rich in varieties of shell fish, and the other is a now abandoned fishing and trading village of Da-pu on the south shore. Da-pu, being one of the closest fishing ports to the Mainland, served also as a trading port for various merchandise such as tea and herbs. The village of austere stone houses sits on a high bluff overlooking the steep and narrow cove below. It is facing south so that it is protected from the cold winter winds from the north, but catches the summer breezes from the south. Because of their respective characteristics in relationship to the landscape, both Fu-cheng and Da-pu have been designated as historic settlements by the local government.

A special feature of the man-made landscape is a British built lighthouse at the northern tip of the island overlooking the village of Fu-jeng. It was built over a hundred years ago by the British to direct the fleets of ships going in and out of the Port of Fuzhou which was one of the treaty ports during the late Ching Dynasty. A large portion of the Chinese tea bound for Britain during this period came through this sea route by Dong-ju Island. The lighthouse is now a major tourist attraction.

Aside from these features, what is equally significant, but less visible, are the military constructions on the island in the form of tunnels dug deep into the rocky cliffs forming a network of underground circulation systems, dramatic unto itself, but otherwise non-visible. Much of this military installation is now abandoned awaiting a new discovery of its use and significance.

THE FIRST STEP: HOW TO UNDERSTAND DONG-JU

The students set a goal of trying to understand Dong-ju as the first task in answering the question of local distinctiveness. In order to know Dong-ju, both from the point of view of the outsider and from the local residents' point of view, it was agreed that a way of combining the role of participant observer with in-depth interviews would be the most appropriate way of gaining access to the residents. The first night in the community, we held a get together to meet the residents. The six students introduced our intent and then individually paired up with members of the community. For the next several days, each student became a shadow to a resident. For example, Xiang-ju, the only male student who is tall, longhaired and somewhat shy, was paired with an elder woman in her fifties. He helped her with her daily chores, and along the way they talked. In answering his questions, she would take him to places that are special to her, such as a spot where she goes to pick wild green onion. By staying close to her for a period of time, he began to see the place through her eyes and her feelings. These are noted down and the six students discussed and consolidated their findings.

Initially, this method of trying to understand place from the view of the residents resulted in the identification of several space-related characteristics. These are briefly: 1) A newly paved road that led from Da-ping to Fu-jeng which is unpleasant as a walking experience so that people prefer to drive. 2) A covered alleyway where it is shady, cool and breezy with a view in all directions. It is a very good place to gather and have conversations in the afternoon with neighbors. 3) In front of the tofu shop where there is a large flat surface with a long view, a good place for people to gather in the evening. 4) The vegetable garden which is a tiered area with small plots for people to grow their own vegetables. From the main road in the village that curves around the garden, people can see each other coming and going. 5) The tides that change everyday which determines the daily routines and living patterns of the island residents. People are profoundly affected by the daily and seasonal changes in the tide actions. 6) People have a habit of strolling with the whole family in the evening after supper from the village of Da-ping along the main road that bends around the vegetable garden and then down to the pier where boats to the other islands are docked. This road is the favorite of the residents.

From these spatial characteristics, an attempt is then made to identify the "specialness" or "uniqueness" of Dong-ju by making individual mental maps. These maps try to record and relate all information gathered through the participant observations and the in-depth interviews. With these, the students held intensive sessions to discuss all of these maps again consolidating them into identifiable spatial characteristics. This time the list grew to twenty-four items with more specific details. The students further grouped these into categories including those dealing with the island as a whole, such as this island is friendlier and more conducive to walking, community information is passed on mostly by face-to-face contact, etc. Other categories include the ecology and geography of the island, military space, landform and man-made form, such as stepped pathways throughout the village, the different types of employment on the island, and what do people do for recreation on the island.

After several rounds of working on the spatial characteristics, the group became aware not only of the spatial attributes, but also the degree to which one knows and understands a space may be quite different from others. Thus in order to construct a collective mental map of the island, one has to begin to fully engage the other so as to reach a common view. Based on this, the second time the group went into the community, they attempted to construct a collective mental map working with

the kids in the village. In the main covered plaza at Da-ping, kids participated in making a large joint map showing their conception of the island as a place.

What was learned from this exercise?

1. Distinctiveness of place is not necessarily spatial. Some unique characteristics may be just interpersonal relationships such as the passing of information. But quite often, specialness and uniqueness do have spatial boundaries.

2. Constructing a collective mental map of distinctiveness tends to focus more on what people have in agreement rather than differences. Differences and varying perspectives are harder to deal with than agreements. Thus, a mental map shows only the common views and not the differences. Then there is a question regarding whether "specialness" is the same as "uniqueness." The uniqueness of place may not be the same as what is special about a place. What's special has more to do with the individual. What's unique is more related to how it is compared to other places. When we seek local distinctiveness, we look for what is special about place to a group of people, the local residents. The outsider may tend to focus on uniqueness, but the resident may be more concerned about specialness.

3. Besides using mental maps, there may be other ways to present specialness. Often, mental maps which show unique characteristics become tourist guide maps which identify points of interests to the tourist, but which may have little meaning to the local residents. Again, how the residents view a place and how the outsiders view the place may be quite different.

4. Due to the limitations of mental maps, some interesting and potential important observations are lost. This is perhaps due to the method of drawing mental maps which tends to focus on the easily identifiable parts and avoids those that do not necessarily have a clear spatial dimension, such as recycling and disposal of waste materials.

5. By working only with kids on constructing the collective mental map, the focus shifted to young people's perspectives. This is a departure from the initial entry into the community when each shadowed one resident for a length of time. The mental map did not account for the previous results. For example, how people feel about the two roads, one from Da-ping to Fu-jeng, and the other from Da-ping down to the pier, does not show up in the mental map. This important understanding is lost.

THE SECOND STEP: SEEKING AN AUTHENTIC/REAL PROBLEM

Having gone through an effort to understand the distinctiveness of Dong-ju, the idea is that the outsider begins to understand the place through the eyes of the local residents, or at least the distance between the outsider and the local is shortened, and thereby we may be more able to see what kind of problems exist in the community that need resolution. Too often, outside professionals go into a community and assume a certain problem is waiting for an answer. For planners and designers, we commonly assume the problem is a space-related one, for example, a building, a park, a garden, a plaza, etc. In this case, as mentioned earlier, the effort to uncover local distinctiveness focused largely on space-related issues even though some were not necessarily space related. For the students from different backgrounds, this was continually a cause for concern, whether space is the basis or whether the issue is the basis.

Thus when the group began the second step of trying to identify a problem, this concern became paramount. What the students felt, based on the previous step, is that while it may be possible to work with the residents in identifying important local distinctiveness, they could not determine any immediate space-related problem that needed to be dealt with. Yet, on the other hand, there was a sense of pending crisis brewing underneath the surface. This potential crisis is an economic one related to the rapidly declining numbers of soldiers on the island. What will the people do when all the soldiers leave. Will they also abandon this island or is there a possible new life for the island in attracting tourists and visitors. Some of the local leaders including teachers who have long been concerned with thinking about the future see this crisis as one of complacency among the residents towards the future. They do not have a vision for the future and do not care to think about collective and public issues regarding the future of the island.

Based on this understanding, the team sought to identify issues that are clearly related to the future and that which would activate the residents in participating. In the next visit to the community, four main issues grew out of an intensive round of interaction with the residents.

Issue 1

The recovery of an old pathway from Da-ping to Da-pu, a distance of perhaps 500 m, is considered an opportunity to both reconstruct the history of the island as well as to provide substance and interest for educational and eco-tourism for the future. This path had been abandoned and overgrown due to the construction of a new road a generation ago, so that young people have no knowledge of it and old people sometimes block their memories due to hardships suffered in the old times. Revealing the pathway by a community work project to clear the overgrown vegetation, the act attracted the interest of the community in different ways. Children and young people were positively attracted to it while some old people joined in. Others, however, remained aloof and detached, watching with curiosity but not joining in the work. As a concrete event that took place,

and as an issue dealing with how people might see the future of this island, the recovery of the old pathway clearly could serve as a focus to initiate and activate participation. Whether the action is directed towards the repair and reconstruction of the pathway, or whether it might be an oral history project with the older people, or whether it involves a study of the native plants along the path, these are all possibilities to generate some thinking about the future.

Issue 2

In the village of Fu-jeng, located towards the upper part below the lighthouse is an old abandoned house that was once a private school in the village. Many residents remember with fondness the time when it was a school. Having been a school and now being vacant, there is history and memory associated with the structure. People in the community have talked about renovating the house and giving it a new use, such as a history museum, a center for the study of marine biology focused on the abundant shell life on the cove below, and another kind of school such as a study camp or a site for holding workshops and training sessions. However, these ideas tend to remain what the public or the government can do with this structure, rather than what the community can do to create a use. While its historic meaning seems apparent, people's enthusiasm towards this issue remains questionable.

Issue 3

During the month of March and April, an unexpected discovery of a type of fire-worm caused substantial interest on the island. Due to the clearing of a plot of land beside the main walking section of the road leading from Da-ping to the pier, many people came into contact with the lovable worm that glowed in the dark. Partly because this stretch of the road is well populated by village residents and their families, especially at dusk when the sun is setting, and as people return from their walk to the pier, they would stop and marvel at these glowing worms. As an environmental protection issue, there is strong interest among the teachers to do something. As a focus of interest for the village residents, this issue seems to be able to attract all age groups. However, there is a question whether there is enough ecological basis for pushing this issue ahead.

Issue 4

The vegetable garden next to Da-ping is of concern to many, including the elected local representative. Right now each plot is owned by individuals and cultivated without much coordination. Even though there is shared water, there is not an overall plan for treating waste and dealing with organic materials. There is also the question of fertilizer. Should they be working out a plan to develop organic gardening? Furthermore, should they be thinking about how to package their produce for the consumption of visitors and tourists? Related to the garden are many potentially complicated issues which include ownership of the plots which may not be easily resolved. While many regard this as a real problem, in the short term, there do not seem to be enough resources to deal with it.

Several rounds of discussions later, and after actually participating in the clearing of the old pathway, the team still arrived at the decision to pursue the glow-worm issue as the most legitimate and most real of the problems. Three specific reasons were given for having made this decision. First, this phenomenon of the glow-worm has become an important aspect of daily life in the village. It is intimately connected to after-dinner strolls, to watching the sunset, and is a topic of interest for all age groups. Second, this glow-worm clearly has ecological and biological significance as a special species on this island. Its potential as an eco-education subject is obvious. Third, there is some danger right now of the grounds being disturbed, and the surrounding areas becoming a dump site for used construction materials such as large chunks of concrete with exposed reinforcing steel bars sticking out. The environment for the proper appreciation of the glow-worms needs to be planned. The team proceeded to implement a plan to deal with this issue.

STEP 3: THE PARTICIPATORY ACTION

1. To get people interested, a large cardboard model was made of the site including the road. This was placed in the middle of the outdoor plaza so that all could see it. The team continued to work on the model while getting people to come and discuss how best to deal with site. This was successful in attracting people especially the school children who got involved in making the model.

2. Gathering opinions regarding the site was not as successful as hoped. There was the problem of how to display an opinion on the model. There was also a problem when people forgot what they had said the day before, thus causing confusion over what is the actual opinion expressed. Furthermore, because the presence of the glow-worm is seasonal, only during the months of March to May, when they are no longer present, it was hard to get people to discuss it.

3. Since differing opinions could not be consolidated, it was difficult to advance collective decisions regarding the specific plan.

4. In terms of on-site construction, the effort to clear away the debris and prepare the site was rewarding with over ten people sharing in the labor of removing the concrete and steel bars from the site. That night, what was done to the site during the day was remade on the model so that people could see the changes that were taking place.

5. Following this, there was a task to find local materials that could be used to create a gathering place on the site. This

included stone, wood, plants, and other used material such as wooden cable spools. School children helped to plant flowers along the path. But due to the slow progress in involving the residents, this part of the implementation was terminated until further consolidation.

REVIEW: HOW CAN TEAM LEARNING BE AS CREATIVE AS COMMUNITY PARTICIPATION?

The purpose of the Dong-ju project is to challenge the traditional studio teaching and learning environments, and provide the substance of "creative learning" experiences for students who are taking community service learning studios. As is defined in the beginning of the paper, "creative learning" refers to "creativity" and "participation."

How can a group of students have creative learning experiences within a community studio that handles a real project? Meanwhile, these students are not only outsiders of a community, but also learning the skills of planning, design, and engaging this community within a short period of time, i.e., a semester. This question underlines my review of the Dong-ju project. My review is based on the six final essays submitted by the National Taiwan University's students (NTU students) at the Graduate Institute of Building and Planning (Deng, 2004; Huang, 200; Li, 2004; Wang, 200; Xu, 2004; and Zou, 2004). The student essays reflected on their personal journeys on Dong-ju Island. They analyzed the steps they went through to understand the villagers and the island, examined the ways of their decision making, and investigated the processes that they initiated to engage the villagers' participation. Their essays answered the three questions posted in the beginning of the paper; how to understand the problems, how to set the goals, and how to engage people from individual students' views and voices. The reflections of each essay not only echoed the work that each student engaged in and the people they encountered during the semester long process, but also the background and the training (i.e., journalism, history, architecture, landscape architecture, sociology, geography etc.) embodied even before they entered the NTU's Building and Planning institute.

As an outsider of the Dong-ju project and a quasi-insider who graduated from the institute and has maintained a decade-long relationship with the group, my review intertwines my personal learning, teaching, and practicing experiences across Taiwan, California, and Maryland in the US. I would like to address my concerns from two viewpoints: 1) professional process: how students learn community participatory design and planning as a professional field, and 2) team-learning process: how students engage each other as professionals within community design process - listen to individual voices as well as make group decisions together. From my reading of the students' final essays, I conclude that there is a gap between how professionals engage the community and how professionals engage each other. I realize that the NTU students applied many creative methods within the three-step process; understanding the people and the place, setting goals, and engaging the community. They, however, confronted the challenge of how to engage their teammates in a less smooth and collaborative way within their internal studio process. Therefore, the question that concerned me the most is: how team learning can be as creative as community participation. With this question in mind, I want to address community design as a professional process first, and then return to the students' team-learning process.

1) Professional processes: how students learn community participatory design and planning as a professional field

Instead of introducing themselves as design professionals, the NTU students chose their role as anthropological researchers and friends of the Dong-ju Islanders. They went through different steps that have been listed earlier in this paper. They addressed the "shadows of residents," "children's collective mental maps," and daily event participations, as the most powerful structures to understand the place and the people from diverse views. These three methods facilitate students to reveal residents' way of life and view of the place within the residents' daily path. It more likely creates a documentary than a thematic film. Students document all the events, chats, and conversations randomly taking place when they interact with their resident-partners, children, and villagers. Information flowed with multiple layers of meanings; contradictory rather than cohesive. Confronting the confusion of their field data and the pressure of time, students were aware of the somehow "immature" judgments that they had to make for the uncertain future of Dong-ju Island. They questioned their role as outsider professionals and self-criticized the legitimacy of making these decisions for/with the Dong-ju Islanders.

The anthropological approaches that the NTU students took are very different than the positivistic methods that have been widely applied in community planning and design processes in the United States. In the US, the common ways of conducting community-based projects are based on quantitative surveys and the opinions that people express during community workshops and public hearings. Within the culture of the western democracy, the minority has to follow the majority. Therefore, numbers and percentages are critical for community decision making processes. Community professionals need to know how many percentages of people agree with certain issues in order to move the project forward. There are strengths and weaknesses of these positivistic methods, but in this section, I prefer to focus on the opportunities and challenges that the anthropological methods open up for the community design and planning profession.

In general, students declared that the anthropological methods help them understand local villagers and Dong-ju Island at a much more in-depth level than other methods might offer. For example, in Wen-juan's essay, she reported that education and health were the critical issues that concerned local residents the most, but these issues were outside the scope of the project (Xu, 2004). While the anthropological methods open up a window for students to understand local villagers ways of life, it strikes me that many students were disturbed by how to neutrally conduct their field data and objectively analyze it. Chun-hui's essay is one example. She asked, "When professionals have their own values and identities which conflict with those of local residents, how can we consider the issues with a neutral stand?" "When professionals interact with local residents, can we honestly express our feelings?" (Huang, 2004). Among all, Yen-ru suggested that, instead of believing professionals can be neutral and objective, "we should initiate the concept of inter-subjectivity" (Li, 2004). Yen-ru feels that the professionals should consider the distinctive quality of Dong-ju Island from both professionals' and local residents' points of view.

Students' responses indicate the crucial issue of how to make decisions for researchers and professionals who apply qualitative methods in their research and professional projects. While numbers are the basis for making judgments within quantitative methods, consensus building is the foundation for decision making within qualitative approaches. In the Dong-ju project, students met, discussed, and negotiated to make decisions. I would like to address this issue as my second point: team learning processes.

2) Team-learning processes: how students engage each other as a professional community within their community design processes, listen to individual voices, and make group decisions together.

Although team learning and building consensus are the critical mechanisms for the NTU team to analyze their field data and determine the future directions for Donj-ju Island, every studio educator knows that there are always problems and crisis projects based on teamwork. Among the NTU students, five out of six were unsatisfied with their group meetings and decision-making, because it seemed to be difficult for their team to build consensus. Jia-ling opened her report with the comment: "We were rather emotional than rational" (Deng, 2004). Yen-ru described the team as, "not many team members, but many problems." She highlighted, "difficult to express opinions; difficult to build consensus" (Lee, 2004). Chi-fan presented similar experiences and suggested that "Maybe we need someone who is more objective and more competent than us to participate in our discussion" (Wang, 2004)

These remarks sound so familiar, somehow like a flash back to me. As I recalled my own experience of taking community studios at the same institute as Chi-fan, Yen-ru, and others dating back to the late 1980s, everyone in my team was often yelling and screaming at each other in our never-ending discussions. In most cases, my teams were falling apart and some teammates never showed up for the conclusion of the semester's teamwork. At that time, I also hoped that we had someone who was more skilled and talented than us to help build consensus. However, bringing in an outside authority is not always the solution, because we still do not learn how to handle our internal dynamics, listen to each others' voices, and integrate our diverse ideas.

From an educator's point of view, how to handle individual team members' personalities, personal values, professional disciplines and group dynamics has, indeed, profoundly impacted students' learning experiences. From a practitioner's experiences, these issues also interfere with the quality of the decisions that the professional team makes for the community that they work with. It is critical to cultivate innovative ways that respect team members' individuality but engage everyone together.

In Dong-ju's case, I suggested that the NTU students apply some important methods they practice with the community, within themselves. These methods might open up new windows for them to perceive each others' view points and help them to listen to each other. For example, maybe, they can be each other's shadow for a weekend and then role-play their counter part when they meet for group discussion next week. In addition to residents' cognitive maps, they can also spend some time doing similar exercises within their team. They can talk about their favorite spots on the island and how these places relate to their environmental autobiography. They can even share their personal values and attachments on the island with Dong-ju villagers. By doing so, the Dong-ju residents can understand the outside professionals' stories and view points of the island. This would facilitate the inter-subjective relationships between the local residents and the outside professionals.

To sum up, it is striking to realize that community professionals, as outsiders of a community, have developed innovative ways to understand and engage the community that they are working with. However, this group of professionals, as insiders of their team, have not found a way to understand and engage themselves within their own teamwork. The NTU students' final essays make me aware that, in most community studio environments, collaborative team learning experiences are not given and can be a struggle. It takes tremendous efforts, from both instructors and students, to nurture a culture of collaboration. It is a challenge and an opportunity.

REFERENCES

Deng, Jia-lin. 2004. Deng Jia-lin's Class Report for Dong-ju Studio. Taipei: Graduate Institute of Building and Planning, National Taiwan University.

Huang, Chun-hui. 2004. Huang Chun-hui's Class Report for Dong-ju Studio. Taipei: Graduate Institute of Building and Planning, National Taiwan University.

Li, Yen-ru. 2004. Li Yen-ru's Class Report for Dong-ju Studio. Taipei: Graduate Institute of Building and Planning, National Taiwan University.

Said, Edward W. 2004. Humanism and Democratic Criticism New York: Columbia U. Press

Wang, Chi-fang. 2004. Wang Chi-fang's Class Report for Dong-ju Studio. Taipei: Graduate Institute of Building and Planning, National Taiwan University.

Xu, Wen-juan. 2004. Xu Wen-juan's Class Report for Dong-ju Studio. Taipei: Graduate Institute of Building and Planning, National Taiwan University.

Li, Yen-ru, et.al. 2004. Dong-Ju: An Educational Seed Program in Architectural Design Creativity. A project funded by the Ministry of Education, Taiwan, Graduate Institute of Building and Planning, National Taiwan University (Unpublished report).

Zuo, Xiang-ju. 2004. Zuo Xiang-ju's Class Report for Dong-ju Studio. Taipei: Graduate Institute of Building and Planning, National Taiwan University.

TOWARD HERITAGE 100 YEARS FROM NOW
An Experience of Forest Management Based on the Partnership Between Government, Local Community and Tourists

Takayoshi Yamamura, Tianxin Zhang and Aijun He

ABSTRACT

The ecosystem in the upper reaches of the Yangzi river basin in Yunnan Province, China (Lijiang area) is suffering a striking decline. With this case as an example, this paper will examine how the partnership between the government, local community and tourists can be developed toward the goal of sustainable forest management, and furthermore, the establishment of a local based global community. These findings are based on the spot inspection carried out by an NGO organized by the authors.

INTRODUCTION

In recent years, there has been a great deal of afforestation activities in China. The primary background to these activities has been the formal launch of "Forest Ecology Programs" such as the "Mountain Afforestation Program" among others, which have been treated as state projects. At present, international cooperation between private NGO groups, tourists from foreign countries, local administrative organizations and inhabitants has been making progress in various areas across China to achieve the goal. However, cooperative enterprises undertaken by such domestic and foreign participants have been largely limited to instances of transient events. The formation of long term collaborations and equal partnerships by a wide range of participants aimed at achieving sustainable forest management is as yet inadequate.

This paper, taking account of the background described above, presents the afforestation activities of "IEGC (Organization for International Exchange of Green-Culture, University of Tokyo, Japan)," an NGO that was established mainly by young researchers and students. This paper attempts to understand the benefits and problems of afforestation endeavors, including tourism, and look into the potential of the formation of a "forest community" through a tripartite collaboration comprising the local administration, local inhabitants, and tourists (offshore residents).

THE ESTABLISHMENT OF IEGC AND ITS PHILOSOPHY

Issues of Forest Management in China and the Establishment of IEGC

Forests play important roles in ecological, economic, and social aspects (Davis et al., 2001). In the past years, assessments of the value of forests have been mostly one-sided-emphasizing their economic value. This results in the overcutting of forests, and therefore resulted in floods and other disasters. This has further led to the frequent occurrence of a wide range of related cultural problems, including great difficulties in the restoration of wooden cultural assets in the cultural heritage areas. Consequently, the nation has come to focus on the public interest functions of forests. In other words, expectations are rising regarding the environmental, social and cultural benefits of forests. The focus on forests is shifting from regarding them as a source of logs to regarding them as a resource stock or even as common social capital (Uzawa, 2000). They are recognized as the foundations for water/soil maintenance and environmental amelioration systems, the foundations to carry on the legacy of wooden cultural assets in a sustainable manner, as recreational resources and tourist targets.

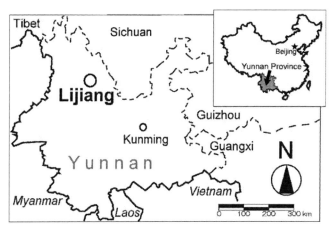

Figure 1. Area Subject to NGO Activities. (Source: map courtesy of Takayoshi Yamamura)

In contrast, very little consideration has been given to the concrete roles of the local inhabitants and tourists concerning forest management. This is so in China partly due to the fact that most policies are carried out in a top-down manner. In order to carry out the appropriate management of natural resources and restore the deteriorating ecological environment in certain areas, there is a need for proper administrative guidance. At the same time local inhabitants and tourists must have a deep understanding of forest management as well as actively and voluntarily participate in it. In the case of areas that do not have such a partnership, there are high expectations for the role of NGOs as "third sector organizations" (Korten,1990), which lead toward the development of a framework of sustainable forest

Figure 2. Traditional wooden buildings have restoration difficulties due to the lack of wood. (Photo: Takayoshi Yamamura)

management based on collaborative management between local administration, local inhabitants, and tourists.

The IEGC, which was established on March 12, 1999, was founded by graduate students of the Graduate School of Tokyo University (including visiting students from China and Japanese students, all in their thirties or younger) who shared a common recognition of such issues. The objectives of IEGC are the "regional development through afforestation activity" and "international interchange between different cultures." The initial members of IEGC decided to focus its main activities on a farm village on the outskirts of Lijiang in Yunnan Province. As of April 2004, the IEGC was only a small student circle with a membership of no more than thirty; however, having received subsidies from Japanese foundations since 1999, the IEGC goes onsite every year in a group of 10-20 people, including foreign tourists in addition to group members, in order to carry out afforestation activities called "Green Hope Project And Environmental Education Undertaking." In addition, the young researchers and graduate students who are the regular IEGC members have made the IEGC a place of interdisciplinary research activities, because they come from a wide range of fields, including agriculture and the humanities, urban engineering, ecology, environmental education, and cultural anthropology. Furthermore, since the beginning of such activities, there has been frequent contact and adequate discussion with local administrative authorities and the local community. Excellent collaboration and partnership has been formed gradually by entrusting them in part with the preparation of afforestation locations, preparations for seeding, and some afforestation activities and the management tasks. In addition to tree-planting activities, there has been an ongoing accumulation of data and interviews, depending on the specialties of each member, information has been accumulated and personal networks built that contribute to the activities.

Approach to the "Participation" of Tourists

As Kant (1803) said, "human beings are the only creatures that cannot exist without education." In addition, "human beings can become human only through education." It is certainly true that the recognition of values is thought to deepen gradually only after passing through the process of education and learning.

In the Belgrade Charter (1975), the targets of environmental education are listed as Awareness, Knowledge, Attitude, Skills, Evaluation Ability, and Participation. In other words, this process, which is considered crucial, begins with interest and concern, followed by understanding and recognition skills, and the ability to make evaluations, and culminating in participation. The key words for the long-term outlook in Japan's environmental master plan also include "participation," in addition to "circulation," "symbiosis," and "international measures" (The International Environmental Education Program (IEEP, 1975).

In fact, it is thought that, before long, one will reach the stage of voluntary, energetic participation if one's recognition of the importance of values deepens, accompanied by actions to resolve environmental problems. In other words, the key targets of environmental education are to instill the proper recognition of the relationship between human beings and the environment and responsibility for one's own actions. Having achieved this, it is possible to create human resources that can participate proactively in the creation of a sustainable society.

The general idea of this "participation" is crucially important in connection with the two following points. The first is that the voluntary participation of the local inhabitants, is the driving force behind the management and development of the region. The second is the participation of others besides the local inhabitants (non-residents), which might include NGO members and tourists. The establishment of a cooperative framework of their participation is a crucial element in realizing the sustainable management of regional resources, and this is a point that has been underlined in recent years by UNESCO and other international organizations (ICCROM Mayors & Decision-Makers' Forum, 2003).

Outline of the Regions Targeted for Activities

In China, afforestation projects have been carried out with the objective of conserving the water and soil of the *Chang Jiang* (*Yangzi* River) catchment basin. A project to protect the forests of the middle and upper reaches of the *Chang Jiang* has been carried out since 1989, with the main objective of alleviating flooding and preventing the sedimentation of the *Sanxia* dam. However, a great flood with serious damage occurred in 1998. It has been pointed out that one of the causes of this flood was the reduction of the forests in the upper reaches of the *Chang Jiang*. In response to this flood, the Chinese government launched a number of projects in earnest, including a program to protect natural forests and the "Mountain Afforestation Program" (the conversion of existing farmlands on steep slopes into forests) (State Forestry Administration, P.R. China, 2001a:

107). Lijiang, which is the district in which IEGC's activities are carried out, belongs to the upper reaches of the *Chang Jiang*. In 1997, the Old Town of Lijiang was registered as a world cultural heritage with UNESCO in recognition of the cultural value of its clusters of traditional wooden buildings. Nonetheless, due to the lack of forested area, it has become impossible to restore and procure wood (Yunnan Pine: *Pinus yunnanensis*) for replacement works in the region. The present situation is that the majority of wood is imported from the neighboring country of Myanmar (Yamamura, 2002).

DESCRIPTION OF THE ACTIVITIES OF IEGC AND COOPERATIVE FRAMEWORK WITH THE REGION

The Setting of Activity Content and Description of Activities

In the Lijiang region, IEGC's activities are known under the title "Green Hope Project" (project to create forests through environmental education). IEGC is carrying out an afforestation project with the cooperation of the local administration, local inhabitants, and elementary and junior high schools. IEGC selected as its site the lands where cultivation has been abandoned, and the riverbeds of four townships (*Longpan, Daju, Shigu, Shitou*) along the *Chang Jiang* under the jurisdiction of the *Yulong Naxi* Autonomous County, Lijiang City of Yunnan Province. The objective of this project is to restore areas that have been devastated, recover the natural ecosystem, and to elevate the environmental awareness of the people by assigning this forest a role in environmental education.

Nonetheless, from the very beginning of the project it has been difficult for participants to gain an understanding regarding the various related targets. In order to eliminate difficulties in theoretical understanding, the initial activity targets were simply defined as "presenting the enjoyment of forest management to children and inhabitants." For this reason, edible fruit trees

Figure 3. Tourists (Japanese University Students) and local residents (Naxi Primary School Children) planting pear trees in agricultural wasteland. (Photo: T. Yamamura)

were chosen for the tree-plantings in the first period so that people would be able to see the concrete benefits of planting commercial trees within a short time. More specifically, chestnuts, pear trees, and walnut trees were chosen. These are regional fruit trees that the local inhabitants were familiar with. These trees produced concrete benefits leading to the short-term goal of bearing fruit within 3 to 4 years, which could be seen by children and participating tourists.

In the process, the tourists paying their own expenses, took part in annual ten-day afforestation tours sponsored by IEGC, in which they contributed their own labor. Besides IEGC members, since 1999, groups of around 20 tourists comprised largely of students and retirees have taken part annually in the tours, and the repeat rate is remarkably high. The repeat rate of university students is particularly high, and some of them are shifting from simply being transient tourists to becoming highly motivated members participating regularly in IEGC's activities.

Sources of Revenue

IEGC is a volunteer organization that basically does not have any activity fees or capital. The funds that are necessary for the afforestation activities are donated by annual grants (around 500,000-1,000,000 yen) from relevant foundations in Japan. Nonetheless, these grants just barely cover expenses for seedlings, expenses for on-site management of afforestation, and land preparation costs. The format used by both domestic and foreign participants (members of IEGC and tourists) who take part in the on-site work is completely voluntary (participants pay their own expenses). This kind of participation, at one's personal expense, has the advantages of instilling a deep understanding of the project in the participants and generating the desire to participate. On the other hand, the amount of funding that can be obtained annually is unstable, and there is the disadvantage that long-term plans of operation may not be set up because of a lack of a stable source of funding.

Benefits of Activities

From 1999 to the end of 2003, the total surface area of land planted with trees amounted to about 30 ha (300,000 sq. meters) in total. All of this land is owned by farmers or villages and was provided voluntarily by parties that approved of the activities of IEGC. After trees have been planted, the farmers, if the land is owned by farmers, or if the land is owned by villages, the village forestry stations, the young people's associations, and elementary and junior high-school students take care of the trees, including watering and fertilizing.

As can be seen from the above description, this project has resulted in the establishment of a cooperative framework consisting of the local administration, local inhabitants and tourists. Its characteristics can be summarized as below:

Figure 4. Local youth member and NGO member carry out a survey for an afforestation project. (Photo: T. Yamamura)

- IEGC, namely, interdisciplinary young researchers, plan their activities from the standpoint of their respective technical specialties while respecting the basic structure of the community, and tourists who approve of this participate in the program at their own expense.

- By securing the support and cooperation of the local administrative bodies, the local inhabitants have become aware that the activities of IEGC are "interdisciplinary, international NGO activities." Consequently, it has become possible for them to be accepted as tourists and members of an NGO by the local community.

Figure 5. Local and Japanese students celebrate after the afforestation activities. (Photo: T. Yamamura)

- Working in collaboration with the local inhabitants, the tourists carry out exactly the same tasks as the inhabitants. Besides such tasks, IEGC frequently arranges meetings with the local inhabitants for exchanging views. Such meetings encourage proper understanding of the local community and forest-related issues. In addition, interchange meetings are also arranged between students. The building of friendly, forward-looking relationships is paving the way for a high percentage of repeaters.

- The project itself has been gaining the support of local administration. The appearance of IEGC on the scene has enabled a format in which work is carried out on the initiative of the local inhabitants as much as possible. In doing so, IEGC listens to the opinions of the inhabitants as much as possible. Things are moving forward in reflection of this, while understanding between local administration

and the inhabitants is developing. Given this situation, a "from the-bottom-up-type project" is taking root, in which the driving force behind the work may be said to be the local inhabitants.

DISCUSSION

An interview survey was carried out on villagers (all adults) in the vicinity of the districts in which the project was conducted in order to understand the "receptivity of the region," which demonstrates an important indicator of the social aspects. The results are as follows: with respect to the "Green Hope Project and Environmental Education Undertaking," the evaluation of 44.6% of the respondents was "very good," 47.3% replied "good," and 1.4% replied "slightly good." In contrast, 6.7% replied, "I thought it was not good" or said they "cannot understand" (study executed in March 2003). In view of these results, it may be said that the local inhabitants have accepted the project and given it a high evaluation. In addition, most of the respondents expressed the following expectations to the role of the project: "land greenification," "resolution of conflict with neighborhood villages," and "environmental education." By seeing and understanding what IEGC and the tourists are doing in the locality, the inhabitants reflect on the formerly destructive development and begin to take interest in tree-planting activities in the familiar forests and rivers and to resuscitate nature. Moreover, this frame of mind having been generated, it may be said that there has been a notable relaxation of disputes between villages and the feelings of dislike formerly associated with forestland are declining.

When overseas participants (tourists) were asked for their impressions, most stated that, by participating in the project and coming into contact with the local history and culture and the lives of the local people, they had come to think about the optimal ways of safeguarding the environment of the earth in the 21st century, the future of international cooperation, and the education of the next generation (study executed in March 2003).

However, certain problems still remain. Here we will raise three topics. The first are the needs in terms of education. The people still cannot be said to have a symbiotic relationship with, nor friendly feelings toward the forest, and their awareness of the

Figure 6. Commemoration monument established by local authorities: NGO staff explain to local children. (Photo: T. Yamamura)

public interest function of the forest and the value of having biodiversity is still inadequate. Secondly, there is vagueness regarding the arrangement of land management. The arrangement of land ownership and usage is vague, especially with respect to land owned by villages. Tree managers are often not present after planting, and in some cases the trees just wither and die. Thirdly, community leadership is lacking. In the future, management of this afforestation project must be transferred from third person organizations like the IEGC to the local community, which is a vehicle for managing original regional resources. Certainly, it is desirable with respect to international cooperation and environmental education for third-person organizations like the IEGC and tourists to take interest regularly in the local community, which would need to manage afforestation over the long term. However, it should be made clear that the inhabitants are the ultimate vehicle for management and the capacity to value this should be instilled into the local inhabitants. It is desirable to build a framework that should be called "the forest community" in the interest of preserving and passing on sustainable regional resources, while the various actors play their respective roles in this way.

The major issue confronted by the activities of IEGC in the future will be to improve the three points covered above. Finding the beginnings of scientific and practicable resolutions to these issues may be suggested as the role to be carried out by the researchers who are the main members of IEGC.

CONCLUSION

This case study has suggested that one of the more effective techniques in permanently maintaining the stock in an area and the forest environment as a flow, is for local administration to take the leadership, with the local inhabitants and tourists participating in a collaborative manner. A variety of problems remain, including confrontations between opposing value systems and difficulties in forming agreements (Kuriyama, 1997). However, from the experiences of IEGC activities, it appears that there is adequate potential for the formation of a "forest community."

It is considered that the following three points are the key to success in the activities of this NGO, and with these characteristics, a partnership continues to be developed between the local government, stakeholders and the local community who form the basis of the forest's administration.

1) Interdisciplinary Research: This NGO was established based on the research know-how contributed by young researchers participating from a variety of fields. All the members are in their thirties or below, and not adhering simply to already existing study fields, makes it possible for them to progress into an interdisciplinary discussion. This factor contributes largely to (2) education.

2) Education: The aim of these afforestation activities is based on the development of an "environment education forest" for children, allowing primary and junior high school pupils in the area to actually take part in the planting work. In this way, the organization succeeds in gathering the attentions of a broad range of people beginning with the parents of the children, teachers and scholars, a comparatively high level of educated society, and domestic and international tourists. Thus, this is linked to the dissemination and enlightenment regarding the importance of forest management.

3) Strategy: Having received the offer from the local government of an abandoned cultivation area within the village, that area became the target of afforestation. In this way, the inhabitants can actually see the effects of plantation. Furthermore, the species of trees planted in the beginning are fruit trees, which have traditionally been used by the local inhabitants for food. This fact links to the creation of a concrete sense of purpose in which some years later, the trees can be harvested for food, thus, in the minds of the tourists and inhabitants, triggering a positive consciousness for the revisit to the forest and the management of it.

In any case, there is a need for environmental planning based on universal theory and scientific foundations, in order to ensure better development of the regional whole. It is the duty of universities, the higher education system, and researchers to spotlight this need. Similarly, it is the role of NGOs, as third person organizations, to be intermediaries between local inhabitants and local administration, providing coordination for theories and plans. The role of tourists who have become repeaters is to make regular visits to the locality while living elsewhere and to provide labor, new information, and other support. The role carried out by the tourists also deserves attention as regards making the inhabitants discover new value systems.

This case study is still in progress. It has experienced a series of trials, errors and failures. However, over time, it is building a relationship of mutual trust with the community (in particular, the youth segment). It will be wonderful if the progress of future studies and research can contribute to the creation of better localities.

REFERENCES

Davis, L. S., Johnson, K. N., Bettinger, P. S. and Howard, T. E. 2001. Forest management: to Sustain Ecological, Economical and Social Values. New York: McGraw-Hill Companies.

He, A. Minowa, M. & Takahashi, Y. 2002. Deriving The Concept Of Capital And Estimating Its Value In Terms Of Sustainable Forest Management. Proceedings of International Symposium on Forest Environmental Value Accounting, ITTO and CAF, 128-132.

Heal, G. M. 2000. Nature And The Marketplace: Capturing the Value of Ecosystem Services. Washington, D. C.: Island Press.

ICCROM Mayors & Decision-Makers' Forum. 2003. ICCROM Mayors & Decision-Makers' Forum Conclusions. A paper prepared for 7th International Symposium of the OWHC 23-26 September 2003. Rhodes, Greece.

Kant, I. 1803. Über Pädagogik. Herausgegeben von D. Friedrich Theodor Rink. Königsberg: Friedrich Nicolovius.

Korten, D. C. 1990. Getting to the 21st Century: Voluntary Action and the Global Agenda. West Hartford, Conn.: Kumarian Press.

Kuriyama, K. 1997. A Critical Analysis of the Public Participation Studies in the Decision Making of the Forest Management: An Approach from Environmental Economics. Japanese Journal of Forest Planning, 29: 1-11.

Minowa, M. 1996. Economic Thought Compared with Forestry One. Proceedings of the Symposium on Forest Inventory and Monitoring in East Asia. Fuchu, Japan: Japan Society of Forest Planning Press: 141-146.

Minowa, M. 1994. Some Characteristics of Modern Thought in Forest Management Science. Proceedings of the IUFRO International Workshop on Sustainable Forest Management. Furano: 451-456.

State Forestry Administration, P. R. China. 2001a. The Chinese Forestry Development Report 2000. Beijing: China Forestry Publishing House.

State Forestry Administration, P. R. China. 2001b. The Chinese Forestry Statistics Almanac 2000. Beijing: China Forestry Publishing House.

Takahashi, Y., Minowa, M. and He, A. 2002. Capital Valuation of Sustainable Forest Management in Collaboration with Public People: A Case Study of Plantation Forests at Upper Reaches of *Chang Jiang* River in China. Environmental Information Science, 33: 13-18

The International Environmental Education Program (IEEP). 1975. Belgrade Charter. UNESCO, Belgrade: United Nations Environment Program (UNEP).

Uzawa, H. 2000. Social capital. Tokyo: Iwanami-Shin-Sho.

Yamamura, T. 2002. Studies in Cultural Tourism as a Method for Regional Development in Developing Countries. Doctoral thesis at The University of Tokyo.

cross-cultural roundtable sessions

MULTI CULTURAL

たしかい文化が

AND

輝やきを

INSPIRATIONAL

CROSS-CULTURAL ANALYSIS OF COMMUNITY DESIGN IN THE NEIGHBORHOOD
A Review and Outlook

Li-Ling Huang, Marcia McNally and Louise Mozingo

ABSTRACT

This paper discusses the planning and design of neighborhood open space in Taipei, Kyoto, Berkeley, Oakland, and Los Angeles. It presents critical questions about the outcomes of the participatory process in neighborhood space design including: the relation between local open space aspirations and design visions for an entire city, the reflection of values in the design of a neighborhood process, the roles of the many players who appear in the production of neighborhoods, and the need for community designers to address the impacts of changing populations and globalized commercialism in neighborhoods. Criteria for evaluating community design in the neighborhood are proposed.

OVERVIEW

The catalyst for this roundtable is our shared interest in the neighborhood as both a concept and an on the ground reality of the city. Our observations are based on teaching, field research, and community design practice in neighborhoods in the San Francisco Bay Area, Los Angeles, Taipei, and Kyoto. They have led us to think closely about the form, components, residents, and conception of the neighborhood in the larger city, and the players who now shape the physical and conceptual neighborhood.

The Neighborhood

Though the neighborhood certainly existed as a daily reality before Clarence Perry, Perry's conception of the neighborhood unit as the basic building block of the city and city planning has had broad and profound influence in the Pacific Rim. Perry's conception of the neighborhood as limited in size (typically 160 acres) and population, and containing essential civic features such as neighborhood parks, schools and retail, displayed the hierarchical and rational precepts of early city planning in response to the advent of the industrial city. At the same time Perry's intent was a humanistic one: to foster a place of belonging through a human scale landscape that contained opportunities for casual yet intimate interaction with neighbors. Perry's neighborhood planning unit countered both the disorienting extent of the early twentieth century city and its tendency to generate anonymity and anomie among its residents.

While Perry's ideas were formulated in the U.S., a quick review of Taipei and Japanese urban history indicates the concepts may have migrated. United Nations experts introduced the neighborhood unit into the planning for new development in Taipei in the 1960s. It is likely, however, that the Japanese, who hugely influenced Taipei's twentieth century urban form, had already laid the groundwork for a neighborhood unit. For example, neighborhood-based primary schools (the centerpiece of Perry's concept) emerge in force in Taipei during Japanese occupation. Some time during this period the *gaku* appeared in Japan. An administrative unit, the *gaku* was determined spatially as the area served by the local primary school, typically with a 400-meter service radius (approximately 160 acres). Japanese occupation of Taiwan parallels the era of "westernization" and the introduction of city planning as a government function in Japan. It is also an era of planning proselytizing in the U.S. – the local histories of many major American cities during this time include a visit by one of the great planning minds of the day, often followed by a report that

Figure 1. The neighborhood as both a concept and a reality. (Sarah Minick)

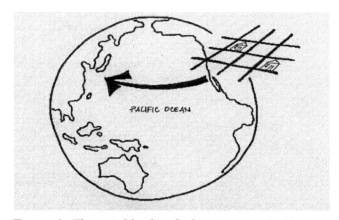

Figure 2. The neighborhood planning unit in its westward migration. (Sarah Minick)

included detailed proposals with small unit circles radiating around schools, playgrounds, and parks. Thus the image of migrating planning units establishing an east-west flyway over the North American continent and one across the Pacific is not farfetched.

While our experience has shown that many of Perry's precepts continue to resonate in Pacific Rim neighborhood form, it also shows that two phenomena of the last thirty years are changing the neighborhood. On the one hand, standardization of neighborhood form has increased. Mass produced housing built by corporate real estate interests and facilitated by local zoning reproduce well worn international building types. Changing consumer preferences replace local retail with international chain stores. Regulation play fields for team sports and liability safe playgrounds dominate neighborhood open spaces. On the other hand, community action to empower residents in neighborhood planning and design decisions is a vibrant and increasing force. Participation in the planning and design of neighborhood parks is common and engages people who typically in other circumstances may not have felt particularly empowered. A foreign nanny in Taipei is the instigator of neighborhood action for open space in Yon Kan. Housewives in Kyoto turned out in force to guide the design of neighborhood mini-parks. In Berkeley, community based design and planning is an expected part of all neighborhood level changes. The neighborhood is evolving as the basic landscape unit of globalization and resistant local action, in parallel. As such it should be a primary field of action for community planners and designers.

The Approach

Our paper discusses approaches to neighborhood community design in the U.S., Japan, and Taiwan. In thinking about how neighborhoods are shaped and reshaped through the community design process, we reviewed our own projects

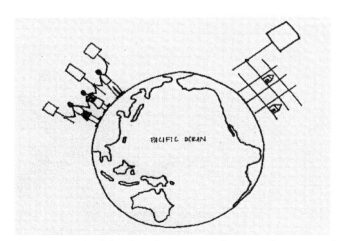

Figure 3. Neighborhoods are simultaneously units of globalization and resistant local action. (Sarah Minick)

and research as well as case studies from previous Pacific Rim conferences. We considered the players, methods, and outcomes and looked at tensions within neighborhood community design with a global-local filter. Using this review we propose a way of evaluating whether or not community design is "good" at the neighborhood level. We conclude with a set of questions and initial answers that will shape our conference panel discussion.

THE PLAYERS: COLLABORATIONS AND COMBINATIONS

In considering the results we must first consider the players. Gone are the simple days of Perry, when these matters were left to rational planners, bureaucracies, and developers. Our research indicates that five sets of actors in *community* based neighborhood design are essential to understand as discrete and interactive entities: academic practitioners, local government, community-based organizations, professional designers, and neighborhood residents.[1]

Today

Though not all of these actors operate in every neighborhood community design process, at a minimum residents do. They can take on a multiplicity of roles. The most obvious is to express their needs in the neighborhood landscape and to evaluate proposals prepared by designers. But they take on expanded roles as well. In many projects residents actively shape the landscape by formulating design proposals themselves. Increasingly, neighbors provide the volunteer labor to construct community open spaces and maintain them. This has worked particularly well in Kyoto and Berkeley. However, democratic neighborhood activity requires assurances – that no member of the neighborhood is excluded; that design and construction have expert supervision from within or outside of the community. Otherwise the product can fall short of the quality needed for public spaces.

The experience of participation at the neighborhood level is the first step in citizen understanding of the larger civic role, and as such has an importance beyond the immediate community design process. In the case of neighborhood parks, for example, the participatory process both produces a place appropriate neighborhood space and catalyzes a wider city attachment and advocacy. This, in and of itself, is an evolution of the original neighborhood park idea that through participation in the activities benevolently provided in the park, community building would happen. The present process builds community by literally building the park, and beyond that wider empowerment.

Regardless of country of origin, local government plays an important role in the production of neighborhood space. Today we find many examples of government supported activity aimed at efficient delivery of services but also at an equitable

Figure 4. Space making and community building as a transactive pair. (Sarah Minick)

distribution of infrastructure to support high quality everyday life. Of course this is not a straightforward pursuit. In the neighborhood local government representatives are usually responding to political pressure from elected officials and from residents while trying to safeguard long-term institutional concerns. Often the individual city staff person regards community participation as a necessary evil, particularly in places like Berkeley where it is required by city policy. For their part neighborhood residents see staff as impediments to their dreams. Yet our research shows that where city staff and residents seem to be naturally, but not insurmountably, diffident of each other, through the community design process staff evolves in their position to the neighborhood and vice versa. In some cases a strong partnership emerges.

Figure 5. Diffidence can become partnership through process. (Sarah Minick)

Beyond these two essential ingredients (residents and government representatives), the players vary. Since the 1960s the role of the academic practitioner in the neighborhood has been to critique norms and to propose innovation for both process and urban form based on the conclusions of research. In the university studio, for example, academic teams of faculty and students marshal extensive resources to provide the many hours of organizational work needed to both systematically analyze existing conditions and involve a broad spectrum of community residents in the design process. In resource strapped cities, the careful analysis necessary for successful neighborhood park design would not be possible

without university involvement. Very often academics take on a strong advocacy role as well – this has consistently been a crucial involvement. In many cases their interests have had a direct influence on politicians and local government officials who, wanting to appear different from their competitors, are naturally interested in innovation, not institutional norms. Through creative neighborhood design and policy planning, local government can appear to be directly responding to their constituent citizens with the support of the academy.

For-fee professional designers are least often involved in community-based design in neighborhoods. Their typical role is often provided by academic practitioners, city officials, or in the case of community construction efforts, residents themselves. The extended commitment of time and effort to complete neighborhood-based design does not fit easily into the strictures of professional practice and the fees are often considered too small for the bother. Most often, professionals enter into the final implementation phase of the process, the construction itself. An exception is a particular hybrid of professional and neighborhood resident, i.e. professional designers, who take an interest in their own neighborhood landscape. In Setagaya, Japan and Berkeley, California there are numerous cases where professionals have taken leadership roles in neighborhood design ensuring a robust community process, design quality, adequate funding, and long-term stewardship.

Our research shows that involvement of community-based organizations (CBO) can be a prerequisite in neighborhood based design processes. These intermediaries can provide outside actors, whether academics, government officials, or professionals, with a way into the neighborhood and connections to key informants and neighborhood activists. They sometimes can bring warring or previously unknown key players to the table, often lending credibility to the outsiders and in turn focusing neighborhood residents on the issues at hand.

Concerns

One issue that is receiving increasing scrutiny is the appropriateness of any intermediary involvement in neighborhood affairs. We saw how in the Kyoto parks initiative the faculty-student team showed citizens and the City how to establish a good relationship. The community process designed by the university created many opportunities for face-to-face, side-by-side communication. We observe, however, that intermediaries are particularly concerned with neighborhood-based community design as an end in itself – they build their own legitimacy through their role in the process. This is fine as long as their interests reach a confluence with those of the neighborhood. We find that if this does not occur, projects can take much longer than needed, are much more costly,

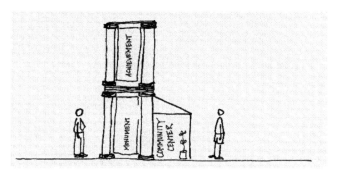

Figure 6. When an intermediary's interests and the interests of the community diverge. (Sarah Minick)

and sometimes the final product (through the multi-layered implementation by too many actors) is far removed from the design agreed upon through the original community process.

One indicator of a good match is a high level of geographic and issue correlation between the intermediary and neighbors. For example in a community design process for Bushrod Park in Oakland, the grassroots organization North Oakland Voters Alliance was able to bring out record numbers of residents to review and evaluate design proposals, while continuing to be active in a range of neighborhood quality of life issues such as traffic calming, clean-ups, and billboard removal. The Alliance also maintains a web site that posts planning analysis and alternative design proposals currently underway.

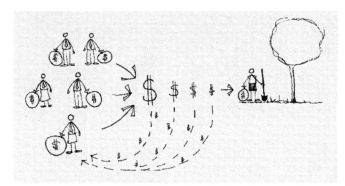

Figure 7. The new cost of doing business in the neighborhood. (Sarah Minick)

Another indicator may be that the scale of the problem is in balance with the scale of the resources expended. In the case of Sanborn Park and Union Point Park (Also in Oakland), the neighborhood-based process was undertaken by faculty-student teams from the University of California, Berkeley in conjunction with the Unity Council, a local but highly sophisticated and well funded CBO. The projects were paid for by monies received from the Lila Wallace Reader's Digest Fund (a national foundation) and federal HUD (Department of Housing and Urban Development) grants, funneled through the university, Trust for Public Land (a national environmental organization), and the City of Oakland. Both cases are

examples of imbalance. In both, large sums of money were paid out long before construction. In both, the designer supervising construction was different than the designers who worked with the community. In one case the design changed completely, and in the other the materials used were compromised. In both cases the projects went on for years. And they were "just" neighborhood parks.

We have begun to research Taipei's Neighborhood Improvement Program and the Citizen Planner system. In recent years Taipei City has invested a lot of money in people-based infrastructure such as neighborhood parks and pedestrianscapes. It has funded white paper research to sort out how best to make government accessible to citizens. The proposed Community Planning Service Center system will hopefully be more consistent with people's natural "life circles" and avoid the pitfalls associated with administrative districts and old political patronage of the *Li* system. The City has also created a training program to activate young professionals to become part of the community design movement. Recent first hand experience with graduates of this program has given us pause, however. In the Shi-lin night market neighborhood we observed the community planners, who work on neighborhood level planning issues (for fees paid by the City), sounding eerily like local *Li* leaders and city district bureaucrats. While too soon to tell, it made us aware of how important it is for this new cadre of planners to develop an identity and working relationship with residents independent of the City, and to take all precautions that they don't become fiduciaries of the status quo.

Figure 8. Value-imbued process produces personality. (Sarah Minick)

METHODS: STANDARD OPERATING PROCEDURE OR LITMUS OF VALUES

One fundamental element of the neighborhood unit conceived by Perry and others is the neighborhood park. Every neighborhood was to have one, and for many that do today, parks provide places in neighborhoods to recreate, express local character, and exercise the democracy of daily life. Using the research on neighborhood parks initiatives in Kyoto, Taipei,

Values	Intention of community design	Technique or method
Japan		
Community and family (citizen value)	Build social capital and diminish old hierarchies	Workshop
Respectful communication	Find a shared vision expressive of shared values	Use humor and cartoon graphics, Goal setting, Good process
Partnership (City value)	Find a way to engage citizens in long term stewardship	Good process
Craft	Overcome alienation through hands on engagement	Work day, Fund raiser
Place as expression of nature and culture	Improve the environment of people's daily lives	Town watching, Producing traditional crafts to express sense of place (postcards, quilts, etc.)
Taiwan		
Community	Help citizens find their voice	Events showcasing local culture
Empowerment	Force institutional reform to give people priority over economy (overcome insufficient public services)	Protest, NEIP, community planner system, community planning service center
Professional knowledge + local wisdom	Create new role and style for planning and design professions	Pattern language (not sure how this actually happens)
Cultural preservation	Resist globalization in built form (city should be a spatial support for local culture)	Events showcasing local culture, pattern language (not sure how this actually happens)
Quality of life	Enhance city livability (city should be a spatial support for daily urban life)	Neighborhood design improvement activities
U.S.		
Community	Create a sense of belonging through process engagement that has long term effects	Anything that brings people together, stewardship projects
Private property rights	Protect property values	Protest
Survival (City value)	Do what it takes to get citizens to sign off	Hire experts
Empowerment and equity	Give voice to those previously excluded	Organizing
Knowledge	Use or acquire skills to have control over technical decisions, develop leadership	Technical training
Quality of life	Improve the environment through active engagement (not passive consumption)	Neighborhood design improvement activities

Table 1.

and Berkeley we would like to zoom in on the methods used by community designers to produce these parks and discuss them in the context of participant values. Table 1 begins to bring these things into focus.

The Assurances of Process

It is our feeling that the real craft of community design method is found in Japan. This is certainly the case in Kyoto, where the City worked with the community directly to develop plans for neighborhood mini-parks known as *hiroba*. This was a government – initiated process, the City's goal being to develop partnerships with citizens where none had previously existed. To that end the City engaged a Kyoto University team of faculty and students to develop a step-by-step method which they then taught city staff. The result was open "machizukuri communication" between participants.

We found that use of the round table workshop – taking off one's shoes, sitting around a table, working on a task in a small group – was key. The workshop was a face-to-face venue where people who didn't know each other (and maybe were apprehensive because of the dictates of old hierarchies) could in fact communicate respectfully and deeply. This should not surprise us because participants in this initiative repeatedly mentioned how important it was to find a setting in which to feel comfortable disagreeing. Venue alone was not enough, however. It was important to weave in techniques such as goal setting that would empower participants to speak their minds because they had the assurances of structured process. Goals yielded a collective, big picture context to work in, making it easier to negotiate the details in a pointed way. The workshop process was powerful enough in one case that neighbors today use it to elect new *jichi-kai* officers.

In all of the Kyoto projects reviewed the hands-on workdays where citizens, city staff, and the university team worked together were effective. They were satisfying practice grounds for overcoming the barriers of traditional rigid, no-touch sense of *machi*. Revisiting some of these sites a few years later we observe that the City's desire to get citizens to take responsibility for the parks on a day-to-day basis may have taken root. Two years after the Yanagatubo Tibikko Hiroba process neighbors were found making a tarp to cover the sandbox at night. In Sakura Hiroba residents continue the annual cycle of propagation, planting, and viewing of flowers grown for the pleasure of neighboring Alzheimer's patients. These activities occur without City assistance or funding.

One aspect of the Kyoto example that is important to discuss is the City's commitment to monitoring the effectiveness of the effort. Today the City has a growing cadre of trained and dedicated staff advancing partnerships in other arenas. In a recent workshop, over 40 participants from the City discussed new collaborations with citizens and with staff in other departments. This is only because the City has been willing to adapt the process, which was immediately imperative because the first year of the *hiroba* initiative was quite painful. Early on staff owned up to being scared of going out to meet the public. The university team had to adjust the method, adding role-playing to show staff how to anticipate and handle confrontational situations. They also created new techniques to reach out to residents who were being excluded, such as children and young mothers.

It is possible that the park partnership process is indicative of a larger movement afoot in Kyoto. One of the City's primary goals was to advance citizen participation in order to decrease the budget by increasing the efficiency of the city, in other words making a better match between citizen needs and city expenditures. As part of the effort to match needs and expenditures in 1999 the City of Kyoto conducted a survey of 3,000 citizens in four languages. According to staff, the most surprising finding was the answer to the question, "What do you think is a good way for citizens to be involved in the city administration." The desire to engage in direct democracy in Kyoto seems to be taking hold, as seen in Table 2.

	Response
Communicate, collaborate, and suggest ideas directly with city administration	35.5%
Represent own opinions and ideas through the *jichi-kai*	34.3%
Represent own opinions and ideas through city council members	12.0%

Table 2. Method of involvement.

The Peculiarities of Place

In Kyoto we found that nearly all of the values of participants were manifest in the park design process. In Taipei the parks created out of the Neighborhood Improvement Program reflect a match between resident desires to improve the quality of their daily living environment and the City's capacity to respond quickly. The result is a neighborhood open space system with a lot of personality. One common community design activity that can be credited is showcasing local cultural resources (puppet theatre, outdoor film viewing, banner making) to inspire imagination and mobilize participants. It is interesting then that in talking about the production of neighborhood parks in Taipei community designers discuss them as a venue for the urban social movement. Instead of design or process detail the tales emphasize the struggle. The use of press conferences, signature drives, and petitions form the main of each story. One observer described it vividly, "...the urgency of a situation often forces devoted members to become effective forces for mobilization for short periods: notifying people, calling meetings, deciding action strategy, dividing the execution of work, and reviewing and discussing results...within a short time, the residents' relationships change from unfamiliar neighbors into familiar comrades in arms."[2]

One would expect the story of the Berkeley parks initiative to be characterized by a well-crafted exercise in democracy. Instead it conveys the pluralism that defines Berkeley politics today (indeed one senior City official has said that there is no such thing as a majority vote in Berkeley – for every citizen there is a different point of view and they are all given equal weight). Perhaps this explains the recent top-down, structure-light design process used by City staff in retrofitting the parks. They knew that no matter what approach they took citizens would make it political. Perhaps this also explains the relative blandness and ubiquitous aesthetic of the parks.

There are several important exceptions. The most exuberant example of intentional process and method is that of Halcyon Commons. It was internally initiated and led by neighborhood activists with professional design degrees. They employed the standard tools of the community design trade – surveys, design charettes, community fact-finding expeditions, consensus building, community workdays. Instead of plurality the goal was to avoid *polarization* (all of those interviewed used the same word). To accomplish this unity the group set up committees to investigate concerns and addressed them one by one. Would a park increase crime? Noise? To answer these questions the group conducted a case study of a similar park nearby. They interviewed people who lived around the park, asking about homeless and criminal behavior. They observed behavior and took measurements of the decibels when kids were playing. Their commitment to consensus paid off, as one person reflected, "We really listened and took concerns seriously no matter how little they seemed. We did reality testing. This really helped – it made us unstoppable. This rarely happens in Berkeley."

Speaking the Unspoken

We wanted to revisit of the conclusions of the Huang-McNally paper from the 2002 Pacific Rim conference, which assert that process tempers the impact of uniformity. Perhaps this should be modified to say value-imbued process produces personality. If we look at the parks designed during this time in all three countries we can conclude that in spite of the neighborhood park being a standardized unit, parks are in some way a place of local expression. On the other hand, it is important to wonder if the process or technique itself is a localizer or globalizer. Maybe both. Japanese and Taiwanese

Figure 9. Value-imbued process produces personality. (Sarah Minick)

Figure 10. Community design process migration. (Sarah Minick)

both use events and activities to draw in citizens by playing on local history, culture, and craft. Americans and Japanese both use processes and workshop techniques that emphasize structure and information. Taiwanese and Americans both use Alinsky-style, confrontational tactics when needed. Everyone makes murals or tiles, has work parties and opening day events. Community design is an expression of culture. It is an expression of designer personality and creativity. It is also the result of process migration.

COMMUNITIES AND GLOBAL CHANGE: NEIGHBORHOOD LANDSCAPES IN AND OUT

During the past four decades of the twentieth century community design served as a tool to help neighborhoods improve the quality of public spaces, empower the grassroots, and encourage the expression of local identities. However, when it enters the new century, the social context and the parameters of shaping our neighborhood landscape have shifted dramatically. We see those phenomena as a reflection at the local level induced by acceleration of the global agenda. These social changes are massive and cut deeply into daily life, and can no more be overlooked by us, community designers, researchers, and planners. Here we argue from three dimensions, including spatial structure, neighborhood economy, and population composition to see their impacts on our neighborhoods.

Spatial Policy

Community is not a self-determined concept nor does it have its own isolated boundary. Local government policy today can have ramifications at many scales within and beyond its borders – regional, global, and neighborhood. This is especially true for communities under high development pressure. For example, Taipei in recent years has accelerated large scale spatial restructuring to push a new urban economy and promote its identity as a global city. The most cited example is the Sin-yi District. As a symbol of Taipei moving towards becoming a global financial center, it has completely revamped its image from a military village, with an historic type of housing rich in its unique community solidarity and characteristic spatial forms, into the site of the world's tallest building and the city's most luxurious residential accommodations.

Another example illustrating the restructuring of space and economy is the idea of developing tourism in the city as the new economy, brought into focus by a recent cross-cultural research exchange between Huang and McNally's students. While studying the neighborhood surrounding the old Shi-lin night market we learned of Taipei City government's plans to promote the area as the biggest night market in Southeast Asia, supported by huge public investment. Despite the fact that the business sector in this area welcomes this policy, most neighborhoods anticipate suffering from problems such as parking, noise, and crowds in the future. The massive change would also alter the neighborhood fabric. The heart of the night market is a set of spatial arrangements composed of traditional cultural, social, and economic elements such as the Tsu-chen Temple square, the river, and shop house streets. Its already tarnished place identity would be further eroded under the strong pressure of development.

Additionally, the new economic activities bring land speculation and destroy the original neighborhood spatial form. Interestingly, the neighborhoods surrounding Shi-lin night market still carry a very livable mixed street network formed by low-to-medium density Ching dynasty housing, Japanese shop houses, and Taiwanese open neighborhood apartments. Yet the success of the MRT makes Shi-lin a 12-minute ride to downtown and vice versa, which has stimulated a new form of high rise, gated community in Shi-lin. It is our expectation that the push to use the city's night markets as a global tourism draw is or will have similar impacts in other night market neighborhoods before the urban design regulation necessary to protect them is in place. Indeed the English language tourism material, from the *Lonely Planet* travel guide to the MRT maps, features them prominently. Community designers beware!

Figure 11. Neighborhoods as the new frontier of the global economy. (Sarah Minick)

Neighborhood Economy and the Civic Spaces

The discussion above leads us to another force altering the neighborhood landscape, the presence and power of non-local capital. This issue is especially significant for neighborhoods in Taiwan and Japan, where residential and commercial land-uses are usually mixed, which means inviting economic activities into the deep reach of people's daily living space. Stated differently, mixed-use neighborhoods with dynamic local economies are the very frontier for the global economy to engage its consumers.

The best example to understand how the organized retailing economy threatens the traditional community economy is to look at the impact on diversified and self-owned shops. Huang lived in the Yon Kan community for almost one year, which allowed her to witness this transition first hand. It was interesting to see the ins and outs after a neighborhood park process made the neighborhood famous. First and foremost, independent grocery stores quickly converted to either convenience stores or venues for higher value craft goods. Cheap dining spots were replaced by chain coffee cafés for customers from elsewhere in the city or even abroad. One small and bustling local hardware store at the corner of the park became an eyewear shop with bright and beautiful interior design.

So we observe the disappearance of barbershops, markets, and tailor shops that used to double as community information centers, chatting rooms, and emergency stations, in other words informal civic space that maintained the social network within the neighborhood. But people nowadays shop less within their communities than before – shopping centers, hyper-marts, and convenience stores are on the rise.[3] With the arrival of global franchise stores, choosing commodities and services now relies on the brand recognition promoted by faceless corporations rather than the trust of the local owners. This new phenomenon begs the attention of community designers, who drink Starbucks coffee, wear Nike shoes, and read books purchased at Borders or Eslite.

Interestingly, Berkeley neighborhoods are vulnerable to the same gentrifying effects of strong local retail, however they have been more successful at fending off chain stores. Indeed city policy promotes neighborhood retail areas for both livability and tourism purposes, but advertises the unique, locally-owned businesses. Parking and traffic are issues. But according to neighborhood studies conducted by McNally's class, the strongest local commercial areas also have the highest rates of residents walking (as opposed to driving) to shopping, and the highest level of satisfaction with the neighborhood generally. In the Elmwood neighborhood shopkeepers sit outside in lawn chairs on sunny days so they can visit with locals, residents report neighboring more at their local cafés than their local parks. Reading the survey data one gets the sense of the commercial district functioning as neighborhood front porch or living room.

New Populations, New Immigrants, and New Users

The final point is to observe how neighborhood needs for public space change along with the changes of the population. Perhaps the most dynamic conditions surround neighborhoods with foreign immigrants and laborers. How they have access to the public space becomes an issue of environmental justice, which we cannot overlook in conducting participatory design. From our Hong Kong planning friends we know the story of how, after a participatory design process, one neighborhood expressed its desire to exclude local Filipino maids from access to 'their' neighborhood park. In a predominantly Latino neighborhood in the San Fernando Valley of Los Angeles, teens try to play soccer in the only park within miles. The City installs boulders and "No Soccer" signs. The youth adapt, using the rocks to delineate goals. In Taipei, in many types of civic spaces, such as MRT stations, urban parks, neighborhood parks, sidewalks, and churches, conflicts occur between local groups and foreign laborers, maids, and new immigrants. One can only expect this tension to rise as in Taiwan one out of eight new babies is born of a foreign spouse, and one out of every three marriages is international (mainly from mainland China and Vietnam). Los Angeles is almost 60% Latino, in fact it is the second largest *Mexican* city in the world. This raises the obvious questions: who are the user groups of neighborhood space and what are their space needs, how do we empower those invisible ones, and how can we create a space to foster dialogue instead of exclusion? We must stress the importance of inclusive planning in neighborhood design to safeguard public spaces for those disadvantaged groups.

DISCUSSION

To write this paper we asked the following question: at the neighborhood scale, and with community design instincts and values, how do we design in the neighborhood and what are the results? Assessment is critical so let us look at a proposed set of criteria for evaluating community design based on the issues discussed (the reader is encouraged to complete the matrix in Table 3).

At the neighborhood scale, good community design…	Yes	No	Irrelevant at this scale
Produces space that is needed			
Produces quality design and construction			
Produces space that fosters neighboring			
Gives all neighbors access to the activity			
Employs techniques that capture local personality and translate it into built form			
Uses methods that match the values and intentions of the participants			
Finds ways for neighbors to have partners to work with (i.e. they don't have to go it alone)			
Makes sure the self interest of the actors find congruence, as opposed to drive the process at the expense of each other			
Ensures that the scale of the problem is in balance with the scale of the effort (including resources expended and players involved)			
Watchdogs that neighborhood intermediaries are advancing the ideals of democratic design (rather than reinforcing the status quo)			
Understands and is addressing the breadth of issues with spatial implications			
Yields a citizen understanding of the broader process of the production of urban space and governance			

Table 3. Community design matrix.

Given the cases discussed we need to ask the question, are the right players at the table? Developers and property and business owners have to be brought into the fold otherwise we'll be eaten alive. They may control economic decisions, which in turn control land use, but we control the making of quality spaces that ensure strong property values and happy local customers. Why not work together?

Perhaps the most fundamental question is–are we working in the right space when we work on neighborhood space? Our research indicates that the neighborhood park's role in the park system is undergoing significant evolution. We should not think of neighborhood parks as fixed elements in the open space landscape but consider their role is to evolve as neighborhoods and urban circumstances evolve; they are funkier and more idiosyncratic. They stand as local place specific symbols of neighborhoods as well as serving user needs. But is park space the only space to consider? Indeed many stated user needs are symbolic rather than actual. The impulse of Taipei City when negotiating with a developer over the reuse of an old mill site in Shi-lin was to lop off 20% of the land for a park to satisfy perceived local needs. The neighborhood studies conducted by the Huang-McNally student research team revealed that resident needs would likely be better served with a number of small spaces in various forms scattered throughout the neighborhood that were linked in such a way to satisfy daily life needs *and* connect to nearby larger systems of urban nature *and* address the pressures of night market tourism takeover.

Thus we conclude that the neighborhood is an appropriate place for flux and change in the urban landscape and an essential means of place identity in an increasingly homogenized and globalized urban landscape. We as community designers, planners, educators, and researchers love it because it is such a perfect scale for us to play with our tools and share them with others. They are undeniably good stepping stone habitat for democratic learning and greater civic engagement. City government should recognize this evolutionary process and formative role much more explicitly and build it into neighborhood management. We would contend that community designers need to take part in this process by taking the time to inventory these conditions and adjust our methods as needed so that when the opportunity (or threat) arises we can guide a process and outcome that makes the best fit.

ENDNOTES

[1] To start we are intentionally excluding a sixth actor, the private business and development sector, but return to this very important force later on in the paper.

[2] Taken from a keynote speech given by Shu-cheng Tseng, Taipei Forum, June 2001. Full text found in: Liu et al (Eds.). 2001. Building Cultural Diversity through Participation. Taipei: Council for Cultural Affairs, The Executive Yuan, 489-93.

[3] According to the statistics, Taiwan presently ranks as the country with the highest density of convenience stores in the world. In the past five years land-use deregulation has further boosted shopping malls in the city and suburban areas. The rise is so prominent that the central government recently designated a shopping mall as the core of the life circle in a plan for a new suburb.

REFERENCES

Asanoumi, Y. 1999. "Consensus Building" Is Not Good Enough. Paper delivered at the 2nd Participatory Community Design in the Pacific Rim conference, Saitama, Japan.

Hsia, C. 1999. Theorizing Community Participatory Design in a Developing Country: The Historical Meaning of Democratic Design in Taiwan. In Hester, R. and Kweskin, C. (Eds.), Democratic Design in the Pacific Rim – Japan, Taiwan and the United States. Mendocino: Ridge Times Press, 14-21.

Huang, L. and McNally, M. 2002. The Production of Neighborhood Space: A Comparison of Taipei, Taiwan and Berkeley, California. Paper delivered at the 4th Participatory Community Design in the Pacific Rim conference, Hong Kong, ROC.

Liu, H. and Lu, B. 1999. Toward a City for Citizens: Two Community Organizations in Taiwan. In Hester, R. and Kweskin, C. (Eds.), Democratic Design in the Pacific Rim – Japan, Taiwan and the United States. Mendocino: Ridge Times Press, 250-57.

Liu, H. and Huang, L. 1999. Participatory Design Process and Community Politics: The Case of Chi-Shan Community in Taipei. Paper delivered at the 2nd Participatory Community Design in the Pacific Rim conference, Saitama, Japan.

Liu, J. 2002. *Kanou Machijin-zukuri* or Kano Neighborhood People: Practicing Community Development at the People Level. Bridging the Grassroots. Japan-U.S. Community Education and Exchange.

McNally, M. and Nagahashi, T. 2001. Challengishimasu! Episodes in the Pursuit of Democratic Design. In Liu et al (Eds.), Building Cultural Diversity through Participation. Taipei: Council for Cultural Affairs, The Executive Yuan, 76-139.

Mozingo, L. 2000. A Century of Neighborhood Parks: Presumptions and Proposals. Proceedings, Does The Neighborhood Landscape Matter?, University of California, Berkeley, Berkeley, California.

Nishimura, Y. 1999. Public Participation in Planning in Japan: The Legal Perspective. In Hester, R. and Kweskin, C. (Eds.), Democratic Design in the Pacific Rim – Japan, Taiwan and the United States. Mendocino, CA: Ridge Times Press, 6-13.

Perry, C. 1929. The Neighborhood Unit: A Scheme of Arrangement for the Family-Life Community. Regional Survey of New York and Its Environs, Volume VII, Neighborhood and Community Planning. Committee on The Regional Plan of New York and Its Environs; New York, NY.

Watanabe, S. 2003. The Challenge of "Machizukuri" in Japan: a Historical Perspective. Proceedings, Urban Forum: International Symposium on Community Architecture, Kaohsiung, Taiwan, City of Kaohsiung, 56-65.

CROSS-CULTURAL COLLABORATION AND COMMUNITY-BASED PLANNING IN QUANZHOU, FUJIAN, CHINA
A Second Look, Based on a Studio Undertaken Summer, 2004

Daniel Abramson and Jeffrey Hou

ABSTRACT

This presentation will follow up on the topic presented at the 4th Pacific Rim Participatory Community Design Conference in December 2002 in Hong Kong. At that time, Prof. Abramson introduced the emergence of opportunities for community-based design and planning in the city of Quanzhou, in Fujian Province China, with the support of a local planning authority that is increasingly open to direct engagement between outside academics, professionals and local residents. By the time the 5th Conference will be held in September 2004 in Seattle, it is expected that an unprecedentedly interdisciplinary and international group of teachers and students[1] will have gathered again in Quanzhou for a "visioning" exercise in which different stakeholder groups in two communities – one in the historic city center, and one in an industrializing peri-urban village – will meet with students to find graphic and text expression for their particular idea of beneficial urban development. The results of this exercise are expected to be mounted in a public exhibition for open discussion of what developmental direction the city should take in neighborhoods such as these. It is also expected that the exhibition may be a centerpiece for a national conference in Quanzhou on "democratization of the urban planning decision-making process in China" sponsored by the Urban Planning Association of China and the Ford Foundation. This presentation will review what actually happens in Summer 2004, by focusing on how field studies by North American students in concert with Chinese students were combined with a grant from a major international NGO to promote community participation in urban planning governance in China. The presentation will also focus on: the format of the design and/or planning "studio," "charrette" and "workshop;" the integration of pedagogical short term studio projects abroad into longer term international professional/research collaborations, and how being integrated into such collaborations can complicate and benefit both pedagogy and local communities; problems relating to the "assymetry" of travel opportunities between studio participants in affluent and in less affluent countries; differences in the way the discipline(s) of planning are defined in host and visiting countries, and how this affects local community involvement and international collaborative student projects; and finally, the relevance of multidisciplinarity itself to the liberalization of planning activities, and the formation of student teams to help overcome barriers in culture and language.

ENDNOTES

[1] The students who participated in the studio include:

National Taiwanese University Building and Planning Foundation, Taipei: Huang Chiung-hui, Masters Student; Hsu Chun-yu , Planner; Lee Yen-ju, Masters Student; Teng Chia-ling, Masters Student

Sichuan University: Xin Jianan, Bachelors Student In Forestry, University Of Washington-sichuan Exchange Program; Assistant Coordinator

Southeast University School of Architecture, Nanjing: Ding Li, Masters Student In Urban Planning; Hu Mingxing, Postdoctoral Researcher; Wu Ping, Masters Student In Architecture; Xu Yehe, Masters Student In Architecture

University of British Columbia School of Community and Regional Planning: Leslie Shieh, Doctoral Student

University of Washington: Will Buckingham, Masters Student In International Studies–china Studies; Sylvia Ya-ting Chan, Masters Student In Urban Planning; Sophia Lan-yin Chen, Masters Student In Urban Planning; Richard Cochrane, Masters Student In Public Affairs And Urban Planning; Andrea Flower, Masters Student In Urban Planning; Katie Idziorek, Masters Student In Architecture; Elizabeth Jackson, Bachelors Student In Art History; Laurie Karlinsky, Masters Student In Urban Planning; Liz Maly, Masters Student In Architecture; Eden Mercer, Masters Student In Public Affairs; Christie O'brien, Masters Student In Urban Planning; Marc Philpart, Masters Student In Public Affairs; Essence Pierce, Masters Student In Public Affairs And China Studies; Jayde Lin Roberts, Doctoral Student In The Built Environment; Studio Teaching Assistant And Facilitator; Lee Roberts, Masters Student In Architecture And Urban Planning; Carl See, Masters Student In Public Affairs; Makie Suzuki, Masters Student In Landscape Architecture; Candy Wang, Masters Student In Architecture

AUTHORS

Daniel Abramson – Assistant Professor, Department of Urban Design and Planning, University of Washington, USA

Satoko Asano – Director, Community Design Center, Osaka, Japan

Hilda Blanco – Chair and Professor, Department of Urban Design and Planning, University of Washington, USA

Christopher Campbell – Assistant Professor, Department of Urban Design and Planning, University of Washington, USA

Shenglin Chang – Assistant Professor, Natural Resource Sciences and Landscape Architecture, University of Maryland, USA

Victoria Chanse – Doctoral candidate, Department of Landscape Architecture and Environmental Planning, University of California, Berkeley, USA

Annie Yung-Teen Chiu – Assistant Professor, Department of Architecture, Shi-Chien University, Taiwan

Jim Diers – Director, South Downtown Foundation, USA

Masato Dohi – Associate Professor, Department of Social Engineering, Tokyo Institute of Technology, Japan

Amy Dryden – MLA/MCP, Department of Landscape Architecture and Environmental Planning and Department of City and Regional Planning, University of California, Berkeley, USA

Patsy Eubanks Owens – Associate Professor, Landscape Architecture Program, University of California, Davis, USA

Mark Francis – Professor, Landscape Architecture Program, University of California, Davis, USA

Haruhiko Goto – Professor, Department of Architecture, Waseda University, Japan

Yuko Hamasaki – Associate Professor, Department of Architecture, Nagasaki International University, Japan

Mayumi Hayashi – Associate Professor, Institute of Natural and Environmental Sciences, Hyogo University/Awaji Landscape Planning and Horticulture Academy, Japan

Yasuyoshi Hayashi – Board Member, Tamagawa Community Development House, Japan

Aijun He – Ph.D., Graduate School of Agricultural and Life Sciences, The University of Tokyo, Japan

Randolph Hester – Professor, Department of Landscape Architecture and Environmental Planning, University of California, Berkeley, USA

Soshi Higuchi – Master's Student, Department of Architecture, Waseda University, Japan

Kristina Hill – Associate Professor, Department of Landscape Architecture, University of Washington, USA

Margarita Hill – Associate Professor, Department of Natural Resource Sciences and Landscape Architecture, University of Maryland, USA

Jeffrey Hou – Assistant Professor, Department of Landscape Architecture, University of Washington, USA

Li-Ling Huang – Assistant Professor, Department of Architecture, Ming-Chuang University, Taiwan

Aaron Isgar – Director, Sonaterra Translation and Consulting, Japan

Julie Johnson – Associate Professor, Department of Landscape Architecture, University of Washington, USA

Min Jay Kang – Assistant Professor, Department of Architecture, Tamkang University, Taiwan

Mintai Kim – Assistant Professor, School of Landscape Architecture, University of Arizona, USA

Naoki Kimura – Tokyo Institute of Technology, USA

Isami Kinoshita – Associate Professor, Department of Environmental Science and Landscape Architecture, Chiba University, Japan

Carey Knecht – Doctoral candidate, Department of Landscape Architecture and Environmental Planning, University of California, Berkeley, USA

Koichi Kobayashi – President, Kobayashi & Associates, Inc.; Affiliate Faculty, University of Washington, USA

Douglas Kot – Master's Student, Department of Landscape Architecture and Environmental Planning and Department of City and Regional Planning, University of California, Berkeley, USA

Shutaro Koyama – Tokyo Institute of Technology, Japan

I-Chun Kuo – MLA, Department of Landscape Architecture and Environmental Planning, University of California, Berkeley, USA

Lichin Kuo – M.S., Graduate Institute of Building and Planning, National Taiwan University, Taiwan.

Ze Li – Graduate student, Department of Architecture, National University of Singapore

Hsing-Rong Liu – Lecturer, Department of Architecture, Tamkang University, Taiwan

John K. C. Liu – Professor, Graduate Institute of Building and Planning, National Taiwan University, Taiwan

Jonathan London – Executive Director, Youth in Focus, USA

Lynne Manzo – Assistant Professor, Department of Landscape Architecture, University of Washington, USA

Milenko Matanovic – Executive Director, the Pomegranate Center, USA

Marcia McNally – Associate Adjunct Professor, Department of Landscape Architecture and Environmental Planning, University of California, Berkeley, USA

Elijah Mirochnik – Assistant Professor, George Mason University, USA

Louise Mozingo – Associate Professor, Department of Landscape Architecture and Environmental Planning, University of California, Berkeley, USA

Shuichi Murakami – Assistant Professor, University of Shiga Prefecture, Japan

Tamesuke Nagahashi – Vice Executive Director, Community Design Center, Osaka, Japan

Sawako Ono – Professor, Department of Environmental Science and Landscape Architecture, Chiba University, Japan

Sergio Palleroni – Associate Professor, Department of Architecture, University of Washington, USA

Michael Rios – Assistant Professor of Architecture and Landscape Architecture, The Pennsylvania State University, USA

Antonio Ishmael Risianto – Triaco Development Consultant, Indonesia

Nancy Rottle – Assistant Professor, Department of Landscape Architecture, University of Washington, USA

Deni Ruggeri – Doctoral candidate, Department of Landscape Architecture and Environmental Planning, University of California, Berkeley, USA

Dennis Ryan – Associate Professor, Department of Urban Design and Planning; Director, Community and Environmental Planning BA Program, University of Washington, USA

Yuichi Sato – Scientific Officer, Pacific Consultants Co., LTD., Japan

Nobuyuki Sekiguchi – Doctoral Candidate, Department of Architecture, Waseda University, Japan

Pao-Chi (Paul) Sung – Doctoral Candidate, The Graduate Institute of Architecture and Urban Design, National Taipei University of Technology, Taiwan

Sanae Sugita – Tokyo Institute of Technology, Japan

Daniel Winterbottom – Associate Professor, Department of Landscape Architecture, University of Washington, USA

Takayoshi Yamamura – Assistant Professor, Department of Tourism Design, Kyoto Saga University of Arts, Kyoto, Japan

Chia-Ning Yang – Ph.D., Department of Landscape Architecture and Environmental Planning, University of California at Berkeley, USA

Ching-Fen Yang – Doctoral student, Graduate Institute of Building and Planning, National Taiwan University, Taiwan.

Perry Yang – Assistant Professor, Department of Architecture, National University of Singapore

Koichiro Yasuba – Director, Community Design Center, Osaka, Japan

Tianxin Zhang – Lecturer, College of Environmental Sciences, Peking University, China

INDEX